WHY WORLD BAND RADIO?

RADIO MOSCOW, VOICE OF AMERICA, RADIO BEIJING, RADIO FRANCE . . . The finest in news, music, sports and entertainment the world has to offer. It's all at your fingertips with world band radio.

Focus on Cairo and Jerusalem for inside perspectives on the Middle East. Or tune to BBC news radio for the best in reporting from the world's juicy hot spots.

Something lighter? Turn to Australian tennis, or Tahiti's island music. Or try for the dozens of other countries on the air.

Nothing else can provide so great a range of news and opinion, so wide a choice, or has a faster growth rate than world band radio. So, turn the page—and enjoy!

1992 PASSPORT TO

Chuichi Nakajima, NHK

Page 27

CONTENTS

WORLD BAND RADIO

Page 123

Ka of Gahan Wilson.

© Anne Hall

About the Cover . . .
Gahan Wilson has been hooked on world band radio for more than three decades. After wandering around Europe for a year, he bought a shortwave radio to keep in touch. "Learning about others really helps you learn who you are," he says.

Favorite stations? "BBC, definitely. They're tops. Also, Radio France Internationale and Deutsche Welle—excellent!"

Wilson, at 60, isn't ready to see himself as a senior citizen. His 16th book, *Still Weird*, is due out in 1992.

Panasonic presents compact portable multi-band radios.

You don't have to travel the world to see it. With a Panasonic portable multi-band radio you can see it like never before . . . with your ears.

So if you're just going as far as the beach, you can still hear what's going on in the gulf. That's because Panasonic's compact multi-band radios are engineered to be small in size, but they're loaded with features for outstanding performance.

RF-B45 — PLL Quartz synthesized tuner with macro computer control.
- Receives Single Side Band
- Up-conversion double super-hetrodyne system
- 6-way multi-tuning system
- DX/local sensitivity selector
- Frequency step (9kHz/10kHz) selectable
- 18-station preset memory
- LCD multi-information readout
- Quartz clock/timer with sleep/standby function
- 10-key direct time setting
- Feather Touch electronic controls
- Power switch light

RF-B65 — Receives Single Side Band
- PLL quartz synthesized tuner with MCC
- FM/MW/LW/SW, Single Side Band
- SSB fine tuning
- 1kHz-step fine tuning for LW/MW/SW
- 6-way multi-tuning system:
- Built-in dual clock/timer keeps time in two zones
- Sleep/standby function
- Multi-function LCD readout with signal strength indicator

So with a Panasonic compact multi-band radio, when it's tea time, you can take the time to tune in the BBC.

SEE THE WORLD THROUGH YOUR EARS

Panasonic®
just slightly ahead of our time.®

ISSN 0897-0157

International Broadcasting Services, Ltd.

PASSPORT TO WORLD BAND RADIO

1992

Editor-in-Chief	Lawrence Magne
Editor	Tony Jones
Features Editor	Rick Booth
Contributing Editors	Jock Elliott, Craig Tyson
Consulting Editors	John Campbell, Don Jensen
Special Contributors	James Conrad, Gordon Darling (Papua New Guinea), Antonio Ribeiro da Motta (Brazil), Ruth Hesch, Konrad Kroszner, Numero Uno/John Herkimer, Toshimichi Ohtake (Japan), Radio Nuevo Mundo/ Tetsuya Hirahara (Japan), Jairo Salazar (Venezuela), Don Swampo (Uruguay), David Walcutt
Database Software	Richard Mayell
Laboratory	Robert Sherwood
Marketing & Production	Mary Kroszner
Administration	Jane Brinker
Cover Artwork	Gahan Wilson
Graphics/Communications	Consultech Communications, Inc.
IBS – North America	Box 300, Penn's Park, Pennsylvania 18943 USA
IBS – Latin America	Casilla de Correo 1844, Asunción, Paraguay
IBS – Japan	5-31-6 Tamanawa, Kamakura 247

Library of Congress Cataloging-in-Publication Data

Passport to world band radio.

    1. Radio, Short wave—Amateurs' manuals.   2. Radio stations, Short wave—Directories
I. Magne, Lawrence, 1941–
TK9956.P27   1991   384.54'5   91–22739
ISBN 0-914941-27-5

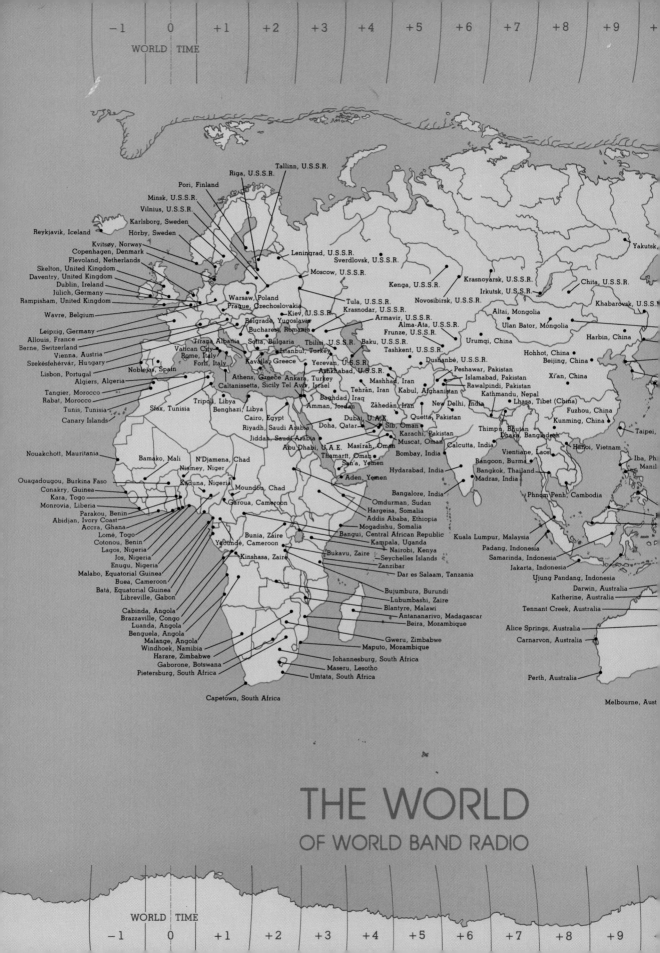

−1 0 +1 +2 +3 +4 +5 +6 +7 +8 +9 +

Tallinn, U.S.S.R.
Riga, U.S.S.R.
Pori, Finland
Minsk, U.S.S.R.
Vilnius, U.S.S.R.
Karlsborg, Sweden
Hörby, Sweden
Reykjavik, Iceland
Kvitsøy, Norway
Copenhagen, Denmark
Flevoland, Netherlands
Skelton, United Kingdom
Daventry, United Kingdom
Dublin, Ireland
Jülich, Germany
Rampisham, United Kingdom
Wavre, Belgium
Leipzig, Germany
Allouis, France
Berne, Switzerland
Vienna, Austria
Székesfehérvár, Hungary
Lisbon, Portugal
Noblejas, Spain
Algiers, Algeria
Tangier, Morocco
Rabat, Morocco
Tunis, Tunisia
Canary Islands
Sfax, Tunisia

Leningrad, U.S.S.R.
Sverdlovsk, U.S.S.R.
Moscow, U.S.S.R.
Warsaw, Poland
Prague, Czechoslovakia
Tula, U.S.S.R.
Krasnodar, U.S.S.R.
Kiev, U.S.S.R.
Belgrade, Yugoslavia
Bucharest, Romania
Sofia, Bulgaria
Tirana, Albania
Vatican City
Rome, Italy
Forli, Italy
Kavalla, Greece
Istanbul, Turkey
Athens, Greece Ankara, Turkey
Caltanissetta, Sicily Tel Aviv, Israel
Yerevan, U.S.S.R.
Ashkhabad, U.S.S.R.
Tbilisi, U.S.S.R. Baku, U.S.S.R.
Armavir, U.S.S.R.
Frunze, U.S.S.R.
Tashkent, U.S.S.R.
Tripoli, Libya
Benghazi, Libya
Cairo, Egypt
Riyadh, Saudi Arabia
Jiddah, Saudi Arabia
Baghdad, Iraq
Amman, Jordan
Dubai, U.A.E.
Doha, Qatar
Sib, Oman
Abu Dhabi, U.A.E.
Masirah, Oman
Thamarit, Oman
Sana, Yemen
Aden, Yemen
Tehran, Iran
Mashhad, Iran
Zahedan, Iran
Kabul, Afghanistan
Muscat, Oman
Karachi, Pakistan
Quetta, Pakistan

Kenga, U.S.S.R.
Krasnoyarsk, U.S.S.R.
Novosibirsk, U.S.S.R.
Irkutsk, U.S.S.R.
Altai, Mongolia
Ulan Bator, Mongolia
Urumqi, China
Dushanbé, U.S.S.R.
Peshawar, Pakistan
Islamabad, Pakistan
Rawalpindi, Pakistan
Kathmandu, Nepal
New Delhi, India
Lhasa, Tibet (China)
Thimpu, Bhutan

Yakutsk,
Chita, U.S.S.R.
Khabarovsk, U.S.S.
Harbin, China
Hohhot, China
Beijing, China
Xi'an, China
Fuzhou, China
Kunming, China
Dhaka, Bangladesh
Taipei,
Hanoi, Vietnam
Iba, Ph.
Manil

Nouakchott, Mauritania
Bamako, Mali
N'Djamena, Chad
Niamey, Niger
Ouagadougou, Burkina Faso
Conakry, Guinea
Kara, Togo
Kaduna, Nigeria
Monrovia, Liberia
Parakou, Benin
Abidjan, Ivory Coast
Accra, Ghana
Lomé, Togo
Cotonou, Benin
Lagos, Nigeria
Jos, Nigeria
Enugu, Nigeria
Malabo, Equatorial Guinea
Buea, Cameroon
Batá, Equatorial Guinea
Libreville, Gabon
Moundou, Chad
Garoua, Cameroon
Yaoundé, Cameroon
Kinshasa, Zaire
Bunia, Zaire
Bukavu, Zaire
Omdurman, Sudan
Hargeisa, Somalia
Addis Ababa, Ethiopia
Mogadishu, Somalia
Bangui, Central African Republic
Kampala, Uganda
Nairobi, Kenya
Seychelles Islands
Zanzibar
Dar es Salaam, Tanzania
Bombay, India
Hydarabad, India
Bangalore, India
Calcutta, India
Rangoon, Burma
Bangkok, Thailand
Madras, India
Vientiane, Laos
Phnom Penh, Cambodia
Kuala Lumpur, Malaysia
Padang, Indonesia
Samarinda, Indonesia
Jakarta, Indonesia
Ujung Pandang, Indonesia

Cabinda, Angola
Brazzaville, Congo
Luanda, Angola
Benguela, Angola
Malange, Angola
Windhoek, Namibia
Harare, Zimbabwe
Gaborone, Botswana
Pietersburg, South Africa
Capetown, South Africa
Bujumbura, Burundi
Lubumbashi, Zaire
Blantyre, Malawi
Antananarivo, Madagascar
Beira, Mozambique
Gweru, Zimbabwe
Maputo, Mozambique
Johannesburg, South Africa
Maseru, Lesotho
Umtata, South Africa

Darwin, Australia
Katherine, Australia
Tennant Creek, Australia
Alice Springs, Australia
Carnarvon, Australia
Perth, Australia
Melbourne, Aust

THE WORLD
OF WORLD BAND RADIO

+11 +12 −11 −10 −9 −8 −7 −6 −5 −4 −3 −2

Nuuk, Greenland

Anchor Point, Alaska

Petropavlovsk-Kamchatskiy, U.S.S.R.
Magadan, U.S.S.R.
Choybalsan, Mongolia
Sapporo, Japan
Vladivostok, U.S.S.R.
Pyongyang, North Korea

Tokyo, Japan
Seoul, South Korea
Hiroshima, Japan

aiwan)

Saipan, Northern Mariana Islands
Guam

ines

Majuro, Marshall Islands

ilippines
balu, Malaysia
g, Malaysia
Biak, Indonesia

Bougainville, Papua New Guinea

Port Moresby, Papua New Guinea

Brisbane, Australia

Auckland, New Zealand

Wellington, New Zealand

Christchurch, New Zealand

Calgary, Canada
Vancouver, Canada

Ottawa, Canada
Montreal, Canada

Toronto, Canada

Scotts Corners, ME, U.S.A.
Halifax, Canada

Salt Lake City, UT, U.S.A.

Chicago, IL, U.S.A.

New York, NY, U.S.A.
Red Lion, PA, U.S.A.
Washington, DC, U.S.A.

San Francisco, CA, U.S.A.
Redwood City, CA, U.S.A.
Delano, CA, U.S.A.
Los Angeles, CA, U.S.A.

Noblesville, IN, U.S.A.
Cincinnati, OH, U.S.A.

Nashville, TN, U.S.A.
Greenville, NC, U.S.A.
Cypress Creek, SC, U.S.A.
Atlanta, GA, U.S.A.
New Orleans, LA, U.S.A.
Okeechobee, FL, U.S.A.
Miami, FL, U.S.A.

Dallas, TX, U.S.A.

Havana, Cuba

México City, Mexico

Managua, Nicaragua

Bonaire, Netherlands Antilles
Caracas, Venezuela
Maturín, Venezuela
Georgetown, Guyana
Paramaribo, Surinam
Cayenne, French Guiana
Montsinéry, French Guiana

Maracaibo, Venezuela
Mérida, Venezuela
Bogotá, Colombia
Cali, Colombia

Quito, Ecuador
Iquitos, Peru

Belem, Brazil
Manaus, Brazil
Recife, Brazil

Pucallpa, Peru

Pôrto Velho, Brazil

Lima, Peru
Cuzco, Peru
Arequipa, Peru
La Paz, Bolivia
Santa Cruz, Bolivia
Sucre, Bolivia
Calama, Chile
Asunción, Paraguay

Cuiabá, Brazil

Salvador, Brazil
Brasília, Brazil

Goiânia, Brazil
Belo Horizonte, Brazil
Rio de Janeiro, Brazil
São Paulo, Brazil
Curitiba, Brazil
Foz do Iguaçú, Brazil
Florianópolis, Brazil
Pôrto Alegre, Brazil
Santa Fé, Argentina
Montevideo, Uruguay
Buenos Aires, Argentina
Córdoba, Argentina
Viedma, Argentina

Tahiti, French Polynesia

Santiago, Chile

Coyhaique, Chile

Base Esperanza, Antarctica

Murdo, Antarctica

+11 +12 −11 −10 −9 −8 −7 −6 −5 −3 −2

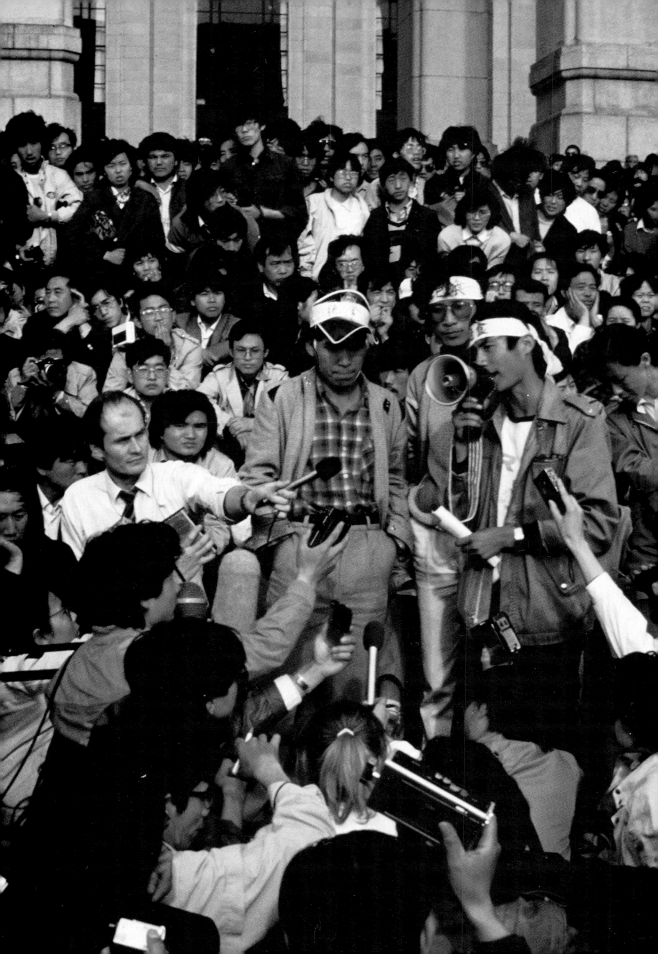

TEN OF THE BEST: TOP SHOWS FOR 1992

What's a good program? Why is it better than others of its kind? How can you fairly compare a discussion on Islam with a concert of Mozart?

Our answer: Select a broad range of programs from which can be chosen ten of the best that include one or more of the following attributes:

- Quality of production
- Sustained listener interest
- Superior program content
- Originality
- Style

Additionally, each year we give slight emphasis to a certain category. This year, it's news and information, since there's more of that on the air these days.

Some of the shows selected are of exceptionally high quality, offering material rarely—if ever—found elsewhere. Herein lies one of the big advantages of world band radio: the unparalleled choice of news, music and other types of entertainment.

So, here are ten of the best shows around. Check through the list, then enjoy!

"Focus"
Voice of America

The VOA has often been accused of being a propaganda outlet for official American policy. No wonder: For years it has carried editorials which "reflect the views of the United States government."

No question, some of what it airs appears to be biased in favor of the official American point of view. But that's some programs. More than anything else, these perceived biases reflect the Voice's attempts to act in accordance with its Charter—a dubious document long overdue for replacement.

But Charter or no Charter, the "Voice" still offers programs of the highest journalistic standards, and which are interesting, to boot. Right up there with the best is *Focus*.

> ## Law or no law, on world band you can legally tune in the VOA.

Comparable to the BBC World Service's *The World Today*, but better. A full 20 minutes are devoted to analyzing any one of a number of contemporary issues, at home or abroad, with ample exposure of contrasting points of view.

Topics cover a wide range of themes, from Western aid for Eastern Europe to the role of women in the American armed forces.

Americans, take note: The Charter that governs the VOA requires that it is not broadcast to Americans. The idea is that this would give the Government too much influ-

---

Wherever there's news, there's the BBC. Correspondent Mark Brayne reports on-the-spot from Beijing's Tian'anmen Square.

ence over citizens' minds. Some Americans think this means their radios can't tune in the Voice, or it's illegal to hear.

No way. As with much legislation, high-sounding rhetoric—and the Charter is Mom's apple pie from top to bottom—has been unencumbered by reality. Law or no law, on world band you can legally tune in the VOA loud and clear—even Congress hasn't found a way to overturn the rules of ionospheric physics. And since you're paying for it, you should.

Focus is broadcast to the Caribbean—also audible in parts of North America—at 1110 World Time, Monday through Saturday, on 6030 (winter) or 15120 (summer), 9590, and 11915 kHz; and to Central and South America Tuesday through Saturday at 0210 on 5995, 9775, 9815, 11580 and 15205 kHz. This broadcast is also well heard in many parts of North America.

Listeners in East Asia and the Pacific may tune in at 1310, Monday through Friday, or Saturday at 1110 on 9760, 15155 and 15425 kHz; additional frequencies 5985, 6110 and 11715 kHz are also available for the 1110 broadcast.

Europeans can hear the program Sundays at 1510 on 15260 kHz.

"Dateline"
Swiss Radio International

It would be unfair to compare directly a news-based program from a medium-sized broadcaster to a similar program from one of the international giants.

Or would it? *Dateline*, SRI's weekday offering to the world, may not have the news gathering or analytical resources of the BBC or Voice of America, but it is near the top of the league when it comes to reliability and professionalism.

> SRI produces the best coverage anywhere of war-torn backwaters.

Experienced Swiss observers give their views not only on major world stories, but also some you would otherwise rarely hear about—in Africa, for example. In part, this may be because the International Committee of the Red Cross has its headquarters in Switzerland. In any event, SRI produces the

best coverage anywhere of events in Ethiopia, Somalia, and other war-torn backwaters otherwise all but ignored by the major Western media.

A combination of information and knowledgeable opinion on a wide variety of topics allows *Dateline* to maintain a consistently high quality. *Dateline* comes on right after the news, roughly eight minutes into the broadcast, and continues until the end of the transmission 20 minutes later. The Saturday edition is shorter, and unfortunately the show isn't aired Sundays.

Listeners in Europe can tune in at 0738 and 2008 World Time on 3985, 6165 and 9535 kHz; also at 1308 on 6165, 9535 and 12030 kHz, as well as at 2238 on 6190 kHz. All times are one hour earlier in summer.

North Americans do best at 0408 on 6135, 9650, 9885 and 12035 kHz, but people living in the South and along the East Coast also have a good opportunity two hours earlier (at 0208) on the same frequencies, plus 6125 and 17730 kHz.

For Australia and parts of East Asia, try 0838 World Time on 9560, 13685, 17670 and 21695 kHz, and at 1108 on 13635, 15570, 17830 and 21770 kHz. Listeners in East Asia can also tune in at 1338, via the Beijing relay, on 7480 and 11695 kHz.

"Science in Action"
BBC World Service

One of the ten programs selected for the 1990 edition of *Passport* was the BBC World Service's *Discovery*. At the time, we referred to it as being "the best science program on radio." It still is. That having been said, we cannot praise too highly its sister program, *Science in Action*.

Variety abounds, with an unbelievable range of topics. The information is concise without being superficial, and the no-frills presentation is easily digestible. The 30-minute program can include just about any scientific or technological topic. One edition started with an item on how trench digging in the desert causes dust storms, then moved on to how ultraviolet filters protect historic paintings, before leaping off on a tangent to discuss the speeding up of enzyme production. The program ended with a talk on computer-aided medicine.

Science in Action is the broadcasting equivalent of stuffing a quart into a pint pot, and doing it superbly.

The Tradition Continues...
FT-990 HF All-Mode Transceiver

The benchmark from which all other HF all-mode transceivers are judged was set with the introduction of the FT-1000. Now, the tradition continues.

Features and Options:

- **High Dynamic Range:** Unsurpassed RF circuit design with quad FET first mixer similar to the FT-1000.

- **Dual Digital Switched Capacitance Filter:** The FT-990 is the **only** HF transceiver to feature a SCF with independent hi/lo-cut controls for skirt selectivity providing unmatched audio reception as never before attained.

- **Built-in Convenience:** Unlike the competition's extras the FT-990 was designed as a true self-contained base station. A switching AC power supply is built-in.

- **CPU Controlled RF FSP (RF Frequency-Shifted Speech Processor):** The RF FSP shifts the SSB carrier point by programming a CPU to change audio frequency response and provide optimum speech processing effect.

- **Dual-VFO's with Direct Digital Synthesis (DDS)**
- **Full and Semi Break-in CW Operation**
- **6 Function Multimeter**
- **Adjustable RF Power**
- **Adjustable Level Noise Blanker**
- **90 Memories**
- **Multimode Selection on Packet/RTTY**
- **Front Panel RX Antenna Selection**

- **Digital Voice Storage DVS-2 Option**
- **Band Stacking VFO System**

- **Accessories/Options:** TCXO-2 (Temperature Compensated Crystal Oscillator), XF-10.9M-202-01 (2nd IF SSB Narrow 2.0kHz), XF-445C-251-01 (3rd IF CW Narrow 250Hz), SP-6 (External Speaker), MD1C8 (Desk Microphone), YH-77ST (Headphones), LL-5 (Phone Patch Module).

YAESU
Performance without compromise.℠

Each Christmas since 1952, the Queen has spoken to her subjects and the world—a tradition dating back to 1932 with King George V. You can hear it over the BBC World Service.

In Europe, *Science in Action* can be heard Fridays at 1615 on 6195, 9410 and 12095 kHz; with a repeat at 2030 on 3955, 6195, 7325 and 9410 kHz. There is a second repeat Sunday morning at 1001 on 5975, 6045, 9750, 12095 and 15070 kHz. Canadian and American listeners can tune in Fridays at 1615 on 9515 (winter), 11775 (summer) and 15260 kHz. The program is beamed to East Asia Fridays at 2030 on 7180 and 15340 kHz, and Sundays at 1001 on 21715 kHz. Australians should listen Fridays at 2030 on 11750 and 15340 kHz.

"Music from China"
Radio Beijing

Just because something is exotic to hear doesn't necessarily mean it's enjoyable. But with Radio Beijing's distinctive *Music from China*, the pleasure's there in spades. Although each individual show is dedicated to the music of one particular type, or from one specific area of China, the regular listener is exposed to a healthy variety of musical styles and instruments.

From traditional Chinese opera to modern compositions played on old Tibetan instruments, there is something for everyone. And what could be more exotic than the two-string erhu, or the horse-bone fiddle?

Music from China is broadcast Saturdays in the listening area, and can be heard during the final 20 minutes of transmission. The actual length of the program varies, but is usually 15-18 minutes long.

Europeans can tune in around 2035 or 2135 on 7315 (winter), 11500 (summer) and 9920 kHz; and again at 2235 on 7170 (winter) and 9740 or 11990 (summer) kHz.

There is no broadcast for East Asia as such, only for Southeast Asia. There, tune in 9670 and 11660 kHz (also try 15285 kHz) at 1235 and 1335 World Time. People in Australia and the South Pacific have four opportunities to enjoy the program—at 0935 and 1035 on 11755, 15440 and 17710 kHz; at 1235 on 11600 and 15450 kHz; and at 1335 on 11600 kHz.

North Americans can hear the broadcast Sundays (Saturday evening in their part of the world) at approximately 0035 on 9770 and 11715, replaced summer by 15285 and 17705 kHz; at 0335 on 9690, 9770 (winter), 11715, and 15285 (summer) kHz; and at 0435 on 11695 (winter) or 11685 (summer) kHz. Listeners in Western North America have an additional transmission on 11840 kHz, summers at 0400 and winters at 0500. Saturday mornings, it's on at 1200 to Eastern North America on 9665 (winter) or 17855 (summer) kHz. To the West Coast winter at 1400, and again at 1500, on 7405 kHz; and summer at 1300, and again at 1400, on 11855 kHz.

"Encounter"
Voice of America

Here is one of the most balanced discussion programs around. The participants, apart from the host, are invariably two highly qualified persons, with lengthy experience in their respective professions. Well-known ex-politicians, bureau chiefs of foreign newspapers, erudite academics—all have been featured at one time or another.

> "Encounter" is not the Oprah Winfrey Show. Discussions are refreshing and civilized.

The topic under discussion—one to each 20-minute program—is always related to a major issue of interest to the United States, or even to the world in general.

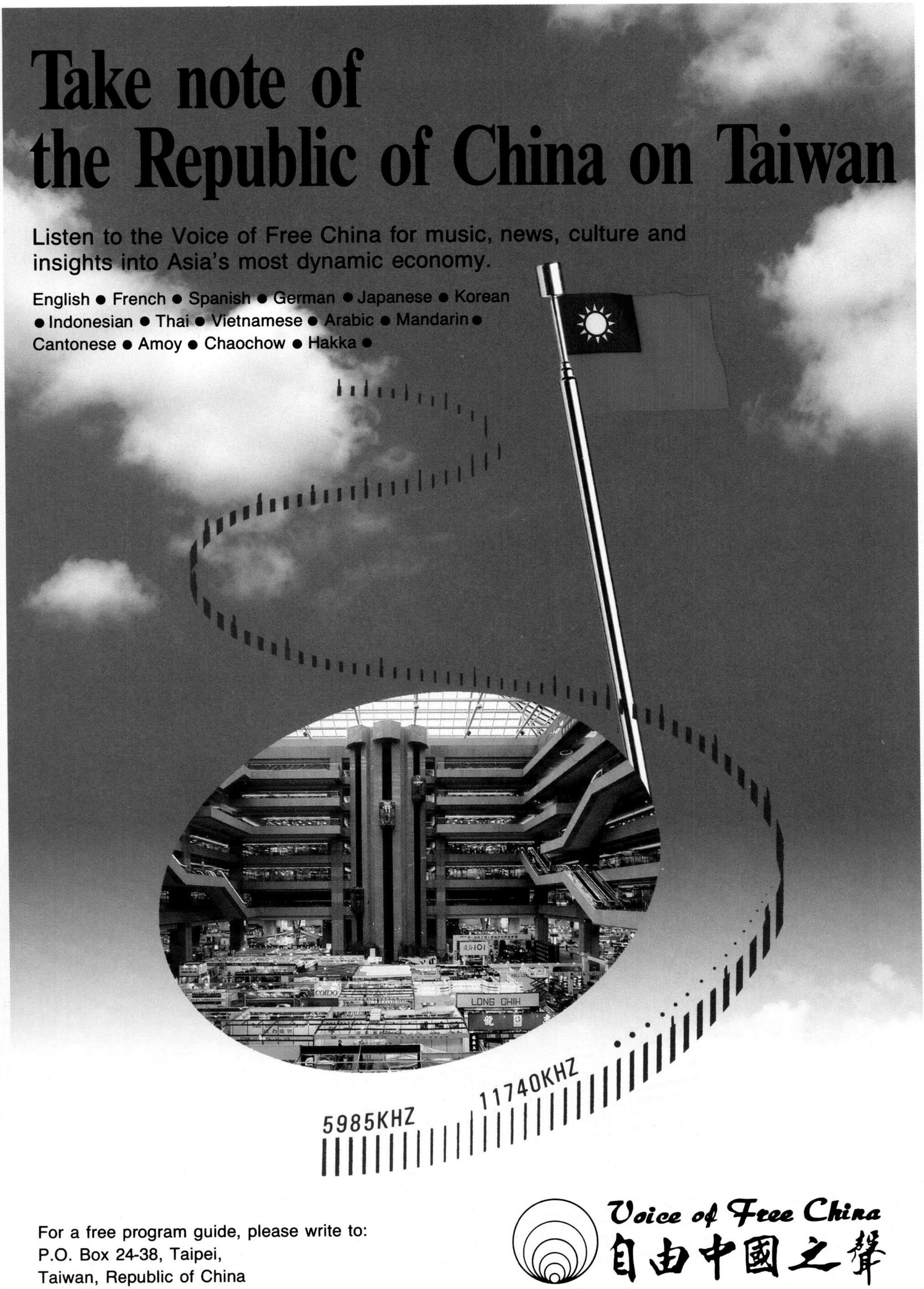

Germany's Deutsche Welle reports on more than politics and conflicts. The Bastei region of Saxony is known not only for its tourist attractions, but also for its special health facilities.

This is not the Oprah Winfrey Show. Discussions are not "pro and con." Rather, they are detailed, collective and learned assessments. And rarely, if ever, does the process degenerate into babbling *ad alta voce*.

Refreshing and civilized.

Encounter is beamed to Europe at 1810 Sundays on 6040, 9760, 11760 and 15205 kHz. Australians can try six hours earlier, at 1210, on 11715 kHz; while listeners in East Asia can also tune in at that time on 9760 and 15155 kHz.

For the Caribbean and South America, as well as much of North America, there is a broadcast at 0010 Mondays (Sunday evening in the Americas) on 5995, 6130, 9455, 9775, 9815, 11695, 11580 and 15205 kHz.

"Research File"
Radio Nederland

The BBC's science programs may be packed with detail, but Radio Nederland's make for easier listening. At its best when devoted to a single subject, *Research File* is part science, part documentary in its presentation.

Outstanding in its treatment of the social sciences, the program excels when handling such topics as gerontology. Not that there isn't any material for the purist. On the contrary, there's something for everyone, although not necessarily in the same weekly program. Astronomy, space exploration, psychology, pollution, medicine, and even scientific ethics all get covered from time to time. All in all, a very good listen, despite inane station jingles worthy of a Sixties "Top Forty" station.

Research File can be heard in Europe at 1152 and 1452 Mondays on 5955 kHz, with the earlier broadcast also being available on 9715 kHz. For listeners in East and Southeast Asia, there are two opportunities to enjoy the program—Mondays at 0852 on 17575 and 21485 kHz, and again three hours later on 17575, 21480 and 21520 kHz. Australians are best served at 0752 on 9630 and 9715 (or 15560) kHz, at 0852 on 9630 kHz, and at 0952 on 11895 kHz.

For Eastern North America, listen Tuesday (Monday evening local time) at 0052 on 6020, 6165 and 11740 (or 15560) kHz; out west, it's three hours later, at 0352 on 6165 and 9590 (or 11720) kHz.

(continued on page 62)

HF-225

Your Gateway to the World

Rugged, reliable, regarded by many as the best receiver they ever used, the HF-225 has shown that there is a new way to provide the listener with all he wants, but without confusing him with a hundred colored buttons and knobs. The HF-225 is technology tamed by the application of common sense. So—what do you get for your money?

High stability, low noise performance, coupled to accurate digital readout for on-the-nose station location.

All filters fitted for every mode—2.2 kHz, 4 kHz, 7 kHz, 10 kHz, as well as a 200 Hz audio filter for CW. No extras to buy.

30 memory channels for your favorite frequencies, with instant access and instant check facilities.

Hot options include a true synchronous AM detector for combatting those deep fades (it also gives you narrow band FM reception as well); an active whip antenna for portable use, and a handsome, rugged carrying case; a battery pack which fits inside the radio; and a keypad for direct frequency entry, about which Larry Magne had this to say:

". . . there's no fooling around with 'enter' keys, 'kHz' keys, leading zeros, decimals—or any of the time wasters found on other keypads. It is, hands down, the best keypad available on any set, regardless of price."

Chris Williams agreed with Larry when he wrote from Massachusetts:

"As a past owner of receivers such as the Sony ICF-2010 and Grundig Satellit 650 and 500, I must say that none compare to your Lowe HF-225. Without question, for hour after hour listening, nothing compares. I especially like the keypad. Why more receivers do not incorporate such intelligent ergonomics is beyond me."

That just about says it all, but in addition to the praise from users, the HF-225 was voted "Receiver of the Year" by World Radio and TV Handbook.

Write now, and find out how the HF-225 can open your own "Gateway to the World."

WHO SAYS YOU CAN'T TAKE IT WITH YOU WHEN YOU GO.
W/MW/SHORT WAVE/PLL SYNTHESIZED RECEIVER
ATS 818
LIGHT
POWER
FM 87.5-108 MHz
MW 520-1620 kHz
LW 150-519 kHz
SW 1621-29999 kHz
102.10 MHz
SLEEP
TIME SET
DUAL TIME
FM
MW
LW
SW
MANUAL / AUTO
DIRECT ACCESS
METER
FREQ
STANDBY
ENTER
STANDBY
BUZZER
RADIO
AM NARR
FM MONO
FM STEREO
AM WIDE
BFO
ON
OFF
TONE
LOW
HIGH
MIN
MAX
A WORLD OF LISTENING

Sangean Portables.
Get away from it all and still
stay in touch.

Whether traveling around the world or across town, Sangean portables keep you informed. Tune into international broadcasters or wake up to your favorite morning DJ, wherever you are. There's no need to leave it all behind, because Sangean goes where you go. . .and further.

Multiple Band. Multiple Choice.

From the full featured ATS-818CS Digital Receiver with programmable built-in cassette recorder, to the world's most popular digital receiver, our highly acclaimed ATS-803A, Sangean's complete line of full featured analog and digital receivers offer the utmost in reliability and performance at a price just right for your budget.

To fully understand the
difference between us and them. . .
just listen.

Only Sangean offers you the features and advanced technology of a high priced communication receiver at a portable price. Features like; PLL Tuning for rock steady short wave listening, tuneable BFO for single sideband reception, dual displayed time systems, up to

45 presets, AM/FM/FM Stereo in addition to all short wave bands, continuously tuneable receivers, snooze/sleep timers, auto-scan and manual tuning, as well as a host of additional features making Sangean the most popular choice of short wave enthusiasts.

All models carry the standard Sangean 1 full year warranty of quality and workmanship; the signature of a company recognized throughout the world as a pioneer and leader in the design and development of multi-band portable radios.

Sangean portables, somehow with them the world seems a little bit smaller.

Call or write for more information.

SANGEAN
AMERICA, INC.
A World Of Listening

2651 Troy Avenue, South El Monte, California 91733
(818) 579-1600   FAX: (818) 579-6806

CRISIS LISTENING

When the Mulch Hits the Ventilator: Getting the Most Out of Your World Band Radio When It Counts

"I found *Passport* very helpful here in Saudi Arabia. Despite the ravings about CNN, shortwave's variety and depth are unbeatable."

—*Capt. Bill Hoadley, 552d AWAC Wing*

Like a big rock dropped in a small pond, the antics of the Baghdad Bandito produced many after-shocks. One was a new awareness of world band radio among the American public.

Where world band radio was once thought to be the preserve of the hobbyist and geopolitically hip, it seemed suddenly everyone wanted one. The sales curve went ballistic, from a respectable 20-25 annual percent to the track of an Atlas-Agena rocket. Smaller Radio Shack dealers, accustomed to selling a single world band radio a month, suddenly sold one a day.

To the cognoscenti, it was no surprise. Between Iraq's annexation of Kuwait and the start of allied bombing, TV told time and again of those who had escaped Kuwait, who in turn told time and again that "the only way we knew what was really going on was the BBC on shortwave."

When the bombing started, it didn't take long to see the similarity in coverage by ABC, NBC and CBS, and that CNN was offering virtually unprocessed information. Not that television news did a bad job, but many people, harkening back to the Vietnam experience, wanted more. They wanted a fresh perspective, a different slant—a variety of information and viewpoints.

> **The only way we knew what was really going on was on shortwave.**

With 1,100 channels available and 150 countries on the air—many with English-language broadcasting—world band radio puts unprecedented power in the hands of an ordinary citizen who wants news in a crisis. Think of it! Suddenly, you are the editor, free to call on a far-flung network of correspondents as you see fit. The challenge is picking the juiciest fruit in this delightful information orchard.

Kuwait's oilfields ablaze. The Gulf conflict was the most recent and dramatic example of how world band radio provides the most comprehensive and varied news during a crisis.

NASA

21

Deutsche Welle

The Berlin Wall has been demolished, but Germany's Deutsche Welle carries daily reports on the much tougher struggle of rebuilding eastern Germany.

Three basic strategies will serve you well in crisis listening: pick your time, pick your target, and scan the airwaves. That's why *Passport's* Worldscan section is arranged in these three ways.

Pick Your Time

If you're like most of us and have other concerns—friends, family, work—picking your listening time is a matter of simple practicality.

If 9 PM is when the kids have settled in for the night and the dog has enjoyed his constitutional, set aside some time for world band listening. Or perhaps you are an early riser; you may want to listen before the rest of the household stirs. The exact details of when you listen aren't critical. What matters is that you pick a time, and back it up with some research.

Research? You bet. In *Passport's* Worldscan section, you'll find the "pick your time" portion is "What's On Tonight," an hour-by-hour listing of world band programs in English.

It's About Time

Remember, *Passport* uses Universal Coordinated Time (UTC), just as do world band stations. UTC is also known as Greenwich Mean Time (GMT), Zulu time, or World Time, a convenient reference keyed to the Greenwich meridian in England and given in a 24-hour mode, like military time. With World Time, a world band broadcaster can announce, "It's now 2300 hours," meaning it is one hour before midnight on the Greenwich meridian. That ends worry about what time it is in the listeners' various local time zones.

You need to know World Time to make sense of *Passport's* listings, and it's explained in "Getting Started with World Band Radio" elsewhere in this book. If you need to

(continued on page 66)

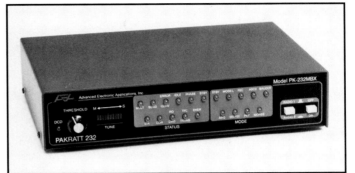

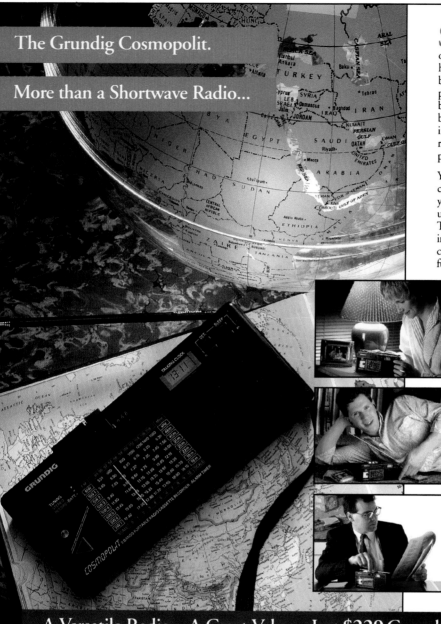

The Grundig Cosmopolit.

More than a Shortwave Radio...

Sure to be the last item you pack, and the first unpacked at home or abroad, the Grundig Cosmopolit has more than enough features to become a required traveling companion. It receives 7 shortwave bands along with AM/FM stereo broadcasts with crisp LED-set tuning, plays your favorite cassettes and records with its built-in microphone, or right off the airwaves.

You can preset the engineered-in clock/timer to start the recording so you won't miss a note, or wake you up for the early morning newscast. The controls have been designed into the top for easy and precise control of the Grundig's many functions.

Rise and Shine... Easily set clock/timer feature allows wake-up to radio, cassette, or alarm; or presetting a recording time for a favorite broadcast. This talking Grundig will even "tell" you the time, or let you "snooze".

All-Round Sound... Learn a new language from tapes or relax with your favorite sounds, The Cosmopolit's stereo headphones keep your tunes to yourself. Cassette features include pause, auto stop, and 3-digit tape counter.

On the Go... The Cosmopolit's cassette features allow you to make verbal notes or dictate an entire manuscript, anywhere you are.
Standard cassette format makes transcription or review easy on any cassette player.

A Versatile Radio.   A Great Value.   Just $229 Complete.

GETTING STARTED WITH WORLD BAND RADIO

Yes, world band radio gives you more perspectives on and news about world events than any other medium. And, yes, there's a greater variety of unusual entertainment and even certain sports than you'll find on ordinary radio or television.

But world band usually doesn't just pop in like ordinary stations. It takes some effort and understanding if you're going to coax the best out of what it has to offer.

What is World Band Radio?

World band is actually just another broadcasting range, like the mediumwave AM and FM bands you're used to. In fact, world band is right between them, in terms of wavelength. If you could tune your AM radio above 1600 kHz, you'd eventually run into it.

There are two main differences. Regular AM and FM stations cannot be heard worldwide, and they use the same channels year in and year out. World band, of course, covers the globe, and its stations change channels—frequencies—much more often.

There's another difference, too: time. World band uses a special worldwide time standard, not a hodgepodge of local times. The box in this article explains this "must" subject.

Finding Your Way Around

World band radio uses 13 groups—"segments," or "bands"—of frequencies within the shortwave portion of the radio spectrum. Shortwave goes long distance, taking music, news and entertainment around the world on a regular basis, although with only Spartan audio fidelity. With a world band radio, it's possible—in fact common—to have a simultaneous choice among stations from London, Moscow, Beijing, Paris, Boston, Berlin or Jerusalem.

The frequencies used by world band stations are measured in either *kiloHertz* (kHz) or *MegaHertz* (MHz). A MegaHertz is equal to 1000 kiloHertz, so 9.58 MHz is the same as 9580 kHz.

> In most cases, operating a world band radio requires only three steps.

You'll hear world band stations announce frequencies both ways, but *Passport* uses only kHz, for uniformity. Some advanced radio sets display the frequency to one-tenth or even one-hundredth of a kHz, but that's splitting hairs. Scientists may need it; you won't.

Hirosaki Park in Aomori is famous for its 5,000 cherry trees. Each spring, people party under the blossoms to mark winter's end. Radio Japan is there to cover the celebrations.

SECRET FREQUENCIES

Why waste valuable time manually twisting that frequency dial looking for interesting transmissions when your computer can do it for you with RCSS™?

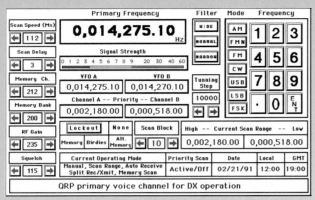

RCSS™ enables full computer control of receiver microprocessor functions through the intuitive graphic user interface shown above. It can be simply operated by keyboard or mouse. RCSS™ runs on IBM compatible and Macintosh computers. The NEW IBM version 4.0 is shown above. Upgrades are available to registered users, call for details. A demo disk is also available.

RCSS™ (Remote Computer Scanning System) takes full control of your radio and automatically scans the airwaves in search of those interesting "secret" transmissions. When a signal is found, RCSS™ automatically logs an entry in the database that includes the frequency, date, time of day, and the length of transmission. Other information may also be added to the record such as class of service, type of unit, callsign, city, and other comments.

RCSS™ can run automatically while you work, sleep, or watch the game on TV. When you return, RCSS™ diligently reports on all receiver activity that was found while you were away, enabling you to choose from among those interesting frequencies for listening. Or, if you prefer, add any standard tape recorder to automatically record the transmissions that RCSS™ finds.

RCSS™ connects to ICOM's R71A, R7000, R9000 and SASI's Seeker-301 receivers for operation. Software, interface and all required cables are included. RCSS™ is the oldest software available of its type (4-years old). It is currently in use in 15 countries and being used by individuals, private corporations and Government agencies.

Seeker 301
A full featured wideband receiver on a half-slot PC card

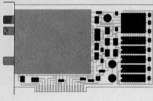

Seeker 301-I
Half-Slot Wideband Receiver compatible with XT and AT busses

Seeker 301-E
External Wideband Receiver for connection to desktop or portables

The Seeker-301 is a wideband receiver mounted on a half-slot PC card. It comes in an internal version (301-I) mounted inside an IBM compatible, and an external version (301-E) convenient for use with portables. RCSS™ software provides full control of Seeker-301 receiver functions.

The Seeker-301 is a rugged field proven receiver with high parametric performance. Frequency coverage is from 100 kHz to 1.3 GHz in FM, AM and SSB options. Its excellent selectivity makes it ideal for use in areas with heavy RF traffic. Connections are provided for antenna (TNC), external audio (RCA) and IF output (BNC). The 301-E also has volume and squelch controls and an RS-232 (DB9) connector for connection to a serial port.

OEMs, Distributors and Government Agencies Take Note:

Both RCSS™ and Seeker can be customized, modified or re-engineered for special applications. A custom labeling program is available for re-marketing. Ruggedized versions are available for field use. Special projects are welcome.

Systems & Software International is a small business and manufactures all equipment in the USA. Please contact us at:
4639 Timber Ridge Drive, Dumfries, Virginia, 22026-1059, USA; (703) 680-3559; Fax (703) 878-1460; Compuserve 74065,1140

THE BEST OF BOTH WORLDS.

The pacesetting IC-R9000 truly reflects ICOM's long-term commitment to excellence. This single-cabinet receiver covers both local area VHF/UHF and worldwide MF/HF bands. It's a natural first choice for elaborate communications centers, professional service facilities and serious home setups alike. Test-tune ICOM's IC-R9000 and experience a totally new dimension in top-of-the-line receiver performance!

Complete Communications Receiver. Covers 100KHz to 1999.8MHz, all modes, all frequencies! The general coverage IC-R9000 receiver uses 11 separate bandpass filters in the 100KHz to 30MHz range and precise-tuned bandpass filters with low noise GaAsFETs in VHF and upper frequency bands. Exceptionally high sensitivity, intermod immunity and frequency stability in all ranges.

Multi-Function Five Inch CRT. Displays frequencies, modes, memory contents, operator-entered notes and function menus. Features a subdisplay area for printed modes such as RTTY, SITOR and PACKET (external T.U. required).

Spectrum Scope. Indicates all signal activities within a +/-25, 50 or 100KHz range of your tuned frequency. It's ideal for spotting random signals that pass unnoticed with ordinary monitoring receivers.

1000 Multi-Function Memories. Store frequencies, modes, and tuning steps. Includes an editor for moving contents between memories, plus an on-screen notepad for all memory locations.

Eight Scanning Modes. Includes programmable limits, automatic frequency and time-mark storage of scanned signals, full, restricted or mode-selected memory scanning, priority channel watch, voice-sense scanning and scanning a selectable width around your tuned frequency. Absolutely the last word in full spectrum monitoring.

Professional Quality Throughout. The revolutionary IC-R9000 features IF Shift, IF Notch, a fully adjustable noise blanker, and more. The Direct Digital Synthesizer assures the widest dynamic range, lowest noise and rapid scanning. Designed for dependable long-term performance. Backed by a full one-year warranty at any one of ICOM's four North American Service Centers!

First in Communications

ICOM America, Inc., 2380-116th Ave. N.E., Bellevue, WA 98004
Customer Service Hotline (206) 454-7619
3150 Premier Drive, Suite 126, Irving, TX 75063 /
1777 Phoenix Parkway, Suite 201, Atlanta, GA 30349
ICOM CANADA, A Division of ICOM America, Inc.,
3071 - #5 Road, Unit 9, Richmond, B.C. V6X 2T4 Canada
All stated specifications are subject to change without notice or obligation. All ICOM radios significantly exceed FCC regulations limiting spurious emissions. 9000489

World band stations can't operate just anywhere within the radio spectrum—chaos would result. Flip through the Blue Pages of *Passport*, and you'll see the answer: most stations are spaced exactly five kHz apart. For example, look at the 15100 to 15600 kHz listings. Typically, stations use frequencies ending in zero or five. The pattern holds in other ranges, too: 5950 to 6200, 7100 to 7300, 9500 to 9900, 11650 to 12050, and 13600 to 13800 kHz.

Advanced world band receivers boast digital frequency display, but old-technology models are *analog*, or slide-rule tuned. The two compare something like digital and conventional clocks. If your radio is analog, finding the station you want takes trial and error. Patience and practice help the analog owner, but digital frequency readout is essential if you value your time. There are, after all, some *1,100* world band channels from which to choose, and finding your way through this thicket is far easier and quicker with digital readout.

Bells and Whistles

Today's world band radios pack an array of knobs and buttons, sliders and switches into a remarkably compact space. The owner's manual should describe your set's controls. However, here's a list of the more common ones. Yours may not have them all, or it may have more.

> Signals are often strongest during your local prime-time evening hours. Nevertheless, there is a wealth of choices during the day.

–**Digital frequency display.** If your radio has a digital readout, it shows the exact frequency the radio is tuned to, either in kHz or MHz. Some display to the nearest kHz, as in 9580 kHz, while others display fractional frequencies, as in 9580.5 kHz.

The Voice of America's talented announcer Leo Sarkasian is also a renowned artist of African scenes. Shown, tribal women dancing in Voinjama, Liberia.

Leo Sarkasian

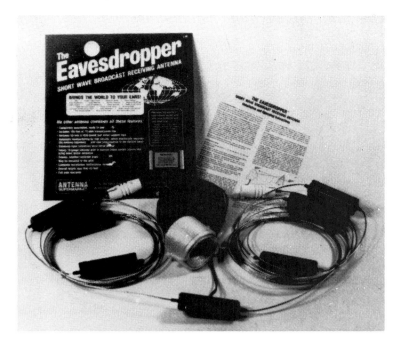

–Tuning knob. No mystery here. Turn it until the frequency of the station you want to hear shows on the display. Or browse through *Passport's* Blue Pages and go "fishing."

Instead of a tuning knob, a few radios have *slewing* controls—elevator-like up/down buttons for tuning. Slewing buttons are fine for your TV or VCR, with reasonably limited channels. But for the vastness of world band radio, slew tuning is a lackluster substitute for a conventional tuning knob.

–Tuning keypad. This works much like the keypad on a Touch-Tone telephone or calculator. Punch in the frequency you want, tap the *enter* or *execute* key, and the radio instantly finds the frequency. For example, if you want 9580 kHz, you would typically press 9-5-8-0, and execute.

Not all keypads operate exactly this way. As most world band stations are on frequencies ending in either zero or five, a few keypads allow only frequencies ending in zero or five. If you try to enter a frequency like 9582 kHz, you'll get either an error message on the display, or a truncated frequency such as 9580 kHz. A handful of models confuse things, making you fiddle with an *AM* key or some other control before entering a frequency. There are other variations, too.

–BFO or SSB control. Single sideband (SSB) is a transmission mode that's used by amateur radio operators and utility stations that operate near world band frequencies. Few world band stations use SSB, so in general it's a good idea to leave this control off or, on some models, set to AM.

–Bandwidth (Wide/Narrow) control. For best audio, leave this in the *wide* position. If there's annoying interference from other stations, try *narrow*. A few top-class radios, mainly tabletop models, offer more than two bandwidths.

–Sensitivity, or attenuator, control. You can often hear weak stations better, and stronger stations with less hiss, by setting this to *high*—or *normal* or *DX*, depending on the manufacturer's nomenclature. However, under certain conditions the high position may cause strong stations to *overload* the radio, resulting in a babble of false signals that dims listening pleasure. In such cases, which with better radios are not common, the *local* position can help.

(continued on page 70)

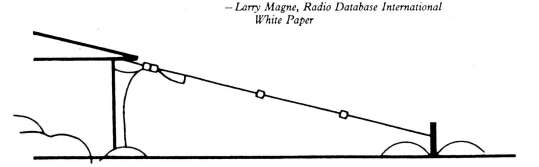

1992'S WINNERS: 20+ BIG SIGNALS

What a year it's been! World band is more popular than ever in some Western countries, and increasingly important in the Middle East. Yet, with the end of the Cold War, world band audiences in much of the former Soviet Bloc are declining, at least for now. The result is we're in the midst of the most exciting period of shuffling, scrambling and changing in decades. Languages, times, budgets—everything is up for grabs.

Of course, with any big change there are winners and losers. A few major operations, such as Radio France Internationale and the BBC World Service, appear to see the decline of Cold War concerns as an opportunity to become mainstream news sources that cut across a wide swath of national, social and class lines. These stations are expanding.

Winning audiences is today's coin of success.

Others, such as Radio Prague, face budgetary contractions, and so have had to cut back on the number of broadcasting hours. Yet, through heads-up administration they've actually managed to become more interesting, easier to hear, or both. A handful—notably Radio Canada International, Israel Radio and RTV Belge—clobbered by severe budgetary cutbacks, bide their time in low gear while working on more satisfactory longer-term solutions.

Those stations know how to respond. Others, looking painfully like tomorrow's losers, are already starting to fade away. A few have shuffled their schedules, only to make things worse. An even larger number plod along as before, watching opportunities and support trickle away—hoping that somehow new technology will rescue them from the need for better management, audience-oriented programs, and wider publicity of what they have to offer.

There is little sign that this ferment is going to let up soon, and it shouldn't. Too many stations continue to operate as if their programs are beamed to their paymasters and some vague "elite" listenership, with catering to broader audience interests being beneath their mandarin dignity. Still, a number of these are at least beginning to give lip service to the concept of democracy inherent in being attuned to audience desires. Whether this is a harbinger of change, or just resistance to change playing for time, remains to be seen.

Yet, the handwriting is up and change is in the air. Stations that excel in programming and quality of delivery do win audiences—and winning audiences is today's coin of success. Broadcasting isn't narrowcasting, and from the BBC World Service onwards, increasingly the word from the top is to reach as many people as pos-

---

Equador's HCJB is one of the few sources of information on Ecuador and the Andes. Exceptional music, too.

Exclusive Licensee & Distributor of Grundig in USA and Canada
Lextronix, Inc.
P.O. Box 2307
Menlo Park, CA 94026
Tel. (415) 361-1611
1 800-872-2228 (USA)
1 800-637-1648 (Canada)

Germany's Best
World Band Receivers From Grundig

With over 45 years of experience, Grundig stands out as a leader in world band radio. Grundig provides you with the most complete range of products to be found worldwide. At the pinnacle of world band radio resides the undisputed best portable shortwave radio, the Grundig Satellit 650.

Microcomputer controlled, PLL tuning with 1.6–30.0 Mhz coverage, known for exceptional selectivity and image rejection, USB/LSB.

sible, at all levels of society, while improving the quality of programming and working tirelessly on the bottom line. It doesn't hurt that, in so doing, stations become more visible and valuable—more likely to be appreciated by their funding agencies.

> ## Finer programs, clearer signals, better radios—we couldn't ask for more.

On the technical side, one plus has been the increasing use of "swap" relay facilities. For example, when Radio Canada International wished to be heard better in Asia, and Radio Japan wanted to come in more clearly in North America, they agreed to use each other's transmission facilities. Now, if you're listening to Radio Japan in Eastern North America, you're probably hearing it via transmitters located in southeastern Canada. That's why it comes in so well and is cited in this article. For broadcasters, these swaps are the cheapest way to produce a first-class signal over world-class distances.

There are many such improvements taking place at radio stations these days. But there's real improvement at the listening end, too. Just take a look at this year's *Passport* "Buyer's Guide." Radios are getting better and cheaper, and there's no end in sight.

Finer programs, clearer signals, better radios—we couldn't ask for more. So that you can dive into all this, here are 20-odd world band outlets that are among the most likely to give you solid reception.

All times used by international broadcasters, and in this book, are World Time. What's that? Flip the pages to "Getting Started with World Band Radio" elsewhere in this *Passport*. You won't understand much about world band radio until you become familiar with this uncommonly straightforward way of keeping track of time worldwide.

EUROPE
Austria

Despite its limited resources, **Radio Austria International** continues to be heard worldwide with its refreshingly enjoyable half-hour blocks in English. A combination of informative programs and friendly presenta-

tion, plus powerful transmitters, provide 30 minutes of very entertaining listening.

Austria is heard in English to North America at 0130-0200 on 9875 and 13730 kHz; 0530-0600 via the Canadian relay on 6015 kHz; and 1130-1200 on 21490 kHz. Europeans can listen at 0530 (winter), 0730 (summer), 0830 (winter), 1130 and 1430 (year around) and 1630 (summer) on 6155 and 13730 kHz; and at 1730 (winter) and 1930 (year around) on 5945 and 6155 kHz. Asians and Australians should try 0830 (winter) and 1030 (summer) on 15450 and 21490 kHz. If you're in East Asia, best bets are 1130 and 1330 on 15430 kHz.

Belgium

Belgische Radio en Televisie, the voice of Belgium's Dutch-speaking population, reaches Europe, Eastern North America, and often well beyond. From the transmitting site at Wavre, close to Brussels, emanate BRT's 25-minute English broadcasts—a mixed bag of Belgian news and features. Although diverse in style from its counterpart in Vienna, BRT and Radio Austria International are two of the friendliest stations on the air.

BRT is heard Sundays at 1230 in North America on 21810 or 21815 kHz; plus daily at 0030 on 9925 (or 13720) and 13655 (or 13675) kHz. In Europe there are daily broadcasts at 0730 on 6035, 9855 (or 9925) and 13695 kHz; 1830 on 5910 or 13675 kHz; and again at 2200 on 5910 and 9925 kHz. The frequency of 9925 kHz is also audible in parts of Eastern North America. There is an additional transmission at 1000, Monday through Saturday, on 6035 and 9855 (or 9925) kHz.

The 0730 broadcast is also directed to Asia and the Pacific on 11695 or 21815 kHz, and again Monday through Saturday at 1400 on 21810 or 21815 kHz.

All broadcasts are one hour earlier during the summer.

Czechoslovakia

Radio Prague International is yet another friendly station to please the ear. In recent months it has emerged successfully from the chaos which followed the sudden leap towards democracy. The programs have a sleeker presentation and more varied content than before, and easily fill the roughly 30-minute broadcast.

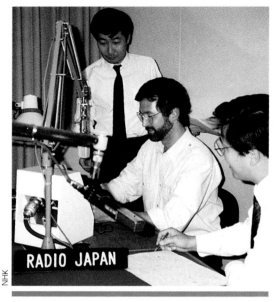

Radio Japan airs top-notch news about Asia. Its economic coverage also makes it a favorite among businessmen.

If you live in North America, tune in at 0000-0030 on 7345, 9540 (11685 summers) and 11990 kHz; and 0100-0130, 0300-0330 and 0400-0430 on 5930, 7345 and 9540 (or 11685) kHz. English is beamed to Europe at 0740-0800, and again at :40 past the hour each hour thereafter until 1300, on 6055, 7345 and 9505 kHz; 1800-1830 on 5930, 6055, 7345 and 9605 kHz; 1930-2000 on 6055 and 9605 kHz; and at 2100-2130 and 2200-2230 on 5930, 6055, 7345 and 9605 kHz (all times are one hour earlier in summer). Listeners in Asia and the Pacific can listen at 0730-0800 on 17840 and 21705 kHz.

France

Radio France Internationale differs from most stations in that its primary aim is to spread French culture and use of the French language. France, after all, was at one time the most powerful nation on earth, and still considers itself to be the most cultured.

Thus, news shares the front seat with these objectives. Absent an overriding importance to disseminate news, RFI feels little need to broadcast in English—even if English has now replaced French as the *lingua franca* of international communication . . . and even though millions of French descent in the United States and elsewhere understand only English.

There was a proposal for an RFI English-language World Service, but this has been put on indefinite hold to avoid France, as one station official put it, "seeming Anglo-Saxon." Indeed, as if to underscore this point, RFI has eliminated its English broadcast to North America evenings, while expanding its operations in other languages.

Whatever the language, though, the level of professionalism at RFI is beyond reproach, and programs are always well prepared. The 55-minute English broadcast for Africa at 1600 has rightfully claimed its place as one of the foremost sources of news and information about a continent otherwise rarely reported on properly.

Too, RFI is in the process of upgrading all its transmitters in continental France to a huge 500 kilowatts each, in addition to installing and improving relays overseas. In the meantime, RFI is still easily audible, notably in French, throughout Europe and much of North America—especially on the North American East Coast.

At Radio France Internationale, programs are always well prepared.

There is one daily English program to Europe and North America, at 1230, but at present it doesn't come in very well in either the United States or Canada. The transmission for Africa and Europe at 1600 is actually better heard in Eastern North America than the one at 1230 nominally beamed there.

At 1230-1300, Europeans can tune in on 9805, 11670, 15155 and 15195 kHz, and North Americans can try listening on 17650, 21635 and 21645 kHz. The 1600-1700 African program is audible in Europe on 6175 kHz, while North American listeners can eavesdrop on 11705, 12015, 15360, 15530, 17620, 17795, 17845 and 17850 kHz. Not all these channels are on the air at any given time—a few are seasonal frequencies.

A transmission to Asia and the Pacific at 1400-1500 is available on 7125 (winter), 11910 (summer), and year-around on 17650 and 21770 kHz.

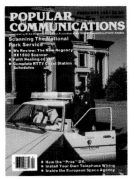

Germany

Deutsche Welle, the official and well-run station of the new united Germany, is easily heard just about anywhere. Not that reception was difficult in the days before unification; it's just that with the additional transmitters inherited from the now-defunct Radio Berlin International there are many more frequencies from which to choose.

Technically speaking, it is possibly the best of all world band broadcasters, and many of its programs are also of the highest standard. Its outlook is similar to that of the BBC World Service: to reach large numbers of listeners, regardless of their ethnic, linguistic or national backgrounds.

Broadcasts to North and Central America can be heard at 0100-0150 on 6040, 6145, 6155, 9565, 11865, 11890, 13610 and 13770 kHz, plus the seasonal frequencies of 6085, 15105, 15425 and 15440 kHz. The first repeat broadcast is at 0300 on 6085, 11890, 13610 and 13770 kHz, with extra winter frequencies being 6040, 6120, 9605 and 15440 kHz. During the summer, these channels are replaced by 6145, 9545, 11810, 15205 and 15245 kHz.

The third and final broadcast goes out at 0500 on 5960, 6120, 9670, 9700 and 13610 kHz. Look for additional seasonal frequencies among 11705, 11890, 11925, 13770, 13790 and 15440 kHz. This slot is best for Western North America.

Surprisingly, there is no specific broadcast in English to Europe, but Deutsche Welle can still be heard by Europeans. In the United Kingdom, reception of 6120 kHz at 0500-0550 is usually excellent. At 0600-0650 try 11765, 13610, 13790 kHz, and in the evening tune in at 1900-1950 on 11810, 13790 and 15350 kHz. Listeners in Asia and the Pacific are catered to at 0900-0950 on 6160, 11915 (or 11740), 17780, 17820, 21465, 21540, 21650 and 21680 kHz; and again at 2100-2150 on 9670, 9765, 11785, 13780 and 15350 kHz.

Holland

Three strategically located transmitter sites—Holland, Madagascar and the Netherlands Antilles—ensure that **Radio Nederland's** punchy signal is reliably heard in most of the station's target areas. Which is as it should be for a station that

Even though Australia doesn't beam to Europe or North America, folks there tune in, anyway. *Passport* readers say Radio Australia is among their favorite stations.

Western Australia Tourist Commission

The United States is still the world's Big Enchilada, and in some respects the Voice of America tells about it better than any other radio or TV station.

provides a fine selection of news and other features. Radio Nederland has long been a favorite with world band listeners, and rightly so. Especially popular is Sunday's refreshing *Happy Station*. This family fun show, complete with barrel-organ music, is the oldest on shortwave, and doesn't contain one minute of news, politics, or doom and gloom.

Radio Nederland is heard well throughout much of North America at 0030-0125 on 6020, 6165 and 11740 (or 15560) kHz; 0330-0425 on 6165 and 9590 (or 11720) kHz; and 1830-1925 on 17605 and 21685 kHz. The 1830 transmission is beamed to Africa, and sometimes contains different programming from what North America hears.

Radio Nederland beams to Europe at 1130-1225 on 5955 and 9715 kHz, and 1430-1525 on 5955 kHz. Best Asian bets are at 0830 on 17575 and 21485 kHz; 1130 on 17575, 21480 and 21520 kHz; and again at 1430 on 13770, 15150, 17575 and 17605 kHz. In the Pacific, try 0730 on 9630 and 9715 (or 15560) kHz; 0830 on 9630 kHz; and 0930 on 11895 kHz.

Many of Radio Nederland's channels now possess improved audio, yet another reason for tuning in.

Switzerland

One of the most news-oriented stations among international broadcasters, **Swiss Radio International** devotes its entire weekday English broadcast lineup to news and news analysis. Even on Saturdays, 20 of the 30 minutes are set aside for news and information. It is only on Sundays that things lighten up a little. Despite the lack of varied programs and an ongoing budget squeeze, SRI is still a top-notch station. You won't be bored!

North American listeners can tune in at 0200 on 6125, 6135, 9650, 9885, 12035 and 17730 kHz; and again at 0400 on 6135, 9650, 9885 and 12035 kHz. In Europe—one hour earlier summers—hear SRI at 0730 and 2000 on 3985, 6165 and 9535 kHz; at 1300 on 6165, 9535 and 12030 kHz; and at 2230 on 6190 kHz. Best bets for Asia and

(continued on page 74)

WHERE IN THE WORLD I:

Atlases for Radio Listeners

remember the first time it happened.
The BBC World Service was warning British subjects to leave Burma because of insurrection there. One moment I was content with a vague understanding that Burma was "somewhere in the Orient." The next moment a burning desire filled me to find out exactly where Burma was.

The geographic bug had bitten my curiosity bone. Within minutes, I had the answer. I had discovered world band radio is more fun, and more informative, with an atlas nearby.

Maps add depth to the radio stories I hear. A newscast tells of a killer typhoon in Bangladesh, the atlas reveals that much of Bangladesh is barely above sea level—no wonder these storms cause such havoc!

A feature story points me to the Isle of Lewis, where Harris tweed is hand-loomed. I turn to a map of the United Kingdom. It shows a lonely place off the Northwest coast of Scotland, cut off when the North Atlantic rages. Seeing the atlas sparks my imagination. I find myself wondering about these faraway places. Who are these people? Is life simpler there, but more harsh? I turn back to world band for more answers. The circle turns: radio, atlas, and back again.

It's clear that an atlas and world band radio complement each other. But what's the best atlas for a world band listener? The answer, I quickly discovered, is no single one. Atlases have personalities, just as people do.

Size? They range from little hand-held books to volumes too large for a lap. Price? You can buy an atlas for less than $5, or for as much as $160. But greater expenditure does not necessarily mean greater satisfaction. It depends on what you are looking for.

It makes sense to divide atlases into two camps: those comfortable for dial-side use, and those not.

About spellings. The world of atlases is divided into those that use British spellings, and those that use American. Mongolia offers a quick check: "Ulan Bator" is American, "Ulaanbaatar" British. We'll use either Ulan Bator or Ulaanbaatar as a kind of shorthand to indicate which spelling convention is used in a particular atlas.

Post Atlases—Instant Reference

Listening post atlases are those small volumes, easily handled and convenient for quick reference at desk, table or bedside listening post. Some can be held in one hand, while others open up no larger than a magazine. They offer ease of access, to be whipped open at a moment's notice while you are listening. What they lack is depth and detail.

When curiosity calls, an atlas adds to listening pleasure. Here are three of our favorites.

★ ★ ★ ½ **Bartholomew Mini World Atlas.**
4.5 × 6.25", 192 pages, $15.95 hardcover,
$10.95 paperback, Ulaanbaatar, 90-page
index.

This tiny atlas has 112 pages of maps showing political boundaries, but no topographic
information; two maps showing world physical and environmental information; a map
of World Time zones; and an index with
some 20,000 entries. Very handy, very
handsome, with regional maps of the
Balkans, Central Africa, Iran and the Gulf,
and so forth. It is detailed enough for casual
home use, yet small enough to sit next to the
radio or to be tucked into a suitcase.

Put together by Bartholomew, the same
cartographers to produce *The Times Atlas*
of the World, it is my personal favorite. One
sits next to my radio and is used all the time.
Splurge for the hardcover, padded with
gilt edges. It will outlast the next ice age.
J. Peterman (2444 Palumbo Drive, Lexington
KY 40509 USA, toll-free in the United States
800/231-7341) offers it by mail with a spectacular guarantee: absolute satisfaction, or
your money refunded. Highly recommended
for home and travel.

★ ★ ★ ½ **NBC News, Rand McNally**
WORLD ATLAS & ALMANAC – 1991
Edition. 8.5 × 11", 192 pages, $9.95
softcover, Ulan Bator, 8-page index.

A hybrid. The first 60 pages summarize
world news events and themes, region by
region. Next is a five-page World Information Table: each country's square miles,
estimated population, form of government
and ruling power, capital, and predominant
languages. Then there are 46 pages of
large, appealing world regional maps
showing political boundaries and mountain
ranges. Each spreads across two pages,
and they give a good feel for how the land
forms and political boundaries interact.
Next is an eight-page map index and five
pages of national flags. The last 62 pages
are a world gazetteer, which individually
profiles the independent nations, each in its
geographic context, followed by information
about the people, politics, economy, land
and history.

Although the maps are light on place-
name information, this annual is fascinating.
No world news junkie should be without
one.

★ ★ ★ **Hammond World Atlas, Gemini**
Edition. 9.5 × 12.5", 200 pages, $12.95
softcover, Ulaanbaatar.

At these dimensions, this atlas has reached
the outer limits of easy manageability. Only
a soft cover saves the *Gemini Edition* from
becoming positively unwieldy.

This atlas takes the same everything-
together approach as the *Hammond Discovery World Atlas* below, but in a more sizable
format, with maps that are larger and easier
to read. Even though it has separate topographic maps, the *Gemini Edition* features
topographic shadowing on the political
maps, which improves presentation. It does
not include the state maps and world thematic maps found in the *Discovery Edition*.
Few world band listeners will miss them.

If you like the Hammond approach,
you'll like this atlas. Personally, I would prefer less clutter and bigger maps.

★ ★ ½ **Hammond PASSPORT TRAVEL-**
MATE and World Atlas. 3.5 × 5.5", 128
pages, $4.95 softcover (also available in a
set with two companion volumes, a U.S.
TRAVELMATE and a TRAVELMATE Diary
for $14.95), Ulaanbaatar, 9-page index.

Think of this micro-volume as "Atlas Lite."
Designed to travel, half its pages are devoted to maps, the rest to information for the
traveler: customs duty rates, foreign
weather, airline toll-free numbers, time
zones and so forth. The nine-page gazetteer
and index includes population and area
information. With only 64 small pages for
maps, detail here is limited, so this is not the
choice for Listener's Home Companion. The
maps show political boundaries, but no
topographic information, and the tiny place
names are hard to read. There is a two-
page world physical map. Nevertheless, the
information crammed into this small volume
is surprising.

> If I were traveling abroad,
> I wouldn't leave town without
> one of these.

If I were traveling abroad, I wouldn't
leave town without one of these—and a tiny
world band radio—tucked in my pocket.
Recommended for the frequent traveler
worried about space and weight.

★ ★ ½ **Hammond Discovery World Atlas.** 8 3/8 × 10 7/8″, 224 pages, hardcover $19.95, $13.95 softcover, Ulaanbaatar, 15-page index, plus index with each map.

This atlas includes a 128-page foreign map collection, 46 pages of state maps, and a collection of thematic world maps that display comparative information about coal production, population, and so forth. The foreign map section takes a different approach to presenting information about a country, or frequently a group of countries. A main map shows political boundaries and place names. On the same page is a separate, smaller topographic map, with flags and a place name index, as well as tables presenting area, population, capital, largest city, highest point, monetary unit, major languages, and major religions for each country on the map. The following page continues the place name index and a map of the area's industry, agriculture, and resources.

It is an interesting presentation that pulls together a lot of information where it is readily accessible, but I find the thematic maps somewhat crude, and the separate topographic maps distracting. Too, the deep color used on the topographic maps occasionally renders the type hard to read. Interesting idea, imperfectly executed.

Reference Atlases—The Big Guns

The heavyweight contenders generally carry price tags to match. Because of their size and thickness, these volumes do not lend themselves to easy reference while you're

> Atlases are used much more frequently when they are easy to handle.

listening. To use most of them effectively usually requires a table or map stand, such as those offered by the specialty firm of Levenger (975 S. Congress, Delray Beach FL 33445 USA; toll-free in US 800/544-0880). In my experience, atlases are used much more frequently when they are easy to handle. Nevertheless, when the need is critical and the place obscure, reference atlases are far more likely to get you the answer. One gross way to measure them is by their index: the bigger, the better.

★ ★ ★ ★ **Rand McNally The New International Atlas, Anniversary Edition.** 11 3/8 × 15″, 560 pages, $125 hardcover, Ulaanbaatar, 200-page index.

This multilingual atlas is spectacular in its beauty. The first 18 pages contain thematic maps on vegetation, minerals, soils, and so forth. The physical relief renderings that follow are truly awe-inspiring in color and execution. The next 266 pages are divided into world regions: Europe, Asia, Africa, North America, South America, and so forth. Most maps are presented in a two-page spread, roughly 11.5 × 19″, showing political boundaries, shadowed relief and roads. Color, when used to represent elevation, is consistent from map to map. Also included are population tables for cities and towns, and one for world population. This last table shows area, density, capital, and political status for countries, states, and territories.

My only, and minor, complaint is that a collection of metropolitan maps is at the extreme end of the map pages, rather than at the end of their respective world regions. Too, for a reader fluent only in English, it's sometimes cumbersome to trudge through the multilingual forest.

This is the kind of atlas that inspires me to thumb through it leisurely, as an armchair explorer. If you enjoy maps, you will delight in this atlas. Very highly recommended.

★ ★ ★ ★ ★ **The Times Atlas of the World, Eighth Edition.** 18 1/8 × 12 1/4″, 520 pages, $159.95 hardcover, Ulaanbaatar, 218-page index/gazetteer.

This atlas is generally considered the most authoritative published in English today, and *Passport's* editorial offices use one as a standard reference. It opens with 47 pages of geographic comparisons, including six breathtaking renderings of the physical planet. There are 122 double-page maps, beginning with thematic renderings of world food, minerals, climate, and so forth, and followed by world maps in sections: the Orient, the USSR, Europe, and so forth. A freestanding laminated key prompts with mapping conventions, and doubles a neat and useful bookmark.

The maps show topographic shading and roads. Color and shade indicate geographic features, and herein lies the rub: the range of colors used to indicate eleva-

THE JAPAN RADIO CO.
NRD-535

THE NEXT GENERATION IN HIGH-PERFORMANCE HF RECEIVERS

Once again JRC breaks new ground in shortwave receiver design. The new NRD-535 has all the features SWLs and amateurs have been waiting for. General coverage from 0.1 to 30 MHz in AM, USB, LSB, CW, RTTY, FAX and Narrow FM modes. Advanced ECSS operation for phase-lock AM reception. Variable bandwidth control (BWC). Tuning accuracy to 1 Hz possible with direct digital synthesis. 200 memory channels with scan and sweep operation. Triple Superheterodyne receiving system. Superb sensitivity, selectivity and image rejection. Dual-width noise blanker eliminates impulse noise. Squelch, RF Gain, Attenuator, AGC and Tone controls. Optional RTTY demodulator available. 24 hour clock/timer. Easy to read vacuum fluorescent display with digital S-meter. AC and DC operation. Plus the most comprehensive computer interface found on any radio to date. Call or write today for a full color brochure, price list and dealer information.

MAIN OFFICE: Akasaka Twin Tower (Main), Akasaka 2-chome, Minato-ku, Tokyo 107, JAPAN
Tel.: (03) 584-8836   Telex: 242-5420 JRCTOK J

IN U.S.A.: 430 Park Avenue (2nd Floor), New York, NY 10022
Tel.: (212) 355-1180   FAX: (212) 319-5227   Telex: 961114 JAPAN RADIO NYK

tion is so broad—from green at sea level to burnt umber at higher elevations—that it sometimes fooled me into thinking the hues represented vegetation instead of elevation. For example, the New York's Adirondack mountains suddenly looked like a dry and brown place (because of their elevation), instead of the forested area it actually is. And, the use of color to represent elevation is not consistent. On the map of Italy, anything above 4,000 meters is rendered white. On a map of the Himalayas, only elevations above 6,000 meters are rendered white, and the other colors are adjusted accordingly. As a result, it is nearly impossible to get a consistent sense of elevation from map to map.

> New York's Adirondack mountains suddenly looked like a dry and brown place instead of the forested area it actually is.

Very highly recommended for its completeness, but with reservations about the use of color.

★ ★ ★ ★ $\frac{1}{2}$ **National Geographic Atlas of the World, Sixth Edition. 18 1/4 × 12 1/4", 280 pages, $66.45 softcover, $82.95 hardcover (includes freestanding pull-out maps and a magnifying glass), Ulaanbaatar, 136-page index.**

This is an extraordinarily ambitious atlas. The first 13 pages consist of two sections: Dynamic Earth and Habitable Earth. A hundred pages of world maps follow, segregated by continent. Each section opens with a false color satellite photograph of the continent, which I didn't find very useful: I had to keep referring to the caption to decipher the false colors' meaning.

Next are thematic maps about the continent: land use/land cover, resources and industry, environmental stress, and population. A beautiful physical map of the continent follows, then a political map and more detailed regional political maps within the continent. These double-page regional maps show topographic shading and roads against a predominantly white background. They sometimes seem positively jammed with place names. After the world maps,

there are sections on the universe, the nations of the world (with the flag and brief information about each), and geographic comparisons.

In all, it is a laudable effort, with one surprise: This is the only reference atlas we reviewed that comes in both hardcover and softcover editions. While both versions have "perfect" binding—that is, the kind used on ordinary paperbacks—the binding is actually hand assembled to enhance durability. National Geographic reports that it hasn't had a single binding failure in the over 200,000 copies sold. Highly recommended for its graphic presentation. It seems likely that the hardcover version (not reviewed), with pull-out maps, and magnifier, would be worth the extra $16.50.

★ ★ ★ ★ **Rand McNally Universal World Atlas, New Revised Edition. 14 3/4 × 11 3/8", 256 pages, $45 hardcover, Ulan Bator, 96-page index.**

This atlas shows topographic shading on political maps. Sixty-four pages of world maps and 61 pages of U.S. state and Canadian provinces represent nearly half the book's thickness. While the world maps are handsomely rendered, the states and provinces are shown in a shade of brown that makes everything look like the Arizona desert. Tables in the back of the volume offer world political and geographic information—mountains, rivers, islands, and so forth—and world population information.

Recommended for those who want a better-than-travel atlas, and need the state and province maps.

★ ★ ★ ★ **Hammond Ambassador World Atlas. 9.5 × 12.5", 524 pages, $49.95 hardcover, Ulaanbaatar, 149-page index.**

This handsome volume, with gilt edges and thumb-notch indexes for different regions of the world, the United States, and Canada, follows in the Hammond tradition of placing all the information about a given area on the same or adjacent pages (i.e., a gazetteer, physical maps, economic maps, flags, locator maps). While this is a nice idea, I keep wishing for less clutter. In all, there are more than 400 color maps—the main political maps include relief shadowing—and charts.

Particularly appealing is a 24-page collection of sculptured physical maps of

UNIVERSAL RADIO & GRUNDIG
ALLOW YOU TO EXPERIENCE 45 YEARS OF LEGENDARY GERMAN ENGINEERING!

GRUNDIG

The Satellit 500

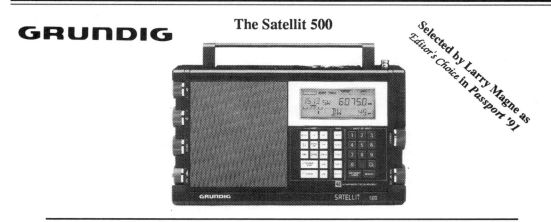

Selected by Larry Magne as Editor's Choice in Passport '91

Already a Classic! **The Satellit 500** offers advanced features for the beginner or serious shortwave listener such as: Direct Keypad Tuning, Alphanumeric Station ID, 42 Station presets, Synchronous Detector, Switchable LSB/USB, and Two Scanning modes. Sound Quality, Sensitivity and Construction are to Exacting German Standards for Excellence! An 18 minute VHS video training manual and the new Grundig Shortwave Listening Guide for North America are included.

The Traveller II

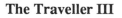

- ✓ Compact AM/FM/SW radio with World Timer/Humane Alarm
- ✓ Five shortwave frequency bands: 49, 41, 31, 25 and 19 meters covering 5.8-15.6 MHz.
- ✓ A "Must Have" for any Traveller!

The Cosmopolit

- ✓ 7-Band Shortwave Receiver with Stereo FM/AM Radio
- ✓ Cassette Player/Recorder with Timer Function
- ✓ Digital Talking Clock with Alarm
- ✓ The Ideal "All In One" Solution

The Traveller III

- ✓ 12-Band With 3.90-21.85 MHz Shortwave, Stereo FM/AM/LW
- ✓ Digital Clock With A Humane Wake-Up Alarm and Sleep Timer
- ✓ Liquid Crystal Display of World Clock and Calendar
- ✓ Great for Short and Long Trips!

The Yachtboy 230

- ✓ 13 Shortwave Bands with Stereo FM, AM and LW
- ✓ Multifunction Digital LCD with World Clock Map
- ✓ Alarm with Dual Wake-Up Times and Radio Sleep Timer
- ✓ Great for the person who wants to hear the world!

Universal Radio, Inc.
1280 Aida Drive *Dept. PP*
Reynoldsburg, Ohio 43068 U.S.A.
Ohio: 614 866-4267 **Toll Free: 800 431-3939**

- ◆ We ship worldwide
- ◆ Visa, MC, Discover
- ◆ Prices & specs. are subject to change.

- ◆ In business since 1942!
- ◆ Used equipment also available.

See full color wire photos

on your computer screen using your shortwave receiver and the new MFJ-1214 computer interface

. . . you'll pick up wire service photos, high resolution weather maps, RTTY, ASCII and Morse Code . . . you get MFJ-1214 interface, software, cables, power supply, comprehensive manual and Fast-Start™ guide -- everything you need for an incredible $149.95!

High resolution weather map received off shortwave with the MFJ-1214

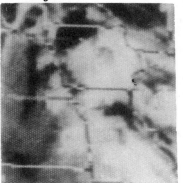

Zoom feature gives you incredible blowups of picture or map details

Watch tomorrow's news today with your shortwave receiver!

See amazing full color news photos as they appear on your computer. Watch them as they're transmitted by shortwave FAX around the world.

Read tomorrow morning's newspaper copy as it is transmitted to newspapers by radioteletype (RTTY).

Is it going to rain? See for yourself when you receive highly detailed weather maps that even show you cloud densities.

Have you ever wondered what hams are doing on their digital modes like RTTY, ASCII and CW? Now you can eavesdrop — the MFJ-1214 will decipher them for you.

You ain't heard nothing yet. You'll also copy military RTTY, ship-to-shore, coast guard CW, distress and safety, dipomatic and embasssy communications, telex, Interpol, utilities, Tass and more.

What do you need to receive these fascinating digital modes? Your shortwave receiver, your computer and the MFJ-1214 package — that's all.

Everything is included. All you do is plug it all in, run the friendly software and tune in a station. Then sit back and watch digital transmissions come to life on your computer screen.

Everything you need is included!

You get the MFJ-1214 multimode, software, computer and radio interface cables (you have to add a connector for your particular radio) and AC power supply. You also get an easy-to-understand comprehensive owner's manual and a Fast Start™ guide.

You also get MFJ's unmatched full one year *No Matter What™* Guarantee.

Receive full color wire photos

You'll see tomorrow's news today when you pick up amazing full color news photos. They look about like the pictures in slick magazines. MFJ-1214 supports the display of up to 4096 colors, depending on your computer.

A timer function lets you set your MFJ-1214 multimode to automatically receive pictures at any time. They can then be automatically saved to disk and/or printed out - even if you're away from your station.

Receive weather maps and wire photos with all 16 gray levels

The MFJ-1214 lets you copy weather maps and news photos with all 16 gray levels. You'll be thrilled when the cloud mass over your house appears on your computer screen. The timer function lets you begin automatic reception with printing to disk or printer at any time.

Radioteletype, ASCII and CW

You'll copy press, weather, ham radio and more over the time-proven and exciting radioteletype (RTTY) mode. It's compatible with all baud rates.

ASCII mode gives you 7 bit ASCII such as Amateur Radio Relay League (ARRL) bulletins from WIAW.

You'll also copy ship to shore Morse code communications as well as amateur radio traffic. No need to learn Morse code — the MFJ-1214 prints it out on your computer screen. Or use it to study Morse code and get your ham license.

Zoom function — gives incredible details of pictures and maps

A special zoom function lets you isolate and enlarge and display any part of a received picture or map.

No Matter What™ Guarantee

Your MFJ Multimode comes with MFJ's unmatched one full year No Matter What™ Guarantee. That means we will repair or replace your MFJ multimode (at our option) *no matter what* happens to it for a full year.

Three models to choose from

MFJ-1214PC works with VGA, EGA or Hercules IBM compatibles with 512K RAM and 8 MHz or faster speed. MFJ- 1214AM works with Amiga. MFJ-1214ST works with Atari ST. Graphics depend on system used. Only **$149.95** each.

Get yours today!

Join the digital SWL fun with the most value packed multimode on the market. Get yours today!

world regions, with political boundaries. This is a spectacularly good idea, and very well executed. Highly recommended for those who prefer to access key information in one spot.

A Wild Card

For the map maniac who demands the most detail about every region in the world, there is *The World Map Directory, 1990-1991*. This $29.95, 300-page book, published by Map Link (805/965-4402), isn't an atlas at all. It's actually a catalogue. But above all, it is an exhaustive reference of sheet maps for nearly every part of the world, including country, city, regional, topographic, and specialty maps. It tells which maps exist, but doesn't show the real maps themselves. Instead, it contains rudimentary outlines of the countries and regions. As a result, you can easily see that map NB35-09 shows the extreme western end of Gabon. You can also see its scale, date—and cost. Every map listed in this book can be ordered directly from Map Link's warehouse in Califor-

nia (25 E. Mason, Santa Barbara CA 93101 USA). Another excellent source for maps is Alfred B. Patton, Inc., Swamp Road & Center, Doylestown PA 18901 USA (215/345-0700).

The Bottom Line

For a world band listener, any atlas is better than none. Each has its own personality, its pros and cons. My experience has shown that a small atlas gets used; a big atlas gathers dust except when the need is critical.

Nevertheless, if money were no object, I'd buy the *Bartholomew Mini World Atlas*, the *NBC News, Rand McNally WORLD ATLAS & ALMANAC*, and the *Rand McNally The New International Atlas, Anniversary Edition*.

Whatever your choice, with the world in your hand and an atlas by your side, the next time the geographic information bug bites your curiosity bone, you'll be ready to scratch.

Prepared by Jock Elliott.

Tune into Com-West

A t Com-West Radio Systems Ltd. our only business is radio. We eat, sleep, and breathe radio so we are always up to date on the latest models, techniques and breakthroughs.

Our knowledgable staff can help you with that critical receiver purchase to ensure you get the maximum effectiveness for your dollar. Or if you are having trouble with your antenna or radio operation, we are ready to help. We want you to get the most out of your radio.

Naturally, we stock many brands of radio equipment, accessories, antenna systems, and publications. And if we don't have it in stock, we'll get it for you, pronto, and ship it anywhere in the world to you.

Just remember us as the one-stop source for all of your radio needs, whether Short Wave, Ham, Commercial, or Marine.

Call or write us today for our new catalog for '92.

Com-West Radio Systems Ltd.

8179 Main Street
Vancouver, B.C.   CANADA V5X 3L2
(604) 321-1833   Fax (604) 321-6560

Canada's Specialty Radio Store

CANADA'S BEST STOCKED
AMATEUR RADIO AND S.W.L. STORE. . . .

Call or write for the best Canadian pricing, immediate delivery and reliable service. . . . . .

Canada's Best Stocked S.W.L. Store

ALLOWS YOU TO EXPERIENCE 45 YEARS OF LEGENDARY GERMAN ENGINEERING !

TEN OF THE BEST

(continued from page 16)

"Concert Hall" et al.
BBC World Service

Concert Hall, International Recital and *From the Proms*: three different concepts of making music, with one common denominator—excellence. Classical music at its very best.

The *Concert Hall* series is just what it says it is—concerts, featuring the finest in music and musicians. The range of styles and periods is more than ample, running the whole gamut of what we know today as classical music.

Although *Concert Hall* runs for several months, the series is occasionally interrupted to give way to *International Recital*, a series of live concerts featuring some of the world's finest musicians. If anything, this series provides an even greater variety of styles than does *Concert Hall*.

Despite the excellence of both these programs, for many listeners the high point of the year is the London season of Promenade Concerts, which takes over the regular classical music spot on the BBC World Service. For those who are unaware of this annual orgy of world-class concerts, *From the Proms* can be summed up in three words—excellence with atmosphere.

World band radio is not the ideal medium for subtle music, but the debut of the Drake R8 receiver (see "Buyer's Guide")

points to a future where shortwave audio fidelity should be more satisfactory. The BBC has also helped by using satellite feeds for its overseas relays, then processing the received audio before retransmitting it. The result fully justifies the effort.

European aficionados of classical music can hear the program Sundays at 1515 on 6195, 9410, 9750 and 12095 kHz, as well as 0815 Tuesdays on 7325, 9410, 12095 and 15070 kHz. Listeners in the United States and Canada can choose 1515 Sundays on 9515 (winter), 11775 (summer) and 15260 kHz, or Tuesdays at 2315 on 5975, 6175, 7325 (winter), 9915 (winter), 9590, and the summer frequencies of 12095 and 15070 kHz.

East Asia is the best served, with three opportunities to tune in: Sundays at 1515 on 7180 kHz; Tuesdays at 0815 on 15280, 15360 and 21715 kHz; and later the same day (Wednesday, local date) at 2315 on 11945, 11955 and 17830 kHz. Australians have to make do with just the one spot, 0815 Tuesdays on 11955 and 17830 kHz.

"Report from Austria"
Radio Austria International

In the film industry, when awards for excellence are handed out, a special "Oscar" is usually given to someone for his or her many years of dedicated service to the industry.

This year, *Passport to World Band Radio* gives a similar nod to *Report from Austria*. Strategically placed in the middle of Central Europe, Radio Austria International, in its own unobtrusive way, has for a long time been providing what is probably the most comprehensive coverage of the area to be found on any international station.

Anyone just happening to stumble across the station won't be bowled over—it's not the kind of program that "impresses." The regular listener, on the other hand, will have access to an audio mirror reflecting many aspects of life not only in Austria, but also in such important neighboring countries as Hungary and Romania. *Report from Austria* is not a national program, it is a regional one—a type of program exceptionally well suited to world band radio.

Not surprisingly, Europeans have the most opportunity to hear it: at 0530 (winter), 0730 (summer), 0830 (winter), 1130 (all year), 1430 (all year) and 1630 (summer) on

The Voice of America's Kelu Chao reports from China. Chao, a talented pianist, also interviews Chinese and Chinese-American artists, such as cellist Yo-Yo Ma.

THE WORLD IS YOURS...

... tuned in and up to date
with MONITORING TIMES

That's because every month **Monitoring Times** brings everything you need to know to make world band listening even more rewarding: the latest information on international broadcasting schedules, frequency listings, station profiles, program commentary, personality interviews, international DX reports, propagation charts, reviews of world band radio products, and tips on how to hear the rare stations.

But **Monitoring Times** doesn't stop there. It also keeps you up to date on what's happening on the airwaves between the international broadcasting bands: information on government, military, police and fire networks; action on the ham bands; and tips on monitoring everything from air-to-ground and ship-to-shore signals to radio-teletype, facsimile and space communications.

Jammed with up-to-date information and concisely written by the top writers in the field, **Monitoring Times** belongs next to your receiver.

Order your subscription today before another issue goes by: only $18 per year in the U.S.; $26 per year for foreign and Canada. For a sample issue, send $2 (foreign, send 5 IRCs). For MC/VISA orders, call 1-704-837-9200.

MONITORING TIMES

*Your authoritative source,
every month.*

P.O. Box 98
Brasstown, N.C. 28902

6155 and 13730 kHz; and 1730 (winter) and 1930 (all year) on 5945 and 6155 kHz. Most editions of the program are daily, but a few are Monday through Friday only. Listeners in East Asia can tune in at 1130 (Monday through Friday) and 1330 (daily) on 15430 kHz, while those in Australia have a daily opportunity at 0830 (winter) and 1030 (summer) on 15450 and 21490 kHz.

The North American audience has a triple choice—0130 (daily) on 9875 and 13730 kHz; 0530 (also daily) on 6015 kHz; and 1130 (Monday through Friday) on 21490 kHz. The 0130 and 1130 broadcasts are beamed to the eastern seaboard, while the 0530 transmission is aimed at the West Coast.

"Focus on Faith"
BBC World Service

Over the past few years, regular listeners will have noticed a considerable increase in the number of religious broadcasts over the international airwaves. Many are poorly produced, "hard sell"—or just downright boring.

Whether or not these broadcasts reflect a resurgence of religious fervor is open to question. But there does seem to be a growing interest in matters concerning religion. Several major international broadcasters now have regular programs which reflect this interest.

Of all the many religious shows on the air, the best is probably *Focus on Faith*, the BBC World Service's weekly spotlight on the world's religions and related matters.

Did you know that stress is the most common illness among missionaries? What about whispers that there is a Vatican conspiracy to prevent publication of the Dead Sea Scrolls?

These and just about anything else can crop up during the course of the 30-minute program. Inter-faith rivalry (or, as in Nigeria, violence), visits of controversial religious figures, church-state relations, or even modern-day mysteries. Politics, archaeology, human interest stories—all can be found here.

In Europe, tune in Thursdays at 1830 on 3955, 6195, 7325, 9410, 12095 and 15070 kHz; with a repeat Fridays at 1001 on 5975, 6045, 9410, 9750, 9760, 12095 and 15070 kHz. Listeners in the United States and Canada have just one opportunity,

0330 Friday (local Thursday evening in North America) on 5975 and 9915 or 12095 kHz. These frequencies are aimed primarily at the western part of the continent, but during winter, at least, those in the eastern half can also tune in on 5975, 6175, 7325 and 9915 kHz.

If you live in Australia, try 1830 Thursdays or 1001 Fridays on 11750 kHz. For East Asia the times are 0330 Friday on 15280 and 21715 kHz, with a repeat at 1001 on 21715 kHz (also on 15360 kHz in summer).

"Man and Environment"
Deutsche Welle

Yet another ecological program? Well, yes, in a way. The German way. In other words, less science and more technology.

Practical matters. Subjects like hydroelectric schemes in the Himalayas; complaints by firefighting American oilmen about the lack of infrastructure in Kuwait. Nuts and bolts. Quite a change from similar programs put out by other international broadcasters.

Not that it's all big projects. There is also information on the British-based Intermediate Technology Group, and information on such down-to-earth topics as drought and starvation on the African continent.

Man and Environment has a special twist in that it is beamed to the developing world, but not the industrialized countries. It can be heard Mondays to Asia and the Pacific at 2134 on 9670, 9765, 11785 and 15350 kHz, plus seasonal frequencies of 6185 (winter), 13780 and 15360 kHz. Europeans aren't served, but can try tuning in to the West African broadcast Saturday mornings at 0634 on 11765, 13610, 13790, 15185, 15205 (or 15435) and 17875 kHz.

There is also a broadcast to South Asia at 0234 Tuesdays on 6035 (winter), 11965 (summer), 7285, 9615, 9690, 11945 and 15235 kHz.

Alas, there is no transmission for North America. Yet, listeners with good receiving equipment can eavesdrop on at least some of those transmissions beamed elsewhere. Experiment to see which comes in best at your location.

Prepared by the staff of Passport to World Band Radio.

Canada's Best Shortwave Store

ICOM R-71A 100 kHz to 30 MHz general coverage receiver with SSB/CW/RTTY/AM modes, FM optional. Dual VFO's and direct keyboard entry; 32 tunable mode and frequency memories. RIT, passband tuning, notch, selectable AGC, noise blanker, tone, squelch, recording jack, built-in speaker. Selectivity: 500 Hz, 2.3 kHz, 6 kHz, 15 kHz bandwidth.

SONY ICF-SW7600 Covers 153 kHz to 29.995 MHz and 76 to 108 MHz; AM/SSB/CW/FM. FM stereo with supplied headphones. Tunes manually, by keyboard entry, memory scan or 10 memory presets. LCD readout, fine tuning, 12/24-hour clock with timer.

YAESU FRG-8800 Covers 150 kHz to 29.99 MHz and 118 to 173.99 MHz with optional VHF converter. Manual tuning and 21-button keyboard for direct entry and programming of 12 memories. LCD with 100 Hz resolution, bargraph S/SINPO indicator. Three scanning modes, dual 24-hour clock/timer.

KENWOOD R-5000 Covers 100 kHz to 30 MHz and 108 to 174 MHz with optional VHF converter; SSB/CW/AM/FM. Dual VFO's, direct keyboard frequency entry. 100 memories store mode, frequency and antenna selection. Scanning, dual noise blankers, selectable AGC, attenuator, dual 24-hour clocks and timer.

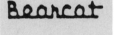

Whether you require advice or are ready to purchase, you can always count on us!

- Experienced Advice
- Competitive Pricing
- Wide Selection
- Customer Satisfaction

NORHAM RADIO INC.

4767 Steeles Ave.W., North York, Ontario M9L 2W1

Mail Order
(416) 745-1000, FAX 24-hours/day: (416) 745-5651

Visit Our Retail Store
Monday: 10-7
Tuesday-Friday: 10-6
Satruday: 10-3
Closed Sunday

check World Time in North America or the Pacific, tune your radio to 5000, 10000 or 15000 kHz, where you will find WWV or WWVH, the U.S. time reference stations broadcasting World Time day and night. WWV, located in Boulder, Colorado, has a male announcer; WWVH, in Hawaii, features a female voice. When conditions are just right, you can hear both on the same frequency, one right after the other.

Checking those frequencies will sketch the range of frequencies that are best heard on that particular day. If, for example, you can barely hear WWV on 15000 kHz, but you can hear it nicely on 5000 kHz—and both WWV and WWVH are coming in well on 10000 kHz—it's a strong indication to listen below 15000 kHz.

Once you know World Time, set the clock on your world band radio, and leave it there. No clock on your radio? Maybe you have a watch with dual-time capability. Failing that, a 24-hour digital clock can be purchased for around ten dollars.

Thanks for the Memories

With World Time under control, you can use "What's On Tonight" to plan your listening for a time that make sense for you. If your radio has memory channels (presets), you can use them to make your crisis listening very convenient. For example, I usually listen in the evening, but I'm never sure exactly when I'll tune in. So, I've programmed my first ten memory channels for stations that are on at 2100 World Time, the next ten for 2200, and so forth. A glance at the World Time clock, and I know which memories to punch.

The payoff for careful time picking can be handsome. On the evening the allied bombing of Iraq began, I found myself switching between TV networks, trying to get as clear a picture as possible of what was going on. Unfortunately, reporting was continually interrupted by interviews with alleged "experts" asked to speculate endlessly. Sometimes another expert would be asked to speculate about the previous expert's speculations.

Thoroughly frustrated with this kind of reporting, I checked my World Time clock,

and selected the correct memory channel for the BBC World Service. In about ten minutes, I had heard a thorough and concise summary of facts as they were then known. Compared to TV's layered speculation, it was a breath of fresh air.

Of course, picking a time to listen will have an impact on what you can hear. For example, most major world band broadcasters (see "1992's Winners: 20+ Big Signals" elsewhere in *Passport*) make an effort to beam English-language broadcasting to North America during prime time evening hours, because that's when most people will be listening. But if you listen at diverse hours of the day or night, you may hear programming intended for other parts of the world. These can offer something quite different in the way of news and perspective.

Dawn may offer the most intriguing time to listen, when the rising sun changes the atmospheric layers that reflect radio waves. You may find signals bouncing in from parts of the globe that are otherwise scarcely heard at your location.

No matter the time, you are bound to hear programming on world band radio that is different and more varied than on your local television or radio.

Pick Your Target

A sensible alternative is to pick your target—that is, decide what stations you want, then go after them regardless of time.

Targets, of course, will depend on the nature of the news event. During the reunification of East and West Germany, the world band stations of the two Germanys were of interest, as were the USSR's, since East Germany was then a Soviet client state. Neighboring states affected by the pending reunification offered interesting listening, too. During the pro-democracy demonstrations in China, Radio Beijing made for a juicy target, as did a number of other major broadcasters, to get a sense of world opinion.

But what if the crisis is in, say, India? Check *Passport's* "Worldwide Broadcasts in English," which is arranged by country. (For other languages in a by-country format, see "Voices from Home.") You'll find that India broadcasts only about seven hours of English-language programming a day, and experience shows it is not easy to hear in certain parts of the world. If you want to discover what India has to say about the

Act Electronics

LETS YOU EXPERIENCE 45 YEARS OF CLASSIC GERMAN DESIGN WITH GRUNDIG SHORTWAVE RADIOS

Grundig Satellit 500
Precision Performance in a Professional Quality International Worldband Receiver

- 42 station memory with alphanumeric station ID
- Two time zone display
- Switchable LSB/USB
- Synchronous detector
- PLL tuning with continuous SW coverage from 1.6–30 MHz
- Illuminated Keypad
- 15 min. instructional video and *Grundig Frequency Guide*
- 7"H x 12"W x 3"D, 4 Pounds

THE CRITICS AGREE ABOUT THE 500:

"Editors Choice..." – Passport To World Band Radio (1991 edition)   *"A Truly Remarkable Radio"* – New York Times

---

The Grundig Yachtboy 230 with its 13 shortwave bands, stereo FM, AM, and LW is sure to please anyone. Also included is an impressive multifunction digital LCD which shows time through a world clock map and acts as an alarm with dual wake-up times and radio sleep timer. Measures 4½"H x 7½"W x 1½"D. Great for the person who wants to hear the world!

The Grundig Traveller III International Receiver is the only 12-band receiver in its class that also includes complete alarm clock features with a Humane wake-up alarm and radio sleep timer, plus a continuous liquid crystal display world clock and calendar. This electronic marvel packs 9 shortwave frequencies from 3.90 - 21.85 MHz, plus stereo FM, AM and LW bands. Just 3¼"H x 5½"W x 1⅛"D. Perfect for people on the go!

ACT ELECTRONICS
2345 East Anaheim St. Long Beach, CA 90804 U.S.A.
(213) 433-0472

Serving Your Electronics Needs For Over 28 Years In The Same Location!

Gary Thomas, VOA correspondent in Islamabad, Pakistan, interviews *mujahedin* leader Haji Din Mohammed on the progress of Afghan rebel fighting.

heaved sighs of relief even before the White House did.

The business of finding and hearing world band broadcasts is not just for current events enthusiasts. Both the United States and British governments think it important enough to spend vast millions every year on professional world band monitoring services. The U.S. Foreign Broadcast Information Service (under the cloak of the CIA) and the kindred BBC Monitoring have listening posts around the world dedicated to eavesdropping on other nations' broadcasts—especially world band—in a variety of languages. The results of their efforts are summarized and placed on the President's and Prime Minister's desks every morning.

In other words, you can hear for free what world leaders spent millions to find out!

crisis, you'll have to arrange your schedule accordingly. You might want to include India's neighbors in your target list. That's when your atlas (see "Where in the World?" elsewhere in *Passport*) will come in handy: where is India, and what are its neighbors? Find out, and you may unearth some surprising insights on world band radio.

On the other hand, the technique of targeting neighbor states can surprise with what they *don't* say. As bombs rained on Iraq, I tuned in Radio Cairo, fully expecting to hear the Egyptian position on the Gulf crisis. Instead, I was amazed to find "Top 40" music—in English!

Another valuable tactic can be seeking major stations of countries less deeply and directly involved in the crisis. A day or two after the Iraq bombing began, I tuned in Radio Nederland. It was airing a discussion of whether the United States had exceeded the letter and spirit of the United Nations' resolutions by directly bombing Iraq, in addition to Kuwait. It was a point that, until then, had not been brought up by American broadcasters.

In radio listening, as in war, picking your target can occasionally produce results truly life-and-death in their importance. During the Cuban missile crisis, when the United States stood at the brink of nuclear war over Soviet ballistic missiles, the first word that missile-laden ships were turning back came not through diplomatic channels, but by an English-language broadcast over Radio Moscow. World band listeners

Scanning the Airwaves

The last technique for crisis listening, "bandscanning," is simple. Yet, it can produce astounding results. In the glossary at the end of this book, you'll find, under "World Band Spectrum" a listing of the frequencies where the various world band segments begin and end, and when they come in best. The next time a news event intrigues you, you can refer to this to find out quickly what's going on.

During the day, you'll probably want to start with a segment above 10000 kHz; evenings, below 10000 kHz will likely be a better bet. For example, in the evening you might want to start at 9995 kHz, the top. Tune slowly enough to identify broadcasts in any language in which you are fluent. When you find one, stop and listen. If it interests you, stay there; if not, note the frequency and keep tuning.

When you get to 9300 kHz, the bottom, you might want to revisit the stations that were broadcasting English to see if the program has changed. Or, you might want to jump down to the next segment. How you scan a segment is entirely up to you; use whatever scheme is comfortable.

As with nearly all crises, the Gulf conflict provided its share of world band discoveries—usually stations that appear just for the occasion. For example, a CIA-run "black" clandestine station, a phoney "Radio Baghdad," operated secretly out of Saudi Arabia. It featured an outrageous fake "Saddam Hussein" making statements the coalition allies hoped would prompt Iraqis to lose confidence in his leadership.

If you scan a segment often enough, each will eventually become a familiar neighborhood street. You will notice when something has changed, just as you'd notice a newly painted house. In the same way, that familiarity with the airwaves which comes from extensive bandscanning can be the key to a breakthrough in crisis listening. Some years back, *Passport* Editor-in-Chief Larry Magne was scanning the 9 MHz segment late one evening when he noticed a carrier (a station on the air, but with no programming yet) on 9009 kHz. This was a frequency used exclusively by Kol Israel—but not, he knew from experience, at this time of night. Given Middle East tension, he thought something might be up, so he stuck with it. A short while later, he was one of the very few in the world to hear the first word of the Israeli commandos' successful raid to free the hostages held at Entebbe Airport.

Very few, yes—but he wasn't alone. A BBC Monitoring employee, scanning at his home in Reading, England, noticed the same thing. He flashed the news to his office, which immediately relayed it to the White House and number 10 Downing Street. It was the first inkling any Western leaders had of the Israeli operation.

Finally, remember that patience pays. If you can't hear a particular station at a particular time, even though it is listed in *Passport*, it doesn't mean your radio is broken or that you are doing something wrong. It probably means that today the radio waves are not bouncing well from there to your part of the world. Keep checking, though, and eventually your persistence may be rewarded. Try the same station at different times, too.

Whether you pick time, pick target, or scan—*Passport's* "Worldscan" section includes all three—one thing is certain: once you've sampled a crisis, you'll come back again and again. Just like the people who scan the airwaves to prepare briefings for the President of the United States and the Prime Minister of Great Britain, the next time some mustachioed martinet sticks his whiskers where they don't belong, you'll be listening.

Prepared by Jock Elliott.

GETTING STARTED

(continued from page 32)

For best results, leave this control switched to high. But if you hear a mishmash of stations that sound as though they're piled atop each other on the same channel, feel free to experiment with the local setting.

–RF (or IF) Gain control. Leave this one on *high*, or perhaps *DX*. With Grundig Satellit series receivers, leave the setting at *AGC*. In practice, this control doesn't do much, but if set improperly—turned down for instance—it can make you think the receiver's dead. It's one of the first places to look when you can't hear anything.

Tuning in Stations

If you're in North America and it's daytime, turn to the Blue Pages in the back of this book to the listing for 15000 kHz. You'll see that stations WWV in Colorado and WWVH in Hawaii both operate there. They are run by the U.S. National Institute of Standards and Technology, and transmit the precise official time and a station identification once each minute. Since they're fairly strong throughout North America, they are good stations to attempt first.

If you're in Europe, try instead the BBC World Service on 9410 or 12095 kHz. In Asia or the Pacific the BBC on 15360 kHz is a good bet. The Blue Pages tell when they're on.

Before tuning, as appropriate, turn the BFO or SSB control to off; set the sensitivity to high; and choose the wide bandwidth. If there is an RF gain control, adjust it to maximum. Extend the telescopic antenna, if it has one, all the way, or attach a wire to the antenna terminals. If you're in a metal-framed building, a high-rise or mobile home, try placing your radio near a window. Metal tends to block radio waves.

Ready?

National Institute of Standards and Technology, Boulder

WWV, which transmits on five frequencies, gives World Time 24 hours a day. Its NBS-6 atomic clock is accurate to three *millionths* of a second per year.

1. Turn your radio on. (A few travel portables require two controls to be switched on, to avoid its happening accidentally in transit.)

2. Turn the tuning knob, or punch in 1-5-0-0-0 on the keypad, to tune in 15000 kHz. (On some sets a band selector or "AM" button may have to be used first.)

3. Adjust the volume to the desired level. On WWV or WWVH, you will hear a time tick each second. On the BBC, you will hear English-language programming.

Those are the basics to get you going. In most cases, operating a world band radio requires only these three steps, but mastery takes time and experience—this is not a medium for the feeble of mind. Initially, try tuning in some of the "easy pickings" stations, or maybe a few of the ten best programs—both described elsewhere in this *Passport*. Become familiar with *Passport*, practice tuning a variety of stations at different times of the day, and with the passage of time the bounty of world band programs will become increasingly within your grasp.

Reception Varies

As you use your radio, you'll soon notice reception on different world band frequencies varies with the time of day. The 5950 to 6200 kHz range is loaded with stations at night, but you'll hear very little there at your

WORLD TIME: THE FIRST THING TO KNOW

You'd like to catch Alistair Cooke's *Letter from America* on the BBC World Service? That's nice, but when does it come on? Is that your time—or British time? After all, there are 24 time zones around the planet, and world band touches every one. How do we know which to use?

World Time is the answer, and you must know this to tune in the world successfully.

You've probably heard of it. It goes by several names: GMT (Greenwich Mean Time), UTC (Coordinated Universal Time), or especially in the military, Zulu time. For the sake of simplicity, we've called it World Time here in *Passport*, and world band radio schedules follow it.

First, get used to the 24-hour format (often called military time, because all the services use it). From midnight to noon, no problem; 24-hour time is the same, for those hours, as 12-hour time. That is, 10:20 AM is just that, 1020 hours, or simply 1020 ("ten-twenty"). After noon, though, 24-hour time doesn't start over, it keeps right on going—1 PM is 1300 ("thirteen hundred"), 2 PM 1400, and so on. Thus, 2400 and 0000 ("zero hours") are the same time (well, practically). Practice a little. It'll save time later.

Converting local to World Time is the next step. See "World Time, Station Addresses and Toll-Free Numbers" elsewhere in this *Passport*. Look under your country to find out how many hours your local time differs from World Time, then add or subtract. Eastern North America, for instance, is five hours earlier (four hours earlier summers) than World Time; or, to look at it the other way, World Time is five hours later than Eastern Time. A program on at 1900 World Time winter thus would be on at 1400 your local time—2 PM.

Live elsewhere? Central Time in the United States and Canada is six hours behind World Time, Mountain seven, and Pacific eight (an hour less—five, six and seven, respectively—if you're on Daylight Saving Time). Let's try somewhere else.

In Continental Western Europe, subtract one hour—two hours summer. In the United Kingdom, World Time is the same as local time except during summer, when you subtract one hour. In Japan, subtract nine hours year-around, and in Western Australia subtract eight.

You only have to figure the difference *once* for your location. Your radio may already have a 24-clock; if not, buy one—they're cheap (MFJ, for example, makes one for less than $10), and worth every penny. Set it once, and that's that.

By the way, World Time also applies to the date. If a BBC drama program is scheduled for 0215 World Time Sunday, in Ohio you would listen at 9:15 PM *Saturday*.

local noon. By contrast, you can hear plenty of stations at noon in the 21450 to 21850 kHz range, but few at your local midnight.

Too, signals are often strongest during your local prime-time evening hours. That's because stations try to beam their signals so they are audible when most people are at home to listen.

Nevertheless, there is still a wealth of choices during the day, even though signals tend to be weaker. For the most fruitful day-time results, a better-than-average radio—one unusually sensitive to reception of weak signals—can be a real plus. Look to *Passport's* Buyer's Guide for what's what here.

There are some notable exceptions to the prime time dictum, though. For example, in much of North America the best time to hear Radio Australia is not in the evening, when its signals are weak and noisy. Rather, it's in the early hours of the morning—on 9580 kHz.

As a loose rule of thumb, the most choice reception is below 10000 kHz during the evening and at night, best above 15000 kHz during the day and early evening, with the 10000 to 15000 kHz range mixed. There are specific tips under "World Band Spectrum" in the Glossary. With the *Passport* schedules and a little experience, you'll soon know exactly which frequencies and times are best for the stations you want to hear. If your radio has station memories, you can set them to these frequencies, like the buttons on a car radio, for easy future access.

Most of us have heard the TV expression, "live via satellite." Signals bounced off space satellites have made our world smaller. Because world band radio bounces signals off the earth's own "natural satellite," the *ionosphere*, reception varies. Like the weather, it varies not only daily, but seasonally. At certain times of the year you can listen to smaller, weaker stations that you otherwise might not be able to hear.

For example, frequencies beginning with threes, fours, fives, sixes and sevens are most vigorous during or near darkness in winter. That's why winter is the best time for Europeans and North Americans to try for stations in Latin America and Africa, as most of these are found in the "low ranges" below 8 MHz.

Spring and fall, on the other hand, are especially good for very distant signals crossing the Equator, such as from Papua New Guinea to New York. Summer evenings are appropriate for long-distance reception above 15000 kHz. So you can take your portable outside and entertain the mosquitos—and yourself—by the barbecue grill.

Most broadcasters adhere to the same schedule year-around. But a few, including some of the biggest, vary by season, especially summer and winter. *Passport* denotes these seasonal schedules with a "J" ("June") for summer and a "D" ("December") for winter.

Another way world band stations differ from local stations is that any number of broadcasters—even a dozen or more—may use a given channel. Because world band signals travel so far, this is more of a problem on world band than on AM or FM. Fortunately, you usually hear only one station at a time. Sometimes, though, an unwanted station makes listening less pleasant, penetrating through to bother the station you're trying to hear.

While listening to specific stations and programs is interesting, don't miss the fun of tuning around with the help of *Passport's* Blue Pages. While most major stations are heard pretty regularly, there are at least as many—some quite worthwhile—that only come in now and then. Too, new stations come on the air, and old ones change frequencies and schedules. This dynamism is part of world band's allure.

Communication doesn't have to be one-way. If you'd like to write some of the stations that broadcast shows you particularly like—or dislike—by all means do so. (*Passport's* address list tells you who and where to write.) Some will provide you with their latest program schedules, calendars, souvenirs and information on their country. Most especially, nearly all are eager to hear what you have to say about their programs.

Prepared by Harry Helms and the staff of Passport to World Band Radio. *Helms is the author of the* Shortwave Listening Guidebook *(HighText Publications).*

—•• •— —— —— •• —   —••• ••— —•—   •—   —••• —— —— —•—

"A hip, concise, astute, accurate, and honest guide. . . very highly recommended!"—Popular Communications magazine

the Pacific are 0830 on 9560, 13685, 17670 and 21695 kHz; plus 1100 and 1330 on 13635, 15570, 17830 and 21770 kHz. There is also a relay via the facilities of Radio Beijing at 1330 on 7480 and 11695 kHz.

United Kingdom

It was left to an announcer at the Voice of America, no less, to put into words what many already knew, anyway—that the **BBC World Service** is the standard by which every other international broadcaster is judged. Who can argue with a daily worldwide audience of more than 120 million listeners?

With a network of transmitter relays stretching from the United States in the west to Hong Kong in the east, and from its home base in the United Kingdom to Ascension Island in the South Atlantic, there is virtually no place on earth which is not within range of "The Beeb."

And if you add a 24-hour service of high-quality programming, who would want to be out of range, anyway? No world band station comes even close to offering a similar choice of programs. Quantity and quality, around the clock.

Expect this to continue. In the past couple of years, the best has been getting better, and the BBC's plans for the future are solid.

> The BBC World Service is quantity and quality, around the clock.

Mornings, the BBC World Service is best heard in Eastern North America at 1100-1400 on 5965, 6195, 9515 or 15220 kHz; and again at 1600 (1500, weekends) to 1745 on 9515, 11775 or 15260 kHz. In

Helga Golz/Deutsche Welle

The reunification of Germany remains a major theme for the Deutsche Welle. Correspondent Michael Lawton reports firsthand from outside the former East German Parliament Building.

Western North America, try 1200-1400 on 9740 kHz, and 1600-1745 on 15260 kHz.

Early evenings in Eastern North America, you can tune in at 2000-2200 on a wealth of frequencies, including 5975 or 15260 kHz. *Caribbean Report* airs at 2115-2130, Monday through Friday, on any two channels from 5975, 9560, 17715 and 21660 kHz—but not on 15260 kHz. It's virtually the only way you can get regular news about that part of the Western Hemisphere.

Throughout the evening, North Americans can listen in at 2200-0815 on a number of frequencies. Best bets are 5975 (to 0730), 6175 (to 0330 or 0430), 9640 (0500 to 0815), and 9915 (to 0330 or 0430).

In Europe, try 6195, 7325, 9410, 9750, 9760, 12095 or 15070 kHz at various times between 0300 and 2315. In East Asia, good choices are 0300-1030 on 15280 and 21715 kHz, 0600-0915 (1115 in winter) on 15360 kHz, 0300-1515 on 9740 and 2200-0030 on 11945, 11955 and 17830 kHz. In Australia and New Zealand, tune to 7150, 9640, 9740, 11750, 11955, 15340 and 17830 kHz at various prime-time hours. Details are in the "Worldscan" section of this book.

USSR

Despite cutbacks and efficiencies brought about by the demise of the Cold War, **Radio Moscow's** 24-hour World Service in English is still the most likely station to appear when the world band listener spins the dial.

Moscow's broadcasts to Europe and North America are virtually continuous, and consist of the North American Service (now restricted to the West Coast only) which operates from 0500 to 0900 (one hour earlier in summer), and the World Service, which operates the rest of the time.

There is an ample choice of programs, ranging from the passable to the exquisite, including news, interviews, political commentary, music and features on life in the Soviet Union. The current affairs programs are a little patchy, depending to a certain extent on the internal political situation existing at the time—but many of the musical offerings are gems.

Where to find them? Nobody broadcasts on as many frequencies, or from as many locations, irrespective of the hour of day or month of the year. Just dial around. You'll find them easily enough.

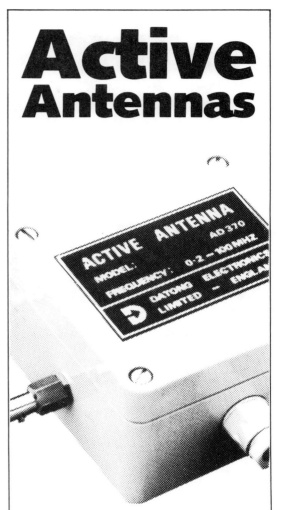

MIDDLE EAST
Israel

Like the Voice of America, **Kol Israel** suffers to a certain extent from a credibility problem. This is not really surprising, taking into account that part of the station's purpose is to explain official Israeli policy to the world outside—and often enough, a hostile one, at that. In spite of this, the station still commands great respect as a valuable source of news and information about the Middle East. Friend and foe alike would rarely dispute the accuracy of the news material broadcast. Kol Israel has one of the most faithful listenerships of any world band station—and they can't all be wrong.

Alas, while listeners are numerous and faithful, the Israeli government seems determined to shoot one of its finest instruments of public contact squarely in the foot. The problem is this: Israel Radio has traditionally been looked upon primarily as a vehicle to attract diaspora Jews to Israel. When waves of immigrants arrived from the Soviet Union and Ethiopia, the need to absorb those immigrants took precedence over the need to attract yet more. Thus, Israel Radio may be unceremoniously cut back to create funding for domestic radio programs oriented to the needs of those new immigrants.

That's reasonable enough if the premise of the station's existence is accepted. But Israel is a modern industrial state and major world power, despite its Lilliputian size, and has a perpetual problem with how the world's peoples perceive its activities. During the Gulf conflict, listenership to Israel Radio soared—the programming was superb, even gripping at times—and this was clearly one of the reasons support for Israel rose in those countries where the station was audible.

> The Israeli government seems determined to shoot Israel Radio squarely in the foot.

Where all this will end is anybody's guess, but for now listeners in Eastern North America can try tuning into the European service. The two transmissions are at 2000 (1900 summers) on 7465 (or 15640), 9435 and 11605 kHz; and at 2230 (2130 summers) on 7465 (or 11588), 9435, 11605,

15640 and 17575 kHz. The timing is awkward, but the quality of reception is reasonable.

Although Israel Radio's programming is dominated by news-related fare, there is also a certain amount of lighter stuff. If you haven't already heard them, they are well worth trying.

As of now, Israel Radio's schedule is up in the air. For the latest information, look within this book's "Worldscan" section, which is prepared only days before the presses roll.

Turkey

The Turkish Radio and Television Corporation's **Voice of Turkey** is currently in the middle of a transmitter expansion program, and it is hoped that the installation of several new 500-kilowatt units will allow its broadcasts to be heard over a wider area than at present.

Long known for its dry, arcane programming, the Voice of Turkey substantially improved its reputation with its reporting of events during *Operation Desert Storm* in early 1991. Hopefully, the program overhaul will have been completed by the time the last new transmitter becomes fully operational.

In the meantime, reception of the station's 50-minute English broadcasts is restricted more or less to Europe, Australia and Eastern North America. Europeans can choose either 2100-2150 on 9795 kHz or 2300-2350 on 9685 kHz, while Australians have an opportunity at 2300 and 0400 (a repeat broadcast) on 17880 kHz. On occasion, this channel can also provide good reception in the western part of North America. For the East Coast, and much more reliable, is 9445 kHz at the same 2300 and 0400 time slots.

During summer all transmissions are one hour earlier.

United Arab Emirates

Many people were deeply disappointed with **UAE Radio's** woeful lack of coverage during the 1991 Gulf conflict. Surprisingly, the Dubai-based station did not alter its programming one iota, and kept its profile very low, much to the chagrin of its listeners.

Whatever its failures as a crisis broadcaster, its regular programs still retain a certain interest, even uniqueness. All

English broadcasts either start or finish with a news bulletin, and the rest of the time is dedicated to features on Arab life and culture, including extracts from Arab literature. A high level of technical competence ensures it is well heard in both Europe and North America.

One of the friendliest stations on the air, UAE Radio can be heard in North America at 0330-0355 on 11945, 13675, 15400 and 15435 kHz. English is beamed to Europe at 1030-1055 and 1330-1355 on 15320, 15435 and 21605; and at 1600-1640 on 11795, 15320, 15435 and 21605 kHz—some of these signals can also be heard in North America. East Asian and Pacific listeners can tune in at 0530-0555 on 15435, 17830 and 21700 kHz.

ASIA
China (People's Republic)

Radio Beijing continues to increase the number of relay arrangements it has with stations in other countries, so there's now better reception than ever before for many of its listeners. That's the good news. The bad news is that there is still some way to go before everyone can listen under the same conditions.

Reception is usually better in Western North America than farther east, although most Canadian and U.S. listeners have a decent chance to hear the English broadcasts. The varied and interesting programs —including exotic music—fully justify the effort.

Radio Beijing broadcasts English six or seven times a day to North America, depending on the season. News is updated for each 55-minute broadcast, but the feature programs remain the same in all transmissions. Try at 0000 winter on 9770 and 11715 kHz; 0000 summer on 15285 and 17705 kHz; 0300 winter on 9690, 9770 and 11715 kHz; 0300 summer on 9690, 11715 and 15285 kHz; 0400 winter on 11695 kHz; 0400 summer on 11685 and 11840 kHz; 0500 winter on 11840 kHz; 1200 on 9665 or 17855 kHz; and 1300 and 1400 on 7405 (winter) and 11855 (summer) kHz.

Europeans can hear Radio Beijing at 2000-2055 and 2100-2155 on 7315 (winter), 11500 (summer) and 9920 kHz; 2200-2255 on 7170 (winter) and 9740 or 11990 (summer) kHz; and via Switzerland at 2200-2225 (2100-2125 summers) on 3985 kHz.

In much of Asia, listeners can tune in at 1200-1255 and 1300-1355 on 9670 and 11660 kHz (also try 15285 kHz). In Australia and New Zealand, one-hour broadcasts can be heard at 0900 and 1000 on 11755, 15440 and 17710 kHz; at 1200 on 11600 and 15450 kHz; and 1300 on 11600 kHz.

China (Taiwan)

Thanks to its relay via the transmitters of Family Radio in Okeechobee, Florida, the interesting **Voice of Free China** is well heard throughout North America. Unfortunately, the same cannot be said for Europe, where reception is iffy.

With the Taiwanese government now encouraging closer links with the People's Republic of China, the coming months could see some interesting programs coming out of Taipei. If you live in North America and happen to miss a favorite program, there's no need to worry—the 0200 broadcast is repeated at 0300 the following evening. It's well worth hearing not only for its unique perspective on the news, but also for traditional Chinese music.

The interesting Voice of Free China is well heard throughout North America.

North American listeners can enjoy a full two-hour show, since both one-hour broadcasts, today's and the repeat of yesterday's, are carried on the same channels—5950 and 9680 kHz.

The Voice of Free China also broadcasts to Asia at 0200 on 11860 and 15345 kHz; to the Pacific at 0200 on 9765 kHz; and to Europe at 2200—winters on 9852.5 and 11805, and summers on 17750 and 21720 kHz.

Japan

One of the major problems facing international broadcasters—apart from where to get money—is one of identity. Do they inform, or entertain? Do they reflect official policy, or maintain an independent posture?

One of the few stations which really seems to know where it is headed is **Radio Japan**. It has embarked on what is virtually a 24-hour service in English and Japanese,

has increased the number of relays overseas, and is looking positively towards the future. This done, Radio Japan plans to leave things pretty much as is for some time to come.

Eastern North America is now amply served via the relay from Radio Canada International's Sackville site. The General Service can be heard at 1100 on 6120 kHz, and again at 0300 (0100 summers) on 5960 kHz. Listeners on the western side of the continent receive their signals direct from Tokyo at 0300 on 11870 (or 15195), 17825 and 21610 kHz; and at 1400, 1700 and 1900 on 11865 kHz.

Europeans can tune in at 0700 on 15325 kHz, and again at 2300 (via the Gabon relay) on 11735 kHz.

Listeners in Australasia can hear Radio Japan's Regional Service at 0900 on 15270 and 17890 kHz. The General Service is aired at 0500 and 0700 on 17890 kHz; 1900 on 11850 kHz; and 2100 on 17890 kHz.

THE PACIFIC
Australia

Radio Australia is on the air around the clock, but officially only to Asia and the Pacific. Fortunately for listeners in other areas, the station's signal reaches well beyond. In survey work at *Passport to World Band Radio*, Radio Australia comes in as one of the most widely listened to stations in North America. It's not the easiest station to hear, but it seems people really like what it has to offer.

In Eastern North America, try in the morning between 0830 and 1500 on 9580 kHz. On the Pacific coast, tune 15160 kHz at 0400-0600; 17795 kHz at 0200-0400; and 21740 kHz at 0030-0300 or later. For a challenge, Eastern North Americans with superior receiving equipment can try those same evening times and frequencies in spring, summer and fall.

People really like what Radio Australia has to offer.

For European listeners, best bets are 13745 kHz at 1530-1900; 15240 kHz at 0800-0930; 17630 kHz at 1300-1800; and 21775 kHz at 0700-1500.

If you live in East Asia, the best all-around frequencies are 17750 kHz at 0000-0300, and 21525 kHz at 0100-0800 and beyond.

LATIN AMERICA
Brazil

Here is one for the loser's column. It was in the later months of 1990 that **Radio Nacional do Brasil**, also known as **Radiobras** (no snickers, please), dealt a bitter blow to its listeners in North America. The timing of its highly entertaining English broadcast to the U.S. and Canada was changed from the prime-time evening slot of 0200 to the morning hour of 1200.

True, the broadcast was then extended from 50 to 80 minutes, but both the time and the frequency are unsuitable for the target area. A bad idea, and worse is that the station doesn't seem to care. A budding BBC World Service this isn't.

Still, for those fortunate Americans who can receive the signal, Radiobras is beamed to North America at 1200-1320 on 11745 kHz.

Listeners in Europe and North Africa, where reception is better, can enjoy chunks of great Brazilian music at 1800-1920 on the better-chosen 15265 kHz.

Cuba

The Brazilian syndrome in reverse—strong in North America, but mediocre in Europe. That's **Radio Habana Cuba**. Some like it, many do not, being mostly to do with how one feels about its political slant. Worth a listen, even if you don't agree; and there's always a good chance you'll be treated to some excellent Cuban music and jazz. After all, Cubans always know how to have a good time.

Another reason to have this station on your checklist is political change. The economy is tired, and after over 30 years so is the regime. Anything can happen down

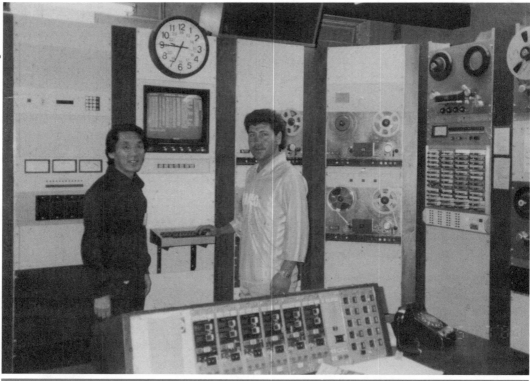

In addition to its popular programs in English, Ecuadorian station HCJB also broadcasts in several other languages, including Japanese.

the road, and the station may provide valuable clues as to where that country is headed.

> ## Radio Habana Cuba may provide valuable clues as to where Cuba is headed.

Broadcasts in English to North America evenings are at 0000-0200 on 11820 or 11950 kHz; 0200-0450 on 9505 (or 15140) and 11820 (or 11950) kHz; 0450-0600 on 11820 (or 11950) kHz; and 0600-0800 on 11760 or 11835 kHz. The initial hour-long broadcast at 0000-0100 repeats at 0200 and 0400, and the 0100-0200 broadcast airs again at 0300 and 0500. Europeans can try their luck at 1900-2100 on 15435 or 17705 kHz.

Ecuador

The granddaddy of South American international broadcasters—and friendly, to boot—

the evangelical station, **HCJB**, in Quito, Ecuador, is well-known to many world band listeners, young and old.

It broadcasts mornings to North America at 1130-1600 on 11740 and 17890 kHz, and 1200-1500 on 15115 kHz. The evening broadcast is at 0030-0430 and 0500-0700 on any two of the following frequencies: 6230, 9745 and 15155 kHz. HCJB also beams to Europe, where it is less clear, at 0700-0830 on 9610, 11835 and 15270 kHz; plus 1900-2000 and 2130-2200 on 15270, 17790 and 21480 kHz. Programs for the South Pacific are broadcast at 0730-1130 on 9745 and 11925 kHz.

If your world band radio operates in the upper sideband mode, you can also listen to many of HCJB's programs on 21455 and 25950 kHz.

Although essentially religious in nature, the station also has several secular programs of interest to the general listener. If you are interested in religious programming, but do not care for a station's approach, tune in to HCJB's locally produced offerings.

Radio Canada International, a long-time favorite of many, is now reduced for the most part to relaying programs of the domestic Canadian Broadcasting Corporation. Budget problems, coupled with a tragic lack of understanding at the government's decision-making level, have robbed millions of some of their best-loved programs.

True, the CBC does produce some excellent material, but most of it is mainly of interest to Canadians—not the world at large. Gone is that friendly, understanding touch that explained Canada so well to the world.

No doubt there are still many—not just Canadians abroad—who are interested in news from the Canadian home front. Even Americans abroad can benefit from Canadian coverage of events in the United States. Yet, one cannot help but mourn the passing of some truly excellent world band fare.

What's ahead? RCI's infrastructure is largely intact, and it is now blessed with superior management. Look well down the road to a reborn RCI that may be finer than ever.

RCI is heard much more clearly in Eastern North America than out west. For now, broadcasts to North America are at 1300-1400 weekdays on 9635, 11855 and 17820 kHz; 1400-1700 Sundays on 11955 and 17820 kHz; with both transmissions being one hour earlier in summer. Evening broadcasts air at 0000-0130 daily, plus 0130-0200 Sundays and Mondays, on 9755 and 5960 kHz. The 0000-0130/0200 transmission features the likes of the Canadian Broadcasting Corporation's excellent news programs, *The World at Six* and *As It Happens*—don't miss these two gems! Summer broadcasts are somewhat differently timed: daily at 2200-2230 and 2330-0030, plus Sundays and Mondays at 0030-0100.

The afternoon transmission to Africa, heard fairly well in North America and sometimes even Europe, begins at 1800 on 13670, 15260 and 17820 kHz, and follows a slightly different format: 1800-1830 and 1900-1930 Mondays through Fridays, and 1800-1900 Saturdays and Sundays.

Europeans now have more options than

Laurie Kassman reports from Paris for the Voice of America. She is fluent not only in French and English, but also Spanish, Portuguese and Italian—useful tongues for covering European Community affairs.

One of the few stations that can make a claim to total global coverage, the **Voice of America** is one of the giants of international broadcasting. Often criticized, but listened to by millions, it is for many a valuable source of news and entertainment.

Probably no other station provides so much regional variation to its worldwide programming as does the VOA. Africa, Latin America, the Caribbean, as well as countries on the Pacific Rim—all have "specials" beamed their way.

The two best times to listen in North America are at 0000-0200 (to 0230 Tuesdays through Saturdays) on 5995, 6130, 9455, 9775, 9815, 11580 and 15205 kHz; and 1000-1200 on 6030 (or 15120), 9590 and 11915 kHz; when the VOA broadcasts to South America and the Caribbean. The African Service is also audible in North America, at 1600-2200 on 15410, 15580, 15600, and 17800 kHz. European listeners can tune in at 0400-0700 on 5995, 6040, 6140 and 7170 kHz; 0400-0600 on 7200 and 15205 kHz; and 1700-2200 on 6040, 9760, 11760 and 15205 kHz.

> Listened to by millions, the Voice of America is a valuable source of news and entertainment.

The popular Pacific Service may be heard at 1900-2000 on 9525, 11870 and 15180 kHz. In East Asia, good bets for the regular VOA English Service include 1100-1400 on 9760 and 15155 kHz; 1400-1500 on 9760 and 15160 kHz; 2200-2400 on 15290, 15305, 17735 and 17820 kHz; and 0000-0100 on 15290, 17735 and 17820 kHz.

before. Try 1500-1530, 1600-1630, 1700-1730, 1800-1900 and 2000-2100, choosing from frequencies such as 5995, 7235, 9555, 11935, 15305, 15315, 15325, 17820, 21545 or 21675 kHz. Generally, the higher frequencies are available earlier in the day, the lower ones later in the evening. There is also a broadcast at 2200-2300 on 9760 and 11745, or 15325 and 17875 kHz. All this is an hour earlier in summer.

Monday through Friday, there is also a morning broadcast for Canadians abroad at 0615-0700 on 6050, 6150, 7155, 9740, 9760 and 11840 kHz; summers one hour earlier on 6050, 6150, 7295, 9750, 11775 and 17840 kHz.

A twice-daily program for East Asia airs at 1330-1400 on 6095, 6150, 9535, 9700 and 11795 kHz; and 2200-2230 on 11705 kHz.

Prepared by the staff of Passport to World Band Radio.

CHOOSING A PREMIUM RECEIVER?

Get premium advice before you buy!

If you could, you'd spend weeks with each receiver. Learning its charms and foibles. Checking the specs. Seeing for yourself how it handles—*before* you spend.

Now, you can do the next best thing—better, some readers insist. *Radio Database International*™ *White Papers,*™ from the *Passport to World Band Radio*™ library of in-depth test reports, put the facts right into your hands.

We run each receiver for you. We put it through comprehensive laboratory and bench tests to find out where it shines. And where it doesn't.

Then our panel takes over: DXers, professional monitors, program listeners—experts all. They're mean, grumpy, hypercritical . . . and they take lots of notes. They spend weeks with each receiver, checking ergonomics and long-run listening quality with all kinds of stations. Living with it day and night.

With *Passport RDI White Papers,* these findings—the good, the bad and the ugly—are yours before you buy. Each report covers one model in depth, and is US$5.95 postpaid in North America, $7.95 airmail outside. Separate reports are

available for each of the following premium radios:

> **Drake R8***
> **Grundig Satellit 500**
> **Grundig Satellit 650**
> **Icom IC-R71**
> **Icom IC-R9000**
> **Japan Radio NRD-93**
> **Japan Radio NRD-525**
> **Japan Radio NRD-535***
> **Kenwood R-5000**
> **Lowe HF-225/HF-235**
> **Sony CRF-V21**
> **Sony ICF-2010/ICF-2001D**
> **Yaesu FRG-8800**

*Available as of 12/91.

Other *Passport RDI White Papers* available:

> **How to Interpret Receiver**
> **Specifications and Lab Tests**
> **Popular Indoor Antennas**
> **Popular Outdoor Antennas**

Available from world band radio dealers or direct. For VISA/Master Card orders call our 24-hour automated order line: 215/794-8252. Or send your check or money order (Pennsylvania add 6%), specifying which report or reports you want, to:

Passport RDI White Papers
Box 300
Penn's Park, PA 18943 USA

1992 BUYER'S GUIDE TO WORLD BAND RADIO

MOTHERS, DON'T LET YOUR SONS GROW UP TO TEST RADIOS

by Lawrence Magne

It used to be so easy.

Fifteen years ago, the best portable was a South African Barlow-Wadley XCR-30 Mark II, and before that the few good tabletops were nearly all made by American manufacturers. Choosing was a snap.

Barlow's doesn't make world band radios any more. Neither does anybody else in the United States or South Africa, except Ohio's R.L. Drake Company. Time marches on, and world band production now has a distinct East Asian accent.

The infrastructure for world band radio has been around for a while—several million years, in fact; back to when the earth's ionosphere that carries radio waves came into being. But until recently, we couldn't do much about it. Granted, world band signals have reached across borders for much of this century, bringing information and ideas to enslaved peoples, and carrying propaganda the other way.

But for those in advanced, free societies, the limitations of technology made world band radio an unpopular choice. Old-technology radios just didn't cut it.

This all changed when Panasonic and Sony introduced a handful of high-quality—if clunky—portables in 1976. In 1980, and again in 1985, Sony introduced high technology to the portable world band marketplace, and the rest we know.

Back then, objective, systematic world band radio reviews were unheard of. But, in 1977, a European-based radio book publisher asked me to test and rate world band radios as a way to boost its fortunes. Finally assured of independence from advertising influence, I agreed. Testing was a strictly one-man operation, and the "Magne Reviews" appeared in its pages every year thereafter, with the exception of 1979.

The reaction was gratifying—and immediate. Once-stagnant circulation jumped 50 percent in a few years. Readers loved it, but manufacturers were mixed. To some, it was a breath of fresh air. To others, a curse. I had acquired unsought-after notoriety, which had its amusing moments.

Take this. One day I walked into a radio store where I was not known, intent on buying a small part. Eyes followed me closely (did I look like a shoplifter?), and a clerk fetched the manager. At the register the manager uttered, "Thank you, Mr. Magne."

So matter-of-factly did he say it that I asked him how he knew me. From under the counter he produced, with understandable reluctance, a kind of "wanted poster" from

Kathleen Nace prepares receiver measurements for *Passport's* Buyer's Guide.

an electronics firm. It didn't say *dead or alive*, but the preference was clear enough. I'd panned one of the company's products, one carried by the store.

I understood their irritation. I had claimed this product had certain serious flaws. Yet, a highly respected consumer publication had given that same model high marks. Obviously, one of us had to be wrong.

That seemed to be the end of that, until something unexpected occurred. Years later, I got a letter from a gentleman who had worked in a well-placed position with this same manufacturer. All along, he revealed, the company had recognized privately that my criticisms were valid - although they obviously had taken the opposite stance publicly.

They had fired the engineer responsible, which turned out to be not such a bad idea. Now, their radios are no longer dogs—they're among the best.

Over time, then, valid reviews help diminish the presence of mediocre products within the marketplace, while boosting the chances of superior models. Advertiser-oriented "reviews" appear to have little such impact.

A different type of case in point. A major manufacturer let me know several years back that it was designing a world band radio based exclusively on my writings over the years. That bothered me. Did they hope to guarantee good press? Did they know that critique differs qualitatively from production? The receiver earned nothing but our usual grouchy, if generally favorable, words.

The kicker? The radio became one of the best-selling world band models of all time. No one was more surprised than we were, even though, in principle, we probably shouldn't have been.

By 1985, what began as a one-man exercise had flowered into a specialized team, including a state-of-the-art laboratory. Too, the worsening strain under the aegis of our original publisher began to take its toll. We parted ways, and that year issued our first world band reviews within our own new and independent publication, *Radio Database International*—the forerunner of today's *Passport to World Band Radio*.

Then, as now, we set forth not so much to do certain things, but to do things in a certain way. I have always had enormous respect for the ethical standards of *Consumer Reports*—and disdain for "reviews" written not to offend manufacturers. For one thing, knowingly impugned truth offends me. And readers aren't fools, for another.

So, that's the way it is here. We're confident in our technical standards to provide meaningful measurements. And with apologies to the U.S. Marines, we have a few good souls thoroughly experienced at hands-on analysis.

Yet, as the cliché goes, figures lie and liars figure. We'd like to think that, in the final analysis, what we're here for is not only to inform the consumer, but also to discourage chicanery in the marketplace. For the latter, let's chalk up two stars . . . and keep pushing for better.

Lawrence Magne is Editor-in-Chief of Passport to World Band Radio *and leads the* Passport Buyer's Guide *review team.*

HOW TO CHOOSE A WORLD BAND RADIO

World band radios, unlike TVs, differ greatly from model to model. Some use old technology and barely function. Others, more advanced, perform superbly. As usual, money talks—but even that's a fickle barometer in this exceptional field.

There's no need to put up with mediocrity.

Exceptional? Think of world band as a jungle, for that's what it is: 1,100 channels, with stations scrunched cheek-by-jowl. This crowding is far greater than on AM or FM, and to make matters worse signals are made weak and quivery by long-haul travel. Coping with all this calls for your radio to perform some extraordinary electronic gymnastics.

The good news? There's no need to put up with mediocrity. The selection of available radios is vast, dozens upon dozens of models, and many perform very well, indeed.

Which ones? Since 1977 we've tested all sorts of world band products. These independent evaluations, which have nothing to do with advertising, include both rigorous hands-on use by veteran listeners and highly specialized laboratory tests. These form the basis of this Buyer's Guide, and are thoroughly detailed in our unabridged *Radio Database International*™ *White Papers*.™

Four Points to Consider

First: How much do you want to spend? Don't fool yourself—world band radios are sophisticated electronic devices. Unless you want a small radio for the road, recognize that an acceptable world band radio costs only slightly less than a video cassette recorder.

Yes, a VCR could sell for $99.95— stripped of counter, timer, clock, channel indicator, and remote control, and susceptible to adjacent-channel interference. But you wouldn't buy something like that, and few others would, either. That's why VCRs don't sell cheap. Use the same reasoning for world band, and avoid disappointment.

An acceptable radio costs only slightly less than a VCR.

Radios as low as $30 can give a coarse idea of what world band's like. But when the novelty wears thin, most people wind up hiding them in the closet. After all, there are good cigars, and there are nickel cigars— but there are no good nickel cigars.

Second: Determine what you feel the minimum performance is you are looking for, then choose a model that surpasses that by a notch or two. This helps ensure against disappointment without wasting money.

If world band is new to you, but you think you'll take it seriously, try a mid-sized or compact portable selling in the $160–$280 range, street price. Most of those are snug enough to take on trips, yet big enough to be daily home companions.

If you just want to gain a nodding acquaintance with world band, the two-and-a-half star sets around $100 can give a taste, of sorts, of what the fuss is about. Still, you're better off making your first radio something good—$180 or more, and another star.

Even if you're experienced with world band, you need to think your needs through. Do you want a few powerful stations? Or do you hanker for softer voices from more exotic lands? Three-and-a-half stars will do nicely for the former, and street prices on some of these start under $200. For the latter, think four stars—perhaps five—and more money.

Third: Consider your location. Signals tend to be strongest in and around Europe, different but almost as good in Eastern North America. If you live in either place, you might get by with less radio. But if you're in Western North America, Australia or New Zealand, you're better off digging deeper: You'll need an unusually sensitive receiver—mentioned under "Advantages" in the

FEATURES TO LOOK FOR ON BETTER MODELS

You can't tell by looking at a world band radio in a store whether it will work better than another model, or how long it will hold up.

But features are another story. That's why sales folks love features: They are relatively free from mystery. If the customer's attention can be focused on "bells and whistles," then performance and reliability usually slide to the back burner. And as if this weren't enough, people pay extra for features whether they do any good or not.

Still, certain performance features can be genuinely useful, and are alluded to under "Advantages" and "Disadvantages" in the Buyer's Guide. For example, a very important performance feature is *multiple conversion*, essential to rejecting spurious signals—unwanted growls, whistles, dih-dah sounds and the like. A power lock also borders on a "must" if you travel frequently with your radio.

Also look for two or more *bandwidths* for superior rejection of stations on adjacent channels; properly functioning *synchronous selectable sideband* for yet greater adjacent-channel rejection, and also to reduce distortion from fading; and continuously tuned bass and treble. For world band reception, *single-sideband* (SSB) reception capability is of only minor use, but it's essential if you want to tune in shortwave utility or "ham" signals.

On heavy-hitting tabletop models, designed to flush out virtually the most stubborn signal, you pay more so you expect more. Additional features to look for include a tunable *notch filter* to zap howls and squeals; *passband offset*, also known as *IF shift*, for superior adjacent-channel rejection and audio contouring; an attenuator, preferably multi-step, to curb overloading; and multiple *AGC decay* rates with selectable *AGC off*. A *noise blanker* sounds like a better idea than it really is, given existing technology—but it doesn't hurt, either.

Highly recommended operating (non-performance) features, for portables and tabletops alike, include digital frequency readout, a virtual *must*; a 24-hour World Time clock, especially one that always shows; and such tuning aids as a keypad, tuning knob, presets (channel memories) and perhaps up/down slewing controls. Useful, but less important, are on/off timing, especially if it can control a tape recorder; illuminated display and controls; a dedicated separate button for each preset (single-keystroke call up), rather than having to call up presets via the keypad (multiple-keystroke call up); numerically displayed seconds on the 24-hour clock; and a good signal-strength indicator.

Buyer's Guide—and maybe an outdoor antenna, too. Central North America and the Caribbean are better, but think twice.

Your first receiver? A good portable will do all but the toughest work. If you decide on a tabletop later, save the portable for trips, even if only to the balcony or backyard.

But if you're an experienced hand and want to play high-stakes games, go for the five-star tabletops. The ante's high, though: Figure around a kilobuck, and the antenna's extra.

Panasonic's RF-B45, just introduced, is the best simple-to-operate portable under $200 or £130.

Unlike TVs and ordinary radios, world band sets rarely test well in stores.

Fourth: What features make sense to you? Separate these into two categories: those that affect performance, and those that don't (see box). Don't rely on performance features alone, though. As our Buyer's Guide tests show, a great deal more besides features goes into performance.

Fifth: Unlike TVs and ordinary radios, world band sets rarely test well in stores, except perhaps in specialty showrooms with the right outdoor antennas at the right time of the day. Even so, given the fluctuations in world band reception, long-term satisfaction is hard to gauge from a spot test. The exceptions are audio quality and ergonomics. Even if a radio can't pick up any world band stations in the store, you can get a thumbnail idea of fidelity by catching some medium-wave AM stations. And by playing with the radio you can get a feel for handiness of operation. Otherwise, whether you buy in the neighborhood or through the mail

makes little difference. Use the same horse sense you would for any other significant appliance.

Repair? Judging from both our experience and reports from *Passport* readers, this tends to correlate with price. At one extreme, some off-brand portables from such places as Hong Kong and the People's Republic of China seem essentially unserviceable, although most outlets will replace a defective unit within warranty. On the other hand, for high-priced tabletop models factory-authorized service is usually available to keep them purring for many years to come. Of course, nothing else quite equals service at the factory itself. So if repair is especially important to you, bend a little towards the home team: Drake in the United States, Grundig in Germany, Lowe in the United Kingdom, and so on.

Finally: A good way to judge a store is by bringing *Passport* when you shop. Reputable dealers welcome it as a sign you are serious and knowledgeable. The rest react accordingly.

Drake's New R8 tabletop receiver, for when only the best will do. It sets a new standard of performance, yet at a price not greater than ordinary tabletops.

OUTDOOR ANTENNAS: DO YOU NEED ONE?

If you're wondering what antenna you'll need for your new radio, in most cases the answer for portables is plain and simple: none. All portables come with built-in telescopic antennas.

Indeed, for use in Eastern North America or Europe nearly all portables perform *less* well evenings with sophisticated outboard antennas than with their built-in ones. But if you listen during the day, or live in the North American Midwest or West, for example, your portable may need more oomph.

For portables, the best solution is the cheapest: $8.49 for Radio Shack's 75' (23 m) "SW Antenna Kit" (#278-758), which comes with insulators and other goodies, plus $1.99 for a claw clip (Radio Shack #270-349 or #270-345). The antenna itself may be a bit too long for your circumstances, but you can always trim it. Alternatively, many electronics and world band specialty firms, such as Universal, sell the necessary parts and wire for you to make your own. An appendix in *Passport's* publication, an *RDI White Paper*, "Popular Outdoor Antennas," gives minutely detailed step-by-step instructions on making and erecting such an antenna.

Basically, you attach the claw clip onto your radio's rod antenna (not the set's external antenna input socket, which may have a desensitizing circuit) and run it out your window as high as is safe and practical to something like a tree. *Keep it clear of any hazardous wiring—the electrical service to your house, in particular—and respect heights.* If you live in an apartment, run it to your balcony or window—as close to the fresh outdoors as possible.

For portables, this "volksantenna" will probably help with most signals. But if it occasionally makes a station sound worse, disconnect the claw clip.

It's a different story with tabletop receivers. They require an external antenna, either electrically amplified (so-called "active") or passive. Active antennas use small wire or rod elements that aren't very efficient, but make up for it with electronic circuitry. For apartment dwellers, they're a godsend—provided they work right.

Choosing a suitable active antenna for your tabletop receiver takes some care. Certain models—notably, those made by McKay Dymek and Datong—are designed better than others, as you'd expect. But sometimes other models perform better in specific locations, which you might not expect, so buy with care. Most sell for under $200; few are more.

If you have space, an outdoor passive wire antenna is better, especially when it's designed for world band frequencies. Besides not needing problematic electronic circuits, good passive antennas also tend to reduce interference from the likes of fluorescent lights and electric shavers—noises which active antennas amplify, right along with the signal. As the *cognoscenti* say, the "signal-to-noise ratio" with passive antennas tends to be better.

With any outdoor antenna, especially if it is high up and out in the open, disconnect it and affix it to something like an outdoor ground rod if there is lightning nearby. Handier, and equally effective except for a direct strike, is a "gas-pill" type lightning protector, such as is made by Alpha Delta. Otherwise, sooner or later the odds are that you will be facing a very expensive repair bill.

Many firms—some large, some tiny—offer world band antennas. Among the best passive models—all under $100—are those made by the Antenna Supermarket and Alpha Delta Communications. Two separate, detailed reports on passive outdoor and active indoor antennas are available as *Radio Database International White Papers*, described elsewhere in this book.

WORLD BAND
PORTABLES FOR 1992

1992 is Year One A.D.S. (After Desert Storm), when each of us read, heard or saw a stream of news reports on shortwave radio. As often as not, these spotlighted serious-looking chaps surrounded by racks of impressive radio hardware.

Yes, there are folks who think nothing of spending half the national debt on radios. If you know archers, for example, you know what we're talking about. Most buy a bow and arrows, then shoot at a target when it strikes their fancy. But there are other types. They scour the continent for the finest materials, make their own arrowheads, shoot target practice at every opportunity. They dream in Comanche.

If you eat, breathe and dream world band radio, stop right now and go to the tabletop section of this Buyer's Guide. If not, this section on portables is the place to start. The best rated among these affordable portables will meet the needs of all but the most exacting listener.

Who are we to judge what's good, and what's not? Another set of "experts" that's going to tell you one day that beef will kill you, the next that it's the best thing the Great Spirit has placed on earth?

A quick backgrounder. Until 1978, reviews of world band equipment were pretty depressing. Some were written to please advertisers, even to the point where the advertiser would write the "review." Others were well-intentioned, but wrong, or focused on things of little import to the real-life needs of the consumer.

Lots of people got badly burned by this "advice," spending good money on radios that couldn't cut the mustard. So in late 1977 we decided to evaluate world band equipment ourselves—but to do it the way we wished it had been done when we were consumers trying to make heads or tails of the marketplace.

We created testing standards for the unusual requirements of world band radio, then proceeded to make enemies with manufacturers by doing our reviews based solely on the needs of the consumer. You didn't do things like that back then, and most in the industry will tell you it still shouldn't be done.

By the fall of 1992, we will have been at this for 15 years. By rough reckoning, figure that a good million people have been exposed to our reviews during that time. The best part is that we still enjoy doing this—it's fun, not just a job—and look forward to another 15 or more years of the same.

Here, then, are the results of this year's hands-on and laboratory testing—evaluations of nearly every widely distributed world band portable currently produced that meets minimum standards. Thus, we exclude, for example, those models, such as the Icom IC-R1 and Kenwood RZ-1, that lack bandwidths narrow enough to qualify for acceptable world band reception.

Models are listed by size; and, within size, in order of world band listening suitability. Unless otherwise indicated:
• Each radio covers the usual 88.7-107.9 MHz FM band.

• AM band (mediumwave) coverage in models with *digital* frequency display includes the forthcoming 1600-1705 kHz segment for the Americas; AM band coverage in models with *analog* frequency display stops short of 1705 kHz.

The longwave band is used for domestic broadcasts in Europe, North Africa, and the USSR. If you live in these parts of the world, or plan to travel there, longwave coverage is a plus. Otherwise, forget it. Keep in mind, though, that when an analog (lacking digital frequency display) model is available with and without longwave coverage, the version with longwave may include that at the expense of some world band coverage.

For the United States and Canada, suggested retail ("list") prices are given. Discounts for most models are common, although those sold under the "Realistic" brand name are usually discounted only during special Radio Shack sales, which are infrequent. As "list" prices are largely a North American phenomenon, observed *selling* prices are generally given in pounds for the United Kingdom and, to have a common benchmark until such time as there is a common currency, U.S. dollars for continental Europe. Prices elsewhere vary widely, with Japan among the highest, and Dubai, Hong Kong, Singapore and parts of Latin America among the lowest.

Duty-free shopping? In some parts of Europe, such as France and Switzerland, it may save you 10 percent or more, *provided* you don't have to declare the radio at your destination. Check on warranty coverage, though. In the United States, where prices are already among the world's lowest, you're better off buying from regular stores.

Canada, too, and to some extent even the United Kingdom.

Naturally, all prices are as we go to press and may fluctuate. Some will probably have changed before the ink dries.

We try to stick to plain English, but some specialized terms have to be used. If you come across something you don't understand, check it out in the Glossary at the back of the book.

What *Passport's* Ratings Mean

Star ratings: ★ ★ ★ ★ ★ is best. We award stars solely for overall performance and meaningful features, both here and in our tabletop model reviews elsewhere in this *Passport* Buyer's Guide. The same star-rating standard applies regardless of price, size or whathaveyou. So you can cross-compare any radio—little or big, portable or tabletop—with any other radio evaluated in *Passport*. A star is a star.

A portable rating of three-and-a-half stars should please most day-to-day listeners. However, for occasional use on trips a small portable with as little as two stars may suffice. Four stars is the best we've given any portable, although a few five-star tabletops really shine. (So, by the way, do their price tags.)

Editor's Choice models are our test team's personal picks of the litter—what we would buy ourselves.

¢: denotes a price-for-performance bargain. It may or may not be a great set, but gives uncommon value for the money.

Models in **(parentheses)** have not been tested by us, but appear to be essentially identical to model(s) tested.

WHAT NOT TO FEAR WHEN TRAVELING

Will airport security devices hurt your world band radio? No. Just leave your radio inside the luggage during inspection.

Headed to Germany? German radio regulations require that world band receivers be unable to tune above about 26.1 MHz—the upper limit of the world band spectrum. Yet, most digitally tuned world band radios sold outside Central Europe cover up to 30 MHz—the upper limit of the shortwave spectrum. (Much of the shortwave spectrum is used for things other than world band radio.)

Fortunately, German customs officials almost never hassle travelers bringing in compact or mini portables that cover the forbidden 26.1-30 MHz range. Not unless you choose to tell them, of course.

MINI-PORTABLES

Great for Travel, Poor for Home

Mini-portables weigh under a pound, or half-kilogram, and are about the size of a hand-held calculator or a bit larger than an audio cassette case. They operate off two to four ordinary little "AA" (UM-3 penlite) batteries. These tiny models do one job well: provide news and entertainment when you're traveling, especially abroad by air. A few will do for day-to-day listening, but only through good headphones—not an attractive prospect, given that none has the full array of Walkman-type features, such as a hidden antenna. Listening to these radios' tiny speakers can be awfully tiring.

Best bet? Sony's ICF-SW1S or ICF-SW1E, if you can stand the sticker shock. No other minis come close. Also look over the large selection of compact models, just after the minis in this Buyer's Guide. They're not much larger than minis, but have more sizable speakers, and so tend to sound better.

Sony's ICF-SW1S, complete with a case full of goodies, is the best mini. Too much to carry? Leave the accessories behind.

★ ★ ★ ½   *Editor's Choice*

Sony ICF-SW1S
Portable Receiving System

Price: $349.95 in the United States, CAN$599.95 in Canada, under £250 in the United Kingdom, $370-480 elsewhere in Europe.

Advantages: Superior overall world band performance for size. High-quality audio when earpieces (supplied) are used. Various helpful tuning features. Unusually straightforward to operate for high-tech model. World Time clock. Alarm/sleep facilities. Travel power lock also disables alarm and display illumination. FM stereo through earpieces. Receives longwave and Japanese FM bands. Amplified outboard antenna (supplied), in addition to usual built-in antenna, enhances weak-signal reception below about 15 MHz. Self-regulating AC power supply, with American and European plugs, adjusts automatically to all local current worldwide. Rugged travel case for radio and accessories.

Disadvantages: Tiny speaker, mediocre audio. No tuning knob. Tunes only in coarse 5 kHz increments. World Time clock readable only when radio is switched off. Volume control at rear, vulnerable to accidental change. For price class, substandard rejection of certain spurious signals ("images"). No meaningful signal-strength indicator. Earpieces less comfortable than foam-padded headphones. Amplified antenna does not switch on and off with radio.

Bottom Line: Although pricey, the Sony ICF-SW1S—the closest thing to a world band "Walkman"—is easily the best mini-portable on the market.

LEAST RISKY RADIOS FOR GLOBETROTTING

Customs inspectors and airport security officials, even in totalitarian countries, rarely give a second glance at everyday small world band portables. But larger, more exotic-looking radios—world band or otherwise—can invite unwelcomed attention, even theft, especially if they contain tape recorders.

When you're flying internationally, then, take along a mini or compact portable that doesn't have a built-in tape recorder. There are lots of models to choose from, and some are cheap enough that you can shrug off their loss, should it come to that.

Sony ICF-SW1E
("Sony ICF-SW1")

Price: *ICF-SW1E:* around £160 in the United Kingdom, $260-340 elsewhere in Europe; *"ICF-SW1":* CAN$449.95.

Identical to Sony ICF-SW1S, less carrying case and most accessories, but not available in North America. "ICF-SW1" is the informal equivalent from Canadian dealer Atlantic Ham Radio.

Sony ICF-SW1E: Same radio as the Sony ICF-SW1S, but cheaper and sans accessories. Not available in all countries.

★ ★ ½   ¢

Sony ICF-SW20

Price: $99.95 in the United States, CAN$169.95 in Canada, around £70 in the United Kingdom, $110-150 elsewhere in Europe.
Advantages: Superior adjacent-channel rejection, similar to pricier ICF-SW1S and ICF-SW1E siblings, for size. Travel power lock.
Disadvantages: No digital frequency display. Limited world band spectrum coverage, omits important 13 MHz segment. Tiny speaker, mediocre audio. No longwave band reception.

Best of the low-tech, low-cost mini portables is the Sony ICF-SW20.

No meaningful signal-strength indicator. Dial not illuminated. No AC power supply.
Bottom Line: Although its circuitry is getting long in the tooth, the ICF-SW20 remains the best low-cost teeny travel radio.

The Sangean MS-103 has mediocre spurious-signal rejection, but good world band coverage.

★ ★

Sangean MS-103
(Sangean MS-103L)

Price: *MS-103:* $99.95 in the United States; *MS-103L:* $75-150 in Europe.
Advantages: Better world band coverage than otherwise-identical MS-101 ($85.95 in the United States). Travel power lock. FM stereo through headphones. *MS-103L:* Receives longwave band.
Disadvantages: No digital frequency display. Slightly limited world band coverage. Mediocre adjacent-channel and spurious-signal ("image") rejection. Inferior audio. Dial not illuminated. No meaningful signal-strength indicator. No AC power supply. *MS-103 and MS-101:* Do not receive longwave band. *MS-103L:* Lacks coverage of world band from 2.3-5.2 MHz.
Bottom Line: Preferable to the cheaper MS-101, but interesting only to the weight- and price-conscious traveler. Also sold under other names, including Goodmans and Siemens.

★ ★

Sangean MS-101

Price: $84.00 in the United States, CAN$99.95 in Canada, $65-125 in Europe.
Advantages: Inexpensive. Travel power lock. FM stereo through headphones.
Disadvantages: No digital frequency display. Limited world band coverage. Mediocre adjacent-channel and spurious- signal ("image") rejection. Inferior audio. Dial not illuminated. No meaningful signal-strength indicator. No AC power supply.

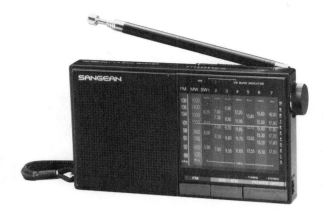

The Sangean MS-101, shown, has less world band coverage than the costlier MS-103.

Bottom Line: A low-priced, plain-vanilla portable of interest almost exclusively to the weight- and price-conscious traveler. Also sold under other names, including Goodmans and Siemens.

★ ★

Sangean SG-789
(Sangean SG-789L)

Price: *SG-789:* $69.95 in the United States, CAN$149.95 in Canada; *SG-789L:* $60-95 in Europe.

Advantages: Inexpensive. FM stereo through headphones. *SG-789L:* Receives longwave band.

Disadvantages: No digital frequency display. Somewhat limited coverage, omits important 13 MHz band. Mediocre adjacent-channel and spurious-signal ("image") rejection. Inferior audio. No meaningful signal-strength indicator. Dial not illuminated. No AC power supply. *SG-789:* Does not receive longwave band. *SG-789L:* Lacks 2.3-5.2 MHz world band coverage.

Bottom Line: Similar to the Sangean MS-101, but with less complete coverage. If this isn't cheap enough for you, try the Sangean SG-796, which lists in the United States for $59.95 —same play, fewer acts.

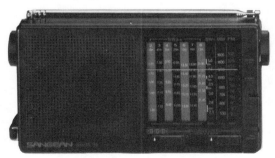

One of Sangean's cheapest models, the lightweight SG-789.

COMPACT PORTABLES

Good for Travel, Fair for Home

Compacts weigh in at 1.0-1.5 pounds, or 0.5-0.7 kg, and are typically sized 8 × 5 × 1.5″, or 20 × 13 × 4 cm. Like minis, they feed off "AA" (UM-3 penlite) batteries—but more of them. They travel almost as well as minis, but sound better and usually receive better, too. For some travelers, they also suffice as home sets—something minis can't really do. However, if you don't travel much by air, you will probably find better value and performance in a mid-sized portable.

Which stand out? Panasonic's RF-B65 and Sony's ICF-SW7600 do a very nice job in locations, such as Europe and Eastern North America, where signal strengths aren't downright feeble. The Sangean ATS-808, Realistic DX-380, Siemens RK 661 and Roberts R808, on the other hand, are the best choices for people living in those parts of the world, such as Central and Western North America, where weaker signals call for a model with superior sensitivity.

Looking for a bargain? Consider the just-released, easy-to-operate, Panasonic RF-B45. It's similar to the RF-B65, but costs less. It's also an excellent choice if you've never owned a world band radio before.

The following three *Editor's Choice* models are of similar overall quality, but tend to perform quite differently depending where you're listening from. Choose accordingly.

★ ★ ★ $\frac{1}{2}$ *Editor's Choice*

Panasonic RF-B65
(Panasonic RF-B65D)
(Panasonic RF-B65L)
(National B65)

Price: *RF-B65:* $269.95-279.95 in the United States, CAN$499.95 in Canada; *RF-B65 and RF-B65D:* around £180 in the United Kingdom, $290-450 elsewhere in Europe. RP-65 120V AC power supply $6.95 in the United States; RP-38 120/220V AC worldwide power supply $14.95 in the United States. (Power supply prices are as provided by Panasonic; actual selling prices in stores are much higher.)

Advantages: Superior overall world band performance for size. Very easy to operate for advanced-technology radio. Pleasant audio. Various helpful tuning features. Signal-strength

The Panasonic RF-B65 combines advanced technology with ease of operation and superior performance.

Sony's ICF-SW7600, the result of a product evolution beginning in 1983 with the ICF-2002.

indicator. World Time clock, plus second time-zone clock. Alarm/sleep facilities. Demodulates single-sideband signals, used by hams and utility stations. Receives longwave band. Travel power lock. AC power supply comes standard (outside North America).

Disadvantages: Cumbersome tuning knob inhibits speed. With built-in antenna, weak-signal sensitivity slightly low. Adjacent-channel rejection (selectivity) slightly broad. Clocks not displayed separately from frequency. Display and keypad not illuminated. AC power supply extra (North America).

Bottom Line: A very nice, easy-to-use portable, especially if you live in Europe or Eastern North America, where world band signals tend to be fairly strong.

★ ★ ★ ½   *Editor's Choice*

Sony ICF-SW7600

Price: $249.95 in the United States, CAN$449.95 in Canada, around £170 in the United Kingdom, $250-400 elsewhere in Europe.

Advantages: Superior overall for size. High-quality audio with supplied earpieces. Easy to operate for level of technology. Helpful tuning features. World Time clock with timer that controls certain tape recorders. Alarm/sleep facilities. Demodulates single sideband, used by hams and utility stations. Illuminated display. Travel power lock also disables display light. Comes with reel-in portable wire antenna, besides built-in telescopic one. Stereo FM, through earpieces, also covers Japanese FM band. Receives longwave band. Comes with AC power supply.

Disadvantages: No tuning knob. No meaningful signal-strength indicator. Earpieces less comfortable than foam-padded headphones. Assembly a bit sloppy on some samples.

Bottom Line: Excellent for globetrotting. Of the three top-rated compact models, this is the one most likely to perform well regardless of where you are in the world.

★ ★ ★ ½   *Editor's Choice*

Sangean ATS-808
(Realistic DX-380)
(Siemens RK 661)
(Roberts R808)

Price: *Sangean:* $259.00 in the United States, CAN$399.95 in Canada; *Realistic:* CAN$299.95 (sold only in Canada for the time being); *Siemens:* 398.00 DM in Germany. *Roberts:* around £120 in the United Kingdom. ADP-808 120V AC power supply $9.95 in the United States.

Advantages: Dual bandwidths, exceptional in this size radio, make for unusually pleasant listening. Easy to operate for high-tech radio. Already-pleasant speaker audio improves with supplied earpieces. Various helpful features.

Sangean's ATS-808 is the best compact for listening in some parts of the world. It's the only model in its size with two bandwidths.

Weak-signal sensitivity above average for size. Keypad has exceptional feel and tactile response. Receives longwave band. 24-hour World Time clock, displayed separately from frequency, and local clock. Alarm/sleep facilities. Signal strength indicator. Travel power lock. Stereo FM via earpieces. Superior FM performance. *Realistic:* 30-day money-back trial period.

Disadvantages: Spurious-signal ("image") rejection only adequate. Fast tuning tends to mute receiver. Tunes only in coarse 5 kHz increments. Display and keypad not illuminated. No carrying strap or handle. Supplied earpieces inferior to comparable foam-padded headphones. AC power supply extra.

Bottom Line: Best compact if you live in Central and Western North America, where weak signals abound—arguably Eastern North America, too. A poorer choice if you're in Europe, North Africa and the Near East, where signals are strong. The only "Editor's Choice" compact that doesn't demodulate single-sideband signals—a disadvantage for some radio enthusiasts, but for world band listening an advantage in that it makes operation less confusing.

New for 1992
★ ★ ★ ½   *Editor's Choice* ¢

Panasonic RF-B45
(Panasonic RF-B45DL)
(National B45)

Price: *RF-B45:* $189.95-199.95 in the United States, CAN$329.95 in Canada; *RF-B45DL:* around £130 in the United Kingdom, $220-320 in Europe. RP-65 120V AC power supply $6.95 in the United States; RP-38 120/220V AC worldwide power supply $14.95 in the United States. Suggested retail prices provided by Panasonic; some reputable dealers insist they are understated.

Advantages: Best performance for price/size category. Easy to operate for advanced-technology radio. A number of helpful tuning features. Signal-strength indicator. World Time clock. Alarm/sleep facilities. Demodulates single-sideband signals, used by hams and utility stations. Has longwave band.

Disadvantages: No tuning knob. Weak-signal sensitivity a bit low. Adjacent-channel rejection (selectivity) a bit broad. Clock not displayed separately from frequency. No display or keypad illumination. AC power supply extra.

Bottom Line: The best buy on the market in a compact portable under $200. Excellent for newcomers and travelers.

Evaluation of New Model: The new Panasonic RF-B45, had it run true to expectations, would have been simply the earlier RF-B40 with

single-sideband reception added. Instead, Panasonic decided to make the 'B45 a variant on the top-of-the-line RF-B65. It's quite a radio.

The 'B45's tuning is fully synthesized, with digital frequency display. Tuning features include keypad, nine memory presets (plus another nine for FM), rudimentary frequency and memory scanning, and up/down slewing buttons like the buttons you use to carousel channels on TV. No tuning knob—the set's biggest drawback—but a function key allows you to scoot right to the desired shortwave band. The 'B45's synthesizer tunes only in coarse 5 kHz increments, but it has a separate analog control for tuning between 5 kHz points.

The 'B45 has only one selectivity position, and it's broader than it should be—the set's only significant weakness. Fortunately, the fine-tuning control helps alleviate this by allowing adjacent-channel interference to be reduced by off-tuning the station slightly.

The 'B45's sensitivity—weak-signal reception—is reasonably good. It's more than adequate for listening in Europe or North America east of the Mountain Time zone, but not equal to the Sangean ATS-808 in its various incarnations if you're listening in the North American West.

Ergonomics? The panel layout is well thought out, including having the zero key where it belongs. The power switch lights up, but there's no display or keypad illumination.

However, the scan button is located just under the up/down slew tuning button. It's easy to hit by mistake, causing the radio to sail merrily up the band on autopilot until you poke the scan button once again to stop it, or it stops at a strong station.

The 'B65's display includes a 24-hour clock and rudimentary three-level signal-strength indicator. The clock appears only with the set off—a major annoyance. When will manufacturers finally understand that we need to know World Time when the radio is on?

Most good world band radios cost over $200 or £130. Here's one that doesn't, Panasonic's new RF-B45. Straightforward to operate, too.

That display also has a battery indicator—no surprise here. But how the set handles weak batteries is: the radio suddenly goes dead, but the clock continues to function and the battery indicator comes on. Pressing the power button brings the radio back to life for a bit longer.

Rudimentary single-sideband reception allows you to listen to hams and utility stations. Its operation—similar to that of the Sony ICF-SW7600, but less "touchy"—is clunky, relying on a fine-tuning knurled thumbwheel, which unfortunately doesn't affect the frequency readout, alongside the set. There's no separate narrow bandwidth, either, nor an LSB/USB switch, and the detector's performance is mediocre. Yet, reception is surprisingly stable. Overall, for the price, it's about as good as you can expect these days.

Traveling? The 'B45 has a "hold" key that maintains the set's status quo by making the other buttons inoperative—a real help in keeping the set from turning on inside your suitcase. For awakening, there is a programmable "on" function, with "off" automatically occurring 90 minutes later. The sleep control switches off the radio after 30, 60 or 90 minutes.

The mediumwave AM band is tuned in either 9 or 10 kHz increments, which allows for reception in any part of the world. There's longwave band coverage, too—useful in such places as Europe and North Africa.

FM is monaural only, with tuning in 50 kHz increments. This allows for FM reception in any part of the world, regardless of regional channel-spacing norms. Audio quality, not surprisingly, is far from ideal for FM, what with this set's modest speaker. The single hi-lo tone switch doesn't help much, either. For world band, though, audio quality is adequate for the radio's size.

The 'B45 has the usual nice touches you expect from Panasonic. Quality of construction appears to be above average. The telescopic antenna base pulls up, and there's complete antenna rotation and swiveling—all of which allow you to use the set on its back, where it belongs. A flip-out elevation panel tilts the set up towards you for handy operation.

The 'B45 comes with no AC power supply. Panasonic's outboard RP-65 supply is optional for use in North America and other places with 120V AC power. Better is Panasonic's RP-38 120/220V AC supply, which works in virtually any country.

Panasonic's new RF-B45 is the best compact radio available under $200, and it doesn't require a degree in particle physics to operate. In the under-$200 category, only the larger, pricier and more complicated Sangean ATS-803A, in its various incarnations, performs better.

Need a scanner and world band radio in one package? Sony's ICF-PRO80 will do the trick. Deplorable ergonomics, though.

★ ★ ★ $\frac{1}{2}$

Sony ICF-PRO80 (Sony ICF-PRO70)

Price: $449.95 in the United States, CAN$689.95 in Canada, around £300 in the United Kingdom, $550-700 elsewhere in Europe.

Advantages: Superior overall performance for size. Above average at bringing in weak world band stations. Helpful tuning features, including scanning, and comes with versatile VHF scanner (reduced coverage in some versions). Demodulates single-sideband signals, used by utility and ham signals. Receives Japanese FM band, longwave band, VHF-TV audio. Illuminated display.

Disadvantages: Awkward to operate—especially outboard scanner module, which requires removal and replacement of antenna and battery pack. Mediocre audio. No tuning knob. Few travel features. No signal-strength indicator. No AC power supply.

Bottom Line: Great for puzzle lovers. Otherwise, of value mainly to weak-signal chasers who need a small world band portable with a VHF scanner.

Sony ICF-SW800
(Sony ICF-SW700)

Price: *ICF-SW800:* $199.95 in the United States; *ICF-SW700:* ¥13,000 (around $100) in Japan. AC-D3M 120V AC/4.5V DC power supply $12.95 in the United States.

Advantages: Innovative card-type tuning system helps newcomers get started. Incorporates a number of other helpful tuning features, too. Unusually obvious how to operate for level of technology. World Time clock. Alarm facility. Highly effective travel power lock. Comes with reel-in portable wire antenna. *ICF-SW700:* Relatively inexpensive for technology provided.

Disadvantages: No tuning knob. Slightly limited world band coverage, including omission of important 21 MHz segment. No longwave band. Adjacent-channel rejection (selectivity) only fair. Tunes only in coarse 5 kHz increments. Keypad uses unorthodox two-row configuration and offers no tactile feedback. Clock not displayed separately from frequency. No display or keypad illumination. No signal-strength indicator. AC power supply extra. Not widely distributed outside Japan at present, but this could change. *ICF-SW800:* No mediumwave AM. *ICF-SW700:* No FM.

Bottom Line: Innovative tuning, respectable performance—but once you become familiar with world band, the ICF-SW800's innovation fades into novelty.

Evaluation of New Model: If only world band radios were foolproof to operate, the reasoning goes, folks would buy them by the carload.

Sony's latest attempt to make the unsimple simple is the ICF-SW800, currently being test marketed in the United States, and the similar ICF-SW700 sold in Japan. The '800 receives FM, but not mediumwave AM; with the '700, it's *vice versa*, with a plus for globetrotters being 9 kHz and 10 kHz channel spacing.

The 'SW800 is in many ways a typical compact digital portable. It has the usual LCD for frequency and 24-hour clock/alarm display, although seconds aren't displayed and, alas, World Time can be read *only* when the radio is switched off. There are also keypad tuning and at least ten presets—plus up/down frequency slew tuning, as in a VCR "clicker," in coarse 5 kHz increments (50 kHz for FM).

There's no tuning knob. However, there is a flip-out tilt panel to angle the radio for handy operation. Additionally, there's a carrying strap, earphone/record/4.5V DC power sockets, a volume control and a power switch with a travel lock built in. That travel lock couldn't be more effective; it works every time you turn the set off, so you can't forget it.

Sony's latest attempts to have world band listening easily grasped are the ICF-SW800 and ICF-SW700. Both are tuned using preprogrammed station cards.

Where the '800/'700 stands apart from the herd is that it may also be tuned by special cards the size of an ordinary credit card. Each side of almost every card is dedicated to frequencies for a single station. So, if you wish to hear, say, Radio Moscow, you pop in the card with "Radio Moscow" on one side—taking care not to let direct sunlight hit the card's sensor—then poke at the various "buttons" on its surface until the station appears.

The radio comes with three station cards, or six sides in all. In the version sold in the United States, there's one side for the Deutsche Welle, another for the BBC World Service, two for the Voice of America and, of course, one for Moscow. The sixth side is for "free memories"—ten presets you can use as you see fit for other stations. The owner's manual says nothing about other station cards being available.

There is also a separate card to allow you to set the 24-hour World Time clock. You *must* have that card to adjust the clock; misplace it, and you'll either have to get another or you will never be able to reset the clock.

Only one card can be used at any given time, but there is a slot on the side for storing a second card. The third station card, along with the "must" clock card, can be stored within the battery cavity. Not terribly handy, but safe.

Interestingly, according to Sony the cards are not magnetically coded, and thus aren't susceptible to deprogramming by the set's speaker magnet. Yet, all preprogrammed station frequencies may be changed at will by the operator. Easily, too. This is important, as most stations change frequencies quite often, and our cards were already partially out of date when we purchased the radio.

There are, however, magnetic memories for the clock/alarm. These use the regular 3xAA power batteries for data backup, and they won't lose that data until some 50 seconds or so after power loss. This not only gives you ample time to replace exhausted batteries, it also ensures that should the batteries lose contact momentarily when the set is jostled, data will remain intact.

Shortwave coverage, 3700-17900 kHz, omits the important 21 MHz world band segment used during the day, as well as the lesser 25 MHz, 3 MHz and 2 MHz segments. (These segments are explained under "World Band Spectrum" in the Glossary.) This isn't bad coverage, but nearly all other models in this price range give you the full shortwave loaf . . . *and* also manage to receive both AM and FM.

World band performance is okay. Sensitivity to weak signals is fairly good, and there's a nifty reel-in "tape measure" outboard antenna to help —although this antenna would be much more effective if its coupling were direct, rather than inductive. Adjacent-channel rejection (selectivity, only one bandwidth) and audio quality are fair, and spurious-signal rejection is good.

Ergonomics are reasonable. The knurled volume control operates nicely, and programming the memories and clock is easy even if the word "programming" scares you. However, the keypad imprinted on each card uses an unorthodox two-row scheme. This layout takes some getting used to. Also, the flat surface of the keypad offers no tactile feedback whatsoever—although there's an aural "beep" each

time a key is depressed—or anything other than a visual indication to tell which key is which. There's virtually no practical way to tune this radio in dim light or the dark, or if you're visually handicapped.

The card-tuning scheme is what makes this model special, and it functions quite well. A total newcomer to world band listening will find this to be nigh foolproof for those first few days when the vagaries of world band might otherwise confuse.

Here's the rub: Once you get the essential hang of shortwave, this initial convenience fades into novelty—even annoyance. After all, while the concept is straightforward, it requires the operator to fiddle about, like a poker dealer, with a bunch of cards just to tune in a station.

Better, it would seem, would have been to have had dedicated pushbuttons, as on the Sony ICF-2010/ICF-2001D—one button per channel. After all, these and a 24-hour clock could always be preprogrammed at the factory to get newcomers off the mark, yet would be far handier than cards for the newcomer and experienced listener, alike.

In the final analysis, world band radios, like personal computers, can be made sensible to operate—and many already are for people who are reasonably adept. But well-meaning recent attempts to make these devices idiot proof have sometimes wound up making things more complex, instead of less. The '800 is a shining example of this.

The Sony ICF-SW800 and sibling '700 perform quite reasonably, and are not overpriced for what they do. They're also great "what will they think of next" conversation starters. If

PORTABLES: WHO'S UP AND WHO'S DOWN

⬆ **SANGEAN.** A few years back, nobody had heard of this tiny firm. Many still haven't, but it's not tiny any more. Annual world band production has soared into the millions of radios—even though most don't appear under the Sangean name—and a second factory is planned. Achilles' heel: weak marketing.

⬆ **RADIO SHACK.** Sleeping giant awakens. Much-improved radios now bring the pleasures of world band to thousands of shopping centers throughout America.

⬆ **GRUNDIG.** Radios are a mixed bag, but American marketing isn't. In a handful of years, Grundig's aggressive promotion and clockwork distribution have helped make world band radio a household term. American sales curve resembles the Matterhorn. Is Europe next?

⬆ **PANASONIC.** This electronics leviathan is still a marketing flyweight—just try to *find* one of their world band models—but its radios keep getting better and more affordable.

⬆ **DAK.** After a bumpy takeoff, this California retailer and its Chinese supplier have redefined the low end of the market.

⬇ **SONY.** Once the IBM of world band radio, now increasingly an also-ran relying on cosmetic redesign and novelty instead of useful innovation. Novel new marketing and PR strategy, too: Treat products as corporate secrets so nobody will know about them. Saving grace: still retains best technical edge in industry.

you've never used a world band radio and are concerned about what it might entail, the '800 may very well appeal to you. If so, go for it.

However, if the simplicity and price of the '800 grab you, but the card-shuffling doesn't, take a look at such models as Panasonic's new RF-B45. These provide slightly more bang for the same buck, and over the longer haul should be more satisfying.

★ ★ ½

Sony ICF-7700
(Sony ICF-7600DA)

Price: *ICF-7700:* $199.95 in the United States, CAN$339.95 in Canada; *ICF-7600DA:* under £150 in the United Kingdom, $230-300 elsewhere in Europe.

Advantages: Very easy to use. World Time clock. Alarm/sleep facilities. Only model featuring digital frequency display complemented by unusual digitalized "analog" tuning scale. Helpful tuning aids include 15 presets—five for world band —and a tuning knob. Travel power lock. Covers longwave and Japanese FM bands.

Disadvantages: Poor adjacent-channel rejection (selectivity). Slightly limited world band coverage. Mediocre unwanted-signal rejection. Coarse 5 kHz tuning increments. No display or "dial" illumination. No meaningful signal-strength indicator. No AC power supply.

Bottom Line: In today's marketplace of rich choices, there's no longer any reason to put up with this model's utter lack of adjacent-channel rejection. In this size and price class, a much better bet for the technically timid is the new Panasonic RF-B45.

Sony's ICF-7700 is digital, but tries to come off as an old-fashioned needle-and-dial set. It's also sold as the ICF-7600DA.

The Magnavox AE 3805, advanced technology made simple. Also sold as the Philips AE 3805.

★ ★ ½   ¢

Magnavox AE 3805
(Philips AE 3805)

Price: *Magnavox:* $149.95 in the United States.

Disadvantages: *Magnavox:* FM and mediumwave AM tuning steps do not conform to channel spacing in much of the world outside the Americas. *Philips:* Mediumwave AM tuning steps do not conform to channel spacing within the Americas.

Bottom Line: Similar, except for layout and lack of stereo earphone output, to Sangean ATS 800, below (see).

★ ★ ½   ¢

Sangean ATS 800
Realistic DX-370
(Siemens RP 647G4)

Price: *Sangean:* $149.00 in the United States. ADP-808 120V AC power supply $7.99 in the United States. *Realistic:* $119.95 at Radio Shack stores in the United States. *Siemens:* About $90 in Europe.

Advantages: Relatively inexpensive for model with digital frequency display and presets. Already-pleasant speaker audio improves with headphones. Five preset buttons retrieve up to ten world band and ten AM/FM stations. Relatively selective for price class. Relatively sensitive, a plus for listeners in Central and Western North America. Simple to operate for radio at this technology level. World Time clock. Timer/ sleep/alarm facilities. Travel power lock. Low

The Sangean ATS 800, also sold as the Realistic DX-370 and Siemens RP 647G4, provides some advanced technology at low cost.

Sony's ICF-7601, the Volkswagen Beetle of the world band radio. Although its circuitry is dated, it remains the best non-digital small portable around.

battery indicator, unusual in price class. Stereo FM via earpieces (supplied in Sangean version). *Realistic:* 30-day money-back trial period.

Disadvantages: Mediocre spurious-signal ("image") rejection. Inferior dynamic range, a drawback for listeners in Europe, North Africa and the Near East. Does not tune 2300-2500, 7300-7600, 9300-9500, 21750-21850 and 25600-26100 kHz world band segments. Tunes world band only in coarse 5 kHz steps. No tuning knob; tunes only via multi-speed up/down slewing buttons. No longwave band. Signal-strength indicator nigh useless. No display or keypad illumination. Clock not displayed separately from frequency. No carrying strap or handle. AC power supply extra. *Sangean:* Supplied earpieces inferior to comparable foam-padded earphones. *Sangean and Realistic:* FM and mediumwave AM tuning steps do not conform to channel spacing in much of the world outside the Americas. *Siemens:* Mediumwave AM tuning steps do not conform to channel spacing within the Americas. *Sangean and Siemens:* Do not receive 1635-1705 kHz portion of forthcoming expanded AM band in Americas, although this could change.

Bottom Line: A popular starter set. Okay for the price, especially for American West Coast listeners who can't afford the Sangean ATS-808 in its various incarnations.

★ ★ ½　　　　　　　　　　　　　　　　　¢

Sony ICF-7601

Price: $129.95 in the United States, CAN$209.95 in Canada, $125-170 in Europe.
Advantages: Weak-signal sensitivity above average for size. Travel power lock. Covers Japanese FM band.
Disadvantages: No digital frequency display. Dial not illuminated. Slightly limited world band coverage. Adjacent-channel rejection only fair. Some crosstalk among adjacent world band segments. No longwave band coverage. No meaningful signal-strength indicator. No AC power supply.
Bottom Line: Honest, reasonable performance at an attractive price, but technology is long in the tooth.

New for 1992

★ ★　　　　　　　　　　　　　　　　　　¢

DAK MR-101s (Pulser)

Price: *DAK:* $49.90 by mail order in the United States. *Pulser:* CAN$59.99 in Canada.
Advantages: Least costly portable tested with digital frequency display. Least costly portable tested with presets (ten for world band, ten for AM/FM). Slightly more selective than usual for price category. Relatively simple to operate for technology class. World Time clock. Alarm/sleep timer. Illuminated display. Available on 30-day money-back basis. FM stereo via optional headphones.
Disadvantages: Unusually lacking in weak-signal sensitivity. No tuning knob; tunes only via presets and multi-speed up/down slewing. Tunes world band only in coarse 5 kHz steps. Mediumwave AM tuning steps do not conform to channel spacing in much of the world outside the Americas. Frequency display in confusing XX.XX/XX.XX5 MHz format. Poor spurious- signal ("image") rejection. Mediocre dynamic range. Does not tune relatively unimportant 6200-7100 and 25600-26100 kHz world band segments. Does not receive longwave band or 1615-1705 kHz portion of forthcoming expanded AM band in the Americas. No signal-strength indicator. No travel power lock switch. No AC power supply. Reportedly

prone to malfunction; flimsy antenna, especially swivel, prone to breakage. Antenna swivels, but does not rotate. Not widely available.

Bottom Line: Audi cockpit, Yugo engine. Nevertheless, in Eastern North America this is the best choice under $90.

Evaluation of New Model: In 1990, the California firm of DAK Industries began selling something really revolutionary: the MR-101, a $49.90 world band portable with digital frequency readout, 20 presets (10 for shortwave), up/down slew tuning, a clock with alarm and sleep features, a dial light, and other goodies—all for a mere $49.90.

Trouble is, it hardly picked up any stations.

Now, the Chinese firm that makes the radio for DAK has introduced a replacement, the MR-101s, also reportedly sold by other firms as the Pulser (not tested) and possibly other names. And, yes—it really is improved.

Start with where it tunes. The old version went from 3200-7300 and 9500-21750 kHz, missing many juicy world band stations. The new version covers 2300-6200 and 7100-21850 kHz, adding the important 7300-9500 and 21750-21850 kHz ranges chocablock with world band catches.

Another positive change is in how the radio tunes. In order to keep costs down, tuning features have been kept to a minimum. Not only is there no tuning knob, there's also no keypad. Instead, on the original MR-101 there was a pair of up/down multi-speed slewing buttons and five programmable channel memories. This original version required some fleet-fingered button pushing and hair-trigger reflexes to get the slewing controls to tune the set properly.

No more. The MR-101s has the same basic tuning configuration, but with three slew buttons—up, down, and fast—instead of the former two. These give the operator much more control over the tuning process, even though the tuning rate is a bit slower.

The DAK MR-101s is substantially improved over last year's MR-101. For some, it's the best radio available under $100.

Nevertheless, one annoying tuning complication remains unchanged: the MR-101s' use of a hoary "SW1 SW2" control. (Better radios have one setting for the entire shortwave spectrum.) For trips abroad, there is yet another drawback—The 10 kHz tuning steps for mediumwave AM are appropriate for the Americas, but not for most other parts of the world, where 9 kHz channel spacing is the norm. So while the MR-101s is in many ways a worthy travel set, it's of limited use for listening to AM outside the Americas.

Further to improvements, the old MR-101's clock used the 12-hour format. That's fine for local time, but incompatible with World Time, or UTC, which uses a 24-hour format. The new MR-101s uses a 24-hour clock with an "off" setting to the timer, which previously had only an "on" setting. This means the radio now cycles itself on and off for one event, like a VCR.

The new MR-101s is definitely less insensitive than the original DAK model, although it's still lacking. Listeners on the North American East Coast or in Europe, for example, now should be able to hear nearly all the stronger international broadcasters. Nevertheless, it is still not sensitive enough for rewarding use in Western North America.

The MR-101s has FM stereo, with pedestrian performance, through optional headphones. The FM stage now tunes in 100, not 200, kHz increments, and thus may be used, albeit with a bit of off-tuning (50 kHz increments are optimum), in nearly any part of the world. For globetrotters and those outside the Americas, that's a big improvement, indeed.

The MR-101s' telescopic antenna swivels, but isn't rotatable, so it's difficult to place the antenna at an optimum angle for FM reception. That lack of rotation also makes it impossible to have the antenna fully vertical—the proper position for world band reception—unless the radio is placed on its tipsy bottom. This means you can't listen properly if this radio is on its back, which is otherwise the most convenient placement of a portable.

Not every change has been for the better. Mediumwave AM coverage stops at 1610 kHz—even worse than the MR-101's upper limit of 1630 kHz—and well below the forthcoming new limit for the Americas of 1705 kHz.

In other respects the radio is pretty much as before. World band tuning is in 5 kHz increments, and the frequency display, in contravention of established norms, simply drops the least-significant zero. Thus, for example, 11990 kHz reads out as 11.99 MHz—an annoyance. The MR-101s' lock switch turns off only the tuning circuitry—not the power, and not even the easily activated dial light. Travelers thus are forced to remove the batteries before packing to ensure they won't be depleted en route.

Also as before is adjacent-channel rejection (selectivity). It's better than that of some sets costing over twice as much, but is still quite broad. Audio quality, while a bit tinny, isn't too bad for a small portable.

The MR-101s has lesser-strength repeats, technically known as "images" (see Glossary), of radio signals that actually operate almost 1 MHz higher. The resulting aural intrusion—whistles, roars, beeps and the like—is one of the major drawbacks of low-cost world band radios, and why they are best avoided.

The MR-101s' quality of construction appears to be below average. Secondhand reports from MR-101 users suggest that this is, indeed, not likely to be a robust set. An obvious mechanical problem continues to be the telescopic antenna's non-rotating swivel, which bends easily. Should that swivel break, it would be harder than most to replace—assuming you can get the part.

No question—the MR-101s is clearly no Sony ICF-2010, nor even a Panasonic RF-B45. But if you live along the North American East Coast or in the Midwest, it is the only set under $90 or so that offers some advanced technology and at least an acceptable level of performance. In Europe and the Near East, this model should be approached with caution not only because of its inappropriate mediumwave AM tuning increments, but also because of its limited ability to cope with the herculean signals commonly heard there.

New for 1992

★ ★

Rodelvox Digital World Band
Rodelsonic Digital World Band

Price: $99.95 plus $6.95 shipping in United States.

Advantages: Relatively inexpensive for a model with digital frequency display and presets (ten for world band, ten for AM/FM). Relatively simple to operate for technology class. Alarm/sleep timer with clock. Illuminated display. FM stereo via optional headphones.

Disadvantages: Mediocre sensitivity to weak signals. No tuning knob; tunes only via presets and multi-speed up/down slewing. Tunes world band only in coarse 5 kHz steps. FM and mediumwave AM tuning steps do not conform to channel spacing in much of the world outside the Americas. Frequency display in confusing XX.XX/XX.XX5 format. Poor spurious-signal ("image") rejection. Mediocre dynamic range. Does not tune popular 7300-9500 and 21750-21850 kHz segments. Does not receive longwave broadcasts or 1635-1705 kHz portion

Simple, but with some advanced technology, is the new Rodelvox, which has presets arranged in an arc. Look for it to appear under other names.

of forthcoming expanded AM band in the Americas. No signal-strength indicator. Clock in 12-hour format. No travel power lock. No AC power supply. Quality of construction appears to be below average. Not widely available.

Bottom Line: Terrible choice for international travel. With the similar DAK model available, why pay double?

Evaluation of New Model: The Chinese-made Rodelvox, sold by the California firm of Haverhills and also known as the Rodelsonic Digital World Band (and probably sold under other names, as well), is in many ways similar to the DAK MR-101s. But here's the rub: It's just a tad less good, especially for traveling; yet, it costs fully twice as much.

Facilities for finding stations are Spartan. There's no tuning knob—no keypad, either—just a pair of up-down slewing buttons and five buttons for programmable channel memories. As these memory buttons, which are spread in an arc, work independently for each of the four "bands," there are actually 20 memories in all: five for mediumwave AM, five for FM, five for "SW1" and five for "SW2."

Those slewing buttons are multi-speed. Although they are a mediocre substitute for a keypad and tuning knob, you get used to them. Indeed, for the first-time listener they have the advantage of being extremely simple to operate.

The set tunes mediumwave AM from 530-1630 kHz only in 10 kHz increments, omitting the 1635-1705 kHz portion of the forthcoming expanded AM band in the Americas. 10 kHz increments are fine for the Americas, but in most of the rest of the world 9 kHz increments are used.

Stereo FM reception, through headphones, is pedestrian. Tuning of the FM band is done in 200 kHz increments. As with AM, this doesn't conform to channel separation norms in most countries outside the Western Hemisphere. There's no longwave band coverage, either—another drawback for listening within certain parts of the world, such as Europe. In all, then, the Rodelvox's AM and FM operation is woefully inappropriate for globetrotting.

World band fares better. "SW1" covers from 3200-7300 kHz, while "SW2" receives 9500-21750 kHz—all in 5 kHz, or one-channel, steps. Missed are the 7305-9495 and 21755-21850 kHz segments. As you can see by glancing at *Passport's* Blue Pages, many worthwhile stations are found within these omitted frequency ranges—particularly 7305-7550 and 9395-9495 kHz.

The Rodelvox's clock/frequency LCD is illuminated for nighttime use. But instead of displaying frequency in the customary XXXXX kHz frequency layout, it reads as XX.XX or XX.XX5 MHz. For frequencies ending in "5", that's fine, even if the half-sized "5" is a bit odd and hard to see. But the last digit is completely dropped when it's a zero. So while 9565 kHz displays as 9.565 MHz, 9560 kHz comes out as 9.56 MHz. Radio Moscow uses this technique, but nearly nobody else does, as it only serves to confuse.

The timer allows for at least some VCR-type hands-off taping. Problem is, its clock uses the 12-hour format—not the 24-hour format required for World Time. And the timer is a simple on-only alarm. That's fine for being awakened, but it is of little use for taping. There's also a sleep-off control.

Ergonomics are quite good, and the antenna rotates on its swivel. This is a real plus over the DAK model, as it allows the set to be operated while laid on its back— the handiest position. There's also a lock switch for the keypad, but this doesn't serve as a power lock to prevent the radio or its dial light from coming on accidentally in transit, running down the batteries.

Performance is a mixed bag. Adjacent-channel rejection (selectivity) is fairly typical for a $100 model—you can hear squeals and other slop from adjacent channels, but it's usually not all that obnoxious. Audio quality, while a bit tinny, is okay. Sensitivity to weak signals, although mediocre, is adequate for reception of most major broadcasters—unless you're listening from the North American West Coast. There, where signals tend to be weak, exceptionally sensitive models, such as the Sangean ATS-808, are preferable. Single-conversion IF circuitry, one of the great remaining curses of cheap radios, means you hear annoying repeats—"images"—of radio signals that actually operate almost 1 MHz away.

The only way to be certain of a given model's reliability is to use numerous samples over long periods of time. As the Rodelvox is a new model, we haven't been able to do that. But looking it over doesn't inspire confidence. Nor does the fact that our sample arrived with a wrinkled antenna.

The Rodelvox lacks the appeal of rock-bottom price found in the DAK model, which costs half as much. Yet, it doesn't have the quality of construction of a variety of similar models within its price class. Additionally, while its performance limits it to being suitable mainly for traveling—not day-after-day listening at home—the channel spacing of its FM and mediumwave AM bands, plus the lack of longwave band coverage, makes it singularly inappropriate for use outside the Americas.

If this set can't hack it as a world travel portable, and just limps by for use at home, then what is it being produced for?

New for 1992

★ ★

Sangean SG-700L
Realistic DX-350

Price: $69.95 in the United States (both models). Realistic #273-1454 120V AC/6V DC power supply $7.95.

Advantages: Inexpensive. Receives longwave band. *Realistic:* 30-day money-back trial period.

Disadvantages: No digital frequency display. Slightly limited world band coverage. Mediocre spurious-signal ("image") rejection. Adjacent-channel rejection (selectivity) only fair. Modest sensitivity to weak signals. Mediocre audio quality. Antenna swivels, but does not rotate. No meaningful signal-strength indicator. Dial not illuminated. AC power supply optional.

Bottom Line: Adequate for use on trips, but a dubious choice for day-to-day listening.

Evaluation of New Model: The '700L's coverage includes the usual FM and mediumwave AM bands; the longwave band; plus world band from roughly 5800-6250, 7050-7550, 9410-9920, 11570-12100, 13550-13900, 15050-15650, 17450-18100, 21450-22050 and 25600-26150 kHz. For a model in this price class, that's reasonable coverage.

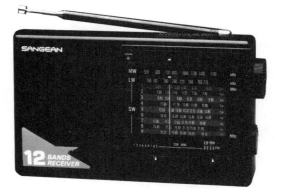

Designed for taking on trips is the new Realistic DX-350, also sold as the Sangean SG-700L.

A plus is that the forthcoming 1600-1705 kHz expanded AM band segment for the Americas is included. Too, in Europe and North Africa you'll appreciate its longwave band coverage.

Where the low cost becomes evident right off is in the old-fashioned analog needle-and-dial tuning circuitry. This means there is no digital frequency readout to tell you precisely where the radio is tuned. Another cost-related shortcoming is obnoxious interference from spurious "image" signals on faraway channels, bothering the signal you're trying to hear.

Features are not the '700L's high card, either. The set is tuned only by a pair of band selectors and a tuning knob, and has a nigh-useless LED signal-strength indicator. There's no travel power lock to prevent the radio switching on accidentally, but the on-off button is not easy to activate accidentally.

Performance is adequate for the sort of listening most travelers do—but precious little else. Adjacent-channel rejection (selectivity) is only fair. Sensitivity to weak signals is also only fair with the built-in telescopic antenna—which, alas, does not rotate on its swivel. This lack of rotation means that the only way for the antenna to be in the proper vertical position for listening to world band stations is to rest the radio vertically, which is unhandy.

Audio has perceptible distortion and no significant bass response, but is adequate for occasional listening. FM performance, overall, is a cut above average for the price/size class.

The bottom line is that the '700L is perfectly adequate for listening to major broadcasters while you're traveling about. And if it's stolen or lost, you can shrug it off.

Still, this is clearly no set for day-in-and-day-out listening. For that, Radio Shack's DX-440, which lists for $199.95—or the essentially identical Sangean ATS-803A in its various incarnations—remains the under-$200, street price, model of choice, along with Panasonic's slightly cheaper new RF-B45. If these are beyond your budget, look over the Realistic DX-370.

Radio Shack will be introducing other new world band models, such as the top-of-the-line DX-390, in the near future. We'll see how these stack up in next year's *Passport*.

★ ★

Panasonic RF-B20L
(Panasonic RF-B20)
(National B20)

Price: CAN$189.95 in Canada, around £70 in the United Kingdom, $120-195 elsewhere. No longer offered in the United States.

Advantages: Good audio for size; continuous tone control. Weak-signal sensitivity slightly above average for class.

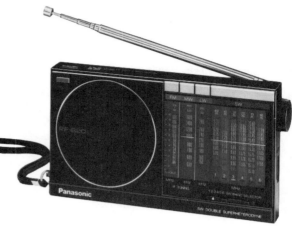

Panasonic's RF-B20 is getting increasingly difficult to find.

Disadvantages: No digital frequency display. Limited world band coverage, omits important 13 and 21 MHz segments. Mediocre adjacent-channel rejection. No meaningful signal-strength indicator. No AC power supply. Not offered in U.S.

Bottom Line: A reasonable performer that would be much better were it to have more complete world band coverage and sort stations out more successfully.

★ ★

Grundig Yacht Boy 230
(Grundig Travel Kit 230)

Price: *Yacht Boy 230:* $199.95 in the United States, CAN$259.95 in Canada, $120-175 in Europe. *Travel Kit 230:* $279.95 in the United States, CAN$399.95 in Canada.

Advantages: Includes World Time and world-wide multi-country clock/alarm/sleep timer with electronic map. Illuminated dial. Receives longwave band. Stereo FM through earphones.

Grundig's Yacht Boy 230 is also available in a travel kit version with pocket knife, alarm clock, pen/pencil set and flashlight.

Extra-cost Travel Kit version, apparently available only in North America, comes with zippered carrying case, pocket knife, alarm clock, pen/pencil set and flashlight.

Disadvantages: No digital frequency display. Slightly limited world band coverage. Mediocre spurious-signal ("image") and adjacent-channel rejection (selectivity). Tricky on-off switch. Pushbutton volume control increases or decreases sound in sizable bites, compromising adjustability. Annoying tuner backlash at lower end of each band. No meaningful signal-strength indicator. No AC power supply.

Bottom Line: A decent, but undistinguished and overpriced, radio of interest mainly for its world map clock.

New for 1992
★ ★

Sangean SG 621
(Sangean SG 631)

Price: *SG 621:* $119.00 in the United States; *SG 631:* $139.00 in the United States.

Advantages: World Time clock, plus second time-zone clock. Alarm/sleep facilities. Self-extinguishing clock light. Stereo FM through earpieces (supplied). Superior FM capture ratio helps in selecting desired station. Smaller than most models in compact category, a plus

Sangean makes a variety of small, low-cost portables. The SG 621 uses digital readout only for its clock—not frequencies.

for traveling. *SG 631:* Clock programmed with local time and date for 260 different cities around the world.

Disadvantages: No digital frequency display. Frequency dial not illuminated. Limited world band coverage. Mediocre spurious and adjacent-channel rejection. Antenna swivels, but does not rotate. No meaningful signal-strength indicator. FM reception sometimes compromised by SCA interference. Does not receive longwave broadcasts. No AC power supply. Lacks carrying strap or handle.

Bottom Line: No surprises, except perhaps the clock, in this latest outdated-technology offering from Sangean. Somewhat overpriced for what it does, which isn't much.

RUBBISH RADIOS: WHY DO THEY SELL?

With all the publicity given to world band radio during the 1991 Gulf conflict, it was inevitable that the Ginsu knife crowd would see a juicy opportunity to make a buck hawking junky shortwave portables. See our review of the "Panashiba FX-298," for example.

The curse of world band radios is that, unlike televisions, you can manufacture them for nearly nothing—provided you don't care how they perform. Rubbish radios like this have been around for years, driving people away from world band with their clumsy operation and screeching performance.

Better advanced-technology models, rated in this Buyer's Guide at three stars or more, perform well but cost more. As most people are not yet familiar enough with world band to understand why they should pay more for one model as opposed to another, these shabby performers continue to sell. Of course, they disappoint. Most get put aside once the novelty wears off.

Dealers don't help, either. Specialty outlets aside, most retailers tend to treat world band as they do refrigerators or VCRs, stressing "price points"—a concept that just doesn't work the same way with world band. This is changing, but slowly, as more dealers begin to realize that offering better radios means fewer returns and greater repeat and step-up sales. Witness the improvement in product quality at Haverhills, DAK and The Sharper Image—three major retailers—just in the last year, and Radio Shack over the past two years.

For traveling, some rubbish radios are okay. Lose one, who cares? But for day-to-day listening, they're like chewing gum—the pleasure doesn't last.

Evaluation of New Model: At first glance, the SG 621 appears to come with digital frequency display, but it's only an LCD clock, nothing more. Lacking a digital frequency display, tuning isn't via precise numbers, but by a vague needle-and-dial.

The '621 covers AM 530-1710 kHz, which means full coverage once the expanded AM band takes root in the Americas. FM has the usual coverage, and as a bonus works in stereo when earpieces (supplied) are used. There's no longwave band coverage, at least in the American version. Should an SG 621L version be introduced, it would almost certainly cover the longwave band, possibly by reducing shortwave coverage; check by looking at the dial.

The '621's world band coverage is from about 5880-6250, 7050-7500, 9470-9950, 11600-12100, 13550-13950, 15010-15700, 17450-18000 and 21450-22050 kHz. Can't argue with that—these are the prime chunks—except that in Europe it's tough to do without such gems as the BBC World Service on 9410 kHz, or Radio France Internationale on 3965 kHz.

The '621's easily adjusted clock covers two time zones, both in 24-hour format. This is ideal for World Time, but the second time zone should use the 12-hour local-time format. There's also a sleep-delay and alarm facility, but no "snooze" shutoff, so it's not really a VCR-type event timer. That clock also comes with a self-extinguishing light, but the frequency dial is unlit.

The antenna swivels from side-to-side, but doesn't rotate. Travel-sized portables are easiest to operate when they're laid on their backs. Do that with the '621—and most other low-cost models—and the telescopic antenna winds up horizontal, like a pencil, flat on the table. Antennas need to be vertical for proper FM and shortwave reception, but to do this on the '621 you have to rest it on its tipsy little bottom, which makes operating the controls a two-handed exercise.

Shortwave performance? No surprises here. Adjacent-channel rejection (selectivity) is adequate, but lets through more interference than is desirable. Sensitivity to weak signals is reasonable, too. However, image "ghosts" dih-dah away to haunt the sturdiest of ears. Audio, too, is in the everyday mold for compacts: somewhat distorted, with precious little low-end response. Fortunately, the supplied earpieces do a much better job than the small speaker.

FM stereo also sounds pretty good, if thin, through those earpieces. But there's no SCA filter, so on some FM stations there are chirps and squeals. Otherwise, superior capture ratio and overall commendable performance allow the '621's FM stage to flush out stations better than do most compact models.

Virtually identical to the '621, except for the clock, is the SG 631 (not tested). The '631's clock, unlike that of the '621, is programmed for the local time and date in 260 cities around the world.

Sangean makes some of the best buys in world band radios. The SG 621, with little besides a clock to make it stand out, isn't one of them.

Changed for 1992
★ ★

Magnavox D1875
Philips D1875

Price: *Magnavox:* $99.95 in the United States; *Philips:* around £50 in the United Kingdom, $85-125 elsewhere in Europe.

Advantages: Receives longwave band.

Disadvantages: No digital frequency display. Limited world band coverage. Mediocre adjacent-channel and spurious- signal ("image") rejection. No meaningful signal-strength indicator. No dial illumination. No AC power supply. Not distributed in Canada.

Bottom Line: A so-so performer whose design is getting long in the tooth.

New for 1992: Although the revised D1875, now made in the People's Republic of China, continues to receive the 25 MHz (11 meter) band, the new dial markings on the radio no longer reflect this coverage. Whether this odd change was made in error, or for some other reason, is unknown.

The Magnavox D1875 is now made in China. Also sold as the Philips D1875.

The Yacht Boy 220 is the best buy among Grundig's small portables. Comes in a travel kit version, too.

★ ★

Grundig Yacht Boy 220 (Grundig Travel Kit 220)

Price: *Yacht Boy 220:* $129.95 in the United States, CAN$169.95 in Canada, around £60 in the United Kingdom, $95-150 in Europe; *Travel Kit 220:* $249.00 in the United States, CAN$344.95 in Canada.

Advantages: Receives longwave band. Travel Kit version, apparently available only in North America, supplied with alarm clock, pocket knife, flashlight, pen/pencil set and calculator.

Disadvantages: No digital frequency display. Dial not illuminated. Limited world band coverage. Mediocre spurious-signal ("images") and adjacent-channel rejection. Pushbutton volume control takes sizable bites, hard to adjust. No meaningful signal-strength indicator. No AC power supply.

Bottom Line: An adequate travel radio, with less dial backlash than its more costly Yacht Boy 230 sibling.

New for 1992

★ ★ 　　　　　　　　　　　　　　　　 ¢

Pomtrex 120-00300

Price: $29.95 plus $4 shipping in the United States; availability and prices elsewhere not yet established.

Advantages: Cheapest radio tested. Sensitivity to weak signals at least average for size. Receives longwave band. 14-day trial period. 30-day exchange privilege if radio "dead on arrival."

Disadvantages: No digital frequency display. Adjacent-channel rejection (selectivity) poor. Mediocre spurious-signal ("image") rejection.

Limited world band coverage, omits important 13 and 21 MHz segments and 11970-12095 kHz portion of 11 MHz segment. Antenna swivels, but does not rotate. Quality of construction appears to be below average, including flimsy battery clips. Batteries awkward to install. Dial not illuminated. Some dial numbering difficult to read. No meaningful signal-strength indicator. Mediumwave AM coverage stops at roughly 1650 kHz, five channels shy of American AM band's forthcoming upper limit. No AC power supply. Apparently not widely distributed in any country. Sole known U.S. vendor charges credit cards immediately, even when shipment is delayed by months. Warranty, only 90 days, written such that it is next to useless.

Bottom Line: Tough on the ears, but its extremely low price makes it worth considering if you're traveling to where it may be lost, damaged or stolen.

Evaluation of New Model: The $30 Pomtrex compact portable, made in China, is sold in the United States by only one firm we know of, "For the People." FTP is a small populist consumers' organization that broadcasts over commercial world band station WWCR in Nashville, Tennessee.

Our Pomtrex from FTP took a full three months to arrive, but reportedly shipments are now being processed within six to eight weeks. Yet, in contravention of American regulations, they charged our credit card immediately when the order was placed—odd behavior, indeed, for an organization that purports to represent consumer interests. Where the Pomtrex may be found outside the United States remains to be seen, but it's likely to pop up here and there in Europe and beyond.

The Pomtrex covers longwave, FM, and mediumwave AM up to around 1650 kHz, so it misses the upper five channels of the forthcoming expanded AM band in the Americas.

King of the throwaways is the new Pomtrex. More than adequate for taking on trips or for a kid's first radio, and it's dirt cheap.

World band coverage is approximately 5800-6300, 7000-7600, 9420-9950, 11400-11970, 15050-15650 and 17400-18200 kHz. For a radio in this price range, that's not bad coverage, but you'll miss the 13600-13800 and 21450-21850 kHz segments, plus the upper 125 kHz or so of the heavily used 11500-12100 kHz segment.

The Pomtrex is a bandspreaded analog model, so you tune using a traditional needle and dial—not a precise digital frequency readout. Its dial is accurate to only about ± 30 kHz. Some of the dial numbers—gold on gray—are hard to read, and there's a single, virtually useless, LED signal-strength indicator.

Sensitivity to weak signals is quite decent for an inexpensive set of this size. Adjacent-channel rejection (selectivity), on the other hand, is poor, with strong stations 10 kHz, or two channels, away sometimes bothering the station you're trying to hear. Dih-dih-dah and other interference from "images," or ghost signals, is also a pain. Audio quality is only fair, and there is a rudimentary hi-lo tone switch.

The telescopic antenna swivels, but doesn't rotate. This is annoying, as the radio can't be laid on its back with the antenna vertical—the proper position for listening to world band and, to a certain extent, FM stations. It also makes the antenna more susceptible to breakage. Another mechanical drawback: The battery clips are disconcertingly flimsy, and it requires patience and manual dexterity to install the four "AA" batteries the set requires. While we have no frequency-of-repair data on this model, other cheap Chinese-made sets have tended to act up more than most.

If a set comes dead on arrival, FTP will exchange it for a new one within 30 days of purchase. Too, if you are not satisfied with the radio for any reason, you can return it for a full refund within 14 days.

Unfortunately, after those first 30 days you're pretty much on your own, as the U.S. distributor's warranty is almost meaningless. The set is warranted by the distributor, MCE Industries, Inc., of Hallandale, Florida, for 90 days which, although brief, is arguably acceptable. But to get the radio fixed during the 60 days between FTP's 30-day exchange period and the expiration of the distributor's 90-day warranty, you have to send in $14, plus pay for shipping and insurance to MCE. That's over half the set's cost just to have it repaired in warranty!

It's hard to recommend any radio without digital tuning, and with inadequate selectivity and image rejection, to boot. Listening to the Pomtrex day in and day out makes for tough sledding, indeed. But if you need a second radio to take on trips, for example, it makes awfully good sense. If the radio gets lost or stolen, or falls into the pool, it's no big deal.

And these days, you have to reckon with the remote possibility that eager airport security personnel may pry open your set and break it.

Finding "For the People" can be frustrating, as they seem to move about. Best bet is to try reaching them via WWCR, whose address is elsewhere in the "Where in the World II" part of this *Passport's* Worldscan section.

New for 1992

★ ★

Magnavox AE 3205
(Philips AE 3205)

Price: $49.95 in the United States.
Advantages: Inexpensive. Receives longwave band.
Disadvantages: No digital frequency display. Adjacent-channel rejection (selectivity) poor. Mediocre spurious-signal ("image") rejection. Limited world band coverage, omits important 13 and 21 MHz segments. Antenna swivels, but does not rotate. Dial not illuminated. No meaningful signal-strength indicator. Medium-wave AM coverage stops at roughly 1620 kHz, eight channels shy of American AM band's forthcoming upper limit. No AC power supply.
Bottom Line: Okay for taking on trips, but there are better choices for the price.
Evaluation of New Model: Magnavox's new AE 3205, available outside the United States as the Philips AE 3205, is now manufactured in the People's Republic of China. It covers the longwave, FM, and mediumwave AM bands up to around 1620 kHz, so it misses the upper eight channels of the forthcoming expanded AM band in the Americas.

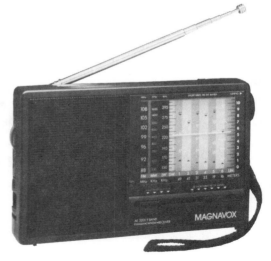

Magnavox's new AE 3205, also sold as the Philips AE 3205, is handy for traveling.

World band coverage is approximately 5900-6250, 7060-7400, 9470-9950, 11600-12100, 15075-15640 and 17550-18200 kHz. For a radio in this price range, that's more or less acceptable, but you'll miss the 13600-13800 and 21450-21850 kHz segments, plus a number of other partial segments—look over this book's Blue Pages for specifics.

The '3205 is a bandspreaded analog model, so you tune using a traditional needle and dial—not a digital frequency readout. Its dial accuracy is only to about ± 40 kHz. Signal strength is given by a nigh-useless single-LED.

Sensitivity is adequate for listening to major broadcasters, but not much more. Adjacent-channel rejection (selectivity) is poor, with strong broadcasters 10 kHz, or two channels, away sometimes bothering the station you're trying to hear. As with virtually all inexpensive models, the '3205 is single-conversion, which means that dih-dih-dah and other interference from "images," or ghost signals, is a real nuisance. Audio quality is only fair.

The telescopic antenna swivels, but doesn't rotate. This is annoying, as the radio can't be laid on its back with the antenna vertical—the proper position for listening to world band and, to a certain extent, FM stations. It also makes the antenna more susceptible to breakage.

The '3205's warranty is only 90 days. After that, the radio is replaced, not repaired, "by a renewed product which meets Philips' high quality standards." Whatever that means.

The '3205 is more or less a commodity radio, not appreciably different from a number of others on the market: low cost, low tech, low performance. For day-to-day listening, none of these satisfies. Yet, for taking outdoors or on trips, they suffice, and you don't need to lose sleep worrying over whether they'll get rained on, lost or ripped off.

New for 1992

★

Panashiba FX-928

Price: $29.95 plus $5.00 shipping in the United States; availability and prices elsewhere not yet established, but may be available in Central Europe.
Advantages: Cheap. Receives longwave band. U.S. vendor claims to provide a 14-day trial period.
Disadvantages: No digital frequency display. Adjacent-channel rejection (selectivity) poor. Mediocre spurious-signal ("image") rejection. Lackluster sensitivity to weak signals. Limited world band coverage, omits important 13 MHz segment and 12010-12095 kHz portion of 11

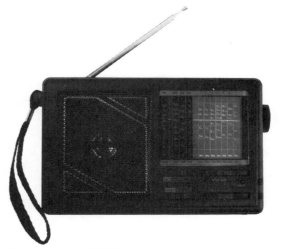

The Panashiba FX-928, one to avoid.

MHz segment. Mediocre automatic-gain control (AGC) causes wide disparity in volume from signal-to-signal. Volume slider control touchy to adjust. Antenna swivels, but does not rotate. Quality of construction appears to be below average. Batteries awkward to install. Dial not illuminated. Dial calibration off as much as 85 kHz. No meaningful signal-strength indicator. Mediumwave AM coverage stops at roughly 1620 kHz, eight channels shy of American AM band's forthcoming upper limit. No AC power supply. Not known to be widely distributed in any country. No written warranty. U.S. vendor has no listed telephone number. U.S. vendor's advertising makes false and misleading claims.
Bottom Line: *Caveat emptor.* For $1 less, you can purchase the two-star Pomtrex.
Evaluation of New Model: With the growth in world band radio sales, all manner of dubious radios have been coming out of the woodwork. Among these is the Chinese-made Panashiba FX-928, advertised by its American vendor as "the voice of the world." "Pana," as in "Panasonic," "shiba" as in "Toshiba." "Voice of the world?" It's a Radio Shack trademark, and the instruction sheet violates yet another trademark. "FX" is the also first part of the model designation for Epson equipment.

No wonder we don't see much of this set in the legitimate marketplace!

Riding on the coattails of other organizations' trusted names isn't limited to the radio itself. In the United States, the Panashiba is sold by one "U.S. Consumer" of Milford, Connecticut. "U.S." as in trustworthy Uncle Sam; "Consumer" as in your dependable friends at *Consumer Reports*.

If this sort of thing doesn't send off alarm bells in your head, the U.S. Consumer ad for the antiquated-tuning-technology Panashiba—"a startling breakthrough in sophisticated electronic tuner design"—should. Quite aside from its misleading claim to have a built-in "radar"

Many do it daily: record television programs on VCRs so they can be enjoyed at a more convenient time. You'd think that with world band radio sales rising for several years, now, history would repeat itself, and there would be a number of world band cassette recorders—WCRs—from which to choose.

Not so. There are a number of "boom box" recorders and the like with some crude coverage of the shortwave spectrum. But there are few worthy world band radios available with recorders built in.

Best Bet for the Moment: Sony's WA-8000MKII and WA-8800

There are some exceptions, though. Take Sony's pricey WA-8000MKII and WA-8800, around £200 in the United Kingdom, ¥50,000 in Japan—that is, about $325-375. (Prices within Continental Europe are, as usual, higher.) Although these are not sterling performers, if you simply must have a WCR, they are the best. Each comes with an auto-reverse stereo cassette recorder and mic, FM stereo, and stereo speakers. There's also a World Time clock with alarm, sleep and timer facilities.

Performance? Two-and-a-half stars, with superior sensitivity to weak signals and spurious-signal ("image") rejection. However, adjacent-channel rejection (selectivity) is only average, and there's no digital frequency display or presets. Without presets, the ability to record different stations automatically at different times—multi-event recording—is unrealized.

The rub for Americans: No Sony WCR is available in the United States or Canada, except perhaps on the gray market. Yanks and Canadians thus have to ferret them out at electronic and airport shops abroad.

Runner Up: Grundig Cosmopolit

In a lesser league of performance is the $249.95 Grundig Cosmopolit—about £100 in the United Kingdom, CAN$299.95 in Canada. It's cleverly constructed to be as small as possible, with the radio's dial serving as the cover for the cassette cavity.

The Cosmo, made in Indonesia, comes with a digital clock that operates from either the 24- or 12-hour standard. But for tuning, there's only an analog needle-and-dial with one-event recording. World band coverage, reasonably adequate, is from about 5850-6300, 7000-7500, 9400-10000, 11500-12150, 13450-13950, 15050-15700 and 17400-18100 kHz.

The Cosmo doesn't offer keypad tuning, presets or any other advanced tuning aids. Its lone tuning device, a thumbwheel, is stiff. There's no travel power lock switch, and—incredible at this price—the telescopic antenna doesn't rotate at its swivel.

World band performance is pedestrian. Sensitivity, selectivity and audio quality are only fair, and spurious signal ("image") rejection is downright poor. In all, this comes across as a $90 radio, which is hardly surprising: Except for the recorder and clock/timer, that's just about what it is. Give Grundig's overpriced Cosmo one cheer: a solid two stars.

Sony WA-6000 Passes Muster . . . If You Can Find It

Something cheaper? Most other available choices are dreadful. An uninspiring, but passable, alternative is the Sony WA-6000. Its coverage of the world band spectrum is limited, as is its performance. For world band, it barely musters two stars.

The WA-6000, not offered in North America and not often found elsewhere, sells for just under half as much as the Sony WA-8000 and WA-8800.

antenna, it lists 22 specific countries, complete with times and frequencies, that supposedly can be heard in the North American Eastern Time Zone "with crystal-clear reception and sound —no matter what station you're listening to."

Of these 22 supposed sure-fire bets—Laos on 7145 kHz at 6:00 PM EST, for example— you'd be lucky to hear just two, neither "crystal-clear" or even close.

Who, then, is "U.S. Consumer?" We tried to reach them by telephone to find out, but directory assistance for Milford, Connecticut, tells us this firm is unknown to them.

Of course, no radio is going to be manufactured just for one unreachable outfit. The Panashiba apparently is also destined for the Central European market, as the German terms "KW" (Kurzwelle) and "UKW" (Ultrakurzwelle) are imprinted on the dial to designate short-wave and FM, respectively. Presumably, then, this radio may also be found in Central Europe and environs.

The Panashiba covers the longwave, FM, and mediumwave AM bands up to around 1620 kHz, so it misses the upper eight channels of the forthcoming expanded AM band in the Americas. World band coverage is approximately 5830-6240, 7000-7520, 9420-10000,

11430-12010, 15090-15530, 17470-18000 and 21450-22000 kHz. For a radio in this price range, that's not bad coverage, but you'll miss the 13600-13800 kHz segment, plus the upper 85 kHz or so of the heavily used 11500-12100 kHz segment and some other bits.

The Panashiba is a bandspreaded analog model, so you tune using a traditional needle and dial—not a digital frequency readout. There's also a single, virtually useless, LED signal-strength indicator. Dial accuracy varies, but can be off by as much as ± 85 kHz—about as bad as you can get these days. And although the tuning mechanism feels snug, there's a degree of play before the radio responds.

Performance is poor, overall. Sensitivity to weak signals, for example, is inferior. So is adjacent-channel rejection (selectivity), with strong stations 10 kHz, or two channels, away sometimes bothering the station you're trying to hear. Dih-dih-dah and other interference from "images," or ghost signals, can be a nuisance, too. Audio quality, however, is not at all unpleasant so long as the volume isn't turned up much.

The telescopic antenna, which is peculiarly short, swivels, but doesn't rotate. This means the radio can't be laid on its back with its an-

Forthcoming Sangean ATS-818CS Looks Promising

For now, the Sony WA-8000MKII and WA-8800 are the best the market has to offer. But there's something exceptionally promising in the offing. By the time you read this, Sangean hopes to have brought on to the market the ATS-818CS single-event WCR, at a suggested retail price in the United States of $329.00. It is described by the factory as being a cross between the ATS-803A and the ATS-808, both very fine receivers, and incorporating single-sideband reception. The tape-recording mechanism is to come from Japan because, Sangean claims, mechanisms made in Taiwan do not as yet equal the standard of quality of those made in Japan.

That there apparently will be only one event is certainly disappointing. The radio's technology would allow for more, so presumably this was a design oversight. Still, given Sangean's record of performance with the ATS-803A and ATS-808, the ATS-818CS WCR may yet prove to be what listeners have been hoping for. Look for an in-depth test in next year's *Passport*.

Grundig's Cosmopolit has a built-in cassette recorder. Not high technology or high performance, but long on creative design.

Forthcoming in 1992 is the Sangean ATS 818CS worldband cassette recorder. Not yet tested, but holds much promise.

tenna vertical—the proper position for listening to world band and, more or less, FM stations. This lack of rotation also makes the antenna more susceptible to breakage. (Do you really expect to get a new antenna from U.S. Consumer?)

Installing the set's four "AA" batteries requires patience and manual dexterity. They tend to leap back out at you, like frogs, and the battery cover is flimsy. While we have no frequency-of-repair data on this model, other cheap Chinese-made sets have tended to act up more than most.

The volume slider control is touchy to adjust so it's not either too loud or too soft. To make matters worse, the miserable automatic-gain control (AGC) performance forces you to fiddle with the volume even more than usual. Another bother is that the set can drift off the tuned frequency if you move where your hand is located when you're holding the set.

Is there a bright side to the "Panashiba?" Yes, sort of. At modest levels of volume, FM performance isn't bad, thanks mainly to FM audio quality that's at least average for this size category.

If you are not satisfied with the radio for any reason, U.S. Consumer claims you can return it for a full refund within 14 days. After that alleged trial period, you're completely on your own, as the set comes with *no written warranty whatsoever*—an outrageous practice, especially as this is not spelled out in the U.S. Consumer's fairyland advertising.

It's hard to recommend any radio without digital tuning, and with inadequate sensitivity, selectivity and image rejection, to boot. Listening to the Panashiba day in and day out is a tiring and frustrating experience. If you need a throwaway radio for trips or for use where damage is likely, then get the two-star Pomtrex. It's not only better—it's a hair cheaper, too.

★

Cougar H-88

Price: $49.95 in the United States, $40-70 in Europe.

Advantages: Inexpensive. Receives longwave band.

Disadvantages: No digital frequency display. Limited world band coverage. Mediocre adjacent-channel and spurious- signal ("image") rejection. Modest sensitivity to weak signals. Tuning knob somewhat stiff. Power switch easily activated by accident, as when radio packed on trips. No dial illumination. No meaningful signal-strength indicator. No AC power supply. Not known to be widely distributed in any country.

Bottom Line: Tinker's toy.

Grundig's Traveller II is the latest incarnation of the Opal OP-35, but with twin earpieces added. No stereo, though.

★

Opal OP-35 (Grundig Traveller II) (Siemens RK 702)

Price: *Opal:* $99.95 in the United States, but the only dealer known to carry it sells them for $47.50-69.95; *Grundig:* $99.95, but sells for up to $119.95, CAN$99.95 in Canada; *Siemens:* $75-160 in Europe.

Advantages: Includes novel World Time and worldwide multi-country clock/timer, what Opal calls the "World Time Handy Humane Wake System." *Opal:* Relatively inexpensive. *Grundig:* Comes with stereo earpieces, even though radio is not stereo.

Disadvantages: No digital frequency display. World band coverage limited to 6, 7, 9, 11 and 15 MHz segments. Inferior adjacent-channel rejection makes for unpleasant listening. Poor spurious-signal ("image") rejection in both in world band and mediumwave AM band. Modest weak-signal sensitivity. Can drift off frequency when held. No signal-strength indicator. Does not receive longwave band. No AC power supply. *Opal:* Not widely distributed.

Bottom Line: Clock in drag.

Overpriced even at $50 or £35 is the Cougar H-88.

MID-SIZED PORTABLES

Good for Home, Fair for Travel

If you're looking for a home set, but also one that can be taken out in the backyard and on the occasional trip, you'll probably gravitate to a mid-sized portable. They're large enough to perform well and sound pretty good; yet compact enough to tote in your suitcase now and then. Most take 3-4 "D" (UM-1) cells, plus a couple of "AA" (UM-3) cells for their fancy computer circuits.

How large? Typically just under a foot wide—that's 30 cm—and weighing in around 3-4 pounds, or 1.3-1.8 kg. For air travel, this is okay if you're a dedicated listener, but a bit much otherwise. Too, larger sets with snazzy controls sometimes attract unwanted attention from customs and security personnel.

Two stand out: the ultra-high-tech Sony ICF-2010, also sold as the ICF-2001D; and the much cheaper Sangean ATS-803A, sold under many names, including Radio Shack's Realistic DX-440. The '2010 is the finest true portable around, and its advanced technology allows it to be used successfully right into the next century, when stations may change over to reduced-carrier single sideband. The '803A is the best buy if you feel the '2010 is too pricey.

World's best affordable portable: Sony's exceptional ICF-2010, also sold as the ICF-2001D.

★ ★ ★ ★   *Editor's Choice*

Sony ICF-2010
Sony ICF-2001D
(Sony ICF-2001DS)

Price: *ICF-2010:* $429.95 in the United States, CAN$689.95 in Canada; *ICF-2001D:* under £330 in the United Kingdom, $500-950 elsewhere in Europe.

Advantages: Superior overall world band performance. High-tech synchronous detector circuit with selectable sideband reduces adjacent-channel interference and fading distortion on world band, longwave band and medium-wave AM band signals; it also provides superior reception of reduced-carrier single-sideband signals. Use of 36 separate preset buttons in neat rows and columns is ergonomically the best to be found—simply pushing one button brings in your station. Numerous other helpful tuning features. Two bandwidths offer superior tradeoff between audio fidelity and adjacent-channel rejection. Tunes in precise 0.1 kHz increments. Separately displayed World Time clock. Alarm/sleep/timer facilities. Some reception of air band signals (most versions). Illuminated display. Best travel-weight portable for single sideband. Travel power lock. Signal-strength indicator. Covers Japanese FM band. AC power supply. In Europe, reportedly available for under $600 in a special "ICF-2001DS" version supplied with Sony AN-1 amplified antenna. Elsewhere, the AN-1 may be purchased separately for around $90.

Disadvantages: Controls and high-tech features, although exceptionally handy once you get the hang of them, initially may intimidate or confuse. Presets and clock/timer facilities sometimes erase when set is jostled. Wide bandwidth somewhat broad for world band reception. Audio quality only average, with mediocre tone control. Synthesizer chuffs a bit. First RF transistor (Q-303) reportedly prone to damage by static electricity, as from nearby lightning strikes, when used with external wire antenna (such antennas should be disconnected with the approach of snow, sand, dry-wind or thunder storms); or when amplified (active) antennas other than Sony AN-1 are used. Telescopic antenna swivel gets slack with use, requiring periodic adjustment of tension screw.

Bottom Line: The Big Enchilada, and fairly priced for all it does so well. Except for audio and the relatively long user learning curve, Sony's very-high-tech offering remains the best-performing travel-weight portable—regardless of where you are—and its use of separate pushbuttons for each preset makes station call-up easier than with virtually any other radio tested.

An *RDI WHITE PAPER* is available for this model.

At Last, a Single Converter Plug for Nearly All Countries

When traveling abroad, most of us simply use batteries to fire up our little portable world band radios. Yet, larger portables can gobble up batteries, making wall sockets look tempting, indeed.

But if you travel abroad with a plug-in device, there's always the problem of what to do about plugging into the local AC power, or mains. Among other things, you have to worry about voltage—120 or 240?—and frequency (is it 50 or 60 Hz?).

But first, your appliance must have a plug that fits, or else you need a suitable converter plug. Franzus, Radio Shack and few other specialty firms have long catered to this need. Cheaply, too: Radio Shack's #273-1405 set of four adapters for Americans going abroad costs only $7.95. Problem is, when you travel widely you have to take along a fistful of these blasted little things.

So, along has come a consummately English inventor to provide us with a single "does-it-all" plug converter, the Globetrotter International Adaptor. It does in one clever unit what all those other converter plugs do in several.

Here's how it works. First, you look at the Globetrotter's side to see the type of socket used, then you push a small slider control to the setting for that type. Next, you reach along both sides of the unit, choose two larger color-coded sliders that also correspond to the plug used, push in hard, then pull those sliders forward until the plug prongs emerge, like a turtle's head, from the plug's body. It works, but the colored slider tabs are thin, and pushing in on them can be downright painful.

The Globetrotter nominally allows you to plug into European, Russian, Chinese, Japanese, American, Australian, New Zealand, Irish and British sockets, plus many in Asia and the Middle East, as well. However, it doesn't fit certain sockets found in India, Pakistan, South Africa, Nepal, Sri Lanka and parts of Malaysia. In reality, it's not quite this straightforward, especially in the hinterland of Third-World countries; but in general these rules apply.

Equally, even though the Globetrotter connects the two main prongs ("hot" and "neutral") of plugs or sockets also having third ("ground" or "earth") prongs, it copes mechanically with, *but doesn't connect electrically to*, those grounds. The manufacturer thus rightly insists that the Globetrotter be used only with non-grounded appliances, and we can but underscore this. An ungrounded appliance designed to be grounded can under certain conditions release a lethal shock. Problem is, the way the Globetrotter is designed it invites going ahead and using grounded appliances, anyway.

Fortunately, virtually no world band portable requires electrical grounding.

The Globetrotter weighs 5 1/2 ounces, or 172 grams, and measures 3 1/8 × 2 1/4" (80 × 57 mm), which some may find a bit much. Too, it does nothing to cope with voltage or frequency standards. It won't, for example, alter European 240V/50 Hz to power American 120V/60 Hz appliances, or *vice versa*. For changing voltage, other, separate devices are needed.

Yet, if you travel widely and are fed up having to worry about the likes of electrical socket standards—and aren't taking along grounded appliances—the Globetrotter should cover nearly all bases nicely. We purchased ours for $32.95, including shipping, from the U.S. firm of Markline, a subsidiary of Artistic Mail Order Fulfillment, Box 1058, Elmira NY 14902. The Globetrotter is also available worldwide, or direct from the manufacturer, Traveller International Products Ltd., 51 Haysmews, London W1, United Kingdom.

★ ★ ★ ★   *Editor's Choice*

Grundig Satellit 500

Price: $699.95 in the United States; CAN$799.95 in Canada; $400-550 in Europe.

Advantages: Superior overall world band performance. Two excellent bandwidths give superior tradeoff between audio fidelity and adjacent-channel rejection. Bandwidth circuitry has best ultimate rejection of any portable tested. Relatively easy to operate, with superior ergonomics. Tunes in precise 0.1 kHz increments. Numerous helpful, well-thought-out tuning features, including 42 presets. Superior tuning knob. Large-character display shows station name in preset mode. Some world band channels factory-programmed. Above average audio for size class, with separate continuous bass and treble tone controls. World Time clock and another 24-hour clock, one of which is displayed separately from frequency. Alarm/sleep/timer, including two-event timer that also controls certain tape recorders. Illuminated keypad and display. One of the best travel-weight portables for single sideband. Signal-strength indicator. Travel power lock disables all functions. Stereo FM through headphones and second speaker (neither supplied). Generally superior FM and mediumwave AM performance. Receives longwave band. Worldwide AC power supply (supplied) and overseas converter plug (sometimes supplied). Built-in NiCd battery charger. Mounting screw holes for securing radio in mobile environments. Telescopic antenna, with spring-loaded detents, unusually rugged.

Disadvantages: Synchronous detector circuit gives neither selectable sideband nor reduced fading distortion, but sometimes causes slight whistle ("heterodyne"). High overall distortion in single-sideband mode at certain audio frequencies. Dynamic range poor at 5 kHz channel spacing. Pushbuttons push hard. Synthesizer chuffs some. AGC control may deaden reception if switched on accidentally. Keypad default is AM mode, which complicates single-sideband tuning. Factory-programmed channels, for German-language broadcasts beamed to Europe, can't be changed (and schedules do). Batteries on our sample sometimes lost contact when set turned on its side, wiping out clock-related data. Otherwise-excellent telescopic antenna tends to flop over from its own weight when adjusted to certain angles. Radio relatively costly in North America.

Bottom Line: Improved since its introduction in 1989, and especially in units with serial numbers above 802000, the '500 is noteworthy for its features, appearance, and ergonomic niceties. Overall performance is, in some ways, the best available in a portable. But the set still

Its shakedown cruise well behind it, the Grundig Satellit 500 is now a superior model, suffering only from a flawed synchronous detector.

suffers from a flawed synchronous detector which, instead of improving reception as it does on the Sony ICF-2010 and ICF-2001D, actually makes matters a bit worse.

 An *RDI WHITE PAPER* is available for this model.

★ ★ ★ ½   *Editor's Choice* ¢

Sangean ATS-803A
Realistic DX-440
(Clairtone PR-291)
(TMR 7602 Hitech Tatung)
(Matsui MR-4099)
(Eska RX 33)
(Siemens RK 651)
(Quelle Universum)

Price: *Sangean:* $249.00 in the United States, CAN$449.95 in Canada, around £100 in the United Kingdom, $150-330 in Europe; *Realistic:* $199.95 plus #273-1455 AC power supply at Radio Shack stores in the United States, CAN$299.00 plus #273-1455 AC power supply in Canada, $230-260 plus AC power supply at Tandy stores in Europe; *Clairtone:* CAN$229.95 in Canada; *Tatung:* under £110 in the United Kingdom; *Matsui:* $160-220 in Europe; *Eska:* Dkr. 1995 (about $315) in Denmark; *Siemens:* $180-250 in Europe; *Quelle Universum:* $180-250 in Europe. #273-1455 Radio Shack 120V AC/9V DC power supply for DX-440: $7.95 in the United States.

Advantages: Superior overall world band performance. Numerous tuning features. Two bandwidths for good fidelity/interference tradeoff. Superior spurious-signal ("image") rejection and good weak-signal sensitivity—a plus for Central or Western North America. Superior reception of utility signals for price class. Illuminated display. Signal-strength indicator. World Time clock. Alarm/sleep/timer.

Best performer for under $200 or £110 is the Sangean ATS-803A, also sold under a variety of other names (see story), including the Realistic DX-440.

Travel power lock. FM stereo through headphones (usually supplied). Separate bass and treble controls. Receives longwave band. Sangean ATS-803A and most other versions supplied with AC adaptor. *Realistic:* 30-day money-back trial period.

Disadvantages: Synthesizer chuffs a little. Audio no prize—only slightly above average. Clock not displayed separately from frequency. *Realistic:* Does not come with tape-recorder jack; AC power supply and headphones are extra.

Bottom Line: A dollar cigar for 75 cents. A nigh-perfect model for getting started, provided all the features don't intimidate. If they do, look over the simpler Panasonic RF-B45.

FULL-SIZED PORTABLES

Very Good for Home, Poor for Travel

Let's call big portables tabletop-type models that run off batteries—usually several "D" (UM-1) cells, plus some "AA" (UM-3) cells for their computer circuitry. Real tabletop models, however, have the advantage of laying flat, and thus are better-suited for everyday home use. Real tabletop models also provide more performance for the money.

Some full-sized portables weigh as much as a stuffed suitcase, and are almost as large. Take one on a worldwide air excursion and you should have your head examined. The first customs or security inspector that sees your radio will probably do it for you.

None of the present full-sized portable crop really excites. However, the Sony CRF-V21 is full of techy goodies, and the Grundig Satellit 650 has clearly superior audio.

★ ★ ★ ★

Sony CRF-V21

Price: $6,500.00 in the United States, under £3,000 in the United Kingdom, $4,500-6,500 elsewhere in Europe.

Advantages: Superior overall world band performance. High-tech synchronous detector circuit with selectable sideband cuts adjacent-channel interference and fading distortion on world band, longwave band and mediumwave AM band. Two bandwidths mean superior tradeoff be-tween audio fidelity and adjacent-channel rejection. Helpful tuning features, including 350 presets. Unusually straightforward keypad. Processes off-the-air narrow-band FM, RTTY (radio teletype) and fax. Covers longwave down to 9 kHz, as well as four satellite fax frequencies. Liquid-crystal video display for various functions, including frequency, station name (in preset mode), separately displayed World Time/Date, and RTTY. Display doubles as spectrum monitor. Built-in thermal printer allows print-screen and fax hard-copy with very high resolution. World Time/Date clock displays seconds numerically. Alarm/sleep/timer/scanner/activity-search can also do hands-off spectrum surveys. Tunes and displays in precise 10 Hz increments. World's best tuning knob, a pure delight. Best portable, barely, for ham and utility signals. Superior weak-signal sensitivity, plus blocking, AGC threshold, dynamic range, ultimate rejection, skirt selectivity, phase noise, spurious-signal ("image") rejection, IF rejection and stability. Very low audio distortion in the AM and synchronous-detection modes. Illuminated display. Precise signal-strength indicator. Amplified antenna, which may be placed up to 15', or 4.5 meters, away. Receives Japanese FM broadcasts. Worldwide AC power supply and rechargeable NiCd battery pack. Except for U.S. version, comes with RS-232C port for computer interface.

Sony's beefy CRF-V21 is the best portable, overall, but five-star tabletop models perform better for far less money.

Disadvantages: Expensive. Complex and generally not user-friendly. Mediocre ergonomics. Video display lacks contrast, very hard to read. Size, weight and no fixed telescopic antenna seriously mar portable operation. Wide bandwidth setting a bit broad for world band. Audio only average. Tuning knob rates are either too slow or too fast. Flip-over night light ineffective —and easily mistaken for carrying handle, and thus broken. Slow-sweep spectrum-occupancy display not real-time. Two of three spectrum-occupancy slices too wide for shortwave use, and the other so narrow it's barely of any use at all. AGC decay much too fast for single sideband. For premium device, only so-so unwanted-sideband suppression. Mediocre front-end selectivity. Does not decode 50 wpm RTTY, AMTOR or CW. RS-232C port not supplied with U.S. version, as it does not meet FCC Part 15 spurious-emission requirements; contrary to Sony's earlier suggestion, the missing port cannot be retrofitted.

Bottom Line: A fax-oriented "portable" with more goodies than Dolly Parton. On world band, however, the CRF-V21 in most respects doesn't equal some tabletops costing a fifth as much, and only modestly exceeds the performance of some portables that are cheaper, yet. According to one *Passport* reader, Sony's customer technical support for this model is abysmal.

 An *RDI WHITE PAPER* is available for this model.

Grundig Satellit 650

Price: $1099.95 in the United States, CAN$1,249.95 in Canada, $700-900 in Europe.

Advantages: Superior world band performance. Excellent audio. Two full bandwidths and a third pseudo-bandwidth give good tradeoff between audio fidelity and adjacent-channel rejection. Superior spurious-signal ("image") rejection. High weak-signal sensitivity. Helpful tuning features. World Time clock, displayed separately. Alarm/timer. Precise signal-strength indicator. Illuminated display. Superior FM reception. Receives longwave band. Built-in worldwide AC power supply.

Disadvantages: Size and weight. Costly, especially in North America. Motorized preselector tuning requires some manual tweaking for best performance and means mechanical complexity. Construction quality below norm for price class.

Bottom Line: Biceps builder's boombox, and not equal to better tabletops for chasing really tough signals. Nevertheless, superior speakers

Excellent audio quality is the Grundig Satellit 650's high card.

and generous, first-rate audio quality make the '650 a favorite for pleasant hour-after-hour listening. Indeed, its only real competition in sound quality comes from the high-tech Drake and Lowe tabletop models—not portables.

 An *RDI WHITE PAPER* is available for this model.

★ ½

Marc II NR-108F1 (Pan Crusader)

Price: $300-550 worldwide.

Advantages: Unusually broad coverage, from 150 kHz longwave to 520 MHz UHF, plus 850-910 MHz UHF (North American/Japanese version). Many helpful tuning features. World

The Marc II, also sold as the Pan Crusader, is the worst buy in a world band radio. Priced as a premium model, it performs more poorly than many low-cost radios.

Time clock, displayed separately from frequency. Sleep/timer. Signal-strength indicator. Illuminated display.

Disadvantages: Marginal overall performance within certain portions of world band, including hissing, buzzing, and serious overloading. Poor adjacent-channel rejection. Poor spurious-signal ("image") rejection. Poorly performing preselector tuning complicates operation. Excessive battery drain. Mediocre construction quality, including casual alignment. Not widely available.

Bottom Line: Rabbit fur at mink prices.

★

Venturer Multiband Rhapsody Multiband (Alconic Series 2959) (MBR7 Mark II)

Price: *Basic model:* $79.95-99.95; *With cassette player:* $129.95; *With cassette player, stereo audio and digital clock:* $159.00.

Advantages: Inexpensive. Covers VHF-TV channels and air/weather bands. Audio at least average. Built-in cassette player (two versions only). Stereo audio (one version only). Digital clock (one version only), displayed separately from frequency. Signal-strength indicator. Rotating ferrite-bar direction finder for mediumwave AM. Built-in AC power supply.

Thanks to heavy advertising, the Alconic Series 2959 is widely sold under various names (see story). It's a miserable performer.

Disadvantages: No acceptable frequency display, so finding a station is a hit-and-miss exercise. World band coverage omits the 2, 3, 13, 15, 17, 21 and 26 MHz segments. Performance inferior in nearly every respect. Does not receive longwave band.

Bottom Line: Pink flamingo. Sold widely throughout North America and Europe under various names—or even no advertised name. Assembled in Hong Kong from China-made components.

★

Electro Brand 2971

Price: $149.95, including cassette player, stereo audio, NiCd batter charger, and digital clock/calendar.

Bottom Line: Essentially identical in performance and features to Alconic Series 2959, above, except for appearance and that Electro Brand is made *and assembled* in the People's Republic of China.

With radios such as the Electro Brand 2971, you have to hunt and peck to find the station you want—and when you finally find it you may wish you hadn't.

OLDIES, SOME GOODIES

The following models reportedly have been discontinued, yet may still be available new at some retail outlets. Cited are typical sale prices in the United States ($) and United Kingdom (£) as *Passport/92* goes to press. Prices elsewhere may differ.

★ ★ ★ ★

Panasonic RF-9000
(National RF-9000)

Excellent overall performance, but too beefy for portable use. Horribly over-priced in London at £1,800.00. For that, you can get two or three top-rated Drake R8 tabletop receivers!

★ ★ ★ $\frac{1}{2}$

Editor's Choice

Magnavox D2935
Philips D2935

One of the very best affordable portables ever. Around $200, but worth more. Virtually impossible to find in North America and most other parts of the world, but still being advertised in London for £119.95. Grab it—you'll love the audio quality!

★ ★ ★ $\frac{1}{2}$

Sony ICF-2003
(Sony ICF-7600DS)
Sony ICF-2002
(Sony ICF-7600D)

Precursors to the current compact Sony ICF-SW7600, they all perform similarly. Under $260, under £140.

★ ★ ★

Panasonic RF-B40
(Panasonic RF-B40DL)
(National B40)

Precursors to the RF-B45 *et al.*, which perform noticeably better. Under $170, around £125.

★ ★ $\frac{1}{2}$

Sony ICF-7600A
(Sony ICF-7600AW)

Similar to the current compact Sony ICF-7601, but 13 MHz coverage omitted. No digital frequency display. Under $100, under £110.

★ ★ $\frac{1}{2}$

Sony ICF-4920
(Sony ICF-4900II)
(Sony ICF-5100)

Identical in all but styling to the current mini Sony ICF-SW20. No digital frequency display. Under $100, under £80.

★ ★

Magnavox D1835
(Philips D1835)

Performance identical to current compact Magnavox D1875 and Philips D1875. No digital frequency display. Still available occasionally for under $70 or £40, but not in Canada.

★ $\frac{1}{2}$

Panasonic RF-B10
(National B10)

Mini with third-rate performance, no digital frequency display, no 13 MHz coverage. Around $70 or £60.

★ $\frac{1}{2}$

Philips D2615

Pleasant audio, but miserable performance and you can't tell tuned frequency. Under £60.

The Passport *equipment review team: Lawrence Magne, along with Jock Elliott and Tony Jones, with laboratory measurements by Robert Sherwood.*

TABLETOP RECEIVERS FOR 1992

For most, a good portable is more than adequate to enjoy the offerings found on world band radio. Others, though, seek something better.

That "better" is a tabletop receiver. Many excel at flushing out the really tough game—faint stations, or those swamped by interference from competing signals. The very best now also provide enhanced-fidelity reception, welcome relief from the aural demerits of shortwave. Still, world band is far from a high-fidelity medium, even with the best of radios. International stations beam over great distances, and you can tell it with your ears.

Tabletop models can be especially useful if you live in a part of the world, such as Central and Western North America, where signals tend to be weak and choppy— a common problem when world band signals have to follow high-latitude paths, paths close to or over the North Pole. To get an idea how much this phenomenon might affect your listening, place a string on a globe (an ordinary map won't do) between where you live and where various signals you like come from. If the string passes near or above latitude 60° N, beware.

Tabletop radios also excel for daytime listening, when signals tend to be weaker, and for listening to stations not beamed to your part of the world. Thanks to the scattering properties of shortwave, you can eavesdrop on some "off-beam" signals, but it's harder.

A good tabletop won't guarantee hearing a favorite daytime or off-beam station, but it will almost certainly help. Tabletops also do unusually well with non-broadcasting signals, such as ham and utility stations —many of which use single sideband and other specialized transmission modes.

Tabletop models are easily found in certain countries, such as the United States, Canada, the United Kingdom, Germany and Japan. At the other extreme, a few countries, such as Saudi Arabia and Singapore, frown upon the importation of tabletop models, which they feel are inimical to their security interests.

Travelers should keep in mind that well-intentioned, if ill-informed, customs agents of almost every nation tend to regard these devices with extreme suspicion, as they resemble transceivers that could be used to communicate with hostile foreign organizations. However, when tabletop models are shipped as part of a household's goods—when an international executive is being transferred, for example—problems are far less likely to arise.

For the most part, tabletop receivers are pricier than portables. Too, most tabletop models also require, and should have, an outboard antenna. Indeed, *tabletop*

Imagine getting paid to enjoy world band radio! Here, Rich Renken, using a new Drake R8 receiver, tunes in the world from his office at Drake's headquarters in Miamisburg, Ohio.

performance is largely determined by antenna quality and placement. A first-rate world band outdoor wire antenna, such as the various models manufactured by Antenna Supermarket and Alpha Delta, usually runs from $60 to $80. These wire antennas are best, and should be used if at all possible. If not, a short amplified antenna, suitable for indoors, and sometimes outdoors when space is at a premium, is the next-best choice. Leading models, such as those made by Datong and McKay Dymek, go for $130-180. Check with the two *RDI White Papers* on antennas for details on performance and installation.

Models new for 1992 are covered at length in this year's Buyer's Guide. Every model, regardless of its introduction year, has taken the various testing hurdles we established and have honed since 1977, when our firm first started evaluating world band equipment.

Each model is thoroughly tested in the laboratory, using criteria developed especially for the strenuous requirements of world band reception. The receiver then undergoes hands-on evaluation, usually for months, before we begin preparing our detailed internal report. That report, in turn, forms the basis for our findings, summarized in this *Passport* Buyer's Guide.

Our unabridged laboratory and hands-on test results are far too exhaustive to reproduce here. However, they are available as *Passport's Radio Database International White Papers*—details on price and availability are elsewhere in this book.

If you listen mainly to weaker stations— or to speech, such as newscasts—audio quality is less important than for music programs over strong, clear stations. Indeed, among some radio enthusiasts there appears to be almost a "real men don't need this" outlook towards audio quality. Too, when shopping, remember that most tabletop models, unlike portables, are available only from electronics and world band specialty outlets.

Service? Tabletops are designed to last and be relatively easy to service. Thus, most firms that sell, distribute or manufacture world band tabletops support them with service that is clearly superior to that for portables, and often continues well after the model has been discontinued. Drake, Lowe, Kenwood and Japan Radio have particularly good track records in this regard.

For the United States and Canada, suggested retail ("list") prices are quoted. However, what manufacturers quote to us and what their sales representatives reportedly quote to dealers do not always agree, so don't treat these figures as holy writ. As the gap between dealer cost and list price tends to be relatively small with world band tabletops, discounts are common, but rarely substantial.

As "list" prices are largely a North American phenomenon, observed *selling* price parameters are given in pounds for the United Kingdom and, to have a common benchmark, U.S. dollars for continental Europe. Prices elsewhere vary widely. World band tabletop models are virtually unavailable at duty-free shops.

Of course, all prices are as of when we

WHAT'S NEW IN TABLETOP MODELS

Here's real evolution. To begin with, the two worst tabletop models, the Heathkit/Zenith SW-7800 and Tunemaster Classic Radio, have been taken off the market. Neither manufacturer plans a replacement.

At the other end of the quality scale, manufacturers are introducing products of unparalleled quality. New for 1992 is the American-made Drake R8, the world's best radio for quality listening to programs from afar. As if that weren't enough, Japan Radio has introduced its NRD-535, the world's best model for DXing—the flushing out of tough, rarely heard stations. And Britain's Lowe has entered this lofty league with its professional-caliber HF-235.

Newer doesn't necessarily mean better, but this year it does. 1992 easily has the best roster of models ever, and it's unlikely that major leaps in quality will materialize in the near future.

go to press and are subject to fluctuation. However, during the past couple of years prices for tabletop models have tended to hold fairly steady.

Receivers are listed in order of suitability for listening to difficult-to-hear world band radio broadcasts, with important but secondary consideration being given to fidelity and ergonomics. Models that are unusually appropriate for hour-after-hour listening to favorite programs are so indicated under "Advantages."

Unless otherwise stated, all tabletop models have:

- digital frequency synthesis and illuminated display;
- a wide variety of helpful tuning features;
- meaningful signal-strength indication;
- the ability to properly demodulate single-sideband and CW (Morse code) signals; and
- full coverage of at least the 155-29999 kHz (155-26099 kHz within Central Europe) longwave, mediumwave AM, and shortwave spectra—including world band.

Unless otherwise stated, all tabletop models do *not*:

- tune the FM broadcast band (87.5-107.9 MHz); and
- come equipped with synchronous selectable sideband.

What *Passport's* Ratings Mean

Star ratings: ★ ★ ★ ★ ★ is best. We award stars solely for overall performance and meaningful features; price, appearance and the like are not taken into account. To facilitate comparison, the same rating system is used for portable models, reviewed elsewhere in this *Passport*. Whether a radio is portable or a tabletop model, a given rating —three stars, say—means essentially the same thing. A star is a star.

Editor's Choice models are our test team's personal picks of the litter—what we would buy ourselves.

¢: Denotes a model that costs appreciably less than usual for the level of performance provided.

Models in **(parentheses)** have not been tested by us, but appear to be essentially identical to the model(s) tested.

PROFESSIONAL MONITOR RECEIVERS

Professional shortwave receivers are made for professional applications, which usually have only some things in common with the needs of world band listening. Realistically, then, for world band listening there is precious little difference—sometimes none of import—between these pricey receivers and regular tabletop models costing a fraction as much.

Nevertheless, if money is no object you should at least consider these models, along with regular tabletop models, when weighing a purchase decision.

★ ★ ★ ★ ★   *Editor's Choice*

Icom IC-R9000

Price: $5,459.00 in the United States, CAN$7,999 in Canada, under £4,000 in the United Kingdom.

Advantages: Unusually appropriate for hour-after-hour world band listening. Exceptional tough-signal performance. Flexible, above-average audio for a tabletop model, when used with suitable outboard speaker. Three AM-mode bandwidths. Tunes and displays frequency in precise 0.01 kHz increments. Video display of radio spectrum occupancy. Sophisticated scanner/timer. Extraordinarily broad coverage of radio spectrum. Exceptional assortment of flexible operating controls and sockets. Very good ergonomics. Superb reception of utility and ham signals. Two 24-hour clocks.

Disadvantages: Very expensive. Power supply runs hot. Both AM-mode bandwidths too broad for most world band applications. Both single-sideband bandwidths almost identical. Dynamic range merely adequate. Reliability, especially when roughly handled, may be wanting. Front-panel controls of only average construction quality.

Top performer, by a hair, for catching rare signals is the costly Icom IC-R9000.

Bottom Line: The Icom IC-R9000, with at least one changed AM-mode bandwidth filter—available from world band specialty firms—is, by a wee margin, the best-performing model we have ever tested for DX reception of faint, tough signals.

An *RDI WHITE PAPER* is available for this model.

★ ★ ★ ★ ★   *Editor's Choice*

Japan Radio NRD-93

Price: $6,850.00 in the United States, $6,000 to $10,000 elsewhere.

Advantages: Professional-quality construction with legendary durability to survive around-the-clock use in punishing environments. Uncommonly easy to repair on the spot. Unusually appropriate for hour-after-hour world band listening. Superb all-around performance. Excellent ergonomics and unsurpassed control feel. Above-average audio. Sophisticated optional scanner, tested. Superb reception of utility and ham signals.

Disadvantages: Very expensive. Designed several years ago, so lacks some advanced-technology tuning aids. Distribution limited to Japan Radio offices and a few specialty organizations, such as shipyards.

Bottom Line: Crafted like a watch, but tough as a tank, the Japan Radio NRD-93 is a breed apart. It is a pleasure to operate for band-scanning hour after hour, but its overall performance is not appreciably different from that of some cheaper tabletop models, and it lacks certain handy advanced-technology features.

An *RDI WHITE PAPER* is available for this model.

For ruggedness and quality of construction, nothing approaches the Japan Radio NRD-93.

New for 1992
★ ★ ★ ★

Lowe HF-235/R
(Lowe HF-235/F)
(Lowe HF-235/H)
(Lowe HF-235)

Editor's Note: As the Lowe HF-235 in its various configurations is based on, and in most performance respects is very similar to, the HF-225, the following writeup concentrates on how the '235 differs from the '225. Detailed information on the many common points may be found in the *RDI White Paper* on the Lowe HF-225.

Price: *HF-235 and HF-235/F:* £950, plus VAT, in the United Kingdom. Up to £350 additional in other configurations.

Advantages over the HF-225: Physically and electrically more rugged, including enhanced capability to handle high-voltage signal input. AGC may be switched off. Rack mounting, preferred for most professional applications. Power supply inboard and dual-voltage (110/220V). IF gain. *HF-235/R:* Scan/search and other remote control via personal computer using RS-232C interface. Allows for computer display of receiver data. *HF-235/F:* Fax capability. *HF-235/H:* Enhanced stability.

Disadvantages over the HF-225: Larger footprint. Lacks tone control and optional mouse-type remote keypad. Built-in AC power supply nominally not suited to voltages in 120-129V range commonly found in the United States (in practice, however, this may not be a problem). *HF-235/F:* Does not receive lower-sideband signals.

Bottom Line: This radio is essentially the highly rated Lowe HF-225 reconfigured for selected professional applications; it's essentially a bare-bones, Lowe-end surveillance receiver. As such, it offers features some professionals require, but lacks certain niceties for home use and bandscanning. World band listeners and manual-bandscanning professionals are better served by the cheaper Lowe HF-225.

Evaluation of New Model: In the world of some professional radio monitoring, as practiced by such organizations as the CIA's Foreign Broadcast Information Service, BBC Monitoring, the U.S. National Security Agency, U.K. General Communications Headquarters (GCHQ), and military organizations worldwide, there is a fundamental principle that is often brought to bear: It is better not to be there when bad things happen in the neighborhood. The idea is to ensure your people aren't around should local unfriendlies overrun your listening post.

Another consideration is that major monitoring sites are often so large and complex that having monitors and their receiving equipment/antennas in proximity to each other is not feasible, or at least practical.

As a result, radios are often placed in some advantageous place and operated remotely; signals thus are fed to where monitors, linguists and analysts toil away. So, for example, if your want to listen to transmissions from East Africa, put the radios in your embassy in Nairobi, Kenya, and feed the signals back to your offices in Reading, England. This is the world the HF-235/R was created for, and in that rarified environment it is considered a genuinely low-cost model.

The Lowe HF-235/R, then, is essentially the Lowe HF-225 reworked for remote monitoring applications. Set up primarily for professional-type rack mounting, and only secondarily for tabletop use, the heavily built cabinet measures 3 5/8" high × 11 1/2" deep × 19" wide (9.2 × 29.2 × 48.3 cm), with two 1 1/8" (2.9 cm) tabs and handles on either side for rack mounting. This makes for an awfully large footprint, and there are no adjustable feet to elevate the front panel for comfortable tabletop operation. On the rear panel are two connectors: a male D-type for providing control, audio and DC power connections; and an RS-232C interface for the R-235 remote control option to give long-distance control of receiver mode and frequency.

Antenna connection is via a BNC connector, widely used by professionals but not the norm for consumer products. On the face of the receiver is a small speaker, just over 2" (5 cm) in diameter, plus a small analog signal-strength indicator, a mode switch (CW, LSB, USB, AM and, with the synchronous detector option, AM synchronous which is not sideband selectable, and FM), an XX.XXX MHz frequency display (resolution is no finer than to the nearest kHz), tuning in precise 8 Hz increments, a tuning knob with fixed (non-rotating) dimple, and a 12-button membrane keypad for entering frequencies. A headphone connector, volume control, IF gain control (also pulls out to turn off AGC), and bank of five buttons for controlling memory functions round out the controls. Unlike the cheaper sibling HF-225 model, the '235 has no tone control.

The membrane keypad is particularly interesting. Each key measures a full 1/2" (1.3 cm) square, and is almost, but not quite, flush mounted with a slightly convex plastic surface.

When fully depressed, each button gives a tactile, inaudible, click to indicate successful entry; no "beep" is used for this purpose.

Unfortunately, as with other membrane keypads, "feel" typically is less than it is on keypads with conventional raised buttons. Panelists, including a seasoned professional band-scanning monitor, greatly preferred the mouse-type remote keypad available on the '225.

The '235 continues in the Lowe tradition of the slickest keypad software around. If you want to hear, say, the BBC on 6175 kHz, press 6 - 1 - 7 - 5, and you've got it. No leading zeros, no periods, no enter keys—what a breath of fresh air! (Well, almost. For frequencies below 3000 kHz, you have to press the ENTER key to let the receiver know that you don't intend to enter another digit.) If you make a mistake, simply press the CANCEL button and start over. Lowe continues to be the keypad software champion of the world.

The '235 has 30 presets. Alas, these are non-tunable and store only the frequency—not such other data as mode. However, the listener can spin through all 30 presets simply by turning the tuning knob. This is handy if you wish to check quickly which channel of a favorite broadcaster sounds best. The software for entering and recalling presets is fairly straightforward, and offers the ability to see what frequencies are stored in which presets while the receiver is tuned to another channel.

In addition, the HF-235 has two VFOs—main tuning circuits—making it convenient to access and tune two different frequencies without fiddling with the presets. Getting from one VFO to another is a bit awkward, though, since it requires pressing two buttons at the same time. Furthermore, there is no indicator to show which VFO is currently in use.

The '235 offers four bandwidths (nominally 10, 7, 4 and 2.2 kHz, but which actually measure 10.9, 8.8, 5.8 and 2.3 kHz), but our panelists found themselves rarely using the "10" and "7" kHz settings. They are simply too wide for nearly all world band listening situations—a pity. Nevertheless, the "4" kHz bandwidth works quite well for AM listening. The optional synchronous detector (tested), which unfortunately lacks selectable sideband, performs smartly, displaying an "L" when locked onto a signal. It works well at reducing fading.

In general, our laboratory measurements of

Lowe's HF-235 is designed for the professional user, but is also purchased by radio enthusiasts.

the '235's performance are similar to those we obtained with our resident '225. However, the dynamic range and related third-order intercept point (IP3) figures for our '235 are poorer than those of the '225. All indications are that this results from a sample anomaly, and that normally the dynamic range/IP3 figures should be at least equal to those of the HF-225.

The Lowe HF-235/R is clearly designed for remote listening applications and other situations of little relevance to the world band listener. One exception, however, is that its AGC may be switched off and the resulting distortion controlled by the IF gain. For tropical station DXing during thunderstorm static, this means the AGC cannot attenuate the desired signal by acting on static peaks.

Too, the '235 has a practical advantage in that its power supply, unlike that of the '225, is inboard. It's also dual-voltage, nominally 100-120 and 200-240V AC. In the United States, the accepted voltage range is 108-126V, with 108V being for brownouts on extremely hot days. Indeed, some major utilities, including Philadelphia Electric, are reluctant to reduce voltage to individual customers unless it is over 129V. We thus ran the '235 for extended periods at 121-126V and found no ill effects.

Many of the '225's excellent audio attributes, including synchronous detection, are present in the '235. However, the '235 is designed for professional shortwave monitoring, in which audio quality is not paramount. Thus, its diminutive speaker, although surprisingly competent for its size, is hardly a "Voice of the Theater." Too, the '235 lacks the interesting and effective tone control found on the '225.

The HF-235/H has enhanced stability, of use for reception of certain modes—especially unattended reception over long periods. However, the display does not read out frequencies to finer than 1 kHz, so the "H" capability cannot be used to enhance frequency measurement.

The HF-235/F is configured, at no extra cost, for fax reception. However, listeners to amateur radio transmissions should note that this fax capability comes at the expense of lower-sideband (LSB) reception.

The '235's detailed and well-written 80-page instruction and maintenance manual makes operation abundantly clear, and gives comprehensive details for taking full advantage of the HF-235/R's remote capabilities. Each receiver also comes with *The Lowe Listener's Guide*, a small manual for radio listening. It's written in a style that is both amusing and informative. Both publications are a refreshing departure from the awkward printed matter turned out by most receiver manufacturers.

Contrary to conventional wisdom, professional shortwave receivers aren't necessarily "better" receivers for world band purposes. However, they are almost certainly better for specific professional applications. Lowe has carefully tailored the HF-235 for just such purposes, and the HF-225 for other, quite different applications.

The upshot is that the Lowe HF-235 is an exceptional buy—a bargain, really—for a number of professional uses. But for world band listening, DXing and bandscanning, it's a different story. Unless you need the special capabilities of the '235, or your lifestyle includes routine meetings with "Q" in the bowels of "The Circus" (I'd like a vodka martini, shaken, not stirred), then you'll get pretty much the same performance—plus handier and more relevant features—from the Lowe HF-225. Less money, too.

By late 1991, the *RDI WHITE PAPER* for the Lowe HF-225 will be revised to include laboratory measurements and other relevant observations concerning the HF-235.

TABLETOP RECEIVERS

If you want a top performer, here is where your money stretches farthest. Five-star models should satisfy even the fussiest, and four-star models are no slouches, either.

The best tabletop models are the Ferraris and Mercedes of the radio world. As with their automotive counterparts, like-ranked receivers may come out of the curve at the same speed, though how they do it can differ greatly from model to model. So, if you're thinking of choosing from the top end, study each contender in detail.

New for 1992
★ ★ ★ ★ ★   *Editor's Choice*

Drake R8

Price: $979.00 in the United States. MS8 accessory speaker not priced as of press time.
Advantages: Unparalleled all-around listening performance. Most appropriate model available for hour-after-hour reception of world band programs. Superior audio quality, especially with suitable outboard speaker. Synchronous selectable sideband for reduced fading and easier rejection of interference. Five bandwidths, four suitable for world band —among the best of any model tested. Highly flexible operating controls, including 100 superb presets, variable notch filter and passband

offset. Superior reception of utility and ham signals. Tunes in precise 0.01 kHz increments. Displays frequency for some modes in those same 0.01 kHz increments. Slow/fast/off AGC. Sophisticated scan functions. Can access all presets quickly via tuning knob and slew buttons. Built-in preamplifier. Accepts two antennas. Two 24-hour clocks, with seconds displayed numerically and timer facilities. Manufacturer has superior track record for providing service.

Disadvantages: Depending on the application, ergonomics vary from okay to awful. Most pushbuttons rock on their centers. XX.XXXXX MHz frequency display format lacks decimal for integers finer than kHz. Neither clock displays for more than three seconds when radio on. Beeps, emitted when keys pressed, can't be turned down. Individual presets not tunable.

Bottom Line: The best of the best for high-quality listening to news, music and entertainment from afar. Superb for reception of faint, tough signals, too. Downside: a pain to operate for DXing.

Evaluation of New Model: Fitted out in matte black finish with white lettering, the R8 has a trim, stealth-like appearance that is scarcely in danger of winning a Las Vegas beauty contest. But, like the stealth fighter, when it comes to sparkling performance the R8 has what it takes —and then some.

The receiver has useful features galore: five bandwidths, synchronous selectable sideband, passband offset, tunable notch filter, two VFOs (tuning circuits), 100 presets, adjustable tuning steps, adjustable slow/fast/off AGC, preamplifier and attenuator, two antenna inputs selectable from the front panel, dual noise blankers (but no level control), tone control, two 24-hour clocks with seconds displayed numerically, all-mode squelch and a timer. For placing the R8 at a proper angle for viewing the display and handling the controls, there's a pair of flip-down feet. Modes the R8 is capable of receiving are AM, FM, CW, RTTY, LSB and USB.

The front panel of the R8 is clean and un-cluttered—too much so, as we shall see. At upper left is an excellent analog signal-strength meter. To its right is a large liquid-crystal display (LCD) that serves as "information central." The midline of the front panel is home for six unmarked dual-function keys, plus buttons for synchronous detector and power. There is also a very useful LED to indicate when the synchronous detector is on.

At lower left is a headphone jack, followed by concentric knobs for controlling tone and notch, a keypad, two slewing buttons, the main tuning knob, concentric knobs for squelch and passband offset, and concentric knobs for volume and RF gain. Compared to some other supersets, such as the Japan Radio NRD-535, that bristle with controls, the R8 seems downright naked.

Maestro of the airwaves, Drake's new R8 is unsurpassed for hour-after-hour listening. Not user friendly, though.

The large LCD makes it easy to find out what's going on, and has full illumination and well-shaped numerals. Frequency is normally displayed to the nearest kilohertz in the AM and FM modes, and to the nearest 0.01 kHz in all other modes. The display also shows which preset is currently ready to be accessed, which VFO is in use, which antenna is being used, the operating mode, the bandwidth in use; as well as the status of the noise blanker, notch, preamplifier, attenuator, scanning of presets and frequency lock. There is even an error message that appears should you press buttons in the wrong sequence. Visually, this LCD is a sensible arrangement that works well.

The R8 tunes in very precise 0.01 kHz increments, and the display reads out to that same degree of precision in most modes. However, for the AM mode, used for virtually all world band broadcasts, readout is only to the nearest kHz. This makes sense, sort of, as to tune more precisely one has to switch to the LSB, USB or CW mode, which creates a whistle sound. This allows for tuning until that whistle disappears— drops to "zero beat" —to determine the precise frequency.

Nevertheless, a user option to have the AM mode read out to the nearest 0.01 kHz would have been helpful as a visual reminder of the exact frequency as derived earlier via zero beat. The rub is that, on our unit, the frequency readout in the CW/LSB/USB modes is off between +0.03 and +0.08 kHz at exact zero beat.

The R8 does allow the operator to alter the display to read out to the nearest 0.1 kHz for AM reception. However, this is not the default setting, and if you change modes the radio will change the readout back to the coarser 1 kHz resolution default when you return to the AM mode.

A related problem is that the frequency readout lacks the decimal customarily used between the kHz and 0.1 kHz integers. Thus, 9750.03 kHz reads out as 9.75003 MHz, not 9.750.03 MHz—something of a jumble, and hardly what we're used to. Gluing a paper decimal onto the display helps alleviate the problem.

Pushbuttons on the R8 are made of a rubbery material that is pleasant to the touch. Problem is, when touched the buttons rock and roll, as though centered on ball joints. When one of these buttons is fully depressed a beep is audible through the speaker or headphones to let you know the keystroke has been successfully executed. If those beeps annoy, they can be switched off—but not down.

The R8 has numerous other and more serious ergonomic quirks, mainly for DX-caliber bandscanning. For example, the chosen bandwidth reverts to default when the mode changes. When you turn the R8 on, each mode has a default bandwidth setting. If you select the AM mode—the mode normally used for world band listening—the 6 kHz bandwidth automatically appears. However, if you change the bandwidth to, say, 4 kHz, then switch into LSB mode for a moment—say, to determine the exact frequency—then return to the AM mode, you'll find that bandwidth has reverted to 6 kHz, the default selection.

The earlier R7 receiver, made by Drake until the mid-1980s, had a much different arrangement. There were no separate USB, LSB, CW or RTTY modes with related default bandwidths. Instead, there was a single on/off button for the BFO and related detection circuitry. The operator selected the sideband via the passband offset, which covered either or both sidebands, and chose the bandwidth and frequency offset as he saw fit. For world band DXing, it was much more satisfactory.

Another ergonomic annoyance is that the bandwidth and mode selection operate on a clockwise-carousel basis. You must press a button to access each one in turn, so to make the full circuit calls for pushing a button five or six times. While these and other carousels keep the main face of the receiver uncluttered, it does slow down operation.

Too, the filter and mode buttons are located close to the plain Jane tuning knob, which lacks the excellent spinning dimple found on the earlier R7. As a result, while you are doing all this button pushing, it is easy to nudge the knob by accident, knocking the radio off frequency. Should the synchronous detector be switched on, that inadvertent bump on the knob will also turn it off.

The R8 uses concentric knobs to give the panel a simplified appearance. Concentric knobs are inherently annoying if you have to handle them often. Nevertheless, the R4245, a model Drake made some years back, had large, knurled concentric knobs that were reasonably easy to grasp. Those on the R8, on the other hand, are relatively clumsy to operate —the under-proportioned rear knobs, in particular. However, they are boldly marked, so it's easy to tell their exact settings.

Drake has been sensitized to the default problem, so improved software may appear shortly—possibly on sets being sold by the time you read this. This won't solve all the ergonomic shortcomings but, depending on the fix, could be a big help. Check with Drake or your dealer for up-to-the-minute information.

The R8 features a pair of VFOs—tuning circuits—that make it possible to enter one frequency on VFO "A" and another frequency on VFO "B," then to switch between the two by pressing a button. This is handy for checking to see if identical programming is on two different frequencies.

Preset storage and retrieval are straightforward. The R8's 100 presets store virtually everything: frequency, mode, bandwidth, AGC setting, RF setting, antenna, notch on/off, noise blanker setting and synchronous detector on/off. This is about as thorough and handy a preset-storage scheme as you could hope for.

To access a preset, just press the MEM button, enter the preset you want and, presto, there it is. Once the receiver is in preset memory mode, you can easily access all preset channels simply by adjusting the tuning knob or by pressing the up/down slewing buttons. This is handy if you wish to check quickly which channel of a favorite broadcaster sounds best. However, when you use the presets you can't tune from a preset frequency to other frequencies without first transferring the preset information in memory into one of the VFOs by pressing the M>V button.

There are two clocks, one for World Time, and either may be made visible whenever the radio is turned off. Yet, neither is automatically visible when the set is on. Instead, only the frequency is displayed. To see the time when the set is on, you must first push two buttons on the keypad. This allows the time to be visible for a scant three seconds, whereupon the display reverts to frequency. There really needs to be a separate, full-time display for the clocks —even if only one of the two clocks shows at any given moment.

Happily, despite its ergonomic foibles, the sheer performance of the R8 as a world band receiver is tall timber, indeed.

Take bandwidths. Proper bandwidths are among the most important variables affecting listening enjoyment—something like gears on a car. A wide bandwidth is best for fidelity, but is prone to let through adjacent-channel interference, if any. A narrow filter reduces interference, but degrades audio fidelity. Because the degree or presence of interference varies markedly from signal to signal, the more choices you have, the better the tradeoff between fidelity and interference rejection for any given station you're trying to enjoy.

Yet, manufacturers of even the costliest receivers rarely install more than two bandwidths, as additional bandwidths are costly. And when there are more than two bandwidths, almost invariably they are not well chosen.

None of this foolishness with the R8. It has fully five bandwidths, four of which are suitable for world band, and they are very well chosen, measuring on our unit 6.3, 4.4, 2.6, 2.0 and 0.5 kHz. The reason Drake was able to incorporate so many bandwidths without pricing the R8 higher is thanks to some heads-up engineering.

How? By perfecting LC (inductance-capacitance) circuitry, Drake has obtained excellent "Q," or selectivity, at low cost. Too, LC bandwidth filters are considered to have the best fidelity response—although in the mediocre-fidelity world of shortwave such nuances are pretty theoretical.

In any event, no other receiver on the market today, other than a proposed new version of the Japan Radio NRD-535D, comes close to the R8 in terms of bandwidth flexibility. For world band listening when adjacent-channel interference is minimal or nonexistent, the 6 kHz bandwidth is just right. If interference is moderate, the 4 kHz bandwidth usually noses out the unwanted racket without degrading fidelity too much. DXers and others going after tough catches will appreciate the 2.3 kHz bandwidth and even occasionally the 1.8 kHz bandwidth.

What a difference this makes in listening pleasure! But as if this weren't enough, the R8 also comes with passband offset, and it works better than similar circuits in competing models. It should, as Drake helped pioneer this circuit 30-odd years back. With passband offset, you can tune away from adjacent-channel interference to some extent, which means you can use a wider bandwidth that would otherwise be the case to keep interference in check. Too, it acts as a sophisticated tone control of sorts.

Not enough? Not if you want enhanced fidelity. So Drake included a synchronous detector, including selectable sideband, to reduce the effects of fading—especially distortion—and to facilitate sideband selection with world band signals. Sometimes this high-tech circuit helps, sometimes not. But if your ear is sensitive to distortion, it's something you'll wonder how you ever did without.

A precious few other models have synchronous detectors, but none except that on the British Liniplex F2 receiver—which is very costly, but has only one bandwidth—works quite so well as that on the R8. Punch it up—no critical tuning is required—then swing the R8's passband offset to the upper or lower side of the signal being received until you get the most pleasant reception. While the synchronous detector will growl and whistle while the passband offset control is being adjusted, it quickly settles down, rumbling slightly, like a full belly, only every now and then.

Any veteran listener will tell you that among the curses of world band radio are howls and squeals—whistles made when two signals operate near each other on the dial. Well, the R8 has a cure for this aural irritant, too.

Most world band stations operate smack on channels 5 kHz apart, which at wide bandwidths can sometimes cause a continuous 5 kHz squeal. Too, sometimes stations are bothered by signals less than 5 kHz away, and these can also create squeals or howls.

The R8 comes with a powerful tunable notch filter within its audio stage to cure this. Although it takes a safecracker's touch and the ears of a bat to operate, its narrow, deep notch slices through a howl or squeal like a Henckels knife through meatloaf.

Overall distortion is low, as well—generally between 0.3 and 3%, averaging around 1%. Although the 4 kHz filter without the synchronous detector has distortion between 0.5-9%, switching in the synchronous detector cleans this up.

While the passband offset acts as a form of tone control, there's also a single conventional audio tone control. Two such controls, as on the Grundig Satellit 650, would have been better, but the one is useful if a good speaker is used.

What all this means is that the combination of five bandwidths, synchronous detection, passband offset, a tunable notch filter and low overall distortion gives the listener a remarkable degree of flexibility in reducing fading and interference, while maximizing fidelity.

Also helping with fidelity, but even more important in snaring faint stations, is that the R8 is relatively quiet. Absent is the persistent background hiss that mars reception on some other models. Switching on the R8's built-in preamplifier helps even more.

All this is music to the ears, and to bring it to fruition Drake plans to offer a high-quality outboard speaker, the MS8, as an option, probably for under $90. We tested the R8 both with its internal speaker and with various outboard speakers—although not the MS8, which was still being designed during our test period. The internal speaker is okay, but using a speaker like this on something like the R8 is like riding a racing bicycle with under-inflated tires. After all, if you don't care about fidelity, why get an R8 in the first place?

Well, one reason might be for its ability to capture faint signals, especially those hemmed in by interference from other signals. Truth is, there are other models that do very well in this regard—notably, the Kenwood R-5000, Icom IC-R71 and anything from Japan Radio. Does the world really need yet another DX hot rod?

Perhaps. By and large, the R8 performs on a par with other top-flight models for tough-signal reception. Pluses include its quietness, which helps improve the audibility of faint signals—especially those more or less "out in the clear." Another DX plus is the ability to switch off the AGC when listening to weak signals during static; otherwise, the AGC tends to respond to static and thus mute the signal. And, of course, there are all those bandwidths.

However, the ergonomic shortcomings of the R8 are most apparent during serious DX bandscanning. Even after weeks of getting used to the R8's operating scheme, our panelists found it to be ergonomically one of the worst sets for DXing up and down the bands—its superb performance notwithstanding. Yet, experience shows that not all DX enthusiasts mind going through ergonomic hoops. It's really a personal thing.

Measurements of tough-signal performance confirm what your ears tell you: this receiver is awfully good. Bandwidth shape factors for the four voice filters measure between 1:1.8 and 1:2.2, which while worthy is hardly enough for you to put a second mortgage on the house. Nearly all other measurements echo this, and what you see when the lab tests are said and done is a receiver that's remarkably consistent in the high quality of its performance. This differs from models that excel in some respects, but are mediocre in others.

What this means is that the R8 is not like, say, a muscle car—a device that does only one or a few things well. It's well rounded, doing everything except ergonomics very well.

Quality of construction? It's too early to tell, but the R8 appears to be about average for a model in its price class, and it runs warm. Traditionally, Drake has provided superior— even legendary—service, with one exception: The earliest samples of their last model, the R7, suffered from persistent frequency-display failures which to this day Drake's service facility has yet to clear up properly.

As with a number of tabletop models, the R8 is designed to be operated via computer, as well as manually. This should make it of interest to intelligence and military organizations, as well as some computer freaks.

If you're interested in the most pleasant reception possible, the Drake R8 is certainly the best choice. Although it's hardly inexpensive, it's quite reasonably priced for all that it does. However, if you're a DX enthusiast primarily interested in logging faint, rarely heard stations, there are other models that are much more straightforward to operate for bandscanning. If you're unsure whether the R8 is what you want, Drake sells the radio direct from the factory with a 15-day return privilege, and some dealers might agree to similar arrangements upon request. Yet, ergonomics or no ergonomics, Drake reports that few receivers sold direct thus far have been returned for refund.

Overall, the Drake R8 is radio for the ears— a generally well thought out package that performs brilliantly, if at times clumsily. If you can accept its ergonomic oddities, its combination of features and performance make it the ultimate radio for listening to programs from around the world.

An *RDI WHITE PAPER* will be made available for this model in late 1991, after a later production sample has been tested.

New for 1992
★ ★ ★ ★ ★

Editor's Choice

Japan Radio NRD-535D (Japan Radio NRD-535)

Editor's Note: Initial production units of the Japan Radio NRD-535 came with a whopping 10.5 kHz wide bandwidth. With this bandwidth, the '535 would earn four stars. However, units now being produced come with a vastly superior 5.8 kHz wide bandwidth.

We tested both versions for this report, but are basing our final recommendations on the newer (5.8 kHz) version. This version clearly earns five stars.

Additionally, Japan Radio informs us just as we are going to press that a revised "D" (deluxe) version with variable bandwidth in the AM mode is shortly to appear on dealers' shelves. This version was not available in time for us to test, but has the potential of eliminating our main criticism of the '535. However, as the performance of this proposed variable bandwidth feature is unconfirmed, we have based the ranking of the '535 on the results of the latest version we have actually tested.

At least in the United States, according to Japan Radio, those who purchased earlier versions of the '535D can obtain free upgrades from Japan Radio's New York office. Upgrading a receiver requires nothing more than a plug-in board swap.

Price: *NRD-535D:* $1,995.00 in the United States; *NRD-535:* £1,115.00 in the United Kingdom, plus £202 for CMF-78 synchronous detector ("ECSS").

Advantages: Best DX receiver tested. Very good ergonomics. Construction quality slightly above average. Computer-type modular plug-in circuit boards ease repair. Highly flexible operating controls, including 200 superb presets, tunable notch filter and passband offset. Superior reception of utility and ham signals. Tunes frequency in exacting 0.001 kHz increments. Displays frequency in precise 0.01 kHz increments. Slow/fast/off AGC. Sophisticated scan functions. World Time clock with timer facilities; displays seconds, albeit only if a wire inside the receiver is cut. *NRD-535D:* Synchronous selectable sideband for reduced fading and easier rejection of interference. Continuously variable bandwidth in single-sideband mode. *NRD-535D (proposed new version):* Continuously variable bandwidth also in AM mode.

Disadvantages: Clock shares display with frequency readout. Clock not visible when receiver off. Front feet do not tilt receiver upwards. Relatively limited dealer network. Also, see "Editor's Note," above.

Bottom Line: Unsurpassed DX performance, superb performance for everyday listening to programs, with worthy ergonomics and superior quality of construction.

Evaluation of New Model: The NRD-535, arguably the handsomest receiver on the market, is laden with useful features: a two-level noise blanker and level control (with LED), all-mode squelch (with LED), tunable notch filter (with annunciator), passband shift control (with annunciator), variable bandwidth control and RF gain control are all located at the lower left of the front panel.

To the upper left is an excellent vacuum fluorescent display that is bright and highly readable—if slightly harsher to the eye than that of the Drake R8. This serves as "information central," and its creative use of color helps keep apples separated from oranges. That display also incorporates a curved digital signal strength indicator with a bright yellow bar moving across a red-and-white scale. It, too, is bright and highly readable, and unlike most such digital indicators does not annoy the eye.

In all modes, the frequency reads out to 0.01 kHz, which should satisfy even the fussiest of technical types. Just as important is that the readout on our units are accurate to within +0.03 kHz—closer than on our Drake R8— and for those requiring greater accuracy there is the $79.95 CGD-135 high-stability crystal oscillator accessory.

Beneath the display are a series of buttons for activating the desired operating mode: RTTY, CW, USB/LSB, AM, FM or fax. Press a function key, however, and these buttons become controls for the dimmer, clock, attenuator and various memory functions.

Just to the right of the '535's center is an excellent large tuning knob with a rubber rim, fixed (non-rotating) tuning dimple and just enough mass for a bit of flywheel effect when you spin the knob. Tuning is in exceptionally exacting 0.001 kHz increments—finer than any other receiver tested—so there is nary a trace of chuffing. Above it are pushbutton controls

The latest in a long tradition of excellence is Japan Radio's ergonomically superior NRD-535. Superior construction, too.

for bandwidth, automatic gain control, synchronous selectable sideband ("ECSS"), tuning rate, frequency lock, frequency control and memory channel. In addition, a couple of push panels can be used to slew the frequency or memory channel up or down.

The keypad at the extreme right-hand side of the receiver has well-spaced keys of reasonable size. Below that are the AF gain (volume) and tone controls. In all, the layout is well thought out and generally easy to use; the tuning and volume controls are set to the right of the set, and the rest of the controls are on the left. Bravo!

Controls on the '535 not only look good, they feel good. Buttons are crisp and positive, and render a beep through the speaker or headphones when pressed. A screw on the bottom of the receiver allows the beep's volume to be regulated or turned off. The knobs are precise and comfortable.

Ergonomically, the '535 behaves quite well. The first-time operator can plunge in and put the set to good use without having to refer to the manual. In addition, LEDs and annunciators on the main display keep the listener up to date on how the controls are being used.

Certain controls, such as the bandwidth, operate via a one-way carousel arrangement, but this can be overcome (the instruction manual explains how). The end result is much handier operation than on the Drake R8.

There are some wrinkles, however. While selecting a frequency is quite straightforward— for example, to tune 6175, you press 6 - 1 - 7 - 5 - Ent/kHz, and you are there—entering a frequency into a memory channel is a bit cumbersome. To enter, say, 6175 kHz into memory 199, you must first select the frequency as above, then press MEMO - Ent/kHz - 1 - 9 - 9 - Ent/kHz.

Still, once set those 200 presets work well. For one thing, they are tunable—an advantage over those of the Drake R8. For another, they store virtually everything. You could hardly ask for more.

Well, almost. If the receiver is in frequency mode—that is, you are entering frequencies directly through the keypad or tuning knob—

and you switch to memory mode (in which you are accessing memory channels), there is no way you can return to the last frequency you were using in the frequency mode. When you exit from a memory channel into frequency mode, the NRD-535 automatically transfers the information from the last memory channel you were using into the frequency mode. As a result, if you are listening to a particular program on, say, 6175 kHz and want to quickly check one of the memory channels and then jump back to the program on 6175 kHz, you can't do it.

In the narrow single-sideband setting, if the receiver is switched from LSB to USB or *vice versa* you have to retune the passband shift control—an annoyance. However, this isn't necessary in the wider bandwidth.

Being able to tilt a receiver upwards tends to make operation handier. The '535 isn't equipped to do this, but it's not hard for operators to devise their own makeshift arrangements to raise the receiver's front feet.

Worse, the NRD-535 is yet another receiver with a "dumb clock" arrangement. If you cut a special jumper wire on one of the circuit boards, the clock displays seconds numerically. There's a timer and scanner as well. So far, so good.

But you can't see the clock and the frequency at the same time. In fact, you can't even see the clock when the radio is turned off. Two thousand bucks, and they can't afford to provide a separate, full-time display for the clock?

The ergonomic quirks of the 535 are not helped by the original instruction manual, which was, we suspect, badly written in Japanese and then badly translated into English. While the general concept and organization of the manual is acceptable, the execution is an affront to the reader.

Fortunately, Japan Radio's New York office has produced a much-improved manual, which is about to be included in all '535s sold with English manuals worldwide. We've had a peek at the initial draft and it looks very encouraging, although an alphabetical index would help.

Performance is fully what you would expect of a world band superset. In particular, as our lab measurements and ears suggest, the '535 is unusually adept at snaring faint, hard-to-catch signals from a recalcitrant ionosphere. Noise is low, sensitivity high, dynamic range good, and so on and on. Like the Drake R8, there are no weak spots in the engineering. It's an exceptionally well-rounded receiver.

Also helpful when DXing, especially tropical stations below 5.1 MHz, is that you can switch off the '535's AGC during periods of thunderstorm static. This prevents the AGC from acting on the static and thus desensitizing the desired signal.

The "ECSS" synchronous selectable sideband—standard on the "D" version sold in North America, optional in the standard version sold elsewhere—works well. Press the "ECSS" button, an LED comes on, and fading distortion is greatly reduced. By pressing the button again, the operator can choose between the upper and lower sidebands to avoid interference from adjacent signals.

The passband shift control can also be used to move the passband of the receiver away from center frequency to avoid adjacent-channel interference and reduce fading. Yet, if the passband is moved too far away from center frequency—more than about half the shift this control is capable of providing—regardless of the bandwidth, the synchronous circuitry begins to protest. That's too bad, because the greater the offset that can be used, the greater the potential for expanding the amount of high audio frequencies heard and avoiding interference.

The Drake R8's synchronous circuit works fine without critical tuning. It tends to lose lock briefly, rumble softly, then regain lock. The '535's circuit, on the other hand, has to be tuned spot-on to function, but once locked in loses lock less often. However, when it does lose lock, it really loses it.

Overall, the nod goes to the R8's synchronous detector.

The great opportunity lost when initially designing the '535 was in the choice of bandwidths. For world band listening, a filter should be like a picture frame—just wide enough to frame the picture and not include parts of other pictures, yet not so narrow that it cuts off parts of the picture people would like to see. Similarly, bandwidth filters should be wide enough to capture the entire signal without picking up interference from other signals; yet, not degrade fidelity excessively.

To do this properly calls for many bandwidth choices, so that the widest bandwidth may be used that does not introduce adjacent-channel interference. Here, the '535 initially missed the boat. In the first units produced, there were three filters, but only two for the AM mode used for world band. The wider filter was 10.5 kHz—much too wide to be of any practical use—whereas the narrower was 2.3 kHz, useful only under conditions of substantial interference. There was nothing between, and the result was mediocre, at best.

That's the bad news. The good news is that after the initial production run, the wide bandwidth was changed to 5.8 kHz—this, we tested. Equally important, the '535D version will shortly be changed to allow the bandwidth to be varied continuously. We haven't tested this, but if it works as promised it will allow the '535D's wide bandwidth to be varied from 5.8-2.3 kHz, and the narrow bandwidth from 2.3-0.5 kHz.

What about the standard '535? It lacks that all-important variable bandwidth, but this option—the CFL-243—may be added for $349.95 from dealers the United States, a bit more from dealers in Europe. Alternatively, some North American dealers will install an accessory bandwidth filter, such as a Collins mechanical, of around 4 kHz—usually for under $200.

Audio quality has never been the hallmark of Japan Radio's consumer-grade receivers. The '535 doesn't fully break with this tradition, but there's no question that this new model sounds much better than its predecessors. Distortion, in particular, is low, ranging from 0.1-3.0%, but typically being just under 2%. For tuning in weak signals, or stations hemmed in by interference, the '535's audio is more than adequate and provides excellent intelligibility. However, for long-term listening to programs—especially those with music—from typical international broadcasters, the Drake R8 is kinder to the ears.

Quality of construction? Japan Radio has always excelled, and the '535 appears to be no exception. Corporate track record aside, there are two other good reasons to expect this model to be good for the long haul: It runs cool, which helps assure long component life, and it's relatively heavy. This is a *real* radio!

Repairs to the '535—and '525—are usually a snap. You usually don't have to ship your receiver, either, thanks to its use of computer-type plug-in circuit boards. Typically all that is needed is to contact a Japan Radio office with a description of symptoms, whereupon they can tell you which board to return for exchange. Nearly any layman can replace a defective board on the '535 in a matter of minutes.

Finally, the '535 is also well equipped to be controlled by computer—a capability of interest mainly to intelligence and military organizations, as well as some computer buffs.

To buy, or not to buy?

On paper, the Japan Radio NRD-535 and Drake R8 appear to be near twins, except for price. However, as our months of testing have shown, they are really aimed at two somewhat different types of listener. Both models are excellent, but the primary emphasis of one is the secondary emphasis of the other, and *vice versa*.

The ergonomically superior, but pricey, '535 is the *ne plus ultra* for chasing weak, tough world band, ham or utility signals. Secondarily, it is quite effective for daily listening to programs from major broadcasters.

The R8, on the other hand, is primarily the ultimate in enhanced-fidelity receivers for listening to news, music and entertainment via world band. It also performs excellently—even if it's clumsy to operate—for reception of weak, tough catches.

Choose accordingly.

 An *RDI WHITE PAPER* will be made available for this model in late 1991, after a later production sample has been tested.

★ ★ ★ ★ ★   *Editor's Choice*

Kenwood R-5000

Price: $1,099.95 in the United States, CAN$1,349.95 in Canada, under £900 in the United Kingdom, $1,000-1,500 elsewhere in Europe.

Advantages: Unusually appropriate for hour-after-hour world band listening. Superb all-around performance. Unusually good audio for a tabletop, provided a suitable outboard speaker is used. Exceptionally flexible operating controls, including tunable notch filter and passband offset. Tunes and displays frequency in precise 0.01 kHz increments. Excellent reception of utility and ham signals. Superior frequency-of-repair record.

Disadvantages: Ergonomics only fair, especially keypad. Mediocre wide bandwidth filter supplied with set; replacement with high-quality YK-88A-1 substitute adds $88.95 to cost. Audio significantly distorted at tape-recording output.

Bottom Line: The Kenwood R-5000's combination of superior tough-signal performance and above-average audio quality makes it an excellent choice in its price class for those who need a receiver for tough-signal DXing, as well as reasonable fidelity for listening to programs.

Comment: Demand for this model sometimes places it in short supply. Waits of up to several weeks are not unheard of.

 An *RDI WHITE PAPER* is available for this model.

Kenwood's R-5000 performs superbly. Sounds good, too.

Japan Radio's proven NRD-525 is a superb performer, except for audio quality.

★ ★ ★ ★ ★   *Editor's Choice*

Japan Radio NRD-525U
(Japan Radio NRD-525E)
(Japan Radio NRD-525J)
(Japan Radio NRD-525G)

Price: $1,275.00 in the United States, under CAN$2,100 in Canada, under £1,100 in the United Kingdom, $1,300-2,000 elsewhere in Europe.

Advantages: Superb all-around performance. Highly flexible operating controls, including tunable notch filter and passband offset. Very good ergonomics. Construction quality slightly above average. Computer-type modular plug-in circuit boards ease repair. Sophisticated scan facilities. Superior reception of utility and ham signals. Slow/fast/off AGC. Tunes and displays frequency in precise 0.01 kHz increments. Two 24-hour clocks with timer facilities.

Disadvantages: Woolly audio, a major drawback for program listening. Dynamic range below par for genre. Relatively limited dealer network.

Bottom Line: A superb performer that's well put together—although hardly like its sibling NRD-93—but lacks audio fidelity. The prominent choice in its price class for listening in diverse modes.

Comment: When tested with Sherwood SE-3 synchronous selectable sideband device fitted to a Realistic Minimus 7 speaker, audio quality improved to excellent.

An *RDI WHITE PAPER* is available for this model.

★ ★ ★ ★ $\frac{1}{2}$

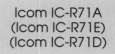

Icom IC-R71A
(Icom IC-R71E)
(Icom IC-R71D)

Price: *IC-R71A:* $999.00 in the United States, CAN$1,559.00 in Canada; *IC-R71E:* under £900 in the United Kingdom; *IC-R71E and IC-R71D:* $1,000-1,600 in continental Europe.

Advantages: Superb reception of weak, hard-to-hear signals. Reception of faint signals alongside powerful competing ones aided by superb ultimate selectivity, as well as excellent dynamic range. Flexible operating controls, including tunable notch filter. Excellent reception of utility and ham signals. Tunes in precise 0.01 kHz increments (reads in 0.1 kHz increments).

Disadvantages: Mediocre audio. Diminutive controls, and otherwise generally substandard ergonomics. Should backup battery die, operating system software erases, requiring re-programming by Icom service center (expected battery life is in excess of 10 years). Units on sale since March, 1989, lack certain helpful operating features found on original version. No longer available in most countries.

Bottom Line: The Icom IC-R71, especially in its original incarnation, has long been a favorite among those seeking faint, hard-to-hear signals. However, the 'R71, now virtually unavailable except in North America, is not equal to some other tabletops for hour-on-hour program listening. The possibility exists, depending upon the outcome of a legal dispute, that this model will be replaced in the United States and Canada by the Icom IC-R72 by the end of 1992.

An *RDI WHITE PAPER* is available for this model.

The Icom IC-R71, which in an earlier version was a favorite for chasing rare signals, is off the market in some countries. Still available in North America, though.

At last, a surge protector that really works. Highly recommended.

NO SHOCKING DEVELOPMENT

For years, an engineer at RCA who helped develop color television was frustrated by the inability of conventional surge arresters to protect his TV set. He lives where there are overhead power lines, and every now and then the inductive surge current from nearby lightning strikes would cause his television to blow.

Curious, he delved into the subject of current-surge protection. The result is the Zero Surge. It's a completely different concept that, instead of trying to shunt most excess current off immediately to ground, fully "stores" the excess, then bleeds it off slowly to neutral. Too, the circuitry used does not become ineffective over time, as it does with most surge or lightning protectors.

At *Passport to World Band Radio*, we are in a zone American Telephone & Telegraph calls "Lightning Alley," and power lines are overhead. We long ago resolved the problem of surge current from our outdoor antennas by using Alpha Delta arresters, which work splendidly. But even though we have been using a wide variety of conventional surge protectors for the power, nearly every year at least one costly item of equipment has fallen victim to whopping surges coming in over the power lines.

Nine months ago, we purchased a Zero Surge and have tested it ever since. It really works. Indeed, we found the results so impressive that we have since purchased five more to protect our regular receiving equipment, test receivers, computers, telephone system and other critical office equipment. Voltage measurements over this test period and the lack of equipment failures—as well as a healthy reduction in computer glitches—show the Zero Surge to be in a league unto itself. It's warranted for 10 years, and any repairs thereafter are guaranteed to run no more than 20% of the purchase price.

The downside? Price. The model ZS900, good for 900 watts, runs $149 (the ZS1800, 1800 watts, is $199). Either model is more than adequate to protect a desk full of radio equipment—receiver, recorder, antenna amplifying gear, RTTY gear and the like.

Zero Surge is currently made to operate only from the 120V power found throughout North America and certain other parts of the world. However, a 220V model is likely to appear, possibly in early 1992. If you live in Europe or elsewhere with 220V as the norm, check directly with Zero Surge Eliminators (103 Claremont Rd., Bernardsville NJ 07924 USA; fax +1 908/766-4144) to see whether the 220V model is ready for sale.

Sturdy design and quality audio are among the hallmarks of the Lowe HF-225, shown in its quasi-portable configuration.

★ ★ ★ ★

Editor's Choice

Lowe HF-225

Price: £429, plus accessories, in the United Kingdom; around $700—including keypad accessory, power supply, shipping and tariff—if sent to the United States.

Advantages: Among the best for listening to world band programs hour after hour. Superior audio with outboard speaker. Straightforward to operate. Generally excellent ergonomics, especially with keypad. Four bandwidths. Tunes in precise, if unusual, 8 Hz increments. Physically rugged with frequency-of-repair record that appears to be somewhat above average. Optional synchronous detector, tested, reduces distortion. Optional field-portable configuration, tested. Small footprint. Attractively priced.

Disadvantages: Limited operational flexibility, including AGC. Two of four bandwidths too wide for most world band applications. Front-end selectivity only fair. In tabletop use, less sensitive to weak signals than top-rated models. Optional portable configuration relatively insensitive to weak signals. Frequency reads in relatively coarse 1 kHz increments. Currently not distributed outside Europe, but this could change during 1992.

Bottom Line: A hardy, easy-to-operate set with superior audio quality. Reasonably priced.

An *RDI WHITE PAPER* is available for this model.

★ ★ ★ ★

Icom IC-R72

Price: £599 (about $1,024) in United Kingdom.

Advantages: Pleasant audio with outboard speaker or headphones. Generally superior ergonomics. Tunes and displays frequency in precise 0.01 kHz increments. World clock/timer. Operates for about one hour off built-in rechargeable battery—useful during power failure. Novel center-tuning LED for world band and certain other signals. Superb image and IF rejection. Small footprint. Smoothly operating tuning knob. Preamplifier.

Disadvantages: Receiver, parts and factory-authorized service currently not available in United States or Canada. Wide bandwidth too broad. Dreadful audio from built-in speaker. Noisy synthesizer. Noise blanker reduces dynamic range. Relatively few features, compared to better models. In our test unit, poor low-frequency audio reproduction in upper-sideband.

Bottom Line: Nice, but nothing special. A number of other models offer better value. The possibility exists, depending upon the outcome of a legal dispute, that this model will replace the better Icom IC-R71 in the United States and Canada before the end of 1992.

Replacing the Icom IC-R71 in some countries is the IC-R72. Less good, but it's priced lower and has battery power backup.

★ ★ ★ ★

Yaesu FRG-8800

Price: $784.00 in the United States, CAN$1,229.00 in Canada, under £650 in the United Kingdom, $800-1,100 elsewhere in Europe.

Advantages: Flexible controls. Slightly above-average audio for tabletop model. Superior sensitivity and related blocking measurements help weak signal reception. Fairly good ergonomics. Two 24-hour clocks. Established circuit design, going back several years, is by now thoroughly proven.

Disadvantages: "Wide" bandwidth too broad for most world band receiving applications. "Narrow" bandwidth somewhat wide for a "narrow," yet rather narrow for a "wide." Spurious signal ("image") rejection only fair. Front-end selectivity only fair. Utility and ham signal reception, though acceptable, below average for tabletop model. Some control settings difficult to see, and a couple of controls are unhandy to reach. Microprocessor reportedly sometimes tends to malfunction.

Bottom Line: The only world band receiver sold by Yaesu, the FRG-8800 is a proven, well-balanced performer very much in need of tighter selectivity.

An *RDI WHITE PAPER* is available for this model.

The only model offered by Japan's Yaesu is the FRG-8800, priced less than most others.

Kenwood's R-2000 is cheaper than its R-5000 brand mate, but the R-5000 is well worth the extra money.

★ ★ ★ $\frac{1}{2}$

Kenwood R-2000

Price: $799.95 in the United States, CAN$1,049.95 in Canada, under £600 in the United Kingdom, $750-1,250 elsewhere in Europe.

Advantages: Straightforward to operate, with generally good ergonomics. Audio slightly above average for tabletop model. Utility and ham reception, although not outstanding, is at least average within its price class. Superior sensitivity makes model relevant to needs of listeners in such places as Western North America and Oceania, where world band signals tend to be weak. Two 24-hour clocks.

Disadvantages: Mediocre dynamic range materially compromises performance by allowing overloading to take place in many parts of the world, such as Europe and even Eastern North America—especially with high-gain antennas. "Wide" bandwidth too broad for most world band applications. Keypad uses nonstandard, unhandy layout.

Bottom Line: This model can be quite pleasurable for listening to the major world band stations—especially if you live in Western North America. But for other, more demanding applications, it is in need of tighter selectivity and better dynamic range.

The Passport *review team: Lawrence Magne, along with Jock Elliott and Tony Jones, with laboratory measurements by Robert Sherwood.*

INDEX TO TESTED RADIOS: 1985-1992

At International Broadcasting Services, we publish three levels of reviews. The most concise are those that appear in *Passport's* Buyer's Guide each year. These run roughly a half page each, and appear annually so long as the reviewed model is still being sold by the manufacturer.

Next in depth are "New for This Year" receiver analyses in the Buyer's Guide. These usually appear just once, the year of model introduction. Those lengthier reviews—they usually run a page or more—serve to detail what's just appeared in the marketplace.

Finally, for premium receivers and antennas there are comprehensive *Passport RDI White Papers*. These usually run 15-30 pages in length, and one *RDI White Paper* thoroughly covers a single model or topic. Each *RDI White Paper*—$5.95 in North America, $7.95 airmail elsewhere—provides the full breadth and depth of our panel's findings and comments during hands-on testing, as well as our laboratory measurements and what these mean to you. These are available from selected dealers, or you may write us or call our 24-hour automated order line (215/794-8252).

Following is the complete list of initial *Passport* reviews and *RDI White Papers*. Longer *Passport* reviews are in **bold**. Please note that back editions of *Passport* are not available from us, but are sometimes found in libraries.

	Passport Edition	RDI White Paper		Passport Edition	RDI White Paper
Alconic Series 2959	1990		Grundig Yacht Boy 210	1989	
Antennas, Indoor (various models)		Yes	Grundig Yacht Boy 215	1989	
Antennas, Outdoor (various models)		Yes	Grundig Yacht Boy 220	1990	
Bearcat/Uniden DX1000	**1985**		Grundig Yacht Boy 650	1987	
Clairtone PR-291	1992		Grundig Yacht Boy 700	1987	
Cougar H-88	1990		Heathkit/Zenith SW-7800	**1985**	
DAK MR-101	**1991**		Heathkit/Zenith SW-7800		
DAK MR-101s	**1992**		(revised version)	1987	
Drake R7/R7A	1987		Icom IC-R71 (all versions)	**1985/1988**	Yes
Drake R8	**1992**	**Yes****	Icom IC-R72	**1991**	
Drake R4245	1987		"Icom IC-R7000HF"	1991	
EEB 4950	1988		Icom IC-R9000	**1990**	Yes
Electro Brand 2971	1991		Japan Radio NRD-93	1987	Yes
Embassy Ambassador 2020	**1988**		Japan Radio NRD-515	**1985**	
Embassy Diplomat 4950	1987		Japan Radio NRD-525	**1987/1988**	Yes
Emerson ATS-803A	1990		Japan Radio NRD-535/535D	**1992**	**Yes****
Emerson PSW4010	1990		Kenwood R-11	1987	
Eska RX99PL	**1985**		Kenwood R-600	1987	
Eskab RX 33	**1988**		Kenwood R-1000	1987	
General Electric World Monitor	**1987**		Kenwood R-2000	1987	
Goodmans ATS-803	1989		Kenwood R-5000	**1988**	Yes
Grundig Cosmopolit	1992		Linaplex F1	**1985**	
Grundig Satellit 300	1987		Lowe HF-125	**1988**	
Grundig Satellit 400	**1988**		Lowe HF-225	**1990**	Yes
Grundig Satellit 500	**1990**		Lowe HF-235 (all versions)	**1992**	Yes
Grundig Satellit 500			Magnavox AE 3205	**1992**	
(revised version)	**1991**	Yes	Magnavox AE 3805	**1991**	
Grundig Satellit 600	**1985**	Yes*	Magnavox D1835	1988	
Grundig Satellit 650	**1988**	Yes	Magnavox D1875	1990/1992	
Grundig Traveller II	1992		Magnavox D2935	**1987**	
Grundig Travel Kit 220	1991		Magnavox D2999	**1987/1988**	
Grundig Travel Kit 230	1991		Marc II	1989	

	Passport Edition	RDI White Paper		Passport Edition	RDI White Paper
Matsui MR-4099	1989		Sangean ATS-803 (revised)/803A	1988	
MBR Mark II	1991		Sangean ATS-808	**1991**	
McKay Dymek DR 33-C	1987		Sangean MS-101	1989	
McKay Dymek DR 101-6	1987		Sangean MS-103/MS-103L	1990	
National B10	1989		Sangean SG 621	**1992**	
National B20	1989		Sangean SG-631	**1992**	
National B40	1990		Sangean SG-700L	**1992**	
National B45	**1992**		Sangean SG-789/SG-789L	1987	
National B50	1989		Sharp FV-310GB	1987	
National B60	**1989**		Sharp FV-610GB	1987	
National B65	1990		Siemens RK 641	1989	
National B300	1989		Siemens RP 647G4	1992	
National B600	1989		Siemens RK 651	1990	
National DR-22	1987		Siemens RK 661		
National DR-29	1987		(Sangean ATS-808)	**1991**	
National DR-31	1987		Siemens RK 702	1989	
National DR-49/RF-4900	1987		Silver XF1900	1987	
National DR-63	1987		Sony CRF-1	1987	
National DR-90	1987		Sony CRF-V21	**1990**	**Yes**
National Micro 00	1987		Sony ICF-2001	1987	
Opal OP-35	1989		Sony ICF-2001D/ICF-2001DS	**1985/1988**	**Yes**
Panashiba FX-928	**1992**		Sony ICF-2002	1988	
Panasonic RF-9/RF-9L	1987		Sony ICF-2003	**1988**	
Panasonic RF-799	1987		Sony ICF-2010	**1985/1988**	**Yes**
Panasonic RF-2200	1987		Sony ICF-4900	1987	
Panasonic RF-2900	1987		Sony ICF-4900 Mark II	1989	
Panasonic RF-3100	1987		Sony ICF-4910	1987	
Panasonic RF-4900	1987		Sony ICF-5100	1989	
Panasonic RF-6300	1987		Sony ICF-6800W	**1987**	
Panasonic RF-9000	1987		Sony ICF-7600A	1987	
Panasonic RF-B10	1989		Sony ICF-7600AW	1987	
Panasonic RF-B20/B20L	1989		Sony ICF-7600D	1988	
Panasonic RF-B40/RF-B40L	1989		Sony ICF-7600DA	**1988**	
Panasonic RF-B45/B45DL	**1992**		Sony ICF-7600DS	**1988**	
Panasonic RF-B50	1987		Sony ICF-7601	1989	
Panasonic RF-B60/B60L	**1988**		Sony ICF-7700	**1988**	
Panasonic RF-B65/B65D/B65L	1990		Sony ICF-PRO70	**1988**	
Panasonic RF-B300	1989		Sony ICF-PRO80	**1988**	
Panasonic RF-B600	1989		"Sony ICF-SW1"	1991	
Pan Crusader	1989		Sony ICF-SW1E	1990	
Philips AE 3205	**1992**		Sony ICF-SW1S	1989	
Philips AE 3805	**1991**		Sony ICF-SW20	1990	
Philips D1835	1987		Sony ICF-SW700	**1992**	
Philips D1875	1990/1992		Sony ICF-SW800	**1992**	
Philips D2615	1990		Sony ICF-SW7600	**1991**	
Philips D2935	**1987/1988**		Sony WA-6000	1990	
Philips D2999	**1987**		Sony WA-8000MKII	1991	
Philips D7476	1989		Sony WA-8800	1990	
Pomtrex 120-00300	**1992**		Supertech SR-16H	1987	
Pulser	**1992**		Ten-Tec RX-325	**1988**	
Quelle Universum	1990		TMR 7602 Hightech Tatung	1991	
Racal RA6790/GM	1987		Toshiba RP-F11	1987	
Realistic DX-350	**1992**		Trio R-11	1987	
Realistic DX-360	1987		Trio R-600	1987	
Realistic DX-370	**1991**		Trio R-1000	1987	
Realistic DX-380	1991		Trio R-2000	1987	
Realistic DX-440	**1988**		Tunemaster Classic Radio	**1990**	
Rhapsody Multiband	1989		Venturer Multiband	1989	
Roberts R808	1992		Yaesu FRG-7700	1987	
Rodelsonic Digital World Band	**1992**		Yaesu FRG-8800	**1985/1988**	**Yes**
Rodelvox Digital World Band	**1992**				
Saisho SW5000	1989				
Sangean ATS 800	**1991**				
Sangean ATS-801	1987		*RDI White Paper* available for Satellit 650, essentially		
Sangean ATS-802	1990		identical to the Satellit 600.		
Sangean ATS-803	**1987/1988**		**Available from 12/91.		

WORLDSCAN

WHAT'S ON TONIGHT?

Passport's Hour-by-Hour Guide to World Band Shows

World band radio has once again come into its own. Last year, millions tuned in for the first time—thousands even depended on it for their lives.

The Gulf conflict underscored world band's vitality when the going gets hot. Stations have reacted by providing better programs in English, especially news. Now, we can sit back and enjoy these upgraded programs, many of which are first rate.

Because there is nearly always something interesting to be heard, day or night, the problem often is when and where to tune. Scratch the surface: There's news on the spot, as it breaks, from people who know what's *really* going on—not instant experts flown in the night before from half a world away. Concertgebouw concerts. Science and technology. Tips for healthy living. The great religions of the world. Financial reports. Farming. Language lessons from Arabic to Vietnamese.

All shows are listed in World Time, also known as Greenwich Mean Time (GMT), Coordinated Universal Time (UTC), and Zulu time—see this *Passport's* glossary, as well as "Getting Started With World Band Radio," for details. Many stations announce World Time at the beginning of each broadcast, on the hour, or both. Use these to set your 24-hour clock so you'll always know the right time.

Schedules in *Passport* consist not only of observed activity, but also that which we have creatively opined will take place throughout 1992. This latter information is original from us, and therefore will not be so exact as factual information. Key channels are given for North America, Western Europe, East Asia and the Pacific, including Australia and New Zealand, with coverage of the Middle East. Information on secondary and seasonal channels, as well as channels for other parts of the world, may be found in the "Worldwide Broadcasts in English" and Blue Pages portions of this Worldscan section.

Unless otherwise noted, "summer" and "winter" refer to seasons in the Northern Hemisphere, even for stations located south of the equator.

¡Buena sintonía!

EVENING PRIME TIME—NORTH AMERICA
0000

BBC World Service. The Queen of the airwaves. First, there's the half-hour *Newsdesk*, which includes both international and British news. This is followed by any one of a wide variety of programs, including *The Ken Bruce Show* (Sunday), *From the Weeklies*

The Voice of America's "Bubble" room processes reports from correspondents around the world. Manager George Keith (seated) receives a feed from VOA's Paris Bureau, while technicians Bob Lindberg (left) and Alan Spector (right) fine tune their equipment.

and *Recording of the Week* (Saturday) and *Comedy Show* (Thursday). On other days you can hear such offerings as *In Praise of God* (Monday), *Omnibus* (Wednesday), or music programs (Tuesday and Friday). Continuous to North America on 5975, 6175, 9590, 9915 and 7325 or 12095 kHz; to East Asia until 0030 on 11945, 11955 and 17830 kHz; and to the Pacific until 0030 on 11955 kHz.

Christian Science Monitor World Service, USA. Considered by many to be North America's best station for news and reasoned analysis. *News*, then *Monitor Radio Worldwide*—news analysis and news-related features with emphasis on international developments. The first part of a two-hour cyclical broadcast repeated throughout the day to different parts of the globe. To North America and Europe Tuesday through Friday (Monday through Thursday, local American date) on 7395 and 9850 kHz.

Radio Sofia, Bulgaria. Winters only at this time. Continues with *news*, features, interviews and music to the Americas on 9655, 9700, 11680, 15370 and 17825 kHz.

Spanish Foreign Radio. *News*, followed most days by *Panorama*, which features commentary, a review of the Spanish press, weather, and comment from the foreign press on matters affecting Spain. The remainder of the program consists of a potpourri of literature, science, music and general programming. Each day's programming has a special emphasis; for instance, the arts on Friday. On weekends the format is varied somewhat, including *Who's Visiting Spain?* and *Radio Club*. Sixty minutes to Eastern North America on 9630 kHz.

Radio Canada International. On weekdays during winter, relays the excellent CBC domestic service *news* programs *World at Six* and *As It Happens*, which feature international stories, Canadian news and general human interest features. On the remaining days, there are relays of other CBC domestic programs. Summer programming is also a relay of CBC domestic fare, but not of quite the same high quality as that which is heard in winter. To North America on 5960 and 9755 kHz (summer weekdays, to 0030 only).

Radio Moscow World Service. Although also beamed to other parts of the world at this hour, most of the programming is aimed at the North American audience.

Available on more than 30 channels, so just tune around. Listeners in Southeast Asia and the Pacific should try the higher frequencies—17 and 21 MHz—but East Asians would do better on the 9 and 11 MHz bands. Listeners in North America, especially in the Eastern part, should dial around on 6, 7, 9 and 11 MHz, as well as trying out the relays via Cuba on 6000 and 6045 kHz (winters) or 11710 and 11850 kHz (summers).

Kol Israel. The Israel Broadcasting Authority has announced that this transmission, and certain others, may be canceled in the near future. Assuming this is not so, you will be able to hear *news*, followed by a variety of feature programs—some of which are aired now, others of which can be heard an hour later or, in summer, an hour earlier. Depending on the time of year, features include *Israel Sound* (latest Israeli pop songs), *Studio Three* (arts in Israel), *Shabbat Shalom* (greetings and music requests), *Calling All Listeners* (replies to questions), *DX Corner* (for radio enthusiasts), *Spotlight* (current events), *Spectrum* (science and technology), *With Me in the Studio* (guest interviews), *This Land* (a travel magazine), *Thank Goodness It's Friday* (Sabbath eve program), *Faith to Faith* (religious affairs), *Israel Mosaic* (a weekly magazine), *Letter from Jerusalem*, *Jewish News Review*, and *Living Here*. A half hour to Eastern North America and Europe on 7465 (or 15640), 9435 and 11605 kHz.

Radio Yugoslavia, located in Serbia. Summers only at this time. *News*, followed by features (see 2100). Forty-five minutes to Eastern North America on 9620 and 11735 kHz.

Radio Prague International, Czechoslovakia. *News*, followed by a lively magazine-style program covering a variety of topics. A half hour to North America on 7345, 9540 (winter), 11685 (summer) and 11990 kHz.

Radio Vilnius, Lithuania, USSR. Winters only at this time. *News* about events in Lithuania, features about the republic's history and culture, and a regrettably small amount of very pleasant Lithuanian music. A half hour to Europe and Eastern North America on 6100, 7400, 9750, 15180, 17690 and 17720 kHz.

Radio Finland. Winters only at this time. See 2230 for program details, though a day later, UTC. Twenty minutes to North

America and East Asia on 9645 and 11755 kHz.

Radio Pyongyang, North Korea. See 1100 for program details. Fifty minutes to the Americas on 13760 and 15115 kHz.

Radio Kiev, Ukraine, USSR. Summers only at this time; see 2100 for program details, though all programs air one day later. Sixty minutes to North America on 11790, 13645, 15180, 15455, 15485 and 15525 kHz.

Voice of America. First hour of VOA's two-hour broadcasts to the Caribbean and Latin America. *News*, followed by split programming Tuesday through Saturday (Monday through Friday evenings in the Americas). Listeners in the Caribbean can tune in to *Caribbean Report* followed by *Music USA*. For Latin America there is *Newsline* and Special English news and features. On Sunday both services carry *On the Line* before splitting into separate programs for the last half hour. Monday's programming is common to both services, consisting of two highly recommended programs—*Encounter* and *Spotlight*. An excellent way to keep in touch with events in the western hemisphere. The service to the Caribbean is on 6130, 9455 and 11695 kHz; and the one to the Americas is on 5995, 9775, 9815, 11580, and 15205 kHz. The final hour of a separate service to East and Southeast Asia and the Pacific (see 2200) can be heard on 7120, 9770, 11760, 15185, 15290, 17735 and 17820 kHz.

Radio Beijing, China. *News*, then *News About China* and *Current Affairs*. These are followed by various feature programs, such as *Culture in China* (Friday), *Listeners' Letterbox* (Monday/Wednesday), *Travel Talk* (Sunday), *Cooking Show* (Sunday) or *In the Third World* (Saturday). The highly recommended *Music from China* is aired Sunday (local Saturday evening in the Americas). One hour to Eastern North America, winter on 9770 and 11715 kHz, summer on 15285 and 17705 kHz.

Radio Habana Cuba. The start of a two-hour cyclical broadcast to North America. *News*, followed by such feature programs as *Newsbreak* (daily except Monday), *Spotlight on Latin America* (Tuesday through Saturday), *DXers Unlimited* (Sunday), *Dateline Havana* (Monday), or *The Jazz Place* (Monday). Interspersed with some good Cuban music. To Eastern North America on 11820 or 11950 kHz.

WRNO, New Orleans, USA. This station broadcasts mostly rock music, plus a little jazz. Offerings to date have included *Crusin' America*, *Rock Over London*, *Profiles of Rock Stars*, and NBC's *The Jazz Show*. To North America throughout much of the evening on 7355 kHz.

0030

Radio Nederland. Tuesday through Sunday there's *News*, followed by *Newsline*, a current affairs program. Then there's a different feature each night, including the excellent *Research File* (Tuesday; science), *Images* (Wednesday; arts in Holland), *Rembrandt Express* (a Saturday magazine program), and the communications program *Media Network* (Friday). Thursday features a documentary or music program, and there are further musical offerings on Sunday. Monday (Sunday evening local time in North America) is devoted to *The Happy Station*, an ever popular program of chat, letters and light music. Fifty-five minutes to Eastern North America on 6020, 6165 and 15315 kHz.

Belgische Radio en Televisie, Belgium. Winters only at this time; see 1730 for program details, although they're one day later, World Time. Twenty-five minutes to Eastern North America on 9925 kHz; also audible on 13655 (or 13675) kHz, though beamed elsewhere. One hour earlier in summer.

HCJB, Ecuador. *Studio 9*, featuring eight minutes of world and Latin American *news*, followed Tuesday through Saturday (Monday through Friday, local American date) by 20 minutes of in-depth reporting on Latin America. The final portion of *Studio 9* is given over to one of a variety of 30-minute features —including *Dateline 90* (Tuesday), *Happiness Is* (Wednesday and Friday) and the excellent *Música del Ecuador* (Saturday). On Sunday (Saturday evening in the Americas) the news is followed by *DX Partyline*, which in turn is replaced Monday by *Saludos Amigos*—HCJB's international friendship program. To North America on 9745 and 15155 kHz.

0100

BBC World Service. Tuesday through Saturday (weekday evenings in North America) it's *News*, followed by *Outlook*, a program of news and human-interest stories. This is succeeded by a variety of features, including *Health Matters* (Tuesday), *Mediawatch* (Wednesday), *Waveguide*, *Book Choice* and *The Farming World* (Thursday), *Global Concerns* (Friday), and *Short Story* (Saturday). There are also 15-minute music programs (jazz, folk or country) on several of these days. On Sunday and Monday (weekends in North America), look for a summary of *news* and longer drama and classical music programs. Continuous to North America on 5975, 6175, 9590, 9915 and 7325 or 12095 kHz. The Sunday program is also available to East Asia on 15280 and 21715 kHz.

Christian Science Monitor World Service, USA. Continuation of 0000 broadcast to North America and Europe. *News*, then *Monitor Radio Worldwide Features* which, as the name suggests, places less emphasis on news, and more on general interest stories. The final half hour includes *Letterbox* (a listener response program) and a religious article from the *Christian Science Monitor*. Tuesday through Thursday on 7395 and 9850 kHz.

Radio Canada International. Winters only. Weekday programming (Tuesday through Saturday World Time) consists of the final 30 minutes of *As It Happens* (see 0000). The broadcasts are extended to one hour at the weekend, and include additional CBC domestic programming. To North America on 5960 and 9755 kHz.

Radio Prague International, Czechoslovakia. *News*, then features, including *Sports Roundup* (Tuesday), *Mailbag* (Thursday), *Ecology* (Friday), *Tip for a Trip* (Saturday) and *Czechoslovakia This Week* (Sunday). Monday (Sunday evening in North America) features the popular *Scrapbook*. Thirty minutes to North America on 5930, 7345 and 9540 (or 11685) kHz.

Radio Argentina al Exterior – R.A.E. Winters only at this time; see 1900 for program details. Fifty-five minutes to North America on 11710 kHz.

Radio Japan. One hour to Eastern North America summers only on 5960 kHz via the powerful relay facilities of Radio Canada International in Sackville, New Brunswick. See 0300 for program details—all programs are one day later.

Kol Israel. *News* at the top of the hour, then various feature programs (see 0000). A half hour to Eastern North America and Europe on 7465 (or 15640), 9435 and 11605 kHz. According to the station, this transmis-

sion may be canceled in the near future.

Spanish Foreign Radio. Repeat of the 0000 transmission. To Eastern North America on 9630 kHz.

Radio Moscow World Service. *News*, followed by features like *Focus on Asia and the Pacific*. Targeted to North America, Asia and the Pacific on more than 30 frequencies, so just dial around to find it.

Radio Sweden. See 1530 for program details. Thirty minutes to Asia and the Pacific on 9765 or 9770 kHz.

Radio Habana Cuba. See 0000 for program details. Continues to North America on 11820 or 11950 kHz.

Radio Yugoslavia, located in Serbia. Winters only at this time. *News*, concentrating mainly on events in the Balkans, then commentary and one of several feature programs, including *Sidewalk Rock* (Saturday; popular music in the Third World), *Science and Ecology Report* (Friday), and *Spotlight on Culture* (Thursday). Unbiased reporting, if somewhat dry. Usually good reception in North America. Forty-five minutes to Eastern North America on 9620 and 11735 kHz, with alternative channels being 5980 and 7215 kHz.

Radio Tashkent, Uzbekistan, USSR. *News* and features reflecting local and regional issues. Thirty minutes to South Asia—occasionally heard in North America—on 7325, 7335 and 9740 kHz, but 11975 kHz is usually best.

HCJB, Ecuador. The second part of *Studio 9* (different programs at the weekend—see 0030), followed by a half hour of mainly religious programming. *Musical Mailbag*—a listener response program—is featured Sunday (Saturday evening in the Americas) at 0130. To North America on 9745 and 15155 kHz.

Voice of America. *News*, then *Report to the Americas*, a series of news features about the United States and other countries in the Americas. This is replaced Sunday by *Press Conference USA*, and Monday by *New Horizons* and *Issues in the News*. To the Americas on 5995, 6130, 9455, 9775, 9815, 11580 and 15205 kHz.

Radio Kiev, Ukraine, USSR. Winters only at this time; see 2100 for program details, although all programs air one day later. One hour directed to Eastern North America on various frequencies, including 7400, 9750, 9800, 15180, 17690 and 17720 kHz.

Deutsche Welle, Germany. *News*, followed weekdays by the comprehensive *European Journal*, which includes commentary, interviews, background reports and analysis. The broadcast ends with *Transatlantic Diary*, a look at cultural, scientific, economic and bilateral developments. Sunday (Saturday night in North America) is given over to *Commentary*, *Mailbag* (or *Nickelodeon*) and *German by Radio*; while Monday brings *Living in Germany* and the popular *Larry's Random Selection*. Very good reception in North America on 6040, 6085, 6145, 6155, 9565, 11865, 11890, 13610 and 13770 kHz; plus seasonal channels of 15205, 15425 and 15440 kHz.

0130

Radio Austria International. *Report from Austria*, which includes a brief bulletin of *news* followed by a series of current events and human interest stories. Ample coverage of national and regional issues, and an excellent source for news of Eastern Europe. Twenty-five minutes to North America on 9870 (actually beamed to South America), 9875 and 13730 kHz.

Voice of Greece. Preceded, and to a lesser extent followed, by lots of delightful Greek music, plus news and features in Greek. There's a ten-minute English *newscast*, more or less at 0130, heard daily except Sunday (Saturday evening local North American date). To Eastern North America on 7430 or 11645 kHz, plus 9395 and 9420 kHz.

0145

BBC World Service for Asia. *South Asia Survey*, 15 minutes of special programming to Asia (Tuesday through Saturday only). Audible in parts of North America and the Pacific as well, on 5965, 7135, 9580 and 11955 kHz.

0200

BBC World Service. Thirty minutes of *Newsdesk*, followed on different days of the week by a variety of features, including *Composer of the Month* (Monday), *People and Politics* (Saturday), *Drama* (Friday), *Sports International* (Tuesday), and *Assignment* (Thursday). Continuous to North America on 5975, 6175, 9590 (to 0230), 9915, and 7325 or 12095 kHz.

Christian Science Monitor World Service, USA. See 0000 for program details. To North America and Europe Monday through Friday on 9850 kHz, with the final half hour also available for North America (Tuesday through Friday) on 9455 and 13760 kHz.

Radio Cairo. A potpourri of exotic Arab music and features reflecting Egyptian life and culture, with *news* and commentary about events in Egypt and the Arab world. There are also quizzes, mailbag shows, and answers to listeners' questions. Ninety minutes of fair reception in North America on 9475 and 9675 kHz.

Voice of America. *News*, then *Focus*—an examination of the major issues of the day. Thirty minutes to the Americas, Tuesday through Saturday, on 5995, 9775, 9815, 11580 and 15205 kHz.

Radio Argentina al Exterior – R.A.E. Summers only at this time. Similar to the 1900 transmission. To North America Tuesday through Saturday (Monday through Friday local American days) on 11710 kHz. One hour earlier in winter.

Radio Budapest, Hungary. This time summers only. *News*, then a variety of fea-

tures, interviews and music. Regular weekly programs include *Music and ...!*, *Letter from Budapest* and *168 Hours* (all on Monday, Tuesday and Friday), *Talk Back* (conversations with controversial personalities, Friday and Sunday), *Briefing* (the best of the week's press conferences, Saturday and Monday) and *Conviction* (open house for those with strong personal beliefs, Monday). There are also regular monthly spots given over to listener participation programs (*Magazine 90* and *What You Say*), as well as to other features like *Reporter* and *Business Partners*. Sixty minutes to North America on 6110, 9835 and 11910 kHz. One hour later in winter.

Kol Israel. Winters only at this time. *News*, followed by various features (see 0000). A half hour to North America on 7465, 9435 and 11605 kHz. According to the station, this transmission may be canceled in the near future.

HCJB, Ecuador. Thirty minutes of religious programming, then a repeat of the first half of *Studio 9* or special weekend programs(see 0030). To North America on 9745 and 15155 kHz.

Voice of Free China, Taiwan. *News*, followed by three different features. The last is *Let's Learn Chinese*, which has a series of segments for beginners, intermediate and advanced learners. Other features include *Focus*, *Jade Bells and Bamboo Pipes*, *Journey into Chinese Culture* and *Kaleidoscope* —a potpourri of business, science, interviews and just about anything else. One hour to North and Central America on 5950, 9680 and 11740 kHz; to East Asia on 15345 kHz; and to the Pacific on 9765 kHz.

Radio Sweden. Repeat of the 1530 transmission. Thirty minutes to North America on 9695 and 11705 kHz.

Radio Moscow World Service. Continuous to Asia, the Pacific and North America. Features *Update*—an excellent source of *news* and information about what is happening in the Soviet Union. On a mass of frequencies—simply dial about.

Radio Habana Cuba. Repeat of the 0000 transmission. To North America on 11820 (or 11950) and 9505 (or 15140) kHz.

Swiss Radio International. *News* and *Dateline* (except Monday)—a thoroughly workmanlike compilation of news and analysis of world and Swiss events. On Sunday, a shorter version of *Dateline* is complemented by *Swiss Shortwave Merry-go-Round*, which

answers technical questions sent in by listeners, and Monday is devoted alternately to *Supplement*, *Roundabout Switzerland* and *The Grapevine*. A half hour to North America on 6125, 6135, 9650, 9885, 12035 and 17730 kHz.

Radio Romania International. *News*, commentary, press review and features on Romania. Not to mention some charming selections of Romanian folk music, although not every evening. Recommended are *Romanian Musicians* (Thursday) and *Skylark* (Friday). Other features include *Youth Club* (Tuesday), *Friendship and Cooperation* (Thursday) and *Cultural Survey* (Saturday). To North America on 5990, 6155, 9510, 9570, 11830 and 11940 kHz.

"Radio Free America," WWCR, Nashville, Tennessee. This time summers only, see 0300 for details. To North America on 7435 or 7520 kHz.

Radio Canada International. Summers only at this time. Thirty minutes of CBC domestic programming targeted to Europe on 6035, 6125, 7230, 7260 and 9650 kHz. You'd have to live in Moscow or be an insomniac to hear this broadcast. One hour later during winter.

0230

Radio Tirana, Albania. The Marxist-Leninist rhetoric may have disappeared, but not the sleep-inducing program content and presentation. *News* and feature programs are now reduced, with more space being given to ethnic Albanian music. Long may the trend continue! To North America on 9580, 9760 or 11825 kHz.

Radio Portugal. *News*—which usually takes up at least half the broadcast—followed by feature programs: *Welcome to Portugal* (Tuesday), *Music Time* (Wednesday), *Challenge of '92* (Thursday), *Portugal past and present* (Friday), and either *Mailbag* or *DX Program* and *Collectors' Corner* (Saturday). There are no broadcasts on Sunday or Monday (Saturday and Sunday evening local North American dates). Only fair reception in Eastern North America —worse to the west—on 9555 (or 9580), 9600, 9705 and 11840 kHz.

0250

Vatican Radio. While concentrating mainly on issues affecting Catholics around the world, this station also features some secularly oriented items such as ecology and the search for peace in areas of armed conflict. There is analysis of the Church's role in a changing world, as well as coverage of the activities of Catholic priests and laity. Weekend programming is of a more religious nature. Twenty minutes to Eastern North America on 9615 and 7305 or 11625 kHz.

Radio Yerevan, Armenia, USSR. Summers only at this time. English consists solely of up to four minutes of *news* of interest mainly to Armenians abroad. To North America on 11675, 11790, 13645, 15180 and 15455 kHz.

0300

BBC World Service. *News,* then *News About Britain,* followed Tuesday through Saturday by *The World Today,* replaced Sunday by *Recording of the Week* and Monday by *Good Books.* Apart from Wednesday, when the science program *Discovery* is aired, the next half hour is taken up by music, quiz shows or religion. Continuous to North America on 5975, 6175 and 9915 kHz; to early risers in parts of Europe on 6195, 9410 and 3955 or 12095 kHz; and to East Asia on 15280 and 21715 kHz.

Christian Science Monitor World Service, USA. See 0100 for program details. Continuation of transmission to North America and Europe Monday through Friday on 9850 kHz. The final 25 minutes are also available for North America, Tuesday through Friday, on 9455 and 13760 kHz.

Voice of Free China, Taiwan. Similar to the 0200 transmission, but with the same programs broadcast on different days of the week. To North and Central America on 5950 and 9680 kHz; to East Asia on 15345 kHz; and to the Pacific on 9765 kHz.

Radio Beijing, China. Repeat of the 0000 transmission. One hour to North America, year-around on 9690 and 11715 kHz; winter on 9770 kHz; and summer on 15285 kHz.

Deutsche Welle, Germany. Repeat of the 0100 broadcast. To North America on 6085, 9545, 11890, 13610 and 13770 kHz, plus seasonal frequencies 6040, 6120, 6145, 9605, 11810, 15205 and 15245 kHz.

Radio Budapest, Hungary. Winters only at this time; see 0200 for program details. Sixty minutes to North America on 6110, 9835 and 11910 kHz. One hour earlier in summer.

Radio Moscow World Service. Continuous to North America, Asia and the Pacific on more than 40 channels. Just tune around and find it.

Radio Habana Cuba. Repeat of the 0100 transmission; see 0000 for program details. To North America on 11820 (or 11950) and 9505 (or 15140) kHz.

HCJB, Ecuador. Continues with *Studio 9* (see 0030 for program details) until 0330, then switches to religious programs. *Musical Mailbag,* a listener response program, is aired Sunday (Saturday evening in North America). To the United States and Canada on 9745 and 15155 kHz.

Radio Japan. On most days *News,* followed by *Radio Japan Magazine Hour,* an umbrella for features like *Out and Around* and *Japan Diary* (Tuesday-Thursday), *Asia Contact* (Wednesday) and *Music Mix* (Friday). Saturday, it's an hour of *This Week,* with *DX Corner* and *Viewpoint* on Sunday. One hour winters to Eastern North America on 5960 kHz. There is also a separate year-round broadcast to the Americas, consisting of *News,* followed by *Let's Learn Japanese* or a feature program. Thirty minutes on 15325, 17825 and 21610 kHz.

Voice of Turkey. Summers only at this time. Repeat of 2200 broadcast. See 2000 for program details. Fifty minutes to North America on 9445 kHz, and to the Pacific (also heard in Western North America) on 17880 kHz.

Radio Prague International, Czechoslovakia. Repeat of the 0100 broadcast. A half hour's pleasant listening targeted to North America on 5930, 7345 and 9540 (or 11685) kHz.

"Radio Free America," WWCR, Nashville, Tennessee. Just about every opinion and perspective imaginable is to be found on world band, and "Radio Free America" underscores this to the hilt. Can you imagine a populist call-in talk show embracing as its friendly guest the Libyan ambassador to the United Nations? And that the host, guest and most callers alike wind up agreeing that the United States was wrong to be involved in the Gulf conflict? Well, this is just one of the many surprises— unvarnished anti-Semitism being another— you can expect on "Radio Free America." This two-hour broadcast, sponsored by the Washington-based Liberty Lobby, is aired via the facilities of WWCR, a relative newcomer to the world band airwaves. Hosted by Tom Valentine, it's heard with a hammer-strong signal throughout much of North America Tuesday through Saturday (Monday through Friday evenings, local American date) from 0300 winters, 0200 summers, on 7435 or 7520 kHz.

Radio Canada International. This time winters only. A half hour of CBC domestic programs targeted to Europe on 5995, 6025, 7260, 7285 and 9615 KHz.

0330

Radio Tirana, Albania. *News* and features in the same mold as the 0230 broadcast, although not necessarily the same ones. To North America on 9480, 9760 or 11825 kHz.

Radio Sweden. Repeat of the 0200 broadcast; see 1530 for program details. Thirty minutes to North America on 9695 and 11705 kHz.

United Arab Emirates Radio, Dubai. Similar to the transmission at 1330, but on 11945, 13675, 15400 and 15435 kHz. Heard best in North America during the warm-weather months. See 1330 transmission for program details.

Radio Nederland. Repeat of the 0030 transmission. Fifty-five minutes to North America on 6165 and 9590 kHz.

BBC World Service for Africa provides separate programs for and about that continent, which otherwise tends to be poorly covered by the international media. Although this special service is beamed only to Africa, it can sometimes be heard in other parts, as well. Try 3255, 6005, 6190, 9600, 11740, 15420 or 17885 kHz.

Voice of Greece. Repeat of the 0130 transmission. Ten minutes of English, surrounded by long periods of Greek music and programming, to North America, except Sunday (Saturday evening local American date), on 9395, 9420, and 11645 kHz.

0350

Radio Yerevan, Armenia, USSR. Winters only at this time. English consists solely of up to four minutes of *news* of interest mainly to Armenians abroad. To North America on 7400, 9750, 15180, 17690 and 17720 kHz.

0400

BBC World Service. Starting off the hour is *Newsdesk*, which airs both international and British news. This is followed, Monday through Friday, by *Off the Shelf*, readings from the best of world literature. Weekends are devoted to music, with Saturday featuring the excellent *Here's Humph* jazz show. The final quarter-hour features a variety of offerings, including *Andy Kershaw's World of Music* (Monday), *Europe's World* (Tuesday), *Country Style* (Wednesday), and jazz or folk on Friday. Continuous to North America on 5975 kHz; to Western Europe on 3955, 6195, 9410 and 12095 kHz; and to East Asia on 15280 and 21715 kHz.

Christian Science Monitor World Service, USA. See 0000 for program details. Monday through Friday to Europe on 9840 kHz, and to East Asia on 17780 kHz. Tuesday through Friday, the second half hour is available for North America on 9455 and 13760 kHz.

Radio Habana Cuba. Repeat of the 0000 broadcast. To North America on 5965, 9505 (or 15140), 11760 and 11820 (or 11950) kHz.

Swiss Radio International. Repeat of the 0200 transmission. To North America on 6135, 9650, 9885 and 12035 kHz.

Radio Prague International, Czechoslovakia. Repeat of the 0000 broadcast. To North America on 5930, 7345 and 9540 (or 11685) kHz.

HCJB, Ecuador. Thirty minutes of religious programming to North America on 9745 and 15155 kHz.

Voice of America. Directed to Europe and North Africa 0400-0700, but widely heard elsewhere. *News,* followed Monday through Friday by *Newsline,* and *VOA Morning*—a conglomeration of popular music, interviews, human interest stories, science digest, sports news, and so on, with news summaries on the half hour. On 5995, 6040, 6140, 7170 and 7200 kHz.

Radio Canada International. *News,* followed Tuesday through Saturday by sports and *As It Happens. Double Exposure* is Sunday's feature, and *Inside Track* is heard on Mondays. Thirty minutes to the Middle East winters on 11925, summers on 15275 kHz.

Radio Beijing, China. Repeat of the 0000 transmission; to North America on 11685 or 11695 kHz plus, summers only, 11840 kHz.

Radio Romania International. An abbreviated version of the 0200 transmission, beginning with national and international *news* and commentary, then the feature program from the first half hour of the 0200 broadcast. To North America on 5990, 6155, 9510, 9570, 11830 and 11940 kHz.

Voice of Turkey. Winters only at this time. Repeat of 2300 broadcast. See 2000 for program details. Fifty minutes to Eastern North America on 9445 kHz, and to the Pacific on 17880 kHz.

Kol Israel. Summers only at this time. *News* for 15 minutes from Israel Radio's domestic network. To Europe and North America on 9435, 11588, 15640 and 17590 kHz, and to Asia and the Pacific on 17575 kHz. According to the station, this broadcast may be canceled in the near future.

Radio Moscow—North American Service. The only truly regional service still produced by Radio Moscow. Beamed to the West Coast on several channels, including 12050 and 15180 kHz. Additional winter frequencies include 9895, 11980, 12010 and 17720 kHz; summers, try 13605, 13645, 15410 and 15595 kHz. This broadcast may be one hour later in winter, depending on whether Moscow resolves the question of standard time within the USSR. In the meantime, the **Radio Moscow World Service** continues to just about every other part of the globe on more than 40 channels. Seek, and ye shall find.

"Radio Free America," WWCR, Nashville, Tennessee. This time winters only. See 0300 for details. To North America on 7435 or 7520 kHz.

0430

BBC World Service for Africa. See 0330. Try 3255, 6005, 6190, 9600, 15400 or 15420 kHz.

0500

BBC World Service. *News,* then *Twenty-Four Hours,* one of the best of the BBC's in-depth news analysis programs. This is followed most days by *Business Review/ Report, Words of Faith,* and another news-analysis program—*The World Today.* The latter is replaced Sunday by Alistair Cooke's popular *Letter from America* and Monday by *Recording of the Week.* Continuous to North America on 5975 kHz; to Western Europe on 3955, 6195, 9410 and 12095 kHz; and to East Asia on 15280 and 21715 kHz.

Christian Science Monitor World Service, USA. See 0100 for program details. Monday through Friday to Europe on 9840 kHz, and to East Asia on 17780 kHz. Tuesday through Friday, the final 25 minutes are available to North America on 9455 and 13760 kHz.

Deutsche Welle, Germany. Repeat of the 0100 transmission to North America, but on 5960, 6120, 9670, 9700 and 13610 kHz, plus additional seasonal frequencies 11705, 11890, 11925, 13770, and 13790 kHz.

HCJB, Ecuador. Repeat of 0030 transmission. To North America on any two of the following: 6230, 9745 or 15155 kHz.

Spanish Foreign Radio. Repeat of the 0000 and 0100 transmissions to North America, but on 9630 kHz only.

Voice of America. Continues with the morning broadcast to Europe and North Africa on the same frequencies as at 0400, plus 11825 and 15205 kHz.

Voice of Nigeria. Usually clearer in winter than in summer, but never brilliant. Opens with *Jamboree* (African popular music and mailbag), followed by *news,* editorials, commentary and more music until 0700, when the station begins its broadcast in other languages. Two hours on 7255 kHz.

Radio Beijing, China. This time winters only. Repeat of the 0000 transmission; to North America on 11840 kHz.

Radio Moscow—North American Service. Continuation of the transmission beamed to the west coast of North America. Tune around to find the best of the numerous Moscow frequencies; 12050 and 15180 are regular year-around channels, so try them first. In the meantime, the **Radio Moscow World Service** continues its broadcast to many parts of the world on more than 30 channels. Dial around, and take your pick.

Kol Israel. Winters only at this time. *News* for 15 minutes from Israel Radio's domestic network. To Europe and North America on 7410, 7465, 9435 and 11605 kHz, and to Asia and the Pacific on 17575 kHz. According to the station, this broadcast may be canceled in the near future.

Radio Habana Cuba. Repeat of the 0100 transmission; see 0000 for program details. Well heard throughout North and Central America on 5965, 11760 and 11820 (or 11950) kHz.

0515

Radio Canada International. Summers only at this time. See 0615 for program details. To Western Europe and Africa on 6050, 6150, 7295, 9750, 11775 and 17840 kHz.

0530

Radio Austria International. *Report from Austria*; see 0130 for more details. To North America on 6015 kHz.

United Arab Emirates Radio, Dubai. See 0330 for program details. To East Asia and the Pacific on 15435, 17830 and 21700 kHz.

EVENING PRIME TIME—EAST ASIA AND THE PACIFIC
0600

BBC World Service. *Newsdesk*, followed Wednesday, Friday and Saturday by *Meridian*, an arts show. *Jazz for the Asking* is aired Sunday, *Counterpoint* on Tuesday, and Thursday is given over to *Omnibus*. Continuous to North America on 5975 and 9640 kHz; to Western Europe on 3955, 6195, 9410 and 12095 kHz; to East Asia on 15280, 15360 and 21715 kHz; and to the Pacific on 7150, 9640, 11955 and 17830 kHz.

Christian Science Monitor World

Service, USA. See 0000 for program details. Monday through Friday to Europe and North America on 9840 kHz; and to East Asia on 17780 kHz.

Radio Habana Cuba. Repeat of the 0000 transmission. To Western North America on 11760 or 11835 kHz.

Voice of America. Final hour of the transmission to Europe and North Africa. See 0400 for program details. On 5995, 6040, 6060, 6095, 7170, and 7325 kHz.

Radio Moscow—North American Service. Another hour of programming to the west coast of North America. Available on a variety of frequencies—winters, try 9505, 9795, 11980 and 17720 kHz; summers, on 12050, 13605, 13645, 15410, 15425 and 15595 kHz.

Radio Korea, South Korea. The hourlong broadcast opens with *news*, followed on most days by commentary, *Seoul Calling* (magazine format), *Let's Learn Korean!*, and features like *Korean Cultural Variety* (Tuesday) and *Pulse of Korea* (Wednesday). On other days, the news is followed by features such as *Sites and Sounds* (Saturday) and *Echoes of Korean Music* (Sunday). To Western North America on 11810 and 15170 kHz.

HCJB, Ecuador. An hour of predominantly religious programming. Popular features include *Music from the Mountains* (Thursday) and *Musical Mailbag* (Sunday). To North America on any two of the following: 6230, 9745 or 15155 kHz.

0615

Radio Canada International. Winters only. Forty-five minutes of programming targeted to Canadians overseas. *News*, followed by a feature: *The Inside Track* (Monday; sports), *Double Exposure* (Tuesday), *Open House* (Wednesday), *Media File* (Thursday), or *Arts Tonight* (Friday). To Western Europe and Africa, Monday through Friday, on 6050, 6150, 7155, 9760, 9740 and 11840 kHz.

0630

BBC World Service for Africa. See 0330. Try 9600, 11860, 11940, 15105 or 15400 kHz.

Radio Finland. Summers only at this time. See 0730 winter transmission for program details. Fifteen minutes to Europe on 6120, 9560 and 11755 kHz.

Swiss Radio International. Summers only at this time. See 0830 for program details. To Europe on 3985, 6165 and 9535 kHz.

Belgische Radio en Televisie, Belgium. Summers only at this time. Weekdays, there's *News* and *Press Review*, followed by *Belgium Today*—a magazine program—and features like *Tourism in Flanders* (Monday), *Around the Arts* (Tuesday and Friday), *Green Society* (Thursday) and *North-South* (Friday). Weekend features include *Record of the Week* and *Radio World* (Saturday) and *Musical Roundabout* (Sunday). Twenty-five minutes to Europe on 6035, 9855 (or 9925) and 11695 kHz; and to the Pacific on 11695 kHz.

0645

Ghana Broadcasting Corporation. Intended for listeners in neighboring countries, so reception is marginal—especially during the summer months. The broadcast begins with West African music, followed by *news*, then a further serving of lively African rhythms. On 6130 kHz.

0700

BBC World Service. News, followed by the in-depth news program *Twenty-Four Hours*. What follows next is very much a mixed bag, depending on the day of the week. Of the regular year-around programs, try Thursday's *Network UK*, a valuable insight into the British way of life. Continuous to North America on 9640 kHz; to Europe on 7325 (winter), 9410, 12095 and 15070 kHz; to East Asia on 15280, 15360 and 21715 kHz; and to the Pacific on 7150, 9640, 11955 and 17830 kHz.

Radio New Zealand International. *News*, followed three days a week by a relay of New Zealand domestic radio—usually a pleasant mix of Easy Listening, jazz and oldies. Non-domestic fare are *Saturday's Scrapbook* and the special programs targeted to the Pacific Islands on Monday and Wednesday. The Thursday programming is also different, being aimed at a more international audience. This includes *Pacific Press Review* and either *Mailbox* or *Travel Pacific*. Part of a longer transmission targeted to the Pacific, and audible in North America on 9700 kHz. One hour later during summer in the Northern Hemisphere.

Christian Science Monitor World Service, USA. See 0100 for program de-

tails. Monday through Friday to Europe and North America on 9840 kHz; and to East Asia on 17780 kHz.

Radio Australia. Part of a 24-hour service to Asia and the Pacific, but which can also be heard at this time in parts of Western Europe. World and Australian *news* is followed—Monday excepted—by *Music of RA*, then any one of a number of features, including *Monitor* (Tuesday; science), *One World* (Saturday; the environment), *Science File* (Thursday), *Innovations* (Friday) and *World of Country Music* (Sunday). To East Asia on 21525 kHz, and audible in Europe on 21775 kHz.

Radio Habana Cuba. Repeat of the 0100 transmission; see 0000 for program details. To Western North America on 11760 or 11835 kHz.

Radio Moscow—North American Service. Continues with programs for West Coast North America on a variety of frequencies. Try 5905, 7175, 7260, 7270, 7345, 9795 and 11980 kHz winters; and 12050, 13605, 13645, 15180, 15410 and 15425 kHz summers.

Radio Moscow World Service. Continuous programming beamed to most parts of the world. Tune around and choose any one of 40 channels.

Voice of Free China, Taiwan. Repeat of the 0200 transmission. Targeted to Central America, but audible in parts of the United States on 5950 kHz.

HCJB, Ecuador. Opens with 30 minutes of religious programming—except for Saturday, when *Musical Mailbag* is on the air. Then comes *Studio 9* (see 0030 for more details), replaced Saturday by *DX Partyline*. Sunday is given over to *Saludos Amigos*—the HCJB international friendship program. To Europe on 9610, 11835 and 15270 kHz; and to the Pacific (from 0730) on 9745 and 11925 kHz.

0730

Radio Finland. Winters only at this time. Monday through Friday it's *News Update*, then *Northern Report* (except for *Business Monday* on the day of that name). Saturday's broadcast is reduced to ten minutes of *Northern Report*, while Sunday's programming is devoted to *Perspectives* and *Backgrounder*. Fifteen minutes (except for Saturday) targeted to Europe on 6120, 9560 and 11755 kHz.

Radio Finland's cheerful Teri Schultz reports to the world on night life in the cafes of central Helsinki.

Radio Prague International, Czechoslovakia. *News,* followed by some of the liveliest fare currently available on the international airwaves. Ecology, economy, comment and culture—these and many more are covered during the course of any one week, with somewhat lighter programming available on weekends. Thirty minutes to Asia and the Pacific on 17840 and 21705 kHz.

Radio Nederland. *News,* followed by *Newsline* and a variety of features (see 0030; all features are one day earlier). Fifty-five minutes to Australasia on 9630 and 9715 or 15560 kHz.

Swiss Radio International. Winters only at this time. See 0830 for program details. To Europe on 3985, 6165 and 9535 kHz.

BBC World Service for Africa. See 0330 for details. Thirty minutes on 9600, 11860 and 15105 kHz.

Ríkisútvarpid, Iceland. Although broadcasting almost exclusively in Icelandic, this station now has a 15-minute weekday *news* bulletin in English during 1991. Audible in Europe at 0730 on 3295, 6100 and 9265 kHz; a tough catch in North America, but worth a try.

Belgische Radio en Televisie, Belgium. Winters only at this time. See 0630 for program details. To Europe on 6035, 9855 (or 9925) and 11695 kHz; and to the Pacific on 11695 kHz.

BBC World Service. *News,* then the religious *Words of Faith,* followed by a wide variety of programming depending on the day of the week. Choice programs include a selection of classical music (Sunday), *Health Matters* and *Anything Goes* (Monday), *Good Books* and *John Peel* (Thursday), and *Music Review* (Friday). Continuous to Western Europe on 7325 (winter), 9410, 12095 and 15070 kHz; to East Asia on 15280, 15360 and 21715 kHz; and to the Pacific on 11955 and 17830 kHz.

Christian Science Monitor World Service, USA. See 0000 for program details. Monday through Friday to Europe and North America on 9840 or 11705 kHz; to East Asia on 9530 or 17755 kHz; and to the Pacific on 15610 or 17755 kHz.

HCJB, Ecuador. Continuous programming to Europe and the Pacific. The final half hour of *Studio 9* (or weekend variations), followed (for the Pacific, only) by 30 minutes of religious fare. To Europe (until 0830) on 9610, 11835 and 15270 kHz; and to the Pacific on 9745 and 11925 kHz.

KNLS, Alaska, USA. Although a religious station, KNLS has some interesting secular fare on offer—such as *American Magazine,* part of the broadcast on Wednesday and Friday. Also of note is the weekday program *The Swinging Years*—one of the few regular sources of Big Band music on international radio. To East Asia, but also well heard in parts of North America, winters on 7365 kHz, and summers on 11715 kHz.

Radio Australia. Begins with *International Report,* followed Monday through Friday by *Stock Exchange Report,* then the daily *Sports Report.* Low on originality, but high on quality. The hour is rounded off (except for Sunday and Thursday, when there are lottery results) with a ten-minute music program. To East Asia, winters only, on 21525 kHz; but audible year-around in Europe on 15240 and 21775 kHz. Listeners in North America can tune in on 9580 kHz, but only from 0830 onwards.

Radio Finland. Summers only at this time; see 0900 for program details. To East Asia and the Pacific on 17800 and 21550 kHz.

Radio Moscow World Service. Continuous to Europe, Asia, Africa and the Pacific. With more than 40 available channels, you cannot miss it. Just dial around.

Radio New Zealand International.
News, then relays from the domestic National Radio network (see 0700), except for Tuesday and Friday (special programs for Fiji and other Pacific Islands) and the weekend *Saturday Scrapbook*. Intended for the Pacific, but also heard in North America, on 9700 kHz. The programs are one hour later during summer in the Northern Hemisphere.

Radio Korea, South Korea. See 0600 for program details. To Europe on 7550 and 13670 kHz.

0830

Radio Austria International. Winters only at this time. The comprehensive *Report from Austria*; see 0130 for more details. To Australia and the Pacific on 15450 and 21490 kHz.

Radio Finland. Summers only at this time; see 0900 for program details. To East Asia and Australia on 17800 and 21550 kHz.

Swiss Radio International. *News*, then *Dateline* (except Sunday). On Saturday, the last 15 minutes are given over to the technically oriented *Swiss Shortwave Merry-go-Round*; Sunday is devoted to *Supplement*, *Roundabout Switzerland* or *The Grapevine* —a listener participation program. Thirty minutes to East Asia and the Pacific on 9560, 13685, 17670 and 21695 kHz.

Radio Nederland. A repeat of the 0730 broadcast, beamed to Australia and the Pacific on 9630 kHz. An identical transmission (except for Friday, when *Asiascan* replaces everything following the news) is beamed to Asia on 17575 and 21485 kHz.

0900

BBC World Service. Starts with *News* and business information (Saturday excepted), and ends with *Sports Roundup*. The remaining time is taken up by a series of short features, the pick of which are *Short Story* (Sunday), *Andy Kershaw's World of Music* (Monday), *Europe's World* (Tuesday), *The Farming World* (Thursday), and *Global Concerns* (Friday). To Europe on 5975, 6045, 7325 (winter), 9750, 9760, 12095, 15070 and 17640 kHz; to East Asia on 21715 kHz, and to the Pacific on 11750 and 17830 (or 15360) kHz.

Christian Science Monitor World Service, USA. See 0100 for program details. Monday through Friday to Europe and

North America on 9840 or 11705 kHz; to East Asia on 9530 or 17755 kHz; and to the Pacific on 15610 or 17555 kHz.

Deutsche Welle, Germany. *News*, followed Monday through Friday by *Newsline Cologne* and *Asia-Pacific Report* (substituted Monday by *Through German Eyes*). These are replaced Saturday by *International Talking Point, Development Forum* and *Religion and Society*; and Sunday by *Arts on the Air* and *German By Radio*. To Asia and the Pacific on 6160, 17780, 17820, 21465, 21650 and 21680 kHz.

Radio New Zealand International.
Relays programs from the domestic National Radio at this time. Continuous to the Pacific on 9700 kHz; also audible in parts of North America.

Belgische Radio en Televisie, Belgium. Monday through Saturday, summers only at this time. See 0630 for program details. To Europe on 9855 (or 9925) and 13675 kHz, and to Africa (also heard elsewhere) on 21810 or 21815 kHz.

HCJB, Ecuador. Sixty minutes of religious programming to the Pacific on 9745 and 11925 kHz.

Radio Moscow World Service. Sixty minutes of continuous programming targeted just about everywhere. Dial around and choose a frequency—there are plenty of them available.

Radio Australia. World and Australian *news*, followed most days by music (replaced Monday by *Back Page*—a sporting feature). Then comes any one of a wide variety of features, including *Connexions* (education issues—even if they can't spell— Monday), *AgriNews* (Tuesday), *Interaction* (Wednesday) and *Points of Law* (Saturday). Thursday, it's *Art Roundabout*; Friday has *Women and Politics*; and Sunday is given over to *Matters of Faith*—an examination of the doctrines and beliefs of Asia and the Pacific. Although beamed elsewhere, it is heard in North America on 9580 kHz, and in Europe on 15240 and 21775 kHz.

Radio Finland. Winters only at this time. The regular programs are *News Update* and *Press Review* (Monday through Friday) and *Northern Report* (Tuesday through Saturday). These are complemented by short features such as *Airmail* (Tuesday), *Sports Fare* (Wednesday) and *Names in the News* (Friday). The Saturday broadcast (five minutes shorter) includes *Finnish History* and *Backgrounder*, while Sunday is given over to *Compass North*, *Perspectives* and *Starting Finnish*. Twenty-five minutes to East Asia and the Pacific on 17800 and 21550 kHz.

0930

Radio Finland. Winters only at this time; the same features as 0900, but not necessarily in the same order. Twenty-five minutes to East Asia and Australia on 15245 and 17800 kHz.

Radio Nederland. Repeat of the 0730 transmission. To Australia on 11895 kHz.

1000

BBC World Service. *News Summary*, followed by some of the *créme de la créme* of the BBC's output (some of which starts at 1030). The list includes *Here's Humph*, *Letter from America* and *People and Politics* (Saturday), *Science in Action* (Sunday), *The Vintage Chart Show* (Monday), *Discovery* and *Sports International* (Tuesday), *Omnibus* and *Jazz for the Asking* (Wednesday), *Assignment* and comedy (Thursday), and *Focus on Faith* (Friday). Tune in any day of the week for some high-quality programming. Continuous to Western Europe on 5975, 6045, 9750, 9760, 12095, 15070 and 17640 kHz; and to East Asia and the Pacific on 15360 kHz (winter only). In summer, 11750 (for Australia) and 21715 kHz (for East Asia) are available until 1030.

Christian Science Monitor World Service, USA. See 0000 for program details. Monday through Friday to North America on 9495 kHz; and to East Asia on 9530 or 17555 kHz.

Radio RSA, South Africa. *News* and comment, followed weekdays by *Africa South*, *Sport RSA* (Monday), *Economic Desk* (Wednesday), *Talking Point* (Friday and Sunday), *Around and About* and *Profile* (Saturday) and *Conversation Corner* (Sunday). Fifty-five minutes aimed at African listeners, but occasionally heard in Europe and beyond on 17835 kHz.

Radio Australia. *International Report*, followed Monday through Friday by *Stock Exchange Report*, then one of several feature programs, including *Arts Roundabout* (Sunday), *Innovations* (Tuesday), *Points of Law* (Wednesday), *Monitor* (Saturday) and *Interaction* (Monday). Heard well in North America on 9580 kHz.

Radio New Zealand International.

Relay of domestic National Radio network. Targeted to the Pacific on 9700 kHz; also heard in North America.

Voice of Vietnam. Much better heard in Europe than in North America. Begins with *news*, then political commentary, interviews, short features, and some very pleasant Vietnamese music. Omnidirectional on 9840 and 12019 or 15010 kHz. Repeats of this transmission can be heard on the same frequencies at 1230, 1330, 1600, 1800, 1900, 2030 and 2330 World Time.

Belgische Radio en Televisie, Belgium. Monday through Saturday, winters only at this time. See 0630 for program details. To Europe on 6035 and 9925, 11695 or 13675 kHz, and to Africa (also heard elsewhere) on 21810 or 21815 kHz.

Swiss Radio International. Repeat of 0830 transmission. To East Asia and the Pacific on 9560, 13685, 17670 and 21695 kHz.

Kol Israel. Summers only at this time. *News* from Israel Radio's domestic network, followed by various features: *Mainstream* (consumer and community affairs, *With Me in the Studio* (guest interviews), *Israel Mosaic* (variety of topics), *Studio Three* (arts in Israel), *This Land* (a travel magazine), and *Thank Goodness It's Friday*. A half hour to Europe—occasionally audible in Eastern North America—on 11588, 17545, 17575, 17590 and 21710 kHz. To Asia and the Pacific on 15650 kHz. According to the station, this broadcast may be canceled in the near future.

Voice of America. The start of VOA's daily broadcasts to the Caribbean. *News*, *Newsline* and *VOA Morning*—a compendium of sports, science, business and features—on 9590, 11915 and 6030 or 15120 kHz. For a separate service to the Pacific, see the next item.

Voice of America. *News*, followed weekdays by *Newsline* and *Magazine Show*. On weekends, there are features such as *Weekend Magazine* (Saturday) and *Critic's Choice* (Sunday). To the Pacific on 5985, 11720, and 15425 kHz.

WHRI, Indiana, USA. WHRI, although essentially a religious broadcaster, has recently been carrying more and more political material (mainly from anti-Castro exiles and Croatian nationalists), which isn't even in English. For listeners seeking inspirational programming, you can try at this hour, with a reasonable chance of actually hearing what you want to hear. To North America (sometimes heard in Europe) on 7315, 7355 or 9780 kHz.

All India Radio. *News*, then a composite program of commentary, press review and features—accompanied by ample servings of highly enjoyable subcontinental music. To the Pacific on 15335 kHz; and to East Asia on 15050, 17387, 17895 and 21735 kHz.

Radio Moscow World Service. A truly worldwide broadcast, beamed to all continents at this time. North Americans can listen to the Cuba relay, on 6000 kHz winters and 11840 kHz summers.

HCJB, Ecuador. Monday through Friday it's *Studio 9*. As 0030, but one day earlier. Weekends, you can hear *DX Partyline* and *Saludos Amigos*. To the Pacific on 9745 and 11925 kHz.

1030

Radio Korea, South Korea. Summers only at this time. Monday through Saturday, *News*, followed by *Seoul Calling* Monday and Tuesday, music Wednesday through Friday, and *From Us to You* Saturday. *Shortwave Feedback* follows *Weekly News in Review* on Sunday. On 11715 kHz via Canadian relay, so this is the best chance for North Americans to tune in the station.

United Arab Emirates Radio, Dubai. *News*, then a feature dealing with aspects of Arab life and culture. Weekends, there are replies to listeners' letters. To Europe on 15320, 15435, 17775 and 21605 kHz.

Radio Austria International. *Report from Austria*; see 0130 for more details. Summers only at this time. Twenty-five minutes to Australia and the Pacific on 15450 and 21490 kHz.

1100

BBC World Service. *Newsdesk*, followed 30 minutes later by the arts program *Meridian* (Wednesday, Friday and Saturday), *The Ken Bruce Show* (Sunday), *Composer of the Month* (Monday), *Megamix* (Tuesday), and drama (Thursday). Continuous to North America on 5965, 6195, 9515, 9740 and 15220 kHz; to Western Europe on 5975, 6045, 9750, 9760, 12095, 15070 and 17640 kHz; and to East Asia and the Pacific on 9740 kHz.

Christian Science Monitor World

Service, USA. See 0100 for program details. Monday through Friday to North America on 9495 kHz; and to East Asia on 9530 or 17555 kHz.

Radio Australia. World and Australian *news*, then music, followed at 1130 by a 30-minute feature, such as *One World* (Sunday), *Land and Culture* (Monday), *Business Horizons* (Tuesday), *Matters of Faith* (Saturday), *AgriNews* (Thursday) or *Science File* (Wednesday). Heard clearly in North America on 9580 kHz.

Voice of Vietnam. Repeat of the 1000 transmission. To Asia on 7420 and 9730 kHz.

HCJB, Ecuador. Thirty minutes of religious programming to the Pacific on 9745 and 11925 kHz.

Voice of America. The second—and final—hour of the morning broadcast to the Caribbean. *News*, followed weekdays by *Focus* and *VOA Morning*. On Saturday there are *American Viewpoints* and *Music U.S.A.*, while Sunday features *Critic's Choice* and *Studio One*. On 6030 (or 15120), 9590 and 11915 kHz. For a separate service to Asia and the Pacific, see the next item.

Voice of America. These programs are different from those to the Caribbean. *News*, followed Saturday by *American Viewpoints* and *Press Conference USA*, Sunday by *New Horizons* and *Issues in the News*, and weekdays by special features and *Music USA*. To East Asia on 9760 and 15155 kHz, and to the Pacific on 5985, 11720 and 15425 kHz.

Radio New Zealand International. Northern summers only at this time. Final hour of transmission. Relay of domestic National Radio network. A pleasant hour's listening, combining agreeable presentation with a variety of musical styles. Intended for the Pacific, but also audible in North America, on 9700 kHz.

Trans World Radio, Netherlands Antilles. The first hour of a transmission which lasts until 1330, and which is predominantly of religious content from 1200 onwards. Monday through Friday it's *Morning Sounds*, 60 minutes of world and Caribbean *news*, weather reports, chat and gospel music. There is also a small amount of religiously oriented talk, but this is kept to a minimum. Weekends, the program is replaced by 30 minutes of *Caribbean Connection*, followed by religious programming. To Eastern North America on 11815 and 15345 kHz.

Radio Moscow World Service. Continuous programming to virtually all parts of the globe. Features the highly informative *Update*, a potpourri of news and comment from (and very much about) the Soviet Union. Forty available channels—just tune around until you find one. North Americans can try the Cuban relay on 6000 kHz (winters) or 11840 kHz (summers).

Swiss Radio International. Repeat of the 0830 transmission. A half hour to Asia and the Pacific on 13635, 15570, 17830 and 21770 kHz.

Radio Japan. On weekdays, opens with *Radio Japan News-Round*, with news oriented to Japanese and Asian affairs. *Radio Japan Magazine Hour* follows, with more feature content, including *Japan Diary* (Monday through Friday), *Crosscurrents* (Monday), *Asia Contact* (Wednesday) and *A Glimpse of Japan* (Friday). *Commentary* and *News* round off the hour. On Saturday, there's *This Week*, and Sunday features *News*, *Hello from Tokyo*, and *Viewpoint*. One hour to North America on 6120 kHz, and to East Asia on 11815 and 11840 kHz.

Radio Beijing, China. See 0000 for program details, but one day earlier at this

hour. To North America winters on 9665 kHz; summers on 17855 kHz.

Radio Pyongyang, North Korea. Lots of patriotic songs and an abundance of political commentary are still not enough to enthuse most listeners. If you're interested in the words and deeds of Comrade Kim, start with the *news* and then listen to the children's choirs. The words of enlightenment come later. Fifty minutes to North America on 6576, 9977 and 11335 kHz.

Voice of Asia, Taiwan. Broadcasts open with features like *Asian Culture* (Monday) and *Touring Asia* (Tuesday), followed by *news*, *Festival Asia*, and *Let's Learn Chinese*. Heard in East Asia and the Pacific— but only occasionally in North America—on 7445 kHz.

1130

Radio Korea, South Korea. Winters only at this time. See 1030 for program details. On 9700 kHz via their Canadian relay, so a good chance for North Americans to tune in the station.

Radio Austria International. Monday through Friday features *Report from Austria* (see 0130 for further details). On Saturday, there's *Austrian Coffeetable*, which consists of light chat and different kinds of music, including classical, popular, jazz, or German and Austrian popular songs from the Twenties and Thirties. On Sunday, it's *Shortwave Panorama* for radio enthusiasts. Thirty minutes to North America on 21490 kHz; to Europe on 6155 and 13730 kHz; and to East Asia on 15430 kHz.

Radio Nederland. *News*, then features. Monday's offering is the first-rate science magazine *Research File*; Tuesday is arts and culture day, with *Images*; Wednesday and Saturday have the accent on music, while Thursday is given over to *Media Network*. Friday's *Asiascan*, a 45-minute live magazine show, presents news and features covering Asia and Europe. On Sunday, it's *Happy Station* time—music, chat and competitions for all the family. Fifty-five minutes to Europe on 5955 and 9715 kHz; and to Asia on 17575, 21480 and 21520 kHz.

HCJB, Ecuador. First 30 minutes of a four-and-a-half-hour block of religious programming to North America. On 11925 kHz.

Belgische Radio en Televisie, Belgium. Summer Sundays only at this time. *News*, followed by *P.O. Box 26* (a mailbag

program) and *Musical Roundabout*. Twenty-five minutes to North America on 21810 kHz.

Kol Israel. Winters only at this time. *News* from Israel Radio's domestic network, followed by various features (see 1000). A half hour to Europe—sometimes heard in Eastern North America—on 11585, 17575, 17590 and 21790 kHz. To Asia and the Pacific on 15650 kHz. According to the station, this transmission may be canceled in the near future.

Radio Sweden. This time summers only; see 1530 for program details. To Asia and the Pacific on 11960, 17740 and 21570 kHz.

EVENING PRIME TIME—ASIA AND WESTERN AUSTRALIA 1200

BBC World Service. Except for Sunday, the hour starts with *News* and *News about Britain*, then *Multitrack* (Tuesday, Thursday, Saturday), *The Farming World* (Wednesday), a quiz, or a special feature. *Sports Roundup* follows at 45 minutes past the hour. This time Sunday there's a *news summary* followed by *Play of the Week*—the epitome of excellence in radio theater. Continuous to North America on 5965, 6195, 9515, 9740 and 15220 kHz; to Europe on 5975, 6045, 9750, 9760, 12095, 15070, and 17640 kHz; and to East Asia and the Pacific on 9740 kHz.

Christian Science Monitor World Service, USA. See 0000 for program details. Monday through Friday to North America on 9495 kHz; and to the Pacific on 9475 kHz.

Radio Canada International. Summers only at this time; see 1300 for program details. Monday through Friday to North and Central America on 9635, 11855 and 17820 kHz.

Radio Tashkent, Uzbekistan, USSR. *News* and commentary, followed by such features as *Life in the Village*, *Youth Program*, and *On the Asian Continent*. Heard better in Asia, the Pacific and Europe than in North America. Thirty minutes winters on 5945, 9540, 9600, 11785 and 15470 kHz; and summers on 7325, 9715, 11785, 15460 and 17740 kHz.

Radio Australia. *International Report*, followed 30 minutes later, Sunday through Thursday, by *Soundabout*—a program of contemporary popular music. On Friday there is a documentary program, *This Aus-*tralia, and Saturday features *Women in Politics*. Well heard in North America on 9580 kHz.

HCJB, Ecuador. Continuous religious programming to North America on 11925, 15115 and 17890 kHz.

Voice of America. *News*, then—week-days—*Newsline* and *Magazine Show*. End-of-week programming consists of features like Saturday's *Weekend Magazine* or Sunday's *Encounter* and *Studio One*. To East Asia on 9760 and 15155 kHz; and to the Pacific on 15425 kHz.

Radio Beijing, China. *News* and various features—see 0000 for specifics, although programs are one day earlier. To North America winters on 9665 kHz, and summers on 17855 kHz; to East Asia on 11600 and 11660 kHz; and to the Pacific on 11600 and 15450 kHz.

Radio Nacional do Brasil (Radiobras), Brazil. Variously titled *Life in Brazil* or *Brazilian Panorama*, Monday through Saturday you can hear a mix of Brazilian music and news, facts and figures about South America's largest and most dynamic country. The *Sunday Special*, on the other hand, is devoted to one particular theme, and often contains lots of stupendous Brazilian music. Eighty minutes to North America on poorly heard 11745 kHz.

Radio Moscow World Service. Continuous programming worldwide. Tune around and choose a channel. Listeners in North America can try the Cuban relay, winters on 6000 and summers on 11840 kHz.

Swiss Radio International. Summers only at this time; see 0830 for program details. To Europe on 6165, 9535 and 12030 kHz.

Radio Yugoslavia, located in Serbia. Summers only at this time. *News*, followed by various features (see 2100). Thirty minutes to Asia, the Pacific and Eastern North America on 17725, 17740 and 21605 kHz.

1215

Radio Cairo. Seventy-five minutes of *News*, comment, culture and authentic Egyptian music; to East Asia on 17595 kHz.

Radio Korea, South Korea. Repeat of the 0800 transmission, but to Eastern North America on 9750 kHz.

1230

Radio France Internationale. *News*, which gives ample coverage of French politics and international events. This is usually followed by a short feature such as *Land of France* (Tuesday), *Science* (Wednesday), or *Arts in France* (Thursday); and if you are interested, tune in Monday for the weekend's sports results. A half hour to North America, usually received with a so-so signal on 17650, 21635 and 21645 kHz; and to Europe on 9805, 11670, 15155 and 15195 kHz.

Radio Sweden. This time winters only; see 1530 for program details. To Asia and the Pacific on 9765 (or 11715), 17740 and 21570 kHz.

Belgische Radio en Televisie, Belgium. Winter Sundays only at this time. See 1130 for program details. Twenty-five minutes to North America on 21810 kHz.

1300

BBC World Service. News and analysis in the incomparable *Newshour*—60 minutes of sheer professionalism. To North America on 5965, 6195, 9515, 9740 or 15220 kHz. Continuous to Europe on 5975, 6045, 9410, 9750, 9760, 12095, 15070 and 17640 kHz; to East Asia on 7180, 9740 and 11820 kHz; and to the Pacific on 9740 kHz.

Christian Science Monitor World Service, USA. See 0100 for program details. Monday through Friday to North America on 9495 kHz; and to the Pacific on 9475 kHz.

Radio Canada International. Winter weekdays only at this time. Relay of CBC domestic network programming. One hour Monday through Friday to North and Central America on 9635, 11855 and 17820 kHz. For an additional service, see next item.

Radio Canada International. Summers only at this time; see 1400 for program details. Sunday only to North and Central America on 11955 and 17820 kHz.

Radio Pyongyang, North Korea. Repeat of the 1100 transmission. To Europe on 9325 and 9345 kHz; and to North America and East Asia on 9640, 13650, and 15230 kHz.

Swiss Radio International. Winters only at this time. See 0830 for program details. To Europe on 6165, 9535 and 12030 kHz.

Radio Nacional do Brasil (Radiobras), Brazil. The final 20 minutes of the broadcast beamed to North America on 11745 kHz.

Belgische Radio en Televisie, Belgium. Summers only at this time, Monday through Saturday. See 0630 for program

details. Twenty-five minutes to Southeast Asia on 21810 or 21815 kHz. One hour later in winter.

Radio Sweden. Summers only at this time; repeat of the 1130 broadcast. Thirty minutes to Asia and the Pacific on 11960, 17740 and 21570 kHz.

Radio Yugoslavia, located in Serbia. Winters only at this time. *News*, followed by various features (see 2100). Thirty minutes to Asia, the Pacific and Eastern North America on 9720, 17725, 21635 and 21715 kHz.

Radio Australia. World and Australian *news*, followed by *Sports Report* and a half hour of music. Beamed elsewhere, but tends to be easily audible in North America on 9580 kHz.

Radio Moscow World Service. Continuous to virtually everywhere; tune around and find a channel that suits you. For North America, try the relay via Cuba; winters on 6000 and summers on 11840 kHz.

HCJB, Ecuador. Sixty minutes of religious broadcasting. Continuous to North America on 11925, 15115 and 17890 kHz.

Voice of America. *News*, followed by *Focus* (weekdays), *On the Line* (Saturday) or *Critic's Choice* (Sunday). The last half hour includes special features. To East Asia on 9760 and 15155 kHz, and to the Pacific on 15425 kHz.

1330

United Arab Emirates Radio, Dubai. *News*, then a feature devoted to Arab and Islamic history and culture. Twenty-five minutes to Europe on 15320, 15435, 17775 and 21605 kHz.

Radio Austria International. *Report from Austria*; see 0130 for more details. Twenty-five minutes to East Asia on 15430 kHz.

Radio Canada International. A 30-minute relay of CBC domestic programming targeted to East Asia on 6095, 6150, 9535, 9700 and 11795 kHz.

Radio Tashkent, Uzbekistan, USSR. Repeat of the 1200 transmission. Heard in Asia, the Pacific, Europe and parts of North America winters on 5945, 9540, 9600, 11785 and 15470 kHz; and summers on 7325, 9715, 11785, 15460 and 17740 kHz.

Swiss Radio International. Repeat of the 0830 transmission. A half hour to Asia and the Pacific on 7480, 11695, 13635, 15570, 17830 and 21695 kHz.

1345

Vatican Radio. Twenty-five minutes of religious and secular programming to Asia and the Pacific on 11830, 15090 and 17535 kHz.

1400

BBC World Service. On weekdays it's *World News*, followed by *Outlook*. On the half hour you can hear *Off the Shelf*, readings from some of the best of world literature. The final 15 minutes are mainly devoted to cultural themes. Continuous to Europe on 5975, 6045, 9410, 9750, 9760, 12095, 15070 and 17640 kHz.

BBC World Service for Asia. Monday through Friday, the BBC World Service airs special programs for the eastern part of that continent, including the highly informative *Dateline East Asia*. To East and South East Asia on 7180, 9740 and 11820 kHz, 9740 also being available for Australia and the Pacific.

Christian Science Monitor World Service, USA. See 0000 for program details. Monday through Friday to Europe and North America on 21670 or 21780 kHz; and to East Asia on 9530 kHz.

Radio France Internationale. *News*, press review and a variety of short features, including *Letterbox* (Sunday) and *Made in France* (Saturday). Fifty-five minutes to Southeast Asia and the Pacific on 7125 (winter), 11910 (summer), 17650 and 21770 kHz.

Radio Australia. *International Report*, followed Monday through Friday by *Stock Exchange Report* and, on the half hour, special feature programs like *Science File* (Friday), *Interaction* (Saturday) and *Lane's Company* (Tuesday). Audible in North America on 9580 kHz, and in Europe on 17630 kHz.

Radio Moscow World Service. Continuous virtually worldwide. There are so many available frequencies, just dial a channel. In North America try 11840 kHz.

Belgische Radio en Televisie, Belgium. Winters only at this time, Monday through Saturday. See 0630 for program details. *News* and *Press Review*, followed by such features as *Belgium Today*, *Focus on Europe* and *Around the Arts*. To Southeast Asia on 17555, 21810 or 21815 kHz.

Radio Finland. Summers only at this time. Actually starts at 1405; see 1500 for program details. Twenty-five minutes to Europe on 6120, 11755 and 11820 kHz. Also available to the Middle East (and heard elsewhere) on 15185 and 21550 kHz.

HCJB, Ecuador. Another hour of religious fare to North America on 11925, 15115 and 17890 kHz.

Voice of America. *News*. This is followed weekdays by *Asia Report*. On Saturday there's jazz, and Sunday is given over to classical music. At 1455, there's a daily editorial. To East Asia on 9760 and 15160 kHz, and to the Pacific on 15425 kHz.

Radio Canada International. This time summers only. A half hour of CBC domestic programming targeted to Europe on 11935, 15305, 15315, 15325, 17795, 17820 and 21545 kHz.

Radio Sweden. Winters only at this time; repeat of 1230 broadcast. To Asia and the Pacific on 9765, 17740 and 21570 kHz.

CFRX-CFRB, Toronto, Canada. Audible throughout much of the northeastern United States and southeastern Canada during the hours of daylight with a modest, but clear, signal on 6070 kHz. With programs for an Ontario audience, this pleasant, friendly station carries news, sports, weather, traffic reports—and, at times, music. Arguably most interesting are talk-show discussions concerning such topics as the status of neighboring Quebec. Call in if you'd like at 514/790-0600—comments from outside Ontario are welcomed.

CFCX-CFCF, Montreal, Canada. Locally oriented programming. Its weak signal is sometimes audible on good radios in parts of the northeastern United States and southeastern Canada during the hours of midday and early afternoon on 6005 kHz.

1430

Radio Nederland. Repeat of the 1130 transmission. Fifty-five minutes to Europe on 5955 kHz, and to Asia on 13770, 15150, 17575 and 17605 kHz.

Radio Austria International. Repeat of 1130 transmission. To Europe on 6155 and 13730 kHz; to Asia on 11780 kHz; and to West Africa (also heard in parts of Europe) on 21490 kHz.

1500

BBC World Service. *World News*, followed Saturday by *Sportsworld* and Sunday by *Concert Hall* (or its substitute). Weekday programming includes a documentary feature (Monday), *A Jolly Good Show* (Tuesday), comedy (Wednesday) and classical music (Thursday and Friday). To Western North America summers on 9740 kHz; to North America weekends on 9515 or 11775 and 15260 kHz; daily to Europe on 6195, 9410, 9750, 12095, 15070 and 17640 kHz; and to East Asia on 7180 and 9740 kHz. Also, until 1515, to the Pacific on 9740 kHz.

Christian Science Monitor World Service, USA. See 0100 for program details. Monday through Friday to Europe and North America on 21670 or 21780 kHz; and to East Asia on 9530 kHz.

KNLS, Alaska, USA. See 0800 for program details. To East Asia and the Pacific; winters on 7355 kHz, and summers on 9615 kHz.

BBC World Service for Africa. See 0330. Try 11860, 15420, 17860 or 21490 kHz.

Radio Canada International. Continuation of CBC domestic program *Sunday Morning.* Sunday only to North and Central America on 11955 and 17820 kHz. For a separate service to Europe, see the next item.

Radio Canada International. Thirty minutes of CBC domestic programs aimed at European listeners. Winters on 9555, 11915, 11935, 15315, 15325, 17820 and 21545 kHz; summers on 11935, 15305, 15325, 17820 and 21545 kHz.

Radio Moscow World Service. Continuous to Europe, Asia, Africa and the Americas. Audible on over 40 channels—it's difficult to miss.

Radio Finland. Winters only at this time. Actually starts at 1505. *News Update* is followed Tuesday through Saturday by *Northern Report*, with *Perspectives* on Sunday, and *Business Monday* (guess when!). Monday through Friday, there is then a daily *Press Review*, replaced Saturday by *Finnish History*, and Sunday by *Starting Finnish.* Other features include such titles as *Airmail* (Tuesday), *Sports Fare* (Wednesday), *Fourth Generation* (Thursday), and *Names in the News* (Friday). Twenty-five minutes to Europe on 6120, 11755 and 11820 kHz. One hour earlier in summer.

Radio Japan. *News* and various features. See 0300 for details. One hour to North America on 9505 or 11865 kHz.

Radio RSA, South Africa. First hour of a three-hour broadcast consisting of *News* and features, including *Historical Almanac* and *Africa South* (weekdays); *Our Wild Heritage* (Sunday, Monday); *Conversation Corner* (Sunday, Monday, Friday); *Black Choirs* (Monday), *Sounds of Soweto* (Tuesday), and *Artist of the Week* (Friday); *Talking About Towns* (Monday); *Women in Africa* (Tuesday, Thursday); *Changing the Face of Africa* (Wednesday); *Medical File* (Wednesday); *Economic Desk* (Wednesday); *Profile* (Thursday); *Not in the Headlines* (Friday); *A Contribution by Colin Jackson* (Saturday); *Kaleidoscope* (Saturday); *Science and Technology* (Sunday); and *Sunday Magazine.* Targeted to Africa (and sometimes heard elsewhere) on 7230 and 15210 (or 15270) kHz. May also be available on 17835 kHz at certain times of the year.

HCJB, Ecuador. Continues with religious programming to North America on 15115 and 17890 kHz.

CFRX-CFRB, Toronto, Canada. See 1400.

1530

Radio Sweden. Each broadcast is called *Weekday, Saturday* or *Sunday,* and begins

with world and Nordic *news*, followed by human interest features and interviews. On Monday, the accent is on sport; Wednesday features *Business Scan*; and Friday's broadcast contains Scandinavian jazz and popular music. On Saturday, there's a look back at the week's events in Scandinavia in *Nordic Newsweek*. Thirty minutes to North America on 17875 and 21500 (or 21665)kHz.

1600

BBC World Service. *World News*, followed by *News About Britain*. Feature programs that follow include sports, drama, science or music. Particularly worthwhile are *Network UK* (Thursday) and *Science in Action* (Friday). At 1645 on Sunday there's Alistair Cooke's popular *Letter from America*, and on weekdays at the same time you can hear a news analysis program, *The World Today*. Continuous to North America on 9515 or 11775 and 15260 kHz; and to Europe on 6195, 9410, 12095 and 15070 kHz. Also, to East Asia until 1615 on 7180 and 9740 kHz.

Christian Science Monitor World Service, USA. *News* and *Monitor Radio Worldwide*—60 minutes of news, analysis and news-related features, with emphasis on international developments. Monday through Friday to Europe on 21640 kHz; and to East Asia on 11580 or 13625 kHz.

Radio France Internationale. This program, formerly called *Paris Calling Africa*, is heard quite well in North America and Europe. Begins with world and African *news*, followed by feature programs, including the *Land of France* (Tuesday), *Arts in France* (Thursday), *Mailbag* (Sunday), *Drumbeat* (Wednesday; African arts), *Spotlight on Africa* (Saturday), and somewhat surprisingly, *Latin American Notes* (Sunday and Wednesday). Fifty-five minutes, audible in Europe and North America, on 6175, 11705, 12015, 15360, 15530, 17620, 17795, 17845 and 17850 kHz.

United Arab Emirates Radio, Dubai. Starts with a feature on Arab history or culture, followed by music at 1615 and a bulletin of *news* at 1630. Answers listeners' letters on weekends. Forty minutes to Europe on 11795, 15320, 15435 and 21605 kHz.

Radio Korea, South Korea. See 0800 for program details. To Asia and beyond on 5975 and 9870 kHz.

Deutsche Welle, Germany. Repeat of the 0900 transmission, except that *Asia-*

Pacific Report replaces *Through German Eyes* on Monday. To Asia on 6170, 7225, 15105, 15595 and 21680 kHz.

Radio RSA, South Africa. Second hour of a three-hour broadcast to the African continent. *News* and features about South Africa, also heard in Europe and parts of Eastern North America on 15210 (or 15270) and 17790 (or 17835) kHz.

Radio Canada International. Winters only. Final hour of CBC's *Sunday Morning*; Sunday only to North and Central America on 11955 and 17820 kHz. For a separate service to Europe, see the next item.

Radio Canada International. A half hour of CBC domestic broadcasting targeted to Europe on 11935, 15305, 15325, 17820 and 21545 kHz.

Voice of America. *News*, followed by *Nightline Africa* —special news and features on African affairs. Heard beyond Africa— including North America—on a number of frequencies, including 15410, 15580, 17800 and 21625 kHz.

CFRX-CFRB, Toronto, Canada. See 1400.

1700

BBC World Service. *World News*, followed by *World Business Report/Review* (Sunday-Friday) or *Personal Choice* (Saturday), then a quiz show, drama, music or sports. There is a daily summary of world sporting news at 1745, in *Sports Roundup*. Until 1745 to North America on 9515 or 11775 and 15260 kHz. Continuous to Western Europe on 6195, 9410, 12095 and 15070 kHz.

BBC World Service for Africa. See 0330. Until 1745, on 6005, 9630, 15400, 15420 and 17880 kHz.

Christian Science Monitor World Service, USA. *News*, then *Monitor Radio Worldwide Features*, followed at 34 minutes past the hour by *Letterbox* (a listener response program) and a religious article from the *Christian Science Monitor*. Monday through Friday to Europe on 21640 kHz, and to East Asia on 11580 or 13625 kHz.

Radio Prague International, Czechoslovakia. Summers only at this time. *News*, then a variety of features with a Czechoslovak slant. Thirty minutes to Europe on 5930, 6055, 7345, and 9605 kHz.

Radio RSA, South Africa. Final hour of three-hour broadcast. *News* and features about South Africa. Fifty-five minutes targeted to the African continent, but also audible in Europe and beyond on 7230, 15210 (or 15270) and 17790 (or 17835) kHz.

Radio Sweden. Summers only at this time; see 1530 for program details. Thirty minutes to Europe on 6065 and 9615 kHz.

Radio Canada International. Thirty minutes of CBC domestic programming for European listeners on 5995 (or 9555), 7235, 15325, 17820 and 21545 kHz.

Voice of America. Programs for Africa. *News,* followed Monday through Friday by *African Panorama*—interviews, current affairs, music and human interest features. Weekend offerings include the excellent *Music Time in Africa* at 1730 Sunday. Audible in many parts of the world on 15410, 15580, 17800 and 21625 kHz.

Kol Israel. Summers only at this time. *News* from Israel Radio's domestic network. To Europe for 15 minutes on 11588 and 11675 kHz.

CFRX-CFRB, Toronto, Canada. See 1400.

1730

Belgische Radio en Televisie, Belgium. Summers only at this time. On weekdays, there's *News, Press Review* and *Belgium Today,* followed by features like *Focus on Europe* (Monday), *Around the Arts* (Tuesday and Friday), *Living in Belgium* (Wednesday) and *North-South* (Thursday). Weekends include features like *Radio World* (Saturday) and *Musical Roundabout* (Sunday). Twenty-five minutes to Europe on 9925 and 11695 or 13675 kHz; also to Africa (and heard elsewhere) on 21810 or 21815 kHz.

Radio Sofia, Bulgaria. Summers only at this time. The first half hour of a 90-minute broadcast. Mostly *news* and news-related items, but includes a fair amount of lively Bulgarian folk music later in the transmission. To Europe and Africa on 11660, 11720, 11765, 15330, 17780 and 17825 kHz.

EVENING PRIME TIME—EUROPE
1800

BBC World Service. Thirty minutes of *Newsdesk,* followed most days by pop, jazz, or classical music. Notable exceptions are the quality science program *Discovery,* broadcast Tuesday at 1830, and the excellent *Focus on Faith,* heard at 1830 Friday. Continuous to Western Europe on 6195,

7325, 9410, 12095 and 15070 kHz; and to the Pacific on 11750 kHz.

Christian Science Monitor World Service, USA. See 1600 for program details. Monday through Friday to Europe and parts of North America on 21640 and 21780 kHz, and to the Pacific on 13625 kHz.

Radio Canada International. Targeted to Africa, but heard quite well in North America. A relay of CBC domestic programming, mainly of interest to Canadians. A half hour weekdays, one hour weekends on 13670, 15260 and 17820 kHz. For a separate service to Europe at this time, see the next item.

Radio Canada International. This time winters only. Thirty minutes of CBC domestic broadcasting aimed at European listeners on 5995, 7235, 11945, 15325 and 17875 kHz.

Radio Prague International, Czechoslovakia. Winters only at this time. *News* and a variety of features dealing with Czechoslovak topics. Thirty minutes to Europe on 5930, 6055, 7345 and 9605 kHz. One hour earlier in summer.

Radio Nacional do Brasil (Radiobras), Brazil. A repeat of the 1200 broadcast. Eighty minutes to Europe on 15265 kHz.

Radio Moscow World Service. Continuous to Europe, Asia, Africa and North America (where it is heard on 11840 kHz). For other areas, tune around—you'll find it easily enough.

Voice of America. *News,* followed by *Focus* (weekdays), *On the Line* (Saturday), and *Encounter* (Sunday). The second half hour is devoted to news and features in "special English"—that is, simplified talk in the American language for those whose mother tongue is other than English. To Europe on 6040, 9760, 11760 and 15205 kHz; to Africa, but often heard elsewhere, on 15410, 15580, 17800 and 21625 kHz.

Radio Argentina al Exterior – R.A.E. Winters only at this time. See 1900 broadcast for program details. Fifty-five minutes to Europe on 15345 kHz.

KNLS, Alaska, USA. See 0800 for program details. To East Asia and the Pacific; winters on 7355 kHz, and summers on 11945 kHz.

Radio Sofia, Bulgaria. Summers, from 1800; winters, from 1830. Part of a 90-minute transmission targeted to Europe and Africa, containing a mixture of news, features, interviews and music. Audible winters on several of the following frequencies: 6070, 9700, 11735, 11765, 11840, 15330 and 15370 kHz; and summers on 11660, 11720, 11765, 15330, 17780 and 17820 kHz.

Kol Israel. Winters only at this time. *News* from Israel Radio's domestic network. To Europe—sometimes audible in Eastern North America—for 15 minutes on 11585 and 11655 kHz. According to the station, this broadcast may be canceled in the near future.

Radio Sweden. Winters only at this time. *News* and features, with a predominantly Nordic slant; see 1530 for program details. To Europe on 6065 and 9615 or 9655 kHz.

Radio Korea, South Korea. *News*, followed by features; see 0800 for program details. One hour to Europe—sometimes also heard in North America—on 15575 kHz.

CFRX-CFRB, Toronto, Canada. See 1400.

1830

Radio Yugoslavia, located in Serbia. Summers only at this time. *News*, followed by various features (see 2100). Thirty minutes for Europe and Africa on 6165 and 15165 kHz.

Belgische Radio en Televisie, Belgium. Winters only at this time; see 1730 for program details. Twenty-five minutes to Europe on 5910 or 9925 kHz.

Radio Prague International, Czechoslovakia. Summers only at this time. *News* and features presented in a magazine-type format. Thirty minutes of pleasant listening for Europeans on 6055 and 9605 kHz.

Radio Finland. Summers only at this time; see 1930 for program details. Twenty-five minutes to Europe and West Africa on 6120, 9550, 11755 and 15185 kHz.

Voice of the Islamic Republic of Iran. Summers only; see 1930 for program details. One hour to Europe on 6035 and 9022 kHz.

BBC World Service for Africa. See 0330. Thirty minutes on 3255, 6005, 6190, 9630, 15400 and 17880 kHz.

1900

BBC World Service. Begins on weekdays with *World News*, then the magazine program *Outlook*. These are followed by just about anything, depending on the day of the week. Choice plums include *Health*

Matters (1945 Monday) and *Omnibus* (1930 Wednesday). The excellent *Play of the Week* can be heard Sunday at this time. Continuous to Western Europe on 6195, 7325, 9410, 12095 and 15070 kHz; and to the Pacific on 11750 kHz.

Christian Science Monitor World Service, USA. See 1700 for program details. Monday through Friday to Europe and parts of North America on 21640 and 21780 kHz, and to the Pacific on 13625 kHz.

Radio Nacional do Brasil (Radiobras), Brazil. Final 20 minutes of 1800 broadcast to Europe on 15265 kHz.

Radio Algiers, Algeria. *News*, then rock and popular music. There are occasional brief features, such as *Algiers in a Week*, which covers the main events in Algeria during the past week. One hour of so-so reception on one or more of the following channels: 9509, 9535, 9640, 9685, 15215 and 17745 kHz.

Kol Israel. Summers only at this time. *News* and features (see 2230). A half hour to Europe—often audible in Eastern North America—on 9435, 11605 and 15640 kHz.

Radio Sofia, Bulgaria. Winters only at this time. Final hour of a 90-minute broadcast (see 1800) targeted to Europe and Africa. Try 6070, 9700, 11735, 11765, 11840, 15330 or 15370 kHz.

HCJB, Ecuador. The first evening transmission for Europe. Repeat of the 1000 broadcast to the Pacific. Weekdays it's *Studio 9*, with *DX Partyline* on Saturday, and *Saludos Amigos* on Sunday. On 15270, 17790 and 21480 kHz.

Deutsche Welle, Germany. This African-oriented transmissions includes *Newsline Cologne* and *African News*, along with such features as *Economic Notebook* (Friday), *Living in Germany* (Wednesday) and *Religion and Society* (Sunday). To West Africa, but heard elsewhere, on 11785, 11810, 13790, 15350, 15390 and 17810 kHz.

Radio Moscow World Service. Continuous to Europe, Africa and North America. Just dial around and find a suitable frequency.

Radio Canada International. A relay of CBC domestic programming. Monday through Friday to Africa—but heard well in parts of North America—on 13670, 15260 and 17820 kHz. For a separate service for European listeners, see the next item.

Radio Canada International. This time summers only. A 60-minute relay of CBC domestic broadcasts targeted to Europe on 5995, 6170, 7235, 9670, 13650, 15325, 17875 and 21675 kHz.

Radio Portugal. Summers only at this time, Monday through Friday. See 0230 for program details; programs in this time slot are one day earlier. Thirty minutes to Europe on 11740 kHz.

Spanish Foreign Radio. *News*, followed by features and Spanish music; see 0000 for program details. To Europe and Africa on 9875, 11790, 15375 and 15395 kHz.

Swiss Radio International. Summers only at this time; see 0830 for program details. To Europe on 3985, 6165 and 9535 kHz.

Voice of America. *News*. For Europe and the Pacific there then follows *Newsline* until 1930. Europeans then get *Magazine Show* (Monday-Friday), *Press Conference USA* (Saturday), and Sunday's *Music USA*. For the Pacific it's *Music USA* Sunday through Friday, replaced Saturday by *Press Conference USA*. Not much doubt about where the programs originate! For listeners in Africa—weekdays—there is *African Panorama* and *Sound of Soul*. Weekend offerings on this service include the second part of the highly entertaining *Music Time in Africa* Sunday at 1930. The European transmission is on 6040, 9760, 11760 and 15205 kHz; the broadcast to the Pacific on 9525, 11870 and 15180 kHz; and the African service (also heard in North America) on 15410, 15580, 17800 and 21625 kHz.

Radio Argentina al Exterior – R.A.E. Monday through Friday only. Lots of mini-features dealing with aspects of life in Argentina, interspersed with examples of the country's various musical styles, from tango to *carnavalito*. Fifty-five minutes to Europe on 15345 kHz. Broadcast an hour earlier during summer in Argentina (winter in the northern hemisphere).

CFRX-CFRB, Toronto, Canada. See 1400.

1920

Voice of Greece. Comparable to the 0130 English transmission, but to Europe on 7430, 9395 or 11645 kHz.

1930

Radio Austria International. *Report from Austria.* See 0130 for complete details. A half hour to Europe and Africa on 5945, 6155 and 13730 kHz.

Voice of the Islamic Republic of Iran. Sixty minutes of *news*, commentary and religion—but not as in the days of the Ayatollah Khomeini! The rhetoric is long gone, and even criticism against the West has been toned down considerably. Anti-western propaganda has been largely replaced by strong support for the Palestinian cause, and more attention is given to matters related to true Islamic principles—ecology, the war against hunger and over-population in the developing world, and the struggle for women's rights in different cultures. Not the lightest of programming, but there are often valid points of view to be heard here. To Europe, winters only, on 9022, plus 6035 or 11895 kHz. One hour earlier in summer.

Radio Yugoslavia, located in Serbia. This time winters only; see 2200. A valuable source of *news* about the region. To Europe and Africa on 6165 and 15165 kHz.

Radio Sweden. See 1530 for program details. To Europe on 6065 and 7265 or 9655 kHz.

Radio Romania International. See 0200 for program details, although programs are one day earlier. Sixty minutes to Europe on any three frequencies from 5955, 5990, 7195, 9690, 9750 and 11810 kHz.

Radio Prague International, Czechoslovakia. This time winters only. A half hour of *News* and features (dealing mostly with Czechoslovak issues). To Europe on 6055 and 9605 kHz.

Radio Finland. Winters only. Monday through Friday, it's *Northern Report* and *Press Review* followed by a ten-minute feature. On weekends there's *News Update*, followed Saturday by *Perspectives* and *Starting Finnish*. Sunday is given over to *Business Monday*—a touch of Finnish-Irish logic? Twenty-five minutes to Europe on 6120, 9550 and 11755 kHz. One hour earlier in summer.

1945

Radio Sofia, Bulgaria. Summers only at this time; see 2045. Forty-five minutes to Europe and Africa on 11765, 17780 and 17825 kHz. One hour later during winter.

2000

BBC World Service. *World News*, then news analysis weekdays on *The World Today*. Saturday, there's *Personal View*, with jazz or folk on Sunday. These are followed

Radio France Internationale has some of the world's most extensive news resources. Reporter Hélène da Costa interviews Kurdish fighters at the Altin Köprü battlefield in the Kurdistan area of Iraq.

by *Words of Faith*, then a quiz or feature program. Recommended at this time are *Meridian* (Tuesday, Thursday, Saturday), *The Vintage Chart Show* (Monday), *Science in Action* (Friday) or *Assignment* (Wednesday). Continuous to most of Eastern North America on 5975 and 15260 kHz; to Western Europe on 3955, 6195, 7325, 9410, 12095 and 15070 kHz; to East Asia on 7180, 11750 or 15340 kHz; and to the Pacific on 11750 and 15340 kHz.

Christian Science Monitor World Service, USA. See 1600 for program details. Monday through Friday to Europe and North America on 13770 and 15610 kHz; to East Asia on 9455 kHz; and to the Pacific on 13625 kHz.

Radio Damascus, Syria. Actually starts at 2005. *News*, ample amounts of Syrian music, a daily press review, and a different feature for each day of the week. These include *Portrait from Our Country*, *Around the World in a Week* and *Reflections on Arab Literature*. Most of the transmission, however, is given over to Syrian and some Western popular music. One hour to Europe, often also audible in Eastern North America, on any two of four frequencies: 9950, 11625, 12085 or 15095 kHz.

Radio Moscow World Service. Part of a 24-hour service for the English-speaking world, but with the accent on Europe at this time of day. Targeted to Europe, North America and the Pacific on scads of frequencies. Dial around to find it.

Radio Canada International. This time winters only. One hour of CBC domestic fare beamed to Europe on 5995, 7235, 11945, 13650, 15140, 15325 and 17875 kHz.

Radio Beijing, China. *News*, then various feature programs; see 0000 for details, although all programs are one day earlier. To Europe winters on 7315 and 9920 kHz, summers on 9920 and 11500 kHz.

Voice of Turkey. Summers only at this time. *News*, followed by *Review of the Turkish Press*, then features on Turkish history, culture and international relations, interspersed with enjoyable selections of the country's popular and classical music. Fifty minutes to Western Europe on 9795 kHz.

KNLS, Alaska, USA. See 0800 for program details. To East Asia and the Pacific; winters on 11880 kHz, summers on 11910 kHz.

Swiss Radio International. Winters only at this time. See 0830 for program details. To Europe on 3985, 6165 and 9535 kHz.

Radio Pyongyang, North Korea. Repeat of the 1100 broadcast. To Europe and beyond on 6576, 9345, 9640 and 9977 kHz.

Radio Portugal. Winters only at this time. *News*, followed by a feature about Portugal; see 1900 for program details. A half hour to Europe Monday through Friday on 11740 kHz.

Kol Israel. Winters only at this time.

News, followed by various features (see 2230). A half hour to Europe—often also audible in Eastern North America—on 7465, 9435 and 11605 kHz.

Voice of America. *News*. Listeners in Europe and North Africa can then hear *Music USA* (jazz on Saturday)—replaced Sunday by *The Concert Hall*—on 6040, 9760, 11760 and 15205 kHz. For the rest of Africa there is the daily *Nightline Africa*—with news, interviews and background reports—on 15410, 15580, 17800, 21425 and 21625 kHz. Both transmissions are also audible elsewhere, including parts of North America.

Radio Prague International, Czechoslovakia. This time summers only. *News*, followed by a variety of features, including politics, economy, ecology, sport and cultural affairs (to name but a few). Thirty minutes to Europe on 5930, 6055, 7345, and 9605 kHz.

CFRX-CFRB, Toronto, Canada. See 1400.

2030

Radio Korea, South Korea. See 0800 for program details. One hour to Europe and beyond on 6480, 7550 and 15575 kHz.

Radio Sweden. See 1530 for program details. Thirty minutes to Europe on 6065 kHz.

2045

All India Radio. Press review, Indian music, regional and international news, commentary, and a variety of talks and features of general interest. Continuous till 2230; to Europe on 7412, 9950 and 11620 kHz; and to the Pacific on 9910, 11715 and 15265 kHz.

Radio Sofia, Bulgaria. This time winters only. Forty-five minutes of *news*, features and music (most of it lively Bulgarian folk rhythms). To Europe and Africa on 7155, 9700, 11735, 11840 or 15370 kHz.

2100

BBC World Service. *Newshour*, and what more need one say? The yardstick for all in-depth news shows from international broadcasters. Sixty minutes of excellence. For the uninitiated, it's available to Western Europe on 3955, 6195, 7325, 9410 and 12095 kHz; to most of Eastern North America on 5975 and 15260 kHz, (except 2115-2130 weekdays on 5975 kHz, see below); and to East Asia and the Pacific on 11750 and 15340 kHz.

Christian Science Monitor World Service, USA. See 1700 for program details. Monday through Friday to Europe and North America on 13770 and 15610 kHz; to East Asia on 9455 kHz; and to the Pacific on 13625 kHz.

Radio Yugoslavia, located in Serbia. Summers only at this time. *News* and features, including well-prepared accounts of events in Eastern Europe. A valuable source of news about the region. Forty-five minutes to Europe on 5960 and 11735 kHz, with the latter frequency also audible in Eastern North America.

Spanish Foreign Radio. Repeat of 1900 transmission. To Europe on 9875 and 11790 kHz.

Radio Kiev, Ukraine, USSR. Summers only at this time. *News*, followed by commentary and *The Ukraine Today*, a show covering all aspects of Ukrainian life, from soccer to politics and just about everything in between. The broadcast ends with a different feature each day, including *Society* (Monday), *Dialogue* (Saturday) and *Sunday with Radio Kiev*—a magazine-type program. Sixty minutes to Europe on 5960 and 9865 kHz. One hour later in winter.

Belgische Radio en Televisie, Belgium. Summers only at this time. Repeat of the 1730 transmission; 25 minutes daily to Europe on 5910 and 9925 kHz.

Radio Prague International, Czechoslovakia. *News*, then a variety of features dealing with various aspects of Czechoslovak life and culture. A half hour to Europe on 5930, 6055, 7345 and 9605 kHz.

Radio Beijing, China. Repeat of the 2000 transmission; see 0000 for details, though programs are one day earlier at this time. To Europe winters on 7315 and 9920 kHz, summers on 9920 and 11500 kHz.

Radio Moscow World Service. Continuous to Europe, North America and the Pacific on a wide variety of frequencies. Look around, and find one that suits you.

Radio Budapest, Hungary. Summers only at this time. *News*, followed by a variety of features, including the thrice-weekly (Monday, Thursday and Sunday) *Music and ...!, Letter from Budapest* and *168 Hours* (the pick of the previous week's news stories). Other regular spots include *Talk Back* (conversation and controversy, Thursday and Saturday), *Briefing* (the pick of the week's press conferences, Friday and Sunday) and *Conviction* (open house for people with strong personal beliefs, Sunday). A number of other features are aired on a monthly basis, including *Magazine 90* and *What You Say* (listener participation programs), *Reporter* and *Business Partners*. Sixty minutes to Europe on 6110, 9835 and 11910 kHz. One hour later in winter.

Deutsche Welle, Germany. *News*, followed Sunday through Thursday by *European Journal* and such features as *Man and Environment* (Monday), *Science and Technology* (Sunday), *Insight* (Tuesday), *Living in Germany* (Wednesday) and *Spotlight on Sport* (Thursday). Friday and Saturday programs include *Panorama* and *Economic Notebook* (Friday), and *Commentary* and *Mailbag Asia* (Saturday). To Asia and the Pacific on 9670, 9765, 11785, 13780 and 15350 kHz.

Radio Japan. Repeat of the 0300 transmission. An hour to East Asia and the Pacific on 11815, 15270 (or 17890), 17765 and 17810 kHz.

Radio Canada International. Summers only at this time. CBC domestic programs for listeners in Europe. Thirty minutes on 5995, 7235 and 13650 kHz; and a full hour on 15325 and 17875 kHz.

Radio Romania International. *News* and commentary, followed by features on Romania—sometimes with some thoroughly enjoyable folk music. A half hour to Europe winters on 5990, 6105, 7105, 7195 and 9690 kHz; summers on 9690, 9750, 11810 and 11940 kHz.

Voice of Turkey. Winters only at this time. See 2000 for program details. To Western Europe on 9795 kHz.

Voice of America. *News*, followed weekdays by *World Report* and on weekends by a variety of features. These depend on the area being served, and include *New Horizons* (Africa, Europe; Sunday), *VOA Pacific* (Sunday), and *Issues in the News* (Africa; Sunday). To Europe on 6040, 11760 and 15205 kHz; to Africa, but often heard elsewhere, on 15410, 15580, 17800, 21485 and 21625 kHz; and to Southeast Asia and the Pacific on 11870, 15185 and 17735 kHz.

Radio Damascus, Syria. Actually starts at 2110. See 2000 for program details. Sixty minutes to North America and the Pacific on 12085 and 9950 or 15095 kHz.

All India Radio. Continues to Europe on 7412, 9950 and 11620 kHz; and to the Pacific on 9910, 11715 and 15265 kHz.

WRNO, USA. Rock music and the like, to North America until around 2400 on 13720 or 15420 kHz.

CFRX-CFRB, Toronto, Canada. See 1400.

2115

BBC World Service for the Caribbean. *Caribbean Report*, although intended for listeners in the area, can also be clearly heard throughout much of Eastern North America. This brief, 15-minute program provides comprehensive coverage of Caribbean economic and political affairs, as well as all-important news of sports. Monday through Friday only, on 6110, 15140 and 17715 kHz.

Radio Cairo. A wide variety of features dealing with Egypt and the Middle East, interlaced with exotic Arab music. These include *Egypt-Europe Weekly Report* (Monday), *Spotlight on the Middle East* (Tuesday), and *Cairo This Week* on Saturday. There are also features on Egyptian history, architecture and tourism. Ninety minutes to Europe on 9900 kHz.

2130

BBC World Service for the Falkland Islands. *Calling the Falklands* is one of the

curiosities of international broadcasting. Chatty and personal, there's probably no other program like it on the international airwaves. Tuesdays and Fridays on 9915 or 13660 kHz—easily heard in North America.

Kol Israel. Summers only at this time. *News*, followed by various features (see 2230). A half hour beamed to Europe and Eastern North America on 9435, 11588, 11605, 15640 and 17575 kHz.

Radio Finland. Summers only at this time. See 2230 for program details. Twenty minutes to Europe on 6120 and 11755 kHz.

Radio Alma-Ata, Kazakhstan, USSR. *News* and commentary, followed by some of the most exotic music to be found on world band radio. Also featured are Kazakh stories and legends—something rarely heard nowadays from international broadcasters, though they were a popular feature 20 or more years ago. These broadcasts are not targeted to any particular part of the world, since the transmitters only use a modest 20 to 50 kilowatts, and the antennas are, in the main, omnidirectional. No matter where you are, try 5960, 5970, 15360, 17715, 17730 and 21490 kHz.

Swiss Radio International. Summers only at this time; see 0830 for program details. To Europe on 6190 kHz.

HCJB, Ecuador. Saturday brings *Musical Mailbag*, Sunday is *Blues, Rags, Jazz*, and the rest of the week is devoted to religious offerings. Thirty minutes to Europe on 17790 and 21480 kHz.

2145

Radio Sofia, Bulgaria. Summers only at this time; the first 15 minutes of a two-and-a-quarter-hour broadcast. See 2200 for program details. To the Americas on 11660, 11710, 15110, 15330, 15370 and 17825 kHz.

2200

BBC World Service. *World News*, followed by any one of a number of features. Worth a mention are *Sports International* (Monday), *Jazz for the Asking* (Saturday), *Global Concerns* and *Network UK* (Thursday), and *People and Politics* (Friday). The hour is rounded off with ten minutes of *Sports Roundup* at 2250. To Eastern North America on 5975, 6175 (winters), 9590, 9915 (or 12095) and 15260 kHz; to Western Europe on 3955, 6195, 7325, 9410 and 12095 kHz; to East Asia on 11955, 15340 and 17830

kHz; and to the Pacific on 11750 (or 11955) and 15340 kHz.

Christian Science Monitor World Service, USA. See 1600 for program details. Monday through Friday to North America on 9465 kHz; to East Asia on 15405 kHz; and to the Pacific on 13625 kHz.

Radio Sofia, Bulgaria. Summers, continuation of 2145 broadcast; winters, does not start until 2245. Two and a quarter hours of news, interviews and features, interspersed with sizable portions of lively Bulgarian folk music. It's not everywhere you can hear an orchestra of 100 bagpipes! To the Americas on 9655 and 9700 (winters), 11660 (summers), 11680 (winters), 15330 (summers), 15370 and 17825 kHz.

Radio Cairo. The second half of a 90-minute broadcast to Europe on 9900 kHz; see 2115 for program details.

Radio Prague International, Czechoslovakia. This time winters only. *News* and features in a magazine-style format. Thirty enjoyable minutes to Europe on 5930, 6055, 7345 and 9605 kHz. Czech it out!

Voice of America. The beginning of a three-hour block of *News*, sports, science, business, music, and features. To East and Southeast Asia on 7120, 9770, 11760, 15185, 15290, 15305, 17735 and 17820 kHz.

Radio Moscow World Service. Another hour of continuous programming, with the accent on Asia and the Pacific. Beamed to North America on 11840 kHz, and to Europe, Asia and the Pacific on a wide variety of channels.

Voice of Free China, Taiwan. See 0200. For Western Europe, winters on 9852.5 and 11805 kHz, and summers on 17850 and 21720 kHz.

Radio Budapest, Hungary. Winters only at this time; see 2100 for program details. Sixty minutes to Europe on 6110, 9835 and 11910 kHz. One hour earlier in summer.

Voice of Turkey. Summers only at this time. See 2000 for program details. Fifty minutes to North America on 9445 kHz; to Europe on 9685 kHz; and to East Asia and the Pacific on 17880 kHz.

Radio Yugoslavia, located in Serbia. This time winters only. *News* and features, providing useful coverage of events in one of the most volatile areas of the world. To Europe on 5955 and 6100 kHz.

Radio Beijing, China. Repeat of the 2000 broadcast. To Europe winters on 7170 kHz, summers on 9740 or 11990 kHz.

Belgische Radio en Televisie, Belgium. Winters only at this time; see 1730 for program details. Twenty-five minutes to Europe on 5910 and 9925 kHz, with the latter frequency also being audible in parts of Eastern North America.

Radio Canada International. Winters only at this time. A relay of CBC domestic fare to Europe. Thirty minutes on 5995, 7135 and 13650 kHz; and one hour on 9760 and 11945 kHz. For a separate summer service to North America, see the next item.

Radio Canada International. Summers only. Monday through Friday, there's CBC's *World at Six*, replaced weekends by other CBC domestic programming. To North America on 5960, 9755, 11905 and 13670 kHz.

Radio Sweden. Repeat of the 1800 transmission; see 1530 for program details. To Europe on 6065 kHz.

Radio Kiev, Ukraine, USSR. Winters only at this time. See 2100 for program details. Sixty minutes to Europe on 6185 kHz.

United Arab Emirates Radio, Abu Dhabi. Begins with *Readings from the Holy Koran*, in which verses are chanted in Arabic, then translated into English. This is followed by a dramatized serialized version of an Arab literary work. The last half hour is a relay of Capital Radio in Abu Dhabi, complete with pop music and local contests. To Eastern North America winters on 9600, 11965 (or 11985) and 13605 kHz, and summers on 13605, 15305 and 17855 kHz.

All India Radio. Final half hour of transmission to Europe on 7412, 9910 and 11620 kHz; and to the Pacific on 7265 and 9550 kHz. Also sometimes audible in Eastern North America on 11620 kHz.

WHRI, Indiana, USA. An hour of religious programming beamed to Western Europe and parts of North America on 13760 and 17830 kHz.

CFRX-CFRB, Toronto, Canada. Live in the northeastern United States or southeastern Canada? Try this pleasant little local station, usually audible for hundreds of miles/kilometers during the hours of daylight. Among the treats: big band and Gaelic music Saturday around 2200-2300 summers on 6070 kHz.

2230

Radio Finland. Winters only at this time. Monday through Friday it's *Northern Report* and *Press Review* followed by a five-minute feature. On Saturdays there's *Perspectives* and a Finnish language lesson, while *Business Monday* is the featured program on the remaining day. Twenty minutes to Europe on 6120 and 11755 kHz.

Kol Israel. Winters only at this time. *News*, followed by a variety of features. These include *Israel Sound* (latest Israeli pop songs), *Studio Three* (arts in Israel), *Shabbat Shalom* (greetings and music requests), *Calling All Listeners* (replies to questions), *DX Corner* (for radio enthusiasts), *Spotlight* (current events), *Spectrum* (science and technology), *With Me in the Studio* (guest interviews), *This Land* (a travel magazine), *Thank Goodness It's Friday* (Sabbath eve program), *Faith to Faith* (religious affairs), *Israel Mosaic* (a weekly magazine), *Letter from Jerusalem*, *Jewish News Review*, and *Living Here*. A half hour to Eastern North America and Europe on 7465, 9435, 11605 and 15640 or 17575 kHz.

Swiss Radio International. Winters only; see 0830 for program details. To Europe on 6190 kHz.

2300

BBC World Service. *News*, then *World Business Report* (Monday-Friday), *World Business Review* (Sunday), or *Words of Faith* (Saturday). The remaining 45 minutes are mainly taken up by music programs like *Multitrack*, *Concert Hall*, *Music Review* or *A Jolly Good Show*, but there are some interesting talks to be found in between. The best of these is Alistair Cooke's *Letter from America*, heard Sunday at 2315. Continuous to North America on 5975, 6175, 9590, 9915 and 7325 or 12095 kHz; to East Asia (till 0030) on 11945, 11955 and 17830 kHz; and to the Pacific (winters only) on 11955 kHz.

Christian Science Monitor World Service, USA. See 1700 for program details. Monday through Friday to North America on 9465 kHz; to East Asia on 15405 kHz; and to the Pacific on 13625 kHz.

Voice of Turkey. Winters only. See 2000 for program details. To Eastern North America on 9445 kHz; to Europe on 9685 kHz; and to Southeast Asia and the Pacific on 17880 kHz. A strong candidate for the "Most Improved Programming" award.

Radio Vilnius, Lithuania, USSR. Summers only at this time. See 0000 for program details. Low key and veridical accounts of events even at the most critical of times. To

Europe and North America on 9710, 11790, 13645, 15180, 15455 and 15485 kHz.

Radio Japan. Similar to the 0300 broadcast, but with *Hello from Tokyo* on Sunday instead of *DX Corner*. One hour to Europe on 11735 kHz; and to East Asia on 11815, 15195 and 17810 kHz.

Radio Sofia, Bulgaria. Continuous programming to the Americas (see 2200) on 9655 and 9700 (winter), 11660 (summer), 11680 (winter), 15330 (summer), 15370 and 17825 kHz.

Radio Pyongyang, North Korea. See 1100 for program details. Fifty minutes to the Americas on 11700 and 13650 kHz.

Radio Moscow World Service. Prime time programming for North America, though also beamed to Asia and the Pacific. An ample choice of frequencies, including 21690 kHz for East and Southeast Asia, and 6045 or 11710 kHz for North America.

Radio Finland. Summers only at this time. See 2230 for program details. Twenty minutes to North America and East Asia on 15185 and 15430 kHz.

United Arab Emirates Radio, Abu Dhabi. The first quarter hour is a review of articles and editorials from the Arab press, which is then followed by a feature with an Islamic slant. The final part of the broadcast is devoted to recordings of Arab music. Heard in Eastern North America winters on 9600, 11965 (or 11985) and 13605 kHz, and summers on 13605, 15305 and 17855 kHz.

Voice of America. *News* and *VOA Morning.* The second hour of programming to East and South East Asia (see 2200) on 7120, 9770, 11760, 15185, 15290, 15305, 17735 and 17820 kHz.

CFRX-CFRB, Toronto, Canada. See 2200.

2305

Radio Polonia, Poland. *News* and commentary, followed by a variety of feature programs, including *Focus* (culture; Thursday), *Panorama* (Wednesday), and *Postbag* (Monday). Fifty minutes to Europe (and sometimes audible in Eastern North America) on 5995, 6135, 7125 and 7270 kHz.

2330

Belgische Radio en Televisie, Belgium. Summers only at this time. See 1730 for program details. Twenty-five minutes to Eastern North America on 13710 or 13720 kHz; also audible on 13655 or 13675 kHz, targeted to South America.

Radio Canada International. Summers only at this time. A relay of CBC's excellent weekday *news* program *As It Happens*, with weekends being given over to alternative programs from the CBC domestic network. To Eastern North America on 5960 and 9755 kHz; also on 13670 kHz Monday through Friday.

Radio Sweden. Repeat of the 1530 transmission. Targeted to Latin America, but also heard in Eastern North America, on 9695 and 11705 kHz.

Radio Tirana, Albania. *News*, followed by such enlightening features as reports on the activities of the Albanian parliament. Fortunately for all concerned, these are interspersed with some pleasant Albanian music. To North America on 6120, 9760 and 11825 kHz.

Prepared by Don Swampo and the staff of Passport to World Band Radio.

WORLDWIDE BROADCASTS IN ENGLISH

Country-by-Country Guide to Best-Heard Stations

Dozens of countries, large and small, reach out to us in English over world band radio. Here are the times and frequencies (channels) where you're most likely to hear them.

Four Helpful Tips

- Best time to listen, in general, is during the late afternoon and evening. This is when most programs are targeted to your location. An exception for North Americans: Some Asian and Pacific stations are strongest around dawn.
- Best times to listen in North America and Europe are in bold—for example, **2200-0430**.
- Best late-afternoon and evening frequencies are usually 5850-12100 kHz, sometimes even 3900-17900 kHz. Earlier in the day, try 9250-21785 kHz, sometimes even 5850-26100 kHz. See *World Band Spectrum* in the glossary at the back of the book for how to tune for best results.
- Best frequencies are often those in bold—say, **6175** —as they are from transmitters that may be located near you.

World Time Simplifies Listening

Times and days of the week are given in World Time, explained in the *Passport* glossary. Midyear, many programs are heard an hour earlier, whereas some in the Southern Hemisphere are heard an hour later.

World Time—a handy concept also known as UTC and GMT—is used to eliminate the potential complication of so many time zones throughout the world. It treats the entire planet as a single zone and is announced regularly on the hour by many world band stations.

For example, if you're in New York and it's 6:00 AM EST, you will hear World Time announced as "11 hours." A glance at your clock shows that this is five hours ahead of your local time. You can either keep this figure in your head or use a separate clock for World Time. A growing number of world band radios come with World Time clocks built in, and separate 24-hour clocks are also widely available.

Schedules Prepared for Entire Year

To be as helpful as possible throughout the year, *Passport's* schedules consist not just of observed activity, but also that which we have creatively opined will take place during the entire year. This latter information is original from us, and therefore, of course, will not be so exact as factual information.

Broadcasts in other than English? Turn to the next section—"Voices from Home." Also, the Blue Pages give detailed information on broadcasts in all languages, including English.

AFGHANISTAN
RADIO AFGHANISTAN
0930-1030	6085 (S Asia & Mideast), 9635 (Mideast & S Asia), **15255**, **15350** & **17655** (S Asia), **17720** (Mideast & S Asia), **21600** (S Asia)
1800-1900	**4915**, **6020**, **7215**, 9635 & **15510** (**Europe**)

ALBANIA
RADIO TIRANA
0230-0300	9580, 9760 & 11825 (**E North Am** & C America)
0330-0400	9580, 9760 & 11825 (**E North Am** & C America)
0530-0600	9500 (**Europe**)
0630-0700	7205 & 9500 (**Europe**)
1130-1200	9480 & 11835 (Australia)
1400-1430	9500 & 11985 (Australia)
1730-1800	9480 (**Europe**)
1830-1900	7120 & 9480 (**Europe**)
1930-2100	9500 (**Europe**)
2130-2200	9480 (**Europe**)
2230-2300	7215 (**W Europe**), 9480 (**Europe**)
2330-2400	6121 (**E North Am**), 9760 & 11825 (**E North Am** & C America)

ALGERIA
RTV ALGERIENNE—(**Europe**)
1900-2000	9509, 9685

ARGENTINA
RADIO ARGENTINA-RAE
0200-0300	Tu-Sa 11710 (**Americas**)
1900-2000	M-F 15345 (**Europe**)

AUSTRALIA
ABC/CAAMA RADIO
2130-0830	4835, 4910

ABC/RADIO RUM JUNGLE
2130-0830	5025

AUSTRALIAN BROADCASTING CORP
24h	9610 (Perth)
24h	9660 (Brisbane)
0900-0100	6140 (Perth)
1900-1400	4920 (Brisbane)
2245-0915	15425 (Perth)

RADIO AUSTRALIA
0000-0100	17630 (E Asia)
0000-0400	17750 (E Asia)
0000-0530	17715 (Pacific)
0000-1030	15240 (Pacific)
0100-0900	21525 (E Asia)
0100-1300	21775 (S Asia)
0330-0430	Sa/Su 15530 (E Asia)
0330-0500	Sa/Su 17630 (E Asia)
0330-0730	21740 (Pacific)
0400-0500	Sa/Su 17750 (E Asia)
0430-0500	17630 (E Asia)
0430-0600	15530 (E Asia)
0430-1000	17630 (E Asia)
0500-0600	17750 (E Asia)
0600-0700	15365 (Pacific)
0630-0800	13705 (Pacific)
0800-0930	6080, 7240 & 9710 (Pacific)
0800-1200	15365 (Pacific)
0800-1330	15160 (Pacific)
0830-1930	9580 (Pacific & **N America**)
0900-1100	25750 (S Asia)
0900-1230	21825 (E Asia)
1000-1100	13605 & 15170 (E Asia)
1000-1230	11800 (Pacific)
1100-1200	11765 & 15170 (E Asia)
1100-1330	21720 (S Asia)
1100-1530	9710 (Pacific)
1100-2100	6080 & 7240 (Pacific)
1100-0930	11930 (Pacific)
1130-2100	5995 (Pacific)
1300-1530	11720 (Pacific)
1330-1800	17630 (S Asia)
1400-1830	11800 (Pacific)
1430-1800	9860 (S Asia), 12000 (E Asia)
1430-2100	13745 (S Asia)
1500-2130	6060 (Pacific)
1600-2030	11910 (Pacific)
1600-2130	13605 (Pacific)
2000-0700	17795 (Pacific)
2030-0200	15465 (Pacific)
2100-0730	15320 (Pacific)
2100-0800	11880 (Pacific)
2130-2200	17715 & 21740 (Pacific)
2130-0700	15160 (Pacific)
2200-2400	15240 & 17715 (Pacific)
2200-0330	21740 (Pacific)
2300-0800	17855 (E Asia)

AUSTRIA
RADIO AUSTRIA INTERNATIONAL
0130-0200	9875 (**N America** & C America), 13730 (**N America**)
0530-0600	**6015** (**N America**), 6155 & 13730 (**Europe**), 15410 & 21490 (Mideast)
0730-0800	6155 & 13730 (**Europe**), 15410 & 21490 (Mideast)
0830-0900	6155 & 13730 (**Europe**), 15450 & 21490 (Australia)
1030-1100	15450 & 21490 (Australia)
1130-1200	6155 & 13730 (**Europe**), 15430 (E Asia), 21490 (**E North Am**)
1330-1400	15430 (E Asia)
1430-1500	6155 (**Europe**), 11780 (S Asia), 13730 (**Europe**)
1630-1700	6155 (**Europe**), 11780 (S Asia), 13730 (**Europe**)
1730-1800	5945 & 6155 (**Europe**), 12010 (Mideast)
1930-2000	5945 & 6155 (**Europe**), 12010 (Mideast)

BAHRAIN
RADIO BAHRAIN
0300-2105	6010 (Mideast)

BANGLADESH
RADIO BANGLADESH
1200-1230	15208 & 17750 (**Europe**)
1745-1900	9578 & 12030 (**Europe**)

BELGIUM
BELGISCHE RADIO & TV
0030-0055	9925 & 13710 (**E North Am**)
0630-0655	6035 (**Europe**), 11695 (**Europe** & Australia), 13675 (**Europe**)
0730-0755	6035 (**Europe**), 11695 (**Europe** & Australia), 13675 (**Europe**)
0900-0925	M-Sa 9925 & M-Sa 13675 (**Europe**)
1000-1025	M-Sa 6035 & M-Sa 13675 (**Europe**)
1130-1155	Su 9925 (**Europe**), Su 21815 (**E North Am**)

1230-1255	Su 21815 (**E North Am**)
1300-1325	M-Sa 21815 (**E North Am**)
1400-1425	M-Sa 21815 (**E North Am**)
1730-1755	9925 & 13675 (**Europe**)
1830-1855	5910 (**Europe**)
2100-2125	5910 & 9925 (**Europe**)
2200-2225	5910 (**Europe**)
2200-2255	9925 (**Europe**)

BHUTAN
BHUTAN BROADCASTING SERVICE

0900-1000	Su 5025 (S Asia)
1415-1500	M-Sa 5025 (S Asia)

BRAZIL
RADIO NACIONAL (RADIOBRAS)

1200-1320	11745 (**N America** & C America)
1800-1920	15265 (**Europe**)

BULGARIA
RADIO SOFIA

1730-1900	11660, 11720, 15330 & 17780 (**Europe**)
1830-2000	7155, 9700, 11765 & 15330 (**Europe**)
1945-2030	17780 (**Europe**)
2045-2130	9700 (**Europe**)
2145-2400	11660 (**Europe** & **E North Am**), 11710 (C America), 15330 (**E North Am**)
2245-0100	9700 & 11680 (**E North Am** & C America)

CANADA
CANADIAN BC CORP—(**E North Am**)

0000-0300	Su 9625
0200-0300	Tu-Sa 9625
0300-0310	M 9625
0330-0610	M 9625
0400-0610	Su 9625
0500-0610	Tu-Sa 9625
1200-1255	M-F 9625
1200-1505	Sa 9625
1200-1700	Su 9625
1700-1805	Sa 9625
1800-2400	Su 9625
2200-2225	M-F 9625
2240-2330	M-F 9625

CFCX-CFCF

24h	6005 (Montréal) (**E North Am**)

CFRX-CFRB

24h	6070 (Toronto) (**E North Am**)

CFVP-CFCN

24h	6030 (Calgary) (**N America**)

CHNX-CHNS

24h	6130 (Halifax) (**E North Am**)

CKFX-CKWX

24h	6080 (Vancouver) (**W North Am**)

CKZN-CBN

0930-0500	6160 (St. John's, Nfld.) (**E North Am**)

CKZU-CBU

24h	6160 (Vancouver) (**W North Am**)

RADIO CANADA INTERNATIONAL

0000-0030	Tu/Sa 13670 (**E North Am**)
0000-0130	5960 & 9755 (**E North Am** & C America)
0030-0100	Su/M 5960 & Su/M 9755 (**E North Am** & C America)
0100-0130	9755 (**E North Am** & C America)
0100-0200	Su/M 11845 (C America)
0130-0200	Su/M 5960 & Su/M 9755 (**E North Am** & C America)
0200-0300	Tu-Sa 9755 (**E North Am** & C America), Tu-Sa 11845 (C America)
0400-0430	**6150** (**Europe**), **9505** (Mideast), **9670** (**Europe**), **11925** & **15275** (Mideast)
0515-0600	M-F **6050**, M-F 6150, M-F **7295** & M-F 9750 (**Europe**)
0615-0700	M-F **6050**, M-F 6150, M-F **7155** & M-F 9760 (**Europe**), M-F **11905** (Mideast)
1200-1300	M-F 17820 (C America)
1200-1400	M-F 11855 (**E North Am**)
1300-1400	Su 11955 (**E North Am**), M-F 17820 (C America)
1300-1600	Su 17820 (C America)
1330-1400	**6095, 6150, 9535, 9700** & **11795** (E Asia)
1400-1430	**11935**, M-Sa 15305, **15315**, **15325**, M-Sa 17795, **17820** & 21545 (**Europe**)
1400-1700	Su 11955 (**E North Am**), Su 17820 (C America)
1430-1500	**6150** (E Asia)
1500-1530	**9555** (**Europe**), **11915** (E Europe), **11935**, M-Sa 13650, M-Sa 15305, M-Sa 15315, **15325** & 21545 (**Europe**)
1600-1630	**9555, 11935**, M-Sa 13650, 15305, M-Sa 15325, **15325**, M-Sa 17820, 17820 & 21545 (**Europe**)
1630-1700	**7150** & **9555** (S Asia)
1700-1730	**5995, 7235, 9555**, 13650, **15325**, 17820 & 21545 (**Europe**)
1800-1830	**5995, 7235**, 11945, 15325 & 17875 (**Europe**)
1900-1930	**5995** & **7235** (**Europe**)
1900-2000	21675 (**Europe**)
1900-2130	13650 (**Europe**)
1900-2200	15325 & 17875 (**Europe**)
1930-2000	**6170** (**Europe**), **9650** (E Asia), **9670** (**Europe**)
2000-2030	**5995** & **7235** (**Europe**)
2000-2100	11945, 15140 & 17820 (**Europe**)
2030-2100	**6010** & **7230** (**Europe**), **9650** (E Asia)
2100-2130	**5995** (**Europe**)
2200-2230	5960 (**E North Am** & C America), **5995** & **7180** (**Europe**), 9755 & 11905 (**E North Am** & C America), 13650 (**Europe**)
2200-2300	9760, 11945 & 13670 (**Europe**)
2300-2330	11730 & 13670 (C America)
2300-2400	9755 (**E North Am** & C America)
2330-2400	5960 (**E North Am** & C America), M-F 13670 (**E North Am**)

CHINA (PR)
RADIO BEIJING

0000-0100	9665 (**E North Am** & C America), **9770** & **11715** (**N America**), 15285 (**E North Am** & C America), 17705 (**E North Am** & C America)
0300-0400	**9690** (**N America** & C America), **9770** & **11715** (**N America**), 15285 (**E North Am** & C America)

0400-0500	11685 & 11695 (**W North Am**), 11840 (**N America**)
0500-0600	9770 & 11840 (**N America**)
0900-1000	11755, 15440 & 17710 (Australia)
1100-1300	9665 (**E North Am** & C America)
1200-1300	17715 (**E North Am**), 17855 (**E North Am** & C America)
1200-1400	11600 (Pacific), 15285 (Australia)
1300-1500	11855 (**W North Am**)
1400-1600	11600 & 15165 (S Asia)
1900-2100	6955, 9440 & 11515 (Mideast)
2000-2100	9785 (Mideast)
2000-2200	6920, 9710, 9820, 9920 & 11500 (**Europe**)
2200-2230	3985 (**Europe**)

CHINA (TAIWAN)
VOICE OF FREE CHINA
0200-0300	5950 (**E North Am**), 11740 (C America)
0200-0400	9680 (**W North Am**), 9765 (Australia), 15345 (E Asia)
0300-0400	5950 (**E North Am** & C America)
0700-0800	5950 (C America)
2200-2300	9852, 11805, 17750 & 21720 (**Europe**)

CLANDESTINE (N AMERICA)
"VOICE OF TOMORROW"—(**E North Am**)
1430-1525	15039 (Irr)
2100-2200	6240 (Irr)
2300-2355	7410 (Irr)

COSTA RICA
ADVENTIST WORLD RADIO—(C America)
1100-1230	9725, 11870
1230-1300	Su-F 9725, Su-F 11870
2300-0100	9725, 11870
FARO DEL CARIBE
| 0300-0355 | 5055, 9645 |
RADIO CASINO
0300-0400	M 5954
0400-0600	5954
1100-1200	5954
RADIO FOR PEACE INTERNATIONAL
0030-1230	Tu-Sa 7375 & Tu-Sa 13630 (C America & **N America**), Tu-Sa 15030 (**N America**)
1800-2000	Sa/Su 7375 (C America), Sa/Su 13630 (C America & **N America**), Sa/Su 15030 (**N America**)
2000-0030	7375 (C America), 13630 (C America & **N America**), 15030 (**N America**)

CUBA
RADIO HABANA
0000-0600	11820 (**E North Am**)
0200-0450	9505 & 15140 (**N America**)
0400-0600	5965 & 11760 (C America)
1900-2100	15435 & 17705 (**Europe**)
2000-2100	11850 (Mideast)
2200-2300	7215 (**W Europe**), 11930 (Europe)

CZECHOSLOVAKIA
RADIO PRAGUE INTERNATIONAL
| 0000-0030 | 7345 (**Americas**), 9540 (**E North Am**), 11685 & 11990 (**Americas**) |

0100-0130	5930 & 7345 (**Americas**), 9540 (**E North Am**), 11685 (**Americas**)
0300-0330	5930 & 7345 (**Americas**), 9540 (**E North Am**), 11685 (**Americas**)
0400-0430	5930 & 7345 (**Americas**), 9540 (**E North Am**), 11685 (**Americas**)
0730-0800	17840 & 21705 (Australia)
0740-0800	6055, 7345 & 9505 (**Europe**)
0840-0900	6055, 7345 & 9505 (**Europe**)
0940-1000	6055, 7345 & 9505 (**Europe**)
1040-1100	6055, 7345 & 9505 (**Europe**)
1140-1200	6055, 7345 & 9505 (**Europe**)
1240-1300	6055, 7345 & 9505 (**Europe**)
1800-1830	5930, 6055, 7345 & 9605 (**Europe**)
1930-2000	6055 & 9605 (**Europe**)
2100-2130	5930, 6055, 7345 & 9605 (**Europe**)
2200-2230	5930, 6055, 7345 & 9605 (**Europe**)

ECUADOR
HCJB-VOICE OF THE ANDES
0030-0430	9745 (C America & **N America**), 15155 (**N America** & C America), 21455 & 25950 (**Europe** & Pacific)
0500-0700	9745 (C America & **N America**), 15155 (**N America** & C America)
0700-0830	6205, 9610, 11835 & 15270 (**Europe**)
0700-1130	21455 & 25950 (**Europe** & Pacific)
0730-1130	9745 (Australia), 11925 (Australia & Pacific)
1130-1500	11925 (C America & **E North Am**)
1200-1600	15115 (**Americas**), 17890 (**N America** & C America), 21455 & 25950 (**Europe** & Pacific)
1630-1715	21480 (Mideast)
1630-1800	21455 & 25950 (**Europe** & Pacific)
1715-1730	M-F 21480 (Mideast)
1730-1800	15270 (**Europe**)
1900-2000	15270 & 17790 (**Europe**), 21455 (**Europe** & Pacific), 21480 (**Europe**), 25950 (**Europe** & Pacific)
2130-2200	15270 & 17790 (**Europe**), 21455 (**Europe** & Pacific), 21480 (**Europe**), 25950 (**Europe** & Pacific)

EGYPT
RADIO CAIRO
0200-0330	9475 (**N America** & C America), 9675 (**N America**)
1215-1330	17595 (S Asia)
2115-2245	9900 (**Europe**)

FINLAND
RADIO FINLAND
0000-0020	9645 & 11755 (**N America**)
0730-0745	6120, 9560 & 11755 (**Europe**)
0830-0855	21550 (E Asia)
0900-0930	17800 & 21550 (Australia)
0930-0955	15245 & 17800 (E Asia)
1230-1250	M-F 15400 & M-F 21550 (**N America**)
1330-1355	M-F 15400 & M-F 21550 (**N America**)
1400-1430	11820 (**E Europe**), 15185 (Mideast), Sa/Su 15400 & Sa/Su 21550 (**N America**), 21550 (Mideast)
1430-1445	15400 & 21550 (**N America**)
1500-1530	6120 & 11755 (**Europe**), 11850 & 15185 (Mideast)

1830-1855	15185 (**Europe**)
1930-2000	6120, 9550 & 11755 (**Europe**)
2230-2250	6120, 9550 & 11755 (**Europe**)
2300-2320	15185 & 15430 (**N America**)

FRANCE
RADIO FRANCE INTERNATIONALE

1230-1300	9805, 11670, 15155 & 15195 (**E Europe**), 17650 & 21635 (**E North Am**), 21645 (**C America**)
1400-1500	**4130** (E Asia), **7125** & **11910** (S Asia), 17650 (Mideast & S Asia), 21765 (S Asia)
1600-1700	6175 (**Europe**), 15360 & 15530 (Mideast)

GERMANY
DEUTSCHE WELLE

0100-0150	**6040** (**N America**), 6085 & 6145 (**N America** & C America), 7120 (**W Europe** & **E North Am**), 9565 (**E North Am** & C America), 9595 (C America), 9640 (**E North Am**), 11865 (**N America** & C America), 11890 (**E North Am** & C America), 13610 (C America), 13770 (**N America**), **15105** (**E North Am** & C America)
0200-0250	6035 & 7285 (S Asia), 9595 (C America), **9615** (S Asia), 9640 (**E North Am**), 9690, 11945, **11965** & 15235 (S Asia)
0300-0350	**6085** (**N America** & C America), 6120 & 6130 (**N America**), 7275 (**W Europe** & **E North Am**), **9545** (**N America** & C America), **9605** (**N America**), 9640 (**E North Am**), 9665 (C America), 11810 & 11890 (**E North Am** & C America), 13610 (C America), 13770 (**N America**), **15205** (**E North Am** & C America)
0400-0450	7275 (**W Europe** & **E North Am**), 9665 & W 9700 (C America), 11890 (**E North Am** & C America), 13610 (C America), 13770 (**N America**)
0500-0550	5960, 6120 & 6185 (**N America**), 7110 (**Europe**), **9670** (**N America**), 9690 (C America), 9700 (**N America**), 11890 (**E North Am** & C America), 13610 (C America), 13790 (**N America**)
0900-0950	**6160** (C America & Australia), **11740**, **11915** & 17780 (Australia), 17780 (E Asia), **17820** (Australia), 21465 (E Asia), 21650 & 21680 (Australia), 21680 (E Asia)
1100-1150	21465 (S Asia)
1500-1550	17735 (Mideast)
1600-1650	**6170**, **7225**, 9615, 11785, 15105, 15415, 15595, **17810** & **21680** (S Asia)
1900-1950	11925 & 13780 (Mideast)
2100-2150	6185, **9670**, 9765 & **11785** (Australia), 13780 (E Asia), 15360 (Australia)

GHANA
GHANA BROADCASTING CORP

| 0525-0905 | 4915 |
| 1200-2305 | 4915 |

GREECE
FONI TIS HELLADAS ("Voice of Greece")

0135-0145	7430, 9395, 9420 & 11645 (**N America**)
0335-0345	7430, 9395, 9420 & 11645 (**N America**)
0835-0845	15265, 17535 & 17550 (Australia)
1035-1050	11645, 15625, 15630 & 17535 (E Asia)
1235-1245	11645 (**N America**), 15625, 15630, 15650, 17535 & 17550 (**N America** & **Europe**)
1535-1545	11645, 15625, 15630 & 17535 (**N America** & **Europe**)
1920-1930	7430, 9395, 9425 & 11645 (**Europe**)

GUAM
ADVENTIST WORLD RADIO

0200-0300	Sa/Su 13720 (E Asia)
1600-1700	11980 (S Asia)
1700-1800	Sa/Su 13720 (S Asia)

KTWR-TRANS WORLD RADIO

0830-1000	11805 (Australia)
1500-1635	11650 (S Asia)
1635-1700	Su 11650 (S Asia)

GUYANA
VOICE OF GUYANA

| 0730-0200 | 5950 (Irr) |

HOLLAND
RADIO NEDERLAND

0030-0125	6020, **6165** & **15560** (**E North Am**)
0330-0425	**6165** & **9590** (**W North Am**)
0730-0825	**9630**, **9715** & **15560** (Australia)
0830-0855	M-Sa **9770** & **15560** (Australia)
0830-0925	**17575** (S Asia), **21485** (Asia)
1030-1125	**6020** (C America), **11890** (Australia)
1130-1225	5955 & 9715 (**Europe**), **17575** (E Asia), 21520 (S Asia)
1430-1525	5955 (**Europe**), 13770, **15150**, **17575** & 17605 (S Asia)

HONDURAS
LA VOZ EVANGELICA

| 0300-0500 | M 4820 |

HUNGARY
RADIO BUDAPEST

| 0300-0400 | 6110, 9835 & 11910 (**N America**) |
| 2200-2300 | 6110, 9835 & 11910 (**Europe**) |

ICELAND
RIKISUTVARPID—(Atlantic & **Europe**)

| 0730-0745 | M-F 6100 & 9265 |

INDIA
ALL INDIA RADIO

| 1845-1945 | 7412 & 11620 (**Europe**) |
| 2045-2230 | 7412 (**Europe**), 9910 (Australia), 9950 & 11620 (**Europe**), 11715 & 15265 (Australia) |

INDONESIA
RADIO REPUBLIK INDONESIA

| 1130-1145 | 5046 |
| 1330-1400 | Sa 4805 |

VOICE OF INDONESIA
0100-0200	11753 (Asia & Pacific), 11785 (Asia)
0800-0900	11753 (Asia & Pacific), 11785 (Asia)
2000-2100	11753 & 11785 (**Europe**)

IRAN
VOICE OF THE ISLAMIC REPUBLIC
1030-1130	7115, 11715, 11930 & 11940 (Mideast)
1130-1230	9525 & 9685 (Mideast), 9705 (S Asia), 11745 (Mideast), 11790 (S Asia)
1930-2030	6035 & 9022 (**Europe**)

ISRAEL
KOL ISRAEL
1430-1500	11587 (**Europe**), 11605 (**E Europe**), 15590 (**Europe**)
1800-1815	11587 (**Europe**), 11675 (**E Europe**), 15590 (**Europe**)
1900-1930	17685 (**Europe, E North Am** & C America)
2000-2030	9435 (**W Europe** & **E North Am**), 11587 & 11605 (**Europe**), 11675 (**E Europe**), 15640 (**Europe**), 17630 (Mideast)
2130-2200	15100 (**E Europe**), 17685 (**Europe, E North Am** & C America)
2230-2300	9435 (**W Europe** & **E North Am**), 11587 (**Europe**), 11605 (**Europe, E North Am** & C America), 15640 (**E North Am** & C America)

ITALY
ADVENTIST WORLD RADIO—(**Europe**)
0830-0900	7230
0900-1000	Su **9670**
1130-1200	7230

EUROPEAN CHRISTIAN RADIO
0700-0730	Su 6210 (**Europe**)

ITALIAN RADIO RELAY—(**Europe**)
0500-0600	Su 9815
0600-0800	M-F 9815
0800-0815	Sa 9815
0815-0930	Sa/Su 9815
0930-1000	Sa 9815
1030-1400	Su 9815
1400-1500	Sa/Su 9815
1500-1600	9815
2030-2200	9815

RTV ITALIANA
0100-0120	9575 (**E North Am**), 11800 (**E North Am** & C America)
0425-0440	5990, 7275 & 9575 (**Europe** & Mideast)
1935-1955	7275, 9710 & 11800 (**Europe**)
2025-2045	7235 (**E Europe** & Mideast), 9575 & 11800 (Mideast)
2200-2225	5990, 9710, 11800 & 15330 (E Asia)
2230-0500	6060 (**Europe** & Mideast)

JAPAN
RADIO JAPAN/NHK
0100-0200	**5960** (**E North Am** & C America), **11840** (S Asia), 15195 & 17835 (E Asia), 17845 (S Asia)
0300-0330	**15325** (C America), 17825 (**W North Am** & C America), 21610 (Pacific)

0300-0400	**5960** (**E North Am** & C America), 15195 (E Asia)
0300-0600	11870 (**W North Am**)
0500-0600	15195 (Pacific & **N America**), 17765 (E Asia), 17825 (**W North Am** & C America), 17890 (Australia)
0700-0800	15325 (**Europe**), 17765 (E Asia), 17890 (Australia), **21690** (**Europe**)
0900-1000	11840 (E Asia), 15270 & 17890 (Australia)
1100-1200	**6120** (**N America**), 11840 (E Asia)
1400-1500	**9535** (S Asia)
1400-1600	9505 & 11865 (Pacific & **W North Am**)
1700-1800	7140 (E Asia), 9505 & 11865 (Pacific & **W North Am**), **15345** (Mideast)
1900-1930	9505 (Pacific & **W North Am**), 9640 & 11850 (Australia), 11865 (Pacific & **W North Am**), 15270 (Australia)
2100-2130	15270 (Australia)
2100-2200	11815 (E Asia), 17890 (Australia)
2300-2400	**11735** (**Europe**), 11815 & 15195 (E Asia)

JORDAN
RADIO JORDAN—(**Europe**)
1200-1415	13655
1420-1730	9560

KOREA (DPR)
RADIO PYONGYANG
0000-0050	13760 & 15115 (C America)
1100-1150	6576, 9977 & 11335 (C America)
1300-1350	9325 (**Europe**), 9345 (**Europe** & Mideast), 9640 (S Asia)
1500-1550	9325 (**Europe**), 9640 (Mideast), 11760 (**Europe**)
1700-1750	9325 (**Europe**), 9640 (Mideast), 11760 (**Europe**)
2000-2050	6576 (**Europe**), 9345 (**Europe** & Mideast), 9640 (Mideast)
2300-2350	11700 & 13650 (C America)

KOREA (REPUBLIC)
RADIO KOREA
0000-0100	15575 (**E North Am**)
0045-0100	7275 (E Asia)
0245-0300	6165 (E Asia)
0600-0700	11810 & 15170 (**N America**)
0800-0900	7550 & 13670 (**Europe**)
0915-0930	13670 (**Europe**)
1030-1100	**11715** (**N America**)
1115-1130	7275 & 11740 (E Asia)
1130-1200	**9700** (**N America**)
1215-1315	9750 (**E North Am**)
1330-1345	7275 & 11740 (E Asia)
1545-1600	7275 (E Asia)
1600-1700	5975 (E Asia), 9870 (Mideast)
1715-1730	9870 (Mideast)
1800-1900	15575 (**Europe**)
2030-2130	6480 (**Europe**), 7550 (Mideast), 15575 (**Europe**)
2045-2100	5975 (E Asia), 9870 (Mideast)

LEBANON
KING OF HOPE
0700-1100	6280 (Mideast), 11530 (**Europe**)
1400-1700	6280 (Mideast), 11530 (**Europe**)

VOICE OF LEBANON
0900-0915   6550
1315-1330   6550
1815-1830   6550

LUXEMBOURG
RADIO LUXEMBOURG
24h   15350 (**E North Am**)

MALAYSIA
RADIO TV MALAYSIA
0100-0500   Su-Th 7295
0500-0600   7295
0600-0900   Sa-Th 7295
0930-1600   7295
2200-0100   7295
VOICE OF MALAYSIA
0555-0825   15295 (Australia)

MALTA
VO MEDITERRANEAN—(**Europe** & Mideast)
0600-0700   9765
1400-1500   11925

MONACO
TRANS WORLD RADIO
0740-0950   9480 (**W Europe**)
0950-1005   Sa 9480 (**W Europe**)
0955-1035   11655 (**Europe**)

MONGOLIA
RADIO ULAANBAATAR
0910-0940   11850 (Australia), W/Th/Sa-M
            12015 (E Asia & Australia), 12015
            (Australia)
1200-1230   W/Th/Sa-M 11850 (E Asia)
1445-1515   M-Sa 9795 & M-Sa 13780 (E Asia)
1940-2010   11850 & 12050 (**Europe**)

MOROCCO
RTV MAROCAINE—(**Europe**)
1530-1700   M-F 17595
1700-1800   Sa 17815
1900-2000   Su 11920

MYANMAR (BURMA)
VOICE OF MYANMAR
0200-0230   7185
0700-0730   9730
1430-1600   5990

NAMIBIA
NAMIBIAN BROADCASTING CORP
0600-1600   7189.5

NEPAL
RADIO NEPAL
0215-0225   5005, 7165
1115-1145   5005 & 7165 (S Asia)
1415-1425   5005, 7165

NETHERLANDS ANTILLES
TRANS WORLD RADIO
0300-0400   9535 & 11930 (**N America**)
1100-1300   11815 & 15345 (**E North Am**)

NEW ZEALAND
RADIO NEW ZEALAND INTL—(Pacific)
0630-1110   9700

1700-2110   Su-F 13785
2105-0630   17770

NIGERIA
FEDERAL RADIO CORP
0400-2305   6025
RADIO NIGERIA
0400-2300   6050
0430-2310   4770, 4990, 9570
1000-1700   7285

NORWAY
RADIO NORWAY INTERNATIONAL
0100-0130   Su/M 9605, Su/M 11925 & Su/M
              15360 (**E North Am** & C America)
0200-0230   Su/M 9615 (**E North Am** & C
              America), Su/M 11730 & Su/M
              11925 (**N America**)
0400-0430   Su/M 11865 (**N America**)
1200-1230   Sa/Su 17820 (Mideast & S Asia),
              Sa/Su 21695 & Sa/Su 25730 (S Asia
              & Australia)
1300-1330   Sa/Su 9590, Sa/Su 11745 & Sa/Su
              11860 (**Europe**)
1500-1530   Sa/Su 17790 (**W North Am**)
1600-1630   Sa/Su 15225 (Mideast & S Asia),
              Sa/Su 21705 & Sa/Su 21730
              (Mideast)
1700-1730   Sa/Su 9655 (**Europe**), Sa/Su 17760
              (**N America**)
1800-1830   Sa/Su 15310 & Sa/Su 17755 (**N
              America**)
1900-1930   Sa/Su 15175 (**Europe**), Sa/Su
              15220 (Australia), Sa/Su 17730 (E
              Asia & Australia), Sa/Su 17730
              (Australia)
2000-2030   Sa/Su 15165 (Atlantic & **E North Am**)
2100-2130   Sa/Su 11850 (Atlantic & **E North Am**)
2200-2230   Sa/Su 21705 (Australia)

PAKISTAN
RADIO PAKISTAN
0230-0245   7095, 7290, 9545, 15114 & 21730
              (S Asia)
0800-0845   17870 & 21520 (**Europe**)
1100-1120   17870 & 21520 (**Europe**)
1600-1630   5905 & 7290 (S Asia), 13665,
              15605, 17555 & 21580 (Mideast)
1700-1800   7305, 9370, 11570 & 15550
              (**Europe**)

PAPUA NEW GUINEA
NBC
1915-1400   4890

PHILIPPINES
FEBC RADIO INTERNATIONAL—(S Asia)
0000-0200   15450
0200-0230   M-F 15450
0900-1100   9800

POLAND
RADIO POLONIA
0630-0700   6135, 7270 & 9675 (**Europe**)
1200-1230   6095, 7285 & 11815 (**Europe**)
1230-1300   9525 (**Europe**), 11840 (**W Europe**)
1430-1455   6135, 7285 & 9540 (**Europe**),
              11815 (**W Europe**)
1600-1630   6135 & 9540 (**Europe**)

1630-1700	9525 (**Europe**), 11840 (**W Europe**)
1830-1855	5995, 6135, 7285 & 9525 (**Europe**), 11840 (**W Europe**)
2000-2030	9525 (**Europe**), 11840 (**W Europe**)
2230-2355	5995, 6135, 7125 & 7270 (**Europe**)

PORTUGAL
RADIO PORTUGAL INTERNATIONAL

0230-0300	Tu-Sa 9555 (**E North Am**), Tu-Sa 9705 (**N America**)
1600-1630	M-F 15425 (Mideast & S Asia)
2000-2030	M-F 11740 (**Europe**)

ROMANIA
RADIO ROMANIA INTERNATIONAL

0200-0300	5990, 6155, 9510, 9570, 11830, 11940 & 15380 (**Americas**)
0400-0430	5990, 6155, 9510, 9570, 11830, 11940 & 15380 (**Americas**)
0645-0715	11940 & 15250 (Australia), 15335 (Asia & Australia), 17720, 17805 & 21550 (Australia)
1200-1230	17720 (S Asia)
1300-1330	11940 (**Europe**)
1300-1400	15365 (**Europe**), 17850 & 21550 (**W Europe**)
1500-1530	11940 (Mideast & S Asia), 15250 (Mideast), 15335 & 17720 (S Asia), 17745 (Mideast & S Asia)
1930-2030	6105, 7105, 7195, 9690, 9750, 11810 & 11940 (**Europe**)
2100-2130	5990, 6105, 7105, 7195, 9690, 9750 & 11940 (**Europe**)

SAUDI ARABIA
BROADCASTING SVC OF THE KINGDOM

1600-2100	9705 (**Europe**)

SEYCHELLES
FAR EAST BROADCASTING ASS'N—(S Asia)

1500-1540	11865
1500-1600	9590, W-Sa 15330
1540-1555	M-Sa 11865
1555-1610	M/Sa 11865
1610-1625	M 11865

SINGAPORE
SINGAPORE BROADCASTING CORP

1000-1600	5010
2200-0100	5010
2200-1605	5052, 11940

SOUTH AFRICA
CAPITAL RADIO

0440-1535	7149.5

RADIO RSA

1500-1755	15210 (Mideast)
1600-1755	17790 or 17835 (Worldwide)

SPAIN
RADIO EXTERIOR DE ESPANA

0000-0200	9630 (**E North Am** & C America)
0500-0600	9630 (**N America** & C America)
1900-2000	9875 & 11790 (**Europe**)
2100-2200	9875 (**Europe**)

SRI LANKA
SRI LANKA BROADCASTING CORP

0030-0430	9720 & 15425 (S Asia)
1030-1130	11835 (Australia), 15120 (E Asia)

1230-1730	6075 & 9720 (S Asia)
2000-2130	9720 & 15120 (**Europe**)

SUDAN
NATIONAL UNITY RADIO

1630-1700	9535

SURINAME
RADIO SURINAME INTERNATIONAL

1730-1740	M-F **17755** or 17835 (**Europe**)

SWEDEN
IBRA RADIO

1930-2000	Sa/Su **7110** (**Europe**)

RADIO SWEDEN (likely to be retired)

0100-0130	9765 (S Asia)
0200-0230	9695 (**N America**), 11705 (**E North Am** & C America)
0330-0400	9695 (**N America**), 11705 (**E North Am** & C America)
1100-1130	21570 (Australia)
1230-1300	9765 (E Asia), 21570 (Australia)
1300-1330	21570 (S Asia)
1400-1430	21570 (S Asia)
1530-1600	17870 (**N America**), 21500 (**E North Am**)
1700-1730	6065 & 9615 (**Europe**)
1800-1830	9655 (**Europe**), 11900 (Mideast)
1800-1900	6065 (**Europe**)
1830-1900	15270 (**Europe** & Mideast)
1930-2000	6065, 7265 & 9655 (**Europe**)
2030-2100	6065 (**Europe**)
2200-2230	6065 (**Europe**)

SWITZERLAND
RED CROSS (airs one week per month)

0310-0330	Tu/F 6135 & Tu/F 9650 (**N America** & C America), Tu/F 9885 & Tu/F 12035 (**N America**)
0740-0800	M/Th 9560, M/Th 13685, M/Th 17670 & M/Th 21695 (Australia)
1040-1100	M/Th 13635 (Australia), M/Th 15570 (E Asia & Australia), M/Th 17830 (Australia), M/Th 21770 (S Asia)
1100-1130	Su 7210 (**Europe**)
1310-1330	M/Th **7480** & M/Th 13635 (E Asia), M/Th 15570, M/Th 17830 & M/Th 21695 (S Asia)
1700-1730	M 7210 (**Europe**)
1710-1730	M/Th 15525 & M/Th 17830 (Mideast)

SWISS RADIO INTERNATIONAL

0200-0230	6125 (C America), 6135 (**N America** & C America), 9650 (C America), 9885 & 12035 (**E North Am** & C America), **17730** (C America & **W North Am**)
0400-0430	6135 & 9650 (**N America** & C America), 9885 & 12035 (**N America**)
0730-0800	3985, 6165 & 9535 (**Europe**)
0830-0900	9560, 13685, 17670 & 21695 (Australia)
1000-1030	9560, 13685, 17670 & 21695 (Australia)
1100-1130	13635 (Australia), 15570 (E Asia & Australia), 17830 (Australia), 21770 (S Asia)

1300-1330	6165, 9535 & 12030 (**Europe**)
1330-1400	**7480** & 13635 (E Asia), 15570, 17830 & 21695 (S Asia)
1530-1600	13685, 15430, 17830 & 21630 (Mideast)
1615-1630	11955 (**E Europe**)
2000-2015	6165 (**Europe**)
2000-2030	3985 & 9535 (**Europe**)
2230-2300	6190 (**W Europe**)

SYRIA
SYRIAN BROADCASTING SERVICE
2005-2105	11625, 12085 & 15095 (**Europe**)
2110-2210	12085 (Australia), 15095 (**N America**)

THAILAND
RADIO THAILAND—(Asia)
0500-0600	9655, 11905
0600-0800	Sa/Su 9655, Sa/Su 11905
1130-1230	9655, 11905
2300-0430	9655, 11905

TOGO
RADIO LOME
1935-1945	5047

TURKEY
VOICE OF TURKEY
0400-0450	9445 (**E North Am**), 17880 (Australia)
1330-1400	9675 (Mideast & S Asia)
2100-2150	9795 (**Europe**)
2300-2350	7225 (Mideast), 9445 (**E North Am**), 9685 (**Europe**), 17880 (Australia)

UNITED ARAB EMIRATES
UAE RADIO (DUBAI)
0330-0400	11945 & 13675 (**E North Am** & C America), 15400 & 15435 (**E North Am**)
0530-0600	15435 (Australia), 17830 (E Asia), 21700 (Australia)
1030-1110	13675, 15435 & 21605 (**Europe**)
1330-1400	13675, 15435 & 21605 (**Europe**)
1600-1640	11795, 13675 & 21605 (**Europe**)

UAE RADIO (ABU DHABI)
2200-2400	6170 (**E North Am** & C America), 9600 (**E North Am**), 11985 (**E North Am** & C America), 13605 (**N America**), 15305 & 17855 (**E North Am** & C America)

UNITED KINGDOM
BBC
0000-0230	**9580** (Mideast), **9580** (S Asia)
0000-0330	7325 (C America)
0000-0430	9915 (**E North Am**)
24h	9410, 12095 & 15070 (**Europe**)
0030-0200	**5965** & **7135** (Mideast)
0030-0230	**9590** (C America), **11955** (S Asia)
0030-0300	**15310** (Mideast)
0100-0300	Su **15280** & Su **21715** (E Asia)
0200-0300	**6110** (C America)
0200-0330	**6195**, **7135** & **9670** (Mideast)
0230-0430	**11955** (Mideast & S Asia)
0300-0400	**6180** (**Europe**)
0300-0730	6195 (**Europe**)

0300-0815	**11760** (Mideast), **15310** (Mideast & S Asia)
0300-0915	**15280** (E Asia)
0300-1030	**21715** (E Asia)
0330-0430	9915 (C America)
0400-0500	**9580** (**Europe**)
0400-0730	3955, **6180** & 7230 (**Europe**), **15590** (**Europe**, Mideast & S Asia)
0400-0945	**15575** (Mideast & S Asia)
0400-1500	**15575** (**Europe**)
0500-0730	7120 (**W Europe**), 9580 (**Europe**)
0500-0815	**9640** (C America)
0600-0815	7150 (Australia), **17790** (S Asia)
0600-1000	**15360** (E Asia)
0600-1030	**17830** (Australia), **17830** (E Asia)
0700-0915	7325 (**Europe**)
0700-1515	5975 & 9760 (**Europe**)
0730-0900	Sa/Su **6180** (**Europe**), Sa/Su **15590** (Mideast & S Asia)
0800-1615	17640 (**Europe**)
0900-0945	**15590** (Mideast & S Asia)
0900-1030	**9740** (S Asia)
0900-1100	**17790** (S Asia)
0900-1330	**11760** (Mideast)
0900-1515	6045, **6180** & **9660** (**Europe**)
0900-1615	9750 (**Europe**), **15310** (Mideast & S Asia)
0900-1700	**11750** (S Asia)
0915-1000	**7180**, **11765** & **11955** (E Asia)
0945-1515	**15575** (Mideast & S Asia)
1030-1515	**9740** (Asia & Australia)
1100-1130	**5965** (**N America**)
1100-1400	**9515** (**N America**)
1100-1430	**6195** (C America), **15220** (**E North Am**)
1130-1200	M-Sa **5965** (**N America**)
1300-1500	**11820** (E Asia)
1300-1615	**7180** (E Asia)
1430-1615	Sa/Su **6195** (C America), **15205** (**E North Am**)
1500-1600	Sa/Su **11775** & Sa/Su **15260** (**N America**)
1500-1700	6195 (**Europe**)
1515-1830	**9740** (S Asia)
1600-1745	**11775** & **15260** (**N America**)
1615-1830	5975 & **15310** (S Asia), 17640 (**Europe**)
1615-2200	7325 (**Europe**)
1700-2200	**6180** & 6195 (**Europe**)
1715-1830	**7160** (Mideast)
1800-2100	**11750** (Australia)
1800-2200	**11955** (Australia)
1800-2300	3955 (**Europe**)
1830-2030	**9740** (Mideast)
1900-2030	**7160** (Mideast)
2000-2100	**15340** (E Asia)
2000-2130	**7180** (E Asia)
2000-2315	**15340** (Australia)
2000-0730	**5975** (C America)
2100-2200	**11750** (E Asia & Australia)
2100-2230	**7180** (E Asia)
2100-2315	**15340** (E Asia)
2100-0030	**9590** & 15070 (**E North Am**)
2115-2130	M-F **6110**, M-F **15140**, M-F **17715** & M-F 21660 (C America)
2200-2300	**11945** (E Asia)
2200-0030	**11955** (E Asia & Australia), 15070 (C America)
2200-0330	9915 (C America)

2200-0430	7325 (**N America** & C America)
2200-0530	12095 (**N America**)
2300-0030	**7145**, **9570** & **11945** (E Asia)
2300-0030	**17830** (E Asia)
2300-0330	**6175** (**E North Am**)

BRITISH FORCES BS—(Mideast, times vary)

0330-0430	6840 (SSB, Irr.)
1300-1500	15670 (SSB, Irr.)
1700-2300	6840 (SSB, Irr.)

USA—All stations audible to some extent within North America, regardless of where they are targeted.

AFRTS-US MILITARY—(Atlantic) (SSB, aired very irregularly on any one or two of the following frequencies:)

24h	**9239**, **9242**, **9244**, **9334**, **9921**, **11207**, **13636**, **13651**, **16041**, **16454**

CHRISTIAN SCIENCE MONITOR

0000-0100	M-Sa 7395 (**E North Am** & C America)
0000-0355	Sa/Su **17865** (E Asia)
0100-0120	7395 (**E North Am** & C America)
0120-0155	Tu-Su 7395 (**E North Am** & C America)
0200-0230	M 9455 (**W North Am** & C America)
0230-0300	9455 (**W North Am** & C America)
0300-0320	M 9455 (**W North Am** & C America)
0330-0355	Tu-F 9455 (**W North Am** & C America)
0400-0430	M 9455 (**W North Am**), M 13760 (C America)
0400-0755	**17780** (E Asia)
0430-0500	9455 (**W North Am**), 13760 (C America)
0500-0520	M 9455 (**W North Am**), M 13760 (C America)
0530-0555	Tu-F 9455 (**W North Am**), Tu-F 13760 (C America)
0600-0630	Su/M 9455 (**W North Am**)
0600-0700	M-F 9840 (**Europe**)
0630-0700	9455 (**W North Am**), M-F 11705 (C America)
0700-0730	Sa/Su 11705 (C America)
0700-0755	9840 (**Europe**)
0730-0755	Tu-Sa 9455 (**W North Am**), 11705 (C America)
0800-0830	Sa/Su 13760 (C America & Australia)
0800-0900	M-F 9840 & M-F 11705 (**Europe**), M-F **15610** (Australia)
0800-1155	**9530** & **17555** (E Asia)
0830-0855	13760 (C America & Australia)
0900-1000	9840 & 11705 (**Europe**), **15610** (Australia)
0930-0955	M-F 13760 (C America & Australia)
1000-1100	**9495** (**E North Am**)
1100-1155	M-F 9495 (**E North Am**)
1200-1305	Su-F **9475** (Australia), 9495 (**E North Am**), Sa/Su 21780 (**Europe**)
1230-1255	M-F 13760 (C America)
1255-1355	**9475** (Australia)
1300-1330	Sa/Su 13760 (C America)
1305-1355	M-F 9495 (**E North Am**)
1330-1355	13760 (C America)
1400-1500	21780 (**Europe**)
1400-1555	**9530** (E Asia)
1400-1755	**13625** (S Asia)

1430-1500	M-F 13760 (**W North Am** & C America)
1500-1530	Sa/Su 13760 (**W North Am** & C America)
1500-1555	Sa/Su 15610 (**E North Am** & C America), M-F 21780 (**Europe**)
1530-1555	13760 (**W North Am** & C America)
1600-1700	Sa/Su 15610 (**E North Am** & C America), Su 17555 (C America & **W North Am**)
1600-1755	**11580** (E Asia)
1700-1720	Sa/Su 17555 (C America & **W North Am**)
1720-1755	Sa 17555 (C America & **W North Am**)
1800-1900	Su-F **13720** (S Asia), Su 15610 (**E North Am** & C America), Su 17555 (C America & **W North Am**), Su-F 21780 (**E North Am**)
1800-1920	Sa/Su 15610 (**E North Am** & C America)
1800-1955	**13625** (S Asia & Australia)
1900-1920	Sa/Su 17555 (C America & **W North Am**), 21780 (**E North Am**)
1900-1955	Su 15610 (**E North Am** & C America)
1920-1955	Sa 15610 (**E North Am** & C America), Sa 17555 (C America & **W North Am**), M-Sa 21780 (**E North Am**)
2000-2100	Su-F **13625** (Australia), 13770 (**Europe**)
2000-2120	Su-F 13770 (**E North Am**), Su-F 15610 (**Europe**)
2000-2155	**9455** (E Asia)
2100-2155	**13625** (Australia), Su-F 13770 (**Europe**)
2120-2155	M-F 13770 (**E North Am**), M-F 15610 (**Europe**)
2200-2300	9465 (**E North Am**)
2200-2355	**15405** (E Asia)
2300-2315	Su-F 9465 (**E North Am**)
2315-2355	M-F 9465 (**E North Am**)

KGEI-VOICE OF FRIENDSHIP

2200-2230	Su 15280 (C America)

KNLS-NEW LIFE STATION

0800-0900	7365 & 11715 (E Asia)
1500-1600	7355 & 9615 (E Asia)
1800-1900	7355 (E Asia), 11945 (E Asia & Australia)
2000-2100	11880 (E Asia & Australia), 11910 (E Asia)

KTBN—(**E North Am**)

0200-1600	7510
1600-0200	15590

KVOH-VOICE OF HOPE—(**W North Am** & C America)

0400-0800	9785
2000-2200	17775

VOA-VOICE OF AMERICA

0000-0100	11695 (C America)
0000-0200	5995, 6130, 9455, 9775, 9815, 11580, 15120 & 15205 (C America)
0100-0300	**7115** & **7205** (S Asia), 7651 (**Europe** & Mideast), **9740** (Mideast & S Asia), **11705**, **15160**, **15250**, **17735** & **21545** (S Asia)
0200-0230	Tu-Sa 5995, Tu-Sa 9775, Tu-Sa 9815, Tu-Sa 11580, Tu-Sa 15120 & Tu-Sa 15205 (C America)

0300-0330	**5965**, **6095**, **11905**, **15160**, **15195**, **17810**, **17865** & **17895** (Mideast)
0300-0500	**21600** (S Asia)
0400-0500	**5995** (**Europe**), **5995** (**E Europe**), **15205** (Mideast & S Asia)
0400-0600	**7200** (**Europe** & Mideast)
0400-0700	**6040** & **6140** (**Europe**), **11725** (Mideast)
0430-0700	**3980** (**Europe**)
0500-0530	**6060** (**E Europe**)
0500-0600	**9670** (**Europe**)
0500-0700	**5995** (**E Europe**), **11825** (Mideast), **15205** (Mideast & S Asia)
0530-0700	**6060** (**E Europe**)
0600-0700	**7325** (**Europe**)
0800-1100	**11735**, **11740**, **15160**, **15195**, **21455**, **21570** & **21615** (Mideast)
1000-1200	5985 (Pacific & Australia), 6095 & 9590 (C America), **11720** (Australia), 11915 & 15120 (C America)
1000-1500	**15425** (S Asia)
1100-1400	**15155** (E Asia)
1100-1700	**9760** (Asia)
1200-1330	**11715** (Australia)
1400-1500	**15160** (E Asia), **15205** (Mideast & S Asia)
1400-1800	**7125** (S Asia), **9645** (E Asia), **15395** (S Asia)
1500-1600	18275 (**Europe**)
1500-1700	15205 (**Europe**)
1500-1800	15260 (Mideast), 18782 (**Europe** & Mideast)
1500-2200	**9700** (Mideast & S Asia)
1600-1630	3980 (**Europe**)
1600-2000	11920 (S Asia)
1630-1700	**6040** & **9760** (**Europe**), **15245** (**E Europe**)
1700-1730	3980 (**Europe**)
1700-2200	**6040**, **9760** & **15205** (**Europe**)
1800-2200	18275 (**Europe**), 18782 (**Europe** & Mideast)
1900-2000	**9525** & **11870** (Australia), **15180** (S Asia)
1900-2200	**11710** (**E Europe**)
2000-2100	**9570** (E Asia)
2100-2200	**11870** (Australia)
2100-2400	**9530** & **11960** (Mideast)
2100-0100	**17735** (Australia)
2200-2400	**6095**, **11905**, **15215** & **15225** (Mideast), **15305** (Australia), **15400**, **17810** & **17885** (Mideast)
2200-0100	**7120** & **9770** (S Asia), **15290**, **17735** & **17820** (E Asia)

WINB-WORLD BROADCASTING—(**Europe**)

1600-2000	15295
2005-2245	15185
2250-2345	15145

WMLK—(**Europe** & Mideast)

0400-0700	Su-F 9465
1700-2000	Su-F 9465

WORLD HARVEST RADIO

0000-0100	Su/M 9495 (C America)
0100-0400	7315 (**E North Am**), M 9495 (C America)
0400-0500	9495 (C America)
0500-0600	Su 7315 (**E North Am**), Su 9495 (C America)
0600-0800	9495 (C America)
0600-1100	7315 (**E North Am**)
0800-1100	7355 (C America)
1100-1130	11790 (C America)
1100-1300	Su 11790 (C America)
1100-1500	9465 (**E North Am**)
1300-1400	11790 (C America)
1400-1600	15105 (C America)
1500-1600	M-Sa 21840 (**E North Am** & **W Europe**)
1600-1700	Su 15105 (C America)
1700-1800	15105 (C America)
1700-2100	13760 (**E North Am** & **W Europe**)
1800-2100	17830 (C America)
2100-2200	M-Sa 13760 (**E North Am** & **W Europe**), M-Sa 17830 (C America)
2200-2300	17830 (C America)
2200-2400	13760 (**E North Am** & **W Europe**)
2300-2400	Sa/Su 9495 (C America)

WRNO WORLDWIDE—(**E North Am**) Transmission hours irregular.

0000-0100	7355
1500-1800	15420
2100-2400	13720
2300-2400	7355

WWCR—(**E North Am** & **Europe**)

0100-1200	7435, 7520
1200-2330	15690

WWV (World Time station, CO)

24h	5000, 10000, 15000, 20000

WWVH (World Time station, HI)

24h	5000, 10000, 15000

WYFR-FAMILY RADIO

0000-0045	5985 (**E North Am**)
0045-0445	6065 (**E North Am**)
0100-0145	11855 (**W North Am**)
0100-0200	9680 (**W North Am**)
0100-0245	15440 (C America)
0100-0445	9505 (**W North Am**)
0500-0545	11725 (**Europe**)
0500-0600	11580 (**Europe**)
0500-0700	5985 (**W North Am**)
0600-0745	7355, 9680 & 13760 (**Europe**)
1000-1400	5950 (**E North Am**)
1100-1245	7355 (**W North Am**)
1100-1700	11580 (**W North Am**)
1200-1445	6015 (**W North Am**)
1200-1500	11830 (**W North Am**)
1200-1700	17640 & 17750 (C America)
1300-1445	9705 (**W North Am**)
1300-2245	13695 (**E North Am**)
1500-1700	11830 & 15215 (**W North Am**)
1600-1700	15355, 15566 & 21615 (**Europe**)
1700-1900	21500 (**Europe**)
1700-1945	17885 (C America)
1900-1945	15355 (**Europe**)
1900-2145	21615 (**Europe**)
1900-2200	15566 (**Europe**)
2000-2145	9455 (**Europe**)
2000-2245	17845 (C America)
2200-0100	11775 (**W North Am**)
2300-0045	9505 (**W North Am**)

USSR—Soviet schedules currently changing often and without notice.
RADIO ALMA-ATA

2130-2200	3955, 4400, 5035, 5260, 5960, 5970, 9505, 15215, 15315, 15360, 15385, 17605, 17715, 17730, 21490

RADIO KIEV

0000-0100	11790 (**E North Am**), 13645 & 15455 (**W North Am**), 15485 (**E North Am**), 15525 (**E North Am** & C America)
0100-0200	7400 & 9750 (**E North Am**), 9800 (**E North Am** & C America), 15180, 17690 & 17720 (**W North Am**)
2100-2200	5960 & 9865 (**Europe**)
2200-2300	6185 (**Europe**)

RADIO MOSCOW

0000-0400	7115 (**E North Am**), 15515 (S Asia)
0000-0600	11850 (**N America**)
0000-0800	15195, 17620 (Pacific)
0000-1000	15140 (S Asia), 15420 (Australia)
0030-0500	11850 (Mideast)
0030-0900	7310 (**E North Am** & C America)
0030-1300	17600 (S Asia)
0100-0400	9700 (**N America**)
0100-0600	12040 (**E North Am**)
0100-0700	15415 (S Asia)
0100-1100	11845 (S Asia)
0130-0800	17850 (Australia)
0200-0400	9575 (Mideast)
0200-0500	12010 (**W North Am**)
0300-0600	15455 (**W North Am**)
0300-0800	11665 (**W North Am**)
0300-1100	15320 (Mideast)
0300-1300	7305 (Mideast)
0300-1500	15540 (Mideast)
0330-1200	17560 (S Asia)
0400-0500	9610 (**Europe**)
0400-0600	15525 (E Asia)
0400-0630	15570 (Mideast)
0400-0700	9750 (**Europe**), 15215, 15245 & 15425 (**W North Am**)
0400-0800	13645, 15180 & 17720 (**W North Am**)
0400-0900	9795 (**Europe**)
0400-1100	17700 (Mideast)
0430-1000	15260 (**Europe**), 15455, 17675 (S Asia)
0430-1200	15155 & 15460 (S Asia), 15595
0500-0700	9520 (C America & **Europe**), 9575 (Mideast)
0500-1000	9450 (**Europe**)
0600-0800	15110 (Mideast), 17605 (**W North Am**)
0600-1100	17765 (S Asia)
0600-1500	21630 (Mideast)
0630-0900	5905 (**W North Am**)
0630-1500	11830 (**Europe**)
0700-1100	15210 (Mideast)
0700-1400	7130 (**Europe**)
0700-1600	13680 (**W Europe** & Atlantic)
0700-1630	11705 (**Europe**)
0730-1200	11710 (Mideast)
0730-1400	15500 (Mideast)
0800-0900	15420 (**Europe**)
0800-0930	15415 (S Asia)
0800-1200	17815 (S Asia)
0830-1200	13690 (Mideast)
0830-1600	11900 (**Europe**)
0900-1000	15110 (Mideast), 17775 (S Asia)
0900-1100	15295 (S Asia)
0900-1400	15490 (S Asia)
1000-1100	15220 (S Asia), 15420 (**Europe**), 17775 (S Asia)
1000-1300	6000 & 9600 (**N America**)
1000-1430	17655 (Mideast)
1000-1530	15150 (**Europe** & Atlantic)
1000-1600	15125 (**Europe**)
1030-1430	11860 (Mideast & S Asia)
1100-1300	11975 (Mideast), 17615 (C America)
1100-1330	9575 (Mideast)
1100-1700	9450 (**Europe**)
1130-1300	15210 (Mideast)
1130-1500	15320 (Mideast), 15420 (**Europe**), 17700 (Mideast)
1200-1500	12025 (S Asia), 12030
1230-1400	15490 (Mideast)
1300-1400	5960, 7315 & 9885 (E Asia), 17560 (S Asia)
1300-1500	7370 (E Asia)
1300-1530	11710 (**W North Am**)
1300-1600	9655 (**W North Am**)
1300-2100	11850 (Mideast)
1300-0800	12050 (Pacific & **W North Am**)
1330-2200	11840 (**N America**)
1400-1430	11720 (S Asia)
1400-1500	15210 (Mideast)
1500-1600	11700 (S Asia), 12010 (**Europe**), 17560 & 17600 (S Asia)
1500-1700	17655 (Mideast)
1500-1800	15500 (Mideast)
1530-1600	9750 & 15370 (Mideast)
1600-1700	11725 (Mideast), 15525 (E Asia)
1600-1800	11765 (Mideast)
1600-2000	11820 (**Europe**)
1600-2100	11950 (**Europe**)
1600-2200	9600 (**W Europe**)
1630-1700	6005 (Mideast), 7330 (**Europe**), 17580 (Mideast)
1630-2100	15150 (**Europe, E North Am** & C America)
1700-1745	15535 (**E Europe**)
1700-1900	17600 (S Asia)
1700-2200	17695 (**W Europe**)
1800-2000	9580 (**W North Am**), 9750 (Mideast), 11755 (**W North Am**), 15480 (Mideast)
1800-2200	7150 (**Europe**)
1800-2300	9685 (**W Europe**)
1800-2400	7195 (**Europe** & **E North Am**)
1900-2000	12010 (**Europe**)
1900-2100	15475 (**W Europe** & **E North Am**)
1930-2030	15425 (**W North Am**)
2000-2200	7330 & 11820 (**Europe**), 15535 (**E Europe**)
2000-2230	7130 (**Europe**)
2030-2300	12060 (**W Europe** & C America), 15500 (C America)
2030-0400	15425 (**W North Am**)
2030-0800	9635 (Pacific & **W North Am**)
2100-2200	5950 (**Europe**), 15175 (**W Europe**)
2100-2230	15285 (S Asia)
2100-2300	9760 (**W Europe**), 11850 (Mideast)
2130-2400	6140 (**Europe**)
2200-2400	15475 (**W Europe** & **E North Am**)
2200-0300	15290 (**E North Am** & C America)
2200-0400	6045, 11710 & 17700 (**N America**)
2200-0600	7150 (**E North Am**)
2230-2400	17850 (Australia)
2230-0200	9650 (S Asia)
2230-0300	17665 (**W North Am**)
2230-0900	17655 (Australia)
2300-2400	17670 (**W Europe** & C America)

2300-0300	9720 (**N America**), 12045 (S Asia), 17605 (**W North Am**)
2300-0400	4895, 9685 (**E North Am** & C America)
2300-0700	11690 (**E North Am** & Europe)
2300-1000	15265 & 15280 (S Asia)
2300-1300	21690 (S Asia)
2330-0700	17860 (Australia)

RADIO RIGA INTERNATIONAL—(**Europe**)

0700-0730	Su 5935
1830-1900	Sa 5935
2130-2140	M-F 5935

RADIO TALLINN

2130-2200	M 5925, M 9560

RADIO TASHKENT

0100-0130	5955, 7195, 7265, 7325 & 7335 (Mideast & S Asia), 11975 (S Asia)
1200-1230	5945 (S Asia & Mideast), 7325, 9540, 9600, 9715, 11785, 15460, 15470 & 17740 (S Asia)
1330-1400	5945 (S Asia & Mideast), 7325, 9540, 9600, 9715, 11785, 15460, 15470 & 17740 (S Asia)

RADIO VILNIUS

0000-0030	7400 (**E North Am**), 9710 (**Europe**), 9750 (**E North Am**), 15180, 17690 & 17720 (**W North Am**)
2230-2300	9675, 9710 (**Europe**)
2300-2330	11790 (**E North Am**), 13645 & 15455 (**W North Am**), 15485 (**E North Am**)

RADIO YEREVAN

0250-0300	11790 (**E North Am**), 13645 & 15455 (**W North Am**), 15485 (**E North Am**)
0350-0400	7400 & 9750 (**E North Am**), 11675, 15180, 17690 & 17720 (**W North Am**)

VATICAN STATE

VATICAN RADIO

0145-0200	7125, 9650, 11750, 11935 & 15090 (S Asia)
0250-0315	7305 (**E North Am** & C America), 9605 (**N America** & C America), 11625 (**E North Am** & C America)

0600-0620	6185 & 6245 (**Europe**)
0700-0800	M-Sa 6185, M-Sa 6245, M-Sa 9645 & M-Sa 11740 (**Europe**), M-Sa 15210 (Mideast)
1130-1200	M-Sa 6245, M-Sa 9645 & M-Sa 11740 (**Europe**), M-Sa 15210 (Mideast)
1345-1415	9615, 11625, 11830 & 17535 (Australia)
1445-1500	6245, 7250, 9645 & 11740 (**Europe**)
1545-1600	11715, 15090 & 17865 (S Asia)
1600-1630	M-Sa 6245, M-Sa 7250, M-Sa 9645 & M-Sa 11740 (**Europe**), M-Sa 15105 (Mideast)
2000-2010	M-Sa 6245 & M-Sa 7250 (**Europe**), M-Sa 15210 (Mideast)
2050-2110	6245 & 7250 (**Europe**)
2245-2315	7125, 11830 & 15105 (Australia)

VIETNAM

VOICE OF VIETNAM

1230-1300	9840, 12018 & 15009 (E Asia & **Americas**)
1330-1400	9840, 12018 & 15009 (E Asia & **Americas**)
1800-1830	9840, 12018 & 15009 (**Europe**)
1900-1930	9840, 12018 & 15009 (**Europe**)
2030-2100	9840, 12018 & 15009 (**Europe**)

YUGOSLAVIA

CROATIAN RADIO

0045-0055	**7315** (**E North Am**), Su/M **9495** (C America)
0445-0455	**7315** (**E North Am**), Su/M **9495** (C America)

RADIO YUGOSLAVIA

0100-0145	9620 & 11735 (**E North Am**)
1200-1230	17740 (**E North Am**), 21605 (S Asia)
1300-1330	17725 (Australia)
1930-2000	6165 (**Europe**)
2100-2145	11735 (**Europe** & **E North Am**)
2200-2245	5960 (**Europe**), 6100 & 9620 (**Europe** & **E North Am**)

For some, the offerings in English on world band radio are merely icing on the cake. Their real interest is in listening to programs aimed at national compatriots. Voices from home.

"Home" may be a place of family origin, or perhaps it's a favorite country you once visited or lived in. Vacationers and business travelers also tune in to keep in touch with events at home. For yet others, it is the perfect way to keep limber in a second tongue.

Schedules Prepared for Entire Year

To be as helpful as possible throughout the year, *Passport's* schedules consist not just of observed activity, but also that which we have creatively opined will take place during the entire year. This latter information is original from us, and therefore, of course, will not be so exact as factual information.

Following are frequencies for the most popular stations that are likely to be heard well beyond their national borders. Some you'll hear, some you won't—which being which depending, among other things, on your location and receiving equipment. Keep in mind that the stations in this "Voices from Home" section often come in weaker than those in English, so better receiving equipment may be required. Those in bold usually come in most strongly, as they are from relay transmitters close to the listening audience.

Reception Sometimes Best Outside Prime Time

Stations in "Voices from Home," unlike those in English, sometimes come in best—or only—outside the usual prime early-evening listening hours. Choice late-afternoon and evening frequencies are usually found in the world band segments between 5850-12100 kHz, sometimes even 3900-17900 kHz. But earlier in the day try 9250-21785 kHz, sometimes even 5850-26100 kHz. See *World Band Spectrum* in the glossary at the back of the book for how to tune for best results.

Times and days of the week are given in World Time, explained in the *Passport* glossary. Midyear, many programs are heard an hour earlier, whereas some in the Southern Hemisphere are heard an hour later. For full details on transmission times and target zones, please refer to The Blue Pages.

ALGERIA
  "VOICE OF PALESTINE"
    Arabic 11715 kHz
  RTV ALGERIENNE
    Arabic/French 6145, 7145, 9509, 9535, 9685, 11715, 15160, 15205, 15215, 17745 kHz

ARGENTINA—Spanish
  RADIO ARGENTINA-RAE
    11710, 15345 kHz
  RADIO NACIONAL
    6060, 9690, 11710, 15345 kHz

AUSTRIA—German
  RADIO AUSTRIA INTERNATIONAL
    5945, **6015**, 6155, 9870, 9875, 11780, 12010, 13730, 15410, 15430, 15450, 21490 kHz

BAHRAIN—Arabic
  RADIO BAHRAIN
    9745 kHz

BELGIUM
  BELGISCHE RADIO & TV
    French 5910, 6035, 9925, 11695, 13655, 13675, 13710, 15515, 17550, 21815 kHz
    Dutch 5910, 6035, 9860, 9925, 11695, 11985, 13655, 13675, 13710, 15515, 17550, 21815 kHz
  RTV BELGE FRANCAISE
    French 7140, 9925, 15540, 17675, 17680, 21460 kHz

BOLIVIA—Spanish
  Very poorly heard.
  RADIO FIDES
    4845, 6155 kHz
  RADIO LIBERTAD
    4808, 5004 kHz
  RADIO PANAMERICANA
    6105 kHz
  RADIO SANTA CRUZ
    6135 kHz

BRAZIL—Portuguese
RADIO BRASIL CENTRAL
4985, 11815 kHz
RADIO INCONFIDENCIA
6010, 15190 kHz
RADIO NACIONAL DA AMAZONIA
6180, 11780 kHz
RADIO BANDEIRANTES
6090, 9645, 11925 kHz
RADIO CULTURA
6170, 9615, 17815 kHz
RADIO EXCELSIOR
9585 kHz
RADIO GAUCHA
6020, 11915 kHz
RADIO GLOBO
6030, 6120, 11805 kHz
RADIO GUAIBA
6000, 11785 kHz
RADIO NACIONAL
4945, 9705, 15265, 17755 kHz
RADIO RECORD
6150, 9505, 11965 kHz

CANADA—French
CANADIAN BROADCASTING CORP
9625 kHz
RADIO CANADA INTERNATIONAL
5960, **5995**, **6025**, **6050**, 6120, 6150, **7155**,
7230, **7235**, **7295**, 9535, 9635, 9650, **9670**,
9740, 9750, 9755, 9760, **11705**, 11730, **11775**,
11845, 11855, 11880, **11905**, **11925**, 11940,
11945, 13650, 13670, 13720, 15150, 15235,
15260, 15325, 15390, 15425, 17820, **17840**,
17875, 21675 kHz

CHINA (PR)—Standard Chinese
CENTRAL PEOPLES BS
5880, 5915, 6095, 6125, 6750, 6840, 6890,
7504, 7770, 7935, 9080, 9170, 9290, 9380,
9455, 9755, 9775, 9800, 10260, 11000, 11040,
11100, 11330, 11630, 11740, 11925, 12120,
15390, 15500, 15550, 15710, 15880, 17605,
17700 kHz
GANSU PEOPLES BS
4865, 6155, 9710 kHz
RADIO BEIJING
6165, 6810, 6975, 6995, 7190, 7315, 7335,
7350, 7420, 7590, 7660, 7780, 7800, 9455,
9480, 9530, 9565, 9575, 9590, 9665, **9690**,
9700, **9745**, 9765, **9770**, 9945, 11445, 11650,
11685, 11695, **11715**, **11790**, 11945, 11975,
12015, 12055, 15100, **15110**, **15130**, 15150,
15165, 15195, 15260, 15320, 15330, 15435,
15455, 17533, 17705, **17715** kHz
VOICE OF THE STRAIT-PLA
4130, 4840, 4900, 5050, 5510, 6000, 6115,
6170, 7280, 9505, 11590 kHz
VOICE OF JINLING
4875, 7215 kHz
XINJIANG PBS
3960, 4501, 6100, 7385, 9560 kHz

CHINA (TAIWAN)—Chinese
BROADCASTING CORP OF CHINA
5950, 9610, **11740**, 11885, 15125, **15440** kHz
VOICE OF FREE CHINA
5950, 6200, 7130, 7445, **9680**, 9765, 9845,
9955, 11745, 11825, **11855**, 11860, 11915,

15130, **15215**, 15270, 15345, 15370, **15440**,
17720, **17750**, **17805**, **17845**, 21720 kHz

CLANDESTINE (CENTRAL AMERICA)—Spanish
"LA VOZ DEL CID"
6305, 7340, 9942, 11635 kHz
"RADIO CAIMAN"
9965 kHz
"RADIO VENCEREMOS"
6400 kHz (Irr)

CLANDESTINE (MIDDLE EAST)
"IRAN FLAG OF FREEDOM RADIO"
Persian 9045, 15100, 15565 kHz
"RADIO IRAN"
Persian 6970, 9400, 15650 kHz
"VOICE OF IRAQ OPPOSITION"
Arabic 9570, 9995, 15605, 17950 kHz

COLOMBIA—Spanish
CARACOL BOGOTA
4755, 5075, 6075, 6150 kHz
LA VOZ DEL LLANO
6116 kHz
LA VOZ DEL CINARUCO
4865 kHz
ONDAS DEL META
4885 kHz (Irr)
RADIO NACIONAL
11822v, 17840-17910v kHz
RADIO CADENA NACIONAL
6160 kHz

COSTA RICA—Spanish
FARO DEL CARIBE
5044, 6175, 9645 kHz
RADIO CASINO
5954 kHz
RADIO FOR PEACE INTERNATIONAL
7375, 13630 kHz
RADIO RELOJ
4832 (Irr), 6005.5 kHz

CUBA—Spanish
RADIO HABANA
9505, 9550, 9590, 9620, 11705, 11760, 11820,
11850, 11875, 11910, 11950, 11970, 12000,
15140, 15220, 15230, 15300, 15340, **15350**,
15415, 15425, **17710**, 17750, 17770, 17795,
17835, **21670** kHz
RADIO REBELDE
3366v, 5025 kHz

DENMARK—Danish
DANMARKS RADIO (Via Radio Norway)
5980, **7160**, **9590**, **9600**, **9605**, **9615**, **9640**, **9645**,
9650, **9655**, **11730**, **11735**, **11745**, **11755**, **11790**,
11840, **11845**, **11850**, **11860**, **11865**, **11870**,
11875, **11925**, **15165**, **15175**, **15220**, **15225**,
15230, **15235**, **15260**, **15310**, **15360**, **17730**,
17740, **17755**, **17760**, **17765**, **17790**, **17820**,
21610, **21695**, **21705**, **21710**, **21730**, **25730** kHz

ECUADOR—Spanish
HCJB-VOICE OF THE ANDES
6050, 6080, 9765, 11835, 11910, 11960, 15270,
17790, 17875, 21455, 21480, 25950 kHz
RADIO NACIONAL ESPEJO
4679.5 kHz

RADIO POPULAR
    4800 kHz
RADIO QUITO
    4920 kHz

EGYPT—Arabic
RADIO CAIRO
    6195, 9455, 9620, 9670, 9700, 9755, 9770, 9805,
    9850, 9900, 9940, 11665, 11785, 11905, 11980,
    12050, 15115, 15175, 15220, 15285, 17670,
    17745, 17770, 17800 kHz

EQUATORIAL GUINEA—Spanish
AFRICA 2000
    6907 kHz
RADIO NACIONAL
    4925, 6250 kHz

FINLAND—Finnish/Swedish
RADIO FINLAND
    6120, 9550, 9560, 9640, 9645, 9670, 9730,
    11755, 11820, 11850, 15185, 15245, 15400,
    15430, 17800, 21550 kHz

FRANCE—French
RADIO FRANCE INTERNATIONALE
    3965, **4890**, 5945, 5990, 5995, 6040, 6045, 6175,
    7120, 7135, 7160, 7175, 7280, 9550, 9605, 9715,
    9745, 9790, 9800, 9805, 9830, 9850, 11660,
    11670, 11685, 11695, 11700, 11705, **11715**,
    11790, 11800, 11845, **11890**, 11965, 11995,
    12025, 15135, 15155, 15180, 15190, 15195,
    15215, **15275**, **15285**, 15300, 15315, 15360,
    15365, 15425, 15435, 15460, 15530, 17620,
    17650, 17695, 17705, **17710**, 17720, 17775,
    17785, 17795, 17800, 17845, 17850, **17860**,
    21520, 21530, 21535, 21580, 21620, 21635,
    21645, 21685, 21730, 21765, **21825**, 25820 kHz

FRENCH GUIANA—French
RFO-GUYANE
    5056, 6170 kHz

FRENCH POLYNESIA—French/Tahitian
RFO-TAHITI
    6135, 9750, 11827, 15171 kHz

GABON—French
AFRIQUE NUMERO UN
    9580, 15475, 17630 kHz
RTV GABONAISE
    4777 kHz

GERMANY—German
BAYERISCHER RUNDFUNK
    6085 kHz
DEUTSCHE WELLE
    3995, 6075, **6085**, 6100, 6115, 6145, 6180, 6185,
    7110, 7130, 7140, 7185, 7225, **7250**, 7275, **9510**,
    9545, 9605, 9640, 9650, 9665, **9690**, 9700, 9715,
    9730, 9735, 9755, **11735**, **11765**, 11785, 11795,
    11810, 11865, **11915**, 11950, **11965**, 11970,
    13610, 13690, 13770, 13780, 15105, 15145,
    15245, **15250**, 15270, 15275, 15350, 15390,
    15410, **15510**, **17715**, 17755, **17810**, 17820,
    17830, 17835, 17845, 17860, 17875, 21540,
    21560, 21600, **21640**, 21680, 25740 kHz
SENDER FREIES BERLIN
    6190 kHz

RUNDFUNK IM AMERIKANISCHEN SEKTOR
    6005 kHz
RADIO BREMEN
    6190 kHz
SUDDEUTSCHER RUNDFUNK
    6030 kHz
SUDWESTFUNK
    7265 kHz

GREECE—Greek
FONI TIS HELLADAS
    7430, 9395, 9420, 9425, 9935, 11645, 12105,
    15625, 15630, 15650, 17535, 17550 kHz
RADIOFONIKOS STATHMOS MAKEDONIAS
    9425, 9935, 11595 kHz

HOLLAND—Dutch
RADIO NEDERLAND
    5955, 6020, **6165**, 7130, **7285**, **9590**, **9630**, 9715,
    9855, 9860, 9895, 11660, 11710, 11730, **11890**,
    11935, 11950, **11955**, 13700, 13770, **15120**,
    15315, **15365**, 15560, **15570**, **17575**, 17605,
    17760, 21480, **21485**, **21515**, 21530, **21685**,
    21745, 25940, 25970 kHz

HONDURAS—Spanish
HRVC-LA VOZ EVANGELICA
    4820 kHz

HUNGARY—Hungarian
RADIO BUDAPEST
    6025, 6110, 7220, 9835, 11910, 15160, 15220
    kHz
RADIO KOSSUTH
    6025 kHz

IRAN—Persian
VOICE OF THE ISLAMIC REPUBLIC
    4985, 5995, 11790, 15084 kHz

IRAQ—Arabic
REPUBLIC OF IRAQ RADIO
    3980, 4600, 7350, 8350, 9722, 15600, 17940 kHz

ISRAEL
KOL ISRAEL
    Arabic 5900, 5915, 9815, 15100, 15480 kHz
    Persian 9435, 11588, 11605, 17590 kHz
    Yiddish 9435, 11588, 11605, 15590, 15640,
    17590 kHz
RASHUTH HASHIDUR (Reshet Bet)
    Hebrew 9388, 11588, 13753, 15617, 17545 kHz

ITALY—Italian
RTV ITALIANA
    3995, 5990, 6060, 7175, 7235, 7275, 7290, 9515,
    9575, 9710, 11800, 11905, 15245, 15330, 15385,
    17780, 17795, 17800, 21515, 21535, 21560,
    21690 kHz

JAPAN—Japanese
RADIO JAPAN/NHK
    5960, 5990, **6120**, 6185, **7125**, 7140, 7210, 9505,
    9535, 9580, 9640, **9645**, 9650, **9675**, **9685**,
    11735, 11815, 11840, 11850, 11865, 11870,
    11875, 15195, 15230, 15270, 15280, 15325,
    15345, **15350**, 15430, 17765, 17810, **17820**,
    17825, 17835, 17845, 17890, 21610, **21635**,
    21640, **21690**, **21700** kHz

RADIO TAMPA
3925, 3945, 6055, 6115, 9595, 9760 kHz

JORDAN—Arabic
RADIO JORDAN
9560, 11810, 11940, 11955, 13655, 15435 kHz

KOREA (DPR)—Korean
KOREAN CENTRAL BS
9665, 11680 kHz
RADIO PYONGYANG
6125, 6540, 6576, 7200, 7250, 9325, 9345, 9505, 9640, 9835, 9977, 11700, 11735, 11760, 11845, 13760, 15115, 15180, 15230, 17765 kHz

KOREA (REPUBLIC)—Korean
RADIO KOREA
5975, 6135, **6145**, 6165, 6480, 7275, 7550, 9570, 9640, **9650**, 9670, 9870, 11740, 13670, 15375, 15575 kHz

LEBANON
KING OF HOPE
Arabic 6280, 11530 kHz
VOICE OF LEBANON
Arabic/French 6550 kHz

LIBYA—Arabic
RADIO JAMAHIRIYA
6185, 9600, 15415, 15450 kHz

LUXEMBOURG—German
RADIO LUXEMBOURG
6090 kHz

MEXICO—Spanish
Rarely heard from afar.
LA HORA EXACTA
9555 kHz
RADIO EDUCACION
6185 kHz
RADIO MIL
6010 kHz
RADIO UNIVERSIDAD
6045, 6115, 9600 kHz
RADIO XEQM
6105 kHz
RADIO XEQQ
9680 kHz
RADIO XEUJ
5982 kHz
RADIO XEUW
6017 kHz

MONACO—Arabic
RADIO MONTE CARLO (via Canada)
5960, 9755 kHz

MOROCCO
RADIO MEDI UN
French 9575 kHz
RTV MAROCAINE
French 11920, 17595, 17815 kHz
Arabic 15105, 15330, 15335, 15345, 15360, 17815 kHz

NORWAY—Norwegian
RADIO NORWAY INTERNATIONAL
5980, 7160, 9590, 9600, 9605, 9615, 9645, 9650, 9655, 11730, 11735, 11745, 11755, 11790, 11840, 11845, 11850, 11860, 11865, 11870, 11875, 11925, 15165, 15175, 15220, 15225, 15230, 15235, 15260, 15270, 15310, 15360, 17730, 17740, 17745, 17755, 17760, 17765, 17790, 17820, 21610, 21640, 21695, 21705, 21710, 21730, 25730 kHz

OMAN—Arabic
RADIO OMAN
6085, 7270, 9735, 11745, 11840, 11890, 17735 kHz

PARAGUAY—Spanish
RADIO ENCARNACION
11945 kHz
RADIO NACIONAL
6025, 9735 kHz

PORTUGAL—Portuguese
RADIO PORTUGAL INTERNATIONAL
6130, 9555, 9600, 9615, 9635, 9705, 9740, 11740, 11750, 11800, 11840, 15140, 15225, 15250, 15285, 15425, 21500, 21700 kHz
RADIO RENASCENCA
9575, 9600, 9680 kHz

QATAR—Arabic
QATAR BROADCASTING SERVICE
11820, 15265, 15395, 17770 kHz

SAUDI ARABIA—Arabic
BS OF THE KINGDOM
6130, 6020, 7150, 7210, 7220, 7250, 7275, 7280, 9570, 9705, 9720, 9870, 9885, 11730, 11780, 11935, 15140, 15170, 15435, 21505, 21670 kHz

SINGAPORE—Chinese
Rarely well heard outside Asia/Pacific.
SINGAPORE BROADCASTING CORP
6000, 9634 kHz

SPAIN—Spanish
RADIO EXTERIOR DE ESPANA
7105, 9580, 9620, 9630, 9650, 9685, 11730, 11790, 11815, 11880, **11910**, 11920, 12035, 15110, 15240, 15325, 15365, 15395, 17715, 17755, 17815, 17845, 17890, 21495, 21555, 21570, 21595 kHz

SWEDEN—Swedish
RADIO SWEDEN (likely to be retimed)
6000, 6065, 7265, 9615, 9655, 9695, 9765, 11705, 11900, 11960, 15230, 15270, 15390, 17740, 17870, 21500, 21570, 21720 kHz

SWITZERLAND
RED CROSS BROADCASTING SERVICE
Airs one week per month.
French 7210 kHz
German 7210 kHz
SWISS RADIO INTERNATIONAL
French 3985, 6135, 6165, **7480**, 9535, 9560, 9650, 9810, 9885, **11695**, 11955, 12030, 12035, 13635, 13685, 15430, 15525, 15570, 17570, 17670, **17730**, 17830, 21630, 21695, 21770 kHz
German 3985, 6125, 6135, 6165, **7480**, 9535, 9560, 9650, 9810, 9885, **11695**, 11955, 12030, 12035, 13635, 13685, 15430, 15525, 15570,

17570, 17670, **17730**, 17830, 21630, 21695,
21770 kHz
Italian 3985, 6125, 6135, 6165, 9535, 9650,
9885, **11695**, 12030, 12035, 13635, 15430,
15525, 15570, 17570, 17830, 21770 kHz

SYRIA—Arabic
SYRIAN BROADCASTING SERVICE
11625, 12085, 15095 kHz

TUNISIA—Arabic
RTV TUNISIENNE
7475, 9675, 11550, 12005, 15450, 17500, 21535
kHz

TURKEY—Turkish
VOICE OF TURKEY
5980, 6140, 9445, 9460, 9665, 9685, 11775,
11925, 11955, 15160, 15220, 15265, 15325,
15365, 15405, 17880 kHz

UNITED ARAB EMIRATES—Arabic
UAE RADIO-Abu Dhabi
6170, 9600, 9695, 9780, 11815, 11965, 11985,
13605, 15305, 15315, 17855, 21515, 21735,
25690 kHz
UAE RADIO-Dubai
11795, 11945, 13675, 15320, 15400, 15435,
17830, 21605, 21700 kHz

UNITED KINGDOM
BBC
Arabic **6030**, 6110, **7140**, 7320, 9825, 11680,
11730, **11740**, 13660, 15180, **15235**, 15245,
15575, **15590**, 17715, **17785** kHz
Persian **5975**, **9590** kHz

USSR
KAZAKH RADIO
Russian, etc. 9780, 11950 kHz
KYRGYS RADIO
Russian, etc. 4010, 4050, 9735, 17785 kHz
LITHUANIAN RADIO
Russian/Lithuanian 6010, 9675, 9710 kHz
RADIO HOPE
Russian 12056 kHz
RADIO KIEV
Ukrainian 5960, 5980, 6010, 6090, 6175, 6185,
7115, 7330, 7400, 9600, 9750, 9800, 9865,
11675, 11790, 13645, 15180, 15455, 15525,
17585, 17690, 17720 kHz
RADIO MOSCOW
Russian **4765**, 7300, 7305, 7310, 7315, 7330,
7335, 7340, 7350, 7355, 7370, 7380, 7390, 7400,

7420, 7440, 9450, 9470, 9480, 9490, 9750, 9775,
9790, 9800, 9810, 9820, 9830, 9865, 9890, 9895,
11510, 11630, 11655, 11670, 11675, 11680,
11690, 11695, 11975, 11990, 12000, 12005,
12015, 12020, 12025, 12030, 12035, 12040,
12045, 12050, 12055, 12060, 12065, 12070,
12100, 13615, 13625, 13630, 13645, 13690,
13700, 13710, 13735, 13745, 13760, 13795,
13820, 15455, 15460, 15470, 15485, 15490,
15495, 15500, 15520, 15525, 15530, 15535,
15550, 15570, 15585, 15590,15595, 15600,
15630, 17560, 17570, 17580,17590, 17595,
17605, 17610, 17615, 17620, 17625, 17635,
17645, 17650, 17660, 17665, 17675, 17680,
17685, 17690, 17695, 17700, 21490, 21515,
21550, 21615, 21750, 21795, 21820 kHz
RADIO RIGA INTERNATIONAL
Russian/Latvian 5935 kHz
RADIO TALLINN
Russian/Estonian 5925 kHz
RADIO YEREVAN
Armenian 6120, 7205, 7400, 9480, 9750, 9775,
11675, 11790, 12050, 12060, 13645, 15180,
15455, 15485, 15510, 17660, 17680, 17690,
17720 kHz
TADJIK RADIO
Russian/Tadjik 4635, 7245, 9785 kHz
TURKMEN RADIO
Russian/Turkmen 4825, 7145, 17635 kHz
UKRAINIAN RADIO
Russian/Ukrainian 4940, 7245, 15385, 17850 kHz
Ukrainian 5950, 6020, 6030, 6080, 6165, 6195,
9560, 9865, 13795 kHz
UZBEK RADIO
Russian, etc. 4850, 5900, 5995, 9595, 17840 kHz

VENEZUELA—Spanish
ECOS DEL TORBES
4980, 9640 kHz
RADIO CONTINENTAL
4939 kHz
RADIO NACIONAL
9540 kHz
RADIO RUMBOS
4970, 9661 kHz
RADIO TACHIRA
4830 kHz
RADIO VALERA
4840 kHz

YUGOSLAVIA—Serbo-Croat
CROATIAN RADIO (via WHRI, USA)
7315, **9495** kHz
RADIO YUGOSLAVIA
6100, 9620, 9720, 11740 kHz

WHERE IN THE WORLD II:

World Time, Station Addresses and Toll-Free Numbers

How to order a Maori T-shirt? Where to write about a program just heard? Who sells Canadian folk records? What's the best way to find lodging in Macas, Ecuador?

Warm up your fingertips! Because multinational audience surveys are so costly, letters are often a station's only link with its listeners. This means that hundreds of stations around the world are eager to hear from you—and some will scratch your back in return. Here's how.

Free Collectibles

To advertise their presence and stimulate listener correspondence, some stations give out souvenirs and tourist literature, as well as the usual complimentary program schedules. These goodies include brochures on national history, exotic calendars, offbeat magazines and newspapers, attractive verification postcards, costume jewelry pins, colorful pennants, T-shirts from places most people have never heard of, stickers and decals, key chains—even, on rare occasion, recordings, weird coins, stamps . . . and, in one case, a doorknob hanger.

If the United States Government and General Motors are operating under shriveling budgets, you can bet that international radio stations are also feeling the economic pinch. So if you want a souvenir, it's usually speak up or be passed up. Specify politely what you'd like; in this section of *Passport*,

we detail what's available, and how. Too, it helps to send along a little souvenir of your own—an autographed photo of your family, or a local tourist brochure or postcard, for example. Of course, especially with photos, keep in mind the religious and cultural sensibilities of the recipient. And, whenever possible, provide constructive, sincere comments on their programs—these are especially welcomed by most stations.

By the Buy

World band stations traditionally have taken the mandarin perspective on earning a profit, and simply given away token items. However, a growing number—notably the Christian Science Monitor, BBC World Service and Radio New Zealand—sell a wide variety of goods by mail, both as a service to listeners and to help offset operating costs. These offerings are detailed in this section.

Many of these products can't be found anywhere else, and are delightful. But there are pitfalls. Americans should remember when buying clothing from other countries to order big, as sizes elsewhere tend to be smaller. Of course, it works in reverse if you're not an American and you're ordering from the United States or Canada. If in doubt, send a life-sized paper cutout of the desired article of clothing in your size. Payment in U.S. dollars is usually okay, provided it's in cash, but charge cards are less chancy. Be sure to take the usual precautions when sending money through the mail.

Tourist Tips Fielding Never Heard of

If you're traveling abroad, here's a little-known secret: World band stations are sometimes willing to provide helpful information to prospective visitors. When writing, especially to smaller stations, appeal to their civic pride and treat them like kindly uncles or aunts from whom you're seeking a favor. After all, catering to tourist inquiries is hardly a requirement of operating most radio stations. (Those stations that do provide tourist literature as a matter of course are so indicated in this section.)

This approach has its limits, especially among that small coterie of central African stations that regards Westerners as sheep to be fleeced. But when it clicks, you can be treated to exceptional information on local cultures, sites, restaurants, places to stay, and events that are nowhere to be found within the pages of any guide book. This is especially true of domestic radio stations, whose primary audiences are in their own backyards—and who know just about all there is to know about those backyards.

How to Visit Stations

Many public and religious stations are delighted to have firsthand visits from listeners, who otherwise may be separated from them by land and sea. Complimentary tours of studios are often given on weekdays by professional guides or other station personnel. A few friendly stations also give separate guided tours of their transmission facilities.

Most commercial stations are not set up to give formal tours. Yet, many are delighted to meet informally with listeners. For example, individual radio enthusiasts from North America, Germany and Japan have been known to fly thousands of miles to embark on pilgrimages to stations in such out-of-the-way places as the Andes mountains or Amazon rain forest.

These visits can have unexpected consequences. According to Tiare Publications' Gerry Dexter, one fellow dropped by to visit a small Latin American station notorious for not responding to listeners' correspondence. While in the men's room, he found several years' worth of unanswered letters in a huge stack . . . being used in lieu of the customary paper roll.

For that reason, in this section the wheat is separated from the chaff. Only the addresses of stations known, or likely, to

respond to listener correspondence, are included.

In general, it's a good idea to write in advance if you wish to tour a public or religious station. Courtesy dictates the same treatment for commercial stations, but with some smaller stations it works best simply to appear, like Lassie, unannounced at the door.

Gift giving? If you're visiting a large international broadcaster outside Africa or Japan, forget it. In Moslem countries avoid cross-gender gift giving, which may be misunderstood. But if you're the guest of a smaller or private station, or one in Africa or Japan, a simple, non-controversial memento—restaurant T-shirt, sports team cap, or other souvenir from where you live or work—can go a long way towards sealing a relationship. Present your gift openly, without ostentation, for best results. Of course, never give money.

Remember, you're a guest, not a customer. You represent your nation's culture and people. Act accordingly, and you will be remembered accordingly.

Will Writing Get You Into Trouble?

No, not these days—at least not in most democratic countries. However, use common sense. If you aspire to be Director of the CIA, don't write sealed letters to Cuba, Libya, Iraq, clandestine stations and such. If in doubt, use a postcard—cheaper, too.

Bunko in Your Mailbox

There are scams in world band. Not many, but they're there.

A few years back, a back-slapping American appeared suddenly on the scene, claiming he was going to build an enormous world band station—something that would have made *Texas Brags* if it had been in Texas. He sent *Passport*, among other publications, impressive-looking press releases, and requested to take out large amounts of advertising space. We were unable to confirm virtually any of his claims, and thus refused to carry his advertising or cover the alleged "story."

Yet, favorable reports and glowing advertising concerning his claimed venture wound up appearing in a variety of other broadcasting publications, as well as over a number of world band stations. Once all this credible-sounding publicity took root, he began selling radios and radio-related items by mail to the public. Trouble is, while charges would appear on customers' credit cards, the ordered products did not always materialize. He got away with this for some time, fooling the mighty and meek alike, then vanished.

The station? No license, no equipment —just vaporware.

A similar situation has existed in recent years in Germany, where a radio book "publisher" has been taking people's money, but not so much as printing the ordered goods—much less sending them. To this day, this firm continues to receive favorable publicity within at least some radio enthusiasts' bulletins and DX programs.

Other scams? For years, listeners who have written certain stations, notably in Nigeria, have found themselves receiving correspondence from "students" or allegedly devout Christians seeking goods, money or sponsorship to emigrate to Western countries. Some are so brazen they will actually specify the brand names and model numbers of the items they want!

In Latin America, correspondence to a handful of stations has been known to generate a smattering of "love letter" replies, sometimes accompanied by comely photos. These usually evolve into pleas for money (often "for sick relatives"), merchandise, "mail-order marriage" or emigration sponsorship.

Not all such correspondence is suspicious. "Pen pal" courtship arrangements, a long-standing tradition in certain countries, exist via some Philippine stations. Those we have come across have been sponsored by legitimate religious institutions, and so have been cloaked in respectability. Nevertheless, pleas for financial and other favors can result as a relationship evolves. If this happens, contact the sponsoring church immediately for advice on how to proceed.

There is, alas, no shortage of tragedy on our planet. If you wish to reach out and touch someone who's suffering, donate to any of the numerous needy charities that exist for this purpose—not world band hustlers.

Address and Toll-Free Numbers

What follows are the addresses and toll-free numbers for stations known to be responding, even if only occasionally, to listener correspondence. Where someone is responsible for listener correspondence, his or her name, or names, is given. Otherwise, simply address your letter to the station itself.

Paying the Postman

Most major stations that reply do so for free. However, some smaller organizations expect, or at least hope for, reimbursement for postage costs. Most effective, especially for Latin American and Indonesian stations, is to enclose return postage; that is, unused (mint) stamps from the *station's* country. These are available from Plum's Airmail Postage, 12 Glenn Road, Flemington NJ 08822 USA (send $1 or a self-addressed, stamped envelope for details); DX Stamp Service, 7661 Roder Parkway, Ontario NY 14519 USA (ditto); and some local private stamp dealers. Unused Brazilian international stamps (10 stamps, good for 10 replies, for $2 or 11 IRCs) are also available from Antonio Ribeiro da Motta, Caixa Postal 949, São José dos Campos—SP, Brazil.

You can also prompt reluctant stations by donating one U.S. dollar, preferably hidden from prying eyes by a piece of foil-covered carbon paper or the like—registration helps, too. Additionally, International Reply Coupons (IRCs), which recipients may exchange locally for air or surface stamps, are available at many post offices worldwide. Thing is, they're relatively costly, aren't all that effective, and aren't accepted by postal authorities in a few countries.

Tips to Optimize Your Results

When writing, remember to make your letter interesting and helpful from the recipient's point of view, and friendly without being excessively personal or forward. Well-thought-out comments on specific programs are almost always appreciated. (If you must use a foreign-language form letter as the basis for your communication, individualize it for each occasion either by writing it out, or by making use of a word processor.)

Writing in the broadcaster's tongue is always a plus—this section of *Passport* indicates when it is a requirement—but English is usually the next best bet. Remember, when writing Spanish-speaking countries, that what gringos think of as the "last name" is actually written as the middle name. Thus Antonio Vargas García, which also can be written as Antonio Vargas G., refers to Sr. Vargas; so your salutation should read, *Estimado Sr. Vargas.*

What's that "García" doing there, then? That's *mamita's* father's family name. Latinos more or less solved the problem of gender fairness in names long before the Anglos.

But, wait—what about Portuguese, used by all those stations in Brazil? Same concept, but in reverse. Mama's father's family name is in the middle, and the "real" last name is where we're used to it, at the end.

Similarly to Spanish, with Chinese the "last" name comes first. However, when writing in English, Chinese names are sometimes reversed for the benefit of *low faan*—foreigners. Use your judgement. For example, "Li" is a common Chinese last name, so if you see "Li Dan," it's "Mr. Li." But if it's "Dan Li," he's already one step ahead of you, and it's still "Mr. Li". If in doubt, fall back on the ever-safe "Dear Sir" or "Dear Madam."

Be patient—replies usually take weeks, sometimes months. Slow responders, those that tend to take six months or more to reply, are cited in this listing, as are erratic repliers.

World Time in Relation to Each Country

Local times are given in terms of hours' difference from World Time, formally known as Coordinated Universal Time (UTC), Greenwich Mean Time (GMT) and Zulu time (Z).

For example, Algeria is World Time +1; that is, one hour later than World Time. So, if World Time is 1200, the local time in Algeria is 1300 (1:00 PM). On the other hand, México City is World Time –6; that is, six hours earlier than World Time. If World Time is 1200, in México City it's 6:00 AM. And so it goes for each country in this section.

For more information on World Time, see the *Passport* Glossary, and the World Time box within *Getting Started with World Band Radio*.

A Rose Is A Rose . . .

Why so many designations for World Time? In simpler days, Greenwich Mean Time was used by civilians, Zulu by military and para-military organizations. When international timekeeping norms were being upgraded, it was decided at an official conference to come up not only with new technical norms, but also a new name. Greenwich Mean Time, referring to the site of an observatory in England, was considered to smack of national chauvinism, and thus to be politically suspect.

Politically proper *Coordinated Universal Time* was agreed upon in its stead. But,

as one frustrated attendee to that conference related afterwards, if the abbreviation chosen had been "CUT," it would have been "CUT" only in English—a manifestation of language chauvinism, and thus once again politically suspect. Thus, "UTC" was agreed upon because it did not conform to the acronym for Coordinated Universal Time in *any* of the world's major languages, and thus was politically proper.

Understandably, this blow against political unenlightenment sailed over more than a few people's heads, including some you'd think would know better. One result is that you'll sometimes find UTC written out or announced in English as "Universal Time Coordinated." Yes, it's wrong—but who can blame them?

At *Passport*, we use the more digestible everyday term, "World Time"—and promise there will be no plenipotentiary conference to change it. Traditionalists, such as the BBC World Service, continue to use GMT.

Tempus Fugit

Has something changed since we went to press? A missing detail? Please let us know. Your update information—particularly photocopied material from stations—is very much welcomed and appreciated at our Editorial Office, IBS, Box 300, Penn's Park, PA 18943 USA (fax 215/598-3794); or IBS, Casilla de Correo 1844, Asunción, Paraguay.

Continuing information on addresses and schedules of rarely heard broadcasters is available each week via the exclusive *Numero Uno* newsletter (Box 54, Caledonia NY 14423 USA), sent to no more than a couple dozen professionals and experienced station chasers who have applied and been accepted for membership. Our thanks to John Herkimer, Editor & Publisher, and Don Jensen, Editor Emeritus, and the members of *NU* for their cooperation in the preparation of this section of *Passport/92*.

Rules of the Road

Unless otherwise stated:
• Only stations that reply to listener correspondence are included.
• Mailing addresses are cited, which in some cases differ from stations' physical locations.
• Stations reply regularly, within six months, to most listeners' letters in English.

- Stations provide, upon request, free station schedules and souvenir verification postcards or letters.
- Stations do not require compensation for return postage costs.
- Correspondence to stations is customarily sent to the headquarters' offices listed herein—not to a transmitter or relay site.

AFGHANISTAN   World Time +4 1/2
Radio Afghanistan, P.O. Box 544, Kabul, Afghanistan.
ALBANIA   World Time +1
Radio Tirana, RTV Shqiptar, International Service, Rrug Ismail Qemali, Tirana, Albania. Contact: Napoleon Roshi, Director. Free tourist literature, stickers, Albanian stamps, pins and other souvenirs.
ALGERIA   World Time +1
RTV Algerienne, 21 Boulevard des Martyrs, Algiers, Algeria. Contact: L. Zaghlami. Replies irregularly to correspondence in French. 1 IRC or return postage helpful.
ANGOLA   World Time +1
Radio Nacional, C.P. 1329, Luanda, Angola. Contact: Sra. Luiza Fancony, Direitora de Programas; or Lourdes de Almeida, Chefe de Secção. Replies occasionally to correspondence, preferably in Portuguese. $1, return postage or 2 IRCs most helpful.
Emissora Provincial—Benguela, C.P. 19, Benguela, Angola. Contact: José Cabral Sande, Direitor. $1 required. Replies to correspondence in Portuguese.
Emissora Provincial—Moxico, C.P. 74, Luena, Angola. Contact: Paulo Cahilo, Direitor. $1 or return postage required. Replies to correspondence in Portuguese.
Other *Emissora Provincial* stations—same address, etc., as Radio Nacional, above.
ANTARCTICA   World Time +13 McMurdo
AFAN McMurdo, U.S. Navy Communication Station COMNAVSUPPOR-ANTARCTICA, McMurdo Station, FPO San Francisco CA 96601 USA.
ARGENTINA   World Time −2 (−3 midyear); with exceptions that include the following: −3 (−4 midyear) La Rioja, San Juan, San Luis and Santiago del Estero
Radio Argentina al Exterior—RAE, Casilla de Correo 2868, 1000 Buenos Aires, Argentina. Contact: Gabriel Iván Barrera, DX Editor. Free paper pennant. Return postage or $1 appreciated.
Radio Belgrano, Uruguay 1237, 1016 Buenos Aires, Argentina. Contact (technical): Carlos A. Tagliapietra, Sub Gerente Técnico. Expected to leave the air permanently before long. Replies to correspondence in Spanish.
Radio Continental, Rivadavia 835, 1002 Buenos Aires, Argentina. Contact: Julio Valles. Stickers and tourist literature; $1 or return postage required. Replies to correspondence in Spanish.
Radio Malargüe, Esquivel Aldao 350, 5613 Malargüe, Argentina. Prefers correspondence in Spanish.
Radio Nacional (when operating, once transmitter parts are obtained), LRA6 Radio Nacional Mendoza, Emilio Civit, 460 Mendoza, Argentina. Contact: Silvana Licciardi.
AUSTRALIA   World Time +11 (+10 midyear) Victoria, Queensland, New South Wales and Tasmania; +10 1/2 (+9 1/2 midyear) South Australia; +9 1/2 Northern Territory; +8 Western Australia
ABC/Caama Radio, P.O. Box 2924, Alice Springs 5740, Northern Territory, Australia. Contact: Rae Allen, Regional Programme Manager; or Sandra McCormack; or Sue Camilleri. 2 IRCs or return postage helpful.
ABC/Radio Rum Jungle, P.O. Batchelor 0845, Northern Territory, Australia. Contact: Andrew Joshua, Chairman, Top End Aboriginal Bush Broadcasting Association. 3 IRCs or return postage helpful.
Australian Broadcasting Corporation, ABC Box 9994, GPO Brisbane 4001, Queensland, Australia. Contact: John Kalinowski, Manager Network Services. Free stickers, "Travellers Guide to ABC Radio." 3 IRCs or return postage helpful.

Australian Broadcasting Corporation, ABC Box 9994, GPO Darwin 5750, Northern Territory, Australia. Contact: Sue Camilleri. Free stickers. Free "Travellers Guide to ABC Radio." 3 IRCs or return postage helpful.
Australian Broadcasting Corporation, ABC Box 9994, GPO Perth 6001, Australia. Contact: Gary Matthews, Head of Broadcast and Technical Department (Radio). Free "Travellers Guide to ABC Radio." 3 IRCs or return postage helpful.
Radio Australia, P.O. Box 755, Glen Waverley VIC 3150, Australia. Contact: Sue Duckworth, Acting Correspondence Officer. Free calendars and tourist literature.
AUSTRIA   World Time +1 (+2 midyear)
Radio Austria International, A-1136 Vienna, Austria. Contact: Paul Lendvai, Director. Free stickers.
BANGLADESH   World Time +6
Radio Bangladesh: Non-technical correspondence to External Services, P.O. Box No. 2204, Dhaka, Bangladesh. Contact: Masudul Hasan, Deputy Director. *Technical correspondence* to National Broadcasting Authority, NBA House, 121 Kazi Nazrul Islam Avenue, Dhaka 1000, Bangladesh. Contact: Mohammed Noor Al-Islam, Station Engineer (Research Wing); or Kazi Rafique.
BELGIUM   World Time +1 (+2 midyear)
Belgische Radio TV, Postbus 26, B-1000 Brussels, Belgium. Replies sometimes take a while.
Radio-Télévision Belge de la Communauté Française, Radio Une (destination outre-mer), B.P. 202, B-1040 Brussels, Belgium.
BELIZE   World Time −6
Belize Radio One, P.O. Box 89, Belize City, Belize. Contact (technical): E.R. Rosado, Chief Engineer.
BENIN   World Time +1
ORT du Bénin, La Voix de la Révolution, B.P. 366, Cotonou, Bénin; this address for Cotonou and Parakou stations. Contact: (Cotonou) Damien Zinsou Ala Hassa; or Leonce Goohouede; (Parakou, non-technical) J. da Matha, Le Chef de la Station, or (Parakou, technical) Léon Donou, Le Chef des Services Techniques. Return postage, $1, return postage or 1 IRC required. Replies irregularly to correspondence in French.
BHUTAN   World Time +6
Bhutan Broadcasting Service, P.O. Box 101, Thimphu, Bhutan. 2 IRCs, return postage or $1 required. Replies irregularly.
BOLIVIA   World Time −4
La Voz del Trópico, "Radiodifusora CVU," Casilla 2494, Villa Tunari, Cochabamba, Bolivia. Contact: Oscar Ustáriz Aranda, Director. Return postage or $1 required. Replies occasionally to correspondence in Spanish.
Radio Abaroa, Casilla 136, Riberalta, Bení, Bolivia. Contact: René Arias Pacheco. Return postage or $1 required. Replies irregularly to correspondence in Spanish.
Radio Animas, Chocaya, Animas, Potosí, Bolivia. Return postage or $1 required. Replies irregularly to correspondence in Spanish.
Radio Brasil Tropical, Cultura, Rua Joaquim Nurtinho, 1456 (Ed. Palácio do Radio), 78015 Cuiabá, Mato Grosso, Brazil. Return postage required. Replies occasionally to correspondence in Portuguese.
Radio Centenario, Casilla 818, Santa Cruz de la Sierra, Bolivia. Contact: Pedro Salces Ruíz, Director. Return postage or $1 required. Replies to correspondence in Spanish.
Radio Cristal, Casilla 5303, La Paz, Bolivia. Contact: Mario Castro M., Director. Return postage or $1 required. Replies irregularly to correspondence in Spanish.
Radio Eco, Av. Brasil, Correo Central, Reyes, Bení, Bolivia. Contact: Carlos Espinoza Cortez, Director Ejecutivo. Free station literature. $1 or return postage required, and financial contributions solicited. Replies irregularly to correspondence in Spanish.
Radio El Mundo, Casilla 1984, Santa Cruz de la Sierra, Bolivia. Contact: Freddy Banegas Carrasco, Gerente. Free sticker. $1 or return postage required. Replies irregularly to correspondence in Spanish.
Radio Galaxia, Guayaramerín, Bení, Bolivia. Contact: Dorián Arias, Gerente; or Jeber Hitachi Banegas, Director. Return postage or $1 required. Replies to correspondence in Spanish.
Radio Illimani, Calle Ayacucho 467, 2° piso, La Paz, Bolivia. Contact: Sra. Gladys de Zamora, Administradora. $1 required, and your letter should be registered and include a tourist brochure or postcard from where you live. Replies irregularly to friendly correspondence in Spanish.

Radio Juan XXIII, San Igancio de Velasco, Santa Cruz, Bolivia. Contact: Manuel Picazo Torres. Return postage or $1 required. Replies occasionally to correspondence in Spanish.
Radio La Cruz del Sur, Casilla 1408, La Paz, Bolivia. Contact: Pastor Rodolfo Moya Jiménez, Director. Pennant for $1 or return postage. Replies slowly to correspondence in Spanish.
Radio La Perla del Acre, Cobija del Acre, Pando, Bolivia. Return postage or $1 required. Replies irregularly to correspondence in Spanish.
Radio Libertad, Casilla 568, Oruro, Bolivia. Return postage or $1 required. Replies irregularly to correspondence in Spanish.
Radio Mamoré, 25 de Mayo, Guayaramerín, Bení, Bolivia. Contact: Lucio Montán E., Director-Proprietario. Return postage or $1 required. Replies irregularly to correspondence in Spanish.
Radio Minería, Casilla 247, Oruro, Bolivia. Contact: Dr. José Carlos Gómez Espinoza, Gerente y Director General. Return postage or $1 required. Replies irregularly to correspondence in Spanish.
Radio Movima, Santa Ana de Yacuma, Bení, Bolivia. Contact: Rubén Serrano López, Director. Return postage or $1 required. Replies irregularly to correspondence in Spanish.
Radio Nacional de Huanuni, Casilla 681, Oruro, Bolivia. Contact: Rafael Linneo Morales, Director-General. Return postage or $1 required. Replies to correspondence in Spanish.
Radio Padilla, Padilla, Chuquisaca, Bolivia. Contact: Moisés Palma Salazar, Director. Return postage or $1 required. Replies to correspondence in Spanish.
Radio Paitití, Casilla 321, Guayaramerín, Bení, Bolivia. Contact: Armando Mollinedo Bacarreza, Director. Return postage or $1 required. Replies irregularly to correspondence in Spanish.
Radio San Gabriel, "La Voz del Pueblo Aymara," Casilla 4792, La Paz, Bolivia. Contact: Hno. José Canut Saurut, franciscano, Director Gerente. $1 or return postage helpful. Free book on station and calendars. Replies fairly regularly to correspondence in Spanish.
Radio San Miguel, Casilla 102, Riberalta, Bení, Bolivia. Contact: Héctor Salas Takaná, Director. Return postage or $1 required. Replies irregularly to correspondence in Spanish.
Radio Santa Ana, Cobija 285 esquina Bolívar, Santa Ana, Bení, Bolivia. Contact: Mario Roberto Suárez, Director. Return postage or $1 required. Replies irregularly to correspondence in Spanish.
Radio Santa Cruz, Emisora del Instituto Radiofónoco Fé y Alegría (IRFA), Casilla 672, Santa Cruz de la Sierra, Bolivia. Contact: Victor Blajot, S.J., Director General. Free pennants. Return postage required. Correspondence in Spanish preferred.
Radio 20 de Setiembre, Bermejo, Tarija, Bolivia. Return postage or $1 required. Replies irregularly to correspondence in Spanish.

BOTSWANA   World Time +2
Radio Botswana, Private Bag 0060, Gaborone, Botswana. Contact: Ted Makgekenene, Chief. Return postage or $1 required. Replies irregularly.

BRAZIL   World Time –1 (–2 midyear) Atlantic Islands; –2 (–3 midyear) Eastern, including Brasília and Rio de Janeiro; –3 (–4 midyear) Western; –4 (–5 midyear) Acre
Note: For Brazilian return postage, see introduction to this article.
Radio Alvorada—Londrina, C.P. 414, 86015 Londrina, Paraná, Brazil. Contact: Raimunda Ribeiro da Silva; or Padre Dilermando Luíz Cozatti, Direitor. Pennants for $1 or return postage. Replies to correspondence in Portuguese.
Radio Alvorada—Parintins, Travessa Leopoldo Neves 503, 69150 Parintins, Amazonas, Brazil. Contact: Raimunda Ribeira da Motta, Direitora. Return postage required. Replies occasionally to correspondence in Portuguese.
Radio Anhanguera—Goiânia, C.P. 13, 74001 Goiânia, Brazil. Contact: Rossana F. da Silva. Return postage required. Replies to correspondence in Portuguese.
Radio Aparecida, C.P. 14664, 03698 São Paulo, Brazil. Contact: Cassiano Macedo; or Antonio C. Moreira, Direitor-General. Return postage required. Replies occasionally to correspondence in Portuguese.
Radio Brasil Tropical, C.P. 405, 78001 Cuiabá, Mato Grosso,

Brazil. Contact: K. Santos. Free stickers. $1 required. Replies to correspondence in Portuguese.
Radio Cabocla (when operating), Rua 4 Casa 9, Conjunto dos Secretários, 69000 Manaus, Amazonas, Brazil. Contact: Francisco Puga, Direitor-General. Return postage required. Replies occasionally to correspondence in Portuguese.
Radio Caiari, C.P. 104, 78901 Porto Velho, Rondônia, Brazil. Contact: Carlos Alberto Diniz Martins, Direitor-General. Free stickers. Return postage required. Replies irregularly to correspondence in Portuguese.
Radio Canção Nova, Estrada Particular alto de Bela Vista s/n, 12630 Cachoeira Paulista, São Paulo, Brazil. Contact: Tadeu Rodrigues Machado, Secretário, Depto. Radiodifusão. Free stickers. $1 or return postage required. Replies to correspondence in Portuguese.
Radio Clube do Pará, C.P. 533, 66001 Belém, Pará, Brazil. Contact: Edyr Paiva Proença, Direitor-General. Return postage required. Replies irregularly to correspondence in Portuguese.
Radio Cultura do Pará, Avenida Almirante Barroso 735, 66065 Belém, Pará, Brazil. Contact: Ronald Pastor; or Augusto Proenca, Direitor. Return postage required. Replies irregularly to correspondence in Portuguese.
Radio Cultura São Paulo, Rua Cenno Sbrighi 378, 05099 São Paulo, Brazil. Contact: Sra. María Luíza A. Kfouri, Chefe de Produção; or José Munhoz, Coordenador. $1 or return postage required. Replies slowly to correspondence in Portuguese.
Radio Difusora Aquidauana, C.P. 18, 79201 Aquidauana, Mato Grosso do Sul, Brazil. Contact: Walter Georg Keppler. Free tourist literature. Return postage required.
Radio Difusora Cáceres, C.P. 297, 78700 Cáceres, Mato Grosso, Brazil. Contact: Sra. Maridalva Amaral Vignardi. $1 or return postage required. Replies occasionally to correspondence in Portuguese.
Radio Difusora Macapá, C.P. 2929, 68901 Macapá, Amapa, Brazil. Contact: Francisco de Paulo Silva Santos. $1 or return postage required. Replies irregularly to correspondence in Portuguese.
Radio Difusora do Maranhão, C.P. 152, 65001 São Luíz, Maranhão, Brazil. Return postage required. Replies occasionally to correspondence in Portuguese.
Radio Difusora Roraima, Rua Capitão Ene Garcez 830, 69300 Boa Vista, Roraima, Brazil. Contact: Geraldo França, Direitor-General; or Francisco Alves Vieira. Return postage required. Replies occasionally to correspondence in Portuguese.
Radio Educação da Bahia, Centro de Rádio, Rua Pedro Gama 413/E, Alto Sobradinho Federação, 40000 Salvador, Bahia, Brazil. Contact: Elza Correa Ramos. $1 or return postage required. Replies to correspondence in Portuguese.
Radio Educação Rural, C.P. 261, 79101 Campo Grande, Mato Grosso do Sul, Brazil. Contact: Aliton Guerra or Diácono Tomás Schwamborn. $1 or return postage required. Replies to correspondence in Portuguese.
Radio Educadora—Bragança, Rua Barão do Rio Branco 1151, 68600 Bragança, Brazil. Contact: José Rosendo de S. Neto. $1 or return postage required. Replies to correspondence in Portuguese.
Radio Educadora da Bahia, Rua Pedro Gama 413/E, Alto Sobradinho Federação, 40000 Salvador, Bahia, Brazil. Contact: Walter Sequieros R. Tanure. Return postage required. Replies irregularly to correspondence in Portuguese.
Radio Emissora Aruanã, C.P. 214, 78601 Barra do Garças, Mato Grosso, Brazil. Contact: Neusa da Costa Ataide. $1 required. Replies slowly and rarely to correspondence in Portuguese.
Radio Gazeta, Avenida Paulista 900, 01310 São Paulo, Brazil. Contact: Ing. Aníbal Horta Figueiredo.
Radio Guarujá, C.P. 45, 88001 Florianópolis, Santa Catarina, Brazil. Contact: Alberto Gonçalves de Sousa, Direitor. Return postage required. Replies to correspondence in Portuguese.
Radio Inconfidência, C.P. 1027, 30001 Belo Horizonte, Minas Gerais, Brazil. Contact: Isaias Lansky, Direitor. $1 or return postage helpful.
Radio Integração, Rua Alagoas 270, lotes 8 e 9, 69980 Cruzeiro do Sul, Acre, Brazil. Contact: Claudio Onofre Ferreiro. Return postage required. Replies to correspondence in Portuguese.
Radio IPB AM, Rua Itajaí 433, Bairro Antonio Vendas, 79050

Campo Grande, Mato Grosso do Sul, Brazil. Contact: Kelly Cristina Rodrigues da Silva, Secretária. Return postage required. Replies to correspondence in Portuguese.
Radio Marajoara, Travessa Campos Sales 370, Centro, 66015 Belém, Pará, Brazil. Return postage required. Replies irregularly to correspondence in Portuguese.
Radio Nacional da Amazônia, C.P. 04/0340, 70323 Brasília, Brazil. Contact: Luís Antonio Alves, Gerente. Free stickers.
Radio Novas de Paz, C.P. 22, 80001 Curitiba, Paraná, Brazil. Contact: Matheus Jensen, Director. $1 or return postage required. Replies irregularly to correspondence in Portuguese.
Radio Pioneira, 24 de Janeiro 150, 64000 Teresina, Piauí, Brazil. Contact: Luíz Eduardo Bastos, or Tony Batista, Direitor. $1 or return postage required. Replies slowly to correspondence in Portuguese.
Radio Portal da Amazônia, Rua Tenente Alcides Duarte de Souza, 533 B° Duque de Caxias, 78010 Cuiabá, Mato Grosso, Brazil; also, C.P. 277, 78001 Cuiabá, Mato Grosso, Brazil. Contact: Arnaldo Medina. Return postage required. Replies occasionally to correspondence in Portuguese.
Radio Progresso, Estrada do Belmont s/n, B° Nacional, 78000 Porto Velho, Rondônia, Brazil. Contact: Angela Xavier, Direitora-General. Return postage required. Replies occasionally to correspondence in Portuguese.
Radio Progresso do Acre, 69900 Rio Branco, Acre, Brazil. Contact: José Alves Pereira Neto, Direitor-Presidente. Return postage or $1 required. Replies occasionally to correspondence in Portuguese.
Radio Record, C.P. 7920, 04084 São Paulo, Brazil. Contact: Mario Luíz Catto. Return postage or $1 required. Replies occasionally to correspondence in Portuguese.
Radio Sentinela, Travessa Ruy Barbosa 142 , 68250 Obidos, Pará, Brazil. Contact: Max Hamoy. Return postage required. Replies occasionally to correspondence in Portuguese.
Radio Transamérica, C.P. 6084, 90031 Porto Alegre, Rio Grande do Sul, Brazil; or C.P. 551, 97100 Santa María, Rio Grande do Sul, Brazil. Contact: Marlene P. Nunes, Secretária. Return postage required. Replies to correspondence in Portuguese.
Radio Tupí, Rua Nadir Dias Figueiredo 1329, 02110 São Paulo, Brazil. Contact: Elia Soares. Return postage required. Replies occasionally to correspondence in Portuguese.
BULGARIA World Time +2 (+3 midyear)
Radio Sofia, 4 Dragan Tsankov Blvd., Sofia, Bulgaria. Contact: Kristina Mihailova, In Charge of Listeners' Letters, English Section; or Ms. Nadezhda Gecheva, Listeners' Letters Department. Free stickers and pennants.
Radio Varna—Same details as Radio Sofia, above.
BURKINA FASO World Time exactly
RTV Burkina, B.P. 7029, Ouagadougou, Burkina Faso. Replies irregularly to correspondence in French. 1 IRC or return postage helpful.
CAMBODIA World Time +7
Radio The Voice of the People of Cambodia, Overseas Service, English Section, Phnom Penh, The State of Cambodia (Kampuchea). Contact: Bory Hem, English Announcer. Free pennants and Cambodian stamps. Replies irregularly and slowly. Do not include stamps, money, IRCs or dutiable items in envelope.
CAMEROON World Time +1
Cameroon Radio TV Corporation—Bafoussam, B.P. 970, Bafoussam (Ouest), Cameroon. Return postage required. Replies irregularly to correspondence in French.
Cameroon Radio TV Corporation—Bertoua—Same details as Douala, below.
Cameroon Radio TV Corporation—Buea, P.M.B., Buea (Sud-Ouest), Cameroon. $1 or return postage required.
Cameroon Radio TV Corporation—Douala, CRTV Feed Back, P.O. Box 986, Douala (Littoral), Cameroon. Contact: James Achanyi-Fontem, Head of Programming. $2 reportedly required, but $1 appears to suffice, as well it should. **Note:** Correspondence to this station may generate "pen pal" replies, including from those seeking favors.
Cameroon Radio TV Corporation—Yaoundé, B.P. 1634, Yaoundé (Centre-Sud), Cameroon. Return postage required. Replies slowly to correspondence in French.
CANADA World Time –3:30 (–2:30 midyear) Newfoundland; –4 (–3 midyear) Atlantic; –5 (–4 midyear) Eastern, including Quebec and Ontario; –6 (–5 midyear) Central; –7 (–6 midyear)

Mountain; –8 (–7 midyear) Pacific, including Yukon
CBC Northern Quebec Shortwave Service—same address as Radio Canada International. Free doorknob hanger.
CFCX-CFCF, 200 McGill College Avenue, Montréal PQ, H3B 4G7 Canada.
CFRX-CFRB, 2 St. Clair Avenue West, Toronto ON, M4V 1L6 Canada. Contact: David Simon, Engineer. Replies are sometimes slow in coming.
CHNX-CHNS, P.O. Box 400, Halifax NS, B3J 2R2 Canada. Contact (technical): K.J. Arsenault, Chief Engineer.
CKZN-CBN, CBC Centre, P.O. Box 12010, Station "A", St. John's NF, A1B 3T8 Canada. Contact (technical): Shawn R. Williams, Regional Engineer.
CKZU-CBU, CBC Centre, P.O. Box 4600, Vancouver BC, VJB 4A2 Canada. Contact: David Newbury.
Radio Canada International, P.O. Box 6000, Montréal PQ, H3C 3A8 Canada. Contact (non-technical): Allan Familiant, Acting Director; (technical) Jacques Bouliane, Assistant to the Chief Engineer. Free stickers and other station souvenirs. Canadian compact disks sold at International Sales, CBC Records, P.O. Box 500, Station "A", Toronto ON, M5W 1E6 Canada (VISA/MC).
CENTRAL AFRICAN REPUBLIC World Time +1
RTV Centrafricaine, B.P. 940, Bangui, Central African Republic. Contact: Jacques Mbilo or Michel Bata. Replies on rare occasion to correspondence in French; return postage required.
CHAD World Time +1
Radiodiffusion Nationale Tchadienne, B.P. 892, N'Djamena, Chad. Contact: Djimadoum Ngoka Kilamian. 2 IRCs or return postage required. Replies slowly to correspondence in French.
Radiodiffusion Nationale Tchadienne, B.P. 122, Moundou, Chad. Contact: Jacques Maimos, Le Chef de la Station Régionale de Radio Moundou.
CHILE World Time –3 (–4 midyear)
Radio Esperanza, Casilla 830, Temuco, Chile. Contact: Eleazar Jara Salazar, Jefe Depto. de Programación. Tourist brochure; $1 or return postage required. Replies to correspondence in Spanish.
Radio Nacional—when station, currently off the air, is operating, use the following address, but don't write "Radio Nacional" on the envelope: Carlos Toledo Verdugo, Casilla 296, San Fernando, VI Region, Chile. Free souvenirs. 3 IRCs required. Replies to correspondence in Spanish.
Radio Santa María, Casilla 1, Coyhaique, Chile. Contact: Pedro Andrade Vera, Dpto. DX. $1 or return postage required. Replies to correspondence in Spanish.
Radio Triunfal Evangélica, Costanera Sur 7209, Comuna de Cerro Navia, Santiago, Chile. Contact: Fernando González Segura, Obispo de la Misión Pentecostal Fundamentalista. 2 IRCs required. Replies to correspondence in Spanish.
CHINA (PR) World Time +6 (+7 midyear) Western; +7 (+8 midyear) Central; +8 (+9 midyear except for Guangdong and Guangxi provinces) Eastern, including Beijing
Note: Radio Beijing, the Central People's Broadcasting Station and certain regional outlets reply regularly to listeners' letters in a variety of languages. If a Chinese regional station does not respond to your correspondence within four months—and many will not, unless your letter is in Chinese or the regional dialect—try writing them c/o Radio Beijing, to the attention of Zhang Yanling.
Central People's Broadcasting Station, Zhongyang Renmin Guanbo Diantai, P.O. Box 4501, Beijing, People's Republic of China.
Fujian People's Broadcasting Station, Fuzhou, Fujian, People's Republic of China. $1 helpful. Replies occasionally.
Guangxi People's Broadcasting Station, No. 12 Min Zu Avenue, Nanning, Guangxi 530022, People's Republic of China. Contact: Li Hai Li, Staffer.
Heilongjiang People's Broadcasting Station, No. 115 Zhongshan Road, Harbin City, Heilongjiang, People's Republic of China. $1 helpful.
Jiangxi People's Broadcasting Station, Nanchang, Jiangxi, People's Republic of China. Replies fairly regularly.
Qinghai People's Broadcasting Station, Xining, Qinghai, People's Republic of China.
Radio Beijing, No. 2 Fuxingmenwai, Beijing 100866, People's Republic of China. Contact: Chen Lifang, English Department;

or Zhang Yanling. Free bi-monthly *The Messenger* magazine, desk calendars, pins and such small souvenirs as handmade papercuts. Two-volume, 820-page set of *Day-to-Day Chinese* language-lesson books for $15, including postage worldwide; contact Mr. Li Yi, English Department.

Sichuan People's Broadcasting Station, Chengdu, Sichuan, People's Republic of China. Replies occasionally.

Voice of Jinling, P.O. Box 268, Nanjing, Jiangsu, People's Republic of China. Free calendars. Replies to correspondence in Chinese and to simple correspondence in English. Return postage helpful.

Voice of Pujiang, P.O. Box 3064, Shanghai, People's Republic of China.

Voice of the Strait, People's Liberation Army Broadcasting Centre, P.O. Box 187, Fuzhou, Fujian, People's Republic of China. Replies very irregularly.

Wenzhou People's Broadcasting Station, Wenzhou, People's Republic of China.

Xilingol People's Broadcasting Station, Abagnar Qi, Xilingol, People's Republic of China.

Xinjiang People's Broadcasting Station, Urümqi, Xinjiang, People's Republic of China.

Xizang People's Broadcasting Station, Lhasa, Tibet, People's Republic of China. Contact: Lobsang Chonphel, Announcer.

Yunnan People's Broadcasting Station, Kunming, Yunnan, People's Republic of China. Replies occasionally.

CHINA (TAIWAN)   World Time +8

Central Broadcasting System, 55 Pei An Road, Taipei, Taiwan, Republic of China. Contact: Lee Ming, Deputy Director. Free stickers.

Voice of Asia, P.O. Box 880, Kao-hsiung, Taiwan, Republic of China. Free stickers.

Voice of Free China, P.O. Box 24-38, Taipei, Taiwan, Republic of China. Contact: Daniel Dong, Deputy Director of International Relations. Free station stickers, *Voice of Free China Journal*, annual diary, booklets and other publications, and Taiwanese stamps.

CLANDESTINE

Note: Clandestine stations, including their addresses and operating schedules, are unusually subject to abrupt change or termination. These stations, being operated by anti-establishment special interest organizations, tend to be suspicious of outsiders' motives. Thus, they are most likely to reply to correspondence from those who write in the station's native tongue, and who are perceived to be at least somewhat favorably disposed to their cause. Most will provide, upon request, printed matter, in their native tongue, on their cause.

"Al Kuds Radio," P.O. Box 10412, Tripoli, Libya. Pro-Palestinian, anti-Israeli government. ("Al Kuds ash Sherif" is the Arab name for Jerusalem.)

"EPRP Radio" (if operating), "Voice of Ethiopia on the Path to Democracy," ESPIC, P.O. Box 710358, Dallas TX 75371 USA; or ESPIC, P.O. Box 2688, Arlington VA 22202 USA; or ESPIC, 46 Rue de Vaugirard, F-75006 Paris, France. *Abyot* newsletter. Radio organ of the Ethiopian People's Revolutionary Party.

"Iran's Flag of Freedom Radio," Post Boks 103, DK-2670 Greve Strand, Denmark; or 20 rue de Concorcet, F-75009 Paris, France. Contact: Sazeman Darferesh Kaviani. Anti-Iranian government; supported by CIA and Egyptian government.

"La Voz de Alpha 66," c/o RMI (expedir, por favor), P.O. Box 526852, Miami FL 33152 USA. Anti-Castro, anti-communist; privately supported.

"La Voz del CID," Apartado de Correo 8130, 1000 San José, Costa Rica; or 10020 SW 37th Terrace, Miami FL 33165 USA. Anti-Castro, anti-communist; privately supported.

"La Voz Popular," Apartado 19619, México City D.F. 03910, Mexico; or Network in Solidarity with the People of Guatemala, 930 "F" Street, NW #720, Washington DC 20004 USA.

"Our Kashmir," Sadai Hurriat-e Kashmir, P.O. Box 102, Muzaffarabad, Azad Kashmir, Pakistan. Favors Azad Kashmiri independence; opposes policies of Indian government.

"Radio Freedom" (while operating), African National Congress, Caixa Postal 3523, Luanda, Angola. Pro ANC, anti-apartheid in South Africa; supported by various governments, international agencies and private organizations.

"Radio Iran," 17, Boulevard Raspail, F-75007 Paris, France. Anti-Iranian government; supported by CIA and Egyptian government.

"Radio Mojahedin of Afghanistan," P.O. Box 204, Peshawar, Pakistan. Pro-Islamic rebels, anti-Afghan government.

"Voice of Democratic Kampuchea," c/o Radio Beijing, No. 2 Fuxingmenwai, Beijing, People's Republic of China; or 212 E. 47th Street #24G, New York NY 10017 USA; or Permanent Mission of Democratic Kampuchea to the United Nations, 747 3rd Avenue, 8th Floor, New York NY 10017 USA. Pro-Khmer Rouge (Pol Pot), anti-Vietnamese; supported by Chinese government.

"Voice of Free Sahara," Sahara Libre, B.P. 10, El Mouradia, Algiers, Algeria; or Sahara Libre, Ambassade de la RASD, 1 Av. Franklin Roosevelt, 16000 Algiers, Algeria; or B.P. 10, Al-Mouradia, Algiers, Algeria. Contact: Mohamed Lamin Abdesalem or Mahafud Zein. Free stickers, booklets, cards, maps, flags and calendars. Pro-Polisario Front; supported by Algerian government.

"Voice of Iraqi Opposition," BSKSA, P.O. Box 61718, Riyadh 11575, Saudi Arabia. Contact: Suliman A. Al-Samnan, Director of Frequency Management. Anti-Saddam Hussein, supported by CIA and allied governments.

"Voice of June Fourth" (last known address, if operating), Independent Federation of Chinese Students in the USA, 1314 E. Hyde Park Blvd. #2, Chicago IL 60615 USA. The future of this struggling station, inactive as we go to press, promoting a cause most governments would just as soon forget about, is in doubt, and with it possibly the Chicago address. (A move to elsewhere in the United States or Canada is being contemplated.) Contact: Sanyuan Li, Director. Financial contribution, or at least return postage, appreciated, but correspondence should be sent via certified or registered mail. Replies irregularly. Supports the Chinese pro-democracy movement. For now, their transmissions via the facilities of the Voice of Free China, Taiwan, have been replaced by the "Voice of China," apparently produced by the Taiwanese government.

"Voice of National Salvation," Tenshin Biru 2, 1-2-1 Hiraga-cho, Chiyoda-ku, Tokyo, Japan; or Kuguk Chonson, Amatsu Blvd., 2-1, Hirakawa 1-chome, Chiyoda-ku, Tokyo, Japan. Free newspaper. Pro-North Korea, pro-Korean unification; supported by North Korean government.

"Voice of Palestine," c/o Said M. Hamad, Assistant Director, Palestine Information Office, 818 18th Street, NW #620, Washington DC 20006 USA. Radio organ of the main, pro-Arafat, faction of the PLO.

"Voice of To-morrow," P.O. Box 314, Clackamas OR 97015 USA. Neo-Nazi "Aryan skinhead" operation that, despite numerous complaints reportedly made to official U.S. Government agencies and Jewish organizations—and notwithstanding that its transmitter location in Maryland has long been known—has operated unmolested for nearly a decade. Authoritative sources imply that were the station to be shut down, the resulting publicity and sympathy for it and what it espouses would outweigh the relatively minor benefit of silencing its message, given that the station is on the air only every now and then.

"Voice of Unity," "Voice of Afghan Unity," Postfach 2605, W-2000 Hamburg 60, Germany. Replies very slowly for 2 IRCs or return postage. Pro-Afghan rebels; supported by CIA and Egyptian government.

"Voice of the Communist Party of Iran"—see "Voice of the Iranian Revolution," below.

"Voice of the Iranian Revolution," OIS, Box 50040, S-104 05 Stockholm, Sweden. Anti-Iranian government.

"Voice of the Khmer," P.O. Box 22-25, Ramindra Post Office, Bangkok 10 220, Thailand. Return postage required. Replies irregularly. Station of the Khmer Nationalist Forces rebels, which consist of two groups: the Khmer People's National Liberation Front, and the National United Front for an Independent, Neutral, Peaceful and Cooperative Cambodia (FUNCINPEC); nominally non-communist and anti-Vietnamese, but Western press reports suggest these groups actually support Khmer Rouge (Pol Pot) forces.

"Voice of the Martyrs," ACA, B.P. 43, F-94210 Fontenay-sous-Bois, France. Anti-Iranian government.

"Voice of the National Salvation," Kankoku Minzoku Minshu Tensen, 1-2-1 Hirakawa-machi, Chiyota-ku, Tokyo, Japan. Pro-Korean unification, pro-North Korea; supported by North Korean government.

"A Voz da Resistência do Galo Negro," Free Angola

Information Service, P.O. Box 65463, Washington DC 20035 USA. Contact: Jaime de Azevedo Vila Santa, Director of Information. Pro-UNITA rebels, supported by South Africa and the United States. This station may leave the air in the near future.

COLOMBIA World Time –5

Note: Colombia, the country, is always spelled with two o's. It is never written as "Columbia."

Caracol Bogotá, Apartado A 8700, Bogotá, Colombia. Contact: Ricardo Alarcón G., Director-General; or J. de Opercindes. Stickers for return postage. Replies infrequently and slowly to correspondence in Spanish.

Caracol Neiva, Apartado A 8700, Bogotá, Colombia. Contact: Luis Eduardo Bejarano J., Jefe de Producción. Free stickers. Replies slowly to correspondence in Spanish.

Ecos Celestiales, Apartado A 8447, Medellín, Colombia. Return postage or $1 required. Replies occasionally to correspondence in Spanish. This station does not appear to be licensed by the Colombian authorities.

Ecos del Atrato, Apartado A 78, Quibdó, Chocó, Colombia. Contact: Oscar Echeverri Mosquera, Director. Return postage or $1 required. Replies rarely to correspondence in Spanish.

Emisora Armonías del Caquetá, HJVK, Florencia, Caquetá, Colombia. Contact: P. Alvaro Serna Alzate, Director. Replies rarely to correspondence in Spanish; return postage required.

La Voz del Cinaruco, Calle 19 No. 19-62, Arauca, Colombia. Pennants for return postage. Replies, rarely, to correspondence in Spanish; return postage required.

La Voz del Guainia, Calle 6 con Carretera 3, Puerto Inírida, Guainia, Colombia. Contact: Luis Fernando Román, Director. Return postage or $1 required. Replies occasionally to correspondence in Spanish.

La Voz del Guaviare (when operating), Carretera 3, Calle 2, San José del Guaviare, Colombia. Contact: José Harley Ramírez Sánchez, Locutor. Free stickers and Colombian stamps. $1 or return postage required. Replies, rarely, to correspondence in Spanish.

La Voz del Río Arauca, Apartado A 16555, Bogotá, Colombia. Contact: Guillermo Pulido, Gerente; Sra. Gloria J. Silvia R.; or Antonio Pardo García, Gerencia de Producción y Programación. Replies at times to correspondence in Spanish; $1 or return postage required.

La Voz de los Centauros, Apartado A 2472, Villavicencio, Meta, Colombia. Contact: Carlos Torres Leyva, Gerencia; or Cielo de Corredor, Administradora. Return postage required. Replies to correspondence in Spanish.

Ondas del Meta, Apartado A 2196, Villavicencio, Meta, Colombia. Contact: Yolanda Plazas de Lozada, Administradora. Return postage required. Replies irregularly and slowly to correspondence in Spanish.

Ondas del Orteguaza, Apartado A 209, Florencia, Caquetá, Colombia. Contact: C.P. Norberto Plaza Vargas, Subgerente. Free stickers. Replies occasionally to correspondence in Spanish; return postage or $1 required.

Radio Melodía, Calle 61, No. 3B-05, Bogotá, Colombia. Contact: Gerardo Páez Mejía, Vicepresidente. Stickers and pennants for $1 or return postage. Replies, rarely, to correspondence in Spanish.

Radio Nacional de Colombia, CAN, Av. El Dorado, Bogotá, Colombia. Contact: Juan Carlos Jaramillo Velosa, Director. Replies irregularly to correspondence in Spanish.

Radio Nueva Vida, Apartado A 402, Cúcuta, Norte de Santander, Colombia. Contact: Marco Antonio Caicedo O., Director. $1 or return postage required. Replies irregularly to correspondence in Spanish.

Radio Santa Fe, Calle 57, No. 17-48, Bogotá, Colombia. Contact: María Luisa Bernal Mahe, Gerente. Free stickers. IRC, $1 or return postage required. Replies to correspondence in Spanish.

COMOROS World Time +4

Radio Comoro, B.P. 250, Moroni, Grande Comore, Comoros. Contact: Ali Hamoi Hissani. Return postage required. Replies very rarely to correspondence in French.

COOK ISLANDS World Time –10

Radio Cook Islands, Avarua, Rarotonga. Contact: (non-technical) Tauraki Rongo Raea; (technical) Orango Tango, Assistant Chief Engineer. Replies irregularly. $1 or return postage required, plus creative token gift helpful.

COSTA RICA World Time –6

Adventist World Radio, Radio Lira Internacional, Radiodifusora Adventista, Apartado 1177, 4050 Alajuela, Costa Rica. Contact: David L. Gregory, General Manager; or Juan Ochoa, Senior Administrator. Stickers, calendars, Costa Rican stamps and pennants for return postage, with $0.50 in unused U.S. stamps also being acceptable. Also, see "USA."

Faro del Caribe, TIFC, Apartado 2710, 1000 San José, Costa Rica; or P.O. Box 620485, Orlando FL 32862 USA. Contact: (Costa Rica) Juan Jacinto Ochoa F., Administrador; (USA) Lim Ortiz. Free stickers. $1 or IRCs helpful for Costa Rica address.

Radio Casino, Apartado 287, 7301 Puerto Limón, Costa Rica. Contact (technical): Ing. Jorge Pardo, Director Técnico.

Radio for Peace International, University for Peace, Apartado 88, Santa Ana, Costa Rica; or P.O. Box 10869-B, Eugene OR 97440 USA; or 2707 College Avenue #109, Berkeley CA 94705 USA; or P.O. Box 2385, Salmon Arm, British Columbia, Canada. Contact (Costa Rica): James L. Latham, Manager. Replies sometimes slow in coming from Costa Rica because of the mail. Free sample newsletter and political literature; quarterly newsletter for $35 annual membership; station T-shirt $15 (VISA/MC). Actively solicits listener contributions. $1, IRCs or return postage appreciated.

Radio Reloj, Sistema Radiofónico H.B., Apartado 341, 1000 San José, Costa Rica. Contact: Francisco Barahona G. $1 required. Replies to correspondence in Spanish.

CUBA World Time –5 (–4 midyear)

Radio Habana Cuba—*Non-technical correspondence:* P.O. Box 7026, Havana, Cuba; *Technical correspondence:* P.O. Box 6240, Havana, Cuba. Contact (Box 7026): Rolando Peláez, Head of Correspondence; Arnie Coro, Director of DX Programming; Milagro Hernández Cuba, General Director. Pocket calendars. Replies slowly, in part because of the mail service.

Radio Rebelde, Apartado 6277, Havana 6, Cuba. Contact: Noemí Cairo, Relaciones Públicas; or Jorge Luis Mas Zabala, Director, Relaciones Públicas.

CYPRUS World Time +2

Cyprus Broadcasting Corporation, P.O. Box 4824, Nicosia, Cyprus.

CZECHOSLOVAKIA World Time +1 (+2 midyear)

Radio Prague International, Czechoslovak Radio, 12099 Prague 2, Vinohradska 12, Czechoslovakia. Contact: Jan Valeska. Free stickers and calendars; free Monitor Club pennants for regular correspondents.

DENMARK World Time +1 (+2 midyear)

Danmarks Radio, DK-1999 Frederiksberg C, Denmark. Contact: Bente Bang. $1 and persistence required, with correspondence in Danish being preferred. Technical details of reception quality may also be sent to the Engineering Department of Radio Norway International (see).

DJIBOUTI World Time +3

RTV de Djibouti, B.P. 97, Djibouti. Return postage helpful. Correspondence in French preferred.

DOMINICAN REPUBLIC World Time –4

La N-103, Apartado Postal 320, Santiago, Dominican Republic.

Radio Amancer, Apartado Postal 1500, Santo Domingo, Dominican Republic. Contact: Rosa O. Alcantara, Secretaria; or Socrates Domínguez. $1 or return postage required. Replies slowly to correspondence in Spanish.

Radio Barahona, HI5V, Apartado 201, Barahona, Dominican Republic; or Gustavo Meija Ricart No. 293, Apto. 2-B, Ens. Quisqueya, Santo Domingo, Dominican Republic. Contact: (non-technical) Rodolfo Z. Lama Jaar, Administrador; (technical) Ing. Roberto Lama Sajour, Administrador General. Letters should be sent via registered mail. $1 or return postage helpful. Replies to correspondence in Spanish.

Radio Norte, Apartado Postal 320, Santiago, Dominican Republic. Contact: Antonio Pérez, Dueño; or Héctor Castillo, Gerente.

ECUADOR World Time –5; –6 Galapagos

Ecos del Oriente, 11 de Febrero y Mariscal Sucre, Lago Agrio, Sucumbios, Ecuador. Contact: Elsa Trene V. $1 or return postage required. Replies to correspondence in Spanish.

Emisoras Gran Colombia, Casilla 2246, Quito, Ecuador. Contact: Matilde Castro Vda. de Cevallos, Presidenta; or César Farah, Lic.-Director General. Return postage or $1 required. Replies to correspondence in Spanish.

Escuelas Radiofónicas, Casilla 4755, Riobamba, Ecuador.

Contact: Juan Pérez S.; or Patricio Muñoz Jacome, Director Ejecutivo de ERPE. Return postage required. Replies to correspondence in Spanish.

HCJB, Casilla 17-01-00691, Quito, Ecuador; or Box 553000, Opa Locka FL 33055 USA. Contact: Glen Voltshadt, Director of Broadcasting (Quito). Religious brochure and calendar; 2 IRCs, unused U.S. or Ecuadorian stamps, or $1 required. *Catch the Vision* book for $8, postpaid. Various items sold via Florida address—catalog available.

La Voz de Caras (when operating), Casilla 628, Bahia de Caráquez, Manabi, Ecuador. Eduardo Rodrigues Coll, Director de Programación. $1 or return postage required. Replies occasionally to correspondence in Spanish.

La Voz de Saquisilí, "Radio Libertador," (when operating) Casilla 669, Saquisilí, Ecuador. Contact: Srta. Carmen Mena Corrales. Return postage required. Replies irregularly and slowly to correspondence in Spanish.

La Voz del Napo, Misión Josefina, Tena, Napo, Ecuador. Contact: Ramiro Cubrero, Director. Free pennants and stickers. $1 or return postage required. Replies occasionally to correspondence in Spanish.

La Voz del Upano, Vicariato Apostólico de Méndez, Misión Salesiana, 10 de Agosto s/n, Macas, Ecuador. Contact: Ramiro Cabrera; or Sor Dolores M. Palacios C., Directora. Free stickers, pennants and calendars. On one occasion, not necessarily to be repeated, sent tape of Ecuadorian folk music for $2. Otherwise, $1 required. Replies to correspondence in Spanish.

Ondas Quevedeñas, 12ma. Calle 207, Quevedo, Ecuador. Contact: Sra. Maruja Jaramillo, Gerente; or Humberto Alvarado P., Director-Dueño. Return postage required. Replies irregularly to correspondence in Spanish.

Radio Católica Nacional, Av. América 1830 y Mercadillo, Quito, Ecuador. Contact: Monseñor Antonio Arregui Y., Director-General; or Yolanda Gorzón Molina, Secretaria. Free stickers. Return postage required. Replies to correspondence in Spanish.

Radio Centro, HCPV6, Casilla 18-01-0574, Ambato, Tungurahua, Ecuador. Contact: (non-technical) Luis A. Gamboa T., Director-Gerente; (technical) Sócrates Domínguez, Ingeniero. Free stickers and sometimes free newspaper. Return postage or $1 required. Replies occasionally to correspondence in Spanish.

Radiodifusora Nacional, c/o HCJB, Casilla 691, Quito, Ecuador. Contact: Rich McVicar. 1 IRC or $1 required.

Radio Federación, Casilla 1422, Quito, Ecuador. Contact: Prof. Albino M. Utitiaj P., Dirigente. Return postage required. Replies irregularly to correspondence in Spanish.

Radio Interoceánica, Casilla de Correo 11294, Quito, Ecuador. $1 or return postage required. Replies occasionally to correspondence in Spanish.

Radio Jesús del Gran Poder, Casilla de Correo 133, Quito, Ecuador. Free pennants and religious material. Return postage required. Replies irregularly to correspondence in Spanish.

Radio Nacional Espejo, Casilla 352, Quito, Ecuador. Contact: Marco Caceido, Gerente; or Mercedes B. de Caceido, Secretaria. Replies to correspondence in Spanish.

Radio Pastaza (when operating), Casilla 728, El Puyo, Pastaza, Ecuador. Contact: Galo Amores, Gerente. Return postage or $1 required. Replies irregularly to correspondence in Spanish. As the station manager is also head of the local taxi drivers' union, printed matter, photos or discussion of this topic may help elicit a response.

Radio Paz y Bien (when operating), Casilla 94, Ambato, Tungurahua, Ecuador. Contact: Padre L. Enrique Pesántez G. Return postage or $1 required. Replies slowly to correspondence in Spanish.

Radio Popular Independiente, Av. Loja 2408, Cuenca, Azuay, Ecuador. Contact: Sra. Manena de Villavicencio, Secretaria. Return postage or $1 required. Replies occasionally to correspondence in Spanish.

Radio Quito, El Comercio, Casilla 57, Quito, Ecuador. Contact: Gonzalo Ruíz Alvarez, Gerente; or José Almeida, Subgerente. Pennants. Return postage required. Replies slowly, but regularly.

Radio Río Amazonas, Casilla 818, El Puyo, Ecuador. Contact: Prof. Marco G. Díaz D., Gerente; or Miriam Marino, Secretaria. Return postage required. Pennants. Replies to correspondence in Spanish.

Radio Zaracay, Casilla 31, Santo Domingo de los Colorados,

Pichincha, Ecuador. Free pennants. Return postage or $1 required. Replies occasionally to correspondence in Spanish.

EGYPT   World Time +2

Radio Cairo, P.O. Box 1186, Cairo, Egypt. Contact: (non-technical) Nivine W. Lawrence; (technical) Hamdy Abdel Hallem, Director of Propagation. Free stickers and calendars. Replies slowly.

EQUATORIAL GUINEA   World Time +1

Radio Africa, Pierce International Communications, 10201 Torre Avenue, Suite 320, Cupertino CA 95014 USA. Contact: Rev. J.W. Ponds. $1 or return postage required.

Radio Nacional Malabo, Apartado 195, Malabo, Equatorial Guinea. $1 or return postage required. Replies irregularly to correspondence in Spanish.

ETHIOPIA   World Time +3

Voice of Ethiopia: P.O. Box 654 (External Service), or P.O. Box 1020 (DS-Domestic Service)—both in Addis Ababa, Ethiopia. A very poor replier to correspondence in recent years, but with the new political structure this could change.

Voice of the Broad Masses of Eritrea, Asmera, Ethiopia; or Eritrean Relief Committee, 475 Rochester Drive, Suite 907, New York NY 10015 USA; or EPLF/Guidance, Information Branch, Sahel Eritrea, P.O. Box 671, Port Sudan, Sudan; or P.O. Box 891, Port Sudan, Sudan.

FINLAND   World Time +2 (+3 midyear)

YLE/Radio Finland

Non-technical: Radio and TV Centre, Box 10, SF-00241 Helsinki, Finland; or P.O. Box 462, Windsor CT 06095 USA; 24-hour toll-free telephone (U.S. only) 800-221-9539. Contact (Helsinki): Riitta Raukko, International Information; or Juhani Niinistö, Head of External Broadcasting. Free *Finnish by Radio* textbook.

Technical: Broadcasting House, P.O. Box 95, SF-00251 Helsinki, Finland. Contact: Kari Ilmonen, Head of International Technical Affairs. Replies to correspondence, but doesn't provide verification cards.

FRANCE   World Time +1 (+2 midyear)

Radio France Internationale—non-technical correspondence: B.P. 9516, F-75016 Paris Cedex 16, France. Contact: (English programs) Simon Najovits, Chief, English Department; (other programs) Denis Louche, Directeur du développement et de la communication. *Technical correspondence:* Télédiffusion de France, 21-27 rue Barbes, F-92542 Montrouge, France. Contact: Daniel Bochent, Chef du service ondes décamétriques. Souvenir keychains, although not normally given out, have been received by some—especially when visiting the headquarters at 116 ave. du Président Kennedy, in the chichi 16th Arrondissement.

FRENCH GUIANA   World Time –3

RFO-Guyane, Cayenne, French Guiana. Replies very rarely to correspondence in French.

FRENCH POLYNESIA   World Time –10 Tahiti

RFO-Tahiti, B.P. 125, Papeete, Tahiti, French Polynesia. Contact (technical or non-technical): Leon Siquin, Services Techniques. 3 IRC, return postage, 5 francs or $1 helpful, but not mandatory.

GABON   World Time +1

Adventist World Radio (via Afrique Numéro Un), P.O. Box 1751, Abidjan 08, Ivory Coast. Contact: Daniel Grisier, Director. Also, see "USA."

Afrique Numéro Un, B.P. 1, Libreville, Gabon. Contact (technical): Mme. Marguerite Bayimbi, Le Directeur [sic] Technique. Free calendars and bumper stickers. $1, 2 IRCs or return postage helpful. Replies very slowly.

GERMANY   World Time +1 (+2 midyear)

Bayerischer Rundfunk, Rundfunkplatz 1, W-8000 Munich, Germany. Free stickers and 250-page program schedule book.

Deutsche Welle, Postfach 10 04 44, W-5000 Cologne 1, Federal Republic of Germany. Contact: (non-technical) Ernst Peterssen, Head of Audience Research and Listeners' Mail; (technical) Peter Senger, Head, Radio Frequency Department. Free pennants, stickers, calendars, *Deutsche—Warum Nicht?* language-course book, and excellent *tune-in* magazine.

Radio in the American Sector (RIAS), Kufsteinerstr. 69, W-1000 Berlin 62, Germany. Contact: Martina Klich. $1 or return postage required. Free stickers and *RIAS Yearbook*. Note that this station may operate under a different name after reorganization planned for January 1, 1992.

Radio Bremen, SFB, Bürgemeister-Spittaallee 45, W-2800 Bremen 33, Germany. Free stickers.
Sender Freies Berlin, Nordostdeutscher Rundfunk, Masurenallee 14, W-1000 Berlin 19, Germany. Free stickers.
Süddeutscher Rundfunk, Postfach 106040, W-7000 Stuttgart 1, Germany. Free stickers.
Südwestfunk, Postfach 820, W-7570 Baden-Baden, Germany. Contact (technical): Dr. Krank, Technical Director.

GHANA   World Time exactly
Radio Ghana, Ghana Broadcasting Corporation, P.O. Box 1633, Accra, Ghana. Contact: Ms. Maud Blankson-Mills, Head, Audience Research. 1 IRC, return postage or $1 helpful.

GREECE   World Time +2 (+3 midyear)
Foni tis Helladas: Non-technical: ERT A.E., ERA-E Program, Voice of Greece, Mesogion 432 Str., Aghia Paraskevi, GR-153 42 Athens, Greece. Contact: Kosta Valetas, Director, Programs for Abroad; or Demetri Vafaas. *Technical:* ERT 5th Program, P.O. Box 60019, GR-153 10 Athens, Greece. Free tourist literature.
Radiophonikos Stathmos Makedonias, Odos Yeorghikis Scholis 129, GR-546 39 Thessaloniki, Greece.

GUAM   World Time +10
Adventist World Radio, KSDA, P.O. Box 7500, Agat, Guam 96928 USA. Contact: Mrs. Andrea Steele. Free pennants, stickers and religious printed matter. 1 IRC or return postage appreciated. Also, see "USA."
Trans World Radio, KTWR, P.O. Box CC, Agana, Guam 96910 USA. Contact: Mrs. Debbie Blosser, Beth Chick, Karen Beck or Susan L. Tag. Also, see "USA."

GUATEMALA   World Time –6 (–5 midyear)
La Voz de Atitlán, Santiago Atitlán, Guatemala. Contact: Juan Atjzip Alvorado. Return postage required. Replies to correspondence in Spanish.
La Voz de Nahualá, Nahualá, Sololá, Guatemala. Contact (technical): Juan Fidel Lepe Juárez, Técnico Auxiliar. Return postage required. Correspondence in Spanish preferred.
Radio Buenas Nuevas, 13020 San Sebastián, Huehuetenango, Guatemala. Contact: Israel Rodas Mérida, Gerente. $1 or return postage helpful. Free religious and station information in Spanish. Replies to correspondence in Spanish.
Radio Chortis, Centro Social, 20004 Jocotán, Chiquimula, Guatemala. Contact: Padre Juan María Boxus, Director. $1 or return postage required. Replies irregularly to correspondence in Spanish.
Radio K'ekchi, TGVC, K'ekchi Baptist Association, 16015 Fray Bartolomé de las Casas, Alta Verapaz, Guatemala. Contact: Gilberto Sun Xicol, Gerente; or Carlos Díaz Araujo, Director; or David Daniel, Media Consultant. Free paper pennant. $1 or return postage required. Replies to correspondence in Spanish.
Radio Mam, Acu'Mam, Cabricán, Quetzaltenango, Guatemala. Contact: José Benito Escalante Ramos, Director. $1 or return postage required. Replies irregularly to correspondence in Spanish.
Radio Maya de Barillas, TGBA, 13026 Barillas, Huehuetenango, Guatemala. Contact: Juan Baltazar, Gerente. Free pennants and pins. $1 or return postage required. Replies occasionally to correspondence in Spanish.
Radio Tezulutlán, Apartado de Correo 19, 16901 Cobán, Guatemala. Contact: Alberto P.A. Macz, Director; or Hno. Antonio Jacobs, Director Ejecutivo. $1 or return postage required. Replies to correspondence in Spanish.
Union Radio-AWR, Radiodifusora Adventista, Apartado de Correo 35-C, Guatemala (City), Guatemala. Contact: Nora Lissette Vásquez R.; or M.J. Castaneda, Sec. Free tourist literature and Guatemalan stamps. Return postage or $1 helpful. Correspondence in Spanish preferred. Also, see "USA."

GUINEA   World Time exactly
RTV Guinéenne, B.P. 391, Conakry, Guinea. Contact: Direction des Services Techniques. Return postage or $1 required. Replies irregularly to correspondence in French.

GUYANA   World Time –3
Voice of Guyana, P.O. Box 10760, Georgetown, Guyana. Contact: Roy Marshall. Replies very irregularly.

HAITI   World Time –5 (–4 midyear)
Radio 4VEH, B.P. 1, Cap-Haïtien, Haiti. Contact: (non-technical) Gaudin Charles, Director; (technical) Mardy Picazo, Development Engineer; or Jean Van Dervort, Verification Secretary. Return postage, IRC or $1 required.

HOLLAND   World Time +1 (+2 midyear)
Radio Nederland Wereldomroep, Postbus 222, NL-1200 JG Hilversum, Holland. Contact: J.C. Veltkamp Helbach, Director of Public Relations.

HONDURAS   World Time –6
La Voz Evangélica, HRVC, Apartado 325, 3252 Tegucigalpa, Honduras. Contact: Orea Eshter Durón Mendoza. Free stickers and pennants. 3 IRCs or $1 required.
Sani Radio, Apartado 113, La Ceiba, Honduras. Contact: Jacinto Molina G., Director. Return postage or $1 required.

HONG KONG   World Time +8
Radio Television Hong Kong, C.P.O. Box 70200, Kowloon, Hong Kong. Contact (technical): W.S. Kong, Engineer.

HUNGARY   World Time +1 (+2 midyear)
Radio Budapest, Bródy Sándor utca 5-7, H-1800 Budapest, Hungary. Contact: Charles Coutts, Len Scott, Ilona Kiss or Anton Réger. Free pennants, stickers and T-shirts, while they last.

ICELAND   World Time exactly
Ríkisútvarpid, Efstaleiti 1, 150 Reykjavik, Iceland. Free stickers. 1 IRC or $1 helpful.

INDIA   World Time +5 1/2
All India Radio, External Services Division, Parliament Street, P.O. Box 500, New Delhi-110 001, India. Contact: The Director; or Audience Relations Officer. Except for stations listed below, correspondence to domestic stations is more likely to be responded to if it is sent via the External Services Division; request that your letter be forwarded to the appropriate domestic station.
All India Radio—Kohima, Kohima-797 001 Nagaland, India. Contact (technical): G.C. Tyagi, Superintending Engineer. Return postage, $1 or IRC helpful.
All India Radio—Port Blair, AIR Ott Dilanipur, Port Blair-744 102, Andaman & Nicobar Islands, India. Contact (technical): Yuvraj Bajaj, Station Engineer. Return postage, $1 or IRC helpful.

INDONESIA   World Time +7 Western: Waktu Indonesia Bagian Barat (Jawa, Sumatera, Bali); +8 Central: Waktu Indonesia Bagian Tengal (Kalimantan, Sulawesi, Nusa Tenggara); +9 Eastern: Waktu Indonesia Bagian Timu (Irian Jaya, Maluku)
Note: Except where otherwise indicated, Indonesian stations will reply to at least some correspondence in English. However, correspondence in Indonesian is more likely to ensure a reply.
Radio Arista, Jalan Timbangan No. 25., Rt. 005/RW06, Kelurahan Kembangan, Jakarta Barat 11610, Indonesia. This station is not legally licensed to operate.
Radio Elkira, Kotak Pos 199, JAT, Jakarta 13001, Indonesia. This station is not legally licensed to operate.
Radio Primadona, Jalan Bintaro Permai Raya No. 5, Jakarta Timur, Indonesia. This station is not legally licensed to operate.
Radio Ribung Subang, Komplek AURI, Subang, Jawa Barat, Indonesia.
Radio Suara Kencana Broadcasting System, Jalan Yos Sudarso Timur, Gombong, Jawa Tengah, Indonesia. This station is not legally licensed to operate.
RPD Berau, Jalan SA Maulana, Tanjungredeb, Kalimantan Timur, Indonesia. Contact: Kus Syariman.
RPD Bima, Jalan Achmad Yani No. 1, Bima (Raba), Sumbawa, Nusa Tenggara Barat, Indonesia. Free stickers. Return postage required. Replies irregularly to correspondence in Indonesian.
RPD Buol-Tolitoli, Jalan Mohamed Ismail Bantilan No. 4, Tolitoli 94511, Sulawesi, Indonesia. Contact: Said Rasjid, Kepala Studio. Return postage required. Replies irregularly to correspondence in Indonesian.
RPD Ende, Jalan Panglima Sudirman, Ende, Flores, Nusa Tenggara Timor, Indonesia. Contact (technical): Thomas Keropong, YC9LHD. Return postage required.
RPD Kabupaten Bima, Jalan A. Yani Atau, Sukarno Hatta No. 2, Nusa Tenggara Barat (NTB), Kode Pos 84116, Indonesia. Contact (technical): Mr. Chairil, Technisi RKPD Dati, II. Free stickers. Replies slowly and irregularly to correspondence in Indonesian; return postage required.
RPD Luwu, Kantor Deppen Kabupaten Luwu, Jalan Diponegoro 5, Palopo, Sulawesi Selatan, Indonesia. Contact: Arman Mailangkay.
RPD Manggarai, Ruteng, Flores, Nusa Tenggara Timor. Contact: Simon Saleh, B.A. Return postage required.

RPD Sambas, Jalan M. Sushawary, Sambas, Kalimantan Barat, Indonesia.

RPD Tapanuli Selatan, Kotak Pos 9, Padang-Sidempuan, Sumatera Utara, Indonesia. Return postage required.

RRI Banda Aceh, Kotak Pos 112, Banda Aceh, Aceh, Indonesia. Contact: S.H. Rosa Kim. Return postage helpful.

RRI Bandung, Stasiun Regional 1, Kotak Pos 155, Bandung, Jawa Barat, Indonesia. Contact: Eem Suhaemi, Chief of Programme Section; or Drs Koeshani, Station Kepala. Return postage or IRCs helpful.

RRI Banjarmasin, Stasiun Nusantara 111, Kotak Pos 117, Banjarmasin 70234, Kalimantan Selatan, Indonesia. Contact: Jul Chaidir, Stasiun Kepala. Return postage or IRCs helpful.

RRI Bengkulu, Stasiun Regional 1, Kotak Pos 13 Kawat, Kotamadya Bengkulu, Indonesia. Contact: Drs. H. Hamdan Syahbeni, Head of RRI Bengkulu. Free picture postcards and tourist literature. Return postage or 2 IRCs helpful.

RRI Bukittinggi, Stasiun Regional 1 Bukittinggi, Jalan Prof. Muhammad Yamin No. 199, Kuning, Bukittinggi, Sumatera Barat, Indonesia. Contact: Mr. Effendi, Sekretaris. Return postage helpful.

RRI Cirebon, Jalan Brigjen. Dharsono/By Pass, Cirebon, Jawa Barat, Indonesia. Contact: Ahmad Sugiarto, Kepala Ceksi Siaran. Return postage helpful.

RRI Díli, Jalan Kaikoli, Díli, Timur, Indonesia. Contact: Paul J. Onelo, Kepala Stasiun. Return postage or $1 helpful.

RRI Fak Fak, Jalan Kapten P. Tendean, Kode Pos 98601, Kotak Pos 54, Fak Fak, Irian Jaya (Bomberai), Indonesia. Contact: A. Rachman Syukur, Kepala Stasiun. Return postage required.

RRI Gorontalo, Jalan Jenderal Sudirman, Gorontalo, Sulawesi Utara, Indonesia. Contact: Saleh S. Thalib. Return postage helpful. Replies occasionally, preferably correspondence in Indonesian.

RRI Jakarta, Stasiun Nasional Jakarta, Kotak Pos 356, Jakarta, Jawa Barat, Indonesia. Contact: Drs R. Baskara, Stasiun Kepala. Return postage helpful. Replies irregularly.

RRI Jambi, Jalan Jendral A. Yani No. 5, Telanaipura (Jambi), Jambi, Indonesia. Contact: Drs. H. Ali Amran; or M. Yazad, B.A. Return postage helpful.

RRI Jayapura, Jalan Tasangkapura No. 23, Jayapura, Irian Jaya, Indonesia. Contact: Harry Liborang, Direktorat Radio. Return postage helpful.

RRI Kendari, Kotak Pos 7, Kendari, Sulawesi Tenggara, Indonesia. Contact: H. Sjahbuddin. Replies slowly for return postage.

RRI Kupang, Jalan Tompello No. 8, Kupang, Timor, Indonesia. Contact: Daud Yusaf Maro, Kepala Seksi Siaran. Return postage helpful.

RRI Madiun, Jalan Mayjend Panjaitan No. 10, Madiun, Jawa Timur, Indonesia. Contact: Imam Soeprapto, Kepala Seksi Siaran. Return postage helpful.

RRI Malang, Kotak Pos 78, Malang 65112, Jawa Timur, Indonesia. Contact: Ml. Mawahib, Kepala Seksi Siaran; or Dra Hartati Soekemi, Mengetahui.

RRI Manado, Jalan TNI 6, No. 12, Manado 95124 Sulawesi Utara, Indonesia. Contact: Daniel Narande or Drs Sonny Kasenda. Return postage helpful.

RRI Manokwari, Regional II, Jalan Merdeka No. 68, Manokwari, Irian Jaya, Indonesia. Contact: Nurdin Mokoginta, P.J. Kepala Stasiun. Return postage helpful.

RRI Mataram, Stasiun Regional I Mataram, Jalan Langko No. 83, Mataram 83114, Nusa Tenggara Barat, Indonesia. Contact: Mr. Soekino, Kepala, Direktorat Radio. Return postage required. With sufficient return postage or small token gift, sometimes sends tourist information and Batik print. Replies to correspondence in Indonesian.

RRI Merauke, Statiun Regional 1, Kotak Pos 11, Merauke, Irian Jaya, Indonesia. Contact: (non-technical) Achmad Ruskaya B.A., Kepala Stasiun; or John Manuputty, Kepala Subseksi Pemancar; (technical) Daf'an Kubangun, Kepala Seksi Tehnik. Return postage helpful.

RRI Nabire, Kotak Pos 11, Nabire 98801, Irian Jaya, Indonesia. Contact: Ismail Saya, Head of Broadcasting Section. Occasional free picture postcards. Return postage or IRCs helpful.

RRI Padang, Kotak Pos 77, Padang, Sumatera Barat, Indonesia. Contact: Drs H. Syamsul Muin Harahap; or M. Nur Darwis, B.A. Return postage helpful.

RRI Palangkaraya, Jalan Husni Thamrin No. 1, Palangkaraya, Kalimantan Tengah, Indonesia. Contact: Drs Amiruddin; Gumer Kamis; or Soedarsono, Kepala Stasiun. Return postage helpful.

RRI Palembang, Jalan Radio No. 2, KM4, Palembang, Sumatera Selatan, Indonesia. Contact: Drs Abdul Roshim; or Iskandar Suradilaga, B.A. Return postage helpful.

RRI Palu, Jalan R.A. Kartini, Palu, Sulawesi (Tg. Karang), Indonesia. Contact: Akson Boole; or M. Hasjim, Head of Programming. Return postage required. Replies slowly to correspondence in Indonesian.

RRI Pekanbaru, Jalan Jend Sudirman No. 440, Tromolpos 51, Pekanbaru, Riau, Indonesia. Contact: Zainal Abbas. Return postage helpful.

RRI Pontianak, Kotak Pos 6, Pontianak, Kalimantan Barat, Indonesia. Contact: Supomo Hadisaputro, Kepala Seksi Siaran; or Muchlis Marzuki B.A. Return postage helpful.

RRI Purwokerto, Stasiun Regional II, Kotak Pos 5, Purwokerto 53116, Jawa Tengah, Indonesia. Contact: Yon Maryono, Stasiun Kepala. Return postage helpful.

RRI Semarang, Kotak Pos 74, Semarang, Jawa Tengah, Indonesia. Contact: M. Mawahib Affandi. Return postage helpful.

RRI Samarinda, Kotak Pos 45, Samarinda, Kalimantan Timor 75001, Indonesia. Contact: Siti Thomah, Kepala Seksi Siaran. Return postage helpful.

RRI Serui, Jalan Pattimura, Serui, Irian Jaya, Indonesia. Contact: Drs. Jasran Abubakar, Kepala Stasiun. Replies occasionally to correspondence in Indonesian. Return postage helpful.

RRI Sibolga, Jalan Ade Irma Suryani, Nasution No. 5, Sibolga, Sumatera Utara, Indonesia. Return postage required. Replies occasionally to correspondence in Indonesian.

RRI Sorong, Jalan Jendral Achmad Yani, Klademak II, Sorong, Irian Jaya, Indonesia. Contact: Mrs. Tien Widarsanto. Return postage helpful.

RRI Sumenep, Jalan Urip Sumoharjo No. 26, Sumenep, Madura, Jawa Timur, Indonesia. Return postage helpful.

RRI Surabaya, Stasiun Regional 1, Kotak Pos 239, Surabaya, Jawa Timur, Indonesia. Contact: Zainal Abbas, Kepala Stasiun; or Drs Agus Widjaja, Kepala Subseksi Programa Siaran; or Ny Koen Tarjadi. Return postage or IRCs helpful.

RRI Surakarta, Kotak Pos 40, Surakarta 57133, Jawa Tengah, Indonesia. Contact: Ton Martono, Head of Broadcasting. Return postage helpful.

RRI Tanjungkarang, Kotak Pos 24, Pahoman, Bandar Lampung, Indonesia. Contact (technical): R. Djaros Nursinggih, Technician Transmission. Return postage helpful.

RRI Tanjung Pinang, Jalan St. Abdel Rachman No. 1, Tanjung Pinang, Riau, Indonesia. Return postage helpful.

RRI Ternate, Jalan Kedaton, Ternate (Ternate), Maluku, Indonesia. Contact (technical): Rusdy Bachmid, Head of Engineering. Return postage helpful.

RRI Ujung Pandang, RRI Nusantara IV, Kotak Pos 103, Ujung Pandang, Sulawesi Selatan, Indonesia. Contact: Drs. H. Harmyn Husein, Kepala Stasiun. Return postage, $1 or IRCs helpful. Replies irregularly.

Voice of Indonesia, Kotak Pos 157, Jakarta, Indonesia.

RRI Wamena, RRI Regional II, Kotak Pos 10, Wamena, Irian Jaya 99501, Indonesia. Contact: Yoswa Kumurawak, Penjab Subseksi Pemancar; or Max Pattimukay, Musik Pa. Return postage helpful.

IRAN   World Time +3 1/2 (+4 1/2 midyear)

Voice of the Islamic Republic of Iran, P.O. Box 19395/3333, Tehran, Iran; or Aria Shahr. 14518, Golnaz Jonubi, St. 29, No. 29, Tehran, Iran. Contact: Hamid Yasamin, Public Affairs. Free magazines and postcards.

IRAQ   World Time +3 (+4 midyear)

Radio Baghdad, P.O. Box 8145, Baghdad, Iraq; or P.O. Box 3044, New Delhi 110003, India.

IRELAND

Radio Dublin International, 58 Inchicore Road, Kilmainham, Dublin 8, Ireland. Contact: Bernard Evans. Free stickers. Replies irregularly.

ISRAEL   World Time +2 (+3 midyear)

Kol Israel, P.O. Box 1082, 91010 Jerusalem, Israel. Contact: (non-technical) Sara Manobla, Head of English Department; or Moshe Sela, Director of Western Broadcasts; (technical) Ben Dalfen, DX Editor. Free quarterly magazine *Kol Israel*, *Israel and the Arab States* booklet of maps, station booklets and stickers, Hebrew-language lesson scripts, pennants and other small souvenirs, and various political, religious, tourist, immigration and language publications.

ITALY   World Time +1 (+2 midyear)
Adventist World Radio, C.P. 383, I-47100 Forlì, Italy. Contact: Gerlindo Cirillo, Secretary; or Lina Lega; or Mrs. Sandy Hodgson. Free stickers. 2 IRCs, $1 or return postage required. Also, see "USA."
European Christian Radio, Postfach 500, A-2345 Brunn, Austria. Contact: John Adams, Director. $1 or 2 IRCs required.
Italian Radio Relay Service, IRRS, P.O. Box 10980, I-20110 Milan MI, Italy. Contact: (non-technical) Alfredo E. Cotroneo, General Manager; (technical) Anna S. Boschett, Verification Manager. Free station literature. 2 IRCs or $1 helpful.
Radio Europe, via Davanzati 8, I-20158 Milan, Italy. Contact: Dario Monferini.
RTV Italiana, Viale Mazzini 14, I-00195 Rome, Italy; or RAI—Radio Division, 21st floor, 1350 Avenue of the Americas, New York NY 10019 USA. Free magazines. Replies from the Italian address tend to be slow and irregular.
Voice of Europe, P.O. Box 26, I-33170 Pordenone, Italy. 1 IRC or $1 helpful.

JAPAN   World Time +9
NHK Osaka, 3-43 Bamba-cho, Higashi-ku, Osaka 540, Japan. Contact: Hideo Ishida, Engineer. IRC or $1 helpful.
NHK Tokyo/Shobu-Kuki, JOAK, 2-2-1 Jinnan, Shibuya-ku, Tokyo, Japan. Contact: Hirso Kakminia. IRC or $1 helpful. Replies occasionally. Correspondence should be sent via registered mail.
Radio Japan/NHK, 2-2-1 Jinnan, Shibuya-ku, Tokyo, Japan. Contact: (non-technical) Ian McFarland, Producer; (technical) Ms. Sumiko Togasaki, DX Producer; or Ms. H. Hishikawa, Verification Secretary. Free station newsletter, stickers, compasses, rulers, and—if you really rate—large, beautiful wall calendars.
Radio Tampa (until around 1997, when scheduled to cease), 9-15 Akasaka 1-chome, Minato-ku, Tokyo 107, Japan. Contact: M. Teshima. Free stickers. 1 IRC or $1 helpful.

JORDAN   World Time +2 (+3 midyear)
Radio Jordan, P.O. Box 909, Amman, Jordan. Contact: Jawad Zada, Director of English Service; Qasral Mushatta; or R. Alkhas. Replies irregularly.

KENYA   World Time +3
Kenya Broadcasting Corporation, P.O. Box 30456, Nairobi, Kenya. Contact: Augustine Kenyanjier Gochui. Replies irregularly.

KIRIBATI   World Time +13
Radio Kiribati, Tarawa, Kiribati.

KOREA (DPR)   World Time +9
Radio Pyongyang, Pyongyang Broadcasting Station, Ministry of Posts and Telecommunications, External Service, Pyongyang, Democratic People's Republic of Korea (not "North Korea"). Free booklets, pennants, calendars, artistic prints and pins. Sometimes replies to mail postmarked from the United States, but frequently replies to correspondence, even from Americans, postmarked outside the United States. Small amounts of cash okay, but do not include dutiable items in envelope.

KOREA (REPUBLIC)   World Time +9
Radio Korea, Overseas Service, Korean Broadcasting System, 46 Yo-ui-do-dong, Yongdungp'o-gu, Seoul 150-790, Republic of Korea. Contact: Che Hong-Pyo, Director of English Section. Free stickers, calendars and a wide variety of other small souvenirs.

KUWAIT   World Time +3 (+4 midyear)
Radio Kuwait, P.O. Box 193, Safat, Kuwait. World band broadcasts are expected to resume by Spring, 1992.

LAOS   World Time +7
Lao National Radio, P.O. Box 310, Vientiane, Laos. Return postage required (IRCs not accepted). Replies slowly and very rarely.

LEBANON   World Time +2 (+3 midyear)
HCJB (via Voice of Hope)—see "Ecuador."
Voice of Hope, P.O. Box 3379, Limassol, Cyprus; or P.O. Box 77, 10292 Metulla, Israel.
Voice of Lebanon, P.O. Box 165271, Al-Ashrafiyah, Beirut, Lebanon. $1 required. Replies irregularly to correspondence in Arabic.

LESOTHO   World Time +2
Radio Lesotho, P.O. Box 552, Maseru, Lesotho.

LIBERIA   World Time exactly
ELBC, Liberian Broadcasting System, P.O. Box 10-0192, 1000 Monrovia, Liberia. Has not replied to correspondence recently, but in light of evolving events may reply in due course.
ELWA (when operating), P.O. Box 192, Monrovia, Liberia. Also, see "Northern Mariana Islands."

LIBYA   World Time +1 (+2 midyear)
Radio Jamahiriya, P.O. Box 17, Hamrun, Malta; or P.O. Box 4677, Tripoli, Libya; or P.O. Box 4396, Tripoli, Libya. Return postage helpful. Replies more consistently from Malta; Arabic preferred for correspondence to Libya. Contact (Tripoli): R. Cachia.

LUXEMBOURG   World Time +1 (+2 midyear)
Radio Luxembourg, 45 Boulevard Pierre Frieden, L-2850 Kirchberg, Luxembourg; or 38 Hertford Street, London W1Y 8BA, United Kingdom. Contact: M. Vaas, Chief, English Service (Luxembourg). Free T-shirts and a wide variety of different stickers.

MADAGASCAR   World Time +3
Radio Madagasikara, B.P. 1202, Antananarivo, Madagascar. Contact: Mlle. R. Soa Herimanitia, Secrétaire de Direction, a young lady who collects stamps. $1 required, and enclosing used stamps from various countries may help. Replies very rarely and slowly, preferably to friendly philatelist gentlemen who correspond in French.

MALAWI   World Time +2
Malawi Broadcasting Corp., Blantyre 3, Malawi. Contact: T.J. Sineta; or H.R. Chirwa, Head of Production.

MALAYSIA   World Time +8
Radio TV Malaysia—Kajang, Angkasapuri, Bukit Putra, 50614 Kuala Lumpur, Peninsular Malaysia, Malaysia. Contact (Radio 4): Santokh Sing Gill, Controller, Radio 4. Return postage required.
Radio TV Malaysia—Kota Kinabalu, 88614 Kota Kinabalu, Sabah, Malaysia. Return postage required. Contact: Benedict Jamil, Manager.
Radio TV Malaysia—Sarawak, Broadcasting House, Jalan Satok, Kuching, Sarawak, Malaysia.
Voice of Malaysia, Box 11272-KL, Kuala Lumpur, Malaysia. Contact (technical): Lin Chew, Director of Engineering. 2 IRCs or return postage helpful. Replies slowly and irregularly.

MALI   World Time exactly
RTV Malienne, B.P. 171, Bamako, Mali. $1 or 1 IRC helpful. Replies slowly and irregularly to correspondence in French.

MALTA   World Time +1 (+2 midyear)
Voice of the Mediterranean, P.O. Box 143, Valletta, Malta. 1 IRC or $1 helpful. Contact: Richard Vella Laurenti, Managing Director. Replies slowly. Station is a joint venture of the Libyan and Maltese governments.

MAURITANIA   World Time exactly
ORT de Mauritanie, B.P. 200, Nouakchott, Mauritania. Rarely replies, and return postage or $1 required.

MEXICO   World Time –6 Central, including México City; –7 Mountain; –8 (–7 midyear) Pacific
La Hora Exacta, XEQK, IMER, Margaritas 18 Col. Florida, México City, D.F. 01030, Mexico. Contact: Gerardo Romero.
La Voz de Veracruz, XEFT, Apartado Postal 21, Veracruz, Ver. 91700, Mexico. Contact: Lic. Juan de Dios Rodríguez Díaz, Director General. Likely to reply to correspondence in Spanish. Return postage, IRC or $1 probably helpful.
Radio Educación, Angel Urraza 662, México City, D.F. 03100 Mexico. Contact (technical): Ing. Gustavo Carreño López, Subdirector, Dpto. Técnico. Replies slowly to correspondence in Spanish. Free station photo. Return postage or $1 required.
Radio Mil, NRM, Insurgentes Sur 1870, Col. Florida, México City, D.F. 01030, Mexico. Contact: Guillermo Salas Vargas, Presidente. $1 or return postage required.
Radio XEQQ, La Voz de la América Latina, Sistema Radiopolis, Ayuntamiento 52, México City D.F. 06070, Mexico; or Ejército Nacional No. 579 (6to piso), 11520 México City D.F., Mexico. Contact: (non-technical) Sra. Martha Aguilar Sandoval; (technical) Ing. Miguel Angel Barrientos, Director Técnico de Plantas Transmisoras. Free pennants. $1, IRC or return postage required. Replies fairly regularly to correspondence in Spanish.
Radio Universidad/UNAM, Apartado de Correo 1817, Hermosillo, Sonora 83000, Mexico. Contact: A. Merino M.,

Director. Free tourist literature. $1 or return postage required. Replies irregularly to correspondence in Spanish.

MONACO   World Time +1 (+2 midyear)

Radio Monte Carlo (when operating), B.P. 128, Monte Carlo, Monaco. Contact: Bernard Poizat, Service Diffusion. Free stickers. Operates on shortwave only under extraordinary circumstances.

Trans World Radio, B.P. 349, Monaco. Free paper pennant. 1 IRC or $1 appreciated. Also, see "USA."

MONGOLIA   World Time +8

Radio Ulaanbaatar, English Department, External Services, C.P.O. Box 365, Ulaanbaatar, Mongolia. Contact: Mr. Bayasa, Mail Editor.

MOROCCO   World Time exactly

Radio Medi Un, B.P. 2055, Tangier, Morocco. 2 IRCs helpful. Free stickers. Correspondence in French preferred.

RTV Marocaine, 1 rue el-Brihi, Rabat, Morocco. Contact: Tanane Mohammed Jamal Eddine, Public Affairs.

MOZAMBIQUE   World Time +2

Radio Moçambique, C.P. 2000, Maputo, Mozambique. Return postage or $1 required. Replies to correspondence in Portuguese.

NAMIBIA   World Time +2

Radio Namibia/NBC, P.O. Box 321, Windhoek 9000, Namibia. Contact: P. Schachtschneider, Manager, Transmitter Maintenance. Free stickers. 1 IRC helpful.

NEPAL   World Time +5:45

Radio Nepal, P.O. Box 634, Singha Durbar, Kathmandu, Nepal. Contact: Ram S. Karki, Divisional Engineer.

NETHERLANDS ANTILLES   World Time –4   •

Trans World Radio, Bonaire, Netherlands Antilles (Caribbean). Contact: (non-technical) Patty Lowell, Sally Rork or Renata Machtigall; (technical): Charles K. Roswell, Frequency Coordinator; or Dave Butler, Chief Engineer. Free calendars and religious material. Also, see "USA."

NEW CALEDONIA   World Time +11

RFO Nouvelle-Calédonie (if reactivated), B.P. G3, Nouméa, New Caledonia. Replies irregularly to correspondence in French.

NEW ZEALAND   World Time +13 (+12 midyear)

Radio New Zealand, Broadcast House, P.O. Box 2092, Wellington, New Zealand. Contact: (non-technical) Rudi Hill, Manager; (technical) Adrian Sainsbury, Frequency Manager; or T. King. Free paper pennants, Maori Tiki good-luck charms and tourist literature. English/Maori T-shirts for US$20; an interesting variety of CD recordings, including Pacific island music, also at $20 each (cassettes $15); plus books and other merchandise (VISA/MC). For a free 40-page catalog, write to *World Band Replay Radio*, c/o the above Wellington address. 3 IRCs helpful.

Print Disabled Radio, P.O. Box 360, Levin 5500, New Zealand. Contact: Ashley Bell.

NICARAGUA   World Time –6

Radio Miskut, Correo Central (Bragman's Bluff), Puerto Cabezas, Nicaragua. Now that this station has once again been legalized, it may reply to listener correspondence.

Radio Nicaragua, Apartado Postal No. 3170, Managua, Nicaragua. Contact: Frank Arana, Gerente.

Radio RICA, Apartado Postal No. 38, Sucursal 14 de Septiembre, Managua, Nicaragua. Contact: Digna Bendaña B., Directora. Free black T-shirts. $1 required. Correspondence in Spanish preferred.

NIGER   World Time +1

La Voix du Sahel, O.R.T.N., B.P. 361, Niamey, Niger. Contact: Yacouba Alwali. **Caution:** Correspondence by males with this station may result in requests for certain unusual types of magazines.

NIGERIA   World Time +1

Caution: Correspondence with Nigerian stations may result in requests from confidence artists for money, free electronic or other products, or immigration sponsorship.

Federal Radio Corporation of Nigeria—Enugu, P.M.B. 1051, Enugu (Anambra), Nigeria. Contact: L. Nnamuchi. 2 IRCs, return postage or $1 required. Replies slowly.

Radio Nigeria, P.O. Box 250, Kaduna (Kaduna), Nigeria. Contact: Johnson D. Alle or Yusuf Garba. $1 or return postage required. Replies slowly.

Radio Nigeria—P.M.B. 12504, Ikoyi, Lagos, Nigeria. Contact: Babatunde Olalekan Raji, Monitoring Unit. 2 IRCs or return

postage helpful. Replies slowly and irregularly.

Voice of Nigeria, P.M.B. 12504, Ikoyi, Lagos, Nigeria. Contact: (non-technical) Alhaji Lawal Saulawa, Director of Programming; or Babatunde Olalekan Raji; (technical) J.O. Kroni, Engineering Services. 2 IRCs or return postage helpful.

NORTHERN MARIANA ISLANDS   World Time +10

Christian Science Monitor, KHBI, P.O. Box 1387, Saipan, Mariana Islands CM 96950 USA; or write to Boston address (see USA). Free stickers. Return postage appreciated if writing to Saipan; no return postage when writing to Boston.

ELWA—see "KFBS Saipan," below, and "Liberia."

KFBS Saipan, Far East Broadcasting Company, Inc., Box 1, 15700 Imperial Highway, La Mirada CA 90637 USA; or P.O. Box 209, Saipan, Mariana Islands CM 96950 USA. Contact: (California) Jim Bowman; (Saipan) Robert Springer.

NORWAY   World Time +1 (+2 midyear)

Radio Norway International, 0340 Oslo 3, Norway. Contact: (non-technical) Sverre Fredheim, Head of External Broadcasting; (technical) Olav Grimdalen, Frequency Manager. Free stickers and flags.

OMAN   World Time +4

Radio Oman, P.O. Box 600, Muscat, Oman. Contact: Rashid Haroon or A. Al-Sawafi. Replies irregularly, but $1, return postage or 3 IRCs helpful.

PAKISTAN   World Time +5

Azad Kashmir Radio, Muzaffarabad, Azad Kashmir, Pakistan. Contact: M. Sajjad Ali Siddiqui, Director of Engineering. Registered mail helpful. Rarely replies to correspondence.

Radio Pakistan, External Services, National Broadcasting House, Constitution Avenue, Islamabad, Pakistan. Contact (technical): Anwar Inayat Khan, Senior Broadcast Engineer. Free stickers, pennants and "Pakistan Calling" magazine.

PAPUA NEW GUINEA   World Time +10

Note: If no reply received directly from station, write Spectrum Management Department, Post & Telecommunication Corp., P.O. Box 1783, Port Moresby, Papua New Guinea. Contact: Gordon M. Darling, Manager.

National Broadcasting Commission of Papua New Guinea, P.O. Box 1359, Boroko, Papua New Guinea. Contact: Timothy Dickson or Bob Kabewa. 2 IRCs or return postage helpful. Replies irregularly.

Radio East New Britain, P.O. Box 393, Rabaul, Papua New Guinea. Contact: Raka D. Saini, Station Manager. If no response, write Esekai Mael, Station Manager, NBC, P.O. Box 1359, Boroko, N.C.D., Papua New Guinea. Return postage required. Replies slowly.

Radio Eastern Highlands, P.O. Box 311, Goroka, Papua New Guinea. Contact: Paia Ottawa, Technician. $1 required. Replies irregularly.

Radio East Sepik, P.O. Box 65, Wewak, E.S.P., Papua New Guinea. Contact: Elias Albert, Acting Station Manager.

Radio Enga, P.O. Box 300, Wabang, Enga Province, Papua New Guinea. Contact (technical): Felix Tumun K., Station Technician.

Radio Gulf, P.O. Box 36, Kerema, Papua New Guinea. Contact: Mark Auhova, Station Manager.

Radio Madang, P.O. Box 2036, Madang, Papua New Guinea. Contact: Simon P. Tiori.

Radio Manus, P.O. Box 359, Lorengau, Papua New Guinea. Contact: Raphael Karahure, Station Manager; or Eliun Sereman, Acting Station Manager.

Radio Milne Bay, P.O. Box 111, Alotau, Papua New Guinea. Contact: Trevor Webumo.

Radio Morobe, P.O. Box 1262, Lae, Papua New Guinea. Contact: Aloysius R. Nase, Station Manager.

Radio New Ireland, P.O. Box 140, Kavieng, Papua New Guinea. Contact: Otto A. Malatana, Station Manager. Return postage or $1 helpful.

Radio Northern, Voice of Oro, P.O. Box 137, Popondetta, Papua New Guinea. Contact: Misael Pendaia, Station Manager. Return postage required.

Radio North Solomons, P.O. Box 35, Kieta, Papua New Guinea. Contact: A.L. Rumina. Replies irregularly.

Radio Sandaun, P.O. Box 37, Vanimo, Papua New Guinea. Contact: Gabriel Deckwalen, Station Manager.

Radio Simbu, P.O. Box 228, Kundiawa, Papua New Guinea. Contact (technical): Gabriel Paiao, Station Technician.

Radio Southern Highlands, P.O. Box 104, Mendi, Papua New

Guinea. Contact: Andrew Meles, Provincial Station Manager. $1 or return postage helpful; or donate a wall poster of a rock band, singer or American landscape.

Radio Western, P.O. Box 23, Daru, Papua New Guinea. $1 or return postage required. Replies irregularly.

Radio West New Britain, P.O. Box 412, Kimbe, Papua New Guinea. Contact: Valuka Lowa, Provincial Station Manager. Return postage required.

PARAGUAY World Time –3 (–4 midyear)

Radio Nacional, Calle Montevideo, esq. Estrella, Asunción, Paraguay. Contact: (non-technical) Lic. Augusto Ocampos Caballero, Director General; (technical) Carlos Montaner, Director Técnico. Tourist literature. $1 or return postage required. Replies to correspondence in Spanish.

PERU World Time –5 year-around at nearly all locations; the few exceptions are –4 (–5 midyear)

Note: Internal unrest and terrorism, widespread cholera, a tottering economy, and devestating earthquakes all combine to make Peruvian broadcasting a perilous affair. Obtaining replies from Peruvian stations thus calls for creativity, tact, patience—and the proper use of Spanish, not form letters and the like. There are nearly 150 world band stations operating from Peru on any given day. While virtually all of these may be reached simply by using as the address the station's city, as given in the Blue Pages, the following are the only stations known to be replying—even if only occasionally—to correspondence from abroad.

Radio Altura, Apartado de Correo 140, Cerro de Pasco, Pasco, Peru. Contact: Oswaldo de la Cruz Vásquez, Gerente-General. Replies to correspondence in Spanish.

Radio Ancash, Apartado de Correo 210, Huáraz. Peru. Contact: Armando Moreno Romero, Gerente-General. $1 required. Replies to correspondence in Spanish.

Radio Atalaya, Teniente Mejía y Calle Iquitos s/n, Atalaya, Depto. de Ucayali, Peru. Replies irregularly to correspondence in Spanish.

Radio Atlántida, Apartado de Correo 786, Iquitos, Loreto, Peru. Contact: Pablo Rojas Bardales, Director QSL DX Oyentes. $1 or return postage required. Replies irregularly to correspondence in Spanish.

Radio Cora, Compañia Radiofónica Lima, S.A., Paseo de la República 144, Centro Cívico, No. 5, Lima 1, Peru. Contact: (non-technical) Juan Ramírez Lazo, Director Gerente; (technical) Ing. Roger Antonio Roldán Mercedes. Free stickers. 2 IRCs or $1 required. Replies slowly to correspondence in Spanish.

Radio Cuzco, Apartado de Correo 251, Cusco, Peru. Contact: Raul Siu Almonte, Gerente. $1 or return postage required. Replies irregularly to correspondence in Spanish. Note that station name continues to be spelled with a "z", even though the city and provincial names were recently changed by decree to an "s".

Radio del Pacífico, Apartado de Correo 4236, Lima 1, Peru. Contact: J. Petronio Allauca, Secretario. Return postage required. Replies occasionally to correspondence in Spanish.

Radio La Hora, Apartado de Correo 540, Cusco, Peru. Contact: Edmundo Montesinos G., Gerente-General. Return postage required. Replies occasionally to correspondence in Spanish.

Radio La Merced, (Tongol) Congoyo, San Miguel, Cajamarca, Peru. $1 or return postage required. Replies irregularly to correspondence in Spanish.

Radio Los Andes, Pasaje Damián Nicolau s/n, Huamachuco, Peru. Contact: Pasio J. Cárdenas Valverde, Gerente-General. Return postage required. Replies occasionally to correspondence in Spanish.

Radio Nor Andina, Jirón Pardo 759, Celendín, Cajamarca, Peru. $1 required. Replies irregularly to correspondence in Spanish.

Radio Oriente, Av. Progreso 112, Yurimaguas, Loreto, Peru. Contact: Prof. Ricardo Arevaldo Flores, Director-Gerente; or Juan Antonio López-Manza Nares Mascunana, Director de Redacción y Programación. Return postage required. Replies occasionally to correspondence in Spanish.

Radio Pomabamba, Pomabamba, Ancash, Peru. $1 or return postage required. Replies occasionally to correspondence in Spanish.

Radio San Antonio de Padua, Difusora Mariana, Arequipa,

Arequipa, Peru. $1 or return postage required. Replies irregularly to correspondence in Spanish.

Radio San Juan, Jirón Pumacahua 528, Caraz, Ancash, Peru. Contact: Víctor Morales. $1 or return postage helpful. Replies occasionally to correspondence in Spanish.

Radio San Martín, Jirón Progreso 225, Tarapoto, San Martín, Peru. Contact: José Roberto Chong, Gerente-General. Return postage required. Replies occasionally to correspondence in Spanish.

Radio San Miguel, Av. Huayna Cápac 146, Huánchac, Cusco, Peru. Replies to correspondence in Spanish.

Radio San Nicolás, Rodriguez de Mendoza, Lambayeque, Peru. Contact: Juan José Grandez Santillán, Director. $1 required. Replies to correspondence in Spanish.

Radio Santa Mónica, Santa Mónica, Santiago de Chuco, La Libertad, Peru. Replies occasionally to correspondence in Spanish.

Radio Satélite E.U.C., Jirón Cutervo No. 570, Cajamarca, Prov. Santa Cruz, Peru. Contact: Sabino Llamo Chávez, Gerente. Free tourist brochure. $1 or return postage required. Replies irregularly to correspondence in Spanish.

Radio Tacna, Casilla de Correo 370, Tacna, Peru. Contact: Vda. Yolanda de Cáceres, Directora; or Alfonso Cáceres, Director Técnico. $1 or return postage required. Replies irregularly to correspondence in Spanish. Caution when considering writing: This station traditionally has been strongly anti-Semetic.

Radio Tarma, Casilla de Correo 167, Tarma, Peru. Contact: Mario Monteverde Poinareda, Gerente-General. $1 or return postage required. Replies irregularly and slowly to correspondence in Spanish.

Radio Tropical, Casilla de Correo 31, Tarapoto, Peru. Contact: Luis F. Mori, Gerente. Return postage required. Replies occasionally to correspondence in Spanish.

PHILIPPINES World Time +8

Note: Males corresponding with Philippine stations may receive publications with lists of Philippine young ladies seeking "pen pal" courtships with foreign men.

Far East Broadcasting Co., Inc., P.O. Box 1, Valenzuela, Metro Manila, Philippines. Contact: (non-technical) Jane J. Colley; or Alida Landman; (technical) Barbara A. Padmore, Verification Secretary. 3 IRCs helpful.

Radio Veritas Asia, P.O. Box 939, Manila, Philippines. Contact: Ms. Cleofe R. Labindao.

POLAND World Time +1 (+2 midyear)

Radio Polonia, P.O. Box 46, 00-950 Warsaw, Poland. Contact: Jacek Detco, Editor of English Section; or María Goc, Editor of English Section. Free stickers.

PORTUGAL World Time (+1 midyear); Azores World Time –1 (World Time midyear)

IBRA Radio—see "Sweden."

Radio Portugal International, Rua São Marçal 1, Lisbon, Portugal. Contact: Ms. Carminda Días da Silva. Free stickers and calendars.

Adventist World Radio (via facilities of Radio Trans Europe), C.P. 2590, P-1114 Lisbon, Portugal. Also, see "USA."

Radio Renascença, Rua Capelo 5, 1294 Lisbon, Portugal. Contact: C. Pabil, Director-Manager.

QATAR World Time +3

Qatar Broadcasting Service, P.O. Box 3939, Doha, Qatar. Contact: Jassem Mohamed Al-Qattan, Head of Public Relations. Rarely replies, but return postage helpful.

ROMANIA World Time +2 (+3 midyear)

Radio Romania International, Str. G-ral Berthelot nr. 60-62, 79756 Bucharest, Romania. Contact: Frederica Dochinoiu, Head of the English Department. Free stickers, pins, Romanian stamps, coasters and other small souvenirs. Replies slowly.

SAUDI ARABIA World Time +3

Broadcasting Service of the Kingdom of Saudi Arabia, P.O. Box 61718, Riyadh 11575, Saudi Arabia. Contact (technical): Suliman A. Al-Samnan, Director of Frequency Management. Free travel information and books. Sometimes replies slowly.

SENEGAL World Time exactly

Office de Radiodiffusion-Télévision du Senegal, B.P. 1765, Dakar, Senegal. Contact: Joseph Nesseim. Return postage or 3 IRCs required. Replies to correspondence in French.

SEYCHELLES World Time +4

Far East Broadcasting Association, P.O. Box 234, Mahé,

Seychelles. Contact: (non-technical) Roger Foyle, Audience Relations Councellor; (technical) Mary Asba, Verification Secretary. $1 or one IRC helpful.

SIERRA LEONE   World Time exactly
Sierra Leone Broadcasting Service (when operating), New England, Freetown, Sierra Leone. Contact (technical): Emmanuel B. Ehirim, Project Engineer.

SINGAPORE   World Time +8
Singapore Broadcasting Corporation, P.O. Box 60, Singapore 9128, Singapore.

SOLOMON ISLANDS   World Time +11
Solomon Islands Broadcasting Corporation, P.O. Box 654, Honiara, Solomon Islands. Contact (technical): Chief Engineer. 1 IRC or $1 helpful.

SOMALIA   World Time +3
Radio Mogadishu, Ministry of Information, Private Postbag, Mogadishu, Somalia. Contact: Mohamed Aden Hirsi, Director; or Dr. Abdel-Qadir Muhammad Mursal, Director, Media Department. Correspondence should be via registered mail.

SOMALILAND   World Time +3
Radio Hargeisa, P.O. Box 14, Hargeisa, Somaliland. Sulayman Abdel-Rahman, announcer. Most likely to respond to correspondence in Somali or Arabic.

SOUTH AFRICA   World Time +2
Radio RSA, Piet Meyer Building, Henley Road, Broadcasting Centre, Johannesburg 2000, Republic of South Africa. Contact: (non-technical) B.R. Leeman, Manager, English External Services; (technical) Lucienne Libotte. Free stickers.
South African Broadcasting Corporation, P.O. Box 91312, Auckland Park 2006, South Africa. Contact: *Radio Five:* Ms. Helena Boshoff, Public Relations Officer; *Radio Oranje:* Hennie Klopper, Announcer; or Christo Olivier. Free stickers.

SPAIN   World Time +1 (+2 midyear)
Radio Exterior de España, Apartado de Correo 156.202, E-28080 Madrid, Spain. Free stickers, calendars and pennants.

SRI LANKA   World Time +5 1/2
Sri Lanka Broadcasting Corporation, P.O. Box 574, Colombo 7, Sri Lanka. $1 required. Replies irregularly.

SUDAN   World Time +2
National Broadcasting Corporation, P.O. Box 572, Omdurman, Sudan. Contact (technical): Technical and Engineering Department.

SURINAME   World Time −3
Radio Suriname International, Postbus 2979, Paramaribo, Suriname. Contact: Saskia de Bruin.

SWAZILAND   World Time +2
Swaziland Commercial Radio, P.O. Box 23114, Joubert Park 2044, South Africa. Replies irregularly.
Trans World Radio, P.O. Box 64, Manzini, Swaziland. Contact: Carol Tatlow. Free stickers. $1, return postage or 1 IRC required. Also, see "USA."

SWEDEN   World Time +1 (+2 midyear)
IBRA Radio, Box 396, S-105 36 Stockholm, Sweden. Free pennants and stickers.
Radio Sweden, S-105 10 Stockholm, Sweden. Contact: Marta Rose Ugirst or Lilian von Arnold. Free stickers; T-shirts for $15.

SWITZERLAND   World Time +1 (+2 midyear)
Red Cross Broadcasting Service, 19 Avenue de la Paix, CH-1202 Geneva, Switzerland. Free stickers and station information.
Swiss Radio International, P.O. Box, CH-3000 Berne 15, Switzerland. Contact: (non-technical) Walter Fankhauser, Press and Public Relations Officer; (technical) Bob Zanotti, DX Editor.

SYRIA   World Time +2 (+3 midyear)
Radio Damascus, Ommayad Square, Damascus, Syria. Free small souvenirs, such as stickers, flags and *The Syria Times* newspaper. Contact: Mr. Afaf, Director General. Replies can be highly erratic, but as of late have been more regular.

TANZANIA   World Time +3
Voice of Tanzania Zanzibar, P.O. Box 1178, Zanzibar, Tanzania. Contact (technical): Nassor M. Suleiman, Maintenance Engineer.

THAILAND   World Time +7
Radio Thailand, External Service, Bangkok 10200, Thailand. Contact: Mrs. Bupha Laemluang, Chief of External Services.

TOGO   World Time exactly
Radio Lomé, Lomé, Togo. Return postage, $1 or IRCs helpful.

TONGA   World Time +13
Tonga Broadcasting Commission, A3Z, P.O. Box 36, Nuku'alofa, Tonga. Contact: Tavake Fusimalohi, General Manager; or M. Indiran.

TURKEY   World Time +2 (+3 midyear)
Turkish Police Radio, T.C. Icisleri Bakanligi, Emniyet Genel Mudurlugu, Ankara, Turkey. Tourist literature for return postage. Replies irregularly.
Turkish Radio-Television Corporation, P.K. 333, 06-443 Ankara, Turkey. Contact: Ms. Semra Eren, Head of English Department. Free stickers, flags and tourist literature.
The *Voice of Meteorology*, T.C. Tarim Bakanligi, Devlet Meteoroloji Isleri, Genel Mudurlugu, P.K. 401, Ankara, Turkey. Contact: Faysal Geyik, Director General of the Turkish State Meteorological Service. Free tourish literature. Return postage helpful.

UGANDA   World Time +3
Radio Uganda, P.O. Box 7142, Kampala, Uganda. Contact: A.K. Mlamizo. $1 or return postage required. Rarely replies.

UNITED ARAB EMIRATES   World Time +4
UAE Radio from Dubai, P.O. Box 1695, Dubai, United Arab Emirates. Contact: (non-technical) Ahmed A. Shouly, Director; (technical) K.F. Fenner, Chief Engineer. Free pennants.
UAE Radio from Abu Dhabi, Ministry of Information & Culture, P.O. Box 63, Abu Dhabi, United Arab Emirates. Contact (technical): Fawzi Saleh, Technical Advisor.

UNITED KINGDOM   World Time exactly (+1 midyear)
BBC World Service, P.O. Box 76, Bush House, Strand, London WC2B 4PH, United Kingdom; or 630 Fifth Avenue, New York NY 10020 USA. Free sample of excellent *London Calling* magazine; write BBC for subscription rate to your location. Numerous audio/video recordings, publications (including *Passport to World Band Radio*), portable world band radios, T-shirts and other BBC souvenirs available by mail from World Band Orders, BBC World Service Shop, at the above London address (VISA/MC/AX/Access). Tapes of BBC programs from BBC Topical Tapes, also at the above London address. World band schedules and weekly *WBI* newsletter for £350 plus air postage per year; audio and teletype feeds for news agencies; and world broadcasting program summaries for researchers; all from BBC Monitoring, Caversham Park, Reading RG4 8TZ, United Kingdom. *BBC English* magazine, to aid in learning English, from BBC English, P.O. Box 96, Cambridge, United Kingdom.
British Forces Broadcasting Service (when operating), Bridge House, North Wharf Road, London W2 1LA, United Kingdom. Contact: Richard Astbury, Station Manager. Free station brochure.

UNITED NATIONS
United Nations Radio/UNESCO (via various stations, such as IRRS/Italy and RFPI/Costa Rica, throughout the world), United Nations S-850, UN Plaza, New York NY 10017 USA; or write the station over which UN Radio was heard.

URUGUAY   World Time −2 (−3 midyear)
Radio Libertad Sport, Soriano 1287, 11100 Montevideo, Uruguay. Contact: Andrea Cruz. $1 or return postage required. Replies irregularly to correspondence in Spanish.
Radio Monte Carlo, Av. 18 de Julio 1224, 11100 Montevideo, Uruguay. Contact: Ana Ferreira de Errázquin, Secretaria. Correspondence in Spanish preferred.
Radio Oriental—Same as Radio Monte Carlo, above.
SODRE, DX Club del Uruguay, Casilla 801, 11000 Montevideo, Uruguay. Contact: Daniel Muñoz Faccioli.

USA   World Time −4 Atlantic, including Puerto Rico and Virgin Islands; −5 (−4 midyear) Eastern, excluding Indiana; −5 Indiana, except northwest and southwest portions; −6 (−5 midyear) Central, including northwest and southwest Indiana; −7 (−6 midyear) Mountain, except Arizona; −7 Arizona, −8 (−7 midyear) Pacific; −9 (−10 midyear) Alaska, except Aleutian Islands; −10 (−11 midyear) Aleutian; −10 Hawaii; −11 Samoa
Adventist World Radio, International Headquarters, 12501 Old Columbia Pike, Silver Spring MD 20904 USA. Contact (non-technical correspondence): Tulio R. Haylock, Director. Pennants and other small souvenirs, with an IRC or $1 appreciated. Technical correspondence should be sent to the country where the transmitter is located—Costa Rica, Gabon, Guam, Italy or Portugal.
Armed Forces Radio and Television Service, AFIS/AFRTS, 601 N. Fairfax, Alexandria VA 22314 USA. Contact: Melvin Russell.

The *Christian Science Monitor, Shortwave World Service,* WCSN/WSHB, P.O. Box 860, Boston MA 02123 USA; 24-hour toll-free telephone (U.S. only) 800-225-7090, extension 2060. Contact: Kate Dearborn, Director of Radio. Free stickers and "Monitor Month" newsletter. Sangean and other world band radios, plus *Passport to World Band Radio* and other publications, available from station's sales office at 6 Ram Ridge Road, Spring Valley NY 10977 USA; toll-free telephone (U.S. only) 800-448-2466.

KGEI—Voice of Friendship, 1400 Radio Road, Redwood City CA 94065 USA. Free religious literature.

KNLS, P.O. Box 473, Anchor Point AK 99556 USA. Contact: Ms. Beverly Jones, Promotions Department. Free pennant, but return postage appreciated.

KTBN, Trinity Broadcasting Network, P.O. Box A, Santa Ana CA 92711 USA. Contact: Ben Miller, WB5TLZ. Religious merchandise sold. Return postage helpful.

KVOH, High Adventure Ministries, 990 Enchanted Way #101, Simi Valley CA 93065 USA; or Box 425, Station "E", Toronto, M6H 4E3 Canada; or BM Box 2575, London WC1N 3XX, United Kingdom. Contact: (non-technical) David Lawrence, International Program Director (U.S.); (technical) Paul Hunter, Chief Engineer.

Radio Free Afghanistan—See "RFE-RL," below.

Radio Marti—See "Voice of America," below.

RFE-RL, Oettingenstrasse 67, D-8000 Munich 22, Federal Republic of Germany; or 1201 Connecticut Avenue, NW, 11th floor, Washington DC 20036 USA; or 1775 Broadway, New York NY 10019 USA. Contact (technical, New York): David Walcutt, Engineering.

Trans World Radio, International Headquarters, P.O. Box 700, Cary NC 27512 USA. Contact (non-technical): Donna Moss, Public Affairs. Free "Towers to Eternity" publication. Technical correspondence should be sent directly to the country where the transmitter is located—Guam, Monaco, Netherlands Antilles or Swaziland.

Voice of America, 330 Independence Avenue, SW, Washington DC 20547 USA; or c/o Apartado 4258, Lisbon 1700, Portugal. Contact (Washington): (non-technical) Mrs. Marie Ciliberti, Room 6-759; (technical) Daniel Ferguson, Frequency Division. Free key chains, booklets on America, stickers and other items to listeners with addresses *outside* the United States. Free "Music Time in Africa" calendar, to non-U.S. addresses only, from Mrs. Rita Rochelle, Africa Division, Room 1728. If you're an American and miffed because you can't receive these goodies from the VOA, don't blame the station—they're only following the law.

WCSN—See "Christian Science Monitor."

WHRI—World Harvest Radio, P.O. Box 12, South Bend IN 46624 USA. Contact: (non-technical) Brad Butler, staff assistant; (technical) James Holycross, Engineer. Return postage appreciated. Carries programs from various expatriate political organizations, such as Cuban and Croatian nationalist groups; these may be contacted via WHRI.

WINB, P.O. Box 88, Red Lion PA 17356 USA. Contact: John W. Norris, Jr., Manager. Return postage helpful outside United States.

WMLK—Assemblies of Yahweh, P.O. Box C, Bethel PA 19507 USA. Contact: Elder Jacob O. Mayer, Manager. Free stickers and religious material. Replies slowly, but enclosing return postage or IRCs helps speed things up.

WRNO, 4539 I-10 Service Road North, Metairie LA 70002 USA. Contact: Joseph Mark Costello III, General Manager. Free stickers. Free tourist literature for correspondence, including return postage, addressed to WRNO World Band Radio, c/o Lt. Gov. Paul Hardy, Louisiana Office of Tourism, P.O. Box 44243, Baton Rouge LA 70804 USA.

WSHB—See "Christian Science Monitor."

WWCR, 4647 Old Hydes Ferry Pike, Nashville TN 37218 USA. Contact: Jay Litton, Public Affairs. Free stickers. Replies irregularly; return postage helpful. Carries various programs that call themselves "Radio" this or that, such as Allan Weiner's "Radio Newyork International" and the Liberty Lobby's "Radio Free America," from organizations lacking their own broadcasting facilities; these organizations may be contacted via WWCR. Those wishing to purchase a Pomtrex radio may also try writing direct to "For the People," Telford Hotel, 3 River Street, White Springs FL 32096 USA; or P.O. Box 15999, Tampa FL 33684 USA.

WWV, Frequency-Time Broadcast Services Section, Time and Frequency Division, NIST, 2000 East County Road 58, Fort Collins CO 80521 USA. Contact: James C. Maxton, Engineer-in-Charge. Free "NBS Time & Frequency Dissemination Services" brochure.

WWVH, NIST, P.O. Box 417, Kekaha, Kauai HI 96752 USA. Contact: Noboru Hironaka, Engineer-in-Charge. Free "NBS Time & Frequency Dissemination Services" brochure.

WYFR—Family Radio, Family Stations, Inc., 290 Hegenberger Road, Oakland CA 94621 USA; toll-free telephone (U.S. only) 800-534-1495. Contact: Thomas A. Schaff, Shortwave Program Manager. Free stickers and pocket diaries.

USSR   Note: As of presstime, the full and changing situation with respect to local time zones within the Soviet Union continues to be unresolved. Following are observed times, plus some predicted times:

World Time +2 (+3 midyear) Moscow, Baltic Republics, Belorusskaya, Moldova, Tatar ASSR, Ukraine; +3, possibly +4 (+4 midyear) Armenia, Azerbaijan; +4 Georgia; +5 Kyrgystan, Tadjikistan, Turkmenistan, Uzbekistan; +6 Kazakhstan; +6 (+7 midyear) Central; +7 (+8 midyear) Eastern Central; +8 (+9 midyear) Near East; +9 (+10 midyear) East; +10 (+11 midyear) Far East; +11 (+12 midyear) Southern Bering; +12 (+13 midyear) Northern Bering

Arkhangel'sk Radio, Dom Radio, ulitsa Popova 2, Arkhangel'sk, Arkhangel'sk, USSR. Replies irregularly to correspondence in Russian.

Armenian Radio—See "Radio Yerevan."

Azerbaijani Radio—See "Radio Baku."

Belorussian Radio—See "Radio Minsk."

Buryat Radio, Dom Radio, ulitsa Erbanova 7, 670000 Ulan-Ude, Buryatskaya ASSR, USSR. Contact: Z.A. Telin.

Chita Radio, Box 45, 672090 Chita, Chitinskaya Oblast, USSR. Contact: V.A. Klimov, Engineer.

Estonian Radio—See "Radio Tallinn."

Georgian Radio—See "Radio Tbilisi."

Kamchatka Radio, RTV Center, Dom Radio, ulitsa Sovietskaya 31 (or 62-G), 683000 Petropavlovsk-Kamchatskiy, Kamchatskaya Oblast, USSR. Contact: A. Borodin, Chief OTK.

Kazakh Radio, ulitsa Mira 175-A, 480013 Alma-Ata, Kazakhstan, USSR; or Do. Vostr., Central Post Office, 101000 Moscow, USSR. Contact: Andrei Nekrasov. Two IRCs required.

Khabarovsk Radio, RTV Center, ulitsa Lenina 71, 680013 Khabarovsk, USSR; or Dom Radio, pl. Slavy, 682632 Khabarovsk, USSR. Contact (technical): V.N. Kononov, Glavnyy Inzhener.

Khanty-Mansiysk Radio, Dom Radio, ulitsa Lenin 21, 626200 Khanty-Mansiysk, Tyumenskaya Oblast, USSR. Contact (technical): Vladimir Sokolov, Engineer.

Krasnoyarsk Radio, RTV Center, Sovietskaja 128, 660017 Krasnoyarsk, Krasnoyarskiy Kray, USSR. May reply to correspondence in Russian. Return postage helpful.

Kyrgys Radio, Prospekt Moloday Gvardil 63, 720300, GSP, Bishkek, Republic of Kyrgystan, USSR. Contact: A.I. Vitshkov or E.M. Abdukarimov.

Latvian Radio, Latvijas Radio, Zakusalas Krastmala 3, 226018 Riga, Latvia, USSR.

Lithuanian Radio—See "Radio Vilnius."

Magadan Radio, RTV Center, ulitsa Kommuny 8/12, 685000 Magadan 13, Magadanskaya Oblast, USSR. May reply to correspondence in Russian. Return postage helpful.

Moghilev Radio—See "Radio Minsk."

Primorsk Radio, RTV Center, ulitsa Uborevieha 20A, 690000 Vladivostok, Primorsk Kray, USSR. Return postage helpful. Replies to correspondence in Russian.

Radio Alma-Ata, ulitsa Mira 175A, 480013 Alma-Ata, Kazakhstan, USSR. Contact: Mr. Usmanov, Editor-in-Chief.

Radio Baku, ulitsa M. Guzeina 1, 370011 Baku, Azerbaijan, USSR. $1 or return postage helpful. Replies occasionally.

Radiocentras, P.O. Box 1792, Vilnius, Lithuania. Return postage or IRC required.

Radio Dushanbé, ulitsa Chapaeva 25, 734015 Dushanbé, Tadjikstan, USSR. Correspondence in Russian preferred.

Radio DVR, P.O. Box 2378, Khabarovsk 8, USSR.

Radio Hope, ulitsa Karl Marx 64, Room 5, 200003 Tallinn, Estoniya SSR, USSR. Likely to prefer correspondence in Russian.

Radio Kiev, ulitsa Kreshchatik 26, 252001 Kiev, Ukraine, USSR. Free stickers and Ukrainian stamps. Seeks financial contributions from correspondents to aid victims of Chernobyl accident.

Radio Minsk, ulitsa Krasnaya 4, 220807 Minsk, Belorusskaya SSR, USSR.

Radio Moscow—Domestic Services, ulitsa Akademika Koroleva 19, 127427 Moscow, USSR. Correspondence in Russian preferred.

Radio Moscow—External Services, ulitsa Pyatnitskaya 25, 113326 Moscow, USSR. Contact: Mrs. Tanya Lavrova; Elena Frolovskaya or Olga Troshina. Free stickers, calendars and booklets, including cookbooks.

Radio Riga International, P.O. Box 266, 226018 Riga, Latvia, USSR. Contact: R. Visnere, Mailbag Editor. Free stickers and pennants.

Radio Station Vedo, Radiostansiya Vedo, Volgograd, USSR. Contact: Andrei Bogdanov. Correspondence in Russian likely to be preferred.

Radio Tallinn, Radio Tallinn DX Club, Eesti Raadio, Lomonossovi 21, 200100 Tallinn, Estonia, USSR. $1 required. Replies occasionally.

Radio Tashkent, ulitsa Khorezmskaya 49, GFP, 700047 Tashkent, Uzbekistan, USSR. Contact: Ms. Nadira Dabadjanova or Mrs. Shodear Burkhan, Correspondence Section. Free wallet calendars and postcards.

Radio Tbilisi, TV-Radio Tbilisi, ulitsa Rostava 68, 380015 Tbilisi, Republic of Georgia, USSR. Contact: Helena Apkhadze, Foreign Editor. Replies occasionally and slowly.

Radio Tikhiy Okean, RTV Center, ulitsa Uborevieha 20A, 690000 Vladivostok, Primorsk Kray, USSR.

Radio Vilnius, Lietuvos Televizija Radijas, Kronarskio 49, 232674 Vilnius, Lithuania, USSR. Contact: Edvinas Butkus, Editor-in-Chief; or Ilonia Rukiene, Head of English Department; or Virginija Budryte, Letterbox. Free stickers and Lithuanian stamps. If no response, or during emergency conditions, address sealed envelope exactly as follows: Sigitas Zilionis, DX Editor, Lithuanian DX Club, A.D. 1646, Vilnius 10, Lithuanian SSR, USSR; correspondence to this address often results in free *Banga* radio club bulletin.

Radio Yerevan, ulitsa Mrovayana 5, 375025 Yerevan, Armenia, USSR. Contact: Olga Iroshina.

Sakhalin Radio, Dom Radio, ulitsa Komsomolskaya 209, 693000, GSP, Yuzhno-Sakhalinsk, Sakhalin Is., USSR. Contact: V. Belyaev, Chairman of Sakhalinsk RTV Committee.

Tadjik Radio—See "Radio Dushanbé."

Tatar Radio, RTV Center, ulitsa 15, 420015 Kazan', Tatar ASSR, USSR. May reply to correspondence in Russian. Return postage helpful.

Tyumen' Radio, RTV Center, ulitsa Permyakova 6, 625013 Tyumen', Tyumenskaya Oblast, USSR. May reply to correspondence in Russian. Return postage helpful.

Ukrainian Radio—See "Radio Kiev."

Uzbek Radio—See "Radio Tashkent."

Yakut Radio, Dom Radio, ulitsa Ordzhonikdze 48, 677007 Yakutsk, Yakutskaya ASSR, USSR. Contact: Alexandra Borisova; or S. Bobev, Letters Dept.

VANUATU World Time +12 (midyear +11)

Radio Vanuatu, P.O. Box 49, Port Vila, Vanuatu. Contact: R. Page.

VATICAN CITY STATE World Time +1 (+2 midyear)

Vatican Radio, Vatican City, Vatican State. Contact: Fr. Federico Lombardi, S.J., Program Manager. Free station stickers. Compact disc musical recordings for $13 each from sales office, Freq. s.r.l.—Edizioni Fonografiche, Via Volturno 80, Edilnord/Portici 1, I-20047 Brugherio MI, Italy.

VENEZUELA World Time –4

Note: Although widely heard, Venezuelan stations are not among the best in responding to listeners' correspondence. Friendly, personalized correspondence in Spanish (Spanish is virtually a "must"), with return postage and some photos or other mementos enclosed, appears to work best in eliciting a reply.

Ecos del Torbes, Apartado 152, San Cristóbal 5001, Táchira, Venezuela. Contact: (non-technical) Gregorio González Lovera, Presidente; (technical) Ing. Iván Escobar S., Jefe Técnico.

Radio Continental, Av. Marqués del Pumar, Barinas, Venezuela. Contact: (non-technical) Angel M. Pérez, Director; (technical) Ing. Santiago San Gil G. $1, return postage or 2 IRCs required. Replies occasionally to correspondence in Spanish.

Radio Frontera, Edificio Radio, San Antonio del Táchira, Táchira, Venezuela. Contact: N. Marchena, Director. May reply to correspondence in Spanish. $1 or return postage suggested.

Radio Los Andes, Apartado 40, Mérida, Venezuela. May reply to correspondence in Spanish. $1 or return postage suggested.

Radio Maracaibo, Calle 67 No. 24-88, Maracaibo, Venezuela. Contact: Máximo Flores Velázquez, Director-Gerente. $1 or return postage required. Replies to correspondence in Spanish.

Radio Nacional, Apartado 3979, Caracas 1010, Venezuela. Contact: Iván Russa Crespo, Jefe; or Mei-Ling Talavera Rojas, Interventora. Stickers and other small souvenirs for 2 IRCs or return postage. Replies irregularly and slowly to correspondence in Spanish.

Radio Rumbos, Apartado 2618, Caracas 1010, Venezuela.

Radio Táchira, Apartado 152, San Cristóbal 5001, Táchira, Venezuela. Contact: Eleázar Silva M., Gerente.

Radio Valera, Av. 10 No. 9-31, Valera, Trujillo, Venezuela.

VIETNAM World Time +7

Hoang Lien Son Broadcasting Station—same address as Voice of Vietnam.

Voice of Vietnam, Overseas Service, 58 Quan Su, Hanoi, Vietnam; or (technical) Office of Radio Reception Quality, Central Department of Radio and Television Broadcast Engineering, Vietnam General Corporation of Posts and Telecommunications, Hanoi, Vietnam. Contact (Overseas Service): Dao Dinh Tuan, Director of External Broadcasting. Free pennant. Replies slowly.

YEMEN World Time +3

Republic of Yemen Radio, Ministry of Information, San'a, Yemen. Contact: (non-technical correspondence in English) English Service; (technical) Abdullah Farhan, Technical Director.

YUGOSLAVIA World Time +1 (+2 midyear)

Radio Yugoslavia, Hilendarska 2/IV, P.O. Box 200, 11000 Belgrade, Yugoslavia. Contact: Aleksandar Georgiev. Replies slowly.

ZAIRE World Time +1 Western, including Kinshasa; +2 Eastern

La Voix du Zaire—Kinshasa, B.P. 3171, Kinshasa-Gombe, Zaire. Contact: Ayimpam Mwan-a-ngo, Directeur des Programmes, Radio. Letters should be sent via registered mail. $1 or 3 IRCs helpful. Correspondence in French preferred.

La Voix du Zaire—Lubumbashi, B.P. 7296, Lubumbashi, Zaire. Contact: Senga Lokavu, Le Chef du Service de l'Audiovisuel; or Bébé Beshelemu, Le Directeur Regional de l'O.Z.R.T; or Mulenga Kanso, Le Chef du Service Logistique. Letters should be sent via registered mail. $1 or 3 IRCs helpful. Correspondence in French preferred.

ZAMBIA World Time +2

Radio Zambia, P.O. Box 50015, Lusaka, Zambia. Contact (technical): W. Lukozu, Project Engineer. $1 required, and correspondence should be sent via registered mail. Replies slowly and irregularly.

Credits: Tony Jones, Craig Tyson, Lawrence Magne, Numero Uno, *Antonio Ribeiro da Motta, David Walcutt and Jo Ann Petrie/DOT.*

THE BLUE PAGES

Channel-by-Channel Guide to World Band Schedules

There are hundreds of channels of news, music and entertainment available on world band radio, with some being shared by several stations. With so much to choose from, it can take some doing just to figure out what is out there.

Schedules at a Glance

Ordinary listings of what's on world band radio are unwieldy, as there are thousands of items of data. That's why *Passport* includes these quick-access Blue Pages. Now, everything—stations, times, languages, targets and more—can be found at a glance. If an abbreviation or something else is not clear, the glossary at the back of the book explains it. There is also a handy key to languages and symbols at the bottom of each pair of Blue Pages.

For example, if you're in North America listening to 6175 kHz at 2300 World Time, you'll see that the BBC World Service is broadcast in English to this area at that hour. The transmitter is located in Canada and operates at a power of 250 kW.

To be as helpful as possible throughout the year, *Passport's* schedules consist not just of observed activity, but also that which we have creatively opined will take place during the entire year. This latter information is original from us, and therefore, of course, will not be so exact as factual information.

World Band Stations Heard Beyond Intended Target

With several hundred stations on the air at the same time, many on the same channels, you can't begin to hear all—or even most. Nevertheless, you can hear some stations even though they're not targeted to your part of the world. Tune around the airwaves, using the Blue Pages as your guide, and you'll discover more variety than ever.

World Time

Times and days of the week are given in World Time, explained in the *Passport* glossary. Midyear, many programs are heard an hour earlier, whereas some in the Southern Hemisphere are heard an hour later.

GUIDE TO BLUE PAGES FORMAT

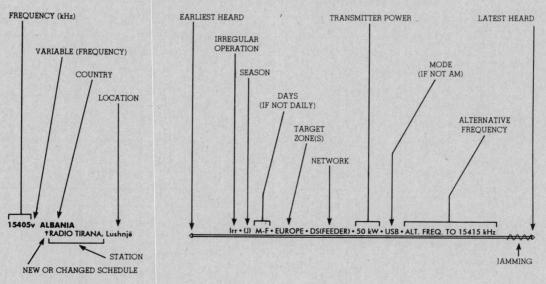

FREQUENCY (kHz)
VARIABLE (FREQUENCY)
COUNTRY
LOCATION
EARLIEST HEARD
IRREGULAR OPERATION
SEASON
DAYS (IF NOT DAILY)
TARGET ZONE(S)
NETWORK
TRANSMITTER POWER
MODE (IF NOT AM)
ALTERNATIVE FREQUENCY
LATEST HEARD

15405v ALBANIA ↑RADIO TIRANA, Lushnjë

STATION
NEW OR CHANGED SCHEDULE

Irr • (J) M-F • EUROPE • DS(FEEDER) • 50 kW • USB • ALT. FREQ. TO 15415 kHz

JAMMING

FREQUENCY   COUNTRY, STATION, LOCATION   TARGET • NETWORK • POWER (kW)   World Time

0 1 2 3 4 5 6 7 8 9 10 11 12 13 14 15 16 17 18 19 20 21 22 23 24

Frequency	Country, Station, Location	Notes
2310	AUSTRALIA / ABC/CAAMA RADIO, Alice Springs	ENGLISH, ETC • DS • 50 kW
2325	AUSTRALIA / ABC/CAAMA RADIO, Tennant Creek	ENGLISH, ETC • DS • 50 kW
2340	CHINA (PR) / FUJIAN PEOPLES BS, Fuzhou	Irr • DS-1, TAIWAN SVC • 10 kW
2350	INDONESIA / †RRI, Yogyakarta, Jawa	DS • 1 kW
2360	GUATEMALA / R MAYA DE BARILLAS, Huehuetenango	DS • 0.5 kW
2376.8	INDONESIA / †RRI, Surabaya, Jawa	DS • 0.5/1 kW
2380	BRAZIL / RADIO EDUCADORA, Limeira	Irr • DS • 0.25 kW
2390	GUATEMALA / LA VOZ DE ATITLAN, Santiago Atitlán	DS-SPANISH, ETC • 1 kW / Su • DS-SPANISH, ETC • 1 kW
	INDONESIA / †RRI, Cirebon, Jawa	DS • 1 kW
	MEXICO / †RADIO HUAYACOCOTLA, Huayacocotla	Tu-Su • DS • 0.5 kW / M-Sa • DS • 0.5 kW
2410	BRAZIL / R TRANSAMAZONICA, Sen'r Guiomard	DS • 1 kW • ALT. FREQ. TO 3255 kHz
	PAPUA NEW GUINEA / RADIO ENGA, Wabag	DS • 10 kW
2415	CHINA (PR) / WENZHOU PEOPLES BS, Wenzhou	DS
2420	BRAZIL / RADIO SAO CARLOS, São Carlos	DS • 0.5 kW
2445	CHINA (PR) / †JIANGXI PEOPLES BS, Nanchang	DS-1 • 10 kW
2460	CHINA (PR) / †YUNNAN PEOPLES BS, Kunming	DS-1 • 15 kW
2473.2	INDONESIA / †RRI, Purwokerto, Jawa	DS-TEMP INACTIVE • 1 kW
2475	CHINA (PR) / ZHEJIANG PBS, Hangzhou	DS-1 • 10 kW
2485	AUSTRALIA / ABC/R RUM JUNGLE, Katherine	DS • 50 kW
2490	BRAZIL / RADIO 8 SETEMBRO, Descalvado	DS • 0.25 kW
	INDONESIA / RRI, Ujung Pandang	DS • 0.5 kW / DS / Sa • DS / Su-F • DS
2495v	MADAGASCAR / †RTV MALAGASY, Antananarivo	Irr • DS-1 • 30/100 kW / Irr • M-F • DS-1 • 30/100 kW
2500	USA / WWV, Ft Collins, Colorado	WEATHER/WORLD TIME • 2.5 kW
	WWVH, Kekaha, Hawaii	WEATHER/WORLD TIME • 5 kW
2560	CHINA (PR) / CENTRAL PEOPLES BS, Urümqi	Irr • DS-MINORITIES • 15 kW
	†XINJIANG PBS, Urümqi	Irr • DS-UIGHUR • 15 kW
2582.4	INDONESIA / RPD TENGAH SELATAN, Soë, Timur	DS • 0.3 kW
2618	INDONESIA / †RPD SAMBAS, Sambas, Kalimantan	DS-TEMP INACTIVE • 0.25 kW
2695	INDONESIA / RPD ENDE, Ende, Flores	DS • 0.5 kW
2850v	KOREA (DPR) / KOREAN CENTRAL BS, Pyongyang	DS • 100 kW
2904.8	INDONESIA / †RPD NGADA, Bajawa, N Tenggara	DS-TEMP INACTIVE • 0.5 kW
2962.7	INDONESIA / †RPD MANGGARAI, Ruteng, Flores	DS • 0.3 kW
3143	INDONESIA / †RPD BELITUNG, Tanjung Pandan, Sum	DS • 0.3 kW
3159	INDONESIA / RPHDI IND HILIR, Tembilahan, Sum	DS • 0.03 kW
3200	SWAZILAND / †TRANS WORLD RADIO, Manzini	S AFRICA • 25 kW
3200.3	BOLIVIA / RADIO 9 DE ABRIL, Pulacayo	Irr • DS / Irr • Tu-Su • DS
3204.4	INDONESIA / †RRI, Bandung, Jawa	DS • 10 kW
3205	BRAZIL / R RIBEIRAO PRETO, Ribeirão Prêto	DS • 1 kW
	R VALE RIO MADEIRA, Humaitá	DS-TEMP INACTIVE • 5 kW
	INDIA / †ALL INDIA RADIO, Lucknow	DS • 10 kW / ENGLISH & HINDI • DS • 10 kW
	PAPUA NEW GUINEA / RADIO SANDAUN, Vanimo	DS • 10 kW
3210v (con'd)	CHINA (PR) / GANNAN PEOPLES BS, Hezuo	Alternative Frequency to 5970v kHz

0 1 2 3 4 5 6 7 8 9 10 11 12 13 14 15 16 17 18 19 20 21 22 23 24

SUMMER ONLY (J)   WINTER ONLY (D)   JAMMING / OR ∧   EARLIEST HEARD ◁   LATEST HEARD ▷   NEW OR CHANGED FOR 1992 †

FREQUENCY   COUNTRY, STATION, LOCATION

TARGET • NETWORK • POWER (kW)

World Time

0 1 2 3 4 5 6 7 8 9 10 11 12 13 14 15 16 17 18 19 20 21 22 23 24

Frequency	Country / Station / Location	Details
3210v (con'd)	MOZAMBIQUE — RADIO MOCAMBIQUE, Maputo	DS • 100 kW
3214.8	INDONESIA — †RRI, Manado, Sulawesi	DS • 10 kW
3215	SOUTH AFRICA — SOUTH AFRICAN BC, Meyerton	ENGLISH & AFRIKAANS • DS-RADIO ORANJE • 100 kW
3220	CHINA (PR) — CENTRAL PEOPLES BS	Irr • DS-1
	ECUADOR — HCJB-VO THE ANDES, Quito	DS-SPANISH, QUECHUA • 10 kW
	PAPUA NEW GUINEA — RADIO MOROBE, Lae	DS • 10 kW
3220v	KOREA (DPR) — KANGWONG PS, Wonsan	DS
3222	TOGO — RADIO KARA, Lama-Kara	DS-FRENCH, ETC • 10 kW
3222.8	INDONESIA — †RRI, Mataram, Lombok	DS • 5 kW
3223	INDIA — ALL INDIA RADIO, Shimla	DS • 2.5 kW / ENGLISH & HINDI • DS • 2.5 kW
3224.8	INDONESIA — †RRI, Tanjungpinang	DS • 10 kW
3230	NEPAL — RADIO NEPAL, Harriharpur	Alternative Frequency to 7165 kHz
3230.3	PERU — R SOL DE LOS ANDES, Juliaca	DS-SPANISH, ETC • 0.5 kW / Irr • DS-SPANISH, ETC • 0.5 kW
3231.8	INDONESIA — †RRI, Bukittinggi, Sumatera	DS • 10 kW
3232	MADAGASCAR — RTV MALAGASY, Antananarivo	Su • DS-2 • 10 kW / DS-2 • 10 kW / Sa/Su • DS-2 • 10 kW
3235	BRAZIL — RADIO CLUBE, Marilia	DS • 0.5 kW
	INDIA — ALL INDIA RADIO, Guwahati	DS-B • 10 kW / Sa • DS-B • 10 kW
	PAPUA NEW GUINEA — R WEST NEW BRITAIN, Kimbe	DS • 10 kW
3240	SWAZILAND — †TRANS WORLD RADIO, Manzini	S AFRICA • 25 kW
3240v	ECUADOR — R ANTENA LIBRE, Esmeraldas	DS • 1 kW
3241.8	INDONESIA — †RRI, Ambon, Maluku	DS-TEMP INACTIVE • 1 kW
3245	BRAZIL — RADIO CLUBE, Varginha	DS • 1 kW / M-Sa • DS • 1 kW
	PAPUA NEW GUINEA — RADIO GULF, Kerema	DS • 10 kW
3249.8	INDONESIA — RRI, Banjarmasin, Kali'n	DS • 10 kW
3250	KOREA (DPR) — RADIO PYONGYANG, Pyongyang	E ASIA • 100 kW
3250v	CLANDESTINE (ASIA) — †"VO THE CRUSADER"	MIDEAST & S ASIA • AFGHAN REBELS
	HONDURAS — RADIO LUZ Y VIDA, Santa Bárbara	DS • 0.8 kW / Su/M • DS • 0.8 kW / Tu-Sa • DS • 0.8 kW
3255	BRAZIL — R EDUCADORA CARIRI, Crato	Tu-Su • DS • 1 kW / DS • 1 kW
	R TRANSAMAZONICA, Sen'r Guiomard	Alternative Frequency to 2410 kHz
	INDIA — †ALL INDIA RADIO, Shillong	DS • 50 kW / ENGLISH & HINDI • DS • 50 kW
	UNITED KINGDOM — †BBC, Via Maseru, Lesotho	S AFRICA • 50 kW
3255v	ECUADOR — LV DEL TRIUNFO, Sto Domingo Clrdos	Irr • DS • 1 kW
	VENEZUELA — †LV DE EL TIGRE, El Tigre	Irr • DS-"RADIO 980" • 1 kW
3259	JAPAN — NHK, Fukuoka	Irr • DS-1 (FEEDER) • 0.6 kW • USB
3259.8	INDONESIA — †RRI, Kupang, Timur	DS • 1 kW
3260	CHINA (PR) — †GUIZHOU PEOPLES BS, Guiyang	DS-1 • 10 kW
	ECUADOR — LV DE RIO CARRIZAL, Calceta	DS • 3 kW
	NIGER — LA VOIX DU SAHEL, Niamey	DS-FRENCH, ETC • 4 kW / Sa • DS-FRENCH, ETC • 4 kW
	PAPUA NEW GUINEA — RADIO MADANG, Madang	DS • 10 kW
	PERU — LA VOZ DE OXAPAMPA, Oxapampa	DS • 2.5 kW / Irr • DS • 2.5 kW

0 1 2 3 4 5 6 7 8 9 10 11 12 13 14 15 16 17 18 19 20 21 22 23 24

ENGLISH ▬   ARABIC ≋   CHINESE ▱▱▱   FRENCH ═   GERMAN ▬   RUSSIAN ═   SPANISH ▬   OTHER ▬

FREQUENCY   COUNTRY, STATION, LOCATION   TARGET • NETWORK • POWER (kW)   World Time

0 1 2 3 4 5 6 7 8 9 10 11 12 13 14 15 16 17 18 19 20 21 22 23 24

Frequency	Country, Station, Location	Schedule Notes
3264.8	INDONESIA †RRI, Bengkulu, Sumatera	DS • 10 kW
3265	CONGO †RTV CONGOLAISE, Brazzaville	Alternative Frequency to 5985 kHz
3265v	INDONESIA †RRI, Gorontalo, Sulawesi	DS • 10 kW
3268	INDIA †ALL INDIA RADIO, Kohima	DS-A • 50 kW
3269.3	ECUADOR ECOS DEL ORIENTE, Lago Agrio	DS
3270	NAMIBIA †NAMIBIAN BC CORP, Windhoek	ENGLISH, GERMAN, ETC • DS • 100 kW
3275	PAPUA NEW GUINEA R SOUTH HIGHLANDS, Mendi	DS • 10 kW
	SWAZILAND †TRANS WORLD RADIO, Manzini	S AFRICA • 25 kW
	VENEZUELA RADIO MARA, Maracaibo	DS-VERY IRREGULAR • 1 kW
3277	INDIA †RADIO KASHMIR, Srinagar	DS-B • 50 kW; Sa • DS-B • 50 kW; ENGLISH, ETC • DS-B • 50 kW
3277.6	INDONESIA †RRI, Jakarta, Jawa	DS • 1 kW
3279.8	ECUADOR LA VOZ DEL NAPO, Tena	DS-SPANISH, ETC • 2.5 kW; Su • DS-SPANISH, ETC • 2.5 kW
3280	CHINA (PR) VOICE OF PUJIANG, Shanghai	E ASIA • CHINESE, ETC
3280v	MOZAMBIQUE EP DE SOFALA, Beira	DS-2 • 100 kW
3280.2	PERU RADIO HUARI, Ayacucho	DS-SPANISH, ETC • 1 kW
3285	BELIZE RADIO BELIZE, Belmopan	DS-ENGLISH, SPANISH • 1 kW
	BRAZIL †RTV SENTINELA, Obidos	DS • 1 kW
3285.8	ECUADOR RADIO RIO TARQUI, Cuenca	DS • 0.36 kW
3286	INDONESIA †RRI, Madiun	DS • 10 kW
3288v	MADAGASCAR RTV MALAGASY, Antananarivo	DS-1 • 10 kW; M-F • DS-1 • 10 kW; Sa/Su • DS-1 • 10 kW
3289.8	ECUADOR RADIO CENTRO, Ambato	DS • 0.5 kW
3290	NAMIBIA †NAMIBIAN BC CORP, Windhoek	DS • 100 kW
	PAPUA NEW GUINEA RADIO CENTRAL, Port Moresby	ENGLISH, ETC • DS • 10 kW
3295	ICELAND †RIKISUTVARPID, Reykjavik	ATLANTIC & EUROPE • DS-1 • 10 kW • USB; M-F • ATLANTIC & EUROPE • DS-1 • 10 kW • USB; Sa/Su • ATLANTIC & EUROPE • DS-1 • 10 kW • USB
3300	GUATEMALA RADIO CULTURAL, Guatemala City	DS • 10 kW; M • DS • 10 kW; Tu-Su • DS • 10 kW; M-Sa • DS • 10 kW; Su • DS • 10 kW
3305	INDIA ALL INDIA RADIO, Ranchi	DS • 2 kW; ENGLISH & HINDI • DS • 2 kW
	PAPUA NEW GUINEA RADIO WESTERN, Daru	ENGLISH, ETC • DS • 10 kW
3305.7	ZIMBABWE ZIMBABWE BC CORP, Gweru	ENGLISH, ETC • DS-TEMP INACTIVE • 10/100 kW; M-Sa • ENGLISH, ETC • DS-TEMP INACTIVE • 10/100 kW
3306v	INDONESIA †RRI, Dili, Timur	DS • 10 kW
3310	CHINA (PR) †JILIN PEOPLES BS, Changchun	Irr • DS • 10 kW; Su • DS • 10 kW
	PERU RADIO BAGUA, Bagua	DS • 1 kW
	RADIO UNIVERSAL, Cusco	DS • 2 kW
3310.3	BOLIVIA RADIO SAN MIGUEL, Riberalta	DS • 1 kW; Tu-Su • DS • 1 kW
3315	ECUADOR RADIO PASTAZA, Puyo	DS • 2.5 kW
	INDIA ALL INDIA RADIO, Bhopal	DS-A • 10 kW; ENGLISH & HINDI • DS-A • 10 kW
	PAPUA NEW GUINEA RADIO MANUS, Lorengau	ENGLISH, ETC • DS • 10 kW
3316	SIERRA LEONE SIERRA LEONE BS, Goderich	ENGLISH, ETC • DS • 10 kW
3320 (con'd)	KOREA (DPR) RADIO PYONGYANG, Pyongyang	E ASIA

FREQUENCY	COUNTRY, STATION, LOCATION	TARGET • NETWORK • POWER (kW)	World Time

FREQUENCY	COUNTRY, STATION, LOCATION	TARGET • NETWORK • POWER (kW)
3320 (con'd)	KOREA (DPR) UNIDENTIFIED	DS
	SOUTH AFRICA †SOUTH AFRICAN BC, Meyerton	ENGLISH & AFRIKAANS • DS-RADIO ORION • 100 kW
		RADIO SUID-AFRIKA • 100 kW
3322.4	ECUADOR RADIO SANGAY, Macas	Irr • DS • 1 kW
3324.8	GUATEMALA R MAYA DE BARILLAS, Huehuetenango	DS • 1 kW
3325	BRAZIL RADIO LIBERAL, Belém	DS • 5 kW
	†RADIO TUPI, Guarulhos	DS • 2.5 kW
	INDONESIA †RRI, Palangkaráya, Kali'n	DS • 10 kW
	PAPUA NEW GUINEA †R NORTH SOLOMONS, Rabaul	ENGLISH, ETC • DS • 8 kW
3325v	ECUADOR ONDAS QUEVEDENAS, Quevedo	Irr • DS • 1.5 kW
3326	NIGERIA RADIO NIGERIA, Lagos	ENGLISH, ETC • DS-1 • 50 kW
3330	COMOROS †RADIO COMORO, Moroni	FRENCH, ETC • DS • 4/60 kW
	PHILIPPINES †FAR EAST BC CO, Bocaue	DS • ALT. FREQ. TO 3345 kHz
	RWANDA †R REP RWANDAISE, Kigali	DS • 20 kW
		Su • DS • 20 kW
3330.4	PERU †ONDAS DEL HUALLAGA, Huánuco	DS • 0.5 kW • ALT. FREQ. TO 3331.2 kHz
		Su • DS • 0.5 kW • ALT. FREQ. TO 3331.2 kHz
3331.2	PERU †ONDAS DEL HUALLAGA, Huánuco	Alternative Frequency to 3330.4 kHz
3335	BRAZIL RADIO ALVORADA, Londrina	DS • 5 kW • ALT. FREQ. TO 4865 kHz
		Tu-Su • DS • 5 kW • ALT. FREQ. TO 4865 kHz
	CHINA (TAIWAN) †CENTRAL BC SYSTEM, T'ai-pei	PRC-5 (HAKKA) • 10 kW
	PAPUA NEW GUINEA RADIO EAST SEPIK, Wewak	DS • 10 kW
3338v	MOZAMBIQUE RADIO MOCAMBIQUE, Maputo	DS • 10 kW
3340	PERU †RADIO ALTURA, Cerro De Pasco	DS • 1 kW
3340.2	BOLIVIA RADIO VILOCO, Viloco	DS-SPANISH, ETC • 1 kW
		Irr • Su/M • DS-SPANISH, ETC • 1 kW
3345	INDIA †RADIO KASHMIR, Jammu	DS-A • 2 kW
		ENGLISH & HINDI • DS-A • 2 kW
	INDONESIA †RRI, Ternate, Maluku	DS • 10 kW
	PAPUA NEW GUINEA RADIO NORTHERN, Popondetta	ENGLISH, ETC • DS • 10 kW
	PHILIPPINES †FAR EAST BC CO, Bocaue	Alternative Frequency to 3330 kHz
3346	ZAMBIA RADIO ZAMBIA-ZBS, Lusaka	DS • 50 kW
3349.8	BOLIVIA RADIO 27 DICIEMBRE, Villa Montes	Irr • DS • 1 kW
		Irr • Tu-Su • DS • 1 kW
3350	GHANA GHANA BC CORP, Accra	Irr • ENGLISH, ETC • DS-1 • 10 kW
	KOREA (DPR) SOUTH PYONGYANG PS, Pyŏngsong	DS
3354v	ANGOLA RADIO NACIONAL, Luanda	DS-A
		S AFRICA
		DS-B
3355	INDIA ALL INDIA RADIO, Kurseong	DS • 20 kW
		ENGLISH & HINDI • DS • 20 kW
	NEW CALEDONIA RFO-N CALEDONIE, Nouméa	FRENCH, ETC • PACIFIC • DS-TEMP INACTIVE • 20 kW
	PAPUA NEW GUINEA RADIO SIMBU, Kundiawa	DS • 10 kW
3355.3	INDONESIA †RRI, Sumenep, Jawa	DS • 1 kW
3356	BOTSWANA †RADIO BOTSWANA, Gaborone	ENGLISH, ETC • DS • 50 kW
		DS-ENGLISH, ETC • 50 kW
3360	GUATEMALA LA VOZ DE NAHUALA, Nahualá	DS-SPANISH, ETC • 0.5/1 kW
		Su • DS-SPANISH, ETC • 0.5/1 kW
3365	BRAZIL RADIO CULTURA, Araraquara	DS • 1 kW
	INDIA †ALL INDIA RADIO, Delhi	DS • 20 kW
(con'd)		ENGLISH & HINDI • DS • 20 kW

ENGLISH ▬ ARABIC ≋ CHINESE ▭▭▭ FRENCH ▭▭ GERMAN ▬ RUSSIAN ═ SPANISH ▬ OTHER ▬

FREQUENCY   COUNTRY, STATION, LOCATION

TARGET • NETWORK • POWER (kW)

World Time

0 1 2 3 4 5 6 7 8 9 10 11 12 13 14 15 16 17 18 19 20 21 22 23 24

Frequency	Country / Station / Location	Details
3365 (con'd)	PAPUA NEW GUINEA — RADIO MILNE BAY, Alotau	ENGLISH, ETC • DS • 10 kW
3366	GHANA — GHANA BC CORP, Accra	DS-2 • 50 kW
3366v	CUBA — †RADIO REBELDE, Havana	DS • 0.5 kW
3370	GUATEMALA — RADIO TEZULUTLAN, Cobán	DS-SPANISH, ETC • 1 kW
3370v	MOZAMBIQUE — EP DE SOFALA, Beira	DS-1 • 10 kW
3374.2	INDONESIA — †RRI, Medan, Sumatera	DS • 7.5 kW
3375	BRAZIL — R NACIONAL, S Gabriel Cachoeira	DS • 5 kW
	RADIO EDUCADORA, Guajará Mirim	DS • 5 kW
	RADIO EQUATORIAL, Macapá	DS-TEMP INACTIVE • 1 kW
	INDIA — †ALL INDIA RADIO, Guwahati	DS-A • 50 kW / ENGLISH & HINDI • DS-A • 50 kW
	PAPUA NEW GUINEA — R WEST HIGHLANDS, Mount Hagen	DS • 10 kW
3375v	ANGOLA — RADIO NACIONAL, Luanda	DS-A • 10 kW
3377.5	JAPAN — NHK, Osaka	Irr • DS-2(FEEDER) • 0.5 kW
3380	GUATEMALA — RADIO CHORTIS, Jocotán	DS-SPANISH, CHORTI • 1 kW / Tu-Su • DS • 1 kW / M-Sa • DS-SPANISH, CHORTI • 1 kW
3380.6	MALAWI — MALAWI BC CORP, Limbe	ENGLISH, ETC • DS • 100 kW / (J) • ENGLISH, ETC • DS • 100 kW
3380.7	INDONESIA — †RRI, Malang, Jawa	DS • 1 kW
3381	ECUADOR — †RADIO IRIS, Quito	DS • 6 kW
3381v	INDONESIA — †RRI, Malang, Jawa	DS • 1 kW
3385	BRAZIL — R EDUCACAO RURAL, Tefé	DS • 1 kW
	FRENCH GUIANA — RFO-GUYANE, Cayenne	DS • 4 kW
	INDONESIA — †RRI, Kupang, Timur	DS • 10 kW / Sa • DS • 10 kW / Su-F • DS • 10 kW
	MALAYSIA — †RTM-SARAWAK, Miri	DS-IBAN • 10 kW
	PAPUA NEW GUINEA — R EAST NEW BRITAIN, Rabaul	DS • 10 kW
3390v	ZAIRE — †RADIO CANDIP, Bunia	FRENCH, ETC • DS • 1 kW / Su • FRENCH, ETC • DS • 1 kW
3390.3	BOLIVIA — RADIO CAMARGO, Camargo	DS • 1 kW
3394.8	ECUADOR — RADIO ZARACAY, Santo Domingo	DS • 5 kW
3395	INDONESIA — †RRI, Tanjungkarang, Sum	DS • 10 kW
	PAPUA NEW GUINEA — R EAST HIGHLANDS, Goroka	DS • 10 kW
3396v	ZIMBABWE — ZIMBABWE BC CORP, Gweru	DS-TEMP INACTIVE • 20/100 kW / M-Sa • DS-TEMP INACTIVE • 20/100 kW
3401v	BRAZIL — RADIO 6 DE AGOSTO, Xapurí	DS • 2 kW / Tu-Su • DS • 2 kW
3447.2	INDONESIA — †RRI, Pontianak, Kalimantan	DS • 1 kW
3460	INDONESIA — †RPD ACEH TIMUR, Langsa, Sumatera	DS
3473v	BOLIVIA — RADIO PADILLA, Padilla	DS • 0.5 kW
3480	CLANDESTINE (ASIA) — "VO NAT SALVATION", Haeju, N Korea	TO SOUTH KOREA • 100 kW
3500.5	PERU — †RADIO CHILLA, Chilla	DS
3520v	BOLIVIA — †RADIO 20 SETIEMBRE, Bermejo	Irr • DS
3569v	BRAZIL — RADIO 3 DE JULHO, Brasiléia	DS • 1.5 kW
3580	INDONESIA — RPD ASAHAN, Kisaran, Sumatera	DS • 0.8 kW
3607.5	JAPAN — NHK, Tokyo-Shobu	Irr • DS-1(FEEDER) • 0.9 kW • USB
3644.7	INDONESIA — RRI, Fak Fak, Irian Jaya	DS • 0.5 kW
3663v	PAKISTAN (AZAD K) — †AZAD KASHMIR RADIO, Muzaffarabad	DS • 1 kW

FREQUENCY   COUNTRY, STATION, LOCATION   TARGET • NETWORK • POWER (kW)   World Time

0 1 2 3 4 5 6 7 8 9 10 11 12 13 14 15 16 17 18 19 20 21 22 23 24

Freq	Country / Station / Location	Schedule details
3778v	**IRAN**	
	VO THE ISLAMIC REP, Tehrän	Irr • MIDEAST • DS • 50 kW
3800	**PERU**	
	†RADIO OYON, Oyón	DS-SPANISH,QUECHUA • 1 kW
		Tu-Su • DS • 1 kW
3811v	**PERU**	
	†RADIO CENTENARIO	DS
3860	**PERU**	
	R SAN NICOLAS, Rodr'z de Mendoza	DS
3890v	**CLANDESTINE (M EAST)**	
	"VO IRAN COMMUNIST, Afghanistan	F • MIDEAST • ANTI-IRANIAN GOVT MIDEAST • ANTI-IRANIAN GOVT
		Sa-Th • MIDEAST • ANTI-IRANIAN GOVT
3900	**CHINA (PR)**	
	HULUNBEI'ER PBS, Hailar	DS
3904.8	**INDONESIA**	
	†RRI, Merauke,Irian Jaya	DS • 1 kW
		Irr • DS • 1 kW
3905	**INDIA**	
	†ALL INDIA RADIO, Delhi	DS • 10 kW
		ENGLISH & HINDI • DS • 10 kW
	PAPUA NEW GUINEA	
	RADIO NEW IRELAND, Kavieng	DS • 10 kW
3912	**CLANDESTINE (ASIA)**	
	†"VO THE PEOPLE", Seoul, S Korea	E ASIA
3915	**UNITED KINGDOM**	
	†BBC, Via Singapore	SE ASIA • 100 kW
		USSR • 100 kW
		(D) • USSR • 100 kW
		(D) • ASIA • 100 kW
3920	**KOREA (DPR)**	
	NORTH PYONGYANG PS, Sinuiju	DS
3925	**CANADA**	
	R CANADA INTL, Via Tokyo, Japan	Sa • E ASIA & PACIFIC • 10/50 kW
	INDIA	
	†ALL INDIA RADIO, Delhi	DS • 20 kW
		ENGLISH & HINDI • DS • 20 kW
		ENGLISH, ETC • DS • 20 kW
	JAPAN	
	RADIO TAMPA, Multiple Locations	DS-1 • 10/50 kW
		Su-F • DS-1 • 10/50 kW
	RADIO TAMPA, Tokyo-Nagara	DS-1 • 50 kW
3927.4	**SOUTH AFRICA**	
	†CAPITAL RADIO, Umtata	DS • 20 kW
3930	**KOREA (REPUBLIC)**	
	KOREAN BC SYSTEM, Hwasung	DS-1 • 5 kW
3934	**INDONESIA**	
	†RRI, Semarang, Jawa	DS • 5/10 kW
3935	**NEW ZEALAND**	
	†PRINT DISABLED R, Levin	M-F • DS • 1 kW
		Su • DS • 1 kW
		Su-F • DS • 1 kW
3935v	**CLANDESTINE (M EAST)**	
	"VO THE MARTYRS", Near Iran	MIDEAST • ANTI-IRANIAN GOVT
3940	**CHINA (PR)**	
	†HUBEI PEOPLES BS, Wuhan	DS-1
		M-Sa • DS-1
3940v	**ETHIOPIA**	
	†VO BROAD MASSES, Asmera	E AFRICA • PLF OF ERITREA
3945	**INDIA**	
	†ALL INDIA RADIO, Gorakhpur	S ASIA • 50 kW
		ENGLISH, ETC • DS • 50 kW DS • 50 kW
	INDONESIA	
	†RRI, Denpasar, Bali	DS • 1/10 kW
	JAPAN	
	RADIO TAMPA, Tokyo-Nagara	DS-2 • 10 kW
	VANUATU	
	RADIO VANUATU, Vila, Efate Island	DS-ENGLISH,FR,ETC • 10 kW
		M-Sa • DS-ENGLISH,FR,ETC • 10 kW
3945.7	**INDONESIA**	
	†RRI, Tanjungkarang	DS • 2.5 kW
3950	**CHINA (PR)**	
	†QINGHAI PEOPLES BS, Xining	DS-1 • 10 kW
3955	**UNITED KINGDOM**	
	†BBC, Multiple Locations	EUROPE • 250/300 kW
	†BBC, Skelton, Cumbria	(D) • EUROPE • 250 kW
	USSR	
	†KAZAKH RADIO	DS-2
	†RADIO ALMA-ATA	
3955v	**PAKISTAN**	
	PAKISTAN BC CORP, Rawalpindi	DS • 10 kW
		F • DS • 10 kW
3959.8	**KOREA (DPR)**	
	CHAGONG PROVINCIAL, Kanggye	DS

0 1 2 3 4 5 6 7 8 9 10 11 12 13 14 15 16 17 18 19 20 21 22 23 24

ENGLISH ▬▬   ARABIC ≋   CHINESE ▭▭▭   FRENCH ▬▬   GERMAN ▬▬   RUSSIAN ══   SPANISH ▬▬   OTHER ──

FREQUENCY   COUNTRY, STATION, LOCATION

TARGET • NETWORK • POWER (kW)   World Time

0 1 2 3 4 5 6 7 8 9 10 11 12 13 14 15 16 17 18 19 20 21 22 23 24

Frequency	Country, Station, Location	Details
3960	**CHINA (PR)** RADIO BEIJING, Beijing	(D) • E ASIA • 10 kW
	†XINJIANG PBS, Urümqi	(D) • DS-CHINESE • 50 kW
	INDONESIA †RRI, Padang, Sumatera	DS • 1 kW
	MONGOLIA †RADIO ULAANBAATAR, Dalandzadgad	DS-1 • 12 kW
	USA †RFE-RL, Via Germany	(D) • WEST USSR • 100 kW
3960.8	**INDONESIA** †RRI, Palu, Sulawesi	DS • 10 kW
3965	**AFGHANISTAN** RADIO AFGHANISTAN, Via USSR	Alternative Frequency to 4975 kHz
	FRANCE †R FRANCE INTL, Issoudun-Allouis	EUROPE • 4 kW
3970	**CAMEROON** CAMEROON RTV CORP, Buea	FRENCH, ENGLISH, ETC • DS • 4 kW
	CHINA (PR) †NEI MONGGOL PBS, Hohhot	DS
	JAPAN NHK, Nagoya	Irr • DS-1 (FEEDER) • 0.3 kW • USB
	NHK, Sapporo	Irr • DS-1 (FEEDER) • 0.6 kW
	KOREA (DPR) NORTH HAMGYONG PS, Ch'öngjin	DS
	USA †RFE-RL, Via Germany	(D) • M-Sa • E EUROPE • 100 kW (D) • E EUROPE • 100 kW
3975	**UNITED KINGDOM** †BBC, Skelton, Cumbria	(D) • EUROPE • 250 kW (J) • EUROPE • 250 kW
3976	**INDONESIA** †RRI, Surabaya, Jawa	DS • 10 kW
3980	**IRAQ** †REP OF IRAQ RADIO	DS
	USA †VOA, Via Germany	EUROPE • 100 kW (D) • EUROPE • 100 kW (J) • EUROPE • 100 kW
3980v	**PAKISTAN** PAKISTAN BC CORP, Islamabad	DS • 100 kW
	PERU RADIO EL PORVENIR, El Porvenir	Irr • DS • 0.5 kW
3985	**CHINA (PR)** RADIO BEIJING, Via Switzerland	EUROPE • 250 kW
	CLANDESTINE (ASIA) †"ECHO OF HOPE", Seoul, South Korea	(D) • E ASIA • 50 kW E ASIA • 50 kW
	SWITZERLAND †SWISS RADIO INTL, Beromünster	EUROPE • 250 kW M-Sa • EUROPE • 250 kW Su • EUROPE • 250 kW
	USA †RFE-RL, Via Germany	(D) • WEST USSR • 100 kW (J) • WEST USSR • 100 kW
3985.8	**INDONESIA** †RRI, Manokwari, Irian Jaya	DS • 1 kW
3990	**CHINA (PR)** CENTRAL PEOPLES BS, Urümqi	(D) • DS-MINORITIES • 50 kW
	VOICE OF PUJIANG, Shanghai	E ASIA • CHINESE, ETC
	†XINJIANG PBS, Urümqi	(D) • DS-UIGHUR • 50 kW
3995	**GERMANY** DEUTSCHE WELLE, Jülich	EUROPE • 100 kW (D) • EUROPE • 100 kW
	ITALY †RTV ITALIANA, Rome	EUROPE, MIDEAST & N AFRICA • DS-3 • 50 kW
	USSR RADIO MOSCOW, Khabarovsk	(D) • DS-MAYAK • 50 kW
	†TUVIN RADIO, Kyzyl	RUSSIAN, ETC • DS • 15 kW
4000v	**CAMEROON** †CAMEROON RTV CORP, Bafoussam	FRENCH, ENGLISH, ETC • DS • 20 kW
4000.2	**INDONESIA** †RRI, Kendari, Sulawesi	DS • 5 kW
4002.7	**INDONESIA** †RRI, Padang, Sumatera	DS • 10 kW Irr • DS • 1 kW
4005v	**CLANDESTINE (M EAST)** "VO IRANIAN REV'N", Afghanistan	MIDEAST • ANTI-IRANIAN GOVT
4008v	**PERU** RADIO GRAU, Huancabamba	Alternative Frequency to 5277v kHz
4010	**USSR** †KYRGYS RADIO, Bishkek	Sa • DS-1 • 50 kW RUSSIAN, ETC • DS-1 • 50 kW Su-F • RUSSIAN, ETC • DS-1 • 50 kW
	†RADIO MOSCOW, Vladivostok	(D) • E ASIA • 100 kW
4011v (con'd)	**PERU** FRECUENCIA POPULAR, Rioja	DS • 0.6 kW

0 1 2 3 4 5 6 7 8 9 10 11 12 13 14 15 16 17 18 19 20 21 22 23 24

SUMMER ONLY (J)   WINTER ONLY (D)   JAMMING / OR ∧   EARLIEST HEARD ◁   LATEST HEARD ▷   NEW OR CHANGED FOR 1992 †

FREQUENCY	COUNTRY, STATION, LOCATION	TARGET • NETWORK • POWER (kW)	World Time

4011v PERU
(con'd) FRECUENCIA POPULAR, Rioja — Tu-Su • DS • 0.6 kW / M-Sa • DS • 0.6 kW
4020 CHINA (PR) RADIO BEIJING, Beijing — E ASIA • FEEDER • 10 kW
4030 USSR †CHUKOT RADIO, Anadyr' — RUSSIAN ETC • DS • 15 kW
4030v CLANDESTINE (M EAST) "VO IRAQI PEOPLE" — MIDEAST • IRAQI COMMUNIST
4035 CHINA (PR) †CENTRAL PEOPLES BS, Lhasa — DS-MINORITIES • 50 kW
 †RADIO BEIJING, Lhasa — S ASIA • 50 kW
 †XIZANG PEOPLES BS, Lhasa — DS-TIBETAN • 50 kW
4039.2 PERU RADIO MARGINAL, Tocache — DS • 1 kW / M-Sa • DS • 1 kW
4040 USSR †ARMENIAN RADIO, Yerevan — RUSSIAN, ETC • DS-1 • 15 kW
 RADIO MOSCOW, Vladivostok — DS-MAYAK • 50 kW
4040v CLANDESTINE (M EAST) "VO KURDISH PEOPLE, Middle East" — Irr • Sa-Th • MIDEAST • ANTI-IRAQI GOVT / Irr • MIDEAST • ANTI-IRAQI GOVT / Irr • F • MIDEAST • ANTI-IRAQI GOVT
4050 USSR †KYRGYS RADIO, Bishkek — Tu • DS-2 • 50 kW / W-M • DS-2 • 50 kW / RUSSIAN, ETC • DS-2 • 50 kW
 †Y-SAKHALINSK R, Yuzhno-Sakhalinsk — DS/TIKHIY OKEAN • 50 kW • USB
4055 USSR †RADIO MOSCOW, Tver — DS-ORFEY
4065v CLANDESTINE (M EAST) "VO IRANIAN KURDS" — MIDEAST • ANTI-IRANIAN GOVT • ALT. FREQ. TO 4200v kHz
4080v MONGOLIA †RADIO ULAANBAATAR, Ulaanbaatar — DS-1 • 50 kW
4110v CLANDESTINE (M EAST) "VO THE MARTYRS", Near Iran — Irr • MIDEAST • ANTI-IRANIAN GOVT
4117v BRAZIL RADIO DIFUSORA, Sena Madureira — DS • 0.25 kW / Tu-Su • DS • 0.25 kW / M-Sa • DS • 0.25 kW
4120v CLANDESTINE (ASIA) "VO NAT SALVATION", Haeju, N Korea — TO SOUTH KOREA • 100 kW
4130 CHINA (PR) RADIO BEIJING, Beijing — E ASIA • FEEDER • 10 kW / (D) • E ASIA • FEEDER • 10 kW / TAIWAN-1 • 10 kW
 †VO THE STRAIT-PLA, Fuzhou
 CLANDESTINE (ASIA) "DEM KAMPUCHEA", Beijing, China (PR) — (D) • PRO-KHMER ROUGE • 50 kW
 FRANCE †R FRANCE INTL, Via Beijing, China — (D) • E ASIA • FEEDER • 10 kW
 SPAIN †R EXTERIOR ESPANA, Via Beijing — (D) • E ASIA • FEEDER • 10 kW • ALT. FREQ. TO 5220 kHz
4160v CLANDESTINE (M EAST) "VO THE MARTYRS", Near Iran — MIDEAST • ANTI-IRANIAN GOVT
 "VO THE WORKER", Near Iran — MIDEAST • ANTI-IRANIAN GOVT
4183v PERU †RADIO CENTENARIO — DS
4185v CLANDESTINE (M EAST) "VO KURD STRUGGLE", Middle East — MIDEAST • ANTI-IRANIAN GOVT
 PERU †RADIO MUNDIAL, Cascas — DS
4190 CHINA (PR) †CENTRAL PEOPLES BS — DS-MINORITIES / (D) • DS-MINORITIES
4194v PERU RADIO UCHIZA, Uchiza — DS
4200 CHINA (PR) RADIO BEIJING, Beijing — E ASIA • FEEDER • 10 kW
4200v CLANDESTINE (M EAST) "VO IRANIAN KURDS" — Alternative Frequency to 4065v kHz
4207 CLANDESTINE (M EAST) †"VO THE SARBEDARAN, Middle East — IRANIAN COMMUNIST
4220 CHINA (PR) CENTRAL PEOPLES BS, Urümqi — DS-MINORITIES
 XINJIANG PBS, Urümqi — DS-MONGOLIAN
4238 PERU RADIO INCA, Baños del Inca — DS
4250v CLANDESTINE (M EAST) "VO THE MARTYRS", Near Iran — Irr • MIDEAST • ANTI-IRANIAN GOVT
4271 ECUADOR RADIO GONZANAMA, Gonzanamá — DS • 1 kW
4299.4 PERU RADIO MODERNA, Celendín — DS • 0.25 kW
4330 CHINA (PR) CENTRAL PEOPLES BS, Urümqi — DS-MINORITIES • 50 kW
 XINJIANG PBS, Urümqi — DS-KAZAKH • 50 kW

ENGLISH ■ ARABIC ≈ CHINESE □□□ FRENCH ═ GERMAN ▬ RUSSIAN ═ SPANISH ═ OTHER ▬

FREQUENCY   COUNTRY, STATION, LOCATION   TARGET • NETWORK • POWER (kW)   World Time

| | | 0 1 2 3 4 5 6 7 8 9 10 11 12 13 14 15 16 17 18 19 20 21 22 23 24 |

Frequency	Country, Station, Location	Target • Network • Power
4340v	CLANDESTINE (M EAST)	Irr • Sa-Th • MIDEAST • ANTI-IRAQI GOVT Irr • MIDEAST • ANTI-IRAQI GOVT
	"VO KURDISH PEOPLE, Middle East	Irr • F • MIDEAST • ANTI-IRAQI GOVT
4360v	CLANDESTINE (M EAST)	
	†"VO THE GUERRILLAS, Middle East	ANTI-IRANIAN GOVT
4395	USSR	
	†KAZAKH RADIO	Alternative Frequency to 4400 kHz
	†RADIO ALMA-ATA	Alternative Frequency to 4400 kHz
	†RADIO MOSCOW, Yakutsk	DS-2/DS-MAYAK • 100 kW
4400	USSR	
	†KAZAKH RADIO	DS-2 • ALT. FREQ. TO 4395 kHz
	†RADIO ALMA-ATA	ALT. FREQ. TO 4395 kHz
4400v	CLANDESTINE (ASIA)	
	"VO NAT SALVATION", Haeju, N Korea	TO SOUTH KOREA • 100 kW
4419v	PERU	
	†FRECUENCIA LIDER, Bambamarca	DS • 0.85 kW
4433	INDONESIA	
	†RRI, Bukittingi, Sumatera	DS
4435	BOLIVIA	DS • 0.25 kW • ALT. FREQ. TO 4747.5 kHz
	†LA VOZ DEL TROPICO, Villa Tunari	M-Sa • DS • 0.25 kW • ALT. FREQ. TO 4747.5 kHz
		Su • DS • 0.25 kW • ALT. FREQ. TO 4747.5 kHz
4453v	CLANDESTINE (ASIA)	
	"VO NAT SALVATION", Haeju, N Korea	TO SOUTH KOREA • 100 kW
4460	CHINA (PR)	DS-1 • 10/15 kW
	†CENTRAL PEOPLES BS, Beijing	
4461.8	PERU	
	RADIO NORANDINA, Celendín	DS
4465	USA	Irr • W EUROPE • (FEEDER) 10 kW • ISU
	RFE-RL, Via Holzkirchen, GFR	Irr • W EUROPE • (FEEDER) 10 kW • ISL
4470v	CLANDESTINE (M EAST)	F • MIDEAST • ANTI-IRANIAN GOVT MIDEAST • ANTI-IRANIAN GOVT
	"VO IRAN COMMUNIST, Afghanistan	Sa-Th • MIDEAST • ANTI-IRANIAN GOVT
4472v	BOLIVIA	DS • 0.25 kW
	RADIO MOVIMA, Santa Ana	Irr • DS • 0.25 kW
4485	PERU	
	†RADIO GRAN PAJATEN, Celendin	DS
	USSR	
	†BASHKIR RADIO, Ufa	DS-RUSSIAN, BASHKIR • 50 kW
	†KAMCHATKA RADIO, Petropavlovsk	DS • 50/100 kW
		DS • 50 kW
	R TIKHIY OKEAN, Petropavlovsk	PACIFIC • MARINERS • 50 kW
		Sa • PACIFIC • MARINERS • 50 kW
		Su-F • PACIFIC • MARINERS • 50 kW
4495	PERU	
	RADIO SAN MATEO, Contumazá	DS
4501.3	CHINA (PR)	DS-CHINESE • 50 kW
	†XINJIANG PBS, Urümqi	
4510	USSR	M-F • DS • 15 kW
	FERGANA RADIO, Fergana	
4510.8	PERU	
	R LAS PALMAS, Nueva Bambamarca	DS
4520	USSR	Sa/Su • DS • 15 kW
	KORYASK RADIO, Palana	Su • DS • 15 kW
		Irr • W/F • DS • 15 kW
	†RADIO MOSCOW, Khanty-Mansiysk	DS-MAYAK • 50 kW
4525	CHINA (PR)	Irr • DS-MINORITIES • 10 kW
	CENTRAL PEOPLES BS, Dongsheng	
	NEI MONGGOL PBS, Dongsheng	Irr • DS-MONGOLIAN • 10 kW
4530.2	BOLIVIA	
	†RADIO HITACHI, Riberalta	DS
4545	USSR	M-F • DS-1 • 50 kW Th-Tu • DS-1 • 50 kW
	†KAZAKH RADIO, Alma-Ata	Sa • DS-1 • 50 kW W • DS-1 • 50 kW
		Sa-M/W • DS-1 • 50 kW
		Sa/Su • DS-1 • 50 kW
		Su-F • DS-1 • 50 kW
		Tu/Th/F • DS-1 • 50 kW
		DS-1/RUSSIAN, ETC • 50 kW
4557v	CLANDESTINE (ASIA)	
	"VO NAT SALVATION", Haeju, N Korea	TO SOUTH KOREA • 100 kW
4560	PERU	
	RADIO HUANDOY, Caraz	DS
4562	BOLIVIA	
	†RADIOEMISORA NORTE	DS
4565 (con'd)	USA	Irr • W EUROPE • (FEEDER) • 10 kW • ISL
	RFE-RL, Via Holzkirchen, GFR	

| | | 0 1 2 3 4 5 6 7 8 9 10 11 12 13 14 15 16 17 18 19 20 21 22 23 24 |

FREQUENCY   COUNTRY, STATION, LOCATION   TARGET • NETWORK • POWER (kW)   World Time

0 1 2 3 4 5 6 7 8 9 10 11 12 13 14 15 16 17 18 19 20 21 22 23 24

4565 (con'd)	USA RFE-RL, Via Holzkirchen,GFR	Irr • W EUROPE • (FEEDER) • 10 kW • ISU
4588	ARGENTINA †RADIO CONTINENTAL, Buenos Aires	Tu-Sa • DS(FEEDER) • 2.5 kW • USB / DS(FEEDER) • 2.5 kW • USB / M-F • DS(FEEDER) • 2.5 kW • USB / Sa/Su • DS(FEEDER) • 2.5 kW • USB
4599.7	BOLIVIA †RADIO VILLA MONTES, Villa Montes	M-Sa • DS / DS
4600	BOLIVIA †R PERLA DEL ACRE, Cobija	DS
	IRAQ †REP OF IRAQ RADIO	DS
4606.6	PERU RADIO AYAVIRI, Ayaviri	DS • ALT. FREQ. TO 5035 kHz / Irr • DS • ALT. FREQ. TO 5035 kHz
4607.3	INDONESIA †RRI, Serui, Irian Jaya	DS • 0.5 kW
4610	USSR †KHABAROVSK RADIO, Khabarovsk	DS-1/DS-2 • 50 kW
4620	CHINA (PR) RADIO BEIJING, Beijing	E ASIA • 10 kW
4625	BOLIVIA †RADIO AGUA DULCE, Mamoré Province	DS
4626v	PERU †RADIO TAYABAMBA, Tayabamba	DS • 1 kW
4635	USSR †TADZHIK RADIO, Dushanbé	RUSSIAN, ETC • DS-1 • 50 kW
4649	BOLIVIA RADIO SANTA ANA, Santa Ana	DS • 1 kW / Irr • DS • 1 kW
4662v	VIETNAM SON LA BC STATION, Son La	DS • ALT. FREQ. TO 4770v kHz
4679.5	ECUADOR †R NACIONAL ESPEJO, Quito	DS • 5 kW
4681v	BOLIVIA RADIO PAITITI, Guayaramerín	DS • 0.75 kW / Tu-Su • DS • 0.75 kW
4700	INDONESIA †RK INFORMASI PER'N, Surabaya, Jawa	DS-TEMP INACTIVE • 2 kW
4700v	BOLIVIA RADIO RIBERALTA, Riberalta	DS • 0.5 kW • ALT. FREQ. TO 4735v kHz / Irr • DS • 0.5 kW • ALT. FREQ. TO 4735v kHz
	PERU RADIO WAIRA, Chota	DS • 1 kW
4705	PERU RADIO ALTO VALLE, Rioja	DS • 0.25 kW
4719.3	INDONESIA †RRI, Ujung Pandang	DS-TEMP INACTIVE • 50 kW
4720v	BOLIVIA RADIO ABAROA, Riberalta	DS • 0.5 kW
4725	MYANMAR (BURMA) †VOICE OF MYANMAR, Yangon	DS-MINORITIES • 50 kW
4730v	PERU RADIO SAN JUAN, Caraz	DS
4735	CHINA (PR) CENTRAL PEOPLES BS, Urümqi	DS-MINORITIES • 50 kW
	†XINJIANG PBS, Urümqi	DS-UIGHUR • 50 kW
4735v	BOLIVIA RADIO RIBERALTA, Riberalta	Alternative Frequency to 4700v kHz
4739v	BOLIVIA †RADIO MAMORE, Guayaramerín	Irr • DS • 0.5 kW / DS • 0.5 kW
4740	AFGHANISTAN RADIO AFGHANISTAN, Via USSR	DS-1 • 100 kW
4747.5	BOLIVIA †LA VOZ DEL TROPICO, Villa Tunari	Alternative Frequency to 4435 kHz
4750	CHINA (PR) CENTRAL PEOPLES BS, Hailar	DS-MINORITIES • 15 kW
	†HULUNBEI'ER PBS, Hailar	DS-MONGOLIAN • 15 kW
	XIZANG PEOPLES BS, Lhasa	DS-CHINESE • 50 kW
	MONGOLIA †RADIO ULAANBAATAR, Olgiy	DS-1 • 12 kW
4750v	CAMEROON †CAMEROON RTV CORP, Bertoua	Irr • FRENCH, ENGLISH, ETC • DS • 20 kW
4751v	ZAIRE LA VOIX DU ZAIRE, Lubumbashi	Irr • DS-FRENCH, ETC • 10 kW
4752v	PERU †RADIO HUANTA 2000, Huanta	DS • 0.5 kW / DS • 1 kW
4753v	INDONESIA †RRI, Ujung Pandang	DS • 50 kW
4755	BRAZIL †R DIF MARANHAO, São Luíz	Irr • DS • 5 kW
	R EDUCACAO RURAL, Campo Grande	DS • 10 kW / M-Sa • DS • 10 kW / Tu-Su • DS • 10 kW
(con'd)		

0 1 2 3 4 5 6 7 8 9 10 11 12 13 14 15 16 17 18 19 20 21 22 23 24

ENGLISH ▬   ARABIC ≋   CHINESE ▭▭▭   FRENCH ═   GERMAN ▬   RUSSIAN ═   SPANISH ▬   OTHER ▬

FREQUENCY   COUNTRY, STATION, LOCATION

TARGET • NETWORK • POWER (kW)   World Time

0 1 2 3 4 5 6 7 8 9 10 11 12 13 14 15 16 17 18 19 20 21 22 23 24

Frequency	Country / Station / Location	Notes
4755 (con'd)	COLOMBIA — CARACOL BOGOTA, Bogota	Irr • DS • 5 kW
	HONDURAS — †SANI RADIO, Puerto Lempira	Alternative Frequency to 6299.3 kHz
4760	CHINA (PR) — †YUNNAN PEOPLES BS, Kunming	DS-1 • 50 kW
	INDIA — †ALL INDIA RADIO, Port Blair	DS • 10 kW / ENGLISH & HINDI • DS • 10 kW / Irr • DS • 10 kW
	†RADIO KASHMIR, Leh	DS • 10 kW / ENGLISH & HINDI • DS • 10 kW
	SWAZILAND — †TRANS WORLD RADIO, Manzini	S AFRICA • 25 kW / Sa/Su • S AFRICA • 25 kW
	USSR — †RADIO MOSCOW, Tbilisi	DS-MAYAK
4760.2	ECUADOR — EMISORA ATALAYA, Guayaquil	DS • 5 kW / Irr • Sa/Su • DS • 5 kW / Tu-Su • DS • 5 kW
4760.8	VENEZUELA — †RADIO FRONTERA, San Antonio	Irr • DS • 1 kW
4765	BRAZIL — RADIO INTEGRACAO, Cruzeiro do Sul	DS • 10 kW / Tu-Su • DS • 10 kW
	RADIO RURAL, Santarém	DS • 10 kW
	CONGO — †RTV CONGOLAISE, Brazzaville	FRENCH, ETC • DS • 50 kW
4765v	BOLIVIA — RADIO HUANAY, Huanay	DS • 0.3 kW
	USSR — RADIO MOSCOW, Via Havana, Cuba	C AMERICA • 10 kW
4770	NIGERIA — RADIO NIGERIA, Kaduna	ENGLISH, ETC • DS-2 • 50 kW
	PERU — RADIO TINGA MARIA, Tinga Maria	Irr • DS • 1 kW
4770v	VIETNAM — SON LA BC STATION, Son La	Alternative Frequency to 4662v kHz
4771v	KOREA (DPR) — RADIO PYONGYANG, Pyongyang	Irr • E ASIA
4774.7	INDONESIA — †RRI, Jakarta, Jawa	DS • 50 kW
4775	AFGHANISTAN — RADIO KABUL, Kabul	DS • 100 kW
	BRAZIL — †PORTAL DA AMAZONIA, Cuiabá	DS • 1 kW
	RADIO CONGONHAS, Congonhas	DS • 1 kW
	INDIA — †ALL INDIA RADIO, Guwahati	DS-B • 10 kW / ENGLISH & HINDI • DS-B • 10 kW
	PERU — RADIO TARMA, Tarma	DS • 1 kW
4775.3	BOLIVIA — RADIO LOS ANDES, Tarija	Tu-Su • DS • 3 kW / DS • 3 kW
4777	GABON — RTV GABONAISE, Libreville	DS • 100 kW / M-Sa • DS • 100 kW / Irr • DS • 100 kW
4780	ANGOLA — EP CUANDO-CUBANGO, Menongue	DS • 5 kW
	DJIBOUTI (JIBUTI) — RTV DE DJIBOUTI, Djibouti	DS • 20 kW / F • DS • 20 kW / Irr • DS-RAMADAN • 20 kW
4783v	MALI — RTV MALIENNE, Bamako	Su • DS • 18 kW / FRENCH, ETC • DS • 18 kW / M-Sa • FRENCH, ETC • DS • 18 kW
4785	BOLIVIA — RADIO BALLIVIAN, San Borja	DS • 0.5 kW
	BRAZIL — †RADIO BRASIL, Campinas	Irr • DS • 1 kW
	RADIO CAIARI, Pôrto Velho	DS • 1 kW
	CHINA (PR) — †ZHEJIANG PBS, Qu Xian	DS-1 • 10 kW
	COLOMBIA — ECOS DEL COMBEIMA, Ibagué	Irr • DS-SUPER • 5 kW
	TANZANIA — RADIO TANZANIA, Dar es Salaam	DS • 50 kW
	USSR — AZERBAIJANI RADIO, Baku	DS-1/RUSSIAN, AZERI • 50 kW
4785.7	PERU — RADIO COOPERATIVA, Satipo	DS • 1 kW
4787v	VIETNAM — †GIA LAI-KON TUM BS, Pleiku	DS
4790 (con'd)	INDIA — †ALL INDIA RADIO, Shillong	DS • 50 kW

0 1 2 3 4 5 6 7 8 9 10 11 12 13 14 15 16 17 18 19 20 21 22 23 24

SUMMER ONLY (J)   WINTER ONLY (D)   JAMMING / OR ∧   EARLIEST HEARD ◁   LATEST HEARD ▷   NEW OR CHANGED FOR 1992 †

FREQUENCY   COUNTRY, STATION, LOCATION   **TARGET • NETWORK • POWER (kW)**   **World Time**

0 1 2 3 4 5 6 7 8 9 10 11 12 13 14 15 16 17 18 19 20 21 22 23 24

Frequency	Country, Station, Location	Target • Network • Power
4790 (con'd)	**INDONESIA** — RRI, Fak Fak, Irian Jaya	DS • 1 kW
	PERU — RADIO ATLANTIDA, Iquitos	DS • 1/3 kW
	SWAZILAND — TRANS WORLD RADIO, Manzini	S AFRICA • 25 kW
4795	**BRAZIL** — †RADIO AQUIDAUANA, Aquidauana	DS • 1 kW
	CAMEROON — †CAMEROON RTV CORP, Douala	FRENCH, ENGLISH, ETC • DS • 100 kW
	USSR — †BURYAT RADIO, Ulan-Ude	DS-RUSSIAN, BURYAT • 50 kW
	†RADIO MOSCOW, Khar'kov	(D) • EUROPE • 100 kW
4795.5	**ECUADOR** — LV DE LOS CARAS, Bahía de Caráquez	DS • 5 kW
4796v	**BOLIVIA** — R NUEVA AMERICA, La Paz	DS • 10 kW
		Tu-Su • DS • 10 kW
		Irr • M-Sa • DS • 10 kW
		Su • DS • 10 kW
		DS-SPANISH, AYMARA • 10 kW
4798v	**VIETNAM** — NGHIA BIN BS, Nghia Binh	DS
		Irr • DS
4799.8	**GUATEMALA** — R BUENAS NUEVAS, San Sebastián	DS • 1 kW
4800	**CHINA (PR)** — †CENTRAL PEOPLES BS	DS-2
		DS-MINORITIES
	DOMINICAN REPUBLIC — †RADIO N-103, Santiago	Irr • DS • 1 kW
	INDIA — †ALL INDIA RADIO, Hyderabad	DS • 10 kW
		ENGLISH & HINDI • DS • 10 kW
		ENGLISH, ETC • DS • 10 kW
	LESOTHO — RADIO LESOTHO, Maseru	DS-ENGLISH, SESOTHO • 100 kW
	USSR — †YAKUT RADIO, Yakutsk	DS-RUSSIAN, YAKUT • 50 kW
4800v	**ECUADOR** — RADIO POPULAR, Cuenca	DS • 5 kW
		Irr • DS • 5 kW
4800.6	**PERU** — RADIO ONDA AZUL, Puno	SPANISH, ETC • DS • 1.5 kW
4804.4	**PERU** — †RADIO HUANCAVELICA, Huancavelica	DS-"R VILLARRICA" • 1 kW • ALT. FREQ. TO 4885.3 kHz
		Irr • DS-"R VILLARRICA" • 1 kW • ALT. FREQ. TO 4885.3 kHz
4805	**BRAZIL** — DIFUSORA AMAZONAS, Manaus	DS • 5 kW
	RADIO ITATIAIA, Belo Horizonte	DS • 0.5 kW
4805.3	**INDONESIA** — †RRI, Kupang, Timor	DS • 0.3 kW
		Sa • DS • 0.3 kW
		Su-F • DS • 0.3 kW
4808.8	**BOLIVIA** — RADIO LIBERTAD, Dist. Santa Fe	DS
		Irr • M-Sa • DS
4810	**SOUTH AFRICA** — †SOUTH AFRICAN BC, Meyerton	RADIO SUID-AFRIKA • 100 kW
	USSR — †ARMENIAN RADIO, Yerevan	RUSSIAN, ETC • DS-1 • 50 kW
	†RADIO MOSCOW	(D) • E ASIA
	†RADIO YEREVAN, Yerevan	MIDEAST • 50 kW
4810.2	**PERU** — RADIO SAN MARTIN, Tarapoto	DS • 3 kW
		Irr • DS • 3 kW M-Sa • DS • 3 kW
4810.4	**ECUADOR** — LV DE GALAPAGOS, San Cristóbal	DS • 5 kW
4815	**BOLIVIA** — RADIO NACIONAL, La Paz	Irr • DS-SPANISH, ETC • 1 kW
	BRAZIL — RADIO CABOCLA, Benjamim Constant	DS • 10 kW
	RADIO DIFUSORA, Londrina	DS • 10 kW
	BURKINA FASO — RTV BURKINA, Ouagadougou	FRENCH, ETC • DS • 50 kW
		M-F • FRENCH, ETC • DS • 50 kW
	CHINA (PR) — †RADIO BEIJING, Togtoh	E ASIA & EAST USSR • RUSSIAN, MONGOLIAN • 10 kW
	PERU — RADIO AMAZONAS, Iquitos	DS • 1 kW
4815v	**PAKISTAN** — PAKISTAN BC CORP, Karachi	(D) • DS-ENGLISH, ETC • 10 kW
4815.4	**COLOMBIA** — RADIO GUATAPURI, Valledupar	Irr • DS • 1 kW

0 1 2 3 4 5 6 7 8 9 10 11 12 13 14 15 16 17 18 19 20 21 22 23 24

ENGLISH ▬   ARABIC ▨   CHINESE ▫▫▫   FRENCH ═   GERMAN ▬▬   RUSSIAN ═   SPANISH ▬   OTHER ─

FREQUENCY   COUNTRY, STATION, LOCATION   TARGET • NETWORK • POWER (kW)   World Time

World Time scale: 0 1 2 3 4 5 6 7 8 9 10 11 12 13 14 15 16 17 18 19 20 21 22 23 24

Frequency	Country, Station, Location	Target • Network • Power
4816v	**VIETNAM** †HA TUYEN BS, Ha Tuyen	DS
4819.7	**ECUADOR** RADIO PAZ Y BIEN, Ambato	Irr • DS-SPANISH, ETC • 1.5 kW; Irr • Tu-Su • DS-SPANISH, ETC • 1.5 kW
4820	**INDIA** ALL INDIA RADIO, Calcutta	DS-A • 10 kW
	USSR †KHANTY-MANSIYSK R, Khanty-Mansiysk	DS • 50 kW
4820.2	**ANGOLA** †EP DA HUILA, Lubango	DS • 25 kW
	HONDURAS †LA VOZ EVANGELICA, Tegucigalpa	DS • 5 kW; M • DS • 5 kW; Tu-Su • DS • 5 kW
4820.8	**PERU** RADIO ATAHUALPA, Cajamarca	DS • 1 kW
4824.5	**PERU** †LV DE LA SELVA, Iquitos	DS • 10 kW
4825	**BRAZIL** †R CANCAO NOVA, Cachoeira Paulista	DS • 10 kW
	RADIO EDUCADORA, Bragança	DS • 10 kW
	GUATEMALA RADIO MAM, Cabricán	DS/SPANISH, ETC • 1 kW
	USSR †RADIO MOSCOW, Star'obel'sk	(D) • E EUROPE & MIDEAST • 100 kW
	†TURKMEN RADIO, Ashkhabad	DS-1/RUSSIAN, ETC • 50 kW
	†YAKUT RADIO, Yakutsk	(D) • DS-RUSSIAN, YAKUT • 50 kW
4826.3	**PERU** RADIO SICUANI, Sicuani	DS-SPANISH, ETC • 0.35 kW
4829v	**MONGOLIA** †RADIO ULAANBAATAR, Altai	DS-1 • 12 kW
4830	**BOLIVIA** RADIO GRIGOTA, Santa Cruz	Tu-Su • DS • 1 kW; DS • 1 kW; Irr • Tu-Su • DS • 1 kW
	BOTSWANA †RADIO BOTSWANA, Gaborone	DS-ENGLISH, ETC • 50 kW
	THAILAND †RADIO THAILAND, Pathum Thani	SE ASIA • 10 kW; Sa/Su • SE ASIA • 10 kW; Tu/Th/Sa • SE ASIA • 10 kW
	VENEZUELA RADIO TACHIRA, San Cristóbal	DS • 10 kW
4831	**PERU** RADIO HUANTA, Huanta	Alternative Frequency to 4890v kHz
4832	**COSTA RICA** RADIO RELOJ, San José	Irr • DS • 3 kW
4835	**AUSTRALIA** ABC/CAAMA RADIO, Alice Springs	DS-ENGLISH, ETC • 50 kW
	GUATEMALA RADIO TEZULUTLAN, Cobán	DS-SPANISH, ETC • 5 kW
	MALAYSIA †RTM-SARAWAK, Kuching-Stapok	DS-MALAY, MELANAU • 10 kW
	PERU RADIO MARANON, Jaén	DS • 1 kW
4835v	**MALI** RTV MALIENNE, Bamako	Su • DS • 18 kW; FRENCH, ETC • DS • 18 kW; M-Sa • FRENCH, ETC • DS • 18 kW
	PAKISTAN PAKISTAN BC CORP, Islamabad	(D) • DS • 100 kW
4839v	**ZAIRE** †RADIO BUKAVU, Bukavu	Alternative Frequency to 4849v kHz
4840	**CHINA (PR)** †HEILONGJIANG PBS, Harbin	DS-CHINESE, KOREAN • 50 kW
	†VO THE STRAIT-PLA, Fuzhou	TAIWAN-1 • 10 kW
	ECUADOR R INTEROCEANICA, Sta Rosa De Quijos	DS • 1 kW
	R INTEROCEANICA, Sta Rosa de Quijos	DS • 1 kW
	INDIA †ALL INDIA RADIO, Bombay	DS-B • 10 kW; ENGLISH, ETC • DS-B • 10 kW
	PERU †RADIO ANDAHUAYLAS, Andahuaylas	DS-SPANISH, QUECHUA • 2 kW
4840.4	**VENEZUELA** †RADIO VALERA, Valera	DS • 1 kW; Tu-Su • DS • 1 kW
4844.4	**GUATEMALA** †RADIO K'EKCHI, San Cristóbal V	SPANISH, ETC • DS • 1.2/5 kW; M-Sa • SPANISH, ETC • DS • 1.2/5 kW; Tu-Su • SPANISH, ETC • DS • 1.2/5 kW; Su • SPANISH, ETC • DS • 1.2/5 kW
4845	**BOLIVIA** †RADIO FIDES, La Paz	Sa/Su • DS • 5 kW; DS • 5 kW; Tu-Su • DS • 5 kW; M-Sa • DS • 5 kW; Su • DS • 5 kW; Irr • DS • 5 kW

(con'd)

0 1 2 3 4 5 6 7 8 9 10 11 12 13 14 15 16 17 18 19 20 21 22 23 24

FREQUENCY   COUNTRY, STATION, LOCATION   TARGET • NETWORK • POWER (kW)   World Time

0 1 2 3 4 5 6 7 8 9 10 11 12 13 14 15 16 17 18 19 20 21 22 23 24

FREQUENCY	COUNTRY, STATION, LOCATION	TARGET • NETWORK • POWER (kW)
4845 (con'd)	BRAZIL	
	†R METEOROLOGIA, Ibitinga	DS • 1 kW
	†RADIO CABOCLA, Manaus	DS • 250 kW
	MALAYSIA	
	RADIO TV MALAYSIA, Kajang	DS-6 (TAMIL) • 50 kW
		Sa/Su • DS-6 (TAMIL) • 50 kW
		Su • DS-6 (TAMIL) • 50 kW
	MAURITANIA	
	†ORT DE MAURITANIE, Nouakchott	Irr • ARABIC, FRENCH, ETC • DS-RAMADAM • 100 kW
		ARABIC, FRENCH, ETC • DS • 100 kW
		Sa-Th • ARABIC, FRENCH, ETC • DS • 100 kW
4845v	COLOMBIA	
	RADIO BUCARAMANGA, Bucaramanga	DS-VERY IRREGULAR • 1 kW
4849v	ZAIRE	
	†RADIO BUKAVU, Bukavu	FRENCH, ETC • DS • 4 kW • ALT. FREQ. TO 4839v kHz
		Su • FRENCH, ETC • DS • 4 kW • ALT. FREQ. TO 4839v kHz
4850	CAMEROON	
	†CAMEROON RTV CORP, Yaoundé	FRENCH & ENGLISH • DS • 100 kW
	INDIA	
	†ALL INDIA RADIO, Kohima	DS-A • 50 kW
		ENGLISH, ETC • DS-A • 50 kW
	MONGOLIA	
	†RADIO ULAANBAATAR, Ulaanbaatar	DS-1 • 100 kW
		DS-1 • 50 kW
	USSR	
	RADIO MOSCOW, Via Mongolia	E ASIA • 50 kW
	†UZBEK RADIO, Tashkent	DS-2/RUSSIAN, UZBEK • 50 kW
	VENEZUELA	
	RADIO CAPITAL, Caracas	Irr • DS • 1 kW
		Irr • Su/M • DS • 1 kW
4851v	ECUADOR	
	RADIO LUZ Y VIDA, Loja	DS • 5 kW
		Irr • DS • 5 kW
4853	YEMEN (REPUBLIC)	
	REP YEMEN RADIO, San'ā	DS • 50 kW
4855	BOLIVIA	
	RADIO CENTENARIO, Santa Cruz	Tu-Sa • DS • 1 kW DS • 1 kW M-F • DS • 1 kW
		Irr • Tu-Sa • DS • 1 kW
	BRAZIL	
	R MUNDO MELHOR, Gov Valadares	DS-TEMP INACTIVE • 1 kW
		M-Sa • DS-TEMP INACTIVE • 1 kW
	†RADIO ARUANA, Barra do Garças	DS • 1 kW
4855v	MOZAMBIQUE	
	RADIO MOCAMBIQUE, Maputo	DS • 20 kW
4855.7	INDONESIA	
	RRI, Palembang, Sumatera	DS • 10 kW
4856v	PERU	
	RADIO PAMPAS, Pampas	DS • 1 kW
4856.8	BOLIVIA	
	RADIO EL CONDOR, Uyuni	DS-SPANISH, ETC
4859.8	PERU	
	RADIO LA HORA, Cusco	DS-SPANISH, QUECHUA • 1 kW
		Tu-Su • DS • 1 kW
4860	INDIA	
	†ALL INDIA RADIO, Delhi	ENGLISH & HINDI • DS • 50 kW S ASIA • 50 kW
		DS • 50 kW
	PERU	
	R COM'L EDUCATIVA, La Peca	DS
	USSR	
	†CHITA RADIO, Chita	DS • 15 kW
	†RADIO MOSCOW, Tver	(D) • FEEDER • 100 kW
	VENEZUELA	
	RADIO MARACAIBO, Maracaibo	Irr • DS • 10 kW
4860v	ANGOLA	
	EP DO LUNDA SUL, Saurimo	DS • 5 kW
4864v	BOLIVIA	
	†RADIO 16 DE MARZO, Oruro	DS
		Irr • Tu-Su • DS M-Sa • DS
4864.3	INDONESIA	
	†RRI, Ambon, Maluku	DS • 10 kW
4865	BRAZIL	
	R VERDES FLORESTAS, Cruzeiro do Sul	DS • 5 kW
	RADIO ALVORADA, Londrina	Alternative Frequency to 3335 kHz
	RADIO SOCIEDADE, Feira de Santana	DS-TEMP INACTIVE • 1 kW
	CHINA (PR)	
	†GANSU PEOPLES BS, Lanzhou	DS-1 • 50 kW
	COLOMBIA	
	LV DEL CINARUCO, Arauca	DS-CARACOL • 5 kW
	MONGOLIA	
	†RADIO ULAANBAATAR, Saynshand	DS-1 • 12 kW
4866v	MOZAMBIQUE	
	RADIO MOCAMBIQUE, Maputo	DS • 20 kW

0 1 2 3 4 5 6 7 8 9 10 11 12 13 14 15 16 17 18 19 20 21 22 23 24

ENGLISH ▬▬   ARABIC ≋≋   CHINESE □□□   FRENCH ══   GERMAN ▬▬   RUSSIAN ══   SPANISH ▬▬   OTHER ──

FREQUENCY   COUNTRY, STATION, LOCATION   TARGET • NETWORK • POWER (kW)   World Time

| 0 1 2 3 4 5 6 7 8 9 10 11 12 13 14 15 16 17 18 19 20 21 22 23 24 |

4866.5 INDONESIA
    †RRI, Wamena, Irian Jaya — DS • 0.5 kW
4870 BENIN
    ORT DU BENIN, Cotonou — M-F • DS-FRENCH, ETC • 30 kW / Irr • DS • 30 kW
    DS-FRENCH, ETC • 30 kW
    Sa/Su • DS-FRENCH, ETC • 30 kW

ECUADOR
    RADIO RIO AMAZONAS, Macuma — DS • 5 kW
    Irr • DS • 5 kW

PERU
    RADIO COSMOS, Lircay — DS
SRI LANKA
    SRI LANKA BC CORP, Colombo-Ekala — DS-SINHALA 2 • 10 kW
4874.6 INDONESIA
    †RRI, Sorong, Irian Jaya — DS • 10 kW
4875 BOLIVIA
    †R LA CRUZ DEL SUR, La Paz — DS • 10 kW / M-F • DS • 10 kW
BRAZIL
    †R DIFUSORA RORAIMA, Boa Vista — DS • 10 kW
    Irr • DS • 10 kW

    R JORNAL DO BRASIL, Rio de Janeiro — DS • 10 kW
CHINA (PR)
    VOICE OF JINLING, Nanjing — E ASIA • 50 kW
USSR
    †GEORGIAN RADIO, Tbilisi — DS-2 • 200 kW
4876v PERU
    RADIO CENTRAL, Bella Vista — DS • 1 kW • ALT. FREQ. TO 4921v kHz
4877.5 MOZAMBIQUE
    EP DE CABO DELGADO, Pemba — DS
4879v PAKISTAN
    PAKISTAN BC CORP, Quetta — DS • 10 kW
    Th-Sa • DS • 10 kW

4880 CLANDESTINE (AFRICA)
    †"AV DO GALO NEGRO", Jamba, Angola — S AFRICA • UNITA
INDIA
    †ALL INDIA RADIO, Lucknow — DS-B • 10 kW
    ENGLISH, ETC • DS-B • 10 kW

4880v BANGLADESH
    RADIO BANGLADESH, Dhaka — DS • 100 kW
4881.7 PERU
    RADIO NUEVO MUNDO, Pucallpa — DS • 0.25/1 kW
4883 CHINA (PR)
    †RADIO BEIJING, Hohhot — (D) • E ASIA & EAST USSR • RUSSIAN, MONGOLIAN • 50 kW
4884v ANGOLA
    EP DO ZAIRE, M'banza Congo — DS • 5 kW
4885 BRAZIL
    R CLUBE DO PARA, Belém — DS • 5 kW

    R DIF ACREANA, Rio Branco — DS • 5 kW

    †RADIO CARAJA, Anápolis — DS • 0.5 kW
COLOMBIA
    ONDAS DEL META, Villavicencio — Irr • DS-SUPER • 5 kW
KENYA
    KENYA BC CORP, Nairobi — M-F • DS-EASTERN • 10 kW
4885v VIETNAM
    THAN HOA BS, Thanh Hoa — DS
4885.3 PERU
    †RADIO HUANCAVELICA, Huancavelica — Alternative Frequency to 4804.4 kHz
4885.6 BOLIVIA
    †RADIO SARARENDA, Camiri — Irr • DS • 0.8 kW
    Irr • M-Sa • DS • 0.8 kW

4889.7 ECUADOR
    CENTINELA DEL SUR, Loja — DS • 2 kW • ALT. FREQ. TO 4899 kHz
    M-Sa • DS • 2 kW • ALT. FREQ. TO 4899 kHz
    Tu-Su • DS • 2 kW • ALT. FREQ. TO 4899 kHz
4890 FRANCE
    R FRANCE INTL, Via Moyabi, Gabon — C AFRICA • 250 kW
PAKISTAN (AZAD K)
    †AZAD KASHMIR RADIO, Via Islamabad — DS • 100 kW
PAPUA NEW GUINEA
    †NBC, Port Moresby — ENGLISH, ETC • DS • 2 kW
4890v PERU
    RADIO CHOTA, Chota — DS

    RADIO HUANTA, Huanta — DS-SPANISH, QUECHUA • 0.5 kW • ALT. FREQ. TO 4831 kHz
    Irr • DS • 0.5 kW • ALT. FREQ. TO 4831 kHz
SENEGAL
    †ORT DU SENEGAL, Dakar — Irr • FRENCH, ETC • DS • 100 kW
    FRENCH, ETC • DS • 100 kW
    M-Sa • FRENCH, ETC • DS • 100 kW

4894v ANGOLA
    EP DO BIE, Bié — Irr • DS • 1 kW
4895 BRAZIL
    †RADIO BARE, Manaus — DS • 1 kW

(con'd)   RADIO IPB AM, Campo Grande — DS • 5 kW

| 0 1 2 3 4 5 6 7 8 9 10 11 12 13 14 15 16 17 18 19 20 21 22 23 24 |

SUMMER ONLY (J)   WINTER ONLY (D)   JAMMING / OR ∧   EARLIEST HEARD ◁   LATEST HEARD ▷   NEW OR CHANGED FOR 1992 †

FREQUENCY	COUNTRY, STATION, LOCATION	TARGET • NETWORK • POWER (kW)	World Time

0 1 2 3 4 5 6 7 8 9 10 11 12 13 14 15 16 17 18 19 20 21 22 23 24

Frequency	Country/Station	Details
4895 (con'd)	COLOMBIA — LV DEL RIO ARAUCA, Arauca	DS-RCN • 10 kW; M-Sa • DS-RCN • 10 kW
	INDIA — †ALL INDIA RADIO, Kurseong	DS • 20 kW; ENGLISH & HINDI • DS • 20 kW
	MALAYSIA — †RTM-SARAWAK, Kuching-Stapok	DS-IBAN • 10 kW
	PERU — RADIO CHANCHAMAYO, La Merced	DS • 0.4 kW; Tu-Su • DS • 0.4 kW; Irr • Tu-Su • DS • 0.4 kW
	USSR — †RADIO MOSCOW, Tver	(D) • FEEDER • 100 kW
	†TYUMEN RADIO, Tyumen	DS • 15 kW
4895v	MONGOLIA — †RADIO ULAANBAATAR, Murun	DS-1 • 12 kW
	VIETNAM — VOICE OF VIETNAM, Hanoi	DS
4899	ECUADOR — CENTINELA DEL SUR, Loja	Alternative Frequency to 4889.7 kHz
4900	CHINA (PR) — †VO THE STRAIT-PLA, Fuzhou	TAIWAN-2 • 10/50 kW
4900v	ECUADOR — RADIO LIBERTADOR, Saquisilí	Irr • DS • 1 kW
	GUINEA — †RTV GUINEENNE, Conakry	M-Sa • FRENCH, ETC • DS • 18 kW; DS • 18 kW; FRENCH, ETC • DS • 18 kW; Su • FRENCH, ETC • DS • 18 kW
4900.6	INDONESIA — †RRI, Surakarta, Jawa	DS • 0.5 kW
4902	SRI LANKA — SRI LANKA BC CORP, Colombo-Ekala	DS-SINHALA 1 • 10 kW
4902.5	BOLIVIA — †R SAN IGNACIO, S Ignacio de Moxos	Irr • DS; DS
4904.5	CHAD — RADIODIF NATIONALE, N'Djamena	FRENCH, ETC • DS • 100 kW; Sa • FRENCH, ETC • DS • 100 kW
4905	BRAZIL — R RELOGIO FEDERAL, Rio de Janeiro	DS • 5 kW
	RADIO ANHANGUERA, Araguaína	DS • 1 kW
4907v	CAMBODIA — VO THE PEOPLE, Phnom Penh	DS • 50 kW; Su • DS • 50 kW
4908v	PERU — RADIO COBRIZA 2000, Pacaycasa	Alternative Frequency to 4925v kHz
4910	AUSTRALIA — ABC/CAAMA RADIO, Tennant Creek	DS-ENGLISH, ETC • 50 kW
4910v	ZAMBIA — RADIO ZAMBIA, Lusaka	DS-ENGLISH, ETC • 50 kW; F/Sa • DS-ENGLISH, ETC • 50 kW
4910.6	PERU — RADIO LIBERTAD, Trujillo	DS • 1 kW
4910.8	PERU — †RADIO TAWANTINSUYO, Cusco	SPANISH, ETC • DS • 5 kW • ALT. FREQ. TO 4977.3 kHz; Irr • DS • 5 kW • ALT. FREQ. TO 4977.3 kHz
4911	ECUADOR — †EM GRAN COLOMBIA, Quito	Irr • DS • 10 kW
4914.6	PERU — RADIO CORA, Lima-Puente Piedra	DS • 10 kW; M-Sa • DS • 10 kW
4915	AFGHANISTAN — RADIO AFGHANISTAN, Via USSR	(D) • EUROPE
	BRAZIL — †RADIO ANHANGUERA, Goiânia	Irr • DS • 10 kW; DS • 10 kW
	RADIO NACIONAL, Macapá	DS • 10 kW
	CHINA (PR) — †GUANGXI PEOPLES BS, Nanning	CHINESE, ETC • DS-1 • 10 kW
	GHANA — GHANA BC CORP, Accra	ENGLISH, ETC • DS-1 • 50 kW; Sa/Su • ENGLISH, ETC • DS-1 • 50 kW
	KENYA — KENYA BC CORP, Nairobi	M-F • DS-CENTRAL • 100 kW
4915v	COLOMBIA — ARMONIAS CAQUETA, Florencia	DS • 3 kW; Tu-Su • DS • 3 kW; M-Sa • DS • 3 kW
4920	AUSTRALIA — AUSTRALIAN BC CORP, Brisbane	DS • 10 kW
	ECUADOR — RADIO QUITO, Quito	DS • 5 kW; Tu-Su • DS • 5 kW; M-Sa • DS • 5 kW
	INDIA — †ALL INDIA RADIO, Madras	DS-A • 10 kW; ENGLISH, ETC • DS-A • 10 kW
(con'd)		

0 1 2 3 4 5 6 7 8 9 10 11 12 13 14 15 16 17 18 19 20 21 22 23 24

ENGLISH ▬   ARABIC ▨   CHINESE ▫▫▫   FRENCH ▬   GERMAN ▬   RUSSIAN ═   SPANISH ▬   OTHER ▬

FREQUENCY   COUNTRY, STATION, LOCATION

TARGET • NETWORK • POWER (kW)   World Time

0 1 2 3 4 5 6 7 8 9 10 11 12 13 14 15 16 17 18 19 20 21 22 23 24

4920	NICARAGUA	
(con'd)	†RADIO RICA, Managua	M-F • C AMERICA • DS • 1.3/10 kW
	USSR	
	†YAKUT RADIO, Yakutsk	DS-RUSSIAN, YAKUT • 50 kW
4921v	PERU	
	RADIO CENTRAL, Bella Vista	Alternative Frequency to 4876v kHz
4922v	PERU	
	ONDAS DEL TITICACA, Puno	DS-SPANISH, ETC • 1 kW
		Tu-Su • DS • 1 kW
4925	BRAZIL	
	RADIO DIFUSORA, Taubaté	DS • 1 kW
	CHINA (PR)	
	HEILONGJIANG PBS, Harbin	DS-CHINESE, KOREAN • 50 kW
	COLOMBIA	
	EM MERIDIANO 70, Arauca	DS • 2.5 kW
4925v	PERU	
	RADIO COBRIZA 2000, Pacaycasa	DS • ALT. FREQ. TO 4908v kHz
		M-Sa • DS • ALT. FREQ. TO 4908v kHz
4925.6	EQUATORIAL GUINEA	
	RADIO NACIONAL, Bata	DS-SPANISH, ETC • 100 kW • ALT. FREQ. TO 5004v kHz
4926v	MOZAMBIQUE	
	RADIO MOCAMBIQUE, Maputo	DS • 10 kW DS • 7.5 kW
4927	INDONESIA	
	RRI, Jambi, Sumatera	DS • 7.5 kW
		Su • DS • 7.5 kW
4930	DOMINICAN REPUBLIC	
	†RADIO BARAHONA, Barahona	DS • 1 kW
	HAITI	
	RADIO STATION 4VEH, Cap Haïtien	Irr • 1.5 kW
		Irr • Sa/Su • 1.5 kW
	USSR	
	†RADIO MOSCOW, Various Locations	DS-MAYAK • 50 kW
4931.7	INDONESIA	
	†RRI, Surakarta, Jawa	DS • 10 kW
4934	KENYA	
	KENYA BC CORP, Nairobi	DS-GENERAL • 100 kW
4935	BRAZIL	
	RADIO DIFUSORA, Jataí	DS • 2.5 kW
4935v	BRAZIL	
	RADIO CAPIXABA, Vitória	DS • 1 kW
	PERU	
	RADIO TROPICAL, Tarapoto	DS • 3 kW
4939.6	VENEZUELA	
	RADIO CONTINENTAL, Barinas	Irr • DS • 1 kW
		Irr • M-Sa • DS • 1 kW
4940	AFGHANISTAN	
	†RADIO AFGHANISTAN, Via USSR	MIDEAST & S ASIA
		DS-1
		DS-2
	CHINA (PR)	
	†QINGHAI PEOPLES BS, Xining	Irr • DS-1 • 10 kW
	INDIA	
	ALL INDIA RADIO, Guwahati	DS-A • 50 kW
	IVORY COAST	
	RTV IVOIRIENNE, Abidjan	DS • 25 kW
	SRI LANKA	
	SRI LANKA BC CORP, Colombo-Ekala	DS • 10 kW
	USSR	
	†UKRAINIAN RADIO, Kiev	RUSSIAN, ETC • DS-2 • 50 kW
	†YAKUT RADIO, Yakutsk	(D) • DS-RUSSIAN, YAKUT • 50 kW
4945	BOLIVIA	
	RADIO ILLIMANI, La Paz	DS • 10 kW
		Tu-Su • DS • 10 kW M-Sa • DS • 10 kW
	BRAZIL	
	RADIO DIFUSORA, Poços de Caldas	DS • 1 kW
		Tu-Su • DS • 1 kW
	RADIO NACIONAL, Pôrto Velho	DS • 50 kW
	VOZ SAO FRANCISCO, Petrolina	DS • 2 kW
	COLOMBIA	
	CARACOL NEIVA, Neiva	DS-CARACOL • 2.5 kW
4950	CHINA (PR)	
	VOICE OF PUJIANG, Shanghai	E ASIA • CHINESE, ETC
	XILINGOL PBS, Abagnar Qi	DS-MONGOLIAN
	ECUADOR	
	RADIO BAHA'I, Otavalo	DS • 1 kW
	INDIA	
	RADIO KASHMIR, Jammu	DS-A • 2 kW
	MALAYSIA	
	†RTM-SARAWAK, Kuching-Stapok	DS • 10 kW
	PAKISTAN	
	PAKISTAN BC CORP, Peshawar	DS • 10 kW
		(D) • DS-ENGLISH, ETC • 10 kW
	PERU	
	†R MADRE DE DIOS, Puerto Maldonado	DS • 5 kW
4950v	ANGOLA	
	RADIO NACIONAL, Luanda	Irr • DS

0 1 2 3 4 5 6 7 8 9 10 11 12 13 14 15 16 17 18 19 20 21 22 23 24

SUMMER ONLY (J)   WINTER ONLY (D)   JAMMING / OR ∧   EARLIEST HEARD ◁   LATEST HEARD ▷   NEW OR CHANGED FOR 1992 †

FREQUENCY   COUNTRY, STATION, LOCATION   TARGET • NETWORK • POWER (kW)   World Time

4955	**BRAZIL**	
	RADIO CLUBE, Rondonópolis	DS-TEMP INACTIVE • 2.5 kW
		M-Sa • DS-TEMP INACTIVE • 2.5 kW
	RADIO CULTURA, Campos	DS • 2.5 kW
4955v	**BRAZIL**	
	RADIO MARAJOARA, Belém	DS • 10 kW
	PERU	
	R CULTURAL AMAUTA, Huanta	DS-SPANISH, ETC • 1 kW
4957.5	**USSR**	
	AZERBAIJANI RADIO, Baku	DS-2 • 50 kW
4960	**CHINA (PR)**	
	RADIO BEIJING, Kunming	E ASIA • 50 kW
	INDIA	
	†ALL INDIA RADIO, Delhi	DS • 10/20 kW
		ENGLISH, ETC • DS • 10/20 kW
4960.3	**PERU**	
	RADIO LA MERCED, La Merced	Tu-Su • DS • 0.5 kW DS • 0.5 kW
		M-Sa • DS • 0.5 kW
4961v	**ECUADOR**	
	†RADIO FEDERACION, Sucúa	DS • 5 kW
4965	**BOLIVIA**	
	†RADIO JUAN XXIII, San Ignacio Velasco	DS • 3 kW M-Sa • DS • 3 kW
		Su • DS • 3 kW
	BRAZIL	
	RADIO ALVORADA, Parintins	DS • 5 kW
	RADIO POTI, Natal	DS-TEMP INACTIVE • 1 kW
	COLOMBIA	
	†RADIO SANTA FE, Bogotá	DS • 5 kW
	SOUTH AFRICA	
	†RADIO RSA, Meyerton	(J) • S AFRICA • 250 kW
4966	**PERU**	
	RADIO SAN MIGUEL, Cusco	DS-SPANISH,QUECHUA • 5 kW
		Tu-Su • DS • 5 kW
4969.8	**ANGOLA**	
	EP DA CABINDA, Cabinda	Irr • DS • 5 kW
4970	**CHINA (PR)**	
	CENTRAL PEOPLES BS, Urümqi	DS-MINORITIES • 50 kW
	XINJIANG PBS, Urümqi	DS-KAZAKH • 50 kW
	MALAYSIA	
	†RTM-KOTA KINABALU, Kota Kinabalu	DS-MALAY • 10 kW
	PERU	
	RADIO IMAGEN, Tarapoto	DS • 1 kW
		Su • DS • 1 kW
		Tu-Su • DS • 1 kW
4970v	**VENEZUELA**	
	RADIO RUMBOS, Villa de Cura	DS • 10 kW
4971	**ECUADOR**	
	RADIO TARQUI, Quito	Irr • DS • 3 kW
4975	**AFGHANISTAN**	
	†RADIO AFGHANISTAN, Via USSR	DS-1 • 50 kW
		DS-1 • ALT. FREQ. TO 3965 kHz
	BRAZIL	
	RADIO TIMBIRA, São Luís	DS • 2.5 kW
	†RADIO TUPI, São Paulo	DS • 1 kW
	CHINA (PR)	
	FUJIAN PEOPLES BS, Jianyang	DS-1 TAIWAN SVC • 10 kW
	PERU	
	†RADIO DEL PACIFICO, Lima	Alternative Frequency to 9675 kHz
	USSR	
	TADZHIK RADIO, Dushanbé	Alternative Frequency to 7245 kHz
4976	**UGANDA**	
	RADIO UGANDA, Kampala	DS-ENGLISH, ETC • 50 kW
		M-F • DS-ENGLISH, ETC • 50 kW
		M-Sa • DS-ENGLISH, ETC • 50 kW
4976v	**COLOMBIA**	
	†ONDAS ORTEGUAZA, Florencia	Irr • DS-TODELAR • 1 kW
		DS-TODELAR • 1 kW
4977v	**ECUADOR**	
	RADIO TARQUI, Quito	Irr • DS • 3 kW
4977.3	**PERU**	
	†RADIO TAWANTINSUYO, Cusco	Alternative Frequency to 4910.8 kHz
4980	**CHINA (PR)**	
	CENTRAL PEOPLES BS, Urümqi	DS-MINORITIES • 50 kW
	XINJIANG PBS, Urümqi	DS-MONGOLIAN • 50 kW
	VENEZUELA	
	†ECOS DEL TORBES, San Cristóbal	DS • 10 kW
4981v	**BOLIVIA**	
	†RADIO MINERIA, Oruro	DS
4985	**BRAZIL**	
	R BRASIL CENTRAL, Goiânia	DS • 10 kW
	IRAN	
	†VO THE ISLAMIC REP, Tehrān	MIDEAST • ALT. FREQ. TO 4990 kHz
4988v	**BOLIVIA**	
	RADIO HORIZONTE, Riberalta	DS • 0.5 kW

ENGLISH ▬   ARABIC ▩   CHINESE ▫▫▫   FRENCH ═══   GERMAN ▭▭▭   RUSSIAN ═══   SPANISH ▬   OTHER ▬

FREQUENCY   COUNTRY, STATION, LOCATION   TARGET • NETWORK • POWER (kW)   World Time

0 1 2 3 4 5 6 7 8 9 10 11 12 13 14 15 16 17 18 19 20 21 22 23 24

Frequency	Country, Station, Location	Target • Network • Power
4990	**CHINA (PR)**	
	†HUNAN PEOPLES BS, Changsha	DS-1 • 10 kW
	INDIA	
	ALL INDIA RADIO, Madras	SE ASIA • 100 kW
	IRAN	
	†VO THE ISLAMIC REP, Tehrān	Alternative Frequency to 4985 kHz
	NIGERIA	
	RADIO NIGERIA, Lagos	ENGLISH, ETC • DS-1 • 50 kW
	USSR	
	†RADIO MOSCOW, Yerevan	DS-1 • 50 kW
	†RADIO YEREVAN, Yerevan	MIDEAST • 50 kW
4990v	**INDONESIA**	
	†RRI, Gorontalo, Sulawesi	Irr • DS 10 kW
4990.2	**BOLIVIA**	
	RADIO ANIMAS, Chocaya	Tu-Su • DS • 1 kW DS • 1 kW M-Sa • DS • 1 kW
4991v	**PERU**	
	RADIO ANCASH, Huáraz	DS 5/10 kW
4995	**MONGOLIA**	
	†RADIO ULAANBAATAR, Choybalsan	DS-1 • 12 kW
4995.8	**PERU**	
	RADIO ANDINA, Huancayo	DS • 1 kW Irr • DS • 1 kW Tu-Su • DS • 1 kW
5000	**CLANDESTINE (ASIA)**	
	†"KASHMIR FREEDOM"	S ASIA • ANTI-INDIAN GOVT
	USA	
	WWV, Ft Collins, Colorado	WEATHER/WORLD TIME • 10 kW
	WWVH, Kekaha, Hawaii	WEATHER/WORLD TIME • 5 kW
	VENEZUELA	
	OBSERVATORIO NAVAL, Caracas	DS • 1 kW
5004v	**EQUATORIAL GUINEA**	
	RADIO NACIONAL, Batá	Alternative Frequency to 4925.6 kHz
5004.8	**BOLIVIA**	
	†RADIO LIBERTAD, La Paz	DS • 1 kW Su • DS • 1 kW
5005	**MALAYSIA**	
	†RTM-SARAWAK, Sibu	DS-IBAN • 10 kW
	NEPAL	
	RADIO NEPAL, Harriharpur	S ASIA • 100 kW DS • 100 kW Sa • DS • 100 kW
5005.7	**SURINAME**	
	RADIO APINTIE, Paramaribo	DS • 0.35 kW Tu-Su • DS • 0.35 kW
5010	**CAMEROON**	
	†CAMEROON RTV CORP, Garoua	FRENCH, ENGLISH, ETC • DS • 100 kW
	CHINA (PR)	
	GUANGXI PEOPLES BS, Nanning	DS-2/CHINESE, ETC • 10 kW
	SINGAPORE	
	SINGAPORE BC CORP, Jurong	DS-1 • 50 kW
5010v	**MADAGASCAR**	
	RTV MALAGASY, Antananarivo	DS-1 • 30/100 kW M-Sa • DS-1 • 30/100 kW
5012	**PERU**	
	RADIO ECO, Iquitos	Irr • DS • 1 kW • ALT. FREQ. TO 5097v kHz
5012v	**ECUADOR**	
	ESCUELAS R'FONICAS, Riobamba	DS • 10 kW
5014.6	**BRAZIL**	
	†RADIO COPACABANA, Rio De Janeiro	DS • 1 kW
	RADIO PIONEIRA, Teresina	DS • 1 kW
5015	**BRAZIL**	
	R BRASIL TROPICAL, Cuiabá	DS • 5 kW
	USSR	
	†ARKHANGELSK RADIO, Arkhangelsk	DS • 50 kW
	†PRIMORSK RADIO, Vladivostok	DS/TIKHIY OKEAN • 50 kW
	†RADIO MOSCOW, Ashkhabad	DS-1 • 50 kW
5015v	**PERU**	
	RADIO TARAPOTO, Tarapoto	DS • 0.7 kW
5020	**CHINA (PR)**	
	†JIANGXI PEOPLES BS, Nanchang	DS-1 • 10 kW
	SOLOMON ISLANDS	
	†SOLOMON ISLANDS BC, Honiara	Su • DS-ENGLISH, PIDGIN • 10 kW Sa • DS-ENGLISH, PIDGIN • 10 kW M-F • DS-ENGLISH, PIDGIN • 10 kW
	SRI LANKA	
	SRI LANKA BC CORP, Colombo-Ekala	DS-TAMIL • 10 kW
5020v	**COLOMBIA**	
	ECOS DEL ATRATO, Quibdó	DS-CARACOL • 2 kW
	NIGER	
	LA VOIX DU SAHEL, Niamey	DS-FRENCH, ETC • 20/100 kW Sa • DS-FRENCH, ETC • 20/100 kW
	VIETNAM	
	VOICE OF VIETNAM, Hanoi	DS

0 1 2 3 4 5 6 7 8 9 10 11 12 13 14 15 16 17 18 19 20 21 22 23 24

SUMMER ONLY (J)   WINTER ONLY (D)   JAMMING / OR /\   EARLIEST HEARD ◁   LATEST HEARD ▷   NEW OR CHANGED FOR 1992 †

FREQUENCY	COUNTRY, STATION, LOCATION	TARGET • NETWORK • POWER (kW) — World Time

0 1 2 3 4 5 6 7 8 9 10 11 12 13 14 15 16 17 18 19 20 21 22 23 24

Freq	Station	Details
5025	**AUSTRALIA**	
	ABC/R RUM JUNGLE, Katherine	DS • 50 kW
	BENIN	
	ORT DU BENIN, Parakou	DS-FRENCH, ETC • 20 kW
	BHUTAN	
	†BHUTAN BC SERVICE, Thimbu	Su • DS • 50 kW M-Sa • DS • 50 kW
	BRAZIL	
	R TRANSAMAZONICA, Altamira	DS • 5 kW
	RADIO BORBOREMA, Campina Grande	DS-TEMP INACTIVE • 1 kW
	RADIO MORIMOTO, Ji-Paraná	DS-TEMP INACTIVE • 5 kW
	PERU	
	RADIO QUILLABAMBA, Quillabamba	DS-SPANISH, ETC • 5 kW
		Tu-Su • DS • 5 kW M-Sa • DS-SPANISH, ETC • 5 kW
5025v	**CUBA**	
	RADIO REBELDE, Havana	DS • 50 kW
5026	**UGANDA**	
	RADIO UGANDA, Kampala	DS-ENGLISH,SWAHILI • 50/250 kW
		M-F • DS-ENGLISH,SWAHILI • 50/250 kW
		M-Sa • DS-ENGLISH,SWAHILI • 50/250 kW
5030	**ECUADOR**	
	RADIO CATOLICA, Quito	DS • 9 kW
	MALAYSIA	
	†RTM-SARAWAK, Kuching-Stapok	DS-BIDAYUTH • 10 kW
	TONGA	
	TONGA BC COMMISS'N, Nuku'alofa	Tu-Su • DS-ENGLISH, TONGAN • 1 kW M-Sa • DS-ENGLISH, TONGAN • 1 kW
5031v	**PERU**	
	RADIO LOS ANDES, Huamachuco	DS • 1 kW
5034	**CENTRAL AFRICAN REP**	
	RTV CENTRAFRICAINE, Bangui	FRENCH, ETC • DS • 100 kW
5035	**BRAZIL**	
	R EDUCACAO RURAL, Coari	DS • 1 kW
	RADIO APARECIDA, Aparecida	DS • 10 kW
	KAMPUCHEA (CAMBODIA)	
	VO THE PEOPLE, Phnom Penh	DS
	PERU	
	RADIO AYAVIRI, Ayaviri	Alternative Frequency to 4606.6 kHz
	RADIO MOYOBAMBA, Moyobamba	DS • 1 kW
	USSR	
	†KAZAKH RADIO, Alma-Ata	DS-2 • 50 kW
	†RADIO ALMA-ATA, Alma-Ata	50 kW
5039	**PERU**	
	†RADIO LIBERTAD, Junín	DS • 1 kW
		Irr • DS • 1 kW
5040	**CHINA (PR)**	
	FUJIAN PEOPLES BS, Fuzhou	DS-1, TAIWAN SVC • 10 kW
	ECUADOR	
	LA VOZ DEL UPANO, Macas	DS • 10 kW
	USSR	
	†GEORGIAN RADIO, Tbilisi	RUSSIAN, ETC • DS-1 • 100 kW
5040v	**ANGOLA**	
	EP DE BENGUELA, Benguela	DS • 1 kW
	VENEZUELA	
	†RADIO MATURIN, Maturín	DS-VERY IRREGULAR • 10 kW
5044.8	**COSTA RICA**	
	†FARO DEL CARIBE, San José	DS • 5 kW
5045	**BOLIVIA**	
	†RADIO ALTIPLANO, La Paz	DS • 5 kW
	BRAZIL	
	R CULTURA DO PARA, Belém	DS • 10 kW
	RADIO DIFUSORA, Presidente Prudente	DS • 0.5 kW
		Tu-Su • DS • 0.5 kW
	PERU	
	RADIO RIOJA, Rioja	DS-TEMP INACTIVE • 1 kW • ALT. FREQ. TO 5049.5 kHz
5045v	**PAKISTAN**	
	PAKISTAN BC CORP, Islamabad	(J) • DS • 10 kW
5046.3	**INDONESIA**	
	†RRI, Yogyakarta, Jawa	DS • 20 kW
5047	**TOGO**	
	RADIO LOME, Lomé-Togblekope	DS • 100 kW DS-FRENCH, ETC • 100 kW
5049.5	**PERU**	
	RADIO RIOJA, Rioja	Alternative Frequency to 5045 kHz
5049.8	**ECUADOR**	
	R JESUS GRAN PODER, Quito	DS • 5 kW
5050	**CHINA (PR)**	
	GUANGXI BC STATION, Nanning	SE ASIA • 50 kW
	GUANGXI BC STATION, Nanning	SE ASIA • 50 kW
	†VO THE STRAIT-PLA, Fuzhou	TAIWAN-1 • 10 kW
	COLOMBIA	
	LA VOZ DE YOPAL, Yopal	DS-CARACOL • 1 kW
		Irr • DS-CARACOL • 1 kW
	INDIA	
(con'd)	†ALL INDIA RADIO, Aizawl	DS • 50 kW

0 1 2 3 4 5 6 7 8 9 10 11 12 13 14 15 16 17 18 19 20 21 22 23 24

ENGLISH ▬   ARABIC ᔕᔕᔕ   CHINESE □□□   FRENCH ▬▬   GERMAN ▬   RUSSIAN ═   SPANISH ▬   OTHER ▬

FREQUENCY	COUNTRY, STATION, LOCATION	TARGET • NETWORK • POWER (kW) / World Time

5050 (con'd) INDIA †ALL INDIA RADIO, Aizawl — ENGLISH, ETC • DS • 50 kW; Sa • DS • 50 kW; Sa • ENGLISH, ETC • DS • 50 kW

PERU RADIO MUNICIPAL, Cangallo — DS • 0.5 kW

TANZANIA RADIO TANZANIA, Dar es Salaam — DS-TEMP INACTIVE • 10 kW

5052 SINGAPORE SINGAPORE BC CORP, Jurong — DS-1 • 50 kW

5055 BRAZIL †RADIO DIFUSORA, Cáceres — DS • 1 kW; M-Sa • DS • 1 kW

SWAZILAND TRANS WORLD RADIO, Manzini — S AFRICA • 25 kW

5055.2 INDONESIA †RRI, Nabire, Irian Jaya — DS • 1 kW

5056 FRENCH GUIANA †RFO-GUYANE, Cayenne — DS • 10 kW

5059 PERU RADIO LIRCAY, Lircay — DS • 1 kW

5060 CHINA (PR) CENTRAL PEOPLES BS, Changji — DS-MINORITIES • 10 kW; XINJIANG PBS, Changji — DS-MONGOLIAN • 10 kW

5060v ECUADOR R NAC PROGRESO, Loja — DS • 5 kW

5062v ANGOLA EP DO HUAMBO, Huambo — DS • 1 kW

5066v ZAIRE RADIO CANDIP, Bunia — FRENCH, ETC • DS • 1 kW; Sa • FRENCH, ETC • DS • 1 kW

5075 COLOMBIA CARACOL BOGOTA, Bogotá — DS • 50 kW • ALT. FREQ. TO 5095 kHz

5080v CLANDESTINE (M EAST) "VO KURD STRUGGLE", Middle East — MIDEAST • ANTI-IRANIAN GOVT

5083v PERU RADIO MUNDO, Cusco — DS-SPANISH, ETC • 1 kW

5090v PAKISTAN PAKISTAN BC CORP, Islamabad — DS • 100 kW

5095 COLOMBIA CARACOL BOGOTA, Bogotá — Alternative Frequency to 5075 kHz

5097v PERU RADIO ECO, Iquitos — Alternative Frequency to 5012 kHz

5110v CLANDESTINE (ASIA) "VO THE WA PEOPLE", Burma — SE ASIA

5125 USA RFE-RL, Via Holzkirchen, GFR — Irr • W EUROPE • (FEEDER) 10 kW • ISU; Irr • W EUROPE • (FEEDER) 10 kW • ISL

5131v PERU RADIO VISION, Juanjuí — DS-SPANISH, QUECHUA • 0.1 kW

5145 CHINA (PR) RADIO BEIJING, Beijing — E ASIA & EAST USSR • RUSSIAN, MONGOLIAN • 120 kW

5147v PERU RADIO ESTRELLA, Huánuco — DS; M-Sa • DS

5156.2 BOLIVIA †RADIO GALAXIA, Guayaramerín — DS • 0.2 kW

5160v PERU R NUEVO CONTINENTE, Cajamarca — DS • 1 kW

5163 CHINA (PR) †CENTRAL PEOPLES BS, Xi'an — DS-2 • 50 kW

5188v PERU RADIO ONDA POPULAR, Bambamarca — DS • 0.25 kW

5192v ANGOLA EP DO MOXICO, Luena — Irr • DS • 5 kW

5220 CHINA (PR) RADIO BEIJING, Beijing — E ASIA • FEEDER • 10 kW; (D) • E ASIA • FEEDER • 10 kW; (J) • E ASIA • FEEDER • 10 kW

SPAIN †R EXTERIOR ESPANA, Via Beijing — Alternative Frequency to 4130 kHz

5235.4 PERU †S ANTONIO DE PADUA, Arequipa — DS • 0.17 kW

5250 CHINA (PR) RADIO BEIJING, Beijing — (D) • E ASIA • FEEDER • 10 kW

SPAIN †R EXTERIOR ESPANA, Via Beijing — (D) • E ASIA • FEEDER • 10 kW

5256.5 INDONESIA †RRI, Sibolga, Sumatera — DS • 1 kW

5260 USSR †KAZAKH RADIO, Alma-Ata — DS-2 • 50 kW; †RADIO ALMA-ATA, Alma-Ata — 50 kW

5260v PERU R NORORIENTAL, S Rosa Huayabamba — DS • 0.5 kW

5263v PERU ESTACION A, Sócota — DS

5275 USA FAMILY RADIO, Via Taiwan — E ASIA • 250 kW

5275.5 PERU RADIO ONDA POPULAR, Bambamarca — DS • 0.25 kW

FREQUENCY   COUNTRY, STATION, LOCATION

TARGET • NETWORK • POWER (kW)   World Time

0 1 2 3 4 5 6 7 8 9 10 11 12 13 14 15 16 17 18 19 20 21 22 23 24

5277v PERU
RADIO GRAU, Huancabamba — DS • 0.5 kW • ALT. FREQ. TO 4008v kHz

5287v CHAD
RADIODIF NATIONALE, Moundou — FRENCH, ARABIC, ETC • DS • 5 kW

5290 USSR
†KRASNOYARSK RADIO, Krasnoyarsk — DS • 100 kW

5295 USA
RFE-RL, Via Holzkirchen,GFR — Irr • W EUROPE • (FEEDER) • 10 kW • ISU
Irr • W EUROPE • (FEEDER) • 10 kW • ISL

5320 CHINA (PR)
†CENTRAL PEOPLES BS, Beijing — DS-1 • 10/15 kW

5323.4 PERU
†RADIO ORIGEN, Huancavelica — DS

5325 PERU
RADIO ACOBAMBA, Acobamba — DS

5408v CLANDESTINE (ASIA)
†"VO NATIONAL ARMY", Southern Laos — SE ASIA • KAMPUCHEAN REBELS

5419.2 PERU
†RADIO SONORAMA, Saposoa — DS

5420 CHINA (PR)
†CENTRAL PEOPLES BS, Beijing — DS-MINORITIES • 10 kW
(D) • DS-MINORITIES • 10 kW

5440 CHINA (PR)
CENTRAL PEOPLES BS, Urümqi — DS-MINORITIES • 50 kW

XINJIANG PBS, Urümqi — DS-KAZAKH • 50 kW

5445 PERU
†R ALTO HUALLAGA, Uchiza — DS

5490 CLANDESTINE (ASIA)
†"VOICE OF UNITY" — S ASIA • PRO-AFGHAN REBELS

5505.3 BOLIVIA
RADIO 2 DE FEBRERO, Rurrenabaque — Irr • DS • 0.5 kW
Irr • Tu-Su • DS • 0.5 kW   Irr • M-Sa • DS • 0.5 kW

5510 CHINA (PR)
VO THE STRAIT-PLA, Fuzhou — TAIWAN-1 • 10 kW

5510v CLANDESTINE (M EAST)
"VO IRAQI KURDS", Middle East — MIDEAST • ANTI-IRAQI GOVT
Irr • MIDEAST • ANTI-IRAQI GOVT

5535 COLOMBIA
†ECOS CELESTIALES, Medellin — DS

5538.7 PERU
FRECUENCIA MODULAR, Celendín — DS
Irr • DS

5567.2 COLOMBIA
RADIO NUEVA VIDA, Tibu — DS • 0.2 kW
Irr • DS • 0.2 kW

5580.2 BOLIVIA
†RADIO SAN JOSE, San José Chiquitos — Irr • DS • 0.5 kW
DS • 0.5 kW

5618v PERU
RADIO ILUCAN, Cutervo — Su • DS • 0.2 kW

5645v PERU
RADIO BAMBAMARCA, Bambamarca — DS • 0.1 kW

5660v VIETNAM
HOANG LIEN SON BS, Hoang Lien Son — DS

VOICE OF VIETNAM, Hoang Lien Son — SE ASIA

5661v PERU
LA VOZ DE CUTERVO, Cutervo — DS • 0.7 kW

5700v PERU
FREC SAN IGNACIO, San Ignacio — DS • 0.1 kW
Irr • DS • 0.1 kW

5720v PERU
R SAN MIGUEL, S Miguel Pallaques — Tu-Su • DS

5725 PERU
R SAN MIGUEL, S Miguel Pallaques — DS

5780 USSR
TASS NEWS AGENCY, Moscow — M-F • DS • 15 kW

5800 CHINA (PR)
CENTRAL PEOPLES BS, Urümqi — DS-MINORITIES • 50 kW

†XINJIANG PBS, Urümqi — DS-UIGHUR • 50 kW

PERU
R NUEVO CAJAMARCA, N Cajamarca — DS • 0.25 kW
Irr • DS • 0.25 kW

5815 USSR
RADIO MOSCOW, Moscow — Irr • (D) • DS-MAYAK (FEEDER) • 15 kW • LSB
Irr • (D) • DS-1 (FEEDER) • 15 kW • LSB

5816 PERU
LV DEL ALTIPLANO, Puno — Irr • DS-SPANISH, QUECHUA • 1 kW

5825 CHILE
†R TRIUNFAL EVANGEL, Santiago — Tu-Th/Sa/Su • DS • 0.05/0.5 kW   M-W/F/Sa • DS • 0.05/0.5 kW

5835.3 PERU
†UNIDENTIFIED — DS

5850 CHINA (PR)
RADIO BEIJING, Beijing — E ASIA & EAST USSR • RUSSIAN, MONGOLIAN • 120 kW

5850v PIRATE (PACIFIC)
†KIWI RADIO, New Zealand — Irr • PACIFIC • 0.05/0.2 kW

5871v KOREA (DPR)
RADIO PYONGYANG, Pyongyang — Irr • E ASIA

0 1 2 3 4 5 6 7 8 9 10 11 12 13 14 15 16 17 18 19 20 21 22 23 24

ENGLISH ▬▬   ARABIC ⧓⧓⧓   CHINESE ⊡⊡⊡   FRENCH ══   GERMAN ▬▬   RUSSIAN ══   SPANISH ▬▬   OTHER ──

FREQUENCY	COUNTRY, STATION, LOCATION	TARGET • NETWORK • POWER (kW)	World Time

Time scale: 0 1 2 3 4 5 6 7 8 9 10 11 12 13 14 15 16 17 18 19 20 21 22 23 24

5875 SAUDI ARABIA
- BS OF THE KINGDOM, Ad Dir'iyah — MIDEAST • DS-GENERAL • 50 kW
- BS OF THE KINGDOM, Jiddah — Alternative Frequency to 6020 kHz

UNITED KINGDOM
- †BBC, Multiple Locations — (D) • C AMERICA & S AMERICA • 300/500 kW
- †BBC, Rampisham — (D) M-F • E EUROPE • 500 kW · E EUROPE • 500 kW
  - (D) • E EUROPE • 500 kW
  - (J) • E EUROPE • 500 kW
  - (J) M-F • E EUROPE • 500 kW · (D) Su • E EUROPE • 500 kW
  - M-Sa • E EUROPE • 500 kW
  - (D) M-Sa • E EUROPE • 500 kW
  - (J) M-Sa • E EUROPE • 500 kW
  - (J) M-Sa • EUROPE & N AFRICA • 500 kW
  - (D) • E EUROPE & MIDEAST • 300 kW
- †BBC, Skelton, Cumbria

5880 CHINA (PR)
- †CENTRAL PEOPLES BS, Beijing — DS-1 • 10 kW

5900 CHINA (PR)
- †SICHUAN PEOPLES BS, Chengdu — CHINESE, ETC • DS-2 • 15 kW

ISRAEL
- KOL ISRAEL, Tel Aviv — MIDEAST • DS-D • 20 kW

USSR
- †UZBEK RADIO, Moscow — RUSSIAN, ETC • DS-1 • 20 kW

5905 USSR
- †ADYGEY RADIO — (D) F • DS · (D) Su • DS
- †KABARDINO-BALKAR R
- †R TIKHIY OKEAN — (D) • PACIFIC & W NORTH AM • MARINERS
- †RADIO MOSCOW — (D) • DS-MAYAK · (D) • W NORTH AM • NORTH AMERICAN SVC · (D) • MIDEAST
- †RADIO MOSCOW, Ryazan' — (D) • EUROPE • 100 kW

5905v PAKISTAN
- PAKISTAN BC CORP, Islamabad — (D) • DS • 10 kW
- PAKISTAN BC CORP, Karachi — (J) • DS-ENGLISH, ETC • 10 kW
- RADIO PAKISTAN, Islamabad — (D) • S ASIA • FEEDER • 10 kW

5910 BELGIUM
- †BELGISCHE RADIO TV, Wavre — (D) • EUROPE • 100 kW
  - (J) • EUROPE • 100 kW
  - (D) M-Sa • EUROPE • 100 kW
  - (J) M-Sa • EUROPE • 100 kW
  - (D) Su • EUROPE • 100 kW
  - (J) Su • EUROPE • 100 kW

USSR
- †RADIO MOSCOW, Moscow — DS-1 • 50 kW

5915 CHINA (PR)
- CENTRAL PEOPLES BS, Beijing — DS-1 • 50 kW

ISRAEL
- †KOL ISRAEL, Tel Aviv — MIDEAST • DS-D

USSR
- RADIO ALMA-ATA, Alma-Ata — ASIA • 100 kW
- RADIO TASHKENT, Alma-Ata — ASIA • 100 kW
- †RADIO VEDO, Volgograd — Sa/Su • DS 20 kW
- †SOVIET BELORUSSIA, Orcha — (D) • EUROPE • 100 kW

5919.5 CHINA (PR)
- †GUANGXI PEOPLES BS, Nanning — CHINESE, ETC • DS-3 • 10 kW

5920 USSR
- LATVIAN RADIO, Moscow — DS-1 • 20 kW
- †RADIO MOSCOW, Orcha — (D) • EUROPE • 100 kW
- †RADIO MOSCOW, Tula — (D) • ATLANTIC • 100 kW

5925 USSR
- †ESTONIAN RADIO, Tallinn — DS-1 • 50 kW
  - M-Sa • DS-1 • 50 kW · Su • DS-1 • 50 kW
- †RADIO TALLINN, Tallinn — Su • 50 kW · M-Sa • 50 kW · 50 kW
  - Su • RUSSIAN, ESTONIAN • 50 kW
  - M • 50 kW
  - Tu-Su • 50 kW

5930 CZECHOSLOVAKIA
- †RADIO PRAGUE INTL — AMERICAS · EUROPE

USSR
- †MURMANSK RADIO, Murmansk — DS • 50 kW
- †RADIO TBILISI, Tbilisi — Tu/Th • MIDEAST • 100 kW · Sa/Su • MIDEAST • 100 kW

5930v PAKISTAN
- PAKISTAN BC CORP, Karachi — DS • 10 kW

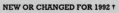

FREQUENCY   COUNTRY, STATION, LOCATION   TARGET • NETWORK • POWER (kW)   World Time

```
                                          0  1  2  3  4  5  6  7  8  9  10 11 12 13 14 15 16 17 18 19 20 21 22 23 24
```

5935   **CHINA (PR)**
RADIO BEIJING, Lhasa   S ASIA • HINDI • 50 kW

XIZANG PEOPLES BS, Lhasa   DS-CHINESE • 50 kW
USSR
†LATVIAN RADIO, Riga   DS-1 • 100 kW

M-Sa • DS-1 • 100 kW   Tu/F • DS-1 • 100 kW   Sa/Su • DS-1 • 100 kW

Su • F • DS-1 • 100 kW

†RADIO RIGA INTL, Riga   EUROPE • 100 kW

Su • EUROPE • 100 kW   Sa • EUROPE • 100 kW

W/Th/Sa-M • EUROPE • 100 kW

M-F • ENGLISH & GERMAN • EUROPE • 100 kW

RADIO TASHKENT   (J) • MIDEAST
5940   **USSR**
†MAGADAN RADIO, Magadan   RUSSIAN, ETC • DS/TIKHIY OKEAN • 50 kW

†RADIO MOSCOW, Petropavlovsk-K   (D) • E ASIA • 100 kW

†RADIO MOSCOW, Serpukhov   (D) • E EUROPE • 120 kW

†RADIO MOSCOW, Sverdlovsk   (D) • DS-1 • 100 kW
5945   **AUSTRIA**
RADIO AUSTRIA INTL, Vienna   EUROPE • 100 kW

(D) • EUROPE • 100 kW

(J) • EUROPE • 100 kW

M-Sa • EUROPE • 100 kW

Su • EUROPE • 100 kW

FRANCE
R FRANCE INTL, Issoudun-Allouis   E NORTH AM • 100 kW   (D) • E NORTH AM • 100 kW
USSR
†GRODNO RADIO, Minsk   RUSSIAN, ETC • DS-1 • 20 kW

RADIO TASHKENT, Bishkek   S ASIA & MIDEAST • 100 kW

(D) • S ASIA & MIDEAST • 100 kW

5950   **CHINA (PR)**
CENTRAL PEOPLES BS, Lhasa   DS-MINORITIES • 50 kW

†HEILONGJIANG PBS, Harbin   CHINESE & KOREAN • DS-2 • 50 kW

XIZANG PEOPLES BS, Lhasa   DS-TIBETAN • 50 kW
CHINA (TAIWAN)
†BC CORP CHINA, Via Okeechobee, USA   E NORTH AM • 100 kW

†VO FREE CHINA, Via Okeechobee, USA   E NORTH AM • 100 kW
E NORTH AM & C AMERICA • 100 kW
C AMERICA • 100 kW

USA
†WYFR-FAMILY RADIO, Okeechobee, Fl   E NORTH AM • 100 kW
USSR
†RADIO MOSCOW, Minsk   (D) • EUROPE • 100 kW

†RADIO MOSCOW, Petropavlovsk-K   (D) • E ASIA & PACIFIC • 100 kW

†SOVIET BELORUSSIA, Minsk   (D) • EUROPE • 100 kW

†UKRAINIAN RADIO, Voronezh, RSFSR   DS-2 • 240 kW
YEMEN (REPUBLIC)
"VO PALESTINE", Via Rep Yemen Radio   PLO • 300 kW

REP YEMEN RADIO, San'ā   DS • 300 kW

F • DS • 300 kW   Irr • DS-RAMADAN • 300 kW

5950.3   **GUYANA**
VOICE OF GUYANA, Georgetown   Irr • DS • 10 kW
5954v   **BOLIVIA**
RADIO PIO DOCE, Llallagua-Siglo XX   SPANISH, ETC • DS • 1 kW
M-Sa • SPANISH, ETC • DS • 1 kW

COSTA RICA
RADIO CASINO, Limón   Irr • DS • 0.7 kW
Irr • M • DS • 0.7 kW
Irr • Tu-Su • DS • 0.7 kW

5954.8   **COLOMBIA**
LA VOZ CENTAUROS, Villavicencio   DS-CARACOL • 5 kW
5955   **BOTSWANA**
†RADIO BOTSWANA, Gaborone   Alternative Frequency to 9600 kHz
BRAZIL
RADIO GAZETA, São Paulo   DS • 7.5 kW
CAMEROON
†CAMEROON RTV CORP, Bafoussam   FRENCH, ENGLISH, ETC • DS • 20 kW
CHINA (PR)
†CENTRAL PEOPLES BS   DS-1
GUATEMALA
RADIO CULTURAL, Guatemala City   Irr • DS • 0.25/10 kW
Irr • M • DS • 0.25/10 kW   Irr • M-Sa • DS • 0.25/10 kW
Irr • Tu-Su • DS • 0.25/10 kW   Irr • Su • DS • 0.25/10 kW

(con'd)

```
0  1  2  3  4  5  6  7  8  9  10 11 12 13 14 15 16 17 18 19 20 21 22 23 24
```

ENGLISH ▬   ARABIC ▧   CHINESE ▯▯▯   FRENCH ▬   GERMAN ▬   RUSSIAN ═   SPANISH ▬   OTHER ▬

FREQUENCY   COUNTRY, STATION, LOCATION   TARGET • NETWORK • POWER (kW)   World Time

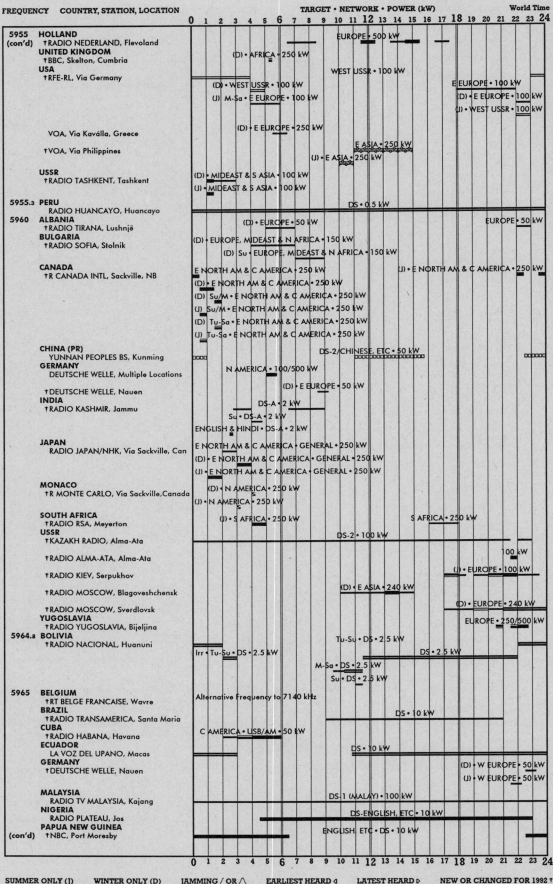

Frequency	Country, Station, Location	Target • Network • Power
5955 (con'd)	**HOLLAND** †RADIO NEDERLAND, Flevoland	EUROPE • 500 kW
	UNITED KINGDOM †BBC, Skelton, Cumbria	(D) • AFRICA • 250 kW
	USA †RFE-RL, Via Germany	WEST USSR • 100 kW; (D) • WEST USSR • 100 kW; E EUROPE • 100 kW; (J) M-Sa • E EUROPE • 100 kW; (D) • E EUROPE • 100 kW; (J) • WEST USSR • 100 kW
	VOA, Via Kaválla, Greece	(D) • E EUROPE • 250 kW
	†VOA, Via Philippines	E ASIA • 250 kW; (J) • E ASIA • 250 kW
	USSR †RADIO TASHKENT, Tashkent	(D) • MIDEAST & S ASIA • 100 kW; (J) • MIDEAST & S ASIA • 100 kW
5955.3	**PERU** RADIO HUANCAYO, Huancayo	DS • 0.5 kW
5960	**ALBANIA** †RADIO TIRANA, Lushnjë	(D) • EUROPE • 50 kW; EUROPE • 50 kW
	BULGARIA †RADIO SOFIA, Stolnik	(D) • EUROPE, MIDEAST & N AFRICA • 150 kW; (D) Su • EUROPE, MIDEAST & N AFRICA • 150 kW
	CANADA †R CANADA INTL, Sackville, NB	E NORTH AM & C AMERICA • 250 kW; (J) • E NORTH AM & C AMERICA • 250 kW; (D) • E NORTH AM & C AMERICA • 250 kW; (D) Su/M • E NORTH AM & C AMERICA • 250 kW; (J) Su/M • E NORTH AM & C AMERICA • 250 kW; (D) Tu-Sa • E NORTH AM & C AMERICA • 250 kW; (J) Tu-Sa • E NORTH AM & C AMERICA • 250 kW
	CHINA (PR) YUNNAN PEOPLES BS, Kunming	DS-2/CHINESE, ETC • 50 kW
	GERMANY DEUTSCHE WELLE, Multiple Locations	N AMERICA • 100/500 kW
	†DEUTSCHE WELLE, Nauen	(D) • E EUROPE • 50 kW
	INDIA †RADIO KASHMIR, Jammu	DS-A • 2 kW; Su • DS-A • 2 kW; ENGLISH & HINDI • DS-A • 2 kW
	JAPAN RADIO JAPAN/NHK, Via Sackville, Can	E NORTH AM & C AMERICA • GENERAL • 250 kW; (D) • E NORTH AM & C AMERICA • GENERAL • 250 kW; (J) • E NORTH AM & C AMERICA • GENERAL • 250 kW
	MONACO †R MONTE CARLO, Via Sackville, Canada	(D) • N AMERICA • 250 kW; (J) • N AMERICA • 250 kW
	SOUTH AFRICA †RADIO RSA, Meyerton	(J) • S AFRICA • 250 kW; S AFRICA • 250 kW
	USSR †KAZAKH RADIO, Alma-Ata	DS-2 • 100 kW
	†RADIO ALMA-ATA, Alma-Ata	100 kW
	†RADIO KIEV, Serpukhov	(J) • EUROPE • 100 kW
	†RADIO MOSCOW, Blagoveshchensk	(D) • E ASIA • 240 kW
	†RADIO MOSCOW, Sverdlovsk	(D) • EUROPE • 240 kW
	YUGOSLAVIA †RADIO YUGOSLAVIA, Bijeljina	EUROPE • 250/500 kW
5964.8	**BOLIVIA** †RADIO NACIONAL, Huanuni	Tu-Su • DS • 2.5 kW; Irr • Tu-Su • DS • 2.5 kW; DS • 2.5 kW; M-Sa • DS • 2.5 kW; Su • DS • 2.5 kW
5965	**BELGIUM** †RT BELGE FRANCAISE, Wavre	Alternative Frequency to 7140 kHz
	BRAZIL †RADIO TRANSAMERICA, Santa Maria	DS • 10 kW
	CUBA †RADIO HABANA, Havana	C AMERICA • USB/AM • 50 kW
	ECUADOR LA VOZ DEL UPANO, Macas	DS • 10 kW
	GERMANY †DEUTSCHE WELLE, Nauen	(D) • W EUROPE • 50 kW; (J) • W EUROPE • 50 kW
	MALAYSIA RADIO TV MALAYSIA, Kajang	DS-1 (MALAY) • 100 kW
	NIGERIA RADIO PLATEAU, Jos	DS-ENGLISH, ETC • 10 kW
	PAPUA NEW GUINEA (con'd) †NBC, Port Moresby	ENGLISH, ETC • DS • 10 kW

SUMMER ONLY (J)   WINTER ONLY (D)   JAMMING / OR ∧   EARLIEST HEARD ◁   LATEST HEARD ▷   NEW OR CHANGED FOR 1992 †

FREQUENCY   COUNTRY, STATION, LOCATION   TARGET • NETWORK • POWER (kW)   World Time

FREQUENCY	COUNTRY, STATION, LOCATION	TARGET • NETWORK • POWER (kW)
5965 (con'd)	SWAZILAND	
	†TRANS WORLD RADIO, Manzini	S AFRICA • 25 kW
	UNITED KINGDOM	
	BBC, Via Maşîrah, Oman	S ASIA • 100 kW
	BBC, Via Sackville, Can	N AMERICA • 250 kW / M-Sa • N AMERICA • 250 kW
	†BBC, Via Zyyi, Cyprus	MIDEAST • 250 kW
	USA	
	†VOA, Via Germany	E EUROPE • 500 kW / (J) • E EUROPE • 500 kW
	†VOA, Via Rhodes, Greece	MIDEAST • 50 kW / (D) • MIDEAST • 50 kW
	†VOA, Via Woofferton, UK	(D) • E EUROPE • 250 kW
	USSR	
	†KHABAROVSK R, Komsomol'sk 'Amure	DS-1/DS-2 • 20 kW
	†MOGHILEV RADIO, Orcha	RUSSIAN, ETC • DS • 20 kW
	†RADIO DVR, Komsomol'sk 'Amure	Tu-Sa • DS • 20 kW / M-F • DS • 20 kW
5969	INDONESIA	
	†RRI, Banjarmasin, Kali'n	DS • 10 kW
5970	BRAZIL	
	RADIO ITATIAIA, Belo Horizonte	DS • 10 kW
	NICARAGUA	
	†RADIO MISKUT, Puerto Cabezas	Irr • DS • 1 kW / DS-SPANISH, MISKITO • 1 kW
	USA	
	†RFE-RL, Via Germany	(D) • WEST USSR • 100 kW / E EUROPE & WEST USSR • 100 kW / (D) • E EUROPE & WEST USSR • 100 kW / (J) • E EUROPE & WEST USSR • 100 kW
	†RFE-RL, Via Portugal	(D) • E EUROPE & WEST USSR • 250 kW
	USSR	
	†KAZAKH RADIO, Alma-Ata	DS-2 • 50 kW
	†RADIO ALMA-ATA, Alma-Ata	50 kW
	†RADIO MOSCOW	Irr • DS-MAYAK • USB
	YEMEN (REPUBLIC)	
	"VO PALESTINE", Via Rep Yemen Radio	MIDEAST • PLO • 100 kW
	†REP YEMEN RADIO, Aden	MIDEAST • DS • 100 kW / F • MIDEAST • DS • 100 kW / Irr • MIDEAST • DS-RAMADAN • 100 kW
5970v	CHINA (PR)	
	GANNAN PEOPLES BS, Hezuo	Irr • DS-CHINESE, TIBETAN • 15 kW • ALT. FREQ. TO 3210v kHz
5975	ALBANIA	
	†RADIO TIRANA, Lushnjë	(J) • EUROPE • 50 kW
	CHINA (PR)	
	RADIO BEIJING, Beijing	E ASIA • 120 kW
	KOREA (REPUBLIC)	
	†RADIO KOREA, Hwasung	E ASIA • 100 kW
	SWEDEN	
	†RADIO SWEDEN, Hörby	Alternative Frequency to 6000 kHz
	UNITED KINGDOM	
	†BBC, Daventry	(D) • EUROPE • 300 kW
	†BBC, Skelton, Cumbria	W EUROPE • 250 kW / AFRICA • 300 kW / (D) • W EUROPE • 250 kW
	†BBC, Various Locations	EUROPE • 250/300/500 kW
	†BBC, Via Antigua	C AMERICA & S AMERICA • 125 kW / C AMERICA • 250 kW
	BBC, Via Maşîrah, Oman	MIDEAST • 100 kW
	†BBC, Via Singapore	S ASIA • 250 kW
	USA	
	†VOA, Via Germany	(D) • E EUROPE • 500 kW
	USSR	
	†RADIO MOSCOW, Leningrad	(D) • E EUROPE • 200 kW
	ZIMBABWE	
	ZIMBABWE BC CORP, Gweru	DS-TEMP INACTIVE • 100 kW / M-Sa • DS-TEMP INACTIVE • 100 kW
5975v	COLOMBIA	
	RADIO MACARENA, Villavicencio	DS • 5 kW / Tu-Su • DS • 5 kW / M-Sa • DS • 5 kW
5979.7	SIERRA LEONE	
	†SIERRA LEONE BS, Goderich	Irr • ENGLISH, ETC • DS • 10 kW
5980	BRAZIL	
	RADIO GUARUJÁ, Florianópolis	DS • 10 kW
	DENMARK	
(con'd)	DANMARKS RADIO, Via Norway	(D) • EUROPE • 500 kW

ENGLISH ▬   ARABIC ≋   CHINESE ▭▭▭   FRENCH ═══   GERMAN ▬▬   RUSSIAN ══   SPANISH ▬▬   OTHER ▬

FREQUENCY   COUNTRY, STATION, LOCATION   TARGET • NETWORK • POWER (kW)   World Time

		0 1 2 3 4 5 6 7 8 9 10 11 12 13 14 15 16 17 18 19 20 21 22 23 24

5980   **ECUADOR**
(con'd)   †RADIO FEDERACION, Sucúa — DS • 5 kW
          GERMANY
          †DEUTSCHE WELLE, Jülich — (D) • WEST USSR • 100 kW
          — (J) • WEST USSR • 100 kW
          — (D) • W EUROPE • 100 kW
          †DEUTSCHE WELLE, Königswusterhausen — (D) • SE ASIA • 500 kW
          †DEUTSCHE WELLE, Wertachtal
          MALAYSIA
          †RTM-KOTA KINABALU, Kota Kinabalu — ENGLISH, ETC • DS • 10 kW
          NORWAY
          †RADIO NORWAY INTL, Kvitsøy — (D) • EUROPE • 500 kW
          TURKEY
          †VOICE OF TURKEY, Ankara — E EUROPE • 250 kW
          UNITED KINGDOM
          BBC, Daventry — AFRICA • 300 kW
          USA
          †VOA, Via Woofferton, UK — (D) • N AFRICA • 300 kW
          USSR
          ESTONIAN RADIO, Ryazan' — DS-1 • 20 kW
          — M-Sa • DS-1 • 20 kW
          †RADIO KIEV, Simferopol' — (D) • EUROPE • 250 kW
          †RADIO MOSCOW, Simferopol' — (D) • EUROPE • 250 kW
          RADIO MOSCOW, Yakutsk — DS-1 • 20 kW
5980v **CHINA (TAIWAN)**
          VOICE OF ASIA, Kao-hsiung — SE ASIA • 10 kW
5981.7 **GUATEMALA**
          UNION RADIO-AWR, Guatemala City — DS • 5 kW
5982v **MEXICO**
          RADIO XEUJ, Linares — Irr • DS • 0.5 kW
5984.2 **INDONESIA**
          †RRI, Pekanbaru, Sumatera — DS • 50 kW
5985   **ALBANIA**
          †RADIO TIRANA, Lushnjë — EUROPE • 50 kW
          — (J) • EUROPE • 50 kW
          CONGO
          †RTV CONGOLAISE, Brazzaville — FRENCH, ETC • DS • 50 kW • ALT. FREQ. TO 3265 kHz
          MEXICO
          RADIO MEXICO INTL, México City — C AMERICA & N AMERICA • 10 kW
          PAPUA NEW GUINEA
          NBC, Port Moresby — ENGLISH, ETC • DS • 10 kW
          TANZANIA
          RADIO TANZANIA, Dar es Salaam — Irr • Sa/Su • S AFRICA • 50 kW
          USA
          †RFE-RL, Via Germany — (J) • WEST USSR • 100 kW — WEST USSR • 100 kW
          — (J) • WEST USSR • 250 kW — E EUROPE • 100 kW
          — (D) • WEST USSR • 100 kW
          — (J) • E EUROPE • 100 kW
          †RFE-RL, Via Portugal — (J) • E EUROPE & WEST USSR • 250 kW
          — (D) • E EUROPE & WEST USSR • 250 kW
          VOA, Delano, California — PACIFIC & AUSTRALIA • 250 kW
          †VOA, Via Germany — (D) • WEST USSR • 500 kW
          VOA, Via Kaválla, Greece — (D) • WEST USSR • 250 kW
          †WYFR-FAMILY RADIO, Okeechobee, Fl — E NORTH AM • 100 kW
          — C AMERICA • 50 kW
          — W NORTH AM • 100 kW
5990   **CLANDESTINE (M EAST)**
          †"AL-QUDS RADIO", Syria — MIDEAST
          ETHIOPIA
          VOICE OF ETHIOPIA, Gedja — DS • 100 kW
          — M-Sa • DS • 100 kW   M-F • DS • 100 kW
          — Su • DS • 100 kW   Sa/Su • DS • 100 kW
          FRANCE
          †R FRANCE INTL, Issoudun-Allouis — E EUROPE • 500 kW
          — (D) • E EUROPE • 500 kW
          — (J) • E EUROPE • 500 kW
          INDIA
          †ALL INDIA RADIO, Bhopal — DS • 10 kW
          — Su • DS • 10 kW
          — ENGLISH & HINDI • DS • 10 kW
          ITALY
          RTV ITALIANA, Rome — (D) • E EUROPE & WEST USSR • 100 kW — EUROPE • 100 kW
          — (D) • EUROPE, N AFRICA & MIDEAST • 100 kW — (D) • N AFRICA • 100 kW — (D) • E ASIA • 100 kW
          — (D) • EUROPE • 100 kW
          JAPAN
          †RADIO JAPAN/NHK, Tokyo-Yamata — (D) • W NORTH AM • GENERAL • 300 kW
          MYANMAR (BURMA)
(con'd)   †VOICE OF MYANMAR, Yangon — DS-ENGLISH, BURMESE • 50 kW

		0 1 2 3 4 5 6 7 8 9 10 11 12 13 14 15 16 17 18 19 20 21 22 23 24

SUMMER ONLY (J)   WINTER ONLY (D)   JAMMING / OR ∧   EARLIEST HEARD ◁   LATEST HEARD ▷   NEW OR CHANGED FOR 1992 †

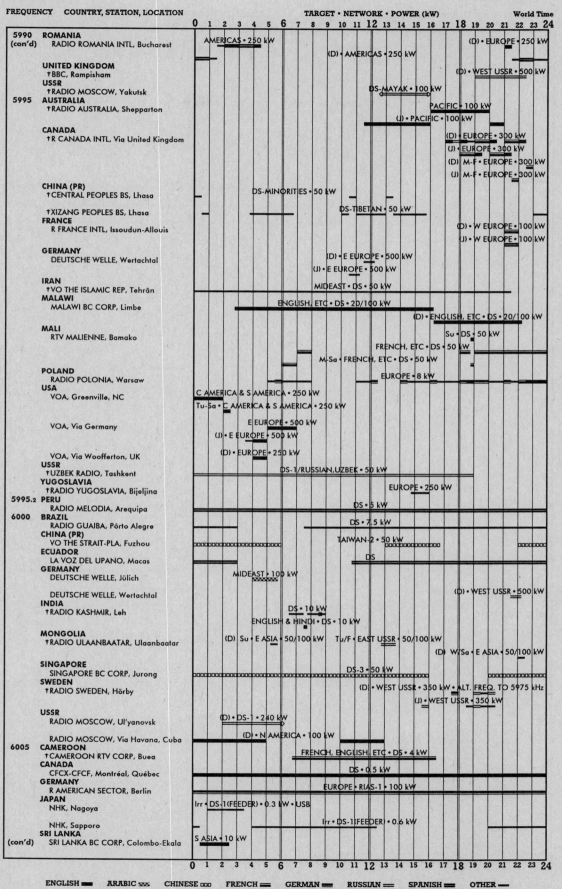

FREQUENCY   COUNTRY, STATION, LOCATION   TARGET • NETWORK • POWER (kW)   World Time

0 1 2 3 4 5 6 7 8 9 10 11 12 13 14 15 16 17 18 19 20 21 22 23 24

5990 **ROMANIA**
(con'd)   RADIO ROMANIA INTL, Bucharest — AMERICAS • 250 kW — (D) • EUROPE • 250 kW

          UNITED KINGDOM
          †BBC, Rampisham
          USSR
          †RADIO MOSCOW, Yakutsk — DS-MAYAK • 100 kW — (D) • WEST USSR • 500 kW
5995 **AUSTRALIA**
          †RADIO AUSTRALIA, Shepparton — PACIFIC • 100 kW — (J) • PACIFIC • 100 kW

          CANADA
          †R CANADA INTL, Via United Kingdom — (D) • EUROPE • 300 kW / (J) • EUROPE • 300 kW / (D) • M-F • EUROPE • 300 kW / (J) • M-F • EUROPE • 300 kW

          CHINA (PR)
          †CENTRAL PEOPLES BS, Lhasa — DS-MINORITIES • 50 kW

          †XIZANG PEOPLES BS, Lhasa — DS-TIBETAN • 50 kW
          FRANCE
          R FRANCE INTL, Issoudun-Allouis — (D) • W EUROPE • 100 kW / (J) • W EUROPE • 100 kW

          GERMANY
          DEUTSCHE WELLE, Wertachtal — (D) • E EUROPE • 500 kW / (J) • E EUROPE • 500 kW

          IRAN
          †VO THE ISLAMIC REP, Tehrān — MIDEAST • DS • 50 kW
          MALAWI
          MALAWI BC CORP, Limbe — ENGLISH, ETC • DS • 20/100 kW / (D) • ENGLISH, ETC • DS • 20/100 kW

          MALI
          RTV MALIENNE, Bamako — Su • DS • 50 kW / FRENCH, ETC • DS • 50 kW / M-Sa • FRENCH, ETC • DS • 50 kW

          POLAND
          RADIO POLONIA, Warsaw — EUROPE • 8 kW
          USA
          VOA, Greenville, NC — C AMERICA & S AMERICA • 250 kW / Tu-Sa • C AMERICA & S AMERICA • 250 kW

          VOA, Via Germany — E EUROPE • 500 kW / (J) • E EUROPE • 500 kW

          VOA, Via Woofferton, UK — (D) • EUROPE • 250 kW
          USSR
          †UZBEK RADIO, Tashkent — DS-1/RUSSIAN, UZBEK • 50 kW
          YUGOSLAVIA
          †RADIO YUGOSLAVIA, Bijeljina — EUROPE • 250 kW
5995.2 **PERU**
          RADIO MELODIA, Arequipa — DS • 5 kW
6000 **BRAZIL**
          RADIO GUAIBA, Pôrto Alegre — DS • 7.5 kW
          CHINA (PR)
          VO THE STRAIT-PLA, Fuzhou — TAIWAN-2 • 50 kW
          ECUADOR
          LA VOZ DEL UPANO, Macas — DS
          GERMANY
          DEUTSCHE WELLE, Jülich — MIDEAST • 100 kW

          DEUTSCHE WELLE, Wertachtal — (D) • WEST USSR • 500 kW
          INDIA
          †RADIO KASHMIR, Leh — DS • 10 kW / ENGLISH & HINDI • DS • 10 kW

          MONGOLIA
          †RADIO ULAANBAATAR, Ulaanbaatar — (D) Su • E ASIA • 50/100 kW / Tu/F • EAST USSR • 50/100 kW / (D) W/Sa • E ASIA • 50/100 kW

          SINGAPORE
          SINGAPORE BC CORP, Jurong — DS-3 • 50 kW
          SWEDEN
          †RADIO SWEDEN, Hörby — (D) • WEST USSR • 350 kW • ALT. FREQ. TO 5975 kHz / (J) • WEST USSR • 350 kW

          USSR
          RADIO MOSCOW, Ul'yanovsk — (D) • DS-1 • 240 kW

          RADIO MOSCOW, Via Havana, Cuba — (D) • N AMERICA • 100 kW
6005 **CAMEROON**
          †CAMEROON RTV CORP, Buea — FRENCH, ENGLISH, ETC • DS • 4 kW
          CANADA
          CFCX-CFCF, Montréal, Québec — DS • 0.5 kW
          GERMANY
          R AMERICAN SECTOR, Berlin — EUROPE • RIAS-1 • 100 kW
          JAPAN
          NHK, Nagoya — Irr • DS-1 (FEEDER) • 0.3 kW • USB

          NHK, Sapporo — Irr • DS-1 (FEEDER) • 0.6 kW
          SRI LANKA
(con'd)   SRI LANKA BC CORP, Colombo-Ekala — S ASIA • 10 kW

0 1 2 3 4 5 6 7 8 9 10 11 12 13 14 15 16 17 18 19 20 21 22 23 24

ENGLISH ▬▬   ARABIC ⌇⌇⌇   CHINESE ▢▢▢   FRENCH ──   GERMAN ▬▬   RUSSIAN ══   SPANISH ▬▬   OTHER ──

complete

FREQUENCY   COUNTRY, STATION, LOCATION   TARGET • NETWORK • POWER (kW)   World Time

0 1 2 3 4 5 6 7 8 9 10 11 12 13 14 15 16 17 18 19 20 21 22 23 24

FREQUENCY	COUNTRY, STATION, LOCATION	TARGET • NETWORK • POWER (kW)
6005 (con'd)	UNITED KINGDOM †BBC, Via Ascension	S AMERICA • 250 kW / C AFRICA & S AFRICA • 250 kW / (D) • W AFRICA • 250 kW / (J) • C AFRICA & S AFRICA • 250 kW
	†BBC, Via Seychelles	E AFRICA • 250 kW
	USSR †KHABAROVSK R, Khabarovsk	DS-2 • 20 kW
	†RADIO MOSCOW, Khabarovsk	DS-MAYAK • 20 kW
	RADIO MOSCOW, Krasnodar	(D) • MIDEAST • 120 kW
	YUGOSLAVIA RADIO YUGOSLAVIA, Bijeljina	WEST USSR • 500 kW
6005.5	COSTA RICA RADIO RELOJ, San José	Irr • DS • 3 kW
6010	BAHRAIN †RADIO BAHRAIN, Abu Hayan	DS • 60 kW
	BRAZIL R INCONFIDENCIA, Belo Horizonte	DS • 25 kW
	CANADA †R CANADA INTL, Via United Kingdom	(D) • EUROPE • 300 kW
	CHINA (PR) †RADIO BEIJING, Kunming	SE ASIA • 50 kW
	CLANDESTINE (ASIA) †"DEM KAMPUCHEA", Kunming, China	SE ASIA • PRO-KHMER ROUGE • 50 kW
	GERMANY †DEUTSCHE WELLE, Königswusterhausen	(D) • WEST USSR • 100 kW
	†DEUTSCHE WELLE, Multiple Locations	(D) • WEST USSR • 100/500 kW
	INDIA ALL INDIA RADIO, Calcutta	DS • 10 kW / ENGLISH & HINDI • DS • 10 kW
	ITALY RTV ITALIANA, Rome	(D) • E EUROPE • 100 kW
	PAKISTAN †RADIO PAKISTAN, Islamabad	MIDEAST • 100 kW
	UNITED KINGDOM BBC, Rampisham	(D) • EUROPE & WEST USSR • 500 kW
	†BBC, Skelton, Cumbria	(D) • EUROPE • 250 kW / (D) • W EUROPE & N AFRICA • 300 kW / (D) • W EUROPE • 300 kW / (J) • EUROPE • 250 kW / (J) • W EUROPE • 250 kW / (D) M-F • EUROPE • 300 kW
	USA VOA, Via Kaválla, Greece	S ASIA • 250 kW
	USSR †LITHUANIAN RADIO, Balashikha	DS-1 • 20 kW
	†RADIO KIEV, Vinnitsa	(D) • EUROPE • 100 kW
	†SOVIET BELORUSSIA, Vinnitsa	(D) M/Tu/Th/F • EUROPE • 100 kW / (D) W/Sa/Su • EUROPE • 100 kW
6010v	MEXICO †RADIO MIL, México City	Irr • DS • 0.25/5 kW
6011v	PERU RADIO AMERICA, Lima	DS • 2.5/5 kW
	VENEZUELA †RADIO LOS ANDES, Mérida	DS • 1 kW
6012	ANTARCTICA AFAN-US MILITARY, McMurdo Base	DS • 1 kW
6014.6	PARAGUAY EMISORAS PARAGUAY, Asunción	DS • 0.3 kW
6015	AUSTRIA RADIO AUSTRIA INTL, Via Sackville, Can	N AMERICA • 250 kW
	GERMANY †DEUTSCHE WELLE, Nauen	(J) • E EUROPE & MIDEAST • 50 kW
	DEUTSCHE WELLE, Wertachtal	(D) • E EUROPE • 500 kW / (J) • E EUROPE • 500 kW
	IVORY COAST RTV IVOIRIENNE, Abidjan	DS • 500 kW
	KOREA (REPUBLIC) KOREAN BC SYSTEM, Hwasung	E ASIA • EDUCATIONAL 1 • 100 kW
	UNITED KINGDOM BBC, Via Zyyi, Cyprus	Su • MIDEAST • 250 kW
	USA †VOA, Via Kaválla, Greece	(D) • MIDEAST & S ASIA • 250 kW / (D) • WEST USSR & MIDEAST • 250 kW / (D) • WEST USSR • 250 kW
	WYFR-FAMILY RADIO, Okeechobee, Fl	(J) • W NORTH AM • 100 kW
	USSR RADIO MOSCOW, Minsk	DS-MAYAK • 100 kW
6015v (con'd)	COLOMBIA †RADIO MIRA, Tumaco	DS • 3 kW

0 1 2 3 4 5 6 7 8 9 10 11 12 13 14 15 16 17 18 19 20 21 22 23 24

SUMMER ONLY (J)   WINTER ONLY (D)   JAMMING / OR ∧   EARLIEST HEARD ◁   LATEST HEARD ▷   NEW OR CHANGED FOR 1992 †

| FREQUENCY | COUNTRY, STATION, LOCATION | TARGET • NETWORK • POWER (kW) | World Time |

Time scale: 0 1 2 3 4 5 6 7 8 9 10 11 12 13 14 15 16 17 18 19 20 21 22 23 24

Frequency	Country / Station / Location	Target • Network • Power
6015v (con'd)	**TANZANIA** VOICE OF TANZANIA, Dole, Zanzibar	DS-SWAHILI • 50 kW
6015.7	**BOLIVIA** RADIO EL MUNDO, Santa Cruz	Su • DS • 10 kW; DS • 10 kW; Irr • Tu-Sa • DS • 10 kW; Tu-Su • DS • 10 kW
6017v	**MEXICO** †RADIO XEUW, Veracruz	Irr • DS • 0.25 kW
6020	**AFGHANISTAN** †RADIO AFGHANISTAN, Via USSR	(D) • EUROPE • 100 kW
	BRAZIL RADIO GAUCHA, Pôrto Alegre	DS • 7.5 kW
	HOLLAND †RADIO NEDERLAND, Flevoland	C AMERICA • 500 kW; E NORTH AM • 500 kW; N AFRICA • 500 kW; EUROPE • 500 kW
	†RADIO NEDERLAND, Via Madagascar	S AFRICA • 300 kW; M-Sa • S AFRICA • 300 kW; Su • S AFRICA • 300 kW
	†RADIO NEDERLAND, Via Neth Antilles	C AMERICA • 300 kW; M-Sa • C AMERICA • 300 kW
	INDIA †ALL INDIA RADIO, Shimla	DS • 2.5 kW; ENGLISH & HINDI • DS • 2.5 kW
	SAUDI ARABIA BS OF THE KINGDOM, Jiddah	MIDEAST • DS-2 • 50 kW • ALT. FREQ. TO 5875 kHz
	SWAZILAND †TRANS WORLD RADIO, Manzini	S AFRICA • 25 kW
	USA †VOA, Greenville, NC	W AFRICA • 250 kW; M-F • W AFRICA • 250 kW
	USSR RADIO MOSCOW, Khabarovsk	(D) • E ASIA & PACIFIC • 50 kW
	†UKRAINIAN RADIO, Kiev	DS-2 • 20 kW
	ZIMBABWE ZIMBABWE BC CORP, Gweru	DS-TEMP INACTIVE • 20/100 kW
6025	**BOLIVIA** RADIO ILLIMANI, La Paz	DS • 10 kW; Tu-Su • DS • 10 kW; M-Sa • DS • 10 kW
	CANADA †R CANADA INTL, Via United Kingdom	(D) • MIDEAST • 300 kW
	CHINA (PR) RADIO BEIJING, Kunming	SE ASIA • 50 kW
	DOMINICAN REPUBLIC RADIO AMANECER, Santo Domingo	DS • 1 kW
	GERMANY DEUTSCHE WELLE, Jülich	(D) • E EUROPE • 500 kW
	DEUTSCHE WELLE, Via Cyclops, Malta	N AFRICA • 250 kW
	HUNGARY †RADIO BUDAPEST	N AMERICA; M • N AMERICA
	RADIO KOSSUTH, Székésfehérvár	EUROPE • DS • 100 kW
	MALAYSIA RADIO TV MALAYSIA, Kajang	DS-5 • 100 kW; Sa/Su • DS-5 • 100 kW
	NIGERIA FEDERAL RADIO CORP, Enugu	DS-ENGLISH, ETC • 10 kW
	PARAGUAY RADIO NACIONAL, Asunción	DS-SPANISH GUARANI • 0.6/2 kW
6025v	**MOZAMBIQUE** EP DE SOFALA, Beira	DS • 10 kW
6029.6	**CHILE** RADIO SANTA MARIA, Coihaique	DS • 10 kW; Tu-Su • DS • 10 kW; M-Sa • DS • 10 kW
6030	**BRAZIL** RADIO GLOBO, Rio de Janeiro	DS • 10 kW
	CANADA CFVP-CFCN, Calgary, Alberta	DS • 0.1 kW
	GERMANY SUDDEUTSCHER RFUNK, Mühlacker	EUROPE • DS-1 • 20 kW
	IRAN †VO THE ISLAMIC REP, Tehrān	Alternative Frequency to 6035 kHz
	PHILIPPINES †FEBC RADIO INTL, Bocaue	SE ASIA • 50 kW
	UNITED KINGDOM †BBC, Multiple Locations	(D) • WEST USSR • 300/500 kW
	†BBC, Rampisham	(D) • EUROPE & WEST USSR • 500 kW; (D) • W EUROPE • 500 kW; (D) M-F • EUROPE & WEST USSR • 500 kW; (J) • W EUROPE • 500 kW
	BBC, Via Maşīrah, Oman	MIDEAST • 100 kW
(con'd)	**USA** †RADIO MARTI, Greenville, NC	C AMERICA • 500 kW

Time scale (bottom): 0 1 2 3 4 5 6 7 8 9 10 11 12 13 14 15 16 17 18 19 20 21 22 23 24

ENGLISH ▬▬ ARABIC ≈≈≈ CHINESE □□□ FRENCH ▬▬ GERMAN ▬▬ RUSSIAN ══ SPANISH ▬▬ OTHER ▬▬

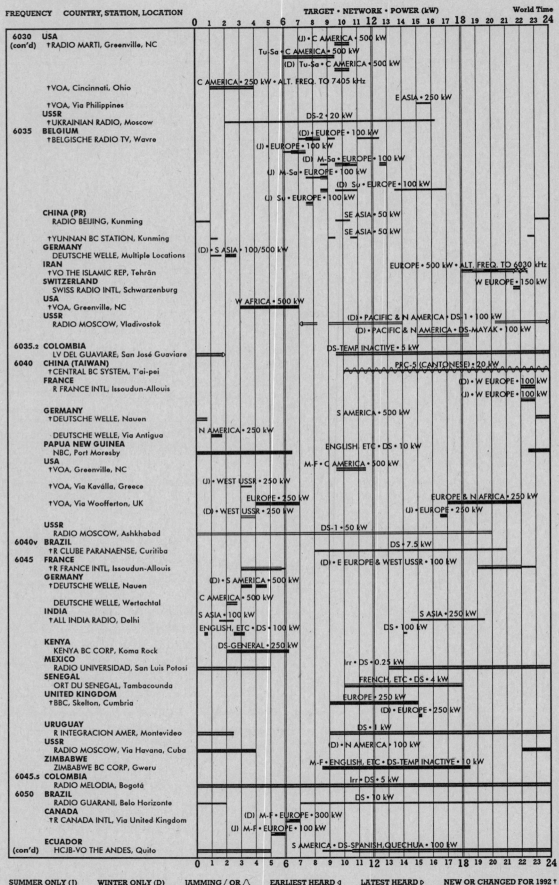

FREQUENCY   COUNTRY, STATION, LOCATION

TARGET • NETWORK • POWER (kW)   World Time

0 1 2 3 4 5 6 7 8 9 10 11 12 13 14 15 16 17 18 19 20 21 22 23 24

Frequency	Country, Station, Location	Target • Network • Power
6030 (con'd)	USA †RADIO MARTI, Greenville, NC	(J) • C AMERICA • 500 kW / Tu-Sa • C AMERICA • 500 kW / (D) Tu-Sa • C AMERICA • 500 kW
	†VOA, Cincinnati, Ohio	C AMERICA • 250 kW • ALT. FREQ. TO 7405 kHz
	†VOA, Via Philippines	E ASIA • 250 kW
	USSR †UKRAINIAN RADIO, Moscow	DS-2 • 20 kW
6035	BELGIUM †BELGISCHE RADIO TV, Wavre	(D) • EUROPE • 100 kW / (J) • EUROPE • 100 kW / (D) M-Sa • EUROPE • 100 kW / (J) M-Sa • EUROPE • 100 kW / (D) Su • EUROPE • 100 kW / (J) Su • EUROPE • 100 kW
	CHINA (PR) RADIO BEIJING, Kunming	SE ASIA • 50 kW
	†YUNNAN BC STATION, Kunming	SE ASIA • 50 kW
	GERMANY DEUTSCHE WELLE, Multiple Locations	(D) • S ASIA • 100/500 kW
	IRAN †VO THE ISLAMIC REP, Tehrān	EUROPE • 500 kW • ALT. FREQ. TO 6030 kHz
	SWITZERLAND SWISS RADIO INTL, Schwarzenburg	W EUROPE • 150 kW
	USA †VOA, Greenville, NC	W AFRICA • 500 kW
	USSR RADIO MOSCOW, Vladivostok	(D) • PACIFIC & N AMERICA • DS-1 • 100 kW / (D) • PACIFIC & N AMERICA • DS-MAYAK • 100 kW
6035.2	COLOMBIA LV DEL GUAVIARE, San José Guaviare	DS-TEMP INACTIVE • 5 kW
6040	CHINA (TAIWAN) †CENTRAL BC SYSTEM, T'ai-pei	PRC-5 (CANTONESE) • 20 kW
	FRANCE R FRANCE INTL, Issoudun-Allouis	(D) • W EUROPE • 100 kW / (J) • W EUROPE • 100 kW
	GERMANY †DEUTSCHE WELLE, Nauen	S AMERICA • 500 kW
	DEUTSCHE WELLE, Via Antigua	N AMERICA • 250 kW
	PAPUA NEW GUINEA NBC, Port Moresby	ENGLISH, ETC • DS • 10 kW
	USA †VOA, Greenville, NC	M-F • C AMERICA • 500 kW
	†VOA, Via Kaválla, Greece	(J) • WEST USSR • 250 kW
	†VOA, Via Woofferton, UK	EUROPE • 250 kW / EUROPE & N AFRICA • 250 kW / (D) • WEST USSR • 250 kW / (J) • EUROPE • 250 kW
	USSR RADIO MOSCOW, Ashkhabad	DS-1 • 50 kW
6040v	BRAZIL †R CLUBE PARANAENSE, Curitiba	DS • 7.5 kW
6045	FRANCE †R FRANCE INTL, Issoudun-Allouis	(D) • E EUROPE & WEST USSR • 100 kW
	GERMANY †DEUTSCHE WELLE, Nauen	(D) • S AMERICA • 500 kW / C AMERICA • 500 kW
	DEUTSCHE WELLE, Wertachtal	
	INDIA †ALL INDIA RADIO, Delhi	S ASIA • 100 kW / S ASIA • 250 kW / ENGLISH, ETC • DS • 100 kW / DS • 100 kW
	KENYA KENYA BC CORP, Koma Rock	DS-GENERAL • 250 kW
	MEXICO RADIO UNIVERSIDAD, San Luis Potosí	Irr • DS • 0.25 kW
	SENEGAL ORT DU SENEGAL, Tambacounda	FRENCH, ETC • DS • 4 kW
	UNITED KINGDOM †BBC, Skelton, Cumbria	EUROPE • 250 kW / (D) • EUROPE • 250 kW
	URUGUAY R INTEGRACION AMER, Montevideo	DS • 1 kW
	USSR RADIO MOSCOW, Via Havana, Cuba	(D) • N AMERICA • 100 kW
	ZIMBABWE ZIMBABWE BC CORP, Gweru	M-F • ENGLISH, ETC • DS-TEMP INACTIVE • 10 kW
6045.5	COLOMBIA RADIO MELODIA, Bogotá	Irr • DS • 5 kW
6050	BRAZIL RADIO GUARANI, Belo Horizonte	DS • 10 kW
	CANADA †R CANADA INTL, Via United Kingdom	(D) M-F • EUROPE • 300 kW / (J) M-F • EUROPE • 100 kW
(con'd)	ECUADOR HCJB-VO THE ANDES, Quito	S AMERICA • DS-SPANISH, QUECHUA • 100 kW

0 1 2 3 4 5 6 7 8 9 10 11 12 13 14 15 16 17 18 19 20 21 22 23 24

SUMMER ONLY (J)   WINTER ONLY (D)   JAMMING / OR ∧   EARLIEST HEARD ◁   LATEST HEARD ▷   NEW OR CHANGED FOR 1992 †

FREQUENCY   COUNTRY, STATION, LOCATION   TARGET • NETWORK • POWER (kW)   World Time

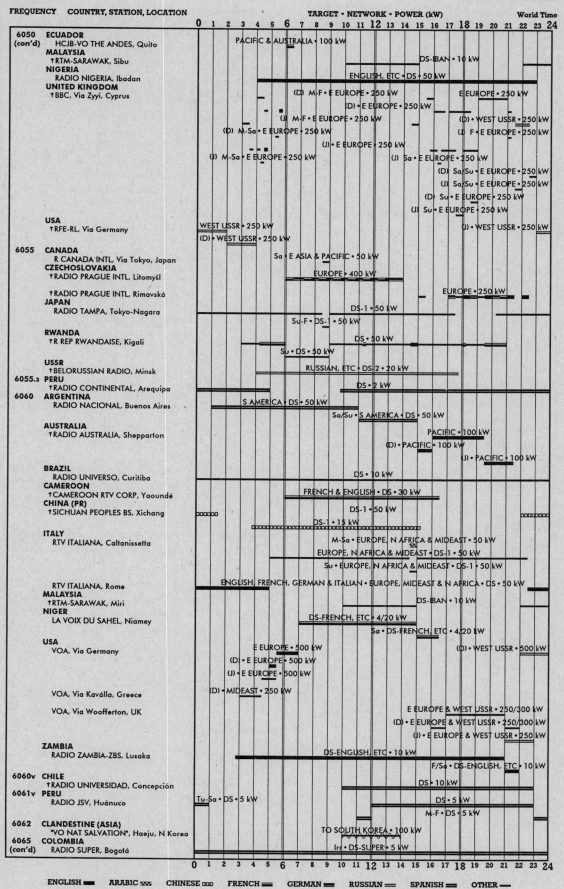

6050	**ECUADOR**	
(con'd)	HCJB-VO THE ANDES, Quito	PACIFIC & AUSTRALIA • 100 kW
	MALAYSIA	
	†RTM-SARAWAK, Sibu	DS-IBAN • 10 kW
	NIGERIA	
	RADIO NIGERIA, Ibadan	ENGLISH, ETC • DS • 50 kW
	UNITED KINGDOM	
	†BBC, Via Zyyi, Cyprus	(D) M-F • E EUROPE • 250 kW E EUROPE • 250 kW
		(D) • E EUROPE • 250 kW
		(J) M-F • E EUROPE • 250 kW (D) • WEST USSR • 250 kW
		(D) M-Sa • E EUROPE • 250 kW (J) F • E EUROPE • 250 kW
		(J) • E EUROPE • 250 kW
		(J) M-Sa • E EUROPE • 250 kW (J) Sa • E EUROPE • 250 kW
		(D) Sa/Su • E EUROPE • 250 kW
		(J) Sa/Su • E EUROPE • 250 kW
		(D) Su • E EUROPE • 250 kW
		(J) Su • E EUROPE • 250 kW
	USA	
	†RFE-RL, Via Germany	WEST USSR • 250 kW
		(D) • WEST USSR • 250 kW (J) • WEST USSR • 250 kW
6055	**CANADA**	
	R CANADA INTL, Via Tokyo, Japan	Sa • E ASIA & PACIFIC • 50 kW
	CZECHOSLOVAKIA	
	†RADIO PRAGUE INTL, Litomyšl	EUROPE • 400 kW
	†RADIO PRAGUE INTL, Rimavská	EUROPE • 250 kW
	JAPAN	
	RADIO TAMPA, Tokyo-Nagara	DS-1 • 50 kW
		Su-F • DS-1 • 50 kW
	RWANDA	
	†R REP RWANDAISE, Kigali	DS • 50 kW
		Su • DS • 50 kW
	USSR	
	†BELORUSSIAN RADIO, Minsk	RUSSIAN, ETC • DS-2 • 20 kW
6055.3	**PERU**	
	†RADIO CONTINENTAL, Arequipa	DS • 2 kW
6060	**ARGENTINA**	
	RADIO NACIONAL, Buenos Aires	S AMERICA • DS • 50 kW
		Sa/Su • S AMERICA • DS • 50 kW
	AUSTRALIA	
	†RADIO AUSTRALIA, Shepparton	PACIFIC • 100 kW
		(D) • PACIFIC • 100 kW
		(J) • PACIFIC • 100 kW
	BRAZIL	
	RADIO UNIVERSO, Curitiba	DS • 10 kW
	CAMEROON	
	†CAMEROON RTV CORP, Yaoundé	FRENCH & ENGLISH • DS • 30 kW
	CHINA (PR)	
	†SICHUAN PEOPLES BS, Xichang	DS-1 • 50 kW
		DS-1 • 15 kW
	ITALY	
	RTV ITALIANA, Caltanissetta	M-Sa • EUROPE, N AFRICA & MIDEAST • 50 kW
		EUROPE, N AFRICA & MIDEAST • DS-1 • 50 kW
		Su • EUROPE, N AFRICA & MIDEAST • DS-1 • 50 kW
	RTV ITALIANA, Rome	ENGLISH, FRENCH, GERMAN & ITALIAN • EUROPE, MIDEAST & N AFRICA • DS • 50 kW
	MALAYSIA	
	†RTM-SARAWAK, Miri	DS-IBAN • 10 kW
	NIGER	
	LA VOIX DU SAHEL, Niamey	DS-FRENCH, ETC • 4/20 kW
		Sa • DS-FRENCH, ETC • 4/20 kW
	USA	
	VOA, Via Germany	E EUROPE • 500 kW
		(D) • E EUROPE • 500 kW (D) • WEST USSR • 500 kW
		(J) • E EUROPE • 500 kW
	VOA, Via Kaválla, Greece	(D) • MIDEAST • 250 kW
	VOA, Via Woofferton, UK	E EUROPE & WEST USSR • 250/300 kW
		(D) • E EUROPE & WEST USSR • 250/300 kW
		(J) • E EUROPE & WEST USSR • 250 kW
	ZAMBIA	
	RADIO ZAMBIA-ZBS, Lusaka	DS-ENGLISH, ETC • 10 kW
		F/Sa • DS-ENGLISH, ETC • 10 kW
6060v	**CHILE**	
	†RADIO UNIVERSIDAD, Concepción	DS • 10 kW
6061v	**PERU**	
	RADIO JSV, Huánuco	Tu-Sa • DS • 5 kW DS • 5 kW
		M-F • DS • 5 kW
6062	**CLANDESTINE (ASIA)**	
	"VO NAT SALVATION", Haeju, N Korea	TO SOUTH KOREA • 100 kW
6065	**COLOMBIA**	
(con'd)	RADIO SUPER, Bogotá	Irr • DS-SUPER • 5 kW

ENGLISH ▬▬   ARABIC ≋≋   CHINESE □□□   FRENCH ══   GERMAN ▬▬   RUSSIAN ══   SPANISH ══   OTHER ▬▬

FREQUENCY   COUNTRY, STATION, LOCATION   TARGET • NETWORK • POWER (kW)   World Time

| | 0 1 2 3 4 5 6 7 8 9 10 11 12 13 14 15 16 17 18 19 20 21 22 23 24 |

6065 **GERMANY**
(con'd) †DEUTSCHE WELLE, Wertachtal — (D) • AFRICA • 500 kW ; (D) • AFRICA • 100 kW

INDIA
†ALL INDIA RADIO, Kohima — DS • 50 kW ; ENGLISH & HINDI • DS • 50 kW

PAKISTAN
PAKISTAN BC CORP, Islamabad — S ASIA • 100 kW

SWEDEN
†RADIO SWEDEN, Hörby — (D) • EUROPE • 350 kW ; (J) • EUROPE • 350 kW ; (D) Sa/Su • EUROPE • 350 kW ; (J) Sa/Su • EUROPE • 350 kW

†RADIO SWEDEN, Karlsborg — (D) M-F • EUROPE • 350 kW ; EUROPE • 350 kW ; (D) • EUROPE • 350 kW ; (J) • EUROPE • 350 kW ; (J) M-F • EUROPE • 350 kW ; (D) Sa/Su • EUROPE • 350 kW ; (J) Sa/Su • EUROPE • 350 kW ; (D) Su • EUROPE • 350 kW ; (J) Su • EUROPE • 350 kW

UNITED KINGDOM
†BBC, Via Singapore — SE ASIA • 250 kW ; (J) • SE ASIA • 250 kW ; (J) • S ASIA • 250 kW ; (J) • S ASIA & SE ASIA • 250 kW ; (J) M-Sa • S ASIA • 250 kW ; (J) Su • S ASIA • 250 kW

†BBC, Via Zyyi, Cyprus — S ASIA • 250 kW

USA
†WYFR-FAMILY RADIO, Okeechobee, Fl — E NORTH AM • 100 kW

USSR
†RADIO MOSCOW, Khabarovsk — E ASIA • 100 kW

RADIO YEREVAN, Yerevan — MIDEAST • 100 kW

6068v **PAKISTAN (AZAD K)**
†AZAD KASHMIR RADIO, Via Islamabad — DS • 10/100 kW

6069.7 **THAILAND**
RADIO THAILAND, Pathum Thani — DS-1 • 10 kW

6070 **BRAZIL**
RADIO CAPITAL, Rio de Janeiro — DS-VERY IRREGULAR • 7.5 kW

BULGARIA
†RADIO SOFIA, Sofia — (D) • EUROPE • 250 kW

†RADIO SOFIA, Stolnik — (D) • EUROPE, MIDEAST & N AFRICA • 150 kW ; (D) Su • EUROPE, MIDEAST & N AFRICA • 150 kW

CANADA
CFRX-CFRB, Toronto, Ontario — DS • 1 kW

INDONESIA
†RRI, Jayapura, Irian Jaya — DS • 20 kW

UNITED KINGDOM
BBC, Via Zyyi, Cyprus — (D) • WEST USSR • 250 kW

USA
†RFE-RL, Via Germany — E EUROPE • 100 kW

USSR
RADIO MOSCOW, Khar'kov — DS-MAYAK • 100 kW

RADIO MOSCOW, Novosibirsk — (D) • DS-1 • 100 kW

6070v **PAKISTAN**
PAKISTAN BC CORP, Peshawar — (J) • DS-ENGLISH, ETC • 10 kW

PAKISTAN BC CORP, Rawalpindi — (D) • DS-ENGLISH, ETC • 10 kW

6075 **COLOMBIA**
CARACOL BOGOTA, Bogotá — Irr • DS • 10 kW

GERMANY
†DEUTSCHE WELLE, Multiple Locations — EUROPE & E NORTH AM • 100/250/500 kW ; EUROPE & AMERICAS • 100/250 kW ; EUROPE & AFRICA • 500 kW ; EUROPE & N AMERICA • 100/250 kW ; EUROPE • 100/250/500 kW

KENYA
KENYA BC CORP, Koma Rock — DS-NATIONAL • 250 kW

SRI LANKA
SRI LANKA BC CORP, Colombo-Ekala — S ASIA • 10 kW

USA
RADIO MARTI, Cincinnati, Ohio — C AMERICA • 250 kW

USSR
†MOLDOVAN RADIO, Tula — RUSSIAN, ETC • DS-1 • 20 kW

6075v **HONDURAS**
LA VOZ DEL JUNCO, Santa Barbara — DS • 3 kW

6078.8 **BOLIVIA**
RADIO SAN GABRIEL, La Paz — Tu-Su • DS • 5 kW ; DS • 5 kW ; M-Sa • DS • 5 kW

| | 0 1 2 3 4 5 6 7 8 9 10 11 12 13 14 15 16 17 18 19 20 21 22 23 24 |

SUMMER ONLY (J)   WINTER ONLY (D)   JAMMING / OR ∧   EARLIEST HEARD ◁   LATEST HEARD ▷   NEW OR CHANGED FOR 1992 †

FREQUENCY   COUNTRY, STATION, LOCATION   TARGET • NETWORK • POWER (kW)   World Time

0 1 2 3 4 5 6 7 8 9 10 11 12 13 14 15 16 17 18 19 20 21 22 23 24

Frequency	Country / Station / Location	Details
6080	ALBANIA †RADIO TIRANA, Lushnjë	EUROPE • 50 kW
	AUSTRALIA †RADIO AUSTRALIA, Shepparton	PACIFIC • 100 kW
	BRAZIL †R NOVAS DE PAZ, Curitiba	DS • 10 kW
	†RADIO ANHANGUERA, Goiânia	Irr • DS • 10 kW DS • 10 kW
	CANADA CKFX-CKWX, Vancouver, BC	DS • 0.01 kW
	CHILE †RADIO PATAGONIA, Coihaique	DS • 1 kW
	ECUADOR HCJB-VO THE ANDES, Quito	DS-SPANISH, QUECHUA • 10 kW
	IRAN †VO THE ISLAMIC REP, Tehrān	(J) • N AFRICA & MIDEAST • 500 kW
	JAPAN †RADIO JAPAN/NHK, Tokyo-Yamata	Alternative Frequency to 6185 kHz
	PAPUA NEW GUINEA NBC, Port Moresby	ENGLISH, ETC • DS • 10 kW
	UNITED KINGDOM †BBC, Via Singapore	SE ASIA & E ASIA • 250 kW SE ASIA • 250 kW (D) • SE ASIA • 250 kW
	USA †VOA, Via Woofferton, UK	(D) • WEST USSR & MIDEAST • 300 kW (J) • E EUROPE • 250 kW
	USSR †BELORUSSIAN RADIO, Minsk	RUSSIAN, ETC • DS-1 • 20 kW
	RADIO MOSCOW, Komsomol'sk 'Amure	DS-1 • 50 kW (D) • DS-1 • 50 kW DS-MAYAK • 50 kW
	RADIO MOSCOW, Novosibirsk	(D) • DS-1 • 100 kW (D) • DS-MAYAK • 100 kW
	†UKRAINIAN RADIO, Kiev	DS-2 • 20 kW
6085	AFGHANISTAN RADIO AFGHANISTAN, Kabul	S ASIA & MIDEAST • 7.5 kW
	BULGARIA †RADIO SOFIA, Stolnik	(J) • EUROPE, MIDEAST & N AFRICA • 150 kW (J) Su • EUROPE, MIDEAST & N AFRICA • 150 kW
	GERMANY BAYERISCHER RFUNK, Ismaning	DS-1, ARD-NACHT • 100 kW
	†DEUTSCHE WELLE, Via Sackville, Can	N AMERICA & C AMERICA • 250 kW
	†DEUTSCHE WELLE, Wertachtal	(D) • N AMERICA & C AMERICA • 500 kW
	INDIA †ALL INDIA RADIO, Delhi	DS • 50 kW ENGLISH, ETC • DS • 50 kW
	OMAN RADIO OMAN, Sīb	MIDEAST & N AFRICA • DS • 100 kW (D) • MIDEAST & N AFRICA • DS • 100 kW Irr • MIDEAST & N AFRICA • DS-RAMADAN • 100 kW
	UNITED KINGDOM †BBC, Via Zyyi, Cyprus	(D) • E EUROPE • 250 kW (D) • E EUROPE & MIDEAST • 250 kW (J) • E EUROPE & MIDEAST • 250 kW (D) Sa/Su • E EUROPE • 250 kW
	USA VOA, Via Kaválla, Greece	(D) • USSR • 250 kW
	†WYFR-FAMILY RADIO, Okeechobee, Fl	C AMERICA • 50 kW C AMERICA • 100 kW
6087	CHINA (TAIWAN) †CENTRAL BC SYSTEM, T'ai-pei	PRC-4 • 50/100 kW
6088.6	CHILE †RADIO ESPERANZA, Temuco	Sa • DS DS
6090	BRAZIL RADIO BANDEIRANTES, São Paulo	DS • 10 kW
		Irr • DS • 10 kW
	CAMBODIA VO THE PEOPLE, Phnom Penh	DS • 50 kW Su • DS • 50 kW
	CHILE †RADIO ESPERANZA, Temuco	M • DS • 1 kW DS • 1 kW Su • DS • 1 kW
	LUXEMBOURG †RADIO LUXEMBOURG, Junglinster	EUROPE • 500 kW
	NIGERIA RADIO NIGERIA, Kaduna	DS-1 • 50/250 kW
	USA VOA, Via Germany	(J) • WEST USSR • 500 kW
	†VOA, Via Portugal	(D) • WEST USSR • 250 kW
(con'd)	USSR †IRKUTSK RADIO, Irkutsk	DS • 50 kW

0 1 2 3 4 5 6 7 8 9 10 11 12 13 14 15 16 17 18 19 20 21 22 23 24

ENGLISH ▬▬   ARABIC ▨▨   CHINESE ▭▭▭   FRENCH ▬▬   GERMAN ▬▬   RUSSIAN ══   SPANISH ▬▬   OTHER ▬▬

FREQUENCY   COUNTRY, STATION, LOCATION   TARGET • NETWORK • POWER (kW)   World Time

6090 **USSR**
(con'd)   †RADIO KIEV, Kiev — (D) • EUROPE • 100 kW

†RADIO MOSCOW, Orenburg — (D) • DS-1 • 100 kW

†SOVIET BELORUSSIA, Kiev — (D) M/Tu/Th/F • EUROPE • 100 kW
(D) W/Sa/Su • EUROPE • 100 kW

6090v **PAKISTAN**
PAKISTAN BC CORP, Islamabad — DS-ENGLISH, ETC • 100 kW
6094v **BOLIVIA** — DS-TEMP INACTIVE • 1 kW
†RADIO COSMOS, Cochabamba — M-Sa • DS-TEMP INACTIVE • 1 kW

6095 **CANADA**
†R CANADA INTL, Via In-Kimjae, Korea — E ASIA • 250 kW
CHINA (PR)
†CENTRAL PEOPLES BS, Nanchang — CHINESE, ETC • TAIWAN-2 • 50 kW
POLAND
RADIO POLONIA, Warsaw — ATLANTIC & N AMERICA • 100 kW / EUROPE • 100 kW
EUROPE & N AFRICA • 100 kW

USA
KNLS-NEW LIFE STN, Anchor Pt, Alaska — (D) • EAST USSR • 100 kW

†RFE-RL, Via Portugal — (D) • WEST USSR • 250 kW

†VOA, Greenville, NC — (D) • C AMERICA • 250 kW

†VOA, Via Rhodes, Greece — (J) • MIDEAST • 50 kW

†VOA, Via Tangier, Morocco — (J) • N AFRICA • 100 kW

VOA, Via Woofferton, UK — (D) • E EUROPE & WEST USSR • 250 kW
USSR
†BELORUSSIAN RADIO, Minsk — RUSSIAN, ETC • DS-2 • 20 kW

RADIO MOSCOW, Kalinin — (D) • DS-1 • 100 kW

RADIO MOSCOW, Serpuhkov — (D) • DS • 100 kW
6100 **AFGHANISTAN**
RADIO AFGHANISTAN, Kabul — DS-2 • 100 kW

RADIO KABUL, Kabul — DS • 100 kW
CENTRAL AFRICAN REP
RTV CENTRAFRICAINE, Bangui — FRENCH, ETC • DS • 20 kW
CHINA (PR)
†XINJIANG PBS, Urümqi — DS-CHINESE • 50 kW
GERMANY
†DEUTSCHE WELLE, Wertachtal — E NORTH AM & C AMERICA • 100/500 kW
ICELAND
†RIKISUTVARPID, Reykjavik — ATLANTIC & EUROPE • DS-1 • 10 kW • USB
M-F • ATLANTIC & EUROPE • DS-1 • 10 kW • USB
Sa/Su • ATLANTIC & EUROPE • DS-1 • 10 kW • USB

KENYA
KENYA BC CORP, Koma Rock — DS-GENERAL • 250 kW
KOREA (DPR)
KOREAN CENTRAL BS, Kanggye — DS • 200 kW
MALAYSIA
VOICE OF MALAYSIA, Kajang — SE ASIA • 100 kW
USSR
†LITHUANIAN RADIO, Kaunas — Alternative Frequency to 9710 kHz

RADIO MOSCOW, Kenga — (D) • E ASIA • 100 kW

†RADIO VILNIUS, Kaunas — Alternative Frequency to 9710 kHz
YUGOSLAVIA
†RADIO YUGOSLAVIA, Bijeljina — EUROPE, N AFRICA & MIDEAST • 250 kW
(D) • EUROPE & E NORTH AM • 500 kW

6105 **BRAZIL**
†R CANCAO NOVA, Cachoeira Paulista — DS • 5 kW

†RADIO CULTURA, Foz do Iguaçú — Irr • DS • 5 kW
ROMANIA
RADIO ROMANIA INTL, Bucharest — (D) • WEST USSR • 250 kW
(D) • EUROPE • 250 kW

TANZANIA
†RADIO TANZANIA, Dar es Salaam — DS-SWAHILI • 100 kW
USA
†RFE-RL, Various Locations — WEST USSR • 100/250 kW
(D) • WEST USSR • 250 kW

WYFR-FAMILY RADIO, Okeechobee, Fl — (D) • S AMERICA • 100 kW
USSR
RADIO MOSCOW, Kalinin — DS-1 • 120 kW
(D) • DS-1 • 120 kW

RADIO MOSCOW, L'vov — (D) • E NORTH AM & C AMERICA • 500 kW
6105v **BRAZIL**
†RADIO CULTURA, Foz do Iguaçú — Irr • DS • 5 kW
MEXICO
RADIO XEQM, Mérida — Irr • DS • 0.25 kW
6105.5 **BOLIVIA**
(con'd) RADIO PANAMERICANA, La Paz — Tu-Sa • DS • 10 kW / DS • 10 kW

0 1 2 3 4 5 6 7 8 9 10 11 12 13 14 15 16 17 18 19 20 21 22 23 24

FREQUENCY   COUNTRY, STATION, LOCATION

TARGET • NETWORK • POWER (kW)

World Time

0 1 2 3 4 5 6 7 8 9 10 11 12 13 14 15 16 17 18 19 20 21 22 23 24

Frequency	Country, Station, Location	Details
6105.5 (con'd)	BOLIVIA RADIO PANAMERICANA, La Paz	Irr • Tu-Sa • DS • 10 kW / M-Sa • DS • 10 kW
6110	BULGARIA †RADIO SOFIA, Sofia	(D) • E EUROPE & MIDEAST • 100 kW
	ECUADOR †HCJB-VO THE ANDES, Quito	S AMERICA • 100 kW
	HUNGARY †RADIO BUDAPEST	N AMERICA / EUROPE / M-Sa • EUROPE / Su • EUROPE
	INDIA †RADIO KASHMIR, Srinagar	DS-B • 50 kW / (J) • DS-B • 50 kW / Su • DS-B • 50 kW / ENGLISH, ETC • DS-B • 50 kW
	UNITED KINGDOM BBC, Multiple Locations	C AMERICA & S AMERICA • 125/250 kW
	†BBC, Skelton, Cumbria	(D) • N AFRICA • 300 kW
	†BBC, Via Antigua	C AMERICA & S AMERICA • 125 kW / (D) • S AMERICA • 250 kW
	†BBC, Via Ascension	(D) • C AMERICA & S AMERICA • 125 kW / M-F • C AMERICA • 250 kW / (J) • S AMERICA • 250 kW
	USA †VOA, Via Philippines	SE ASIA • 250 kW / (D) • E ASIA • 250 kW
	†VOA, Via Tangier, Morocco	(D) • N AFRICA • 50 kW
	USSR RADIO BAKU, Baku	MIDEAST • ARABIC, PERSIAN, ETC • 200 kW
	RADIO MOSCOW, Baku	MIDEAST • DS-MAYAK • 200 kW
	RADIO MOSCOW, Novosibirsk	(D) • E ASIA • 100 kW
6112v	MOZAMBIQUE RADIO MOCAMBIQUE, Maputo	Irr • DS • 100 kW
6115	CHINA (PR) †VO THE STRAIT-PLA, Fuzhou	TAIWAN-1 • 50 kW
	GERMANY †DEUTSCHE WELLE, Königswusterhausen	EUROPE • 50 kW / (J) • EUROPE • 50 kW / (D) • EUROPE • 50 kW
	†DEUTSCHE WELLE, Nauen	(D) • EUROPE • 100 kW / (D) • WEST USSR • 100 kW
	INDIA †ALL INDIA RADIO, Madras	DS • 100 kW
	JAPAN RADIO TAMPA, Tokyo-Nagara	DS-2 • 50 kW
	MEXICO RADIO UNIVERSIDAD, Hermosillo	DS • 1 kW
	PERU RADIO UNION, Lima	DS • 10 kW / M-Sa • DS • 10 kW / Su • DS • 10 kW
	USA †RFE-RL, Via Germany	(D) • E EUROPE • 100 kW
	†RFE-RL, Via Portugal	(J) • WEST USSR • 250 kW
	USSR †BELORUSSIAN RADIO, Orcha	RUSSIAN, ETC • DS-2 • 20 kW
	†RADIO KUDYMKAR, Sverdlovsk	M-Sa • DS • 20 kW
	†RADIO MOSCOW, Khabarovsk	EAST USSR & PACIFIC • DS-1/TIKHIY OKEAN • 100 kW
	†RADIO MOSCOW, Sverdlovsk	DS-1 • 20 kW / Su • DS-1 • 20 kW
	†RADIO NOVAYA VOLNA, Novosibirsk	Irr • DS • 20 kW
	†RADIO PERM, Sverdlovsk	DS • 20 kW
	†TATAR RADIO, Zhigulevsk	DS-RUSSIAN, TATAR • 20 kW
6116	COLOMBIA LA VOZ DEL LLANO, Villavicencio	DS • 2/10 kW
6120	BRAZIL RADIO GLOBO, São Paulo	Irr • DS • 7.5 kW / DS • 7.5 kW
	CANADA R CANADA INTL, Sackville, NB	Su/M • E NORTH AM • 250 kW
	FINLAND †RADIO FINLAND, Pori	EUROPE • 100 kW
	GERMANY †DEUTSCHE WELLE, Jülich	(D) • N AMERICA • 100 kW
	†DEUTSCHE WELLE, Multiple Locations	N AMERICA • 100/500 kW
	INDIA ALL INDIA RADIO, Hyderabad	DS • 10 kW / Su • DS • 10 kW
(con'd)		

0 1 2 3 4 5 6 7 8 9 10 11 12 13 14 15 16 17 18 19 20 21 22 23 24

ENGLISH ▬   ARABIC ⬚⬚⬚   CHINESE □□□   FRENCH ▬   GERMAN ▬   RUSSIAN ═   SPANISH ▬   OTHER ▬

FREQUENCY   COUNTRY, STATION, LOCATION   TARGET • NETWORK • POWER (kW)   World Time

		0 1 2 3 4 5 6 7 8 9 10 11 12 13 14 15 16 17 18 19 20 21 22 23 24

6120 **INDIA**
(con'd)   ALL INDIA RADIO, Hyderabad — ENGLISH & HINDI • DS • 10 kW
           JAPAN
           RADIO JAPAN/NHK, Via Sackville, Can — N AMERICA • GENERAL • 250 kW
           (D) • N AMERICA • GENERAL • 250 kW
           (J) • N AMERICA • GENERAL • 250 kW

           USSR
           †BELORUSSIAN RADIO, Minsk — RUSSIAN, ETC • DS-2 • 20 kW
           RADIO MOSCOW, Moscow — (D) • E EUROPE & W AFRICA • 250 kW
           †RADIO YEREVAN — (D) • EUROPE / (D) M-Sa • EUROPE / (D) Su • EUROPE

6121v **ALBANIA**
           †RADIO TIRANA, Krujë — S AMERICA • 100 kW   E NORTH AM • 100 kW
6125 **ALBANIA**
           †RADIO TIRANA, Lushnjë — EUROPE • 50 kW
           CHINA (PR)
           CENTRAL PEOPLES BS, Shijiazhuang — DS-1 • 50 kW
           KOREA (DPR)
           †RADIO PYONGYANG, Pyongyang — E ASIA • 200 kW
           SWITZERLAND
           †RED CROSS BC SVC, Schwarzenburg — Irr • Tu/F • C AMERICA & S AMERICA • 150 kW
           †SWISS RADIO INTL, Schwarzenburg — C AMERICA & S AMERICA • 150 kW
           M • C AMERICA & S AMERICA • 150 kW
           Tu-Su • C AMERICA & S AMERICA • 150 kW

           UNITED KINGDOM
           †BBC, Daventry — EUROPE • 300 kW
           Su • EUROPE & N AFRICA • 300 kW

           †BBC, Skelton, Cumbria — EUROPE • 250 kW
           EUROPE • 250 kW
           †BBC, Via Zyyi, Cyprus — E EUROPE & MIDEAST • 250 kW
           M-Sa • E EUROPE & MIDEAST • 250 kW
           Sa/Su • EUROPE • 250 kW

           USA
           VOA, Cincinnati, Ohio — N AFRICA • 250 kW
           †VOA, Via Philippines — (D) • SE ASIA • 250 kW
           †VOA, Via Woofferton, UK — (D) • E EUROPE • 250 kW
           (J) • E EUROPE • 300 kW

           USSR
           †KAZAKH RADIO, Various Locations — DS-2 • 20 kW
           †MARIY RADIO, Yoshkar Ola — DS • 20 kW
6127 **INDONESIA**
           †RRI, Nabire, Irian Jaya — DS • 0.5 kW
6130 **CANADA**
           CHNX-CHNS, Halifax, NS — DS • 0.5 kW
           GERMANY
           DEUTSCHE WELLE, Jülich — (D) • N AMERICA • 100 kW
           †DEUTSCHE WELLE, Königswusterhausen — (D) • E EUROPE & MIDEAST • 50 kW
           DEUTSCHE WELLE, Wertachtal — (D) • WEST USSR • 500 kW   (D) • E EUROPE • 500 kW   (D) • W EUROPE • 500 kW
           (J) • E EUROPE • 500 kW   (J) • W EUROPE • 500 kW

           GHANA
           RADIO GHANA, Accra — W AFRICA • 100 kW
           JAPAN
           NHK, Fukuoka — Irr • DS-1 (FEEDER) • 0.6 kW • USB
           PORTUGAL
           R PORTUGAL INTL, Lisbon — M-F • EUROPE • 100 kW
           SAUDI ARABIA
           †BS OF THE KINGDOM — MIDEAST • DS-GENERAL
           USA
           VOA, Greenville, NC — C AMERICA & S AMERICA • 500 kW
           †WYFR-FAMILY RADIO, Okeechobee, Fl — (D) • EUROPE • 100 kW
           USSR
           RADIO MOSCOW, Moscow — EUROPE • 240 kW
           RADIO MOSCOW, Novosibirsk — (D) • DS-MAYAK • 100 kW
           RADIO MOSCOW, Star'obel'sk — (J) • EUROPE • 100 kW
6130v **LAOS**
           LAO NATIONAL RADIO, Vientiane — DS • 10 kW
           PAKISTAN
           PAKISTAN BC CORP, Islamabad — (D) • DS • 100 kW   DS-ENGLISH, ETC • 100 kW
           PAKISTAN BC CORP, Rawalpindi — Th-Sa • DS • 10 kW
           DS-ENGLISH, ETC • 10 kW

6134 **INDONESIA**
           †RRI, Samarinda, Kalimantan — DS • 1 kW
6135 **BOLIVIA**
(con'd)   RADIO SANTA CRUZ, Santa Cruz — DS-SPANISH, ETC • 10 kW

		0 1 2 3 4 5 6 7 8 9 10 11 12 13 14 15 16 17 18 19 20 21 22 23 24

SUMMER ONLY (J)   WINTER ONLY (D)   JAMMING / OR ∧   EARLIEST HEARD ◁   LATEST HEARD ▷   NEW OR CHANGED FOR 1992 †

| FREQUENCY | COUNTRY, STATION, LOCATION | TARGET • NETWORK • POWER (kW) | World Time |

Time scale: 0 1 2 3 4 5 6 7 8 9 10 11 12 13 14 15 16 17 18 19 20 21 22 23 24

6135
(con'd)
BOLIVIA
  RADIO SANTA CRUZ, Santa Cruz — Irr • DS • 10 kW | M-Sa • DS-SPANISH, ETC • 10 kW
BRAZIL
  RADIO APARECIDA, Aparecida — DS • 7.5 kW
BULGARIA
  †RADIO SOFIA, Plovdiv — (D) • MIDEAST • 500 kW
KOREA (REPUBLIC)
  KOREAN BC SYSTEM, Hwasung — E ASIA • EDUCATIONAL-2 • 10 kW
  RADIO KOREA, Hwasung — E ASIA • 10 kW
MADAGASCAR
  RTV MALAGASY, Antananarivo — DS-1 • 100 kW
POLAND
  RADIO POLONIA, Warsaw — W AFRICA, ATLANTIC & S AMERICA • 100 kW | EUROPE • 100 kW
  W EUROPE & N AFRICA • 100 kW
  (D) • EUROPE • 100 kW
SWITZERLAND
  RED CROSS BC SVC, Schwarzenburg — Irr • Tu/F • N AMERICA & C AMERICA • 150 kW
  SWISS RADIO INTL, Schwarzenburg — N AMERICA & C AMERICA • 150 kW
  M • N AMERICA & C AMERICA • 150 kW
  Tu-Su • N AMERICA & C AMERICA • 150 kW
USA
  †RFE-RL, Via Germany — WEST USSR • 100/250 kW
  (D) • WEST USSR • 100/250 kW
  (J) • WEST USSR • 100/250 kW
  †RFE-RL, Via Portugal — (D) • WEST USSR • 500 kW
USSR
  AZERBAIJANI RADIO, Baku — DS-2 • 100 kW
  RADIO ALMA-ATA, Alma-Ata — (D) • E ASIA • 100 kW
  RADIO BAKU, Baku — MIDEAST • ARABIC, PERSIAN ETC • 100 kW
  RADIO TASHKENT, Alma-Ata — (D) • E ASIA • 100 kW
YEMEN (REPUBLIC)
  REP YEMEN RADIO, San'ā — E AFRICA • DS • 300 kW
  F • E AFRICA • DS • 300 kW

6135.4
FRENCH POLYNESIA
  †RFO-TAHITI, Papeete — DS-FRENCH, TAHITIAN • 4 kW
6140
AUSTRALIA
  AUSTRALIAN BC CORP, Perth — DS • 10 kW
BURUNDI
  LA VOIX DE LA REV, Gitega — DS • 100 kW | Su • DS • 100 kW
  Su • DS-FRENCH, ETC • 100 kW | M-F • DS • 100 kW
  Sa/Su • DS • 100 kW
  DS-FRENCH, ETC • 100 kW
  M-F • DS-FRENCH, ETC • 100 kW
  M-Sa • DS-FRENCH, ETC • 100 kW
  Sa/Su • DS-FRENCH, ETC • 100 kW
CHINA (PR)
  RADIO BEIJING, Baoding — EAST USSR • 120 kW
  RADIO BEIJING, Kunming — SE ASIA • 50 kW
CLANDESTINE (ASIA)
  †"AFGHAN MOJAHEDIN" — MIDEAST & S ASIA • ANTI-AFGHAN GOVT
GERMANY
  DEUTSCHE WELLE, Wertachtal — (D) • E EUROPE & MIDEAST • 500 kW
  (J) • E EUROPE & MIDEAST • 500 kW
INDIA
  †ALL INDIA RADIO, Delhi — S ASIA • 50 kW
  DS • 50 kW
  ENGLISH & HINDI • DS • 50 kW
  ALL INDIA RADIO, Ranchi — DS-A • 2 kW
  Su • DS-A • 2 kW
  ENGLISH & HINDI • DS-A • 2 kW
PAPUA NEW GUINEA
  NBC, Port Moresby — ENGLISH, ETC • DS • 10 kW
PERU
  RADIO HUAYLLAY, Huayllay — DS • 1 kW
  M-Sa • DS • 1 kW
TURKEY
  VOICE OF TURKEY, Ankara — E EUROPE • 250 kW
URUGUAY
  RADIO MONTE CARLO, Montevideo — DS • 1.5 kW
  RADIO ORIENTAL, Montevideo — Irr • DS • 1.5 kW
USA
  †VOA, Via Kaválla, Greece — (D) • WEST USSR & MIDEAST • 250 kW
  VOA, Via Woofferton, UK — EUROPE • 250 kW | (D) • WEST USSR • 250 kW
  (J) • WEST USSR • 300 kW

(con'd)

Time scale: 0 1 2 3 4 5 6 7 8 9 10 11 12 13 14 15 16 17 18 19 20 21 22 23 24

ENGLISH ▬   ARABIC ░░░   CHINESE ▫▫▫   FRENCH ▬▬   GERMAN ▬▬   RUSSIAN ══   SPANISH ▬▬   OTHER ▬

FREQUENCY   COUNTRY, STATION, LOCATION   TARGET • NETWORK • POWER (kW)   World Time

```
                                                    0  1  2  3  4  5  6  7  8  9 10 11 12 13 14 15 16 17 18 19 20 21 22 23 24
```

Frequency	Country, Station, Location	Target • Network • Power (kW)
6140 (con'd)	**USSR** RADIO MOSCOW, Voronej	DS-1 • 100 kW
	RADIO MOSCOW, Zhigulevsk	(D) • EUROPE • 100 kW
6140v	**BOLIVIA** R LUIS DE FUENTES, Tarija	Irr • DS • 1 kW
	PERU †RADIO CONCORDIA, Arequipa	DS • 1 kW
6145	**ALGERIA** RTV ALGERIENNE, Algiers	N AFRICA • DS • 50 kW
	GERMANY DEUTSCHE WELLE, Jülich	(D) • WEST USSR • 100 kW
	†DEUTSCHE WELLE, Multiple Locations	N AMERICA & C AMERICA • 100/500 kW (D) • MIDEAST • 100/500 kW
	†DEUTSCHE WELLE, Nauen	(J) • S AMERICA • 500 kW
	†DEUTSCHE WELLE, Wertachtal	C AMERICA & S AMERICA • 500 kW
		(D) • N AMERICA • 500 kW
	KOREA (REPUBLIC) RADIO KOREA, Via Sackville, Can	E NORTH AM • 250 kW
	USSR †RADIO MOSCOW, Moscow	(D) • EUROPE • 100 kW
6150	**BRAZIL** RADIO RECORD, São Paulo	Irr • DS • 7.5 kW DS • 7.5 kW
	CANADA R CANADA INTL, Sackville, NB	(D) M-F • EUROPE • 250 kW (J) M-F • EUROPE • 250 kW
	R CANADA INTL, Via In-Kimjae, Korea	E ASIA • 250 kW
	†R CANADA INTL, Via Sines, Portugal	EUROPE • 250 kW
	†R CANADA INTL, Via Tokyo, Japan	(D) • E ASIA • 300 kW (J) • E ASIA • 300 kW (D) • E ASIA • 120 kW
	†R CANADA INTL, Via Xi'an, China(PR)	
	CHINA (PR) HEILONGJIANG PBS, Qiqihar	DS-CHINESE, KOREAN • 50 kW
	CLANDESTINE (S AMER) *LV DE RESISTENCIA, Colombia	Su • S AMERICA • USB
	COLOMBIA CARACOL BOGOTA, Bogotá	DS • 10 kW
	FRANCE R FRANCE INTL, Issoudun-Allouis	EUROPE • 500 kW
	IRAN †VO THE ISLAMIC REP, Tehrān	(D) • MIDEAST • 500 kW
	KENYA †KENYA BC CORP, Koma Rock	DS-NATIONAL • 250 kW Sa/Su • DS-NATIONAL • 250 kW
	USA †VOA, Via Tangier, Morocco	N AFRICA • 100 kW (J) • WEST USSR • 100 kW
	VOA, Via Woofferton, UK	(D) • E EUROPE • 300 kW (J) • E EUROPE • 300 kW
	USSR †BELORUSSIAN RADIO, Serpukhov	RUSSIAN, ETC • DS-1 • 20 kW
6150v	**CYPRUS** RADIO BAYRAK, Yeni Iskele	DS-2 • 7.5 kW Th-Tu • DS-2 • 7.5 kW W • DS-2 • 7.5 kW
6152v	**ANGOLA** ER DE BENGUELA, Benguela	DS • 1 kW
6154.8	**PERU** RADIO PUCALLPA, Pucallpa	DS • 1 kW M-Sa • DS • 1 kW
6155	**AUSTRIA** RADIO AUSTRIA INTL, Vienna	EUROPE • 300 kW (D) • EUROPE • 300 kW (J) • EUROPE • 300 kW M-Sa • EUROPE • 300 kW Su • EUROPE • 300 kW
	BOLIVIA †RADIO FIDES, La Paz	Sa/Su • DS • 10 kW DS • 10 kW Tu-Su • DS • 10 kW M-Sa • DS • 10 kW Irr • DS • 10 kW Su • DS • 10 kW
	CHINA (PR) †GANSU PEOPLES BS, Lanzhou	DS-1 • 15 kW
	GERMANY †DEUTSCHE WELLE, Nauen	(D) • S AMERICA • 500 kW
	INDIA †ALL INDIA RADIO, Delhi	S ASIA • 100 kW
	ROMANIA (con'd) RADIO ROMANIA INTL, Bucharest	(D) • AMERICAS • 250 kW

```
                                                    0  1  2  3  4  5  6  7  8  9 10 11 12 13 14 15 16 17 18 19 20 21 22 23 24
```

SUMMER ONLY (J)   WINTER ONLY (D)   JAMMING / OR ∧   EARLIEST HEARD ◁   LATEST HEARD ▷   NEW OR CHANGED FOR 1992 †

FREQUENCY   COUNTRY, STATION, LOCATION

TARGET • NETWORK • POWER (kW)

World Time

0 1 2 3 4 5 6 7 8 9 10 11 12 13 14 15 16 17 18 19 20 21 22 23 24

Frequency	Country, Station, Location	Target • Network • Power
6155 (con'd)	SINGAPORE	
	SINGAPORE BC CORP, Jurong	DS-2/MALAY • 50 kW
	SWAZILAND	
	†SWAZI COMMERCIAL R, Sandlane	S AFRICA • 50 kW / M-F • S AFRICA • 50 kW / M-F • S AFRICA • PARALELO 27 • 10 kW / Sa/Su • S AFRICA • PARALELO 27 • 10 kW / M-F • S AFRICA • 10 kW
	TOGO	
	RADIO KARA, Lama-Kara	FRENCH, ETC • DS • 10 kW / Sa/Su • FRENCH, ETC • DS • 10 kW
	USSR	
	RADIO MOSCOW, Nikolayevsk 'Amure	DS-MAYAK • 50 kW
6160	BRAZIL	
	†RADIO RIO MAR, Manaus	DS • 10 kW / Sa • DS • 10 kW / Su-F • DS • 10 kW
	BULGARIA	
	†RADIO SOFIA, Sofia	(D) • E EUROPE • 250 kW
	CANADA	
	CKZN-CBN, St John's, Nfld	DS • 0.3 kW
	†CKZU-CBU, Vancouver, BC	DS • 0.5 kW
	GERMANY	
	DEUTSCHE WELLE, Via Antigua	C AMERICA & AUSTRALIA • 250 kW
	USA	
	†RFE-RL, Via Portugal	(D) • MIDEAST & WEST USSR • 500 kW
	†VOA, Various Locations	MIDEAST • 50/500 kW / N AFRICA & W AFRICA • 250 kW
	VOA, Via Kaválla, Greece	(D) • S ASIA • 250 kW / (D) • MIDEAST • 250 kW / (D) • WEST USSR • 250 kW
	†VOA, Via Woofferton, UK	(D) • WEST USSR • 300 kW / (D) • E EUROPE • 300 kW / (J) • WEST USSR • 300 kW
	USSR	
	RADIO MOSCOW, Kazan'	(D) • DS-MAYAK • 100 kW
6160.3	COLOMBIA	
	RCN BOGOTA, Bogotá	Irr • DS-RCN • 10 kW
6160.6	ARGENTINA	
	RADIO MALARGUE, Malargüe	Irr • DS • 0.3 kW
6165	CHINA (PR)	
	RADIO BEIJING, Via Switzerland	EUROPE • 250 kW
	HOLLAND	
	†RADIO NEDERLAND, Via Neth Antilles	E NORTH AM • 300 kW / C AMERICA & S AMERICA • 300 kW / W NORTH AM • 300 kW / C AMERICA • 300 kW
	KOREA (REPUBLIC)	
	RADIO KOREA, In-Kimjae	E ASIA • 100 kW
	MEXICO	
	LV AMERICA LATINA, México City	Irr • DS • 0.5/10 kW
	SWITZERLAND	
	†SWISS RADIO INTL, Sarnen	EUROPE & N AFRICA • 250 kW / M-Sa • EUROPE & N AFRICA • 250 kW / Su • EUROPE & N AFRICA • 250 kW
	USSR	
	†RADIO MOSCOW, Khabarovsk	E ASIA • 100 kW
	†RADIO MOSCOW, Moscow	(D) • EUROPE • 200 kW / (D) • EUROPE • 100 kW
	†SOVIET BELORUSSIA, Kiev	
	†UKRAINIAN RADIO, Khar'kov	DS-2 • 20 kW
	YUGOSLAVIA	
	†RADIO YUGOSLAVIA, Bijeljina	EUROPE • 500 kW
	ZAMBIA	
	RADIO ZAMBIA-ZBS, Lusaka	DS-ENGLISH, ETC • 50 kW / F/Sa • DS-ENGLISH, ETC • 50 kW
6170	BRAZIL	
	RADIO CULTURA, São Paulo	DS • 7.5 kW
	CANADA	
	†R CANADA INTL, Via United Kingdom	(J) • EUROPE • 300 kW
	CHINA (PR)	
	†VO THE STRAIT-PLA, Fuzhou	TAIWAN-1 • 15 kW
	COLOMBIA	
	LA VOZ DE LA SELVA, Florencia	DS • 2 kW
	FRENCH GUIANA	
	RFO-GUYANE, Cayenne	DS • 4 kW
	GERMANY	
	DEUTSCHE WELLE, Via Sri Lanka	S ASIA & SE ASIA • 250 kW
	DEUTSCHE WELLE, Wertachtal	(J) • E EUROPE • 500 kW
	INDIA	
(con'd)	†ALL INDIA RADIO, Delhi	S ASIA • 100 kW

0 1 2 3 4 5 6 7 8 9 10 11 12 13 14 15 16 17 18 19 20 21 22 23 24

ENGLISH ▬ ARABIC ⋙ CHINESE ▭▭▭ FRENCH ═══ GERMAN ▬ RUSSIAN ══ SPANISH ▬ OTHER ▬

| FREQUENCY | COUNTRY, STATION, LOCATION | TARGET • NETWORK • POWER (kW) | World Time |

World Time scale: 0 1 2 3 4 5 6 7 8 9 10 11 12 13 14 15 16 17 18 19 20 21 22 23 24

6170
(con'd) **MADAGASCAR**
  RTV MALAGASY, Antananarivo — Su • DS-2 • 100 kW
UNITED ARAB EMIRATES
  †UAE RADIO, Abu Dhabi — (D) • E NORTH AM & C AMERICA • 500 kW
  (D) • MIDEAST & S ASIA • 500 kW • ALT. FREQ. TO 7280 kHz
USA
  †RFE-RL, Via Germany — WEST USSR • 100 kW
  (D) • WEST USSR • 100/250 kW
  (J) • E EUROPE • 100 kW
  DS-1 • 100 kW
USSR
  RADIO MOSCOW, Armavir
6174 PERU
  RADIO TAWANTINSUYO, Cusco — DS-SPANISH, QUECHUA • 5 kW
  Irr • DS • 5 kW
6175 COSTA RICA
  FARO DEL CARIBE, San José — DS • 2.5 kW
FRANCE
  R FRANCE INTL, Issoudun-Allouis — EUROPE & N AFRICA • 100 kW
JAPAN
  NHK, Tokyo-Shobu — Irr • DS-1 (FEEDER) • 0.9 kW • USB
MALAYSIA
  VOICE OF MALAYSIA, Kajang — SE ASIA • 50 kW
UNITED KINGDOM
  †BBC, Via Sackville, Can — E NORTH AM • 250 kW
USA
  †WYFR-FAMILY RADIO, Okeechobee, Fl — S AMERICA • 100 kW
  (D) • S AMERICA • 100 kW
  (J) • S AMERICA • 100 kW
USSR
  †RADIO KIEV, Kiev — (D) • EUROPE • 100 kW
  †SOVIET BELORUSSIA, Kiev — (D) • M/Tu/Th/F • EUROPE • 100 kW
  (D) • W/Sa/Su • EUROPE • 100 kW
6176 CHINA (PR)
  SHAANXI PEOPLES BS, Xi'an — DS-1 • 15 kW
6180 BRAZIL
  R NAC DA AMAZONIA, Brasília — DS • 250 kW
CHINA (TAIWAN)
  CENTRAL BC SYSTEM, T'ai-pei — PRC-2 • 50/100 kW
CYPRUS
  †CYPRUS BC CORP, Zyyi — (D) • F-Su • EUROPE • 250 kW
GERMANY
  †DEUTSCHE WELLE, Jülich — (D) • S ASIA • 100 kW
SENEGAL
  ORT DU SENEGAL, Ziguinchor — FRENCH, ETC • DS • 4 kW
UNITED KINGDOM
  †BBC, Via Zyyi, Cyprus — EUROPE • 100/300 kW   EUROPE • 100/250 kW
  (J) • EUROPE • 250 kW
  (J) Sa/Su • EUROPE • 250 kW   (J) • S ASIA • 250 kW
  (J) M-F • SE ASIA • 250 kW
USA
  †VOA, Greenville, NC — W AFRICA • 250 kW
  M-F • W AFRICA • 250 kW
  †VOA, Via Kaválla, Greece — MIDEAST • 250 kW
  †VOA, Via Portugal — (D) • WEST USSR • 250 kW
  †VOA, Via Woofferton, UK — (J) • WEST USSR • 250 kW   (D) • WEST USSR • 300 kW
USSR
  KAZAKH RADIO, Alma-Ata — M-F • DS-1 • 100 kW   Th-Tu • DS-1 • 100 kW
  Sa • DS-1 • 100 kW   W • DS-1 • 100 kW
  Sa/Su • DS-1 • 100 kW
  Su-F • DS-1 • 100 kW
  Tu/Th/F • DS-1 • 100 kW
  RUSSIAN, ETC • DS-1 • 100 kW
  Sa-M/W • RUSSIAN, ETC • DS-1 • 100 kW
VENEZUELA
  RADIO TURISMO, Valera — Irr • DS • 1 kW
6185 GERMANY
  †DEUTSCHE WELLE, Jülich — (D) • SE ASIA & AUSTRALIA • 100 kW
  †DEUTSCHE WELLE, Königswusterhausen — (D) • N AMERICA • 100 kW
  †DEUTSCHE WELLE, Multiple Locations — (D) • ASIA • 100/500 kW
JAPAN
  †RADIO JAPAN/NHK, Tokyo-Yamata — (D) • E ASIA • 100 kW • ALT. FREQ. TO 6080 kHz
  (D) • E ASIA • GENERAL • 100 kW • ALT. FREQ. TO 6080 kHz
LIBYA
  RADIO JAMAHIRIYA, Tripoli — Irr • DS-RAMADAN • 100 kW
  DS • 100 kW
MEXICO
  †RADIO EDUCACION, México City — DS • 1 kW
USSR
(con'd) †RADIO KIEV — (D) • EUROPE

Bottom scale: 0 1 2 3 4 5 6 7 8 9 10 11 12 13 14 15 16 17 18 19 20 21 22 23 24

FREQUENCY   COUNTRY, STATION, LOCATION

TARGET • NETWORK • POWER (kW)

World Time

	0 1 2 3 4 5 6 7 8 9 10 11 12 13 14 15 16 17 18 19 20 21 22 23 24
6185 **USSR**	
(con'd) †SOVIET BELORUSSIA	(J) • EUROPE
VATICAN STATE	
†VATICAN RADIO, Sta Maria di Galeria	EUROPE • 100 kW
	M-Sa • EUROPE • 100 kW W EUROPE & N AFRICA • 100 kW
	(D) • E EUROPE & WEST USSR • 100 kW
	M-Sa • ENGLISH, FRENCH, SPANISH & ITALIAN • EUROPE • 100 kW (D) • EUROPE • 100 kW
6187 **INDONESIA**	
†RRI, Manokwari, Irian Jaya	DS-TEMP INACTIVE • 1 kW
6190 **GERMANY**	
FREIES BERLIN-SFB, Bremen	EUROPE • DS • 10 kW
	Sa • EUROPE • DS • 10 kW
	Su-F • EUROPE • DS • 10 kW
RADIO BREMEN, Bremen	Sa • EUROPE • DS • 10 kW
	Su-F • EUROPE • DS • 10 kW
INDIA	
†ALL INDIA RADIO, Delhi	DS • 10 kW
	ENGLISH & HINDI • DS • 10 kW
INDONESIA	
†RRI, Padang, Sumatera	DS • 10 kW
JAPAN	
NHK, Osaka	Irr • DS-2 (FEEDER) • 0.5 kW
ROMANIA	
RADIO ROMANIA INTL, Bucharest	(D) • EUROPE • 250 kW
SWITZERLAND	
SWISS RADIO INTL, Schwarzenburg	W EUROPE • 150 kW
UNITED KINGDOM	
†BBC, Via Maseru, Lesotho	C AFRICA & S AFRICA • 100 kW
	S AFRICA • 50 kW
	Sa/Su • S AFRICA • 50 kW
USA	
VOA, Greenville, NC	C AMERICA & S AMERICA • 500 kW
USSR	
RADIO MOSCOW, Bishkek	MIDEAST • 100 kW
RADIO MOSCOW, Omsk	DS-MAYAK • 100 kW
6190v **PERU**	DS • 1.5 kW
†RADIO ORIENTE, Yurimaguas	Irr • DS • 1.5 kW M-Sa • DS • 1.5 kW
6190.8 **INDONESIA**	
†RRI, Padang, Sumatera	DS • 10 kW
6191.7 **PERU**	
†RADIO CUZCO, Cusco	DS-SPANISH, QUECHUA • 1 kW
6195 **EGYPT**	
RADIO CAIRO, Kafr Silim-Abis	N AMERICA • 250 kW
UNITED KINGDOM	
†BBC, Daventry	(J) • EUROPE & WEST USSR • 300 kW
†BBC, Multiple Locations	EUROPE • 250/300/500 kW
	(J) • EUROPE • 250/300 kW
†BBC, Via Antigua	C AMERICA • 125 kW
	(D) • C AMERICA • 125 kW
	(D) Sa/Su • C AMERICA • 125 kW
†BBC, Via Singapore	SE ASIA • 125 kW
†BBC, Via Zyyi, Cyprus	(D) • MIDEAST • 250 kW
USSR	
RADIO MOSCOW, Baku	DS-MAYAK • 50 kW
RADIO MOSCOW, Via Havana, Cuba	(D) • C AMERICA • 50/100 kW
†UKRAINIAN RADIO, Kiev	DS-2 • 20 kW
6200 **CHINA (TAIWAN)**	
VO FREE CHINA, T'ai-pei	E ASIA • 50/100 kW
6201v **PERU**	
LA VOZ DE HUAMANGA, Ayacucho	DS • 2 kW
6205 **ECUADOR**	
†HCJB-VO THE ANDES, Quito	(D) • EUROPE • 500 kW
	M-F • WEST USSR • 500 kW
	(D) M-F • EUROPE • 500 kW
	(D) Sa/Su • EUROPE • 500 kW
PIRATE (EUROPE)	
†"RADIO FAX", Ireland	Irr • Sa/Su • W EUROPE • 0.23 kW
6206v **PIRATE (EUROPE)**	
"R ORANG UTAN", Holland	Irr • Su • W EUROPE • 0.1 kW
6210 **ITALY**	
†EURO CHRISTIAN R, Pordenone	Su • EUROPE • 7 kW M-F • EUROPE • 7 kW
PIRATE (EUROPE)	
†"FREE RADIO LONDON", England	Irr • Su • W EUROPE • 0.1 kW • ALT. FREQ. TO 7425 kHz
6220 **PIRATE (EUROPE)**	
†"MIDLANDS MUSIC R", England	Irr • Su • W EUROPE
†"RAINBOW R GERMANY, Germany	Irr • Su • W EUROPE • 0.08 kW

0 1 2 3 4 5 6 7 8 9 10 11 12 13 14 15 16 17 18 19 20 21 22 23 24

ENGLISH ▬▬   ARABIC ≈≈≈   CHINESE □□□   FRENCH ══   GERMAN ▬▬   RUSSIAN ══   SPANISH ══   OTHER ▬

FREQUENCY   COUNTRY, STATION, LOCATION   TARGET • NETWORK • POWER (kW)   World Time

Freq	Country / Station / Location	Notes
6220v	**PAKISTAN** — PAKISTAN BC CORP, Rawalpindi	(J) • DS-ENGLISH, ETC • 10 kW
6229v	**PIRATE (EUROPE)** — †"JOLLY ROGER R", Ireland	Sa/Su • W EUROPE
6230	**ECUADOR** — †HCJB-VO THE ANDES, Quito	Alternative Frequency to 15155 kHz
	EGYPT — RADIO CAIRO, Abu Za'bal	MIDEAST • 100 kW
	MONACO — †TRANS WORLD RADIO, Monte Carlo	(J) • EUROPE • 500 kW
6233	**PIRATE (EUROPE)** — †"R PAMELA INTL", England	Irr • Su • W EUROPE • 0.02 kW
6233.5	**PIRATE (EUROPE)** — †"RADIO MI AMIGO", England	Irr • Sa • W EUROPE
6234	**PIRATE (EUROPE)** — †"RADIO ZENITH", England	Su • W EUROPE • 0.025 kW
6234v	**PIRATE (EUROPE)** — †"BRITAIN R INTL", Germany (FR)	Irr • Su • ENGLISH & GERMAN • W EUROPE • 0.05 kW
6235	**PIRATE (EUROPE)** — †"RADIO MARABU", Germany (FR)	Alternative Frequency to 7485 kHz
	†"RADIO POGO 104", Germany	Irr • Su • W EUROPE
6235v	**PIRATE (EUROPE)** — "RADIO GEMINI", England	Irr • Su • W EUROPE • 0.15 kW
6240	**CLANDESTINE (N AMER)** — "VOICE OF TOMORROW, Virginia, USA	Irr • E NORTH AM • NEO-NAZI PARTY
	PIRATE (EUROPE) — †"RADIO MERLIN INTL", England	Irr • Sa/Su • W EUROPE
6242	**PERU** — RADIO MUNICIPAL, Calca	Irr • DS • 0.12 kW
6245	**VATICAN STATE** — †VATICAN RADIO, Sta Maria di Galeria	EUROPE • 100 kW
		Su • EUROPE • 100 kW
		M-Sa • ENGLISH, FRENCH & SPANISH • EUROPE • 100 kW
		M-Sa • ENGLISH, FRENCH, SPANISH & ITALIAN • EUROPE • 100 kW
6250	**EQUATORIAL GUINEA** — RADIO NACIONAL, Malabo	SPANISH, ETC • DS • 10 kW
6250v	**KOREA (DPR)** — RADIO PYONGYANG, Pyongyang	E ASIA • 50/100 kW
6252v	**VIETNAM** — LAI CHAU BS, Lai Chau	DS
6260	**CHINA (PR)** — †QINGHAI PEOPLES BS, Xining	DS-1 • 10 kW
	PERU — RADIO SAPOSOA, Saposoa	DS • 0.3 kW
6261v	**PERU** — RADIO JUANJUI, Juanjui	DS
6266	**PIRATE (EUROPE)** — †"RADIO ORION", England	Alternative Frequency to 6290v kHz
6270v	**CLANDESTINE (S AMER)** — †"PUEBLO RESPONDE", Colombia	Alternative Frequency to 6315v kHz
	†"R PATRIA LIBRE", Colombia	Alternative Frequency to 6315v kHz
6272.4	**PIRATE (EUROPE)** — †"N IRELAND RELAY", Northern Ireland	Irr • Su • W EUROPE • 0.2 kW
6273	**PIRATE (EUROPE)** — "TRIANGLE NIGHT FM, N Ireland	Irr • Sa/Su • W EUROPE • 0.2 kW Irr • Sa • W EUROPE • 0.2 kW
		Irr • Su • W EUROPE • 0.2 kW
6275	**PIRATE (EUROPE)** — †"W & N KENT RADIO", England	Irr • Su • W EUROPE • 0.018 kW • ALT. FREQ. TO 6315 kHz
6280	**PIRATE (EUROPE)** — †"OZONE RADIO INTL", Ireland	Su • W EUROPE • 0.08 kW
6280.2	**LEBANON** — †KING OF HOPE, Marjayoûn	MIDEAST • 12 kW
		MIDEAST & WEST USSR • 12 kW
6282	**PIRATE (EUROPE)** — †"LIVE WIRE RADIO", England	Su • W EUROPE • 0.1 kW • ALT. FREQ. TO 6310 kHz
6290	**PIRATE (EUROPE)** — †"WEEKEND MUSIC R", Scotland	Irr • Su • W EUROPE • 0.1 kW • ALT. FREQ. TO 6305 kHz
6290v	**PIRATE (EUROPE)** — †"RADIO ORION", England	Sa/Su • W EUROPE • 0.018 kW • ALT. FREQ. TO 6266 kHz
		Irr • Sa/Su • W EUROPE • 0.018 kW • ALT. FREQ. TO 6266 kHz
6295	**PAKISTAN** — PAKISTAN BC CORP, Islamabad	(D) • MIDEAST • DS • 100 kW
6295v	**VIETNAM** — †SON LA BC STATION, Son La	DS
6299.3	**HONDURAS** — †SANI RADIO, Puerto Lempira	SPANISH, ETC • DS • 10 kW • ALT. FREQ. TO 4755 kHz
6300	**USA** — FAMILY RADIO, Via Taiwan	E ASIA • 250 kW
6304.5	**PERU** — RADIO ACARI, Caravelí	DS
6305	**CLANDESTINE (C AMER)** — "LA VOZ DEL CID", Guatemala	C AMERICA • ANTI-CASTRO
	PIRATE (EUROPE) — †"WEEKEND MUSIC R", Scotland	Alternative Frequency to 6290 kHz
6310	**PIRATE (EUROPE)** — †"LIVE WIRE RADIO", England	Alternative Frequency to 6282 kHz
6315 (con'd)	**PIRATE (EUROPE)** — †"PIRATE FREAKS BC", Germany	Irr • Su • ENGLISH & GERMAN • W EUROPE

FREQUENCY   COUNTRY, STATION, LOCATION

TARGET • NETWORK • POWER (kW)

World Time

0 1 2 3 4 5 6 7 8 9 10 11 12 13 14 15 16 17 18 19 20 21 22 23 24

Frequency	Country, Station, Location	Schedule / Notes
6315 (con'd)	PIRATE (EUROPE) †"W & N KENT RADIO", England	Alternative Frequency to 6275 kHz
6315v	CLANDESTINE (S AMER) †"PUEBLO RESPONDE", Colombia	Irr • S AMERICA • ANTI-GUERRILLA • ALT. FREQ. TO 6270v kHz
	†"R PATRIA LIBRE", Colombia	Irr • S AMERICA • ELN REBELS • ALT. FREQ. TO 6270v kHz
6320v	CLANDESTINE (M EAST) "VO IRANIAN KURDS"	Alternative Frequency to 7365v kHz
	PIRATE (EUROPE) †"RADIO STELLA", Scotland	Alternative Frequency to 11416v kHz
6323.6	PERU ESTACION C, Moyobamba	Tu-Su • DS • 0.8 kW / DS • 0.8 kW / Irr • Tu-Su • DS • 0.8 kW
6325	CLANDESTINE (ASIA) "VO THE KHMER", Kampuchea/Thailand	SE ASIA • PRO-REBEL STATION / Su • SE ASIA • PRO-REBEL STATION
6325.8	PERU RADIO ABANCAY, Abancay	DS-SPANISH, QUECHUA • 1 kW / M-Sa • DS-SPANISH, QUECHUA • 1 kW
6348	CLANDESTINE (ASIA) †"ECHO OF HOPE", Seoul, South Korea	E ASIA • 50 kW / (J) • E ASIA • 50 kW
6381v	PERU RADIO SAN MIGUEL, Huánchac	Irr • DS
6390	USSR RADIO MOSCOW	(D) • DS-1 (FEEDER) • ISL / (D) • DS-1 (FEEDER) • ISU
6400v	CLANDESTINE (C AMER) †"RADIO VENCEREMOS", El Salvador	Irr • C AMERICA • PRO-FMLF
	KOREA (DPR) RADIO PYONGYANG, Pyongyang	E ASIA • 50 kW
6435v	CLANDESTINE (M EAST) "VO IRANIAN REV'N", Afghanistan	MIDEAST • ANTI-IRANIAN GOVT
6440v	CLANDESTINE (M EAST) "VO IRAN COMMUNIST, Afghanistan	F • MIDEAST • ANTI-IRANIAN GOVT / MIDEAST • ANTI-IRANIAN GOVT / Sa-Th • MIDEAST • ANTI-IRANIAN GOVT
6451v	VIETNAM VOICE OF VIETNAM, Hanoi	DS
6480	KOREA (REPUBLIC) RADIO KOREA, In-Kimjae	EUROPE • 250 kW
6500	CHINA (PR) †QINGHAI PEOPLES BS, Xining	DS-TIBETAN • 10 kW / Irr • DS-TIBETAN • 10 kW
6540	IRAQ †REP OF IRAQ RADIO	DS
	KOREA (DPR) RADIO PYONGYANG, Pyongyang	E ASIA • 100 kW / MIDEAST & N AFRICA • 200 kW
6550v	LEBANON VOICE OF LEBANON, Beirut-Ashrafiyah	DS-PHALANGE • 8 kW
6560	KOREA (DPR) RADIO PYONGYANG, Pyongyang	E ASIA • 100 kW
6570	MYANMAR (BURMA) †DEFENSE FORCES BC, Taunggyi	DS
6571v	PERU RADIO TACNA, Tacna	M-F • DS • 0.18 kW
6571.8	ARGENTINA RADIO COLON, San Juan	Irr • DS (FEEDER) • USB
6575v	VIETNAM CAO BANG BS, Cao Bang	DS / Irr • DS
6576	KOREA (DPR) †RADIO PYONGYANG, Kujang-dong	C AMERICA • 400 kW
	RADIO PYONGYANG, Pyongyang	WEST USSR & EUROPE • 200 kW
6590v	VIETNAM †HOANG LIEN SON BS, Hoang Lien Son	DS
	†VOICE OF VIETNAM, Hoang Lien Son	SE ASIA
6595	KOREA (DPR) RADIO PYONGYANG, Pyongyang	E ASIA • 100 kW
6600v	CLANDESTINE (ASIA) †"VO THE PEOPLE", Seoul, S Korea	E ASIA
6617v	VIETNAM BAC THAI BS, Bac Thai	DS
6620	PERU †RADIO TRADICION, Huanta	DS
6627v	PERU RADIO SAN ANTONIO, Cajamarca	DS • 0.5 kW
6670.2	PERU †R SANTA MONICA, Santiago de Chuco	DS
6691	PERU RADIO CUTERVO, Cutervo	DS • 1 kW
6724v	PERU RADIO SATELITE, Santa Cruz	DS • 1 kW
6750	CHINA (PR) CENTRAL PEOPLES BS	DS-1
6754.7	PERU RADIO LA MERCED, Cajamarca	DS
6770	USSR TASS NEWS AGENCY, Moscow	M-F • DS • 15 kW

0 1 2 3 4 5 6 7 8 9 10 11 12 13 14 15 16 17 18 19 20 21 22 23 24

ENGLISH ▬ ARABIC ▨ CHINESE ▫▫ FRENCH ═ GERMAN ▬ RUSSIAN ＝ SPANISH ▬ OTHER ▬

FREQUENCY   COUNTRY, STATION, LOCATION   TARGET • NETWORK • POWER (kW)   World Time

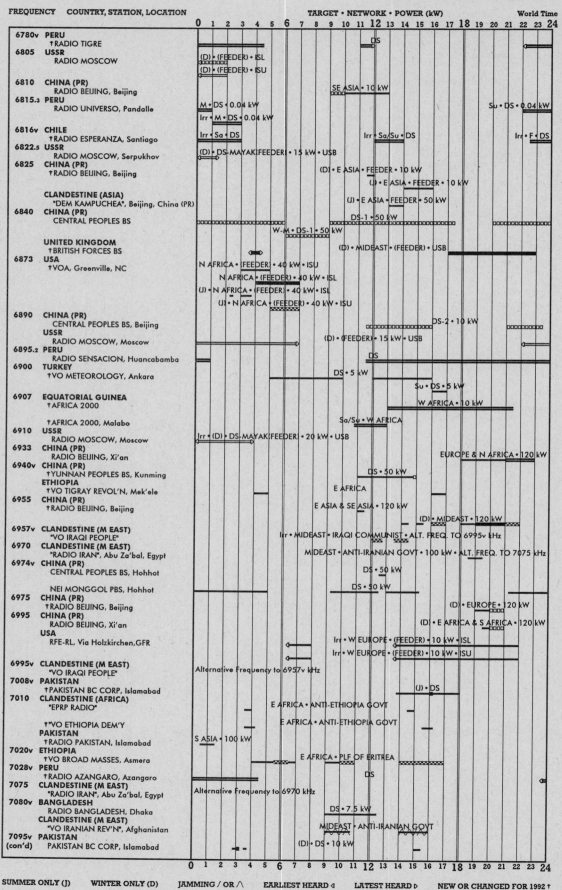

SUMMER ONLY (J)   WINTER ONLY (D)   JAMMING / OR ∧   EARLIEST HEARD ◁   LATEST HEARD ▷   NEW OR CHANGED FOR 1992 †

FREQUENCY   COUNTRY, STATION, LOCATION

TARGET • NETWORK • POWER (kW)

World Time

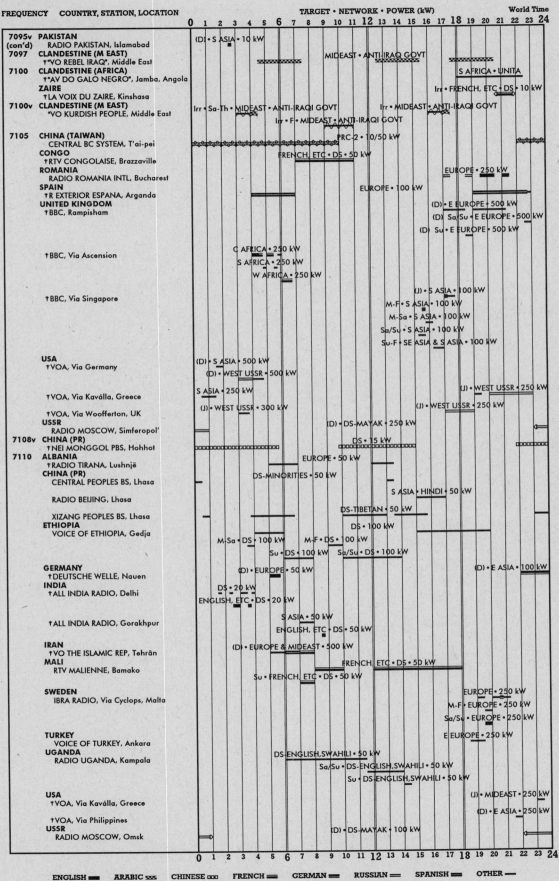

7095v	**PAKISTAN**
(con'd)	RADIO PAKISTAN, Islamabad — (D) • S ASIA • 10 kW
7097	**CLANDESTINE (M EAST)**
	†"VO REBEL IRAQ", Middle East — MIDEAST • ANTI-IRAQ GOVT
7100	**CLANDESTINE (AFRICA)**
	†"AV DO GALO NEGRO", Jamba, Angola — S AFRICA • UNITA
	ZAIRE
	†LA VOIX DU ZAIRE, Kinshasa — Irr • FRENCH, ETC • DS • 10 kW
7100v	**CLANDESTINE (M EAST)**
	"VO KURDISH PEOPLE, Middle East — Irr • Sa-Th • MIDEAST • ANTI-IRAQI GOVT Irr • MIDEAST • ANTI-IRAQI GOVT
	Irr • F • MIDEAST • ANTI-IRAQI GOVT
7105	**CHINA (TAIWAN)**
	CENTRAL BC SYSTEM, T'ai-pei — PRC-2 • 10/50 kW
	CONGO
	†RTV CONGOLAISE, Brazzaville — FRENCH, ETC • DS • 50 kW
	ROMANIA
	RADIO ROMANIA INTL, Bucharest — EUROPE • 250 kW
	SPAIN
	†R EXTERIOR ESPANA, Arganda — EUROPE • 100 kW
	UNITED KINGDOM
	†BBC, Rampisham — (D) • E EUROPE • 500 kW
	(D) • Sa/Su • E EUROPE • 500 kW
	(D) • Su • E EUROPE • 500 kW
	†BBC, Via Ascension — C AFRICA • 250 kW
	S AFRICA • 250 kW
	W AFRICA • 250 kW
	†BBC, Via Singapore — (J) • S ASIA • 100 kW
	M-F • S ASIA • 100 kW
	M-Sa • S ASIA • 100 kW
	Sa/Su • S ASIA • 100 kW
	Su-F • SE ASIA & S ASIA • 100 kW
	USA
	†VOA, Via Germany — (D) • S ASIA • 500 kW
	(D) • WEST USSR • 500 kW
	†VOA, Via Kaválla, Greece — S ASIA • 250 kW (J) • WEST USSR • 250 kW
	†VOA, Via Woofferton, UK — (J) • WEST USSR • 300 kW (J) • WEST USSR • 250 kW
	USSR
	RADIO MOSCOW, Simferopol' — (D) • DS-MAYAK • 250 kW
7108v	**CHINA (PR)**
	†NEI MONGGOL PBS, Hohhot — DS • 15 kW
7110	**ALBANIA**
	†RADIO TIRANA, Lushnjë — EUROPE • 50 kW
	CHINA (PR)
	CENTRAL PEOPLES BS, Lhasa — DS-MINORITIES • 50 kW
	RADIO BEIJING, Lhasa — S ASIA • HINDI • 50 kW
	XIZANG PEOPLES BS, Lhasa — DS-TIBETAN • 50 kW
	ETHIOPIA
	VOICE OF ETHIOPIA, Gedja — DS • 100 kW
	M-Sa • DS • 100 kW M-F • DS • 100 kW
	Su • DS • 100 kW Sa/Su • DS • 100 kW
	GERMANY
	†DEUTSCHE WELLE, Nauen — (D) • EUROPE • 50 kW (D) • E ASIA • 100 kW
	INDIA
	†ALL INDIA RADIO, Delhi — DS • 20 kW
	ENGLISH, ETC • DS • 20 kW
	†ALL INDIA RADIO, Gorakhpur — S ASIA • 50 kW
	ENGLISH, ETC • DS • 50 kW
	IRAN
	†VO THE ISLAMIC REP, Tehrān — (D) • EUROPE & MIDEAST • 500 kW
	MALI
	RTV MALIENNE, Bamako — FRENCH, ETC • DS • 50 kW
	Su • FRENCH, ETC • DS • 50 kW
	SWEDEN
	IBRA RADIO, Via Cyclops, Malta — EUROPE • 250 kW
	M-F • EUROPE • 250 kW
	Sa/Su • EUROPE • 250 kW
	TURKEY
	VOICE OF TURKEY, Ankara — E EUROPE • 250 kW
	UGANDA
	RADIO UGANDA, Kampala — DS-ENGLISH, SWAHILI • 50 kW
	Sa/Su • DS-ENGLISH, SWAHILI • 50 kW
	Su • DS-ENGLISH, SWAHILI • 50 kW
	USA
	†VOA, Via Kaválla, Greece — (J) • MIDEAST • 250 kW
	†VOA, Via Philippines — (D) • E ASIA • 250 kW
	USSR
	RADIO MOSCOW, Omsk — (D) • DS-MAYAK • 100 kW

ENGLISH ▬   ARABIC ⋙   CHINESE ▭▭▭   FRENCH ═══   GERMAN ▬▬▬   RUSSIAN ══   SPANISH ▬▬   OTHER ───

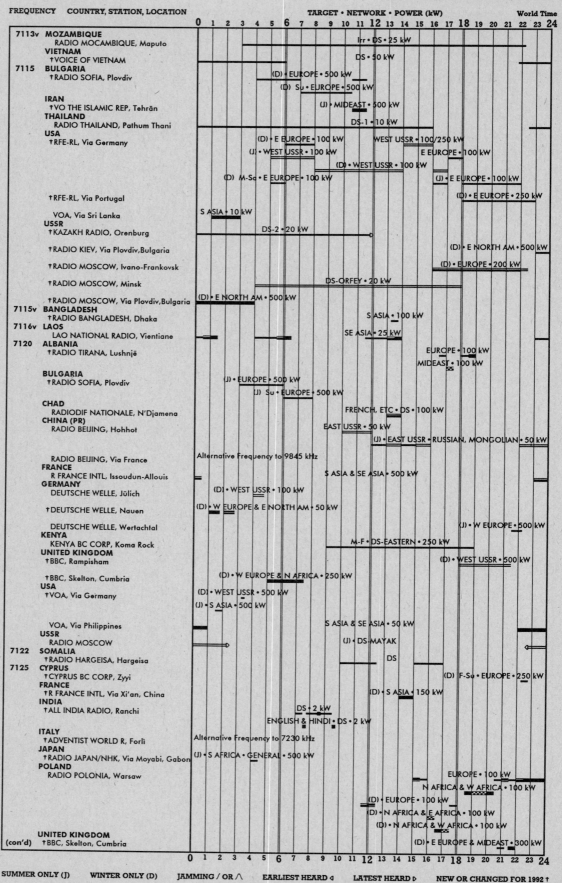

FREQUENCY   COUNTRY, STATION, LOCATION   TARGET • NETWORK • POWER (kW)   World Time

7113v MOZAMBIQUE
          RADIO MOCAMBIQUE, Maputo   Irr • DS • 25 kW
       VIETNAM
          †VOICE OF VIETNAM   DS • 50 kW
7115   BULGARIA
          †RADIO SOFIA, Plovdiv   (D) • EUROPE • 500 kW
                                                            (D) Su • EUROPE • 500 kW
       IRAN
          †VO THE ISLAMIC REP, Tehrān   (J) • MIDEAST • 500 kW
       THAILAND
          RADIO THAILAND, Pathum Thani   DS-1 • 10 kW
       USA
          †RFE-RL, Via Germany   (D) • E EUROPE • 100 kW   WEST USSR • 100/250 kW
                                                            (J) • WEST USSR • 100 kW   E EUROPE • 100 kW
                                                            (D) • WEST USSR • 100 kW
                                                            (D) M-Sa • E EUROPE • 100 kW   (J) E EUROPE • 100 kW

          †RFE-RL, Via Portugal   (D) • E EUROPE • 250 kW

          VOA, Via Sri Lanka   S ASIA • 10 kW
       USSR
          †KAZAKH RADIO, Orenburg   DS-2 • 20 kW

          †RADIO KIEV, Via Plovdiv, Bulgaria   (D) • E NORTH AM • 500 kW

          †RADIO MOSCOW, Ivano-Frankovsk   (D) • EUROPE • 200 kW

          †RADIO MOSCOW, Minsk   DS-ORFEY • 20 kW

          †RADIO MOSCOW, Via Plovdiv, Bulgaria   (D) • E NORTH AM • 500 kW
7115v BANGLADESH
          †RADIO BANGLADESH, Dhaka   S ASIA • 100 kW
7116v LAOS
          LAO NATIONAL RADIO, Vientiane   SE ASIA • 25 kW
7120   ALBANIA
          †RADIO TIRANA, Lushnjë   EUROPE • 100 kW
                                                            MIDEAST • 100 kW

       BULGARIA
          †RADIO SOFIA, Plovdiv   (J) • EUROPE • 500 kW
                                                            (J) Su • EUROPE • 500 kW

       CHAD
          RADIODIF NATIONALE, N'Djamena   FRENCH, ETC • DS • 100 kW
       CHINA (PR)
          RADIO BEIJING, Hohhot   EAST USSR • 50 kW
                                                            (J) • EAST USSR • RUSSIAN, MONGOLIAN • 50 kW

          RADIO BEIJING, Via France   Alternative Frequency to 9845 kHz
       FRANCE
          R FRANCE INTL, Issoudun-Allouis   S ASIA & SE ASIA • 500 kW
       GERMANY
          DEUTSCHE WELLE, Jülich   (D) • WEST USSR • 100 kW

          †DEUTSCHE WELLE, Nauen   (D) • W EUROPE & E NORTH AM • 50 kW

          DEUTSCHE WELLE, Wertachtal   (J) • W EUROPE • 500 kW
       KENYA
          KENYA BC CORP, Koma Rock   M-F • DS-EASTERN • 250 kW
       UNITED KINGDOM
          †BBC, Rampisham   (D) • WEST USSR • 500 kW

          †BBC, Skelton, Cumbria   (D) • W EUROPE & N AFRICA • 250 kW
       USA
          †VOA, Via Germany   (D) • WEST USSR • 500 kW
                                                   (J) • S ASIA • 500 kW

          VOA, Via Philippines   S ASIA & SE ASIA • 50 kW
       USSR
          RADIO MOSCOW   (J) • DS-MAYAK
7122   SOMALIA
          †RADIO HARGEISA, Hargeisa   DS
7125   CYPRUS
          †CYPRUS BC CORP, Zyyi   (D) F-Su • EUROPE • 250 kW
       FRANCE
          †R FRANCE INTL, Via Xi'an, China   (D) • S ASIA • 150 kW
       INDIA
          †ALL INDIA RADIO, Ranchi   DS • 2 kW
                                                   ENGLISH & HINDI • DS • 2 kW

       ITALY
          †ADVENTIST WORLD R, Forlì   Alternative Frequency to 7230 kHz
       JAPAN
          †RADIO JAPAN/NHK, Via Moyabi, Gabon   (J) • S AFRICA • GENERAL • 500 kW
       POLAND
          RADIO POLONIA, Warsaw   EUROPE • 100 kW
                                                            N AFRICA & W AFRICA • 100 kW
                                                   (D) • EUROPE • 100 kW
                                                   (D) • N AFRICA & E AFRICA • 100 kW
                                                   (D) • N AFRICA & W AFRICA • 100 kW
       UNITED KINGDOM
(con'd)   †BBC, Skelton, Cumbria   (D) • E EUROPE & MIDEAST • 300 kW

FREQUENCY	COUNTRY, STATION, LOCATION	TARGET • NETWORK • POWER (kW)	World Time

Time scale: 0 1 2 3 4 5 6 7 8 9 10 11 12 13 14 15 16 17 18 19 20 21 22 23 24

7125 UNITED KINGDOM
(con'd) †BBC, Skelton, Cumbria — (D) • M-Sa • E EUROPE & MIDEAST • 300 kW
USA
VOA, Via Kaválla, Greece — (D) • WEST USSR • 250 kW
†VOA, Via Portugal — (D) • MIDEAST & S ASIA • 250 kW
VOA, Via Sri Lanka — S ASIA • 10 kW
VOA, Via Woofferton, UK — (J) • E EUROPE • 300 kW
USSR
⚓GEORGIAN RADIO, Moscow — RUSSIAN, ETC • DS-1 • 20 kW
†RADIO VEDO, Volgograd — Sa/Su • DS • 20 kW
VATICAN STATE
†VATICAN RADIO, Sta Maria di Galeria — (D) • S ASIA • 500 kW; (D) • E ASIA • 500 kW; (D) • E ASIA & SE ASIA • 500 kW; (D) • AUSTRALIA • 500 kW

7125v CLANDESTINE (ASIA)
"DEMOCRACY BC STN", Taiwan — Irr • E ASIA
7130 CHINA (TAIWAN)
†VO FREE CHINA, T'ai-pei — SE ASIA • 50/100 kW; E ASIA • 50/100 kW
GERMANY
DEUTSCHE WELLE, Jülich — (D) • E EUROPE • 100 kW; (J) • E EUROPE • 100 kW
†DEUTSCHE WELLE, Königswusterhausen — (D) • E EUROPE • 100 kW; (D) • W EUROPE • 50 kW; (D) • WEST USSR • 50 kW; (J) • E EUROPE • 50 kW; (J) • W EUROPE • 50 kW; (J) • WEST USSR • 50 kW
†DEUTSCHE WELLE, Nauen — (D) • E EUROPE • 100 kW
†DEUTSCHE WELLE, Wertachtal — N AFRICA • 500 kW; (D) • E EUROPE • 500 kW; (D) • SE ASIA • 500 kW
HOLLAND
†RADIO NEDERLAND, Flevoland — EUROPE • 500 kW; (D) • EUROPE • 500 kW
MONACO
†TRANS WORLD RADIO, Monte Carlo — EUROPE • 100 kW
USA
†RFE-RL, Via Germany — (D) • WEST USSR • 250 kW
†VOA, Via Kaválla, Greece — (D) • WEST USSR • 250 kW; (D) • E EUROPE • 250 kW; (J) • E EUROPE • 250 kW; (J) • MIDEAST & S ASIA • 250 kW
USSR
†ADYGEY RADIO — (J) • F
†KABARDINO-BALKAR R — (J) • F
RADIO MOSCOW, Krasnodar — (D) • EUROPE • 100 kW
RADIO MOSCOW, Minsk — MIDEAST • 100 kW; (D) • MIDEAST • 100 kW; (D) • EUROPE • 100 kW; (D) • DS-MAYAK • 100 kW
RADIO MOSCOW, Serpuhkov — DS-MAYAK • 100 kW
RADIO MOSCOW, Yerevan — S ASIA • 100 kW
7135 ALBANIA
RADIO TIRANA, Lushnjë — EUROPE • 100 kW
AUSTRALIA
†RADIO AUSTRALIA, Various Locations — SE ASIA • 250 kW
FRANCE
R FRANCE INTL, Issoudun-Allouis — E EUROPE • 500 kW; (D) • E EUROPE • 500 kW; (J) • E EUROPE • 500 kW
†R FRANCE INTL, Multiple Locations — AFRICA • 100/500 kW
UNITED KINGDOM
†BBC, Via Zyyi, Cyprus — MIDEAST • 100 kW; (J) • MIDEAST • 100 kW
USSR
RADIO MOSCOW, Komsomol'sk 'Amure — (D) • E ASIA • 500 kW
RADIO MOSCOW, Moscow — DS-MAYAK • 240 kW
7139 INDONESIA
†RRI, Ambon, Maluku — DS • 10/100 kW
7140 AUSTRALIA
†RADIO AUSTRALIA, Carnarvon — (J) • SE ASIA • 250 kW
†RADIO AUSTRALIA, Darwin — (J) • E ASIA • 250 kW
BELGIUM
†RT BELGE FRANCAISE, Wavre — (D) • EUROPE • DS-1 • 100 kW • ALT. FREQ. TO 5965 kHz; (D) • M-F • EUROPE • DS-1 • 100 kW • ALT. FREQ. TO 5965 kHz

(con'd)

Time scale: 0 1 2 3 4 5 6 7 8 9 10 11 12 13 14 15 16 17 18 19 20 21 22 23 24

ENGLISH ▬   ARABIC ▨   CHINESE ▢▢▢   FRENCH ═   GERMAN ▬   RUSSIAN ═   SPANISH ▬   OTHER ▬

FREQUENCY   COUNTRY, STATION, LOCATION   TARGET • NETWORK • POWER (kW)   World Time

World Time scale: 0 1 2 3 4 5 6 7 8 9 10 11 12 13 14 15 16 17 18 19 20 21 22 23 24

Frequency	Country, Station, Location	Target • Network • Power
7140 (con'd)	**CHINA (PR)** RADIO BEIJING, Xi'an	WEST USSR • 120 kW
	GERMANY †DEUTSCHE WELLE, Königswusterhausen	(D) • W EUROPE & ATLANTIC • 100 kW
	DEUTSCHE WELLE, Wertachtal	(J) • WEST USSR • 500 kW
	INDIA †ALL INDIA RADIO, Delhi	S ASIA • 100 kW
	ALL INDIA RADIO, Hyderabad	DS • 10 kW / Sa/Su • DS • 10 kW / Su • DS • 10 kW
	JAPAN †RADIO JAPAN/NHK, Tokyo-Yamata	E ASIA • GENERAL • 300 kW
	†RADIO JAPAN/NHK, Via Moyabi, Gabon	(J) • S AFRICA • 500 kW
	KENYA KENYA BC CORP, Nairobi	DS-NATIONAL • 100 kW
	UNITED KINGDOM †BBC, Via Zyyi, Cyprus	E AFRICA • 100 kW
	USSR †GRODNO RADIO, Minsk	RUSSIAN, ETC • DS • 20 kW
	RADIO MOSCOW, Kazan'	(J) • E EUROPE • 100 kW
	†YAKUT RADIO, Yakutsk	DS-RUSSIAN, YAKUT • 50 kW
7140v	**ITALY** RADIO ITALIA INTL, Spoleto	DS • 0.5 kW
7145	**ALGERIA** RTV ALGERIENNE, Algiers	N AFRICA & MIDEAST • DS • 100 kW / N AFRICA & MIDEAST • DS-1 • 100 kW
	FRANCE R FRANCE INTL, Issoudun-Allouis	EUROPE • 500 kW
	GERMANY †DEUTSCHE WELLE, Königswusterhausen	(D) • WEST USSR • 100 kW
	†DEUTSCHE WELLE, Leipzig	(J) • E EUROPE • 100 kW
	MALAYSIA RTM-SARAWAK, Kuching-Stapok	DS-MALAY, MELANAU • 10 kW
	POLAND RADIO POLONIA, Warsaw	EUROPE • 100 kW / W EUROPE & W AFRICA • 100 kW
	SAUDI ARABIA BS OF THE KINGDOM, Riyadh	EAST USSR • 350 kW
	UNITED KINGDOM †BBC, Via Singapore	E ASIA • 100 kW
	USA †RFE-RL, Via Germany	WEST USSR • 100/250 kW / (D) • WEST USSR • 100/250 kW / (J) • WEST USSR • 250 kW
	†RFE-RL, Via Portugal	(D) • WEST USSR • 250 kW / (D) • E EUROPE • 250 kW
	USSR †RADIO MOSCOW, Orcha	DS-MAYAK • 20 kW
	RADIO MOSCOW, Tula	(D) • DS-1 • 100 kW
	TURKMEN RADIO, Tula	DS-1/RUSSIAN, ETC • 20 kW
7149v	**SOUTH AFRICA** CAPITAL RADIO, Umtata	DS • 20 kW
7150	**CAMEROON** CAMEROON RTV CORP, Douala	FRENCH, ENGLISH, ETC • DS • 100 kW
	CANADA †R CANADA INTL, Via Xi'an, China(PR)	S ASIA • 120 kW
	GERMANY DEUTSCHE WELLE, Jülich	AFRICA • 100 kW / (D) • E EUROPE • 100 kW / (J) • E EUROPE • 100 kW
	†DEUTSCHE WELLE, Nauen	(D) • E EUROPE • 50 kW
	DEUTSCHE WELLE, Wertachtal	(D) • E EUROPE • 500 kW / (J) • E EUROPE • 500 kW
	INDIA ALL INDIA RADIO, Guwahati	DS-B • 10 kW / Su • DS-B • 10 kW
	SAUDI ARABIA BS OF THE KINGDOM, Riyadh	EUROPE • DS-GENERAL • 350 kW
	UNITED KINGDOM †BBC, Rampisham	AUSTRALIA • 500 kW / W EUROPE • 500 kW / AFRICA • 500 kW
	USSR RADIO MOSCOW, L'vov	(D) • E NORTH AM • 500 kW / (D) • EUROPE • 500 kW
	ZAIRE RADIO CANDIP, Bunia	FRENCH, ETC • DS • 1 kW / Sa/Su • FRENCH, ETC • DS • 1 kW / Su • FRENCH, ETC • DS • 1 kW
7152v	**ANGOLA** †EP DO LOBITO, Lobito	DS • 1 kW

SUMMER ONLY (J)   WINTER ONLY (D)   JAMMING / OR ∧   EARLIEST HEARD ◁   LATEST HEARD ▷   NEW OR CHANGED FOR 1992 †

FREQUENCY   COUNTRY, STATION, LOCATION

TARGET • NETWORK • POWER (kW)

World Time

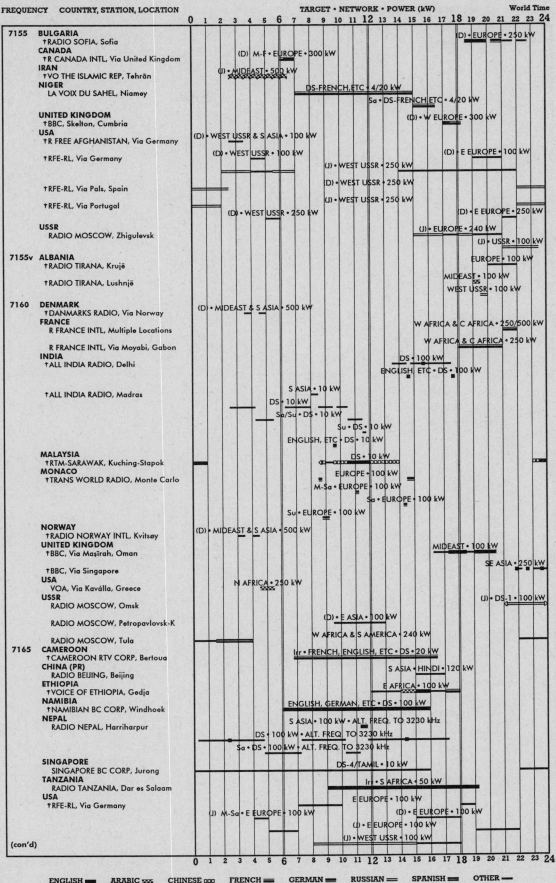

FREQUENCY	COUNTRY, STATION, LOCATION	Notes
7155	**BULGARIA** †RADIO SOFIA, Sofia	(D) • EUROPE • 250 kW
	CANADA †R CANADA INTL, Via United Kingdom	(D) • M-F • EUROPE • 300 kW
	IRAN †VO THE ISLAMIC REP, Tehrān	(J) • MIDEAST • 500 kW
	NIGER LA VOIX DU SAHEL, Niamey	DS-FRENCH, ETC • 4/20 kW; Sa • DS-FRENCH, ETC • 4/20 kW
	UNITED KINGDOM †BBC, Skelton, Cumbria	(D) • W EUROPE • 300 kW
	USA †R FREE AFGHANISTAN, Via Germany	(D) • WEST USSR & S ASIA • 100 kW
	†RFE-RL, Via Germany	(D) • WEST USSR • 100 kW; (D) • E EUROPE • 100 kW; (J) • WEST USSR • 250 kW
	†RFE-RL, Via Pals, Spain	(D) • WEST USSR • 250 kW
	†RFE-RL, Via Portugal	(J) • WEST USSR • 250 kW; (D) • WEST USSR • 250 kW; (D) • E EUROPE • 250 kW
	USSR RADIO MOSCOW, Zhigulevsk	(J) • EUROPE • 240 kW; (J) • USSR • 100 kW
7155v	**ALBANIA** †RADIO TIRANA, Krujë	EUROPE • 100 kW
	†RADIO TIRANA, Lushnjë	MIDEAST • 100 kW; WEST USSR • 100 kW
7160	**DENMARK** †DANMARKS RADIO, Via Norway	(D) • MIDEAST & S ASIA • 500 kW
	FRANCE R FRANCE INTL, Multiple Locations	W AFRICA & C AFRICA • 250/500 kW
	R FRANCE INTL, Via Moyabi, Gabon	W AFRICA & C AFRICA • 250 kW
	INDIA †ALL INDIA RADIO, Delhi	DS • 100 kW; ENGLISH, ETC • DS • 100 kW
	†ALL INDIA RADIO, Madras	S ASIA • 10 kW; DS • 10 kW; Sa/Su • DS • 10 kW; Su • DS • 10 kW; ENGLISH, ETC • DS • 10 kW
	MALAYSIA †RTM-SARAWAK, Kuching-Stapok	DS • 10 kW
	MONACO †TRANS WORLD RADIO, Monte Carlo	EUROPE • 100 kW; M-Sa • EUROPE • 100 kW; Sa • EUROPE • 100 kW; Su • EUROPE • 100 kW
	NORWAY †RADIO NORWAY INTL, Kvitsøy	(D) • MIDEAST & S ASIA • 500 kW
	UNITED KINGDOM †BBC, Via Maṣīrah, Oman	MIDEAST • 100 kW
	†BBC, Via Singapore	SE ASIA • 250 kW
	USA VOA, Via Kaválla, Greece	N AFRICA • 250 kW
	USSR RADIO MOSCOW, Omsk	(J) • DS-1 • 100 kW
	RADIO MOSCOW, Petropavlovsk-K	(D) • E ASIA • 100 kW
	RADIO MOSCOW, Tula	W AFRICA & S AMERICA • 240 kW
7165	**CAMEROON** †CAMEROON RTV CORP, Bertoua	Irr • FRENCH, ENGLISH, ETC • DS • 20 kW
	CHINA (PR) RADIO BEIJING, Beijing	S ASIA • HINDI • 120 kW
	ETHIOPIA †VOICE OF ETHIOPIA, Gedja	E AFRICA • 100 kW
	NAMIBIA †NAMIBIAN BC CORP, Windhoek	ENGLISH, GERMAN, ETC • DS • 100 kW
	NEPAL RADIO NEPAL, Harriharpur	S ASIA • 100 kW • ALT. FREQ. TO 3230 kHz; DS • 100 kW • ALT. FREQ. TO 3230 kHz; Sa • DS • 100 kW • ALT. FREQ. TO 3230 kHz
	SINGAPORE SINGAPORE BC CORP, Jurong	DS-4/TAMIL • 10 kW
	TANZANIA RADIO TANZANIA, Dar es Salaam	Irr • S AFRICA • 50 kW
	USA †RFE-RL, Via Germany	E EUROPE • 100 kW; (J) • M-Sa • E EUROPE • 100 kW; (D) • E EUROPE • 100 kW; (J) • E EUROPE • 100 kW; (J) • WEST USSR • 100 kW

(con'd)

FREQUENCY   COUNTRY, STATION, LOCATION

TARGET • NETWORK • POWER (kW)

World Time

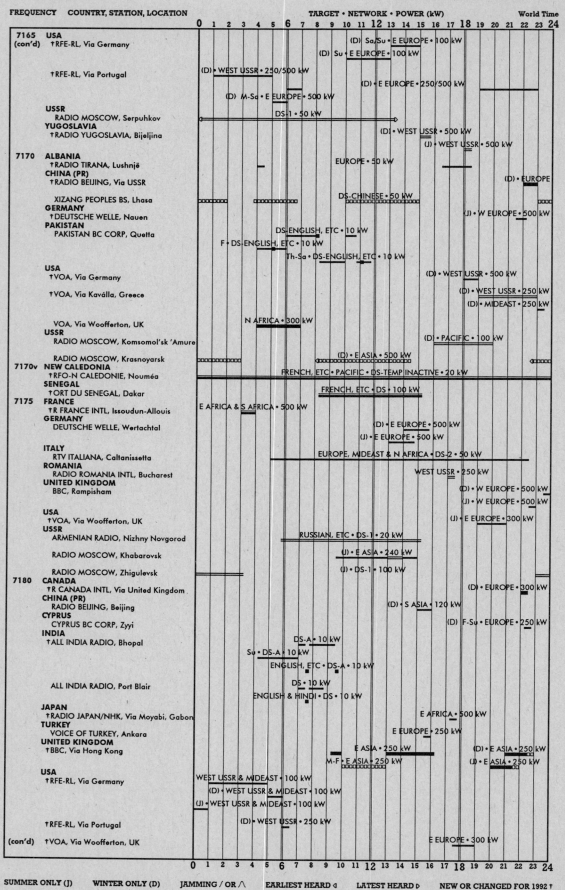

7165 **USA**	
(con'd) †RFE-RL, Via Germany	(D) • Sa/Su • E EUROPE • 100 kW
	(D) • Su • E EUROPE • 100 kW
†RFE-RL, Via Portugal	(D) • WEST USSR • 250/500 kW
	(D) • E EUROPE • 250/500 kW
	(D) • M-Sa • E EUROPE • 500 kW
USSR	
RADIO MOSCOW, Serpuhkov	DS-1 • 50 kW
YUGOSLAVIA	
†RADIO YUGOSLAVIA, Bijeljina	(D) • WEST USSR • 500 kW
	(J) • WEST USSR • 500 kW
7170 ALBANIA	
†RADIO TIRANA, Lushnjë	EUROPE • 50 kW
CHINA (PR)	
†RADIO BEIJING, Via USSR	(D) • EUROPE
XIZANG PEOPLES BS, Lhasa	DS-CHINESE • 50 kW
GERMANY	
†DEUTSCHE WELLE, Nauen	(J) • W EUROPE • 500 kW
PAKISTAN	
PAKISTAN BC CORP, Quetta	DS-ENGLISH, ETC • 10 kW
	F • DS-ENGLISH, ETC • 10 kW
	Th-Sa • DS-ENGLISH, ETC • 10 kW
USA	
†VOA, Via Germany	(D) • WEST USSR • 500 kW
†VOA, Via Kaválla, Greece	(D) • WEST USSR • 250 kW
	(D) • MIDEAST • 250 kW
VOA, Via Woofferton, UK	N AFRICA • 300 kW
USSR	
RADIO MOSCOW, Komsomol'sk 'Amure	(D) • PACIFIC • 100 kW
RADIO MOSCOW, Krasnoyarsk	(D) • E ASIA • 500 kW
7170v NEW CALEDONIA	
†RFO-N CALEDONIE, Nouméa	FRENCH, ETC • PACIFIC • DS-TEMP INACTIVE • 20 kW
SENEGAL	
†ORT DU SENEGAL, Dakar	FRENCH, ETC • DS • 100 kW
7175 FRANCE	
†R FRANCE INTL, Issoudun-Allouis	E AFRICA & S AFRICA • 500 kW
GERMANY	
DEUTSCHE WELLE, Wertachtal	(D) • E EUROPE • 500 kW
	(J) • E EUROPE • 500 kW
ITALY	
RTV ITALIANA, Caltanissetta	EUROPE, MIDEAST & N AFRICA • DS-2 • 50 kW
ROMANIA	
RADIO ROMANIA INTL, Bucharest	WEST USSR • 250 kW
UNITED KINGDOM	
BBC, Rampisham	(D) • W EUROPE • 500 kW
	(J) • W EUROPE • 500 kW
USA	
†VOA, Via Woofferton, UK	(J) • E EUROPE • 300 kW
USSR	
ARMENIAN RADIO, Nizhny Novgorod	RUSSIAN, ETC • DS-1 • 20 kW
RADIO MOSCOW, Khabarovsk	(J) • E ASIA • 240 kW
RADIO MOSCOW, Zhigulevsk	(J) • DS-1 • 100 kW
7180 CANADA	
†R CANADA INTL, Via United Kingdom	(D) • EUROPE • 300 kW
CHINA (PR)	
RADIO BEIJING, Beijing	(D) • S ASIA • 120 kW
CYPRUS	
CYPRUS BC CORP, Zyyi	(D) • F-Su • EUROPE • 250 kW
INDIA	
†ALL INDIA RADIO, Bhopal	DS-A • 10 kW
	Su • DS-A • 10 kW
	ENGLISH, ETC • DS-A • 10 kW
ALL INDIA RADIO, Port Blair	DS • 10 kW
	ENGLISH & HINDI • DS • 10 kW
JAPAN	
†RADIO JAPAN/NHK, Via Moyabi, Gabon	E AFRICA • 500 kW
TURKEY	
VOICE OF TURKEY, Ankara	E EUROPE • 250 kW
UNITED KINGDOM	
†BBC, Via Hong Kong	E ASIA • 250 kW
	(D) • E ASIA • 250 kW
	M-F • E ASIA • 250 kW
	(J) • E ASIA • 250 kW
USA	
†RFE-RL, Via Germany	WEST USSR & MIDEAST • 100 kW
	(D) • WEST USSR & MIDEAST • 100 kW
	(J) • WEST USSR & MIDEAST • 100 kW
†RFE-RL, Via Portugal	(D) • WEST USSR • 250 kW
(con'd) †VOA, Via Woofferton, UK	E EUROPE • 300 kW

SUMMER ONLY (J)   WINTER ONLY (D)   JAMMING / OR /\   EARLIEST HEARD ◁   LATEST HEARD ▷   NEW OR CHANGED FOR 1992 †

FREQUENCY   COUNTRY, STATION, LOCATION   TARGET • NETWORK • POWER (kW)   World Time

0 1 2 3 4 5 6 7 8 9 10 11 12 13 14 15 16 17 18 19 20 21 22 23 24

Frequency	Country, Station, Location	Target • Network • Power
7180 (con'd)	**USA** †VOA, Via Woofferton, UK	(D) • WEST USSR • 300 kW; (D) • E EUROPE • 300 kW; (J) • E EUROPE • 300 kW
7185	**GERMANY** †DEUTSCHE WELLE, Nauen	EUROPE & AFRICA • 100 kW
	MYANMAR (BURMA) VOICE OF MYANMAR, Yangon	DS-ENGLISH, BURMESE • 50 kW
	TURKEY †VOICE OF TURKEY, Ankara	(D) • MIDEAST • 250 kW
	USSR †RADIO MOSCOW, Minsk	DS-2 • 20 kW
	†RADIO MOSCOW, Novosibirsk	(D) • E ASIA • 100 kW
	†RADIO MOSCOW, Volgograd	DS-1 • 20 kW
	TATAR RADIO, Sverdlovsk	DS-RUSSIAN, TATAR • 20 kW
7189.5	**NAMIBIA** †NAMIBIAN BC CORP, Windhoek	DS • 100 kW
7190	**ALBANIA** †RADIO TIRANA, Lushnjë	EUROPE • 50 kW
	BENIN ORT DU BENIN, Parakou	FRENCH, ETC • DS • 20 kW
	CHINA (PR) RADIO BEIJING, Kunming	SE ASIA • 50 kW
	INDIA †ALL INDIA RADIO, Shillong	DS • 50 kW; ENGLISH & HINDI • DS • 50 kW
	IRAN †VO THE ISLAMIC REP, Tehrän	MIDEAST • 500 kW
	SRI LANKA †SRI LANKA BC CORP, Colombo-Ekala	S ASIA • 10 kW; Su • S ASIA • 10 kW
	USA †RFE-RL, Via Germany	WEST USSR • 100 kW; E EUROPE & WEST USSR • 100 kW; (J) • WEST USSR • 100 kW; (D) • WEST USSR • 100 kW; (D) • E EUROPE & WEST USSR • 100 kW; (J) • E EUROPE • 100 kW; (J) • E EUROPE & WEST USSR • 100 kW
	†RFE-RL, Via Portugal	E EUROPE • 250/500 kW; (D) • WEST USSR • 500 kW; (D) • E EUROPE • 250/500 kW; (J) • E EUROPE • 250 kW
	†VOA, Via Portugal	(D) • WEST USSR • 250 kW
	YEMEN (REPUBLIC) "VO PALESTINE", Via Rep Yemen Radio	MIDEAST • PLO • 100 kW
	†REP YEMEN RADIO, Aden	MIDEAST • DS • 100 kW; F • MIDEAST • DS • 100 kW; Irr • MIDEAST • DS-RAMADAN • 100 kW
7190v	**EQUATORIAL GUINEA** †RADIO AFRICA, Batá	W AFRICA • 50 kW • ALT. FREQ. TO 7203v kHz; Sa/Su • W AFRICA • 50 kW • ALT. FREQ. TO 7203v kHz
7190.8	**INDONESIA** †RRI, Yogyakarta, Jawa	DS • 50 kW
7195	**CHINA (PR)** CENTRAL PEOPLES BS, Urümqi	(J) • DS-MINORITIES • 15 kW
	†XINJIANG PBS, Urümqi	(J) • DS-UIGHUR • 15 kW
	FRANCE †R FRANCE INTL, Issoudun-Allouis	(D) • N AFRICA • 100 kW
	ROMANIA RADIO ROMANIA INTL, Bucharest	(D) • EUROPE • 250 kW
	UGANDA RADIO UGANDA, Kampala	DS-ENGLISH, ETC • 20 kW; Sa/Su • DS-ENGLISH, ETC • 20 kW; Su • DS-ENGLISH, ETC • 20 kW
	USSR RADIO MOSCOW, Komsomol'sk 'Amure	(J) • E ASIA & SE ASIA • 100 kW
	RADIO MOSCOW, Tula	(D) • EUROPE & E NORTH AM • 100 kW
	†RADIO TASHKENT, Tashkent	(D) • MIDEAST & S ASIA • 100 kW
7198v	**SOMALIA** †RADIO MOGADISHU, Mogadishu	DS • 100 kW; F • DS • 100 kW; Sa-Th • DS • 100 kW; Su-Th • DS • 100 kW
7199v	**AFGHANISTAN** RADIO AFGHANISTAN, Kabul	DS-1 • 50 kW
7200	**KOREA (DPR)** †RADIO PYONGYANG, Pyongyang	E ASIA & EAST USSR • 200 kW; E ASIA & SE ASIA • 200 kW
(con'd)	**SWAZILAND** †TRANS WORLD RADIO, Manzini	S AFRICA • 25 kW

0 1 2 3 4 5 6 7 8 9 10 11 12 13 14 15 16 17 18 19 20 21 22 23 24

ENGLISH ▬ ARABIC ▨ CHINESE □□□ FRENCH ▬ GERMAN ▬ RUSSIAN ▬ SPANISH ▬ OTHER —

FREQUENCY   COUNTRY, STATION, LOCATION   TARGET • NETWORK • POWER (kW)   World Time

Time scale: 0 1 2 3 4 5 6 7 8 9 10 11 12 13 14 15 16 17 18 19 20 21 22 23 24

7200 SWAZILAND
(con'd) †TRANS WORLD RADIO, Manzini
- (J) • S AFRICA • 25 kW
- M-F • S AFRICA • 25 kW

USA
†RFE-RL, Via Germany
- (D) • WEST USSR • 100/250 kW

†RFE-RL, Via Portugal
- (D) • WEST USSR • 250 kW

†VOA, Via Philippines
- E ASIA • 100 kW
- (D) • E ASIA • 100 kW

†VOA, Via Woofferton, UK
- EUROPE & MIDEAST • 250/300 kW

USSR
†BELORUSSIAN RADIO, Minsk
- RUSSIAN, ETC • DS-2 • 20 kW

RADIO MOSCOW, Vladivostok
- (D) • DS-MAYAK • 50 kW
- DS-MAYAK • 50 kW

RADIO MOSCOW, Zhigulevsk
- DS-1 • 100 kW
- (D) • DS-1 • 100 kW

†YAKUT RADIO, Yakutsk
- DS-RUSSIAN, YAKUT • 100 kW

7203v EQUATORIAL GUINEA
†RADIO AFRICA, Batá
- Alternative Frequency to 7190v kHz

ZAIRE
†LA VOIX DU ZAIRE, Lubumbashi
- DS-FRENCH, ETC • 10 kW
- Sa/Su • DS-FRENCH, ETC • 10 kW
- Su • DS-FRENCH, ETC • 10 kW

7205 ALBANIA
†RADIO TIRANA, Lushnjë
- WEST USSR • 100 kW
- MIDEAST • 100 kW
- EUROPE • 100 kW

AUSTRALIA
†RADIO AUSTRALIA, Carnarvon
- Alternative Frequency to 7240 kHz

CYPRUS
†CYPRUS BC CORP, Zyyi
- (J) F-Su • EUROPE • 250 kW

USA
†VOA, Via Kaválla, Greece
- S ASIA • 250 kW
- (J) • WEST USSR • 250 kW
- (D) • S ASIA • 250 kW

VOA, Via Rhodes, Greece
- (D) • MIDEAST • 50 kW

USSR
RADIO MOSCOW, Armavir
- EUROPE & ATLANTIC • 100 kW

RADIO MOSCOW, Kiev
- (D) • ATLANTIC & C AMERICA • 100 kW

RADIO MOSCOW, Krasnoyarsk
- (D) • S ASIA • 500 kW

†RADIO YEREVAN
- (D) • EUROPE
- (D) M-Sa • EUROPE
- (D) Su • EUROPE
- (J) • EUROPE • 100 kW

†SOVIET BELORUSSIA, Orcha

7210 CANADA
†R CANADA INTL, Via Sines, Portugal
- (D) • MIDEAST • 250 kW

INDIA
ALL INDIA RADIO, Calcutta
- DS • 10 kW
- Irr • DS • 10 kW
- ENGLISH & HINDI • DS • 10 kW

†ALL INDIA RADIO, Delhi
- S ASIA • 100 kW
- ENGLISH & HINDI • DS • 20 kW
- DS • 20 kW
- ENGLISH, ETC • DS • 100 kW

JAPAN
†RADIO JAPAN/NHK, Tokyo-Yamata
- E ASIA • 100 kW
- (J) • E ASIA • 100 kW
- E ASIA • GENERAL • 100 kW
- SE ASIA • GENERAL • 100 kW

SAUDI ARABIA
BS OF THE KINGDOM, Riyadh
- EUROPE • DS-GENERAL • 350 kW

SWITZERLAND
RED CROSS BC SVC, Beromünster
- Irr • M • EUROPE & N AFRICA • 1ST OR LAST MONDAY • 250 kW
- Irr • Su • EUROPE & N AFRICA • 1ST OR LAST SUNDAY • 250 kW

UNITED KINGDOM
†BBC, Rampisham
- (D) • WEST USSR • 500 kW
- E EUROPE • 500 kW
- (D) • EUROPE • 500 kW
- (D) • E EUROPE • 500 kW
- (D) M-F • E EUROPE • 500 kW
- (J) M-F • E EUROPE • 500 kW
- (D) Sa/Su • E EUROPE • 500 kW

USA
†VOA, Via Kaválla, Greece
- (D) • WEST USSR • 250 kW

†VOA, Via Portugal
- (J) • WEST USSR & S ASIA • 250 kW

†VOA, Via Woofferton, UK
- (J) • E EUROPE • 300 kW
- (D) • WEST USSR • 250 kW

USSR
(con'd) †KHABAROVSK RADIO, Khabarovsk
- DS-1/TIKHIY OKEAN • 50 kW

Time scale: 0 1 2 3 4 5 6 7 8 9 10 11 12 13 14 15 16 17 18 19 20 21 22 23 24

SUMMER ONLY (J)   WINTER ONLY (D)   JAMMING / OR ∧   EARLIEST HEARD ◁   LATEST HEARD ▷   NEW OR CHANGED FOR 1992 †

FREQUENCY   COUNTRY, STATION, LOCATION   TARGET • NETWORK • POWER (kW)   World Time

0 1 2 3 4 5 6 7 8 9 10 11 12 13 14 15 16 17 18 19 20 21 22 23 24

Frequency	Country, Station, Location	Target • Network • Power
7210 (con'd)	USSR RADIO MOSCOW, Moscow	DS-1 • 100 kW
7210v	CHINA (PR) †YUNNAN PEOPLES BS, Kunming	DS-1 • 50 kW
7215	AFGHANISTAN †RADIO AFGHANISTAN, Via USSR	(D) • EUROPE • 100 kW
	ALBANIA †RADIO TIRANA, Lushnjë	W EUROPE • 100 kW
	CHINA (PR) VOICE OF JINLING, Nanjing	E ASIA • 50 kW
	CUBA RADIO HABANA, Via USSR	(D) • W EUROPE • 500 kW
	IRAN VO THE ISLAMIC REP, Tehrān	MIDEAST • 500 kW
	IVORY COAST †RTV IVOIRIENNE, Abidjan	DS • 20 kW
	PAKISTAN †RADIO PAKISTAN, Islamabad	MIDEAST • 100 kW
	SEYCHELLES †FAR EAST BC ASS'N, North Pt, Mahé Is	S ASIA • 100 kW
7215v	ANGOLA RADIO NACIONAL, Luanda	DS-B • 10 kW
7220	HUNGARY †RADIO BUDAPEST	Su • EUROPE M-Sa • EUROPE
	SAUDI ARABIA BS OF THE KINGDOM, Riyadh	MIDEAST • DS-GENERAL • 350 kW
	USA †RFE-RL, Various Locations	WEST USSR • 100/250/500 kW
	USSR RADIO MOSCOW, Chita	E ASIA & SE ASIA • 500 kW
	†RADIO MOSCOW, Sverdlovsk	DS-2 • 100/240 kW
	YUGOSLAVIA †RADIO YUGOSLAVIA, Bijeljina	EUROPE & N AFRICA • 250 kW
7220v	ZAMBIA RADIO ZAMBIA-ZBS, Lusaka	DS-ENGLISH, ETC • 50 kW
7225	CHINA (PR) †SICHUAN PEOPLES BS, Chengdu	DS-1 • 15 kW
	GERMANY †DEUTSCHE WELLE, Jülich	(D) • S ASIA • 100 kW
	DEUTSCHE WELLE, Via Cyclops, Malta	(D) • MIDEAST • 250 kW
	DEUTSCHE WELLE, Via Kigali, Rwanda	C AFRICA & S AFRICA • 250 kW
	DEUTSCHE WELLE, Via Sri Lanka	S ASIA • 250 kW
	INDIA ALL INDIA RADIO, Aligarh	S ASIA • 250 kW
	†ALL INDIA RADIO, Delhi	DS • 100 kW ENGLISH, ETC • DS • 100 kW
	MONACO †TRANS WORLD RADIO, Monte Carlo	Alternative Frequency to 7230 kHz
	ROMANIA RADIO ROMANIA INTL, Bucharest	EUROPE • 250 kW (D) • EUROPE • 250 kW
	TURKEY †VOICE OF TURKEY, Ankara	(J) • MIDEAST • 250 kW
7230	BURKINA FASO †RTV BURKINA, Ouagadougou	FRENCH, ETC • DS • 50 kW Th/Sa/Su • FRENCH, ETC • DS • 50 kW
	CANADA †R CANADA INTL, Via United Kingdom	(D) • EUROPE • 300 kW (D) M-F • EUROPE • 300 kW
	INDIA ALL INDIA RADIO, Kurseong	S ASIA • 20 kW DS • 20 kW ENGLISH, ETC • DS • 20 kW
	INDONESIA †RRI, Fak Fak, Irian Jaya	DS • 0.5 kW
	IRAN †VO THE ISLAMIC REP, Tehrān	(D) • MIDEAST • 500 kW
	ITALY †ADVENTIST WORLD R, Forlì	EUROPE • 3 kW • ALT. FREQ. TO 7125 kHz Sa/Su • EUROPE • 3 kW • ALT. FREQ. TO 7125 kHz
	KOREA (DPR) †RADIO PYONGYANG, Pyongyang	E ASIA & SE ASIA • 200 kW
	MONACO †TRANS WORLD RADIO, Monte Carlo	(D) • E EUROPE • 100 kW • ALT. FREQ. TO 7290 kHz (J) • E EUROPE • 100 kW • ALT. FREQ TO 7225 kHz
	SOUTH AFRICA †RADIO RSA, Meyerton	S AFRICA • 250 kW S AFRICA • 100 kW (D) • S AFRICA • 250 kW (J) • W AFRICA & S AFRICA • 250/500 kW • ALT. FREQ. TO 9570 kHz
	UNITED KINGDOM †BBC, Skelton, Cumbria	EUROPE • 250 kW
	USSR RADIO MOSCOW, Kiev	(D) • EUROPE, W AFRICA & ATLANTIC • 240 kW EUROPE • 240 kW
(con'd)		

0 1 2 3 4 5 6 7 8 9 10 11 12 13 14 15 16 17 18 19 20 21 22 23 24

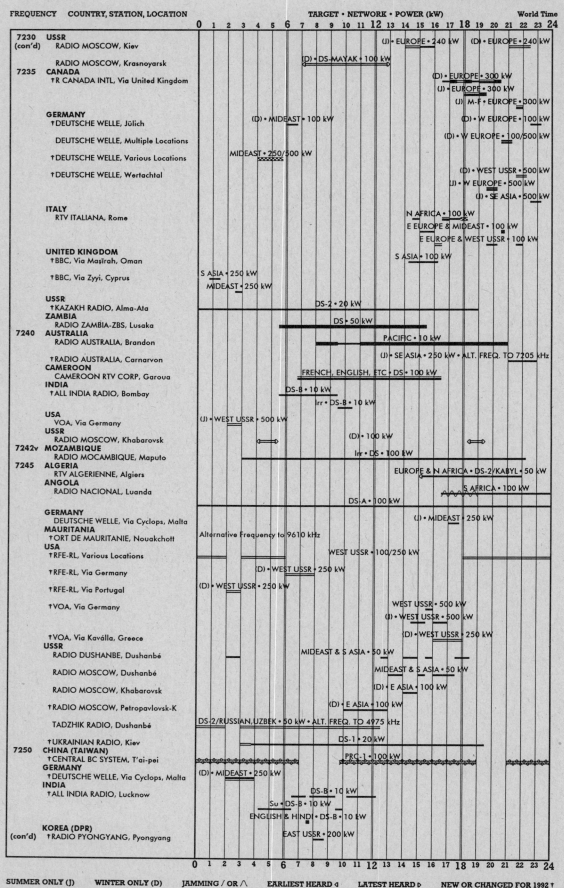

FREQUENCY   COUNTRY, STATION, LOCATION   TARGET • NETWORK • POWER (kW)   World Time

0 1 2 3 4 5 6 7 8 9 10 11 12 13 14 15 16 17 18 19 20 21 22 23 24

7230 **USSR** (con'd)
    RADIO MOSCOW, Kiev   (J) • EUROPE • 240 kW   (D) • EUROPE • 240 kW
    RADIO MOSCOW, Krasnoyarsk   (D) • DS-MAYAK • 100 kW

7235 **CANADA**
    †R CANADA INTL, Via United Kingdom   (D) • EUROPE • 300 kW
    (J) • EUROPE • 300 kW
    (J) • M-F • EUROPE • 300 kW

    GERMANY
    †DEUTSCHE WELLE, Jülich   (D) • MIDEAST • 100 kW   (D) • W EUROPE • 100 kW
    DEUTSCHE WELLE, Multiple Locations   (D) • W EUROPE • 100/500 kW
    †DEUTSCHE WELLE, Various Locations   MIDEAST • 250/500 kW
    †DEUTSCHE WELLE, Wertachtal   (D) • WEST USSR • 500 kW
    (J) • W EUROPE • 500 kW
    (J) • SE ASIA • 500 kW

    ITALY
    RTV ITALIANA, Rome   N AFRICA • 100 kW
    E EUROPE & MIDEAST • 100 kW
    E EUROPE & WEST USSR • 100 kW

    UNITED KINGDOM
    †BBC, Via Maṣīrah, Oman   S ASIA • 100 kW
    †BBC, Via Zyyi, Cyprus   S ASIA • 250 kW
    MIDEAST • 250 kW

    USSR
    †KAZAKH RADIO, Alma-Ata   DS-2 • 20 kW
    ZAMBIA
    RADIO ZAMBIA-ZBS, Lusaka   DS • 50 kW

7240 **AUSTRALIA**
    RADIO AUSTRALIA, Brandon   PACIFIC • 10 kW
    †RADIO AUSTRALIA, Carnarvon   (J) • SE ASIA • 250 kW • ALT. FREQ. TO 7205 kHz
    CAMEROON
    CAMEROON RTV CORP, Garoua   FRENCH, ENGLISH, ETC • DS • 100 kW
    INDIA
    †ALL INDIA RADIO, Bombay   DS-B • 10 kW
    Irr • DS-B • 10 kW

    USA
    VOA, Via Germany   (J) • WEST USSR • 500 kW
    USSR
    RADIO MOSCOW, Khabarovsk   (D) • 100 kW

7242v MOZAMBIQUE
    RADIO MOCAMBIQUE, Maputo   Irr • DS • 100 kW

7245 **ALGERIA**
    RTV ALGERIENNE, Algiers   EUROPE & N AFRICA • DS-2/KABYL • 50 kW
    ANGOLA
    RADIO NACIONAL, Luanda   S AFRICA • 100 kW
    DS-A • 100 kW

    GERMANY
    DEUTSCHE WELLE, Via Cyclops, Malta   (J) • MIDEAST • 250 kW
    MAURITANIA
    †ORT DE MAURITANIE, Nouakchott   Alternative Frequency to 9610 kHz
    USA
    †RFE-RL, Various Locations   WEST USSR • 100/250 kW
    †RFE-RL, Via Germany   (D) • WEST USSR • 250 kW
    †RFE-RL, Via Portugal   (D) • WEST USSR • 250 kW
    †VOA, Via Germany   WEST USSR • 500 kW
    (J) • WEST USSR • 500 kW
    †VOA, Via Kaválla, Greece   (D) • WEST USSR • 250 kW
    USSR
    RADIO DUSHANBE, Dushanbé   MIDEAST & S ASIA • 50 kW
    RADIO MOSCOW, Dushanbé   MIDEAST & S ASIA • 50 kW
    RADIO MOSCOW, Khabarovsk   (D) • E ASIA • 100 kW
    †RADIO MOSCOW, Petropavlovsk-K   (D) • E ASIA • 100 kW
    TADZHIK RADIO, Dushanbé   DS-2/RUSSIAN, UZBEK • 50 kW • ALT. FREQ. TO 4975 kHz
    †UKRAINIAN RADIO, Kiev   DS-1 • 20 kW

7250 **CHINA (TAIWAN)**
    †CENTRAL BC SYSTEM, T'ai-pei   PRC-1 • 100 kW
    GERMANY
    †DEUTSCHE WELLE, Via Cyclops, Malta   (D) • MIDEAST • 250 kW
    INDIA
    †ALL INDIA RADIO, Lucknow   DS-B • 10 kW
    Su • DS-B • 10 kW
    ENGLISH & HINDI • DS-B • 10 kW

    KOREA (DPR) (con'd)
    †RADIO PYONGYANG, Pyongyang   EAST USSR • 200 kW

0 1 2 3 4 5 6 7 8 9 10 11 12 13 14 15 16 17 18 19 20 21 22 23 24

FREQUENCY　COUNTRY, STATION, LOCATION　　　　　　TARGET • NETWORK • POWER (kW)　　　World Time

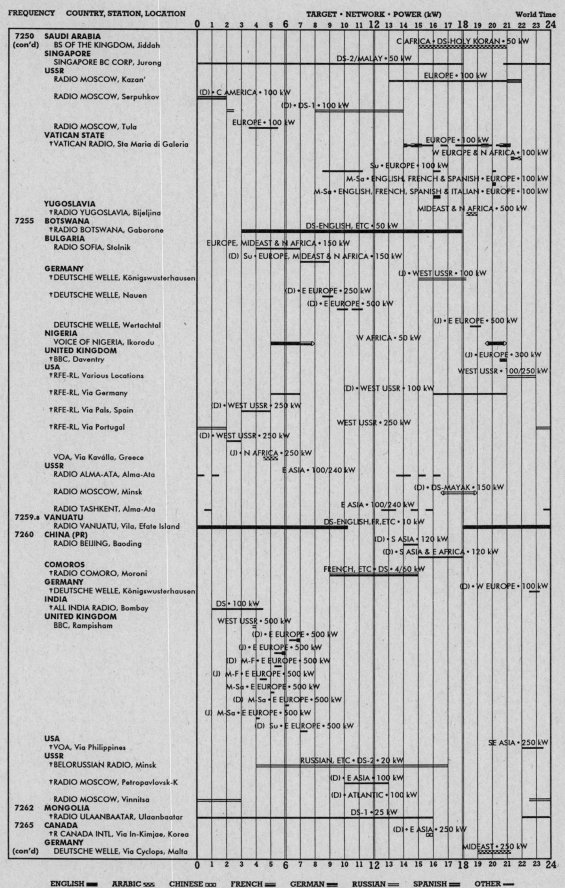

Freq	Country / Station / Location	Target • Network • Power
7250 (con'd)	**SAUDI ARABIA** BS OF THE KINGDOM, Jiddah	C AFRICA • DS-HOLY KORAN • 50 kW
	SINGAPORE SINGAPORE BC CORP, Jurong	DS-2/MALAY • 50 kW
	USSR RADIO MOSCOW, Kazan'	EUROPE • 100 kW
	RADIO MOSCOW, Serpuhkov	(D) • C AMERICA • 100 kW; (D) • DS-1 • 100 kW
	RADIO MOSCOW, Tula	EUROPE • 100 kW
	VATICAN STATE †VATICAN RADIO, Sta Maria di Galeria	EUROPE • 100 kW; W EUROPE & N AFRICA • 100 kW; Su • EUROPE • 100 kW; M-Sa • ENGLISH, FRENCH & SPANISH • EUROPE • 100 kW; M-Sa • ENGLISH, FRENCH, SPANISH & ITALIAN • EUROPE • 100 kW
	YUGOSLAVIA †RADIO YUGOSLAVIA, Bijeljina	MIDEAST & N AFRICA • 500 kW
7255	**BOTSWANA** †RADIO BOTSWANA, Gaborone	DS-ENGLISH, ETC • 50 kW
	BULGARIA RADIO SOFIA, Stolnik	EUROPE, MIDEAST & N AFRICA • 150 kW; (D) Su • EUROPE, MIDEAST & N AFRICA • 150 kW
	GERMANY †DEUTSCHE WELLE, Königswusterhausen	(J) • WEST USSR • 100 kW
	†DEUTSCHE WELLE, Nauen	(D) • E EUROPE • 250 kW; (D) • E EUROPE • 500 kW
	DEUTSCHE WELLE, Wertachtal	(J) • E EUROPE • 500 kW
	NIGERIA VOICE OF NIGERIA, Ikorodu	W AFRICA • 50 kW
	UNITED KINGDOM †BBC, Daventry	(J) • EUROPE • 300 kW
	USA †RFE-RL, Various Locations	WEST USSR • 100/250 kW
	†RFE-RL, Via Germany	(D) • WEST USSR • 100 kW
	†RFE-RL, Via Pals, Spain	(D) • WEST USSR • 250 kW
	†RFE-RL, Via Portugal	WEST USSR • 250 kW
	†RFE-RL, Via Portugal	(D) • WEST USSR • 250 kW
	VOA, Via Kaválla, Greece	(J) • N AFRICA • 250 kW
	USSR RADIO ALMA-ATA, Alma-Ata	E ASIA • 100/240 kW
	RADIO MOSCOW, Minsk	(D) • DS-MAYAK • 150 kW
	RADIO TASHKENT, Alma-Ata	E ASIA • 100/240 kW
7259.8	**VANUATU** RADIO VANUATU, Vila, Efate Island	DS-ENGLISH, FR, ETC • 10 kW
7260	**CHINA (PR)** RADIO BEIJING, Baoding	(D) • S ASIA • 120 kW; (D) • S ASIA & E AFRICA • 120 kW
	COMOROS †RADIO COMORO, Moroni	FRENCH, ETC • DS • 4/60 kW
	GERMANY †DEUTSCHE WELLE, Königswusterhausen	(D) • W EUROPE • 100 kW
	INDIA †ALL INDIA RADIO, Bombay	DS • 100 kW
	UNITED KINGDOM BBC, Rampisham	WEST USSR • 500 kW; (D) • E EUROPE • 500 kW; (J) • E EUROPE • 500 kW; (D) M-F • E EUROPE • 500 kW; (J) M-F • E EUROPE • 500 kW; M-Sa • E EUROPE • 500 kW; (D) M-Sa • E EUROPE • 500 kW; (J) M-Sa • E EUROPE • 500 kW; (D) Su • E EUROPE • 500 kW
	USA †VOA, Via Philippines	SE ASIA • 250 kW
	USSR †BELORUSSIAN RADIO, Minsk	RUSSIAN, ETC • DS-2 • 20 kW
	†RADIO MOSCOW, Petropavlovsk-K	(D) • E ASIA • 100 kW
	RADIO MOSCOW, Vinnitsa	(D) • ATLANTIC • 100 kW
7262	**MONGOLIA** †RADIO ULAANBAATAR, Ulaanbaatar	DS-1 • 25 kW
7265	**CANADA** †R CANADA INTL, Via In-Kimjae, Korea	(D) • E ASIA • 250 kW
	GERMANY	
(con'd)	DEUTSCHE WELLE, Via Cyclops, Malta	MIDEAST • 250 kW

ENGLISH ▬　ARABIC ⬚⬚⬚　CHINESE ⬚⬚⬚　FRENCH ══　GERMAN ▬▬　RUSSIAN ══　SPANISH ──　OTHER ▬

FREQUENCY   COUNTRY, STATION, LOCATION

TARGET • NETWORK • POWER (kW)   World Time

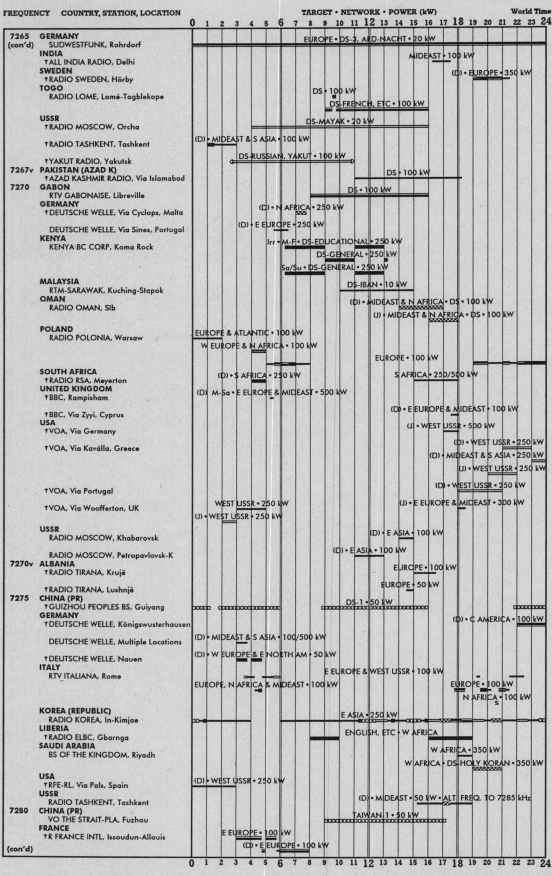

Frequency	Country / Station / Location	Schedule
7265 (con'd)	**GERMANY** SUDWESTFUNK, Rohrdorf	EUROPE • DS-3, ARD-NACHT • 20 kW
	INDIA †ALL INDIA RADIO, Delhi	MIDEAST • 100 kW
	SWEDEN †RADIO SWEDEN, Hörby	(D) • EUROPE • 350 kW
	TOGO RADIO LOME, Lomé-Togblekope	DS • 100 kW / DS-FRENCH, ETC • 100 kW
	USSR †RADIO MOSCOW, Orcha	DS-MAYAK • 20 kW
	†RADIO TASHKENT, Tashkent	(D) • MIDEAST & S ASIA • 100 kW
	†YAKUT RADIO, Yakutsk	DS-RUSSIAN, YAKUT • 100 kW
7267v	**PAKISTAN (AZAD K)** †AZAD KASHMIR RADIO, Via Islamabad	DS • 100 kW
7270	**GABON** RTV GABONAISE, Libreville	DS • 100 kW
	GERMANY †DEUTSCHE WELLE, Via Cyclops, Malta	(D) • N AFRICA • 250 kW
	DEUTSCHE WELLE, Via Sines, Portugal	(D) • E EUROPE • 250 kW
	KENYA KENYA BC CORP, Koma Rock	Irr • M-F • DS-EDUCATIONAL • 250 kW / DS-GENERAL • 250 kW / Sa/Su • DS-GENERAL • 250 kW
	MALAYSIA RTM-SARAWAK, Kuching-Stapok	DS-IBAN • 10 kW
	OMAN RADIO OMAN, Sīb	(D) • MIDEAST & N AFRICA • DS • 100 kW / (J) • MIDEAST & N AFRICA • DS • 100 kW
	POLAND RADIO POLONIA, Warsaw	EUROPE & ATLANTIC • 100 kW / W EUROPE & N AFRICA • 100 kW / EUROPE • 100 kW
	SOUTH AFRICA †RADIO RSA, Meyerton	(D) • S AFRICA • 250 kW / S AFRICA • 250/500 kW
	UNITED KINGDOM †BBC, Rampisham	(D) M-Sa • E EUROPE & MIDEAST • 500 kW
	†BBC, Via Zyyi, Cyprus	(D) • E EUROPE & MIDEAST • 100 kW
	USA †VOA, Via Germany	(J) • WEST USSR • 500 kW
	†VOA, Via Kaválla, Greece	(D) • WEST USSR • 250 kW / (D) • MIDEAST & S ASIA • 250 kW / (J) • WEST USSR • 250 kW
	†VOA, Via Portugal	(D) • WEST USSR • 250 kW
	†VOA, Via Woofferton, UK	WEST USSR • 250 kW / (J) • WEST USSR • 250 kW / (J) • E EUROPE & MIDEAST • 300 kW
	USSR RADIO MOSCOW, Khabarovsk	(D) • E ASIA • 100 kW
	RADIO MOSCOW, Petropavlovsk-K	(D) • E ASIA • 100 kW
7270v	**ALBANIA** †RADIO TIRANA, Krujë	EUROPE • 100 kW
	†RADIO TIRANA, Lushnjë	EUROPE • 50 kW
7275	**CHINA (PR)** †GUIZHOU PEOPLES BS, Guiyang	DS-1 • 50 kW
	GERMANY †DEUTSCHE WELLE, Königswusterhausen	(D) • C AMERICA • 100 kW
	DEUTSCHE WELLE, Multiple Locations	(D) • MIDEAST & S ASIA • 100/500 kW
	†DEUTSCHE WELLE, Nauen	(D) • W EUROPE & E NORTH AM • 50 kW
	ITALY RTV ITALIANA, Rome	E EUROPE & WEST USSR • 100 kW / EUROPE, N AFRICA & MIDEAST • 100 kW / EUROPE • 100 kW / N AFRICA • 100 kW
	KOREA (REPUBLIC) RADIO KOREA, In-Kimjae	E ASIA • 250 kW
	LIBERIA †RADIO ELBC, Gbarnga	ENGLISH, ETC • W AFRICA
	SAUDI ARABIA BS OF THE KINGDOM, Riyadh	W AFRICA • 350 kW / W AFRICA • DS-HOLY KORAN • 350 kW
	USA †RFE-RL, Via Pals, Spain	(D) • WEST USSR • 250 kW
	USSR RADIO TASHKENT, Tashkent	(D) • MIDEAST • 50 kW • ALT FREQ. TO 7285 kHz
7280	**CHINA (PR)** VO THE STRAIT-PLA, Fuzhou	TAIWAN-1 • 50 kW
	FRANCE †R FRANCE INTL, Issoudun-Allouis	E EUROPE • 100 kW / (D) • E EUROPE • 100 kW
(con'd)		

| FREQUENCY | COUNTRY, STATION, LOCATION | TARGET • NETWORK • POWER (kW) | World Time |

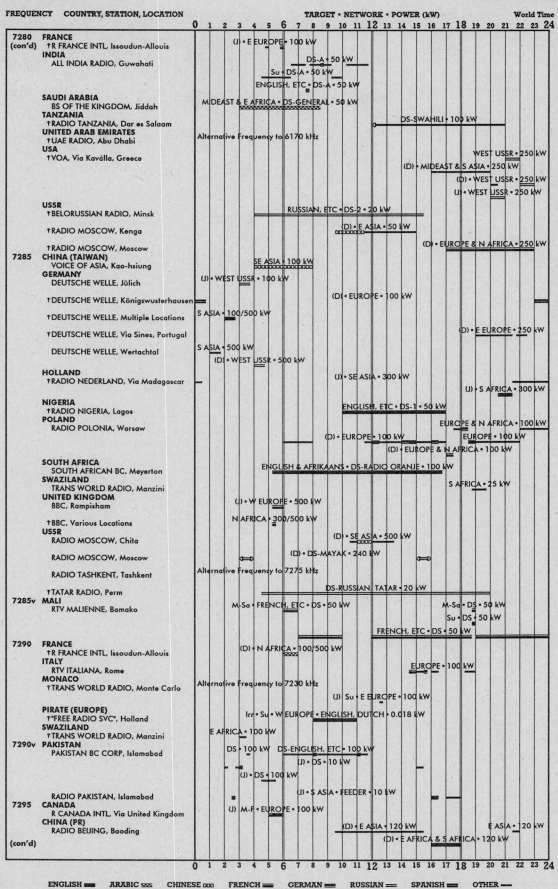

7280
(con'd) **FRANCE**
         †R FRANCE INTL, Issoudun-Allouis   (J) • E EUROPE • 100 kW
         INDIA
         ALL INDIA RADIO, Guwahati   DS-A • 50 kW
                                                 Su • DS-A • 50 kW
                                                 ENGLISH, ETC • DS-A • 50 kW
         SAUDI ARABIA
         BS OF THE KINGDOM, Jiddah   MIDEAST & E AFRICA • DS-GENERAL • 50 kW
         TANZANIA
         †RADIO TANZANIA, Dar es Salaam   DS-SWAHILI • 100 kW
         UNITED ARAB EMIRATES
         †UAE RADIO, Abu Dhabi   Alternative Frequency to 6170 kHz
         USA
         †VOA, Via Kaválla, Greece   WEST USSR • 250 kW
                                                 (D) • MIDEAST & S ASIA • 250 kW
                                                 (D) • WEST USSR • 250 kW
                                                 (J) • WEST USSR • 250 kW
         USSR
         †BELORUSSIAN RADIO, Minsk   RUSSIAN, ETC • DS-2 • 20 kW
         †RADIO MOSCOW, Kenga   (D) • E ASIA • 50 kW
         †RADIO MOSCOW, Moscow   (D) • EUROPE & N AFRICA • 250 kW

7285   **CHINA (TAIWAN)**
         VOICE OF ASIA, Kao-hsiung   SE ASIA • 100 kW
         GERMANY
         DEUTSCHE WELLE, Jülich   (J) • WEST USSR • 100 kW
         †DEUTSCHE WELLE, Königswusterhausen   (D) • EUROPE • 100 kW
         †DEUTSCHE WELLE, Multiple Locations   S ASIA • 100/500 kW
         †DEUTSCHE WELLE, Via Sines, Portugal   (D) • E EUROPE • 250 kW
         DEUTSCHE WELLE, Wertachtal   S ASIA • 500 kW
                                                 (D) • WEST USSR • 500 kW
         HOLLAND
         †RADIO NEDERLAND, Via Madagascar   (J) • SE ASIA • 300 kW
                                                 (J) • S AFRICA • 300 kW
         NIGERIA
         †RADIO NIGERIA, Lagos   ENGLISH, ETC • DS-1 • 50 kW
         POLAND
         RADIO POLONIA, Warsaw   EUROPE & N AFRICA • 100 kW
                                                 (D) • EUROPE • 100 kW   EUROPE • 100 kW
                                                 (D) • EUROPE & N AFRICA • 100 kW
         SOUTH AFRICA
         SOUTH AFRICAN BC, Meyerton   ENGLISH & AFRIKAANS • DS-RADIO ORANJE • 100 kW
         SWAZILAND
         TRANS WORLD RADIO, Manzini   S AFRICA • 25 kW
         UNITED KINGDOM
         BBC, Rampisham   (J) • W EUROPE • 500 kW
         †BBC, Various Locations   N AFRICA • 300/500 kW
         USSR
         RADIO MOSCOW, Chita   (D) • SE ASIA • 500 kW
         RADIO MOSCOW, Moscow   (D) • DS-MAYAK • 240 kW
         RADIO TASHKENT, Tashkent   Alternative Frequency to 7275 kHz
         †TATAR RADIO, Perm   DS-RUSSIAN, TATAR • 20 kW

7285v   **MALI**
         RTV MALIENNE, Bamako   M-Sa • FRENCH, ETC • DS • 50 kW   M-Sa • DS • 50 kW
                                                                                      Su • DS • 50 kW
                                                 FRENCH, ETC • DS • 50 kW

7290   **FRANCE**
         †R FRANCE INTL, Issoudun-Allouis   (D) • N AFRICA • 100/500 kW
         ITALY
         RTV ITALIANA, Rome   EUROPE • 100 kW
         MONACO
         †TRANS WORLD RADIO, Monte Carlo   Alternative Frequency to 7230 kHz
                                                 (J) Su • E EUROPE • 100 kW
         PIRATE (EUROPE)
         †"FREE RADIO SVC", Holland   Irr • Su • W EUROPE • ENGLISH, DUTCH • 0.018 kW
         SWAZILAND
         †TRANS WORLD RADIO, Manzini   E AFRICA • 100 kW
7290v   **PAKISTAN**
         PAKISTAN BC CORP, Islamabad   DS • 100 kW   DS-ENGLISH, ETC • 100 kW
                                                 (J) • DS • 10 kW
                                                 (J) • DS • 100 kW
         RADIO PAKISTAN, Islamabad   (J) • S ASIA • FEEDER • 10 kW
7295   **CANADA**
         R CANADA INTL, Via United Kingdom   (J) M-F • EUROPE • 100 kW
         CHINA (PR)
         RADIO BEIJING, Baoding   (D) • E ASIA • 120 kW   E ASIA • 120 kW
                                                 (D) • E AFRICA & S AFRICA • 120 kW
(con'd)

ENGLISH ▬▬   ARABIC ≈≈≈   CHINESE □□□   FRENCH ▬▬   GERMAN ▬▬   RUSSIAN ══   SPANISH ▬▬   OTHER ▬

FREQUENCY   COUNTRY, STATION, LOCATION   TARGET • NETWORK • POWER (kW)   World Time

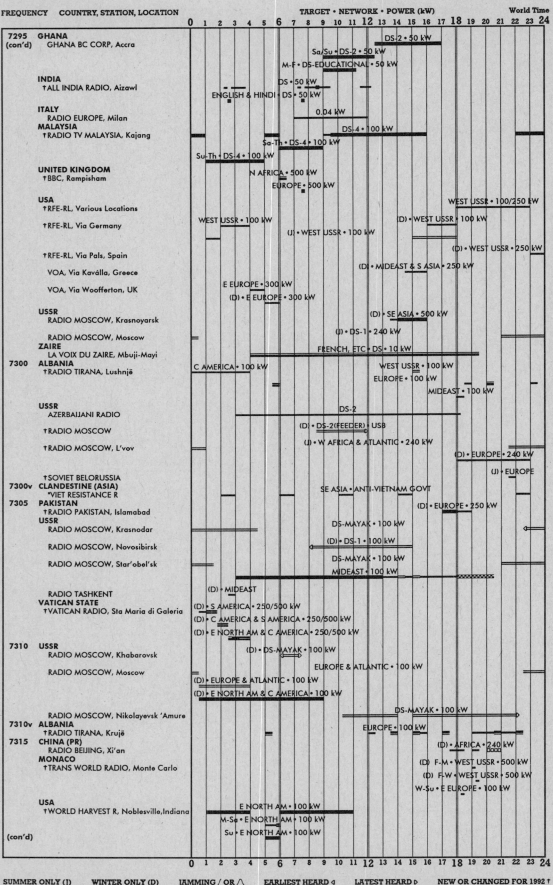

FREQUENCY	COUNTRY, STATION, LOCATION	TARGET • NETWORK • POWER (kW)
7295 (con'd)	GHANA — GHANA BC CORP, Accra	DS-2 • 50 kW / Sa/Su • DS-2 • 50 kW / M-F • DS-EDUCATIONAL • 50 kW
	INDIA — †ALL INDIA RADIO, Aizawl	DS • 50 kW / ENGLISH & HINDI • DS • 50 kW
	ITALY — RADIO EUROPE, Milan	0.04 kW
	MALAYSIA — †RADIO TV MALAYSIA, Kajang	DS-4 • 100 kW / Sa-Th • DS-4 • 100 kW / Su-Th • DS-4 • 100 kW
	UNITED KINGDOM — †BBC, Rampisham	N AFRICA • 500 kW / EUROPE • 500 kW
	USA — †RFE-RL, Various Locations	WEST USSR • 100/250 kW
	†RFE-RL, Via Germany	WEST USSR • 100 kW / (D) • WEST USSR • 100 kW / (J) • WEST USSR • 100 kW
	†RFE-RL, Via Pals, Spain	(D) • WEST USSR • 250 kW
	VOA, Via Kaválla, Greece	(D) • MIDEAST & S ASIA • 250 kW
	VOA, Via Woofferton, UK	E EUROPE • 300 kW / (D) • E EUROPE • 300 kW
	USSR — RADIO MOSCOW, Krasnoyarsk	(D) • SE ASIA • 500 kW
	RADIO MOSCOW, Moscow	(J) • DS-1 • 240 kW
	ZAIRE — LA VOIX DU ZAIRE, Mbuji-Mayi	FRENCH, ETC • DS • 10 kW
7300	ALBANIA — †RADIO TIRANA, Lushnjë	C AMERICA • 100 kW / WEST USSR • 100 kW / EUROPE • 100 kW / MIDEAST • 100 kW
	USSR — AZERBAIJANI RADIO	DS-2
	†RADIO MOSCOW	(D) • DS-2(FEEDER) • USB
	†RADIO MOSCOW, L'vov	(J) • W AFRICA & ATLANTIC • 240 kW / (D) • EUROPE • 240 kW
	†SOVIET BELORUSSIA	(J) • EUROPE
7300v	CLANDESTINE (ASIA) — "VIET RESISTANCE R	SE ASIA • ANTI-VIETNAM GOVT
7305	PAKISTAN — †RADIO PAKISTAN, Islamabad	(D) • EUROPE • 250 kW
	USSR — RADIO MOSCOW, Krasnodar	DS-MAYAK • 100 kW
	RADIO MOSCOW, Novosibirsk	(D) • DS-1 • 100 kW
	RADIO MOSCOW, Star'obel'sk	DS-MAYAK • 100 kW / MIDEAST • 100 kW
	RADIO TASHKENT	(D) • MIDEAST
	VATICAN STATE — †VATICAN RADIO, Sta Maria di Galeria	(D) • S AMERICA • 250/500 kW / (D) • C AMERICA & S AMERICA • 250/500 kW / (D) • E NORTH AM & C AMERICA • 250/500 kW
7310	USSR — RADIO MOSCOW, Khabarovsk	(D) • DS-MAYAK • 100 kW
	RADIO MOSCOW, Moscow	EUROPE & ATLANTIC • 100 kW / (D) • EUROPE & ATLANTIC • 100 kW / (D) • E NORTH AM & C AMERICA • 100 kW
	RADIO MOSCOW, Nikolayevsk 'Amure	DS-MAYAK • 100 kW
7310v	ALBANIA — †RADIO TIRANA, Krujë	EUROPE • 100 kW
7315	CHINA (PR) — RADIO BEIJING, Xi'an	(D) • AFRICA • 240 kW
	MONACO — †TRANS WORLD RADIO, Monte Carlo	(D) F-M • WEST USSR • 500 kW / (D) F-W • WEST USSR • 500 kW / W-Su • E EUROPE • 100 kW
	USA — †WORLD HARVEST R, Noblesville, Indiana	E NORTH AM • 100 kW / M-Sa • E NORTH AM • 100 kW / Su • E NORTH AM • 100 kW
(con'd)		

FREQUENCY   COUNTRY, STATION, LOCATION   TARGET • NETWORK • POWER (kW)   **World Time**

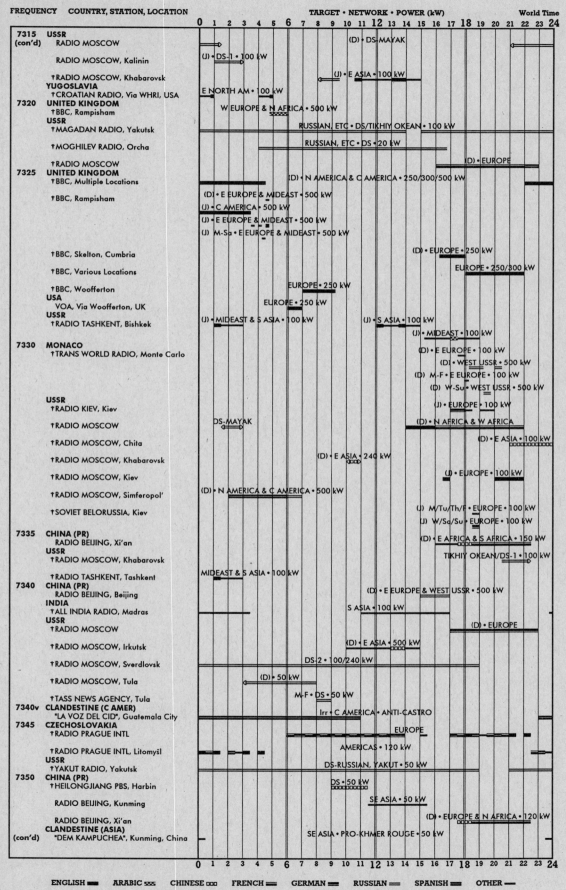

7315   **USSR**
(con'd)   RADIO MOSCOW — (D) • DS-MAYAK
           RADIO MOSCOW, Kalinin — (J) • DS-1 • 100 kW
           †RADIO MOSCOW, Khabarovsk — (J) • E ASIA • 100 kW
    YUGOSLAVIA
           †CROATIAN RADIO, Via WHRI, USA — E NORTH AM • 100 kW

7320   **UNITED KINGDOM**
           †BBC, Rampisham — W EUROPE & N AFRICA • 500 kW
    USSR
           †MAGADAN RADIO, Yakutsk — RUSSIAN, ETC • DS/TIKHIY OKEAN • 100 kW
           †MOGHILEV RADIO, Orcha — RUSSIAN, ETC • DS • 20 kW
           †RADIO MOSCOW — (D) • EUROPE

7325   **UNITED KINGDOM**
           †BBC, Multiple Locations — (D) • N AMERICA & C AMERICA • 250/300/500 kW
           †BBC, Rampisham — (D) • E EUROPE & MIDEAST • 500 kW
                      (J) • C AMERICA • 500 kW
                      (J) • E EUROPE & MIDEAST • 500 kW
                      (J) M-Sa • E EUROPE & MIDEAST • 500 kW
           †BBC, Skelton, Cumbria — (D) • EUROPE • 250 kW
           †BBC, Various Locations — EUROPE • 250/300 kW
           †BBC, Woofferton — EUROPE • 250 kW
    USA
           VOA, Via Woofferton, UK — EUROPE • 250 kW
    USSR
           †RADIO TASHKENT, Bishkek — (J) • MIDEAST & S ASIA • 100 kW   (J) • S ASIA • 100 kW
                      (J) • MIDEAST • 100 kW

7330   **MONACO**
           †TRANS WORLD RADIO, Monte Carlo — (D) • E EUROPE • 100 kW
                      (D) • WEST USSR • 500 kW
                      (D) M-F • E EUROPE • 100 kW
                      (D) W-Su • WEST USSR • 500 kW
    USSR
           †RADIO KIEV, Kiev — (J) • EUROPE • 100 kW
           †RADIO MOSCOW — DS-MAYAK   (D) • N AFRICA & W AFRICA
           †RADIO MOSCOW, Chita — (D) • E ASIA • 100 kW
           †RADIO MOSCOW, Khabarovsk — (D) • E ASIA • 240 kW
           †RADIO MOSCOW, Kiev — (J) • EUROPE • 100 kW
           †RADIO MOSCOW, Simferopol' — (D) • N AMERICA & C AMERICA • 500 kW
           †SOVIET BELORUSSIA, Kiev — (J) M/Tu/Th/F • EUROPE • 100 kW
                      (J) W/Sa/Su • EUROPE • 100 kW

7335   **CHINA (PR)**
           RADIO BEIJING, Xi'an — (D) • E AFRICA & S AFRICA • 150 kW
    USSR
           †RADIO MOSCOW, Khabarovsk — TIKHIY OKEAN/DS-1 • 100 kW
           †RADIO TASHKENT, Tashkent — MIDEAST & S ASIA • 100 kW

7340   **CHINA (PR)**
           RADIO BEIJING, Beijing — (D) • E EUROPE & WEST USSR • 500 kW
    INDIA
           †ALL INDIA RADIO, Madras — S ASIA • 100 kW
    USSR
           †RADIO MOSCOW — (D) • EUROPE
           †RADIO MOSCOW, Irkutsk — (D) • E ASIA • 500 kW
           †RADIO MOSCOW, Sverdlovsk — DS-2 • 100/240 kW
           †RADIO MOSCOW, Tula — (D) • 50 kW
           †TASS NEWS AGENCY, Tula — M-F • DS • 50 kW

7340v **CLANDESTINE (C AMER)**
           "LA VOZ DEL CID", Guatemala City — Irr • C AMERICA • ANTI-CASTRO

7345   **CZECHOSLOVAKIA**
           †RADIO PRAGUE INTL — EUROPE
           †RADIO PRAGUE INTL, Litomyšl — AMERICAS • 120 kW
    USSR
           †YAKUT RADIO, Yakutsk — DS-RUSSIAN, YAKUT • 50 kW

7350   **CHINA (PR)**
           †HEILONGJIANG PBS, Harbin — DS • 50 kW
           RADIO BEIJING, Kunming — SE ASIA • 50 kW
           RADIO BEIJING, Xi'an — (D) • EUROPE & N AFRICA • 120 kW
    CLANDESTINE (ASIA)
(con'd)   "DEM KAMPUCHEA", Kunming, China — SE ASIA • PRO-KHMER ROUGE • 50 kW

ENGLISH ▬   ARABIC ∿∿∿   CHINESE ▭▭▭   FRENCH ═══   GERMAN ▬▬   RUSSIAN ══   SPANISH ▬▬   OTHER ▬

FREQUENCY   COUNTRY, STATION, LOCATION   TARGET • NETWORK • POWER (kW)   World Time

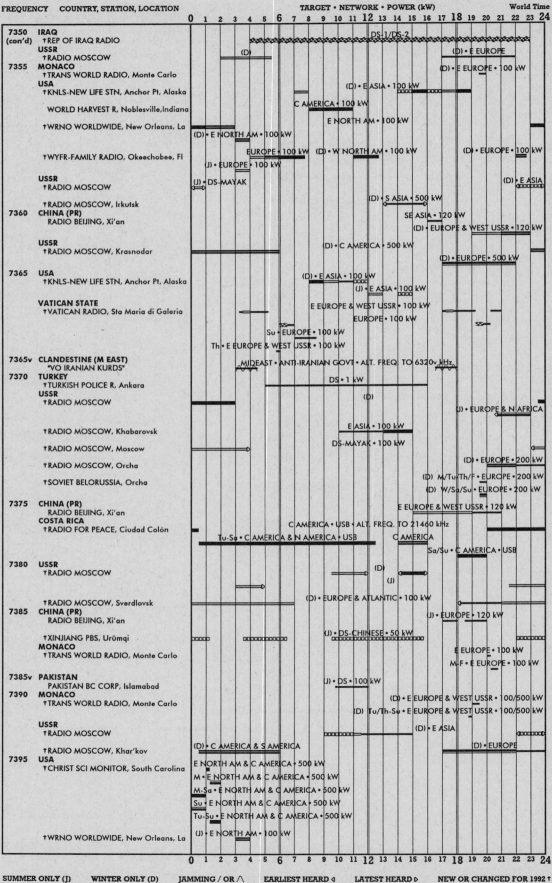

FREQUENCY	COUNTRY, STATION, LOCATION	TARGET • NETWORK • POWER (kW)
7350 (con'd)	IRAQ †REP OF IRAQ RADIO	DS-1/DS-2
	USSR †RADIO MOSCOW	(D) • E EUROPE
7355	MONACO †TRANS WORLD RADIO, Monte Carlo	(D) • E EUROPE • 100 kW
	USA †KNLS-NEW LIFE STN, Anchor Pt, Alaska	(D) • E ASIA • 100 kW
	WORLD HARVEST R, Noblesville, Indiana	C AMERICA • 100 kW
		E NORTH AM • 100 kW
	†WRNO WORLDWIDE, New Orleans, La	(D) • E NORTH AM • 100 kW
	†WYFR-FAMILY RADIO, Okeechobee, Fl	EUROPE • 100 kW (D) • W NORTH AM • 100 kW (D) • EUROPE • 100 kW
		(J) • EUROPE • 100 kW
	USSR †RADIO MOSCOW	(J) • DS-MAYAK (D) • E ASIA
	†RADIO MOSCOW, Irkutsk	(D) • S ASIA • 500 kW
7360	CHINA (PR) RADIO BEIJING, Xi'an	SE ASIA • 120 kW (D) • EUROPE & WEST USSR • 120 kW
	USSR †RADIO MOSCOW, Krasnodar	(D) • C AMERICA • 500 kW (D) • EUROPE • 500 kW
7365	USA †KNLS-NEW LIFE STN, Anchor Pt, Alaska	(D) • E ASIA • 100 kW (J) • E ASIA • 100 kW
	VATICAN STATE †VATICAN RADIO, Sta Maria di Galeria	E EUROPE & WEST USSR • 100 kW EUROPE • 100 kW
		Su • EUROPE • 100 kW
		Th • E EUROPE & WEST USSR • 100 kW
7365v	CLANDESTINE (M EAST) "VO IRANIAN KURDS"	MIDEAST • ANTI-IRANIAN GOVT • ALT. FREQ. TO 6320v kHz
7370	TURKEY †TURKISH POLICE R, Ankara	DS • 1 kW
	USSR †RADIO MOSCOW	(D) (J) • EUROPE & N AFRICA
	†RADIO MOSCOW, Khabarovsk	E ASIA • 100 kW
	†RADIO MOSCOW, Moscow	DS-MAYAK • 100 kW
	†RADIO MOSCOW, Orcha	(D) • EUROPE • 200 kW
	†SOVIET BELORUSSIA, Orcha	(D) M/Tu/Th/F • EUROPE • 200 kW (D) W/Sa/Su • EUROPE • 200 kW
7375	CHINA (PR) RADIO BEIJING, Xi'an	E EUROPE & WEST USSR • 120 kW
	COSTA RICA †RADIO FOR PEACE, Ciudad Colón	C AMERICA • USB • ALT. FREQ. TO 21460 kHz C AMERICA
		Tu-Sa • C AMERICA & N AMERICA • USB
		Sa/Su • C AMERICA • USB
7380	USSR †RADIO MOSCOW	(D) (J)
	†RADIO MOSCOW, Sverdlovsk	(D) • EUROPE & ATLANTIC • 100 kW
7385	CHINA (PR) RADIO BEIJING, Xi'an	(J) • EUROPE • 120 kW
	†XINJIANG PBS, Urümqi	(J) • DS-CHINESE • 50 kW
	MONACO †TRANS WORLD RADIO, Monte Carlo	E EUROPE • 100 kW M-F • E EUROPE • 100 kW
7385v	PAKISTAN PAKISTAN BC CORP, Islamabad	(J) • DS • 100 kW
7390	MONACO †TRANS WORLD RADIO, Monte Carlo	(D) • E EUROPE & WEST USSR • 100/500 kW (D) Tu/Th-Su • E EUROPE & WEST USSR • 100/500 kW
	USSR †RADIO MOSCOW	(D) • E ASIA
	†RADIO MOSCOW, Khar'kov	(D) • C AMERICA & S AMERICA (D) • EUROPE
7395	USA †CHRIST SCI MONITOR, South Carolina	E NORTH AM & C AMERICA • 500 kW
		M • E NORTH AM & C AMERICA • 500 kW
		M-Sa • E NORTH AM & C AMERICA • 500 kW
		Su • E NORTH AM & C AMERICA • 500 kW
		Tu-Su • E NORTH AM & C AMERICA • 500 kW
	†WRNO WORLDWIDE, New Orleans, La	(J) • E NORTH AM • 100 kW

SUMMER ONLY (J)   WINTER ONLY (D)   JAMMING / OR ∧   EARLIEST HEARD ◁   LATEST HEARD ▷   NEW OR CHANGED FOR 1992 †

FREQUENCY	COUNTRY, STATION, LOCATION	TARGET • NETWORK • POWER (kW) — World Time

0 1 2 3 4 5 6 7 8 9 10 11 12 13 14 15 16 17 18 19 20 21 22 23 24

7400 USSR
 †RADIO KIEV, Kiev — (D) • E NORTH AM • 100 kW
 †RADIO MOSCOW, Kiev — (D) • E NORTH AM • 100 kW ; E NORTH AM • 100 kW
 †RADIO MOSCOW, Moscow — (J) • EUROPE • 120 kW
 †RADIO MOSCOW, Volgograd — (J) • DS-MAYAK • 50 kW
 †RADIO VILNIUS, Kiev — (D) • E NORTH AM • 100 kW
 †RADIO YEREVAN, Kiev — (D) • E NORTH AM • 100 kW
 †SOVIET BELORUSSIA, Kiev — (D) • E NORTH AM • 100 kW

7405 USA
 †VOA, Cincinnati, Ohio — Alternative Frequency to 6030 kHz

7410 CLANDESTINE (N AMER)
 "VOICE OF TOMORROW, Virginia, USA — Irr • E NORTH AM • NEO-NAZI PARTY

7412 INDIA
 †ALL INDIA RADIO, Aligarh — SE ASIA • 250 kW ; S ASIA & E ASIA • 250 kW ; EUROPE • 250 kW ; MIDEAST • 250 kW ; DS • 250 kW

7416v VIETNAM
 VOICE OF VIETNAM — SE ASIA

7420 CHINA (PR)
 RADIO BEIJING, Beijing — (D) • S AMERICA • 240 kW ; (D) • WEST USSR & EUROPE • 240 kW
 USSR
 †RADIO MOSCOW, Minsk — (D) • EUROPE • 100 kW
 †RADIO MOSCOW, Moscow — DS-1 • 100 kW
 †SOVIET BELORUSSIA, Minsk — (D) • M/Tu/Th/F • EUROPE • 100 kW ; (D) • W/Sa/Su • EUROPE • 100 kW
 TASS NEWS AGENCY, Ul'yanovsk — M-F • DS • 100 kW

7425 PIRATE (EUROPE)
 †"FREE RADIO LONDON, England — Alternative Frequency to 6210 kHz ; Irr • Sa • W EUROPE
 †"RADIO MI AMIGO", England — Irr • Su • W EUROPE • 0.23 kW

7425v CLANDESTINE (S AMER)
 "LV DE RESISTENCIA, Colombia — Su • S AMERICA • USB

7430 GREECE
 FONI TIS HELLADAS, Athens — MIDEAST • 100 kW ; (D) • E EUROPE • 100 kW ; (D) • N AMERICA • 100 kW ; (D) • AUSTRALIA • 100 kW ; (D) • MIDEAST • 100 kW ; (D) • FRENCH & GERMAN • EUROPE • 100 kW ; (D) • EUROPE • 100 kW

7435 USA
 †WWCR, Nashville, Tennessee — E NORTH AM & EUROPE • 100 kW

7440 USSR
 †RADIO MOSCOW — (D) ; (D) • DS-1 ; (D) • W EUROPE & W AFRICA • 250 kW
 †RADIO MOSCOW, Moscow

7443 UNITED NATIONS
 UNITED NATIONS R, Via Switzerland — F • WEST USSR • 15 kW • USB

7445 CHINA (TAIWAN)
 VO FREE CHINA, T'ai-pei — E ASIA • 50 kW
 VOICE OF ASIA, Kao-hsiung — SE ASIA • 100 kW

7450 PIRATE (EUROPE)
 †"RADIO WAVES INTL", France — Irr • Su • ENGLISH & FRENCH • W EUROPE • 0.015 kW

7470 CHINA (PR)
 RADIO BEIJING, Xi'an — WEST USSR & E EUROPE • 500 kW ; EUROPE & N AFRICA • 500 kW

7475 TUNISIA
 †RTV TUNISIENNE, Sfax — Irr • DS-RAMADAN • 100 kW ; (D) • DS • 100 kW

7480 CHINA (PR)
 RADIO BEIJING, Beijing — E ASIA • 100 kW
 SWITZERLAND
 †RED CROSS BC SVC, Via Beijing, China — Irr • M/Th • E ASIA • 120 kW
 †SWISS RADIO INTL, Via Beijing, China — E ASIA • 120 kW ; M-Sa • E ASIA • 120 kW ; Su • E ASIA • 120 kW

7485 PIRATE (EUROPE)
 †"RADIO MARABU", Germany (FR) — Irr • Su • GERMAN & ENGLISH • W EUROPE • ALT. FREQ. TO 6235 kHz

7490v ETHIOPIA
 †VO BROAD MASSES, Asmera — E AFRICA • PLF OF ERITREA

7504 CHINA (PR)
 CENTRAL PEOPLES BS, Xi'an — DS-1 • 120 kW ; W-M • DS-1 • 120 kW

7510 USA
 †KTBN, Salt Lake City, Utah — E NORTH AM • 100 kW

7520 USA
 †WWCR, Nashville, Tennessee — E NORTH AM & EUROPE • 100 kW

0 1 2 3 4 5 6 7 8 9 10 11 12 13 14 15 16 17 18 19 20 21 22 23 24

ENGLISH ▬ ARABIC ≋ CHINESE ▫▫▫ FRENCH ═ GERMAN ▬ RUSSIAN ═ SPANISH ▬ OTHER ▬

FREQUENCY   COUNTRY, STATION, LOCATION   TARGET • NETWORK • POWER (kW)   World Time

0 1 2 3 4 5 6 7 8 9 10 11 12 13 14 15 16 17 18 19 20 21 22 23 24

Frequency	Country, Station, Location	Target • Network • Power (kW)
7538v	ITALY	
	VOICE OF EUROPE, Forni Alto	Irr • W EUROPE • 1 kW • ALT. FREQ. TO 13710 kHz
7550	KOREA (REPUBLIC)	
	RADIO KOREA, In-Kimjae	EUROPE • 250 kW MIDEAST & AFRICA • 250 kW
7565	USSR	
	KAZAKH TELEGRAPH, Alma-Ata	M/W/F • DS-NEWSCAST • 15 kW
7580	KOREA (DPR)	
	RADIO PYONGYANG, Pyongyang	E ASIA • 100 kW
7590	CHINA (PR)	
	RADIO BEIJING, Kunming	SE ASIA • 120 kW
		SE ASIA & S ASIA • 120 kW
7615	USSR	
	RADIO MOSCOW, Moscow	Irr • (FEEDER) • 20 kW • LSB
7651	USA	
	†VOA, Greenville, NC	EUROPE & MIDEAST • (FEEDER) • 40 kW • ISL
		(D) • EUROPE & MIDEAST • (FEEDER) • 40 kW • ISU
		(D) • EUROPE & MIDEAST • (FEEDER) • 40 kW • ISL
		(J) • EUROPE & MIDEAST • (FEEDER) • 40 kW • ISU
		(J) • EUROPE & MIDEAST • (FEEDER) • 40 kW • ISL
7660	CHINA (PR)	
	RADIO BEIJING, Xi'an	WEST USSR & EUROPE • 120 kW
7670	BULGARIA	
	BULGARIAN RADIO, Stolnik	DS-1 • 15 kW
7680	USSR	
	RADIO MOSCOW	(D) • (FEEDER) • USB
7695	USSR	
	RADIO MOSCOW	(D) • (FEEDER) • USB
7700	CHINA (PR)	
	RADIO BEIJING, Kunming	E EUROPE • 50 kW
7768.5	USA	
	VOA, Greenville, NC	N AFRICA • 40 kW • LSB
7770	CHINA (PR)	
	†CENTRAL PEOPLES BS, Kunming	DS-2 • 50 kW
7780	CHINA (PR)	
	RADIO BEIJING, Kunming	(D) • EUROPE • 50 kW
7800	CHINA (PR)	
	RADIO BEIJING, Kunming	(D) • EUROPE & N AFRICA • 50 kW
7820	CHINA (PR)	
	RADIO BEIJING, Beijing	USSR • 120 kW
		(D) • S AMERICA • 120 kW
		(D) • E EUROPE & WEST USSR • 120 kW
		(J) • E EUROPE • 120 kW
7820v	ETHIOPIA	
	†VO TIGRAY REVOL'N, Mek'ele	E AFRICA
7925	USSR	
	RADIO MOSCOW, Moscow	Irr • DS-MAYAK(FEEDER) • 20 kW • ISL
		Irr • DS-1(FEEDER) • 20 kW • ISU
7935	CHINA (PR)	
	†CENTRAL PEOPLES BS, Beijing	DS-1 • 15 kW
8005	USSR	
	RADIO MOSCOW, Moscow	Irr • DS-1(FEEDER) • 20 kW • ISU
		Irr • DS-MAYAK(FEEDER) • 20 kW • ISU
		Irr • DS-MAYAK(FEEDER) • 20 kW • ISL
		Irr • (D) • DS-MAYAK(FEEDER) • 20 kW • ISL
		Irr • (D) • DS-MAYAK(FEEDER) • 20 kW • ISU
		Irr • (J) • DS-MAYAK(FEEDER) • 20 kW • ISL
8140	USSR	
	†RADIO MOSCOW	(J) • DS-1(FEEDER) • USB
8260	CHINA (PR)	
	RADIO BEIJING, Beijing	E ASIA • FEEDER • 10 kW
		(D) • E ASIA • FEEDER • 10 kW
8345	CHINA (PR)	
	RADIO BEIJING, Beijing	(J) • E ASIA • FEEDER • 10 kW
	CLANDESTINE (ASIA)	
	"DEM KAMPUCHEA", China (PR)	(D) • SE ASIA • PRO-KHMER ROUGE
8350.3	IRAQ	
	†REP OF IRAQ RADIO	DS
8425	CHINA (PR)	
	RADIO BEIJING, Beijing	E ASIA • FEEDER • 100 kW
		(D) • E ASIA • FEEDER • 100 kW
	FRANCE	
	†R FRANCE INTL, Via Beijing, China	E ASIA • FEEDER • 100 kW
8450	CHINA (PR)	
	RADIO BEIJING, Beijing	E ASIA • FEEDER • 100 kW (J) • E ASIA • FEEDER • 100 kW
	CLANDESTINE (ASIA)	
	†"DEM KAMPUCHEA", China (PR)	SE ASIA • PRO-KHMER ROUGE
8566	CHINA (PR)	
	†CENTRAL PEOPLES BS	DS-MINORITIES
8660	CHINA (PR)	
	RADIO BEIJING, Beijing	E ASIA • FEEDER • 10 kW
8962	CLANDESTINE (M EAST)	
	†"GULF RADIO"	MIDEAST • ANTI-SADDAM • USB
9022	IRAN	
	†VO THE ISLAMIC REP, Tehrān	Irr • EUROPE • DS-RAMADAN • 500 kW • ALT. FREQ. TO 9790 kHz
		C AMERICA • 500 kW EUROPE & WEST USSR • 500 kW
		EUROPE • 500 kW
9045	CLANDESTINE (M EAST)	
	"IRAN FREEDOM FLAG, Egypt	MIDEAST • ANTI-IRANIAN GOVT • 100 kW

0 1 2 3 4 5 6 7 8 9 10 11 12 13 14 15 16 17 18 19 20 21 22 23 24

| FREQUENCY | COUNTRY, STATION, LOCATION | TARGET • NETWORK • POWER (kW) | World Time |

Time scale: 0 1 2 3 4 5 6 7 8 9 10 11 12 13 14 15 16 17 18 19 20 21 22 23 24

Frequency	Country, Station, Location	Target • Network • Power
9080	CHINA (PR) †CENTRAL PEOPLES BS, Beijing	DS-1 • 50 kW
9090	USSR KAZAKH TELEGRAPH, Alma-Ata	M/W/F • DS-NEWSCAST • 15 kW
9105	USSR RADIO MOSCOW	(D) • (FEEDER) • USB
9115	ARGENTINA †RADIO CONTINENTAL, Buenos Aires	Tu-Sa • DS(FEEDER) • 10 kW • USB; DS(FEEDER) • 10 kW • USB; M-F • DS(FEEDER) • 10 kW • USB; Sa/Su • DS(FEEDER) • 10 kW • USB
9145	USSR RADIO MOSCOW	(J) • (FEEDER) • USB
9150	USSR RADIO MOSCOW, Moscow	(J) • DS-1(FEEDER) • 20 kW • ISL; (J) • DS-1(FEEDER) • 20 kW • ISU
9170	CHINA (PR) CENTRAL PEOPLES BS, Beijing	CHINESE, ETC • TAIWAN-2 • 10 kW
9180	USSR †RADIO MOSCOW	WORLD SERVICE(FEEDER) • USB; (D) • WORLD SERVICE(FEEDER) • USB
	†RADIO MOSCOW, Khabarovsk	(J) • DS-MAYAK(FEEDER) • 15 kW • USB
9210	USSR †RADIO MOSCOW	(J) • DS-2(FEEDER) • USB
9239.3	USA AFRTS-US MILITARY, Via Barford, UK	Irr • ATLANTIC • DS-ABC/CBS/NBC/NPR(FEEDER) • 4 kW • USB
9242.3	USA AFRTS-US MILITARY, Via Barford, UK	Irr • ATLANTIC • DS-ABC/CBS/NBC/NPR(FEEDER) • 4 kW • LSB
9244.3	USA AFRTS-US MILITARY, Via Barford, UK	Irr • ATLANTIC • DS-ABC/CBS/NBC/NPR(FEEDER) • 4 kW • LSB
9250	USSR RADIO MOSCOW	(J) • (FEEDER) • USB
9265	ICELAND †RIKISUTVARPID, Reykjavik	ATLANTIC & EUROPE • DS-1 • 10 kW • USE; M-F • ATLANTIC & EUROPE • DS-1 • 10 kW • USB; Sa/Su • ATLANTIC & EUROPE • DS-1 • 10 kW • USB
9280	CHINA (TAIWAN) †VOICE OF ASIA, Kao-hsiung	E ASIA • 250 kW
	USA †FAMILY RADIO, Via Taiwan	E ASIA • 250 kW
9290	CHINA (PR) †CENTRAL PEOPLES BS, Beijing	DS-1 • 50 kW; W-M • DS-1 • 50 kW
9320	USSR RADIO MOSCOW	(D) • (FEEDER) • USB
9325	KOREA (DPR) RADIO PYONGYANG, Pyongyang	EUROPE & WEST USSR • 200 kW
9334.3	USA AFRTS-US MILITARY, Via Barford, UK	Irr • ATLANTIC • DS-ABC/CBS/NBC/NPR(FEEDER) • 4 kW • LSB
9345	KOREA (DPR) †RADIO PYONGYANG, Pyongyang	E ASIA • 200 kW; USSR, EUROPE & MIDEAST • 200 kW
9350	USA †VOA, Delano, California	SE ASIA • (FEEDER) • 50 kW • ISU; SE ASIA • (FEEDER) • 50 kW • ISL; (D) • SE ASIA • (FEEDER) • 50 kW • ISU; (D) • SE ASIA • (FEEDER) • 50 kW • ISL; (J) • SE ASIA • (FEEDER) • 50 kW • ISU; (D) M-F • SE ASIA • (FEEDER) • 50 kW • ISU
9365	CHINA (PR) RADIO BEIJING, Xi'an	S AMERICA • 120 kW; EUROPE & WEST USSR • 120 kW; (J) • EUROPE & WEST USSR • 120 kW
9369.3	PAKISTAN †RADIO PAKISTAN, Karachi	S ASIA • 50 kW
9370	PAKISTAN †RADIO PAKISTAN, Islamabad	(D) • EUROPE • 250 kW
9375	ALBANIA †RADIO TIRANA, Lushnjë	EUROPE • 100 kW
9380	CHINA (PR) †CENTRAL PEOPLES BS, Beijing	CHINESE, ETC • TAIWAN-1 • 10 kW
9388	ISRAEL †RASHUTH HASHIDUR, Tel Aviv	(D) • EUROPE • DS-B • 50/100 kW; (D) Su-F • EUROPE • DS-B • 50/100 kW
9395	GREECE FONI TIS HELLADAS, Athens	N AMERICA • 100 kW; EUROPE • 100 kW; MIDEAST • 100 kW; AUSTRALIA • 100 kW • ALT. FREQ. TO 9400 kHz; S AMERICA • 100 kW; (D) • E EUROPE & WEST USSR • 100 kW; FRENCH, ETC • EUROPE • 100 kW
9400	CLANDESTINE (AFRICA) "EPRP RADIO"	E AFRICA • ANTI-ETHIOPIA GOVT
	CLANDESTINE (M EAST) "RADIO IRAN", Abu Za'bal, Egypt	MIDEAST • ANTI-IRANIAN GOVT • 100 kW
	GREECE FONI TIS HELLADAS, Athens	Alternative Frequency to 9395 kHz

Time scale (bottom): 0 1 2 3 4 5 6 7 8 9 10 11 12 13 14 15 16 17 18 19 20 21 22 23 24

ENGLISH ▬ ARABIC ▩ CHINESE ▭▭▭ FRENCH ▬ GERMAN ▬ RUSSIAN ═ SPANISH ▬ OTHER ▬

FREQUENCY   COUNTRY, STATION, LOCATION

TARGET • NETWORK • POWER (kW)   World Time

0 1 2 3 4 5 6 7 8 9 10 11 12 13 14 15 16 17 18 19 20 21 22 23 24

Frequency	Country, Station, Location	Target • Network • Power
9410	UNITED KINGDOM	
	†BBC, Multiple Locations	EUROPE • 250/300/500 kW
9420	GREECE	
	FONI TIS HELLADAS, Kaválla	N AMERICA • 250 kW
9425	GREECE	
	FONI TIS HELLADAS, Athens	MIDEAST • 100 kW AUSTRALIA • 100 kW
	FONI TIS HELLADAS, Kaválla	MIDEAST • 250 kW E EUROPE • 250 kW WEST USSR • 250 kW
		EUROPE • 250 kW
		AUSTRALIA • 250 kW
		C AMERICA & S AMERICA • 250 kW
		(D) • EUROPE • 250 kW
		(D) • FRENCH & GERMAN • EUROPE • 250 kW
		(J) • EUROPE • DS • 250 kW
	RS MAKEDONIAS, Kaválla	(D) • EUROPE • 100 kW
9430	ALBANIA	
	†RADIO TIRANA, Lushnjë	
9435	ISRAEL	
	†KOL ISRAEL, Tel Aviv	MIDEAST • 300 kW
		E EUROPE & WEST USSR • 300 kW
		EUROPE • 300 kW
		(D) • W EUROPE & E NORTH AM • 300 kW
		(D) • E EUROPE & WEST USSR • 300 kW
		(J) • E EUROPE & WEST USSR • 300 kW
	MONACO	
	†TRANS WORLD RADIO, Monte Carlo	(J) • E EUROPE • 100 kW
		(J) Tu/Th-Su • WEST USSR • 100 kW
		(J) W-Su • E EUROPE • 100 kW
9440	CHINA (PR)	
	RADIO BEIJING, Beijing	MIDEAST & N AFRICA • 120 kW
	RADIO BEIJING, Xi'an	SE ASIA • 120 kW
	CLANDESTINE (ASIA)	
	"DEM KAMPUCHEA", Xi'an, China (PR)	SE ASIA • PRO-KHMER ROUGE • 120 kW
9445	TURKEY	
	†VOICE OF TURKEY, Ankara	E NORTH AM • 500 kW
		EUROPE • 250 kW
9450	CLANDESTINE (AFRICA)	
	"VO LIBYAN PEOPLE", Southern Chad	Alternative Frequency to 9480 kHz
	USSR	
	RADIO MOSCOW	(D) • E ASIA
		W AFRICA & ATLANTIC • 240 kW
	RADIO MOSCOW, Moscow	(D) • EUROPE • 240 kW (D) • W AFRICA • 240 kW
		(J) • E EUROPE • 240 kW
	RADIO MOSCOW, Novosibirsk	(D) • E ASIA • 250 kW
		DS-1 • 50 kW
	RADIO MOSCOW, Yerevan	W AFRICA • 120 kW
9455	CHINA (PR)	
	†CENTRAL PEOPLES BS, Kunming	CHINESE, ETC • TAIWAN-1 • 50 kW
	RADIO BEIJING, Kunming	(D) • S ASIA & S AFRICA • 50 kW
	EGYPT	
	RADIO CAIRO, Kafr Silim-Abis	N AFRICA • DS-GENERAL • 250 kW
	USA	
	†CHRIST SCI MONITOR, South Carolina	W NORTH AM & C AMERICA • 500 kW
		W NORTH AM • 500 kW
		S AMERICA • 500 kW
		S AMERICA • 500 kW • ALT. FREQ. TO 13760 kHz
		M • W NORTH AM & C AMERICA • 500 kW
		M • W NORTH AM • 500 kW
		M-F • S AMERICA • 500 kW
		M-F • S AMERICA • 500 kW • ALT. FREQ. TO 13760 kHz
		Sa-M • W NORTH AM & C AMERICA • 500 kW
		Sa-M • W NORTH AM • 500 kW
		Sa/Su • S AMERICA • 500 kW
		Sa/Su • S AMERICA • 500 kW • ALT. FREQ. TO 13760 kHz
		Su/M • W NORTH AM • 500 kW
		Tu-F • W NORTH AM & C AMERICA • 500 kW
		Tu-F • W NORTH AM • 500 kW
		Tu-Sa • W NORTH AM • 500 kW
		Tu-Su • W NORTH AM & C AMERICA • 500 kW
		Tu-Su • W NORTH AM • 500 kW
	CHRIST SCI MONITOR, Via Saipan	E ASIA • 100 kW
(con'd)	VOA, Greenville, NC	C AMERICA & S AMERICA • 500 kW (D) • S AMERICA • 500 kW

0 1 2 3 4 5 6 7 8 9 10 11 12 13 14 15 16 17 18 19 20 21 22 23 24

SUMMER ONLY (J)   WINTER ONLY (D)   JAMMING / OR ∧   EARLIEST HEARD ◁   LATEST HEARD ▷   NEW OR CHANGED FOR 1992 †

FREQUENCY   COUNTRY, STATION, LOCATION

TARGET • NETWORK • POWER (kW)

World Time

0 1 2 3 4 5 6 7 8 9 10 11 12 13 14 15 16 17 18 19 20 21 22 23 24

Freq	Country / Station / Location	Schedule
9455 (con'd)	**USA**	
	VOA, Greenville, NC	(J) • C AMERICA & S AMERICA • 500 kW
	WYFR-FAMILY RADIO, Okeechobee, Fl	(D) • EUROPE • 100 kW
9460	**TURKEY**	
	VOICE OF TURKEY, Ankara	EUROPE • 500 kW
9465	**NORTHERN MARIANA IS**	
	†KFBS-FAR EAST BC, Saipan Island	WEST USSR • 100 kW
		Sa • WEST USSR • 100 kW
		Su-F • WEST USSR • 100 kW
	USA	
	CHRIST SCI MONITOR, South Carolina	E NORTH AM • 500 kW
		M-F • E NORTH AM • 500 kW
		Sa • E NORTH AM • 500 kW
		Sa/Su • E NORTH AM • 500 kW
		Su-F • E NORTH AM • 500 kW
	FAMILY RADIO, Via Taiwan	E ASIA • 250 kW
	VOA, Delano, California	C AMERICA & S AMERICA • 250 kW
	WMLK, Bethel, Pa	Su-F • EUROPE & MIDEAST • 50 kW
	†WORLD HARVEST R, Noblesville, Indiana	E NORTH AM • 100 kW
		M-Sa • C AMERICA • 100 kW
9470	**USSR**	
	†RADIO MOSCOW, Irkutsk	(D) • DS-1 (FEEDER) • 15 kW • LSB
	†RADIO MOSCOW, Minsk	(J) • DS-MAYAK DS-MAYAK
	†RADIO MOSCOW, Ul'yanovsk	(D) • S AMERICA • 100 kW
		(D) • W AFRICA • 100 kW
		(J) • E EUROPE • 100 kW
		(J) • S AMERICA • 100 kW
9475	**EGYPT**	
	RADIO CAIRO, Kafr Silim-Abis	N AMERICA & C AMERICA • 250 kW
	USA	
	†CHRIST SCI MONITOR, Via Saipan	(J) • AUSTRALIA • 100 kW
		(J) Sa • AUSTRALIA • 100 kW
		(J) Su-F • AUSTRALIA • 100 kW
9480	**ALBANIA**	
	†RADIO TIRANA, Lushnjë	C AFRICA & S AFRICA • 100 kW (D) • WEST USSR • 100 kW
		SE ASIA & AUSTRALIA • 100 kW
		(D) • C AFRICA & S AFRICA • 100 kW
		MIDEAST • 100 kW
		(D) • EUROPE • 100 kW
		(J) • EUROPE • 100 kW
		(J) • WEST USSR • 100 kW
	CHINA (PR)	
	RADIO BEIJING, Beijing	SE ASIA & E ASIA • 120 kW
	RADIO BEIJING, Xi'an	MIDEAST • 120 kW
		(D) • MIDEAST • 120 kW
	CLANDESTINE (AFRICA)	
	"VO LIBYAN PEOPLE", Southern Chad	Irr • N AFRICA • ANTI-QADDAFI • ALT. FREQ. TO 9450 kHz
	"VO THE PEOPLE", Southern Chad	Irr • N AFRICA • ANTI-QADDAFI
	MONACO	
	†TRANS WORLD RADIO, Monte Carlo	W EUROPE • 100 kW
		Sa • W EUROPE • 100 kW
	USSR	
	RADIO MOSCOW	(D)
	RADIO MOSCOW, Novosibirsk	E ASIA • 250 kW
		(D) • E ASIA • 250 kW
	RADIO MOSCOW, Yerevan	MIDEAST & E AFRICA • 120 kW
		(D) • N AFRICA • 120 kW
	†RADIO YEREVAN, Yerevan	(D) • S AMERICA • 120 kW
9485	**MONACO**	
	†TRANS WORLD RADIO, Monte Carlo	Sa • WEST USSR • 100 kW
9486	**PERU**	
	RADIO TACNA, Tacna	Su • DS • 0.18 kW
9490	**CHINA (PR)**	
	RADIO BEIJING, Lhasa	S ASIA • 50 kW
	XIZANG PEOPLES BS, Lhasa	DS-CHINESE • 50 kW
	MONACO	
	†TRANS WORLD RADIO, Monte Carlo	(J) F-M • E EUROPE • 100 kW
		(J) • E EUROPE • 100 kW
		(J) M-Sa • E EUROPE • 100 kW
		(J) Sa/Su • E EUROPE • 100 kW
		(J) Su • E EUROPE • 100 kW

(con'd)

0 1 2 3 4 5 6 7 8 9 10 11 12 13 14 15 16 17 18 19 20 21 22 23 24

ENGLISH ▬   ARABIC ⩩   CHINESE ▭▭▭   FRENCH ═   GERMAN ▬   RUSSIAN ═   SPANISH ▬   OTHER ▬

FREQUENCY   COUNTRY, STATION, LOCATION

TARGET • NETWORK • POWER (kW)   World Time

Time scale: 0 1 2 3 4 5 6 7 8 9 10 11 12 13 14 15 16 17 18 19 20 21 22 23 24

Frequency	Country / Station / Location	Target • Network • Power
9490 (con'd)	USSR — RADIO MOSCOW, Nikolayev	S AMERICA • 500 kW
		(J) • W AFRICA • 500 kW
		(D) • W AFRICA • 500 kW
		(D) • S AMERICA • 500 kW
	†RADIO MOSCOW, Ul'yanovsk	DS-1/MAYAK/POLAR • 240 kW
9495	GUAM — ADVENTIST WORLD R, Agat	(D) • E ASIA • 100 kW
	MONACO — †TRANS WORLD RADIO, Monte Carlo	(D) • E EUROPE • 100 kW
		(D) • MIDEAST • 500 kW
		(D) • F-M • E EUROPE • 100 kW
		(J) • WEST USSR • 500 kW
		(J) • E EUROPE • 100 kW
		(D) • M-F • MIDEAST • 500 kW
		(J) • M-F • E EUROPE • 100 kW
		(D) • M-Sa • E EUROPE • 100 kW
		(J) • W-Su • WEST USSR • 500 kW
		(D) • Sa/Su • E EUROPE • 100 kW
		(D) • Su • E EUROPE • 100 kW
	NORTHERN MARIANA IS — †KFBS-FAR EAST BC, Saipan Island	E ASIA • 100 kW • ALT. FREQ. TO 12025 kHz
		E ASIA • 100 kW
		W AFRICA • RELAY ELWA • 100 kW
	PHILIPPINES — FEBC RADIO INTL, Bocaue	SE ASIA • 50 kW
	USA — CHRIST SCI MONITOR, South Carolina	E NORTH AM • 500 kW
		M-F • E NORTH AM • 500 kW
		Sa/Su • E NORTH AM • 500 kW
	†WORLD HARVEST R, Noblesville, Indiana	C AMERICA • 100 kW
		M • C AMERICA • 100 kW
		M-F • C AMERICA • 100 kW
		Sa/Su • C AMERICA • 100 kW
		M-Sa • C AMERICA • 100 kW
		Su • C AMERICA • 100 kW
		Su/M • C AMERICA • 100 kW
		Tu-Sa • C AMERICA • 100 kW
		Tu-Su • C AMERICA • 100 kW
	YUGOSLAVIA — †CROATIAN RADIO, Via WHRI, USA	Irr • Su/M • C AMERICA • 100 kW
9500	ALBANIA — †RADIO TIRANA, Lushnjë	(D) • S AMERICA • 100 kW
		SE ASIA & AUSTRALIA • 100 kW
		(J) • WEST USSR • 100 kW
		AFRICA • 100 kW
		(D) • WEST USSR • 100 kW
		(D) • MIDEAST • 100 kW
		(D) • EUROPE • 100 kW
		(J) • MIDEAST • 100 kW
		(J) • EUROPE • 100 kW
	USSR — MAGADAN RADIO, Chita	DS-1 • 50 kW
	RADIO MOSCOW	DS-1
	RADIO MOSCOW, Armavir	MIDEAST & E AFRICA • 100 kW
9505	AUSTRALIA — †RADIO AUSTRALIA, Carnarvon	(J) • SE ASIA • 100 kW
	BRAZIL — RADIO RECORD, São Paulo	Irr • DS • 7.5 kW
		DS • 7.5 kW
	CANADA — †R CANADA INTL, Via Germany	(D) • MIDEAST • 500 kW
	CHINA (PR) — †VO THE STRAIT-PLA, Fuzhou	TAIWAN-2 • 50 kW
	CUBA — †RADIO HABANA, Havana	N AMERICA • 50 kW
		C AMERICA • 75 kW
	CZECHOSLOVAKIA — †RADIO PRAGUE INTL, Velké Kostolany	EUROPE • 120 kW
	JAPAN — RADIO JAPAN/NHK, Tokyo-Yamata	(D) • PACIFIC & W NORTH AM • GENERAL • 300 kW
	KOREA (DPR) — †RADIO PYONGYANG, Pyongyang	E ASIA • 200 kW
	PERU — RADIO TACNA, Tacna	Tu-Su • DS • 0.18 kW
		M-Sa • DS • 0.18 kW
	UNITED ARAB EMIRATES — †UAE RADIO, Abu Dhabi	Alternative Frequency to 9600 kHz
	UNITED KINGDOM — †BBC, Daventry	(J) • WEST USSR • 300 kW
	†BBC, Via Zyyi, Cyprus	(D) • WEST USSR • 250 kW
	USA — †RFE-RL, Via Germany	(D) • WEST USSR • 100 kW
		WEST USSR • 250 kW
		(J) • WEST USSR • 100/250 kW
	†RFE-RL, Via Pals, Spain	(J) • WEST USSR • 250 kW
(con'd)	†RFE-RL, Via Portugal	(D) • WEST USSR • 250/500 kW

SUMMER ONLY (J)   WINTER ONLY (D)   JAMMING / OR ∧   EARLIEST HEARD ◁   LATEST HEARD ▷   NEW OR CHANGED FOR 1992 †

FREQUENCY	COUNTRY, STATION, LOCATION	TARGET • NETWORK • POWER (kW) / World Time
9505 (con'd)	USA	
	†RFE-RL, Via Portugal	(J) • WEST USSR • 250 kW
	†VOA, Via Philippines	SE ASIA • 100 kW
	†VOA, Via Tangier, Morocco	(J) • WEST USSR • 100 kW
	†WYFR-FAMILY RADIO, Okeechobee, Fl	(D) • W NORTH AM • 100 kW / W NORTH AM • 100 kW
	USSR	
	†KAZAKH RADIO, Alma-Ata	DS-2 • 120 kW
	†RADIO ALMA-ATA, Alma-Ata	120 kW
	ZAMBIA	
	RADIO ZAMBIA-ZBS, Lusaka	S AFRICA • 50 kW / F/Sa • S AFRICA • 50 kW
9509	ALGERIA	
	RTV ALGERIENNE, Algiers	EUROPE & N AFRICA • 50 kW
9510	ALBANIA	
	†RADIO TIRANA, Lushnjë	(J) • C AFRICA & S AFRICA • 100 kW
	GERMANY	
	†DEUTSCHE WELLE, Königswusterhausen	(D) • S AMERICA • 100 kW
	†DEUTSCHE WELLE, Via Sri Lanka	S ASIA • 250 kW
	ROMANIA	
	RADIO ROMANIA INTL, Bucharest	AMERICAS • 250 kW
		EUROPE • 250 kW / (D) • EUROPE • 250 kW / (D) • AMERICAS • 250 kW
	UNITED KINGDOM	
	†BBC, Various Locations	W EUROPE & N AFRICA • 100/500 kW
	USA	
	VOA, Via Philippines	SE ASIA • 250 kW
	USSR	
	RADIO MOSCOW, Vladivostok	(D) • E ASIA • 100 kW / (J) • E ASIA • 100 kW
9510v	PERU	
	RADIO AMERICA, Lima	Irr • DS • 5/10 kW
9515	BRAZIL	
	†R NOVAS DE PAZ, Curitiba	DS • 10 kW
	GERMANY	
	DEUTSCHE WELLE, Jülich	(J) • W EUROPE • 100 kW
	DEUTSCHE WELLE, Via Cyclops, Malta	MIDEAST • 250 kW
	ITALY	
	RTV ITALIANA, Caltanissetta	M-Sa • EUROPE, N AFRICA & MIDEAST • 50 kW / EUROPE, N AFRICA & MIDEAST • DS-1 • 50 kW
		Su • EUROPE, N AFRICA & MIDEAST • DS-1 • 50 kW
	KOREA (REPUBLIC)	
	RADIO KOREA, In-Kimjae	MIDEAST & AFRICA • 250 kW
	MEXICO	
	LV AMERICA LATINA, México City	Irr • DS • 0.5 kW
	NETHERLANDS ANTILLES	
	†TRANS WORLD RADIO, Bonaire	S AMERICA • 50 kW
	SWAZILAND	
	†TRANS WORLD RADIO, Manzini	S AFRICA • 25 kW
	UNITED KINGDOM	
	†BBC, Via Delano, USA	C AMERICA & S AMERICA • 250 kW
	†BBC, Via Sackville, Can	N AMERICA • 250 kW
	USSR	
	RADIO MOSCOW, Kazan'	(J) • MIDEAST & E AFRICA • 240 kW
	RADIO MOSCOW, Leningrad	(D) • N AFRICA & MIDEAST • 240 kW
	RADIO MOSCOW, Yerevan	(J) • E AFRICA • 100 kW
9520	BULGARIA	
	†RADIO SOFIA, Plovdiv	(D) • C AMERICA • 500 kW / (D) • EUROPE • 500 kW
		(D) • Su • EUROPE • 500 kW
	PHILIPPINES	
	†RADIO VERITAS ASIA, Palauig	E ASIA • 250 kW / SE ASIA • 250 kW / S ASIA & SE ASIA • 250 kW
	SWAZILAND	
	†TRANS WORLD RADIO, Manzini	S AFRICA • 25 kW / S AFRICA • 100 kW / Sa/Su • S AFRICA • 100 kW
	USA	
	†RFE-RL, Various Locations	WEST USSR • 100/250/500 kW
	USSR	
	RADIO MOSCOW, Irkutsk	(J) • E ASIA • 240 kW
	RADIO MOSCOW, Krasnodar	(D) • C AMERICA • 500 kW / (D) • C AMERICA & EUROPE • 500 kW
	RADIO MOSCOW, Moscow	ATLANTIC • 240 kW
9525 (con'd)	IRAN	
	†VO THE ISLAMIC REP, Tehrān	(D) • MIDEAST • 500 kW

FREQUENCY   COUNTRY, STATION, LOCATION

TARGET • NETWORK • POWER (kW)   World Time

0 1 2 3 4 5 6 7 8 9 10 11 12 13 14 15 16 17 18 19 20 21 22 23 24

9525 POLAND
(con'd) RADIO POLONIA, Warsaw
- EUROPE, ATLANTIC & N AMERICA • 100 kW
- EUROPE & W AFRICA • 100 kW
- EUROPE & N AFRICA • 100 kW

USA
†RADIO MARTI, Cincinnati, Ohio
- C AMERICA • 250 kW
- Tu-Sa • C AMERICA • 250 kW
- M-F • C AMERICA & S AMERICA • 250 kW

VOA, Cincinnati, Ohio
- (D) • MIDEAST • 500 kW

VOA, Via Germany
- AUSTRALIA • 100 kW

†VOA, Via Philippines

9530 CHINA (PR)
RADIO BEIJING, Baoding
- (D) • SE ASIA • 120 kW

RADIO BEIJING, Xi'an
- (D) • SE ASIA • 150 kW

GUAM
†ADVENTIST WORLD R, Agat
- (D) • EAST USSR • 100 kW

UNITED KINGDOM
†BBC, Via Zyyi, Cyprus
- (J) • EUROPE • 100 kW

USA
†CHRIST SCI MONITOR, Via Saipan
- (D) • E ASIA • 100 kW   E ASIA • 100 kW

†RFE-RL, Via Pals, Spain
- (D) • WEST USSR • 250 kW

VOA, Greenville, NC
- W AFRICA • 500 kW

†VOA, Via Germany
- (J) • S ASIA • 500 kW
- MIDEAST • 500 kW
- (D) • MIDEAST • 500 kW
- (J) • MIDEAST • 500 kW

†VOA, Via Kavália, Greece
- (J) • WEST USSR • 250 kW

†VOA, Via Portugal
- (D) • WEST USSR • 250 kW

VOA, Via Tangier, Morocco
- (D) • E EUROPE • 100 kW

†VOA, Via Woofferton, UK
- (D) • WEST USSR • 300 kW
- (J) • WEST USSR • 250 kW
- (J) • E EUROPE • 250 kW

USSR
†MAGADAN RADIO, Okhotsk
- RUSSIAN, ETC • DS/TIKHIY OKEAN • 100 kW

RADIO MOSCOW, Irkutsk
- (J) • 50 kW

RADIO MOSCOW, Moscow
- (J) • AFRICA • 240 kW

9534.8 ANGOLA
RADIO NACIONAL, Luanda
- S AFRICA • 100 kW
- DS-B • 100 kW

9535 ALGERIA
RTV ALGERIENNE, Algiers
- AFRICA • 50 kW

CANADA
†R CANADA INTL, Sackville, NB
- (D) • S AMERICA • 250 kW
- Su/M • S AMERICA • 250 kW
- (D) Su/M • S AMERICA • 250 kW
- Tu-Sa • S AMERICA • 250 kW
- (D) Tu-Sa • S AMERICA • 250 kW
- (D) M-F • S AMERICA • 250 kW
- (D) Sa/Su • S AMERICA • 250 kW

†R CANADA INTL, Via Xi'an, China(PR)
- E ASIA • 120 kW

GERMANY
†DEUTSCHE WELLE, Via Sri Lanka
- (D) • E ASIA • 250 kW

INDIA
†ALL INDIA RADIO, Madras
- DS • 100 kW

JAPAN
NHK, Fukuoka
- Irr • DS-1 (FEEDER) • 0.6 kW • USB

NHK, Osaka
- Irr • DS-2 (FEEDER) • 0.5 kW

NHK, Sapporo
- Irr • DS-1 (FEEDER) • 0.6 kW

†RADIO JAPAN/NHK, Tokyo-Yamata
- E AFRICA • 300 kW
- S ASIA • GENERAL • 300 kW

†RADIO JAPAN/NHK, Via Sri Lanka
- S ASIA • 300 kW
- S ASIA • GENERAL • 300 kW

NETHERLANDS ANTILLES
†TRANS WORLD RADIO, Bonaire
- N AMERICA • 50 kW
- C AMERICA • 50 kW

SUDAN
†NATIONAL UNITY R, Omdurman
- Irr

SWITZERLAND
†SWISS RADIO INTL, Lenk
- EUROPE & N AFRICA • 250 kW
- M-Sa • EUROPE & N AFRICA • 250 kW
- Su • EUROPE & N AFRICA • 250 kW

USA
(con'd) VOA, Via Kavália, Greece
- (D) • WEST USSR • 250 kW

0 1 2 3 4 5 6 7 8 9 10 11 12 13 14 15 16 17 18 19 20 21 22 23 24

SUMMER ONLY (J)   WINTER ONLY (D)   JAMMING / OR ∧   EARLIEST HEARD ◁   LATEST HEARD ▷   NEW OR CHANGED FOR 1992 †

FREQUENCY   COUNTRY, STATION, LOCATION   TARGET • NETWORK • POWER (kW)   World Time

		0 1 2 3 4 5 6 7 8 9 10 11 12 13 14 15 16 17 18 19 20 21 22 23 24

9535   **USSR**
(con'd)   †ECHO OF MOSCOW — DS
      Sa/Su • DS

9540   **BRAZIL**
     †R EDUCADORA BAHIA, Salvador — DS • 10 kW
     CLANDESTINE (AFRICA)
      "VO ETHIOPIA UNITY, Sudan — Irr • E AFRICA • ALT. FREQ. TO 9550 kHz

      †"VO OROMO LIBER'N", Sudan — E AFRICA
     CZECHOSLOVAKIA
      †RADIO PRAGUE INTL, Velké Kostolany — (D) • E NORTH AM • 120 kW
     POLAND
      RADIO POLONIA, Warsaw — EUROPE • 100 kW
     USA
      R FREE AFGHANISTAN, Via Germany — (D) • WEST USSR & S ASIA • 100 kW

      †RFE-RL, Via Germany — (D) • WEST USSR • 100 kW

      †RFE-RL, Via Pals, Spain — (D) • WEST USSR • 250 kW

      VOA, Via Kaválla, Greece — (J) • MIDEAST & S ASIA • 250 kW

      †VOA, Via Rhodes, Greece — (J) • MIDEAST • 50 kW
     USSR
      RADIO MOSCOW, Moscow — (J) • DS-1 • 100 kW

      RADIO TASHKENT, Tashkent — MIDEAST • 100 kW
      — (D) • S ASIA • 100 kW

     VENEZUELA
      †RADIO NACIONAL, Caracas — SPANISH, ENGLISH, FRENCH, GERMAN, ETC • C AMERICA • 50 kW
9545   **ALBANIA**
      †RADIO TIRANA, Lushnjë — (J) • EUROPE • 100 kW
     GERMANY
      †DEUTSCHE WELLE, Jülich — (J) • EUROPE • 100 kW

      †DEUTSCHE WELLE, Multiple Locations — (D) • C AMERICA & S AMERICA • 100/500 kW
      — EUROPE • 100/250/500 kW
      — EUROPE & MIDEAST • 100/250/500 kW

      DEUTSCHE WELLE, Via Antigua — N AMERICA & C AMERICA • 250 kW

      DEUTSCHE WELLE, Via Brasília, Brazil — S AMERICA & C AMERICA • 250 kW

      †DEUTSCHE WELLE, Via Sackville, Can — N AMERICA • 250 kW

      †DEUTSCHE WELLE, Wertachtal — (J) • S AMERICA • 500 kW
      — (D) • MIDEAST • 500 kW

     MEXICO
      †LV DE VERACRUZ, Veracruz — Irr • DS • 0.25 kW
     SOLOMON ISLANDS
      †SOLOMON ISLANDS BC, Honiara — Su • DS-ENGLISH, PIDGIN • 10 kW
      — Sa • DS-ENGLISH, PIDGIN • 10 kW
      — M-F • DS-ENGLISH, PIDGIN • 10 kW

     USA
      †VOA, Via Philippines — (D) • E ASIA • 250 kW
      — E ASIA • 250 kW
      — (J) • E ASIA • 250 kW

     USSR
      RADIO MOSCOW, Khabarovsk — (J) • DS-MAYAK • 50 kW
9545v   **PAKISTAN**
      PAKISTAN BC CORP, Islamabad — DS • 10 kW

      RADIO PAKISTAN, Islamabad — S ASIA • 10 kW
9550   **CLANDESTINE (AFRICA)**
      "VO ETHIOPIA UNITY, Sudan — Alternative Frequency to 9540 kHz
     CUBA
      †RADIO HABANA, Havana — S AMERICA • 100 kW
     FINLAND
      †RADIO FINLAND, Pori — EUROPE & W AFRICA • 500 kW
     FRANCE
      †R FRANCE INTL, Issoudun-Allouis — MIDEAST • 100 kW
      — (D) • MIDEAST • 100 kW

     INDIA
      †ALL INDIA RADIO, Aligarh — S ASIA • 250 kW

      †ALL INDIA RADIO, Delhi — SE ASIA • 50 kW
      — ENGLISH & HINDI • DS • 50 kW

     JAPAN
      NHK, Tokyo-Shobu — Irr • DS-1 (FEEDER) • 0.9 kW • USB
     USA
      WYFR-FAMILY RADIO, Okeechobee, Fl — (J) • S AMERICA • 100 kW
9552   **INDONESIA**
      †RRI, Ujung Pandang — DS • 10 kW
9555   **CANADA**
      †R CANADA INTL, Via United Kingdom — (D) • EUROPE • 300 kW
      — (J) • EUROPE • 300 kW

      †R CANADA INTL, Via Xi'an, China(PR) — S ASIA • 120 kW
     CYPRUS
(con'd)   †CYPRUS BC CORP, Zyyi — (D) • F-Su • EUROPE • 250 kW

		0 1 2 3 4 5 6 7 8 9 10 11 12 13 14 15 16 17 18 19 20 21 22 23 24

ENGLISH ▬   ARABIC ≈   CHINESE ∘∘∘   FRENCH ═   GERMAN ▬   RUSSIAN =   SPANISH ▬   OTHER —

FREQUENCY   COUNTRY, STATION, LOCATION

TARGET • NETWORK • POWER (kW)   World Time

FREQUENCY	COUNTRY, STATION, LOCATION	Schedule / Notes
9555 (con'd)	MEXICO LA HORA EXACTA, México City	Irr • DS • 1 kW
	PHILIPPINES †RADIO VERITAS ASIA, Palauig	S ASIA & SE ASIA • 250 kW SE ASIA • 250 kW E ASIA • 250 kW S ASIA • 250 kW
	PORTUGAL †R PORTUGAL INTL, Lisbon	E NORTH AM • 100 kW Su/M • E NORTH AM • 100 kW Tu-Sa • E NORTH AM • 100 kW
	SOUTH AFRICA †RADIO RSA, Meyerton	S AFRICA • 100 kW
	USA †RFE-RL, Via Germany	(J) • WEST USSR • 100/250 kW (D) • WEST USSR • 250 kW (D) • WEST USSR • 250 kW
	†RFE-RL, Via Pals, Spain	(D) • WEST USSR • 250 kW (D) • WEST USSR & MIDEAST • 250 kW (J) • E EUROPE • 250 kW
	†RFE-RL, Via Portugal	(J) • E EUROPE • 300 kW
	†VOA, Via Woofferton, UK	
	WYFR-FAMILY RADIO, Okeechobee, Fl	(D) • S AMERICA • 100 kW
	USSR RADIO MOSCOW, Tula	DS-MAYAK • 100 kW
9560	CHINA (PR) †XINJIANG PBS, Urümqi	Su • DS-CHINESE • 50 kW Sa • DS-CHINESE • 50 kW
	ETHIOPIA †VOICE OF ETHIOPIA, Gedja	E AFRICA • 100 kW
	FINLAND †RADIO FINLAND, Pori	EUROPE & W AFRICA • 500 kW
	JORDAN RADIO JORDAN, Qasr el Kharana	EUROPE • 500 kW EUROPE • 500 kW • ALT. FREQ. TO 9835 kHz
	PHILIPPINES RADIO VERITAS ASIA, Palauig	(D) • SE ASIA • 100 kW E ASIA • 100 kW
	SWITZERLAND RED CROSS BC SVC, Schwarzenburg	Irr • M/Th • AUSTRALIA • 150 kW
	SWISS RADIO INTL, Schwarzenburg	AUSTRALIA • 150 kW M-Sa • AUSTRALIA • 150 kW Su • AUSTRALIA • 150 kW
	UNITED KINGDOM †BBC, Via Antigua	(J) • S AMERICA • 250 kW
	†BBC, Via Ascension	(D) • S AMERICA • 250 kW
	†BBC, Via Zyyi, Cyprus	(D) M-F • EUROPE • 250 kW (D) • EUROPE • 250 kW (J) M-F • EUROPE • 250 kW (J) • EUROPE • 250 kW (D) Sa/Su • EUROPE • 250 kW
	USSR †ESTONIAN RADIO, Serpukhov	DS-1 • 20 kW Su • DS-1 • 20 kW
	†RADIO DVR, Khabarovsk	Tu-Sa • DS • 20 kW M-F • DS • 20 kW
	RADIO MOSCOW, Serpukhov	(J) • W AFRICA & ATLANTIC • 240 kW
	†RADIO TALLINN, Serpukhov	M-Sa • 20 kW 20 kW M • 20 kW Tu-Su • 20 kW
	†UKRAINIAN RADIO, L'vov	DS-2 • 240 kW
9565	BRAZIL RADIO UNIVERSO, Curitiba	DS • 7.5 kW
	CHINA (PR) RADIO BEIJING, Xi'an	S ASIA & E AFRICA • 150 kW
	GERMANY †DEUTSCHE WELLE, Multiple Locations	E NORTH AM & C AMERICA • 100/250/500 kW (D) • E ASIA • 100/500 kW
	†DEUTSCHE WELLE, Nauen	(D) • E ASIA • 500 kW
	†DEUTSCHE WELLE, Via Kigali, Rwanda	S AFRICA • 250 kW C AFRICA & E AFRICA • 250 kW
	INDIA †ALL INDIA RADIO, Delhi	DS • 50 kW ENGLISH & HINDI • DS • 50 kW
	SEYCHELLES FAR EAST BC ASS'N, North Pt, Mahé Is	C AFRICA & S AFRICA • 100 kW F-M • C AFRICA & S AFRICA • 100 kW
(con'd)		

SUMMER ONLY (J)   WINTER ONLY (D)   JAMMING / OR ∧   EARLIEST HEARD ◁   LATEST HEARD ▷   NEW OR CHANGED FOR 1992 †

FREQUENCY   COUNTRY, STATION, LOCATION

TARGET • NETWORK • POWER (kW)

World Time

0 1 2 3 4 5 6 7 8 9 10 11 12 13 14 15 16 17 18 19 20 21 22 23 24

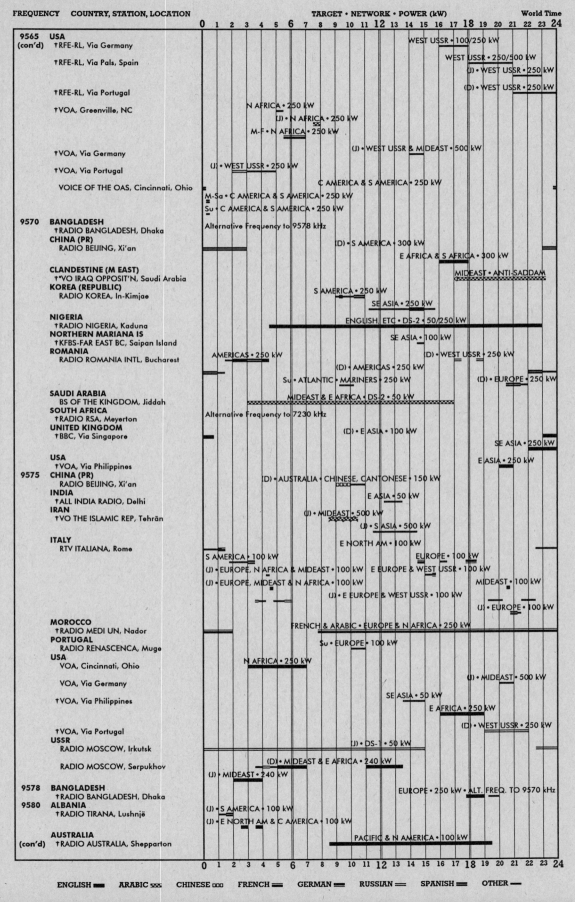

Frequency	Country, Station, Location	Target • Network • Power
9565 (con'd)	**USA**	
	†RFE-RL, Via Germany	WEST USSR • 100/250 kW
	†RFE-RL, Via Pals, Spain	WEST USSR • 250/500 kW
		(J) • WEST USSR • 250 kW
	†RFE-RL, Via Portugal	(D) • WEST USSR • 250 kW
	†VOA, Greenville, NC	N AFRICA • 250 kW
		(J) • N AFRICA • 250 kW
		M-F • N AFRICA • 250 kW
	†VOA, Via Germany	(J) • WEST USSR & MIDEAST • 500 kW
	†VOA, Via Portugal	(J) • WEST USSR • 250 kW
	VOICE OF THE OAS, Cincinnati, Ohio	C AMERICA & S AMERICA • 250 kW
		M-Sa • C AMERICA & S AMERICA • 250 kW
		Su • C AMERICA & S AMERICA • 250 kW
9570	**BANGLADESH** †RADIO BANGLADESH, Dhaka	Alternative Frequency to 9578 kHz
	CHINA (PR) RADIO BEIJING, Xi'an	(D) • S AMERICA • 300 kW
		E AFRICA & S AFRICA • 300 kW
	CLANDESTINE (M EAST) †*VO IRAQ OPPOSIT'N, Saudi Arabia	MIDEAST • ANTI-SADDAM
	KOREA (REPUBLIC) RADIO KOREA, In-Kimjae	S AMERICA • 250 kW
		SE ASIA • 250 kW
	NIGERIA †RADIO NIGERIA, Kaduna	ENGLISH, ETC • DS-2 • 50/250 kW
	NORTHERN MARIANA IS †KFBS-FAR EAST BC, Saipan Island	SE ASIA • 100 kW
	ROMANIA RADIO ROMANIA INTL, Bucharest	AMERICAS • 250 kW
		(D) • WEST USSR • 250 kW
		(D) • AMERICAS • 250 kW
		Su • ATLANTIC • MARINERS • 250 kW
		(D) • EUROPE • 250 kW
	SAUDI ARABIA BS OF THE KINGDOM, Jiddah	MIDEAST & E AFRICA • DS-2 • 50 kW
	SOUTH AFRICA †RADIO RSA, Meyerton	Alternative Frequency to 7230 kHz
	UNITED KINGDOM †BBC, Via Singapore	(D) • E ASIA • 100 kW
		SE ASIA • 250 kW
	USA †VOA, Via Philippines	E ASIA • 250 kW
9575	**CHINA (PR)** RADIO BEIJING, Xi'an	(D) • AUSTRALIA • CHINESE, CANTONESE • 150 kW
	INDIA †ALL INDIA RADIO, Delhi	E ASIA • 50 kW
	IRAN †VO THE ISLAMIC REP, Tehrān	(J) • MIDEAST • 500 kW
		(J) • S ASIA • 500 kW
	ITALY RTV ITALIANA, Rome	E NORTH AM • 100 kW
		S AMERICA • 100 kW
		EUROPE • 100 kW
		(J) • EUROPE, N AFRICA & MIDEAST • 100 kW E EUROPE & WEST USSR • 100 kW
		(J) • EUROPE, MIDEAST & N AFRICA • 100 kW MIDEAST • 100 kW
		(J) • E EUROPE & WEST USSR • 100 kW
		(J) • EUROPE • 100 kW
	MOROCCO †RADIO MEDI UN, Nador	FRENCH & ARABIC • EUROPE & N AFRICA • 250 kW
	PORTUGAL RADIO RENASCENCA, Muge	Su • EUROPE • 100 kW
	USA VOA, Cincinnati, Ohio	N AFRICA • 250 kW
	VOA, Via Germany	(J) • MIDEAST • 500 kW
	†VOA, Via Philippines	SE ASIA • 50 kW
		E AFRICA • 250 kW
	†VOA, Via Portugal	(D) • WEST USSR • 250 kW
	USSR RADIO MOSCOW, Irkutsk	(J) • DS-1 • 50 kW
	RADIO MOSCOW, Serpukhov	(D) • MIDEAST & E AFRICA • 240 kW
		(J) • MIDEAST • 240 kW
9578	**BANGLADESH** †RADIO BANGLADESH, Dhaka	EUROPE • 250 kW • ALT. FREQ. TO 9570 kHz
9580	**ALBANIA** †RADIO TIRANA, Lushnjë	(J) • S AMERICA • 100 kW
		(J) • E NORTH AM & C AMERICA • 100 kW
	AUSTRALIA (con'd) †RADIO AUSTRALIA, Shepparton	PACIFIC & N AMERICA • 100 kW

0 1 2 3 4 5 6 7 8 9 10 11 12 13 14 15 16 17 18 19 20 21 22 23 24

ENGLISH ▬   ARABIC ⋙   CHINESE ▭▭▭   FRENCH ▭▭   GERMAN ▬▬   RUSSIAN ══   SPANISH ▬   OTHER ▬

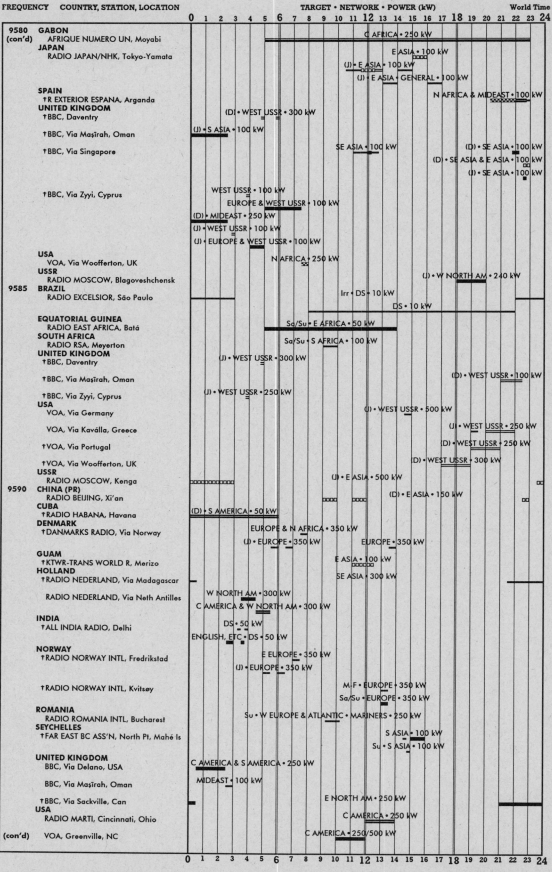

FREQUENCY   COUNTRY, STATION, LOCATION

FREQUENCY	COUNTRY, STATION, LOCATION	TARGET • NETWORK • POWER (kW)
9580 (con'd)	GABON — AFRIQUE NUMERO UN, Moyabi	C AFRICA • 250 kW
	JAPAN — RADIO JAPAN/NHK, Tokyo-Yamata	E ASIA • 100 kW
		(J) • E ASIA • 100 kW
		(J) • E ASIA • GENERAL • 100 kW
	SPAIN — †R EXTERIOR ESPANA, Arganda	N AFRICA & MIDEAST • 100 kW
	UNITED KINGDOM — †BBC, Daventry	(D) • WEST USSR • 300 kW
	†BBC, Via Maṣīrah, Oman	(J) • S ASIA • 100 kW
	†BBC, Via Singapore	SE ASIA • 100 kW / (D) • SE ASIA • 100 kW
		(D) • SE ASIA & E ASIA • 100 kW
		(J) • SE ASIA • 100 kW
	†BBC, Via Zyyi, Cyprus	WEST USSR • 100 kW
		EUROPE & WEST USSR • 100 kW
		(D) • MIDEAST • 250 kW
		(J) • WEST USSR • 100 kW
		(J) • EUROPE & WEST USSR • 100 kW
	USA — VOA, Via Woofferton, UK	N AFRICA • 250 kW
	USSR — RADIO MOSCOW, Blagoveshchensk	(J) • W NORTH AM • 240 kW
9585	BRAZIL — RADIO EXCELSIOR, São Paulo	Irr • DS • 10 kW
		DS • 10 kW
	EQUATORIAL GUINEA — RADIO EAST AFRICA, Batá	Sa/Su • E AFRICA • 50 kW
	SOUTH AFRICA — RADIO RSA, Meyerton	Sa/Su • S AFRICA • 100 kW
	UNITED KINGDOM — †BBC, Daventry	(J) • WEST USSR • 300 kW
	†BBC, Via Maṣīrah, Oman	(D) • WEST USSR • 100 kW
	†BBC, Via Zyyi, Cyprus	(J) • WEST USSR • 250 kW
	USA — VOA, Via Germany	(J) • WEST USSR • 500 kW
	VOA, Via Kaválla, Greece	(J) • WEST USSR • 250 kW
	†VOA, Via Portugal	(D) • WEST USSR • 250 kW
	†VOA, Via Woofferton, UK	(D) • WEST USSR • 300 kW
	USSR — RADIO MOSCOW, Kenga	(J) • E ASIA • 500 kW
9590	CHINA (PR) — RADIO BEIJING, Xi'an	(D) • E ASIA • 150 kW
	CUBA — †RADIO HABANA, Havana	(D) • S AMERICA • 50 kW
	DENMARK — †DANMARKS RADIO, Via Norway	EUROPE & N AFRICA • 350 kW
		(J) • EUROPE • 350 kW / EUROPE • 350 kW
	GUAM — †KTWR-TRANS WORLD R, Merizo	E ASIA • 100 kW
	HOLLAND — †RADIO NEDERLAND, Via Madagascar	SE ASIA • 300 kW
	RADIO NEDERLAND, Via Neth Antilles	W NORTH AM • 300 kW
		C AMERICA & W NORTH AM • 300 kW
	INDIA — †ALL INDIA RADIO, Delhi	DS • 50 kW
		ENGLISH, ETC • DS • 50 kW
	NORWAY — †RADIO NORWAY INTL, Fredrikstad	E EUROPE • 350 kW
		(J) • EUROPE • 350 kW
	†RADIO NORWAY INTL, Kvitsøy	M-F • EUROPE • 350 kW
		Sa/Su • EUROPE • 350 kW
	ROMANIA — RADIO ROMANIA INTL, Bucharest	Su • W EUROPE & ATLANTIC • MARINERS • 250 kW
	SEYCHELLES — †FAR EAST BC ASS'N, North Pt, Mahé Is	S ASIA • 100 kW
		Su • S ASIA • 100 kW
	UNITED KINGDOM — BBC, Via Delano, USA	C AMERICA & S AMERICA • 250 kW
	BBC, Via Maṣīrah, Oman	MIDEAST • 100 kW
	†BBC, Via Sackville, Can	E NORTH AM • 250 kW
	USA — RADIO MARTI, Cincinnati, Ohio	C AMERICA • 250 kW
(con'd)	VOA, Greenville, NC	C AMERICA • 250/500 kW

FREQUENCY	COUNTRY, STATION, LOCATION	TARGET • NETWORK • POWER (kW) / World Time

0 1 2 3 4 5 6 7 8 9 10 11 12 13 14 15 16 17 18 19 20 21 22 23 24

9590 (con'd)	**USA**	
	VOA, Via Philippines	S ASIA • 250 kW
9595	**CANADA**	
	R CANADA INTL, Via Tokyo, Japan	Sa • E ASIA & PACIFIC • 50 kW
	ETHIOPIA	
	"RADIO FREEDOM", Via Vo Ethiopia	S AFRICA • ANC/ENGLISH, ETC • 100 kW
	GERMANY	
	†DEUTSCHE WELLE, Leipzig	(D) • C AMERICA • 100 kW
	JAPAN	
	RADIO TAMPA, Tokyo-Nagara	DS-1 • 50 kW
		Su-F • DS-1 • 50 kW
	UNITED KINGDOM	
	BBC, Via Seychelles	S AFRICA • 250 kW
	†BBC, Via Singapore	(D) • SE ASIA • 250 kW
	URUGUAY	
	RADIO MONTE CARLO, Montevideo	DS • 1.5 kW
	USA	
	†RFE-RL, Via Germany	(D) • WEST USSR • 100/250 kW
		(J) • WEST USSR • 100 kW
	†RFE-RL, Via Pals, Spain	(D) • WEST USSR • 250 kW
	†RFE-RL, Via Portugal	(J) • WEST USSR • 250 kW
	USSR	
	RADIO MOSCOW, Novosibirsk	E ASIA • 100 kW · (J) • E ASIA • 100 kW
	UZBEK RADIO, Serpukhov	DS-2/RUSSIAN, UZBEK • 20 kW
9600	**BOTSWANA**	
	†RADIO BOTSWANA, Gaborone	DS-ENGLISH, ETC • 50 kW • ALT. FREQ. TO 5955 kHz
	DENMARK	
	†DANMARKS RADIO, Via Norway	(J) • EUROPE • 500 kW
	GERMANY	
	DEUTSCHE WELLE, Via Sri Lanka	(D) • MIDEAST • 250 kW
	LIBYA	
	RADIO JAMAHIRIYA, Benghazi	MIDEAST • DS • 100 kW
	NORWAY	
	†RADIO NORWAY INTL, Kvitsøy	(J) • EUROPE • 500 kW
	PORTUGAL	
	†R PORTUGAL INTL, Lisbon	S AMERICA • 100 kW
		Su/M • S AMERICA • 100 kW
		Tu-Sa • S AMERICA • 100 kW
	RADIO RENASCENCA, Muge	S AMERICA • 100 kW
	SWAZILAND	
	†TRANS WORLD RADIO, Manzini	(J) • E AFRICA • 100 kW
	UNITED ARAB EMIRATES	
	†UAE RADIO, Abu Dhabi	(D) • E NORTH AM • 500 kW • ALT. FREQ. TO 9505 kHz · (D) • E NORTH AM • 500 kW
	UNITED KINGDOM	
	†BBC, Daventry	(D) • EUROPE • 300 kW
		(J) • EUROPE • 300 kW
	BBC, Rampisham	(J) • EUROPE • 500 kW
	†BBC, Via Ascension	S AFRICA • 250 kW
		W AFRICA • 250 kW
		(J) • S AFRICA • 250 kW
		(J) • W AFRICA • 250 kW
	†BBC, Via Maṣīrah, Oman	S ASIA • 100 kW
	†BBC, Via Singapore	SE ASIA & S ASIA • 250 kW
	USSR	
	†MAGADAN RADIO, Okhotsk	RUSSIAN, ETC • DS/TIKHIY OKEAN • 100 kW
	†RADIO KIEV, Kiev	(J) • EUROPE • 100 kW
	†RADIO MOSCOW, Kiev	(J) • EUROPE • 100 kW
	RADIO MOSCOW, Moscow	(J) • W EUROPE • 240 kW
	RADIO MOSCOW, Via Havana, Cuba	(J) • N AMERICA • 100 kW
	RADIO TASHKENT, Tashkent	(D) • S ASIA • 100 kW
	†SOVIET BELORUSSIA, Kiev	(J) • M/Tu/Th/F • EUROPE • 100 kW
		(J) • W/Sa/Su • EUROPE • 100 kW
	VATICAN STATE	
	†VATICAN RADIO, Sta Maria di Galeria	USSR • 500 kW
		SE ASIA • 500 kW
9600v	**MEXICO**	
	RADIO UNIVERSIDAD, México City	Irr • DS • 0.25/1 kW
9600.7	**CLANDESTINE (ASIA)**	
	†"CPBS"	Irr • E ASIA • FAKE CHINESE STN
9605	**CHINA (PR)**	
	RADIO BEIJING, Kunming	SE ASIA • 50 kW
	CZECHOSLOVAKIA	
	†RADIO PRAGUE INTL, Litomyšl	EUROPE • 120 kW
	DENMARK	
(con'd)	†DANMARKS RADIO, Via Norway	(D) • E NORTH AM & C AMERICA • 350 kW

0 1 2 3 4 5 6 7 8 9 10 11 12 13 14 15 16 17 18 19 20 21 22 23 24

ENGLISH ▬ ARABIC ▨ CHINESE ▫▫▫ FRENCH ▭ GERMAN ▬ RUSSIAN ▭ SPANISH ▬ OTHER ▬

FREQUENCY   COUNTRY, STATION, LOCATION   TARGET • NETWORK • POWER (kW)   World Time

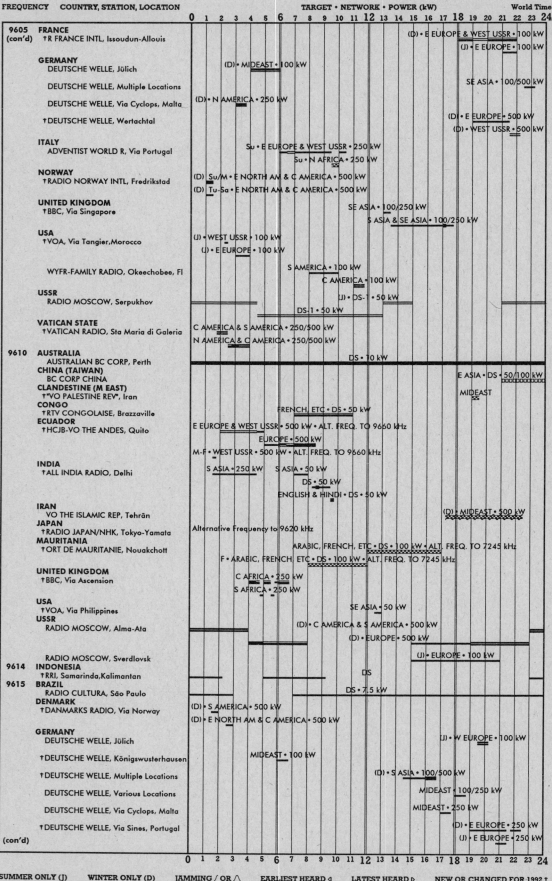

FREQUENCY	COUNTRY, STATION, LOCATION	TARGET • NETWORK • POWER (kW)	World Time

World Time scale: 0 1 2 3 4 5 6 7 8 9 10 11 12 13 14 15 16 17 18 19 20 21 22 23 24

9615 GERMANY
(con'd)   DEUTSCHE WELLE, Via Sri Lanka — S ASIA • 250 kW

DEUTSCHE WELLE, Wertachtal — (J) • MIDEAST & S ASIA • 500 kW

INDIA
↑ALL INDIA RADIO, Bombay — DS • 100 kW

↑ALL INDIA RADIO, Delhi — DS • 50 kW / ENGLISH & HINDI • DS • 50 kW

NORWAY
↑RADIO NORWAY INTL, Sveio — (D) Su/M • S AMERICA • 500 kW
(D) Su/M • E NORTH AM & C AMERICA • 500 kW
(D) Tu-Sa • S AMERICA • 500 kW
(D) Tu-Sa • E NORTH AM & C AMERICA • 500 kW

PHILIPPINES
RADIO VERITAS ASIA, Palauig — E ASIA • 100 kW

PORTUGAL
R PORTUGAL INTL, Sines — Sa/Su • EUROPE • 250 kW

SWEDEN
↑RADIO SWEDEN, Hörby — EUROPE • 350 kW
(D) • EUROPE • 350 kW
(J) • EUROPE • 350 kW

USA
↑KGEI-VO FRIENDSHIP, Redwood City, Ca — C AMERICA & S AMERICA • 50 kW

↑KNLS-NEW LIFE STN, Anchor Pt, Alaska — (J) • E ASIA • 100 kW

↑RFE-RL, Via Germany — (J) • E EUROPE • 100 kW

↑VOA, Via Kaválla, Greece — (D) • WEST USSR • 250 kW

↑VOA, Via Tangier, Morocco — (D) • E EUROPE • 100 kW

USSR
RADIO MOSCOW, Zhigulevsk — (J) • DS-MAYAK • 100 kW

VATICAN STATE
↑VATICAN RADIO, Sta Maria di Galeria — S AMERICA • 250/500 kW / AUSTRALIA • 250/500 kW

9616 MONGOLIA
RADIO ULAANBAATAR, Ulaanbaatar — Alternative Frequency to 11850 kHz

9618v MOZAMBIQUE
RADIO MOCAMBIQUE, Maputo — S AFRICA • 100 kW / DS • 100 kW

PHILIPPINES
DZFM, Marulas — Irr • DS • 2.5 kW

9620 CUBA
↑RADIO HABANA, Havana — C AMERICA • 75 kW / Su • C AMERICA • 75 kW

EGYPT
RADIO CAIRO, Abu Za'bal — N AFRICA • DS-GENERAL • 100 kW

INDIA
↑ALL INDIA RADIO, Aligarh — (D) • WEST USSR • 250 kW

JAPAN
↑RADIO JAPAN/NHK, Tokyo-Yamata — MIDEAST & N AFRICA • 300 kW • ALT. FREQ. TO 9610 kHz

SPAIN
↑R EXTERIOR ESPANA, Arganda — EUROPE • 100 kW

↑R EXTERIOR ESPANA, Via Beijing — E ASIA • 120 kW

USA
↑VOA, Via Philippines — SE ASIA • 50 kW / SE ASIA • 250 kW / (J) • SE ASIA • 50 kW

YUGOSLAVIA
↑RADIO YUGOSLAVIA, Bijeljina — E NORTH AM • 500 kW / EUROPE • 250 kW
(D) • ATLANTIC & E NORTH AM • 500 kW / (D) • WEST USSR • 500 kW
Su • EUROPE • 250 kW / (D) • N AFRICA • 250 kW
(D) • EUROPE & E NORTH AM • 500 kW

9620.2 URUGUAY
SODRE, Montevideo — DS • 0.3 kW

9625 CANADA
CANADIAN BC CORP, Sackville, NB — M • DS-NORTHERN • 100 kW / M-F • DS-NORTHERN • 100 kW
Tu-Sa • DS-NORTHERN • 100 kW / Sa • DS-NORTHERN • 100 kW
Su • DS-NORTHERN • 100 kW

CHINA (PR)
RADIO BEIJING, Kunming — E AFRICA & S AFRICA • 120 kW / (J) • S ASIA • 120 kW

GABON
ADVENTIST WORLD R, Moyabi — M-Sa • W AFRICA • VIA AFRIQUE NR UN • 500 kW

GERMANY
DEUTSCHE WELLE, Multiple Locations — (D) • MIDEAST • 100/250 kW

ROMANIA
RADIO ROMANIA INTL, Bucharest — EUROPE • 250 kW

USA
↑RFE-RL, Via Germany — (D) • WEST USSR • 100 kW / (D) • E EUROPE • 100 kW / (J) • WEST USSR • 100 kW

↑RFE-RL, Via Pals, Spain — (J) • WEST USSR • 250 kW

↑RFE-RL, Via Portugal — (D) • WEST USSR • 250 kW / (D) • E EUROPE • 250 kW

(con'd)

World Time scale: 0 1 2 3 4 5 6 7 8 9 10 11 12 13 14 15 16 17 18 19 20 21 22 23 24

ENGLISH ▬ ARABIC ∞∞ CHINESE □□□ FRENCH ══ GERMAN ▬▬ RUSSIAN ══ SPANISH ▬▬ OTHER ──

FREQUENCY   COUNTRY, STATION, LOCATION   TARGET • NETWORK • POWER (kW)   World Time

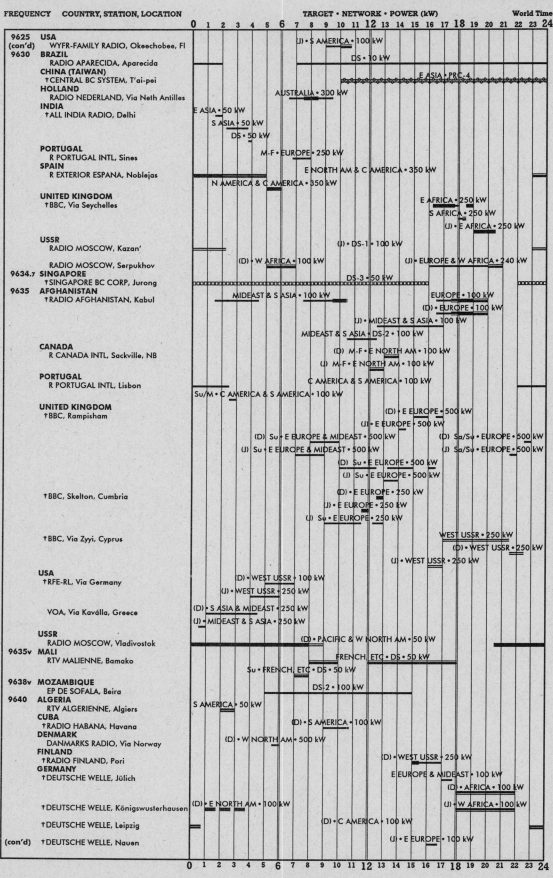

0 1 2 3 4 5 6 7 8 9 10 11 12 13 14 15 16 17 18 19 20 21 22 23 24

Frequency	Country, Station, Location	Target • Network • Power
9625 (con'd)	USA — WYFR-FAMILY RADIO, Okeechobee, Fl	(J) • S AMERICA • 100 kW
9630	BRAZIL — RADIO APARECIDA, Aparecida	DS • 10 kW
	CHINA (TAIWAN) — †CENTRAL BC SYSTEM, T'ai-pei	E ASIA • PRC-4
	HOLLAND — RADIO NEDERLAND, Via Neth Antilles	AUSTRALIA • 300 kW
	INDIA — †ALL INDIA RADIO, Delhi	E ASIA • 50 kW / S ASIA • 50 kW / DS • 50 kW
	PORTUGAL — R PORTUGAL INTL, Sines	M-F • EUROPE • 250 kW
	SPAIN — R EXTERIOR ESPANA, Noblejas	E NORTH AM & C AMERICA • 350 kW / N AMERICA & C AMERICA • 350 kW
	UNITED KINGDOM — †BBC, Via Seychelles	E AFRICA • 250 kW / S AFRICA • 250 kW / (J) • E AFRICA • 250 kW
	USSR — RADIO MOSCOW, Kazan'	(J) • DS-1 • 100 kW
	RADIO MOSCOW, Serpukhov	(D) • W AFRICA • 100 kW / (J) • EUROPE & W AFRICA • 240 kW
9634.7	SINGAPORE — †SINGAPORE BC CORP, Jurong	DS-3 • 50 kW
9635	AFGHANISTAN — †RADIO AFGHANISTAN, Kabul	MIDEAST & S ASIA • 100 kW / EUROPE • 100 kW / (D) • EUROPE • 100 kW / (J) • MIDEAST & S ASIA • 100 kW / MIDEAST & S ASIA • DS-2 • 100 kW
	CANADA — R CANADA INTL, Sackville, NB	(D) M-F • E NORTH AM • 100 kW / (J) M-F • E NORTH AM • 100 kW
	PORTUGAL — R PORTUGAL INTL, Lisbon	C AMERICA & S AMERICA • 100 kW / Su/M • C AMERICA & S AMERICA • 100 kW
	UNITED KINGDOM — †BBC, Rampisham	(D) • E EUROPE • 500 kW / (J) • E EUROPE • 500 kW / (D) Su • E EUROPE & MIDEAST • 500 kW / (J) Su • E EUROPE & MIDEAST • 500 kW / (D) Su • E EUROPE • 500 kW / (J) Su • E EUROPE • 500 kW / (D) Sa/Su • EUROPE • 500 kW / (D) Sa/Su • EUROPE • 500 kW
	†BBC, Skelton, Cumbria	(D) • E EUROPE • 250 kW / (J) • E EUROPE • 250 kW / (J) Su • E EUROPE • 250 kW
	†BBC, Via Zyyi, Cyprus	WEST USSR • 250 kW / (D) • WEST USSR • 250 kW / (J) • WEST USSR • 250 kW
	USA — †RFE-RL, Via Germany	(D) • WEST USSR • 100 kW / (J) • WEST USSR • 250 kW
	VOA, Via Kaválla, Greece	(D) • S ASIA & MIDEAST • 250 kW / (J) • MIDEAST & S ASIA • 250 kW
	USSR — RADIO MOSCOW, Vladivostok	(D) • PACIFIC & W NORTH AM • 50 kW
9635v	MALI — RTV MALIENNE, Bamako	FRENCH, ETC • DS • 50 kW / Su • FRENCH, ETC • DS • 50 kW
9638v	MOZAMBIQUE — EP DE SOFALA, Beira	DS-2 • 100 kW
9640	ALGERIA — RTV ALGERIENNE, Algiers	S AMERICA • 50 kW
	CUBA — †RADIO HABANA, Havana	(D) • S AMERICA • 100 kW
	DENMARK — DANMARKS RADIO, Via Norway	(D) • W NORTH AM • 500 kW
	FINLAND — †RADIO FINLAND, Pori	(D) • WEST USSR • 250 kW
	GERMANY — †DEUTSCHE WELLE, Jülich	E EUROPE & MIDEAST • 100 kW / (D) • AFRICA • 100 kW / (J) • W AFRICA • 100 kW
	†DEUTSCHE WELLE, Königswusterhausen	(D) • E NORTH AM • 100 kW
	†DEUTSCHE WELLE, Leipzig	(D) • C AMERICA • 100 kW
(con'd)	†DEUTSCHE WELLE, Nauen	(J) • E EUROPE • 100 kW

0 1 2 3 4 5 6 7 8 9 10 11 12 13 14 15 16 17 18 19 20 21 22 23 24

SUMMER ONLY (J)   WINTER ONLY (D)   JAMMING / OR ∧   EARLIEST HEARD ◁   LATEST HEARD ▷   NEW OR CHANGED FOR 1992 †

| FREQUENCY | COUNTRY, STATION, LOCATION | TARGET • NETWORK • POWER (kW) | World Time |

Time scale: 0 1 2 3 4 5 6 7 8 9 10 11 12 13 14 15 16 17 18 19 20 21 22 23 24

9640 (con'd)

GERMANY
  DEUTSCHE WELLE, Wertachtal — MIDEAST • 500 kW
JAPAN
  †RADIO JAPAN/NHK, Tokyo-Yamata — (J) • AUSTRALIA • 100 kW
KOREA (DPR)
  †RADIO PYONGYANG, Pyongyang — S ASIA • 200 kW / MIDEAST & AFRICA • 200 kW

KOREA (REPUBLIC)
  RADIO KOREA, In-Kimjae — SE ASIA • 250 kW

SAUDI ARABIA
  BS OF THE KINGDOM, Riyadh — MIDEAST • 350 kW
UNITED KINGDOM
  BBC, Via Antigua — C AMERICA • 125/250 kW
USSR
  RADIO MOSCOW, Armavir — (D) • S AMERICA • 500 kW
  S AMERICA • 250 kW

  RADIO MOSCOW, Moscow — (J) • EUROPE • 240 kW
VENEZUELA
  ECOS DEL TORBES, San Cristóbal — DS • 10 kW
  Su • DS • 10 kW

9645

AUSTRALIA
  †RADIO AUSTRALIA, Carnarvon — (D) • SE ASIA • 100 kW
BRAZIL
  RADIO BANDEIRANTES, São Paulo — DS • 7.5 kW
  Irr • DS • 7.5 kW

COSTA RICA
  FARO DEL CARIBE, San José — DS • 0.5 kW
DENMARK
  †DANMARKS RADIO, Via Norway — (D) • N AMERICA • 500 kW / (D) • E NORTH AM & C AMERICA • 500 kW
FINLAND
  †RADIO FINLAND, Pori — (D) • N AMERICA • 500 kW
JAPAN
  †RADIO JAPAN/NHK, Via Moyabi, Gabon — (D) • S AFRICA • 500 kW
NORWAY
  †RADIO NORWAY INTL, Sveio — (D) • N AMERICA • 500 kW / (D) • E NORTH AM & C AMERICA • 500 kW
USA
  †RFE-RL, Via Pals, Spain — (D) • WEST USSR • 250 kW

  VOA, Via Sri Lanka — E ASIA • 35 kW
USSR
  RADIO MOSCOW, Sverdlovsk — (J) • DS-1 • 240 kW
VATICAN STATE
  †VATICAN RADIO, Sta Maria di Galeria — C AMERICA • 500 kW / EUROPE • 100 kW / N AFRICA • 100 kW
    Su • EUROPE • 100 kW / Su • N AFRICA • 100 kW
    M-Sa • ENGLISH, FRENCH & SPANISH • N AFRICA • 100 kW
    M-Sa • ENGLISH, FRENCH, SPANISH & ITALIAN • EUROPE • 100 kW

9645v

PAKISTAN
  PAKISTAN BC CORP, Islamabad — (J) • DS • 10 kW

  RADIO PAKISTAN, Islamabad — S ASIA • FEEDER • 10 kW
9650
CANADA
  R CANADA INTL, Sackville, NB — (D) • M-F • E NORTH AM • 250 kW
    (J) • M-F • E NORTH AM • 250 kW

  †R CANADA INTL, Via Tokyo, Japan — (D) • E ASIA • 300 kW
    (J) • E ASIA • 300 kW

DENMARK
  †DANMARKS RADIO, Via Norway — (D) • MIDEAST & E AFRICA • 500 kW
    (D) • E AFRICA • 350 kW

FRANCE
  †R FRANCE INTL, Via Tokyo, Japan — (D) • E ASIA • 300 kW
GERMANY
  †DEUTSCHE WELLE, Jülich — (J) • E NORTH AM • 100 kW

  †DEUTSCHE WELLE, Nauen — (D) • S ASIA • 500 kW / (J) • E EUROPE • 50 kW
    (J) • WEST USSR • 100 kW

  DEUTSCHE WELLE, Via Cyclops, Malta — (J) • MIDEAST • 250 kW

  DEUTSCHE WELLE, Via Sines, Portugal — (D) • E EUROPE • 250 kW
    (J) • E EUROPE • 250 kW

  †DEUTSCHE WELLE, Wertachtal — (D) • WEST USSR • 500 kW / (D) • MIDEAST • 500 kW
    (D) • E EUROPE • 500 kW
    (J) • E EUROPE • 500 kW

GUAM
  ADVENTIST WORLD R, Agat — E ASIA • 100 kW
JAPAN
  †RADIO JAPAN/NHK, Tokyo-Yamata — (D) • E ASIA • GENERAL • 100 kW
KOREA (DPR)
  RADIO PYONGYANG, Pyongyang — E ASIA • 200 kW
KOREA (REPUBLIC)
  RADIO KOREA, Via Sackville, Can — E NORTH AM • 250 kW
MONACO
  TRANS WORLD RADIO, Monte Carlo — EUROPE • 100 kW
NORWAY
(con'd) †RADIO NORWAY INTL, Fredrikstad — (D) • E AFRICA • 350 kW

Time scale: 0 1 2 3 4 5 6 7 8 9 10 11 12 13 14 15 16 17 18 19 20 21 22 23 24

ENGLISH ▪▪▪ ARABIC ≈≈≈ CHINESE □□□ FRENCH ══ GERMAN ▬▬ RUSSIAN ══ SPANISH ══ OTHER ──

FREQUENCY	COUNTRY, STATION, LOCATION	TARGET • NETWORK • POWER (kW)	World Time

World Time scale: 0 1 2 3 4 5 6 7 8 9 10 11 12 13 14 15 16 17 18 19 20 21 22 23 24

9650
(con'd)
NORWAY
  †RADIO NORWAY INTL, Kvitsøy — (D) • MIDEAST & E AFRICA • 500 kW
SPAIN
  R EXTERIOR ESPANA, Noblejas — AUSTRALIA • 350 kW
SWAZILAND
  †TRANS WORLD RADIO, Manzini — S AFRICA • 25 kW
SWITZERLAND
  †RED CROSS BC SVC, Sottens — Irr • Tu/F • C AMERICA • 500 kW
  — Irr • Tu/F • N AMERICA & C AMERICA • 500 kW

  †SWISS RADIO INTL, Sottens — C AMERICA • 500 kW
  — N AMERICA & C AMERICA • 500 kW
  — M • C AMERICA • 500 kW
  — M • N AMERICA & C AMERICA • 500 kW
  — Tu-Su • C AMERICA • 500 kW
  — Tu-Su • N AMERICA & C AMERICA • 500 kW

UNITED KINGDOM
  †BBC, Daventry — (D) • E EUROPE • 300 kW
USA
  †VOA, Via Portugal — (D) • WEST USSR • 250 kW
  †VOA, Via Tangier, Morocco — (D) • E EUROPE • 100 kW
  †VOA, Via Woofferton, UK — (J) • E EUROPE • 250/300 kW
USSR
  RADIO MOSCOW, Bishkek — (D) • C AMERICA & S AMERICA • 500 kW
  RADIO MOSCOW, Moscow — (J) • S ASIA & SE ASIA • 250 kW
  RADIO MOSCOW, Zhigulevsk — (J) • E EUROPE • 100 kW
VATICAN STATE
  VATICAN RADIO, Sta Maria di Galeria — S ASIA • 250 kW

9655
BRAZIL
  †RADIO NACIONAL, Brasilia — Alternative Frequency to 9745 kHz
BULGARIA
  †RADIO SOFIA, Sofia — Alternative Frequency to 11870 kHz
DENMARK
  †DANMARKS RADIO, Via Norway — (D) • N AMERICA • 350 kW / EUROPE • 350 kW
  — (D) • W NORTH AM & PACIFIC • 500 kW
NORWAY
  †RADIO NORWAY INTL, Fredrikstad — (D) • N AMERICA • 350 kW / M-F • EUROPE • 350 kW
  — Sa/Su • EUROPE • 350 kW

  †RADIO NORWAY INTL, Sveio — (D) • W NORTH AM & PACIFIC • 500 kW
SWAZILAND
  †TRANS WORLD RADIO, Manzini — S AFRICA • 25 kW
  — (D) • S AFRICA • 25 kW
  — Sa/Su • S AFRICA • 25 kW

SWEDEN
  †RADIO SWEDEN, Hörby — (D) • EUROPE • 350 kW
  — (D) • EUROPE & AFRICA • 350 kW
  — (J) • EUROPE • 350 kW

THAILAND
  †RADIO THAILAND, Pathum Thani — ASIA • 100 kW
  — Sa/Su • ASIA • 100 kW / Tu/Th/Sa • MIDEAST • 100 kW

USSR
  †BELORUSSIAN RADIO, Orcha — RUSSIAN, ETC • DS-1 • 20 kW
  RADIO MOSCOW, Kazan' — (D) • MIDEAST & S ASIA • 100 kW
  RADIO MOSCOW, Komsomol'sk 'Amure — (J) • W NORTH AM • 240 kW / (D) • E ASIA • 100 kW
  RADIO MOSCOW, Orcha — (J) • E NORTH AM & C AMERICA • 100 kW

9660
AUSTRALIA
  AUSTRALIAN BC CORP, Brisbane — DS • 10 kW
CANADA
  †R CANADA INTL, Via Tokyo, Japan — (D) • E ASIA • 300 kW
ECUADOR
  †HCJB-VO THE ANDES, Quito — Alternative Frequency to 9610 kHz
PHILIPPINES
  †FEBC RADIO INTL, Bocaue — SE ASIA • 50 kW
UNITED KINGDOM
  †BBC, Via Zyyi, Cyprus — EUROPE • 100 kW
  — (D) • EUROPE • 100/250 kW
  — (J) • M-F • EUROPE • 100 kW
  — Sa/Su • EUROPE • 100/250 kW
  — (D) • Sa/Su • EUROPE • 250 kW

USA
  †RFE-RL, Via Germany — (J) • WEST USSR • 100/250 kW
  — WEST USSR • 250 kW
  — (D) • WEST USSR • 250 kW

  †RFE-RL, Via Pals, Spain — (D) • WEST USSR • 250 kW
(con'd)
  †RFE-RL, Via Portugal — WEST USSR • 250 kW

World Time scale: 0 1 2 3 4 5 6 7 8 9 10 11 12 13 14 15 16 17 18 19 20 21 22 23 24

FREQUENCY　　COUNTRY, STATION, LOCATION　　　　　　TARGET • NETWORK • POWER (kW)　　　World Time

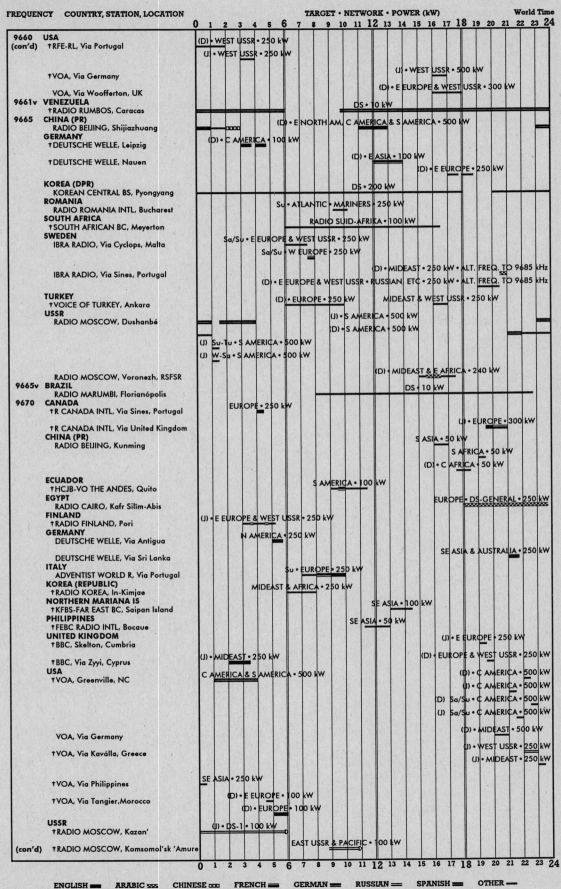

0 1 2 3 4 5 6 7 8 9 10 11 12 13 14 15 16 17 18 19 20 21 22 23 24

9660 **USA**
(con'd)　　†RFE-RL, Via Portugal　　　　(D) • WEST USSR • 250 kW
　　　　　　　　　　　　　　　　　　(J) • WEST USSR • 250 kW

　　　†VOA, Via Germany　　　　　　　　　　　　　　(J) • WEST USSR • 500 kW
　　　　VOA, Via Woofferton, UK　　　　　　　　　(D) • E EUROPE & WEST USSR • 300 kW
9661v **VENEZUELA**　　　　　　　　　　　　　　　　DS • 10 kW
　　　†RADIO RUMBOS, Caracas
9665 **CHINA (PR)**　　　　　　　(D) • E NORTH AM, C AMERICA & S AMERICA • 500 kW
　　　　RADIO BEIJING, Shijiazhuang
　　GERMANY　　　　　　　(D) • C AMERICA • 100 kW
　　　†DEUTSCHE WELLE, Leipzig

　　　†DEUTSCHE WELLE, Nauen　　　　　　(D) • E ASIA • 100 kW
　　　　　　　　　　　　　　　　　　　　(D) • E EUROPE • 250 kW

　　KOREA (DPR)　　　　　　　　　　DS • 200 kW
　　　　KOREAN CENTRAL BS, Pyongyang
　　ROMANIA　　　　　　　Su • ATLANTIC • MARINERS • 250 kW
　　　　RADIO ROMANIA INTL, Bucharest
　　SOUTH AFRICA　　　　　RADIO SUID-AFRIKA • 100 kW
　　　†SOUTH AFRICAN BC, Meyerton
　　SWEDEN　　　　Sa/Su • E EUROPE & WEST USSR • 250 kW
　　　　IBRA RADIO, Via Cyclops, Malta　　Sa/Su • W EUROPE • 250 kW

　　　　　　　　　　　　　　　(D) • MIDEAST • 250 kW • ALT. FREQ. TO 9685 kHz
　　　　IBRA RADIO, Via Sines, Portugal　(D) • E EUROPE & WEST USSR • RUSSIAN, ETC • 250 kW • ALT. FREQ. TO 9685 kHz

　　TURKEY　　　　　　(D) • EUROPE • 250 kW　　　MIDEAST & WEST USSR • 250 kW
　　　†VOICE OF TURKEY, Ankara
　　USSR　　　　　　　　　　　(J) • S AMERICA • 500 kW
　　　　RADIO MOSCOW, Dushanbé　　　(D) • S AMERICA • 500 kW

　　　　　　　　　　(J) • Su-Tu • S AMERICA • 500 kW
　　　　　　　　　　(J) • W-Sa • S AMERICA • 500 kW

　　　　RADIO MOSCOW, Voronezh, RSFSR　　　(D) • MIDEAST & E AFRICA • 240 kW
9665v **BRAZIL**　　　　　　　　　　　　　　DS • 10 kW
　　　　RADIO MARUMBI, Florianópolis
9670 **CANADA**　　　　EUROPE • 250 kW
　　　†R CANADA INTL, Via Sines, Portugal

　　　†R CANADA INTL, Via United Kingdom　　　　(J) • EUROPE • 300 kW
　　CHINA (PR)　　　　　　　　　　S ASIA • 50 kW
　　　　RADIO BEIJING, Kunming　　　　　　S AFRICA • 50 kW
　　　　　　　　　　　　　　　(D) • C AFRICA • 50 kW

　　ECUADOR　　　　　　　S AMERICA • 100 kW
　　　†HCJB-VO THE ANDES, Quito
　　EGYPT　　　　　　　　　　EUROPE • DS-GENERAL • 250 kW
　　　　RADIO CAIRO, Kafr Silim-Abis
　　FINLAND　　(J) • E EUROPE & WEST USSR • 250 kW
　　　†RADIO FINLAND, Pori
　　GERMANY　　N AMERICA • 250 kW
　　　　DEUTSCHE WELLE, Via Antigua

　　　　DEUTSCHE WELLE, Via Sri Lanka　　　　SE ASIA & AUSTRALIA • 250 kW
　　ITALY　　　　Su • EUROPE • 250 kW
　　　　ADVENTIST WORLD R, Via Portugal
　　KOREA (REPUBLIC)　　MIDEAST & AFRICA • 250 kW
　　　†RADIO KOREA, In-Kimjae
　　NORTHERN MARIANA IS　　　　SE ASIA • 100 kW
　　　†KFBS-FAR EAST BC, Saipan Island
　　PHILIPPINES　　　　　SE ASIA • 50 kW
　　　†FEBC RADIO INTL, Bocaue
　　UNITED KINGDOM　　　　　　(J) • E EUROPE • 250 kW
　　　†BBC, Skelton, Cumbria
　　　†BBC, Via Zyyi, Cyprus　(J) • MIDEAST • 250 kW　(D) • EUROPE & WEST USSR • 250 kW
　　USA　　　　C AMERICA & S AMERICA • 500 kW
　　　†VOA, Greenville, NC　　　　　　　　　(D) • C AMERICA • 500 kW
　　　　　　　　　　　　　　　　　　　　(J) • C AMERICA • 500 kW
　　　　　　　　　　　　　　　　　　(D) Sa/Su • C AMERICA • 500 kW
　　　　　　　　　　　　　　　　　　(J) Sa/Su • C AMERICA • 500 kW

　　　　VOA, Via Germany　　　　　　　　　　(D) • MIDEAST • 500 kW
　　　†VOA, Via Kaválla, Greece　　　　　　　(J) • WEST USSR • 250 kW
　　　　　　　　　　　　　　　　　　　　(J) • MIDEAST • 250 kW

　　　†VOA, Via Philippines　　SE ASIA • 250 kW
　　　†VOA, Via Tangier, Morocco　(D) • E EUROPE • 100 kW
　　　　　　　　　　　　　(D) • EUROPE • 100 kW

　　USSR　　　　(J) • DS-1 • 100 kW
　　　†RADIO MOSCOW, Kazan'
(con'd)　†RADIO MOSCOW, Komsomol'sk 'Amure　EAST USSR & PACIFIC • 100 kW

0 1 2 3 4 5 6 7 8 9 10 11 12 13 14 15 16 17 18 19 20 21 22 23 24

ENGLISH ▬　ARABIC ≋　CHINESE ▭▭▭　FRENCH ═　GERMAN ═　RUSSIAN ═　SPANISH ═　OTHER ▬

FREQUENCY　　COUNTRY, STATION, LOCATION　　　　　　TARGET • NETWORK • POWER (kW)　　　World Time

0 1 2 3 4 5 6 7 8 9 10 11 12 13 14 15 16 17 18 19 20 21 22 23 24

FREQUENCY	COUNTRY, STATION, LOCATION	TARGET • NETWORK • POWER (kW)
9670 (con'd)	USSR †RADIO MOSCOW, Komsomol'sk 'Amure	DS-MAYAK • 100 kW
9675	BRAZIL †R CANCAO NOVA, Cachoeira Paulista	DS • 10 kW
	EGYPT RADIO CAIRO, Kafr Silim-Abis	N AMERICA • 250 kW
	INDIA ALL INDIA RADIO, Delhi	S ASIA • 100 kW / ENGLISH & HINDI • DS • 100 kW
	INDONESIA †VOICE OF INDONESIA, Padang Cermin	ASIA • 250 kW / EUROPE • 250 kW
	JAPAN †RADIO JAPAN/NHK, Via French Guiana	S AMERICA • 500 kW / S AMERICA • GENERAL • 500 kW
	PERU †RADIO DEL PACIFICO, Lima	DS • 4 kW • ALT. FREQ. TO 4975 kHz / DS • 4 kW / M-Sa • DS • 4 kW
	POLAND RADIO POLONIA, Warsaw	(J) • EUROPE • 100 kW
	SOUTH AFRICA †RADIO RSA, Meyerton	C AFRICA • 250 kW
	TUNISIA RTV TUNISIENNE, Sfax	(D) • MIDEAST • DS • 100 kW
	TURKEY †VOICE OF TURKEY, Ankara	MIDEAST & S ASIA • 500 kW / MIDEAST • 250 kW
	USSR †LITHUANIAN RADIO, Balashikha	DS-1 • 20 kW
	RADIO MOSCOW	(D)
	RADIO MOSCOW, Tashkent	S AMERICA • 500 kW
	†RADIO VILNIUS, Balashikha	20 kW
9680	CHINA (TAIWAN) VO FREE CHINA, Via Okeechobee,USA	W NORTH AM • 100 kW
	GERMANY †DEUTSCHE WELLE, Nauen	(J) • E EUROPE • 250 kW
	INDONESIA †RRI, Jakarta, Jawa	DS • 50/100 kW
	PORTUGAL RADIO RENASCENCA, Muge	EUROPE • 100 kW / Sa/Su • EUROPE • 100 kW
	SWITZERLAND SWISS RADIO INTL, Schwarzenburg	W EUROPE • 150 kW
	TURKEY †VOICE OF TURKEY, Ankara	Alternative Frequency to 15220 kHz
	UNITED KINGDOM †BBC, Via Singapore	(D) • S ASIA • 250 kW / (D) M-F • S ASIA • 250 kW / (D) Sa/Su • S ASIA • 250 kW
	USA †RFE-RL, Via Germany	(J) • WEST USSR & MIDEAST • 100 kW / (J) • WEST USSR • 250 kW
	†RFE-RL, Via Portugal	(D) • WEST USSR & MIDEAST • 250 kW / (D) • E EUROPE • 250 kW
	†VOA, Via Kaválla, Greece	MIDEAST & S ASIA • 250 kW / (D) • MIDEAST • 250 kW
	†VOA, Via Philippines	(D) • SE ASIA • 50 kW
	WYFR-FAMILY RADIO, Okeechobee, Fl	(D) • W NORTH AM • 100 kW / (D) • EUROPE • 100 kW
9680v	MEXICO RADIO XEQQ, México City	Irr • DS • 0.5 kW
9684v	TANZANIA RADIO TANZANIA, Dar es Salaam	S AFRICA • 50 kW / DS • 50 kW
9685	ALGERIA RTV ALGERIENNE, Algiers	EUROPE & N AFRICA • 100 kW / EUROPE & N AFRICA • DS • 100 kW
	CANADA †R CANADA INTL, Via Tokyo, Japan	(J) • E ASIA • 300 kW
	GERMANY †DEUTSCHE WELLE, Königswusterhausen	(D) • WEST USSR • 50 kW
	IRAN †VO THE ISLAMIC REP, Tehrān	(D) • MIDEAST • 500 kW
	JAPAN RADIO JAPAN/NHK, Via French Guiana	S AMERICA • GENERAL • 500 kW
	SPAIN †R EXTERIOR ESPANA, Arganda	EUROPE • 100 kW
	SWEDEN IBRA RADIO, Via Sines, Portugal	Alternative Frequency to 9665 kHz
	TURKEY VOICE OF TURKEY, Ankara	EUROPE • 250 kW
	USSR RADIO MOSCOW, Irkutsk	(D) • E ASIA & SE ASIA • 500 kW / (J) • SE ASIA • 500 kW / (J) • E ASIA & SE ASIA • 500 kW
(con'd)		

0 1 2 3 4 5 6 7 8 9 10 11 12 13 14 15 16 17 18 19 20 21 22 23 24

FREQUENCY   COUNTRY, STATION, LOCATION | TARGET • NETWORK • POWER (kW) | World Time

0 1 2 3 4 5 6 7 8 9 10 11 12 13 14 15 16 17 18 19 20 21 22 23 24

Frequency	Country, Station, Location	Target • Network • Power
9685 (con'd)	USSR — RADIO MOSCOW, Moscow	(D) • E NORTH AM & C AMERICA • 100 kW
		(D) • W EUROPE • 100 kW
9685.2	BRAZIL — †RADIO GAZETA, São Paulo	DS • 7.5 kW
9690	ARGENTINA — R ARGENTINA-RAE, Buenos Aires	Tu-Sa • S AMERICA • 25 kW
	RADIO NACIONAL, Buenos Aires	Su/M • S AMERICA • DS • 25 kW
	CHINA (PR) — RADIO BEIJING, Kunming	W EUROPE • 120 kW
	RADIO BEIJING, Via Noblejas, Spain	N AMERICA & C AMERICA • 350 kW
	CHINA (TAIWAN) — †CENTRAL BC SYSTEM, T'ai-pei	E ASIA • PRC-5 (CANTONESE) • 10 kW
	GERMANY — DEUTSCHE WELLE, Jülich	(D) • WEST USSR • 100 kW
		(J) • WEST USSR • 100 kW
	†DEUTSCHE WELLE, Leipzig	(D) • C AMERICA • 100 kW
	†DEUTSCHE WELLE, Multiple Locations	S ASIA • 100/500 kW
		(J) • MIDEAST & N AFRICA • 100/500 kW
		(D) • MIDEAST & S ASIA • 100/500 kW
	DEUTSCHE WELLE, Via Antigua	AUSTRALIA & C AMERICA • 250 kW
	DEUTSCHE WELLE, Via Cyclops, Malta	(J) • MIDEAST • 250 kW
	DEUTSCHE WELLE, Wertachtal	S ASIA & SE ASIA • 500 kW
	MADAGASCAR — RTV MALAGASY, Antananarivo	Irr • DS-1 • 10 kW
	ROMANIA — RADIO ROMANIA INTL, Bucharest	EUROPE • 250 kW
		MIDEAST • 250 kW
		WEST USSR • 250 kW
		(D) • MIDEAST • 250 kW
		(D) • EUROPE • 250 kW
		(J) • WEST USSR • 250 kW
	SPAIN — †R EXTERIOR ESPANA, Noblejas	F • E NORTH AM & C AMERICA • 350 kW
	UNITED KINGDOM — †BBC, Via Delano, USA	C AMERICA • 250 kW
	USA — VOA, Via Kaválla, Greece	E AFRICA • 250 kW
	†VOA, Via Portugal	(D) • WEST USSR • 250 kW
	†VOA, Via Woofferton, UK	(D) • USSR • 300 kW
	USSR — †KAZAKH RADIO, Tula	DS-2 • 20 kW
9695	BRAZIL — †RADIO RIO MAR, Manaus	DS • 7.5 kW
		Sa • DS • 7.5 kW
		Su-F • DS • 7.5 kW
	SWEDEN — †RADIO SWEDEN, Hörby	S AMERICA • 350 kW
		N AMERICA • 350 kW
		(D) • WEST USSR • 350 kW
		(J) • WEST USSR • 350 kW
	UNITED ARAB EMIRATES — UAE RADIO, Abu Dhabi	MIDEAST & S ASIA • 120 kW
	USA — †RFE-RL, Via Portugal	E EUROPE • 250 kW
		(D) • WEST USSR • 250 kW
		(D) • E EUROPE • 250 kW
		(J) • E EUROPE • 250 kW
	USSR — LATVIAN RADIO, Moscow	DS-1 • 20 kW
9700	BULGARIA — †RADIO SOFIA, Sofia	(D) • E NORTH AM & C AMERICA • 250 kW
		(D) • C AMERICA • 250 kW
		(J) • E EUROPE • 250 kW
		(D) • EUROPE • 250 kW
		(J) • EUROPE • 250 kW
	†RADIO SOFIA, Stolnik	(D) • EUROPE, N AFRICA & MIDEAST • 150 kW
		(J) • EUROPE, N AFRICA & MIDEAST • 150 kW
		(D) • Su • EUROPE, N AFRICA & MIDEAST • 150 kW
		(J) • Su • EUROPE, N AFRICA & MIDEAST • 150 kW
	CANADA — †R CANADA INTL, Via In-Kimjae, Korea	E ASIA • 250 kW
		(J) • E ASIA • 250 kW
	CHINA (PR) — RADIO BEIJING, Xi'an	(D) • MIDEAST & S ASIA • 150 kW
		(D) • EUROPE & N AFRICA • 150 kW
	CLANDESTINE (AFRICA) — †"AV DO GALO NEGRO", Jamba, Angola	S AFRICA • UNITA
	EGYPT — RADIO CAIRO, Abu Za'bal	N AFRICA • DS-VO THE ARABS • 100 kW
(con'd)		

0 1 2 3 4 5 6 7 8 9 10 11 12 13 14 15 16 17 18 19 20 21 22 23 24

ENGLISH ▬   ARABIC ⧓⧓   CHINESE □□□   FRENCH ══   GERMAN ▬▬   RUSSIAN ══   SPANISH ▬▬   OTHER ▬

FREQUENCY   COUNTRY, STATION, LOCATION   TARGET • NETWORK • POWER (kW)   World Time

0 1 2 3 4 5 6 7 8 9 10 11 12 13 14 15 16 17 18 19 20 21 22 23 24

Frequency	Country, Station, Location	Target • Network • Power
9700 (con'd)	**GERMANY**	
	†DEUTSCHE WELLE, Jülich	(J) • N AMERICA • 100 kW
	†DEUTSCHE WELLE, Königswusterhausen	(D) • C AMERICA & S AMERICA • 100 kW
	DEUTSCHE WELLE, Multiple Locations	C AMERICA & S AMERICA • 100/500 kW
	DEUTSCHE WELLE, Wertachtal	C AMERICA & S AMERICA • 500 kW
	INDIA	
	†ALL INDIA RADIO, Aligarh	S ASIA • 250 kW
	KOREA (REPUBLIC)	
	RADIO KOREA, Via Sackville, Can	(D) • N AMERICA • 250 kW
	NEW ZEALAND	
	†R NEW ZEALAND INTL, Rangitaiki	ENGLISH, ETC • PACIFIC • 100 kW
		Irr • Sa/Su • E ASIA • TESTS • 100 kW
	USA	
	VOA, Via Kaválla, Greece	(D) • MIDEAST • 250 kW
		MIDEAST & S ASIA • 250 kW
		(D) • N AFRICA & W AFRICA • 250 kW
	USSR	
	RADIO MOSCOW	(D) • N AMERICA
9705	**BRAZIL**	
	RADIO NACIONAL, Rio de Janeiro	DS • 10 kW
		Irr • DS • 10 kW
	IRAN	
	†VO THE ISLAMIC REP, Tehrãn	S ASIA • 500 kW
	MEXICO	
	RADIO MEXICO INTL, México City	C AMERICA • 10 kW
	NIGER	
	LA VOIX DU SAHEL, Niamey	DS-FRENCH, ETC • 100 kW
		Sa • DS-FRENCH, ETC • 100 kW
	PORTUGAL	
	R PORTUGAL INTL, Lisbon	N AMERICA • 100 kW
		Su/M • N AMERICA • 100 kW
		Tu-Sa • N AMERICA • 100 kW
	SAUDI ARABIA	
	BS OF THE KINGDOM, Jiddah	EUROPE • 50 kW
		EUROPE • DS-GENERAL • 50 kW
	USA	
	†RFE-RL, Via Germany	(J) • E EUROPE & WEST USSR • 100 kW
	†RFE-RL, Via Portugal	(D) • WEST USSR • 250 kW
		E EUROPE • 250 kW
		(J) • E EUROPE • 250 kW
		(D) • E EUROPE • 250 kW
	VOA, Via Kaválla, Greece	MIDEAST & S ASIA • 250 kW
	†WYFR-FAMILY RADIO, Okeechobee, Fl	C AMERICA • 50 kW
		(D) • W NORTH AM • 100 kW
	USSR	
	KAZAKH RADIO, Tashkent	DS-2 • 20 kW
9706.4	**ETHIOPIA**	
	†VOICE OF ETHIOPIA, Gedja	DS • 100 kW
		M-Sa • DS • 100 kW M-F • DS • 100 kW
		Su • DS • 100 kW Sa/Su • DS • 100 kW
9710	**AUSTRALIA**	
	†RADIO AUSTRALIA, Shepparton	PACIFIC • 100 kW
	CHINA (PR)	
	GANSU PEOPLES BS, Lanzhou	Irr • DS-1 • 15 kW
	RADIO BEIJING, Xi'an	(D) • EUROPE • 120 kW
	ITALY	
	RTV ITALIANA, Rome	E EUROPE & WEST USSR • 100 kW
		=
		E EUROPE & MIDEAST • 100 kW E ASIA • 100 kW
		N AFRICA & W AFRICA • 100 kW
		N AFRICA • 100 kW
		N AFRICA & MIDEAST • 100 kW
		EUROPE • 100 kW
		(J) • N AFRICA • 100 kW
		Su • EUROPE • 100 kW
	PHILIPPINES	
	†FEBC RADIO INTL, Bocaue	SE ASIA • 50 kW
	†RADIO VERITAS ASIA, Palauig	E ASIA • 250 kW
	TURKEY	
	†VOICE OF TURKEY, Ankara	E ASIA • 500 kW
	USSR	
	†LITHUANIAN RADIO, Kaunas	DS-1 • 50/100 kW • ALT. FREQ. TO 6100 kHz
		DS-1 • 50/100 kW
	RADIO MOSCOW, Kiev	(J) • EUROPE • 100 kW
	†RADIO VILNIUS, Kaunas	EUROPE • 50/100 kW • ALT. FREQ. TO 6100 kHz
9715	**FRANCE**	
	R FRANCE INTL, Issoudun-Allouis	S AMERICA • 500 kW
	R FRANCE INTL, Via French Guiana	S AMERICA • 500 kW
	GERMANY	
(con'd)	†DEUTSCHE WELLE, Jülich	(D) • E EUROPE • 100 kW

0 1 2 3 4 5 6 7 8 9 10 11 12 13 14 15 16 17 18 19 20 21 22 23 24

SUMMER ONLY (J)   WINTER ONLY (D)   JAMMING / OR ∧   EARLIEST HEARD ◁   LATEST HEARD ▷   NEW OR CHANGED FOR 1992 †

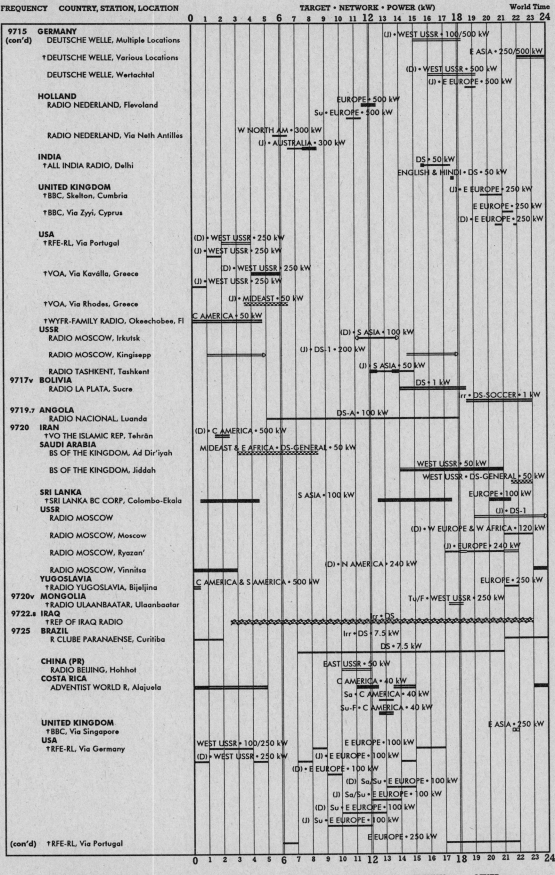

FREQUENCY   COUNTRY, STATION, LOCATION   TARGET • NETWORK • POWER (kW)   World Time

9715 **GERMANY**
(con'd)   DEUTSCHE WELLE, Multiple Locations   (J) • WEST USSR • 100/500 kW
    †DEUTSCHE WELLE, Various Locations   E ASIA • 250/500 kW
    DEUTSCHE WELLE, Wertachtal   (D) • WEST USSR • 500 kW
      (J) • E EUROPE • 500 kW

    HOLLAND
    RADIO NEDERLAND, Flevoland   EUROPE • 500 kW
      Su • EUROPE • 500 kW
    RADIO NEDERLAND, Via Neth Antilles   W NORTH AM • 300 kW
      (J) • AUSTRALIA • 300 kW

    INDIA
    †ALL INDIA RADIO, Delhi   DS • 50 kW
      ENGLISH & HINDI • DS • 50 kW

    UNITED KINGDOM
    †BBC, Skelton, Cumbria   (J) • E EUROPE • 250 kW
    †BBC, Via Zyyi, Cyprus   E EUROPE • 250 kW
      (D) • E EUROPE • 250 kW

    USA
    †RFE-RL, Via Portugal   (D) • WEST USSR • 250 kW
      (J) • WEST USSR • 250 kW
    †VOA, Via Kaválla, Greece   (D) • WEST USSR • 250 kW
      (J) • WEST USSR • 250 kW
    †VOA, Via Rhodes, Greece   (J) • MIDEAST • 50 kW
    †WYFR-FAMILY RADIO, Okeechobee, Fl   C AMERICA • 50 kW
    USSR
    RADIO MOSCOW, Irkutsk   (D) • S ASIA • 100 kW
    RADIO MOSCOW, Kingisepp   (J) • DS-1 • 200 kW
    RADIO TASHKENT, Tashkent   (J) • S ASIA • 50 kW

9717v **BOLIVIA**
    RADIO LA PLATA, Sucre   DS • 1 kW
      Irr • DS-SOCCER • 1 kW

9719.7 **ANGOLA**
    RADIO NACIONAL, Luanda   DS-A • 100 kW
9720 **IRAN**
    †VO THE ISLAMIC REP, Tehrān   (D) • C AMERICA • 500 kW
    SAUDI ARABIA
    BS OF THE KINGDOM, Ad Dir'iyah   MIDEAST & E AFRICA • DS-GENERAL • 50 kW
    BS OF THE KINGDOM, Jiddah   WEST USSR • 50 kW
      WEST USSR • DS-GENERAL • 50 kW

    SRI LANKA
    †SRI LANKA BC CORP, Colombo-Ekala   S ASIA • 100 kW   EUROPE • 100 kW
    USSR
    RADIO MOSCOW   (J) • DS-1
    RADIO MOSCOW, Moscow   (D) • W EUROPE & W AFRICA • 120 kW
    RADIO MOSCOW, Ryazan'   (J) • EUROPE • 240 kW
    RADIO MOSCOW, Vinnitsa   (D) • N AMERICA • 240 kW
    YUGOSLAVIA
    †RADIO YUGOSLAVIA, Bijeljina   C AMERICA & S AMERICA • 500 kW   EUROPE • 250 kW
9720v **MONGOLIA**
    †RADIO ULAANBAATAR, Ulaanbaatar   Tu/F • WEST USSR • 250 kW
9722.8 **IRAQ**
    †REP OF IRAQ RADIO   Irr • DS
9725 **BRAZIL**
    R CLUBE PARANAENSE, Curitiba   Irr • DS • 7.5 kW
      DS • 7.5 kW

    CHINA (PR)
    RADIO BEIJING, Hohhot   EAST USSR • 50 kW
    COSTA RICA
    ADVENTIST WORLD R, Alajuela   C AMERICA • 40 kW
      Sa • C AMERICA • 40 kW
      Su-F • C AMERICA • 40 kW

    UNITED KINGDOM
    †BBC, Via Singapore   E ASIA • 250 kW
    USA
    †RFE-RL, Via Germany   WEST USSR • 100/250 kW   E EUROPE • 100 kW
      (D) • WEST USSR • 250 kW   (J) • E EUROPE • 100 kW
      (D) • E EUROPE • 100 kW
      (D) Sa/Su • E EUROPE • 100 kW
      (J) Sa/Su • E EUROPE • 100 kW
      (D) Su • E EUROPE • 100 kW
      (J) Su • E EUROPE • 100 kW

(con'd)   †RFE-RL, Via Portugal   E EUROPE • 250 kW

ENGLISH ▬   ARABIC ▨   CHINESE ▭▭▭   FRENCH ▬   GERMAN ▬   RUSSIAN ▬   SPANISH ▬   OTHER ▬

FREQUENCY	COUNTRY, STATION, LOCATION	TARGET • NETWORK • POWER (kW)	World Time

0 1 2 3 4 5 6 7 8 9 10 11 12 13 14 15 16 17 18 19 20 21 22 23 24

Freq	Station	Details
9725 (con'd)	**USA** †RFE-RL, Via Portugal	(D) • E EUROPE • 250 kW
		(J) • E EUROPE • 250 kW
		(D) M-Sa • E EUROPE • 250 kW
		(J) M-Sa • E EUROPE • 250 kW
9730	**FINLAND** †RADIO FINLAND, Pori	(D) • MIDEAST • 500 kW
	GERMANY †DEUTSCHE WELLE, Nauen	E NORTH AM & C AMERICA • 500 kW
	MYANMAR (BURMA) VOICE OF MYANMAR, Yangon	Sa/Su • DS • 50 kW
		DS-ENGLISH,BURMESE • 50 kW
	SAUDI ARABIA BS OF THE KINGDOM, Riyadh	EAST USSR • 350 kW
	USSR RADIO MOSCOW	(J) • EUROPE
	RADIO MOSCOW, Dushanbé	(D) N AFRICA & MIDEAST • 500 kW
	RADIO MOSCOW, Irkutsk	(D) • SE ASIA • 500 kW
	TASS NEWS AGENCY, Ul'yanovsk	M-F • DS • 100 kW
9731v	**VIETNAM** †VOICE OF VIETNAM, Hanoi	SE ASIA • 15 kW
9735	**CYPRUS** †CYPRUS BC CORP, Zyyi	(J) F-Su • EUROPE • 250 kW
	GERMANY †DEUTSCHE WELLE, Jülich	(J) • WEST USSR • 100 kW
		(J) • MIDEAST • 100 kW
	DEUTSCHE WELLE, Multiple Locations	N AMERICA & C AMERICA • 250/500 kW
	DEUTSCHE WELLE, Via Kigali, Rwanda	C AFRICA & E AFRICA • 250 kW
		AFRICA • 250 kW
	DEUTSCHE WELLE, Wertachtal	AUSTRALIA & C AMERICA • 500 kW
	OMAN RADIO OMAN, Sīb	(D) • MIDEAST & N AFRICA • DS • 100 kW MIDEAST & N AFRICA • DS • 100 kW
		(J) • MIDEAST & N AFRICA • DS • 100 kW
	RADIO OMAN, Thamarīt	(D) • MIDEAST & N AFRICA • DS • 100 kW
	PARAGUAY RADIO NACIONAL, Asunción	S AMERICA, C AMERICA & E NORTH AM • DS-SPANISH,GUARANI • 40/100 kW
	UNITED KINGDOM †BBC, Via Zyyi, Cyprus	(D) • E EUROPE • 250 kW
	USA †VOA, Via Woofferton, UK	(D) • E EUROPE & MIDEAST • 250 kW
	USSR †KYRGYS RADIO, Tula	Sa • DS-1 • 20 kW
		RUSSIAN, ETC • DS-1 • 20 kW
		Su-F • RUSSIAN, ETC • DS-1 • 20 kW
	RADIO MOSCOW, Armavir	(J) • W AFRICA & ATLANTIC • 100 kW
		(J) • EUROPE • 100 kW
	RADIO MOSCOW, Irkutsk	(J) • E ASIA & SE ASIA • 500 kW
	RADIO MOSCOW, Novosibirsk	(J) • E ASIA • 200 kW
9740	**CANADA** R CANADA INTL, Via United Kingdom	(D) M-F • AFRICA • 300 kW
	EGYPT RADIO CAIRO, Kafr Silim-Abis	C AMERICA • 250 kW
	PORTUGAL †R PORTUGAL INTL, Lisbon	EUROPE • 100 kW
		Sa/Su • EUROPE • 100 kW
	UNITED KINGDOM †BBC, Via Singapore	S ASIA & SE ASIA • 125/250 kW S ASIA • 100/250 kW
		ASIA & AUSTRALIA • 100/125/250 kW
		S ASIA & SE ASIA • 100/250 kW
	†BBC, Via Zyyi, Cyprus	(D) Su • E EUROPE & MIDEAST • 250 kW MIDEAST • 100 kW
		(J) Su • E EUROPE & MIDEAST • 250 kW
	USA VOA, Via Kaválla, Greece	(D) • MIDEAST & S ASIA • 250 kW
		(J) • MIDEAST • 250 kW
		(J) • N AFRICA & E AFRICA • 250 kW
	†VOA, Via Portugal	(J) • WEST USSR • 250 kW
	VOA, Via Rhodes, Greece	(D) • MIDEAST • 50 kW
	USSR RADIO MOSCOW, Moscow	(J) • DS-1 • 240 kW
		(J) • EUROPE • 240 kW
	†RADIO TASHKENT, Tashkent	(J) • MIDEAST & S ASIA • 100 kW
9743	**INDONESIA** †RRI, Sorong, Irian Jaya	DS

0 1 2 3 4 5 6 7 8 9 10 11 12 13 14 15 16 17 18 19 20 21 22 23 24

SUMMER ONLY (J)   WINTER ONLY (D)   JAMMING / OR ∧   EARLIEST HEARD ◁   LATEST HEARD ▷   NEW OR CHANGED FOR 1992 †

FREQUENCY   COUNTRY, STATION, LOCATION   TARGET • NETWORK • POWER (kW)   World Time

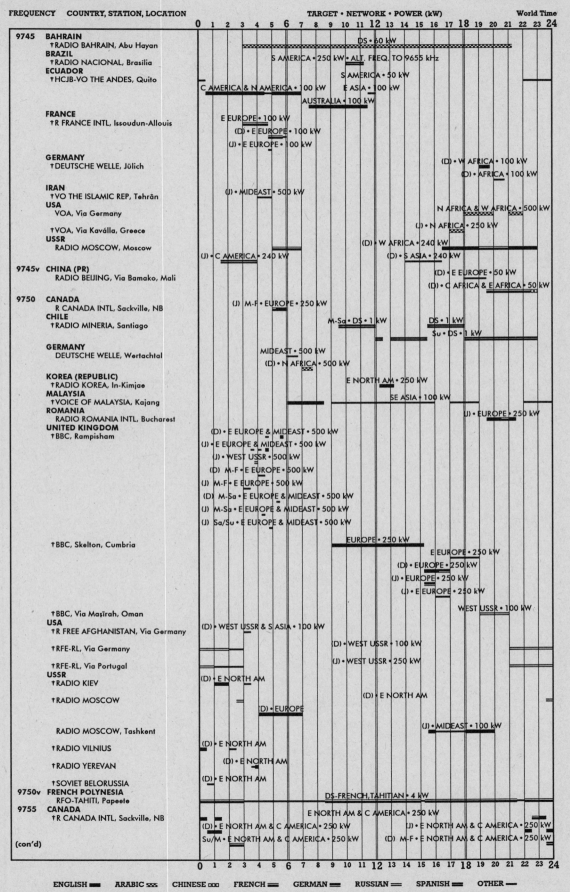

FREQUENCY	COUNTRY, STATION, LOCATION	TARGET • NETWORK • POWER (kW)
9745	**BAHRAIN** †RADIO BAHRAIN, Abu Hayan	DS • 60 kW
	BRAZIL †RADIO NACIONAL, Brasília	S AMERICA • 250 kW • ALT. FREQ. TO 9655 kHz
	ECUADOR †HCJB–VO THE ANDES, Quito	S AMERICA • 50 kW / C AMERICA & N AMERICA • 100 kW / E ASIA • 100 kW / AUSTRALIA • 100 kW
	FRANCE †R FRANCE INTL, Issoudun-Allouis	E EUROPE • 100 kW / (D) • E EUROPE • 100 kW / (J) • E EUROPE • 100 kW
	GERMANY †DEUTSCHE WELLE, Jülich	(D) • W AFRICA • 100 kW / (D) • AFRICA • 100 kW
	IRAN †VO THE ISLAMIC REP, Tehrān	(J) • MIDEAST • 500 kW
	USA VOA, Via Germany	N AFRICA & W AFRICA • 500 kW
	†VOA, Via Kaválla, Greece	(J) • N AFRICA • 250 kW
	USSR RADIO MOSCOW, Moscow	(D) • W AFRICA • 240 kW / (J) • C AMERICA • 240 kW / (D) • S ASIA • 240 kW
9745v	**CHINA (PR)** RADIO BEIJING, Via Bamako, Mali	(D) • E EUROPE • 50 kW / (D) • C AFRICA & E AFRICA • 50 kW
9750	**CANADA** R CANADA INTL, Sackville, NB	(J) • M-F • EUROPE • 250 kW
	CHILE †RADIO MINERIA, Santiago	M-Sa • DS • 1 kW / DS • 1 kW / Su • DS • 1 kW
	GERMANY DEUTSCHE WELLE, Wertachtal	MIDEAST • 500 kW / (D) • N AFRICA • 500 kW
	KOREA (REPUBLIC) †RADIO KOREA, In-Kimjae	E NORTH AM • 250 kW
	MALAYSIA †VOICE OF MALAYSIA, Kajang	SE ASIA • 100 kW
	ROMANIA RADIO ROMANIA INTL, Bucharest	(J) • EUROPE • 250 kW
	UNITED KINGDOM †BBC, Rampisham	(D) • E EUROPE & MIDEAST • 500 kW / (J) • E EUROPE & MIDEAST • 500 kW / (J) • WEST USSR • 500 kW / (D) M-F • E EUROPE • 500 kW / (J) M-F • E EUROPE • 500 kW / (D) M-Sa • E EUROPE & MIDEAST • 500 kW / (J) M-Sa • E EUROPE & MIDEAST • 500 kW / (J) Sa/Su • E EUROPE & MIDEAST • 500 kW
	†BBC, Skelton, Cumbria	EUROPE • 250 kW / E EUROPE • 250 kW / (D) • EUROPE • 250 kW / (J) • EUROPE • 250 kW / (J) • E EUROPE • 250 kW
	†BBC, Via Maşīrah, Oman	WEST USSR • 100 kW
	USA †R FREE AFGHANISTAN, Via Germany	(D) • WEST USSR & S ASIA • 100 kW
	†RFE-RL, Via Germany	(D) • WEST USSR • 100 kW
	†RFE-RL, Via Portugal	(J) • WEST USSR • 250 kW
	USSR †RADIO KIEV	(D) • E NORTH AM
	†RADIO MOSCOW	(D) • E NORTH AM / (D) • EUROPE
	RADIO MOSCOW, Tashkent	(J) • MIDEAST • 100 kW
	†RADIO VILNIUS	(D) • E NORTH AM
	†RADIO YEREVAN	(D) • E NORTH AM
	†SOVIET BELORUSSIA	(D) • E NORTH AM
9750v	**FRENCH POLYNESIA** RFO-TAHITI, Papeete	DS-FRENCH,TAHITIAN • 4 kW
9755	**CANADA** †R CANADA INTL, Sackville, NB	E NORTH AM & C AMERICA • 250 kW / (D) • E NORTH AM & C AMERICA • 250 kW / (J) • E NORTH AM & C AMERICA • 250 kW / Su/M • E NORTH AM & C AMERICA • 250 kW / (D) M-F • E NORTH AM & C AMERICA • 250 kW

(con'd)

ENGLISH ▬ ARABIC ▨ CHINESE ▫▫▫ FRENCH ▭▭ GERMAN ▬▬ RUSSIAN ▭▭ SPANISH ▭ OTHER ▬

FREQUENCY   COUNTRY, STATION, LOCATION   TARGET • NETWORK • POWER (kW)   World Time

0 1 2 3 4 5 6 7 8 9 10 11 12 13 14 15 16 17 18 19 20 21 22 23 24

9755   **CANADA**
(con'd)   ↑R CANADA INTL, Sackville, NB
- (D) Su/M • E NORTH AM & C AMERICA • 250 kW
- (J) Su/M • E NORTH AM & C AMERICA • 250 kW
- Tu-Sa • E NORTH AM & C AMERICA • 250 kW
- (D) Tu-Sa • E NORTH AM & C AMERICA • 250 kW
- (J) Tu-Sa • E NORTH AM & C AMERICA • 250 kW
- (J) Tu/Sa • E NORTH AM & C AMERICA • 250 kW

CHINA (PR)
   ↑CENTRAL PEOPLES BS, Baoji — DS-2 • 50 kW
EGYPT
   RADIO CAIRO, Cairo-Mokattam — N AFRICA & MIDEAST • DS-KORAN • 100 kW
   F • N AFRICA & MIDEAST • DS-KORAN • 100 kW

GERMANY
   ↑DEUTSCHE WELLE, Königswusterhausen — (D) • AFRICA • 100 kW
MONACO
   ↑R MONTE CARLO, Via Sackville, Canada
- (D) • N AMERICA • 250 kW
- (J) • N AMERICA • 250 kW

USA
   VOA, Via Philippines — E ASIA • 250 kW
VATICAN STATE
   ↑VATICAN RADIO, Sta Maria di Galeria — WEST USSR • 250 kW
   Su • WEST USSR • 250 kW

9760   **ALBANIA**
   ↑RADIO TIRANA, Lushnjë — E NORTH AM & C AMERICA • 100 kW
   (D) • E NORTH AM & C AMERICA • 100 kW

CANADA
   R CANADA INTL, Sackville, NB — (D) M-F • EUROPE • 250 kW   (D) • EUROPE • 250 kW
JAPAN
   RADIO TAMPA, Tokyo-Nagara — DS-2 • 50 kW
UNITED KINGDOM
   ↑BBC, Rampisham
- (J) M-F • E EUROPE • 500 kW
- (J) M-Sa • E EUROPE • 500 kW

   ↑BBC, Skelton, Cumbria — (D) • EUROPE • 250 kW

   ↑BBC, Various Locations — EUROPE • 250/300 kW
USA
   VOA, Via Kaválla, Greece — (D) • N AFRICA • 250 kW

   VOA, Via Philippines — ASIA • 250 kW

   ↑VOA, Via Tangier, Morocco — (D) • WEST USSR • 100 kW

   ↑VOA, Via Woofferton, UK
- (J) • WEST USSR • 300 kW   EUROPE • 250 kW
- (D) • EUROPE • 250 kW

USSR
   RADIO MOSCOW, Ivano-Frankovsk — ATLANTIC • 100 kW
   (D) • W EUROPE & W AFRICA • 100 kW

   ↑RADIO MOSCOW, Kenga — (J) • DS-1 • 100 kW
9765   **CHINA (PR)**
   RADIO BEIJING, Beijing — (J) • WEST USSR & E EUROPE • 500 kW
CHINA (TAIWAN)
   ↑VO FREE CHINA, T'ai-pei — AUSTRALIA • 50/100 kW
ECUADOR
   ↑HCJB-VO THE ANDES, Quito — S AMERICA • 100 kW
GERMANY
   ↑DEUTSCHE WELLE, Multiple Locations — AFRICA • 100/500 kW

   DEUTSCHE WELLE, Wertachtal — SE ASIA & AUSTRALIA • 500 kW
MALTA
   VO MEDITERRANEAN, Cyclops — EUROPE, N AFRICA & MIDEAST • 250 kW
SWEDEN
   ↑RADIO SWEDEN, Hörby — S ASIA • 350 kW   (D) • USSR & E ASIA • 350 kW • ALT. FREQ. TO 11715 kHz
   (D) • USSR & SE ASIA • 350 kW

9770   **AUSTRALIA**
   ↑RADIO AUSTRALIA, Shepparton — SE ASIA • 250 kW
   SE ASIA • 100 kW

CYPRUS
   ↑CYPRUS BC CORP, Zyyi — (D) F-Su • EUROPE • 250 kW
EGYPT
   RADIO CAIRO, Kafr Silîm-Abis — N AFRICA & MIDEAST • DS-VO THE ARABS • 250 kW
GERMANY
   DEUTSCHE WELLE, Jülich
- (D) • E EUROPE • 100 kW
- (J) • E EUROPE • 100 kW

   ↑DEUTSCHE WELLE, Königswusterhausen — (D) • S AMERICA • 100 kW

   DEUTSCHE WELLE, Wertachtal
- (D) • E EUROPE • 500 kW
- (J) • E EUROPE • 500 kW

HOLLAND
   ↑RADIO NEDERLAND, Via Neth Antilles — (J) M-Sa • AUSTRALIA • 300 kW
SEYCHELLES
   ↑FAR EAST BC ASS'N, North Pt, Mahé Is — S ASIA • 100 kW   E AFRICA • 100 kW
   Su-W • S ASIA • 100 kW
   Th-Su • S ASIA • 100 kW

(con'd)

0 1 2 3 4 5 6 7 8 9 10 11 12 13 14 15 16 17 18 19 20 21 22 23 24

FREQUENCY   COUNTRY, STATION, LOCATION
TARGET • NETWORK • POWER (kW)
World Time

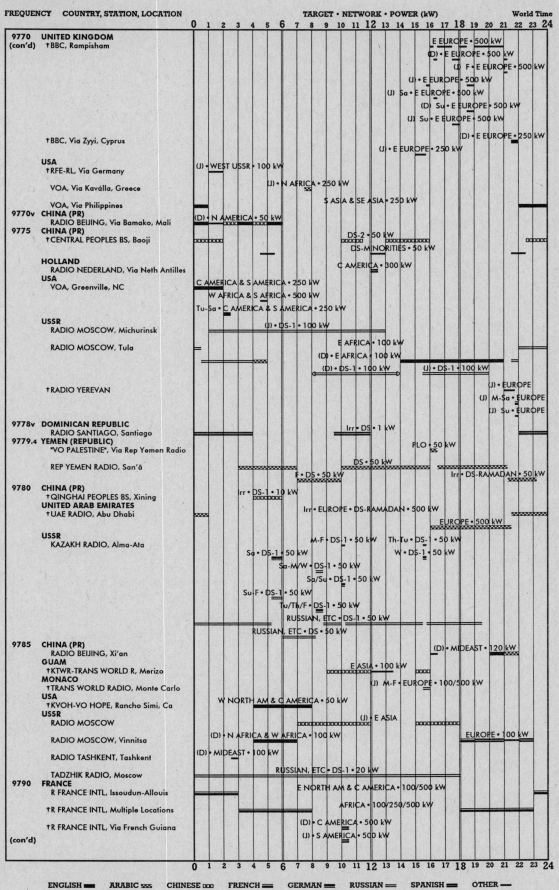

9770 UNITED KINGDOM
(con'd) †BBC, Rampisham
- E EUROPE • 500 kW
- (D) • E EUROPE • 500 kW
- (J) F • E EUROPE • 500 kW
- (J) • E EUROPE • 500 kW
- (J) Sa • E EUROPE • 500 kW
- (D) Su • E EUROPE • 500 kW
- (J) Su • E EUROPE • 500 kW
- (D) • E EUROPE • 250 kW

†BBC, Via Zyyi, Cyprus
- (J) • E EUROPE • 250 kW

USA
†RFE-RL, Via Germany — (J) • WEST USSR • 100 kW
VOA, Via Kaválla, Greece — (J) • N AFRICA • 250 kW
VOA, Via Philippines — S ASIA & SE ASIA • 250 kW

9770v CHINA (PR)
RADIO BEIJING, Via Bamako, Mali — (D) • N AMERICA • 50 kW

9775 CHINA (PR)
†CENTRAL PEOPLES BS, Baoji
- DS-2 • 50 kW
- DS-MINORITIES • 50 kW

HOLLAND
RADIO NEDERLAND, Via Neth Antilles — C AMERICA • 300 kW
USA
VOA, Greenville, NC
- C AMERICA & S AMERICA • 250 kW
- W AFRICA & S AFRICA • 500 kW
- Tu-Sa • C AMERICA & S AMERICA • 250 kW

USSR
RADIO MOSCOW, Michurinsk — (J) • DS-1 • 100 kW
RADIO MOSCOW, Tula
- E AFRICA • 100 kW
- (D) • E AFRICA • 100 kW
- (D) • DS-1 • 100 kW
- (J) • DS-1 • 100 kW

†RADIO YEREVAN
- (J) • EUROPE
- (J) M-Sa • EUROPE
- (J) Su • EUROPE

9778v DOMINICAN REPUBLIC
RADIO SANTIAGO, Santiago — Irr • DS • 1 kW
9779.4 YEMEN (REPUBLIC)
"VO PALESTINE", Via Rep Yemen Radio — FLO • 50 kW
REP YEMEN RADIO, San'ā
- DS • 50 kW
- F • DS • 50 kW
- Irr • DS-RAMADAN • 50 kW

9780 CHINA (PR)
†QINGHAI PEOPLES BS, Xining — Irr • DS-1 • 10 kW
UNITED ARAB EMIRATES
†UAE RADIO, Abu Dhabi
- Irr • EUROPE • DS-RAMADAN • 500 kW
- EUROPE • 500 kW

USSR
KAZAKH RADIO, Alma-Ata
- M-F • DS-1 • 50 kW
- Th-Tu • DS-1 • 50 kW
- Sa • DS-1 • 50 kW
- W • DS-1 • 50 kW
- Sa-MW • DS-1 • 50 kW
- Sa/Su • DS-1 • 50 kW
- Su-F • DS-1 • 50 kW
- Tu/Th/F • DS-1 • 50 kW
- RUSSIAN, ETC • DS-1 • 50 kW
- RUSSIAN, ETC • DS • 50 kW

9785 CHINA (PR)
RADIO BEIJING, Xi'an — (D) • MIDEAST • 120 kW
GUAM
†KTWR-TRANS WORLD R, Merizo — E ASIA • 100 kW
MONACO
†TRANS WORLD RADIO, Monte Carlo — (J) M-F • EUROPE • 100/500 kW
USA
†KVOH-VO HOPE, Rancho Simi, Ca — W NORTH AM & C AMERICA • 50 kW
USSR
RADIO MOSCOW — (J) E ASIA
RADIO MOSCOW, Vinnitsa
- (D) • N AFRICA & W AFRICA • 100 kW
- EUROPE • 100 kW
RADIO TASHKENT, Tashkent — (D) • MIDEAST • 100 kW
TADZHIK RADIO, Moscow — RUSSIAN, ETC • DS-1 • 20 kW

9790 FRANCE
R FRANCE INTL, Issoudun-Allouis — E NORTH AM & C AMERICA • 100/500 kW
†R FRANCE INTL, Multiple Locations — AFRICA • 100/250/500 kW
†R FRANCE INTL, Via French Guiana
- (D) • C AMERICA • 500 kW
- (J) • S AMERICA • 500 kW

(con'd)

ENGLISH ▬   ARABIC ⠶⠶⠶   CHINESE ▭▭▭   FRENCH ▰▰▰   GERMAN ▬   RUSSIAN ═══   SPANISH ▬   OTHER ▬

FREQUENCY	COUNTRY, STATION, LOCATION	TARGET • NETWORK • POWER (kW) World Time

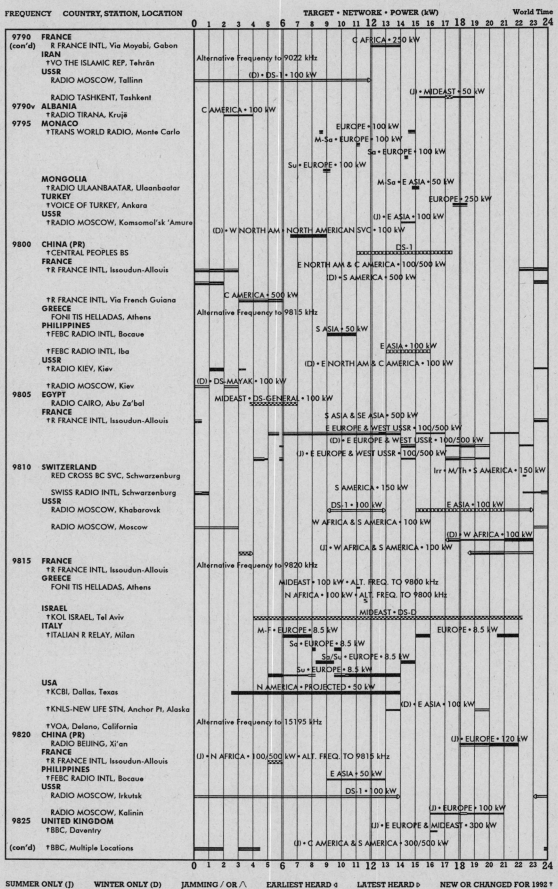

9790
(con'd)   **FRANCE**
    R FRANCE INTL, Via Moyabi, Gabon   C AFRICA • 250 kW
   IRAN
    †VO THE ISLAMIC REP, Tehrān   Alternative Frequency to 9022 kHz
   USSR
    RADIO MOSCOW, Tallinn   (D) • DS-1 • 100 kW
    RADIO TASHKENT, Tashkent   (J) • MIDEAST • 50 kW

9790v **ALBANIA**
    †RADIO TIRANA, Krujë   C AMERICA • 100 kW

9795 **MONACO**
    †TRANS WORLD RADIO, Monte Carlo   EUROPE • 100 kW
    M-Sa • EUROPE • 100 kW
    Sa • EUROPE • 100 kW
    Su • EUROPE • 100 kW

   MONGOLIA
    †RADIO ULAANBAATAR, Ulaanbaatar   M-Sa • E ASIA • 50 kW
   TURKEY
    †VOICE OF TURKEY, Ankara   EUROPE • 250 kW
   USSR
    †RADIO MOSCOW, Komsomol'sk 'Amure   (J) • E ASIA • 100 kW
    (D) • W NORTH AM • NORTH AMERICAN SVC • 100 kW

9800 **CHINA (PR)**
    †CENTRAL PEOPLES BS   DS-1
   FRANCE
    †R FRANCE INTL, Issoudun-Allouis   E NORTH AM & C AMERICA • 100/500 kW
    (D) • S AMERICA • 500 kW
    †R FRANCE INTL, Via French Guiana   C AMERICA • 500 kW
   GREECE
    FONI TIS HELLADAS, Athens   Alternative Frequency to 9815 kHz
   PHILIPPINES
    †FEBC RADIO INTL, Bocaue   S ASIA • 50 kW
    †FEBC RADIO INTL, Iba   E ASIA • 100 kW
   USSR
    †RADIO KIEV, Kiev   (D) • E NORTH AM & C AMERICA • 100 kW
    †RADIO MOSCOW, Kiev   (D) • DS-MAYAK • 100 kW

9805 **EGYPT**
    RADIO CAIRO, Abu Za'bal   MIDEAST • DS-GENERAL • 100 kW
   FRANCE
    †R FRANCE INTL, Issoudun-Allouis   S ASIA & SE ASIA • 500 kW
    E EUROPE & WEST USSR • 100/500 kW
    (D) • E EUROPE & WEST USSR • 100/500 kW
    (J) • E EUROPE & WEST USSR • 100/500 kW

9810 **SWITZERLAND**
    RED CROSS BC SVC, Schwarzenburg   Irr • M/Th • S AMERICA • 150 kW
    SWISS RADIO INTL, Schwarzenburg   S AMERICA • 150 kW
   USSR
    RADIO MOSCOW, Khabarovsk   DS-1 • 100 kW   E ASIA • 100 kW
    RADIO MOSCOW, Moscow   W AFRICA & S AMERICA • 100 kW
    (D) • W AFRICA • 100 kW
    (J) • W AFRICA & S AMERICA • 100 kW

9815 **FRANCE**
    †R FRANCE INTL, Issoudun-Allouis   Alternative Frequency to 9820 kHz
   GREECE
    FONI TIS HELLADAS, Athens   MIDEAST • 100 kW • ALT. FREQ. TO 9800 kHz
    N AFRICA • 100 kW • ALT. FREQ. TO 9800 kHz
   ISRAEL
    †KOL ISRAEL, Tel Aviv   MIDEAST • DS-D
   ITALY
    †ITALIAN R RELAY, Milan   M-F • EUROPE • 8.5 kW   EUROPE • 8.5 kW
    Sa • EUROPE • 8.5 kW
    Sa/Su • EUROPE • 8.5 kW
    Su • EUROPE • 8.5 kW
   USA
    †KCBI, Dallas, Texas   N AMERICA • PROJECTED • 50 kW
    †KNLS-NEW LIFE STN, Anchor Pt, Alaska   (D) • E ASIA • 100 kW
    †VOA, Delano, California   Alternative Frequency to 15195 kHz

9820 **CHINA (PR)**
    RADIO BEIJING, Xi'an   (J) • EUROPE • 120 kW
   FRANCE
    †R FRANCE INTL, Issoudun-Allouis   (J) • N AFRICA • 100/500 kW • ALT. FREQ. TO 9815 kHz
   PHILIPPINES
    †FEBC RADIO INTL, Bocaue   E ASIA • 50 kW
   USSR
    RADIO MOSCOW, Irkutsk   DS-1 • 100 kW
    RADIO MOSCOW, Kalinin   (J) • EUROPE • 100 kW

9825 **UNITED KINGDOM**
    †BBC, Daventry   (J) • E EUROPE & MIDEAST • 300 kW
(con'd)   †BBC, Multiple Locations   (J) • C AMERICA & S AMERICA • 300/500 kW

FREQUENCY   COUNTRY, STATION, LOCATION   TARGET • NETWORK • POWER (kW)   World Time

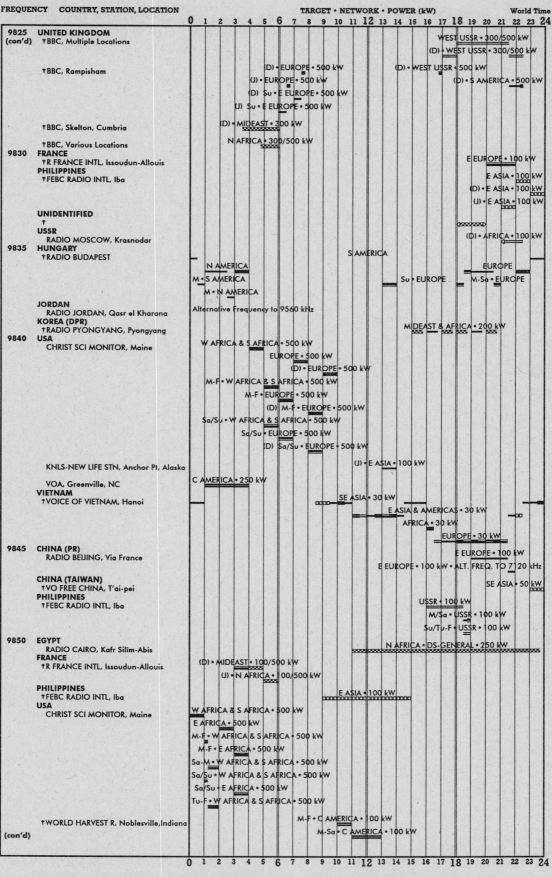

9825	**UNITED KINGDOM**
(con'd)	†BBC, Multiple Locations
	†BBC, Rampisham
	†BBC, Skelton, Cumbria
	†BBC, Various Locations
9830	**FRANCE**
	†R FRANCE INTL, Issoudun-Allouis
	PHILIPPINES
	†FEBC RADIO INTL, Iba
	UNIDENTIFIED
	†
	USSR
	RADIO MOSCOW, Krasnodar
9835	**HUNGARY**
	†RADIO BUDAPEST
	JORDAN
	RADIO JORDAN, Qasr el Kharana
	KOREA (DPR)
	†RADIO PYONGYANG, Pyongyang
9840	**USA**
	CHRIST SCI MONITOR, Maine
	KNLS-NEW LIFE STN, Anchor Pt, Alaska
	VOA, Greenville, NC
	VIETNAM
	†VOICE OF VIETNAM, Hanoi
9845	**CHINA (PR)**
	RADIO BEIJING, Via France
	CHINA (TAIWAN)
	†VO FREE CHINA, T'ai-pei
	PHILIPPINES
	†FEBC RADIO INTL, Iba
9850	**EGYPT**
	RADIO CAIRO, Kafr Silim-Abis
	FRANCE
	†R FRANCE INTL, Issoudun-Allouis
	PHILIPPINES
	†FEBC RADIO INTL, Iba
	USA
	CHRIST SCI MONITOR, Maine
	†WORLD HARVEST R, Noblesville, Indiana
(con'd)	

ENGLISH ▬   ARABIC ▨   CHINESE ▦   FRENCH ▬   GERMAN ▬   RUSSIAN ═   SPANISH ▬   OTHER ─

FREQUENCY   COUNTRY, STATION, LOCATION   TARGET • NETWORK • POWER (kW)   World Time
0 1 2 3 4 5 6 7 8 9 10 11 12 13 14 15 16 17 18 19 20 21 22 23 24

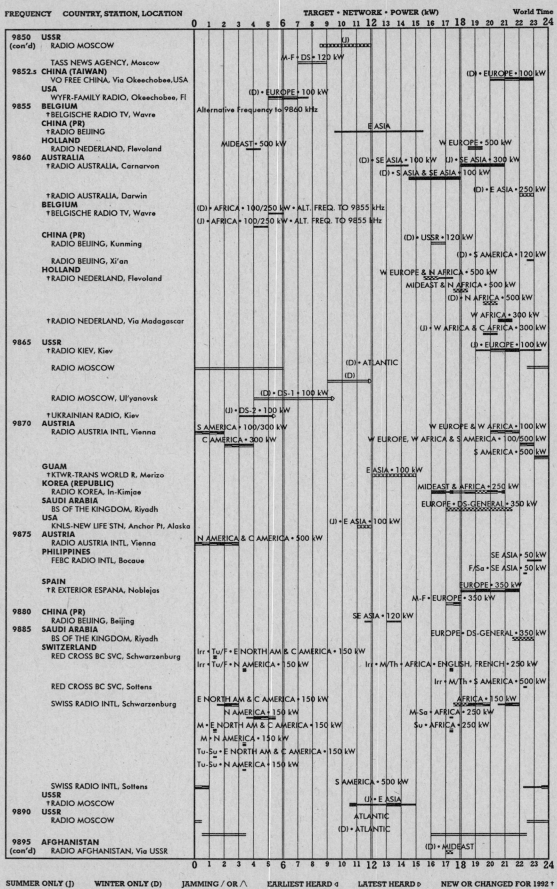

Frequency	Country, Station, Location	Target • Network • Power (kW)
9850 (con'd)	USSR — RADIO MOSCOW	(J) / M-F • DS • 120 kW
	TASS NEWS AGENCY, Moscow	
9852.5	CHINA (TAIWAN) — VO FREE CHINA, Via Okeechobee, USA	(D) • EUROPE • 100 kW
	USA — WYFR-FAMILY RADIO, Okeechobee, Fl	(D) • EUROPE • 100 kW
9855	BELGIUM — †BELGISCHE RADIO TV, Wavre	Alternative Frequency to 9860 kHz
	CHINA (PR) — †RADIO BEIJING	E ASIA
	HOLLAND — RADIO NEDERLAND, Flevoland	MIDEAST • 500 kW / W EUROPE • 500 kW
9860	AUSTRALIA — †RADIO AUSTRALIA, Carnarvon	(D) • SE ASIA • 100 kW (J) • SE ASIA • 300 kW / (D) • S ASIA & SE ASIA • 100 kW
	†RADIO AUSTRALIA, Darwin	(D) • E ASIA • 250 kW
	BELGIUM — †BELGISCHE RADIO TV, Wavre	(D) • AFRICA • 100/250 kW • ALT. FREQ. TO 9855 kHz / (J) • AFRICA • 100/250 kW • ALT. FREQ. TO 9855 kHz
	CHINA (PR) — RADIO BEIJING, Kunming	(D) • USSR • 120 kW
	RADIO BEIJING, Xi'an	(D) • S AMERICA • 120 kW
	HOLLAND — †RADIO NEDERLAND, Flevoland	W EUROPE & N AFRICA • 500 kW / MIDEAST & N AFRICA • 500 kW / (D) • N AFRICA • 500 kW
	†RADIO NEDERLAND, Via Madagascar	W AFRICA • 300 kW / (J) • W AFRICA & C AFRICA • 300 kW
9865	USSR — †RADIO KIEV, Kiev	(J) • EUROPE • 100 kW
	RADIO MOSCOW	(D) • ATLANTIC / (D)
	RADIO MOSCOW, Ul'yanovsk	(D) • DS-1 • 100 kW
	†UKRAINIAN RADIO, Kiev	(J) • DS-2 • 100 kW
9870	AUSTRIA — RADIO AUSTRIA INTL, Vienna	S AMERICA • 100/300 kW / W EUROPE & W AFRICA • 100 kW / C AMERICA • 300 kW / W EUROPE, W AFRICA & S AMERICA • 100/500 kW / S AMERICA • 500 kW
	GUAM — †KTWR-TRANS WORLD R, Merizo	E ASIA • 100 kW
	KOREA (REPUBLIC) — RADIO KOREA, In-Kimjae	MIDEAST & AFRICA • 250 kW
	SAUDI ARABIA — BS OF THE KINGDOM, Riyadh	EUROPE • DS-GENERAL • 350 kW
	USA — KNLS-NEW LIFE STN, Anchor Pt, Alaska	(J) • E ASIA • 100 kW
9875	AUSTRIA — RADIO AUSTRIA INTL, Vienna	N AMERICA & C AMERICA • 500 kW
	PHILIPPINES — FEBC RADIO INTL, Bocaue	SE ASIA • 50 kW / F/Sa • SE ASIA • 50 kW
	SPAIN — †R EXTERIOR ESPANA, Noblejas	EUROPE • 350 kW / M-F • EUROPE • 350 kW
9880	CHINA (PR) — RADIO BEIJING, Beijing	SE ASIA • 120 kW
9885	SAUDI ARABIA — BS OF THE KINGDOM, Riyadh	EUROPE • DS-GENERAL • 350 kW
	SWITZERLAND — RED CROSS BC SVC, Schwarzenburg	Irr • Tu/F • E NORTH AM & C AMERICA • 150 kW / Irr • Tu/F • N AMERICA • 150 kW / Irr • M/Th • AFRICA • ENGLISH, FRENCH • 250 kW
	RED CROSS BC SVC, Sottens	Irr • M/Th • S AMERICA • 500 kW
	SWISS RADIO INTL, Schwarzenburg	E NORTH AM & C AMERICA • 150 kW / AFRICA • 150 kW / N AMERICA • 150 kW / M-Sa • AFRICA • 250 kW / M • E NORTH AM & C AMERICA • 150 kW / Su • AFRICA • 250 kW / M • N AMERICA • 150 kW / Tu-Su • E NORTH AM & C AMERICA • 150 kW / Tu-Su • N AMERICA • 150 kW
	SWISS RADIO INTL, Sottens	S AMERICA • 500 kW
	USSR — †RADIO MOSCOW	(J) • E ASIA
9890	USSR — RADIO MOSCOW	ATLANTIC / (D) • ATLANTIC
9895 (con'd)	AFGHANISTAN — RADIO AFGHANISTAN, Via USSR	(D) • MIDEAST

0 1 2 3 4 5 6 7 8 9 10 11 12 13 14 15 16 17 18 19 20 21 22 23 24

SUMMER ONLY (J)   WINTER ONLY (D)   JAMMING / OR ∧   EARLIEST HEARD ◁   LATEST HEARD ▷   NEW OR CHANGED FOR 1992 †

FREQUENCY   COUNTRY, STATION, LOCATION   TARGET • NETWORK • POWER (kW)   World Time

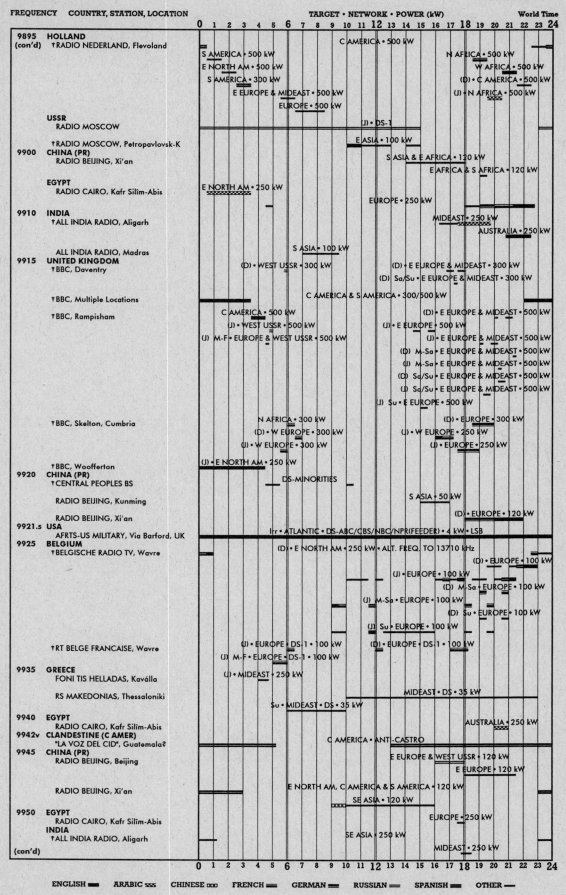

Freq	Country / Station / Location	Schedule
9895 (con'd)	HOLLAND †RADIO NEDERLAND, Flevoland	C AMERICA • 500 kW; S AMERICA • 500 kW; E NORTH AM • 500 kW; S AMERICA • 300 kW; E EUROPE & MIDEAST • 500 kW; EUROPE • 500 kW; N AFRICA • 500 kW; W AFRICA • 500 kW; (D) • C AMERICA • 500 kW; (J) • N AFRICA • 500 kW
	USSR RADIO MOSCOW	(J) • DS-1
	†RADIO MOSCOW, Petropavlovsk-K	E ASIA • 100 kW
9900	CHINA (PR) RADIO BEIJING, Xi'an	S ASIA & E AFRICA • 120 kW; E AFRICA & S AFRICA • 120 kW
	EGYPT RADIO CAIRO, Kafr Silîm-Abis	E NORTH AM • 250 kW; EUROPE • 250 kW
9910	INDIA †ALL INDIA RADIO, Aligarh	MIDEAST • 250 kW; AUSTRALIA • 250 kW
	ALL INDIA RADIO, Madras	S ASIA • 100 kW
9915	UNITED KINGDOM †BBC, Daventry	(D) • WEST USSR • 300 kW; (D) • E EUROPE & MIDEAST • 300 kW; (D) Sa/Su • E EUROPE & MIDEAST • 300 kW
	†BBC, Multiple Locations	C AMERICA & S AMERICA • 300/500 kW
	†BBC, Rampisham	C AMERICA • 500 kW; (J) • WEST USSR • 500 kW; (J) M-F • EUROPE & WEST USSR • 500 kW; (D) • E EUROPE & MIDEAST • 500 kW; (J) • E EUROPE • 500 kW; (D) M-Sa • E EUROPE & MIDEAST • 500 kW; (J) M-Sa • E EUROPE & MIDEAST • 500 kW; (D) Sa/Su • E EUROPE & MIDEAST • 500 kW; (J) Sa/Su • E EUROPE & MIDEAST • 500 kW; (J) Su • E EUROPE • 500 kW
	†BBC, Skelton, Cumbria	N AFRICA • 300 kW; (D) • W EUROPE • 300 kW; (J) • W EUROPE • 300 kW; (D) • EUROPE • 300 kW; (J) • W EUROPE • 250 kW; (J) • EUROPE • 250 kW
	†BBC, Woofferton	(J) • E NORTH AM • 250 kW
9920	CHINA (PR) †CENTRAL PEOPLES BS	DS-MINORITIES
	RADIO BEIJING, Kunming	S ASIA • 50 kW
	RADIO BEIJING, Xi'an	(D) • EUROPE • 120 kW
9921.5	USA AFRTS-US MILITARY, Via Barford, UK	Irr • ATLANTIC • DS-ABC/CBS/NBC/NPR(FEEDER) • 4 kW • LSB
9925	BELGIUM †BELGISCHE RADIO TV, Wavre	(D) • E NORTH AM • 250 kW • ALT. FREQ. TO 13710 kHz; (D) • EUROPE • 100 kW; (J) • EUROPE • 100 kW; (D) M-Sa • EUROPE • 100 kW; (J) M-Sa • EUROPE • 100 kW; (D) Su • EUROPE • 100 kW; (J) Su • EUROPE • 100 kW
	†RT BELGE FRANCAISE, Wavre	(J) • EUROPE • DS-1 • 100 kW; (D) • EUROPE • DS-1 • 100 kW; (J) M-F • EUROPE • DS-1 • 100 kW
9935	GREECE FONI TIS HELLADAS, Kaválla	(J) • MIDEAST • 250 kW
	RS MAKEDONIAS, Thessaloniki	MIDEAST • DS • 35 kW; Su • MIDEAST • DS • 35 kW
9940	EGYPT RADIO CAIRO, Kafr Silîm-Abis	AUSTRALIA • 250 kW
9942v	CLANDESTINE (C AMER) "LA VOZ DEL CID", Guatemala?	C AMERICA • ANTI-CASTRO
9945	CHINA (PR) RADIO BEIJING, Beijing	E EUROPE & WEST USSR • 120 kW; E EUROPE • 120 kW
	RADIO BEIJING, Xi'an	E NORTH AM, C AMERICA & S AMERICA • 120 kW; SE ASIA • 120 kW
9950	EGYPT RADIO CAIRO, Kafr Silîm-Abis	EUROPE • 250 kW
	INDIA †ALL INDIA RADIO, Aligarh	SE ASIA • 250 kW; MIDEAST • 250 kW
(con'd)		

ENGLISH ▬▬   ARABIC ﹏﹏   CHINESE ▢▢▢   FRENCH ▭▭   GERMAN ▬▬   RUSSIAN ══   SPANISH ▬▬   OTHER ──

FREQUENCY   COUNTRY, STATION, LOCATION   TARGET • NETWORK • POWER (kW)   World Time

FREQUENCY	COUNTRY, STATION, LOCATION	TARGET • NETWORK • POWER (kW)
9950 (con'd)	INDIA †ALL INDIA RADIO, Aligarh	N AFRICA • 250 kW
	†ALL INDIA RADIO, Delhi	DS • 50 kW EUROPE • 50/250 kW
		ENGLISH, ETC • DS • 50 kW
	SYRIA †SYRIAN BC SERVICE, Adhra	(D) • N AMERICA • 500 kW
9955	CHINA (TAIWAN) †VO FREE CHINA, T'ai-pei	MIDEAST & N AFRICA • 50/100 kW
	USA FAMILY RADIO, Via Taiwan	USSR • 250 kW E ASIA • 250 kW
9965	CHINA (PR) RADIO BEIJING, Beijing	EUROPE, MIDEAST & N AFRICA • 120 kW
		(D) • WEST USSR • 120 kW
	CLANDESTINE (C AMER) "RADIO CAIMAN", Guatemala City	C AMERICA • ANTI-CASTRO
9977	KOREA (DPR) RADIO PYONGYANG, Pyongyang	C AMERICA • 400 kW AFRICA • 200 kW
		SE ASIA • 200 kW
9985	CHINA (PR) RADIO BEIJING	E EUROPE
		(D) • E EUROPE & WEST USSR
	PIRATE (EUROPE) "QUALITY RADIO", Scandinavia	Irr • Su • W EUROPE • 0.4 kW
9995	CLANDESTINE (M EAST) †"VO IRAQ OPPOSIT'N, Saudi Arabia	MIDEAST • ANTI-SADDAM
10000	USA WWV, Ft Collins, Colorado	WEATHER/WORLD TIME • 10 kW
	WWVH, Kekaha, Hawaii	WEATHER/WORLD TIME • 10 kW
10009v	VIETNAM VOICE OF VIETNAM, Hanoi	E ASIA • 30 kW SE ASIA • 30 kW
10059v	VIETNAM VOICE OF VIETNAM, Hanoi	DS • 30 kW
10200v	CLANDESTINE (ASIA) "R LAO LIBERATION", Northern Laos	SE ASIA • ANTI-LAO GOVT • 0.1 kW
10235	USA VOA, Greenville, NC	N AFRICA • (FEEDER) • 40 kW • USB (D) • N AFRICA • (FEEDER) • 40 kW • USB
10260	CHINA (PR) †CENTRAL PEOPLES BS, Beijing	DS-MINORITIES • 15 kW DS-2 • 15 kW
10275	USSR RADIO MOSCOW, Sverdlovsk	(J) • DS-1 (FEEDER) • 20 kW • LSB
10330	INDIA †ALL INDIA RADIO, Delhi	DS • 50 kW ENGLISH, ETC • DS • 50 kW
10380	USA †VOA, Greenville, NC	EUROPE & MIDEAST • (FEEDER) • 40 kW • LSB
10420	USA RFE-RL, Via Holzkirchen, GFR	Irr • W EUROPE • (FEEDER) • 10 kW • ISL Irr • W EUROPE • (FEEDER) • 10 kW • ISU
10690	USSR †RADIO MOSCOW	DS-2 (FEEDER) • USB
10855	USSR †RADIO MOSCOW, Sverdlovsk	(J) • DS-MAYAK (FEEDER) • 15 kW • ISU (J) • DS-1 (FEEDER) • 15 kW • ISL
10860	USA †RFE-RL, Via Germany	Irr • (J) • W EUROPE • (FEEDER) • 10 kW • LSB
11000	CHINA (PR) †CENTRAL PEOPLES BS	CHINESE, ETC • TAIWAN-2 Th-Tu • CHINESE, ETC • TAIWAN-2
11020	USSR RADIO MOSCOW	(D) • (FEEDER) • USB
11040	CHINA (PR) †CENTRAL PEOPLES BS	DS-2 Th/Sa-Tu • DS-2
11090	USA †VOA, Delano, California	SE ASIA • (FEEDER) • 50 kW • ISU SE ASIA • (FEEDER) • 50 kW • ISL (D) • SE ASIA • (FEEDER) • 50 kW • ISL (D) • SE ASIA • (FEEDER) • 50 kW • ISU
11100	CHINA (PR) †CENTRAL PEOPLES BS, Beijing	CHINESE, ETC • TAIWAN-1 • 120 kW
11207	USA AFRTS-US MILITARY, Via Barford, UK	Irr • ATLANTIC • DS-ABC/CBS/NBC/NPR (FEEDER) • 4 kW • LSB
11330	CHINA (PR) †CENTRAL PEOPLES BS	DS-1 W-M • DS-1
11335	KOREA (DPR) †RADIO PYONGYANG, Kujang-dong	C AMERICA • 400 kW
	†RADIO PYONGYANG, Pyongyang	USSR • 200 kW
11365	CHINA (PR) RADIO BEIJING, Xi'an	(J) • EUROPE • 120 kW

FREQUENCY	COUNTRY, STATION, LOCATION	TARGET • NETWORK • POWER (kW) — World Time

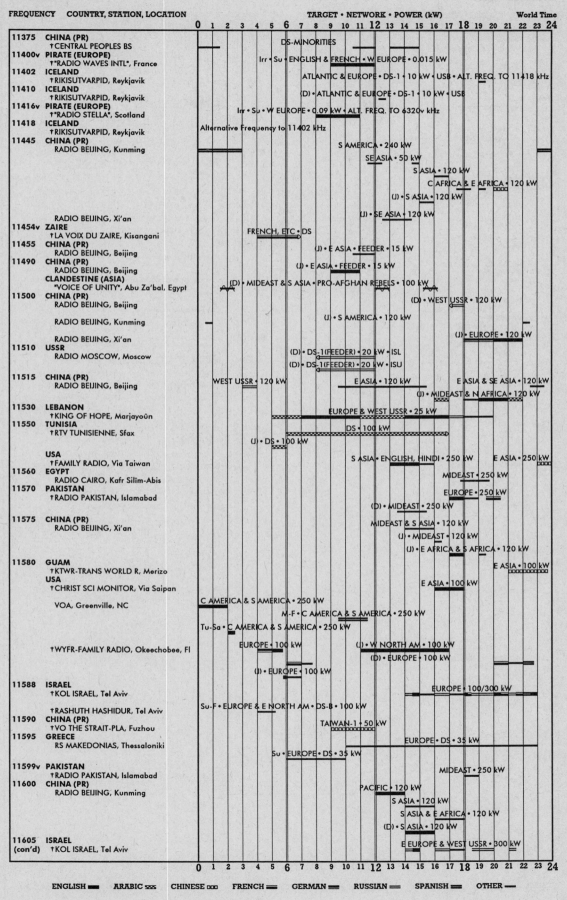

11375	**CHINA (PR)**	
	†CENTRAL PEOPLES BS	DS-MINORITIES
11400v	**PIRATE (EUROPE)**	
	†"RADIO WAVES INTL", France	Irr • Su • ENGLISH & FRENCH • W EUROPE • 0.015 kW
11402	**ICELAND**	
	†RIKISUTVARPID, Reykjavik	ATLANTIC & EUROPE • DS-1 • 10 kW • USB • ALT. FREQ. TO 11418 kHz
11410	**ICELAND**	
	†RIKISUTVARPID, Reykjavik	(D) • ATLANTIC & EUROPE • DS-1 • 10 kW • USB
11416v	**PIRATE (EUROPE)**	
	†"RADIO STELLA", Scotland	Irr • Su • W EUROPE • 0.09 kW • ALT. FREQ. TO 6320v kHz
11418	**ICELAND**	
	†RIKISUTVARPID, Reykjavik	Alternative Frequency to 11402 kHz
11445	**CHINA (PR)**	
	RADIO BEIJING, Kunming	S AMERICA • 240 kW
		SE ASIA • 50 kW
		S ASIA • 120 kW
		C AFRICA & E AFRICA • 120 kW
		(J) • S ASIA • 120 kW
	RADIO BEIJING, Xi'an	(J) • SE ASIA • 120 kW
11454v	**ZAIRE**	
	†LA VOIX DU ZAIRE, Kisangani	FRENCH, ETC • DS
11455	**CHINA (PR)**	
	RADIO BEIJING, Beijing	(J) • E ASIA • FEEDER • 15 kW
11490	**CHINA (PR)**	
	RADIO BEIJING, Beijing	(J) • E ASIA • FEEDER • 15 kW
	CLANDESTINE (ASIA)	
	"VOICE OF UNITY", Abu Za'bal, Egypt	(D) • MIDEAST & S ASIA • PRO-AFGHAN REBELS • 100 kW
11500	**CHINA (PR)**	
	RADIO BEIJING, Beijing	(D) • WEST USSR • 120 kW
	RADIO BEIJING, Kunming	(J) • S AMERICA • 120 kW
	RADIO BEIJING, Xi'an	(J) • EUROPE • 120 kW
11510	**USSR**	
	RADIO MOSCOW, Moscow	(D) • DS-1(FEEDER) • 20 kW • ISL
		(D) • DS-1(FEEDER) • 20 kW • ISU
11515	**CHINA (PR)**	
	RADIO BEIJING, Beijing	WEST USSR • 120 kW E ASIA • 120 kW E ASIA & SE ASIA • 120 kW
		(J) • MIDEAST & N AFRICA • 120 kW
11530	**LEBANON**	
	†KING OF HOPE, Marjayoûn	EUROPE & WEST USSR • 25 kW
11550	**TUNISIA**	
	†RTV TUNISIENNE, Sfax	DS • 100 kW
		(J) • DS • 100 kW
	USA	
	†FAMILY RADIO, Via Taiwan	S ASIA • ENGLISH, HINDI • 250 kW E ASIA • 250 kW
11560	**EGYPT**	
	RADIO CAIRO, Kafr Silîm-Abis	MIDEAST • 250 kW
11570	**PAKISTAN**	
	†RADIO PAKISTAN, Islamabad	EUROPE • 250 kW
		(D) • MIDEAST • 250 kW
11575	**CHINA (PR)**	
	RADIO BEIJING, Xi'an	MIDEAST & S ASIA • 120 kW
		(J) • MIDEAST • 120 kW
		(J) • E AFRICA & S AFRICA • 120 kW
11580	**GUAM**	
	†KTWR-TRANS WORLD R, Merizo	E ASIA • 100 kW
	USA	
	†CHRIST SCI MONITOR, Via Saipan	E ASIA • 100 kW
	VOA, Greenville, NC	C AMERICA & S AMERICA • 250 kW
		M-F • C AMERICA & S AMERICA • 250 kW
		Tu-Sa • C AMERICA & S AMERICA • 250 kW
	†WYFR-FAMILY RADIO, Okeechobee, Fl	EUROPE • 100 kW (J) • W NORTH AM • 100 kW
		(D) • EUROPE • 100 kW
		(J) • EUROPE • 100 kW
11588	**ISRAEL**	
	†KOL ISRAEL, Tel Aviv	EUROPE • 100/300 kW
	†RASHUTH HASHIDUR, Tel Aviv	Su-F • EUROPE & E NORTH AM • DS-B • 100 kW
11590	**CHINA (PR)**	
	†VO THE STRAIT-PLA, Fuzhou	TAIWAN-1 • 50 kW
11595	**GREECE**	
	RS MAKEDONIAS, Thessaloniki	EUROPE • DS • 35 kW
		Su • EUROPE • DS • 35 kW
11599v	**PAKISTAN**	
	†RADIO PAKISTAN, Islamabad	MIDEAST • 250 kW
11600	**CHINA (PR)**	
	RADIO BEIJING, Kunming	PACIFIC • 120 kW
		S ASIA • 120 kW
		S ASIA & E AFRICA • 120 kW
		(D) • S ASIA • 120 kW
11605 (con'd)	**ISRAEL**	
	†KOL ISRAEL, Tel Aviv	E EUROPE & WEST USSR • 300 kW

ENGLISH ▬ ARABIC ⧖ CHINESE ▭▭▭ FRENCH ▭▭ GERMAN ▬▬ RUSSIAN ══ SPANISH ▬▬ OTHER ▬

FREQUENCY   COUNTRY, STATION, LOCATION   TARGET • NETWORK • POWER (kW)   World Time

0 1 2 3 4 5 6 7 8 9 10 11 12 13 14 15 16 17 18 19 20 21 22 23 24

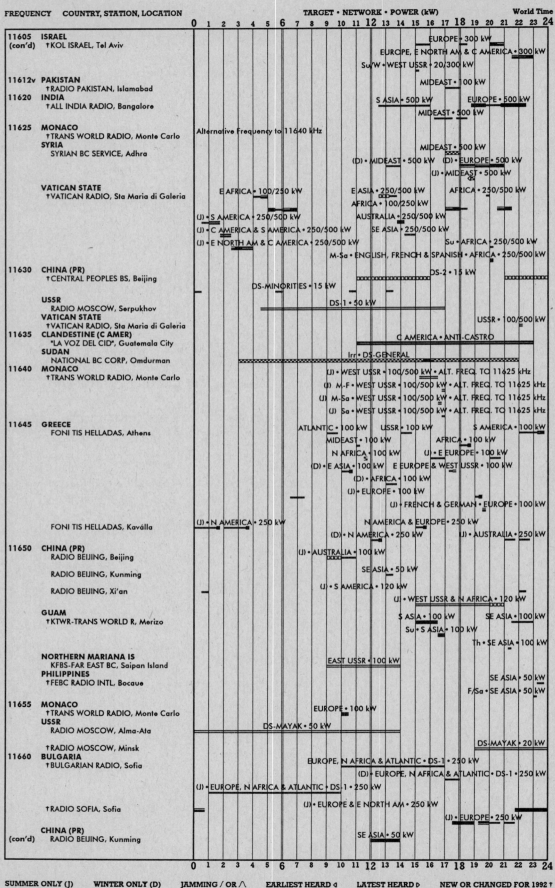

11605   **ISRAEL**
(con'd)   †KOL ISRAEL, Tel Aviv
- EUROPE • 300 kW
- EUROPE, E NORTH AM & C AMERICA • 300 kW
- Su/W • WEST USSR • 20/300 kW

11612v   **PAKISTAN**
    †RADIO PAKISTAN, Islamabad
- MIDEAST • 100 kW

11620   **INDIA**
    †ALL INDIA RADIO, Bangalore
- S ASIA • 500 kW
- EUROPE • 500 kW
- MIDEAST • 500 kW

11625   **MONACO**
    †TRANS WORLD RADIO, Monte Carlo   Alternative Frequency to 11640 kHz

     SYRIA
    SYRIAN BC SERVICE, Adhra
- MIDEAST • 500 kW
- (D) • MIDEAST • 500 kW   (D) • EUROPE • 500 kW
- (J) • MIDEAST • 500 kW

     VATICAN STATE
    †VATICAN RADIO, Sta Maria di Galeria
- E AFRICA • 100/250 kW
- E ASIA • 250/500 kW   AFRICA • 250/500 kW
- AFRICA • 100/250 kW
- (J) • S AMERICA • 250/500 kW   AUSTRALIA • 250/500 kW
- (J) • C AMERICA & S AMERICA • 250/500 kW   SE ASIA • 250/500 kW
- (J) • E NORTH AM & C AMERICA • 250/500 kW   Su • AFRICA • 250/500 kW
- M-Sa • ENGLISH, FRENCH & SPANISH • AFRICA • 250/500 kW

11630   **CHINA (PR)**
    †CENTRAL PEOPLES BS, Beijing
- DS-2 • 15 kW
- DS-MINORITIES • 15 kW

     USSR
    RADIO MOSCOW, Serpukhov
- DS-1 • 50 kW

     VATICAN STATE
    †VATICAN RADIO, Sta Maria di Galeria
- USSR • 100/500 kW

11635   **CLANDESTINE (C AMER)**
    "LA VOZ DEL CID", Guatemala City
- C AMERICA • ANTI-CASTRO

     SUDAN
    NATIONAL BC CORP, Omdurman
- Irr • DS-GENERAL

11640   **MONACO**
    †TRANS WORLD RADIO, Monte Carlo
- (J) • WEST USSR • 100/500 kW • ALT. FREQ. TO 11625 kHz
- (J) M-F • WEST USSR • 100/500 kW • ALT. FREQ. TO 11625 kHz
- (J) M-Sa • WEST USSR • 100/500 kW • ALT. FREQ. TO 11625 kHz
- (J) Sa • WEST USSR • 100/500 kW • ALT. FREQ. TO 11625 kHz

11645   **GREECE**
    FONI TIS HELLADAS, Athens
- ATLANTIC • 100 kW   USSR • 100 kW   S AMERICA • 100 kW
- MIDEAST • 100 kW   AFRICA • 100 kW
- N AFRICA • 100 kW   (J) • E EUROPE • 100 kW
- (D) • E ASIA • 100 kW   E EUROPE & WEST USSR • 100 kW
- (D) • AFRICA • 100 kW
- (J) • EUROPE • 100 kW
- (J) • FRENCH & GERMAN • EUROPE • 100 kW

    FONI TIS HELLADAS, Kaválla
- (J) • N AMERICA • 250 kW   N AMERICA & EUROPE • 250 kW
- (D) • N AMERICA • 250 kW   (J) • AUSTRALIA • 250 kW

11650   **CHINA (PR)**
    RADIO BEIJING, Beijing
- (J) • AUSTRALIA • 100 kW

    RADIO BEIJING, Kunming
- SE ASIA • 50 kW

    RADIO BEIJING, Xi'an
- (J) • S AMERICA • 120 kW
- (J) • WEST USSR & N AFRICA • 120 kW

     GUAM
    †KTWR-TRANS WORLD R, Merizo
- S ASIA • 100 kW   SE ASIA • 100 kW
- Su • S ASIA • 100 kW
- Th • SE ASIA • 100 kW

     NORTHERN MARIANA IS
    KFBS-FAR EAST BC, Saipan Island
- EAST USSR • 100 kW

     PHILIPPINES
    †FEBC RADIO INTL, Bocaue
- SE ASIA • 50 kW
- F/Sa • SE ASIA • 50 kW

11655   **MONACO**
    †TRANS WORLD RADIO, Monte Carlo
- EUROPE • 100 kW

     USSR
    RADIO MOSCOW, Alma-Ata
- DS-MAYAK • 50 kW

    †RADIO MOSCOW, Minsk
- DS-MAYAK • 20 kW

11660   **BULGARIA**
    †BULGARIAN RADIO, Sofia
- EUROPE, N AFRICA & ATLANTIC • DS-1 • 250 kW
- (D) • EUROPE, N AFRICA & ATLANTIC • DS-1 • 250 kW
- (J) • EUROPE, N AFRICA & ATLANTIC • DS-1 • 250 kW

    †RADIO SOFIA, Sofia
- (J) • EUROPE & E NORTH AM • 250 kW
- (J) • EUROPE • 250 kW

     CHINA (PR)
(con'd)   RADIO BEIJING, Kunming
- SE ASIA • 50 kW

0 1 2 3 4 5 6 7 8 9 10 11 12 13 14 15 16 17 18 19 20 21 22 23 24

SUMMER ONLY (J)   WINTER ONLY (D)   JAMMING / OR ∧   EARLIEST HEARD ◁   LATEST HEARD ▷   NEW OR CHANGED FOR 1992 †

FREQUENCY   COUNTRY, STATION, LOCATION   TARGET • NETWORK • POWER (kW)   World Time

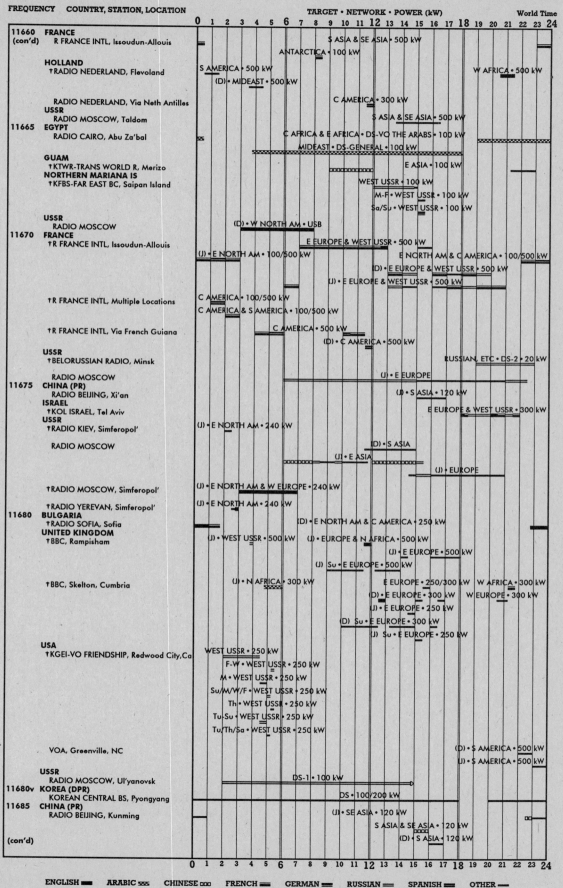

11660 **FRANCE**	
(con'd) R FRANCE INTL, Issoudun-Allouis	S ASIA & SE ASIA • 500 kW / ANTARCTICA • 100 kW
HOLLAND †RADIO NEDERLAND, Flevoland	S AMERICA • 500 kW / W AFRICA • 500 kW / (D) • MIDEAST • 500 kW
RADIO NEDERLAND, Via Neth Antilles	C AMERICA • 300 kW
USSR RADIO MOSCOW, Taldom	S ASIA & SE ASIA • 500 kW
11665 **EGYPT** RADIO CAIRO, Abu Za'bal	C AFRICA & E AFRICA • DS-VO THE ARABS • 100 kW / MIDEAST • DS-GENERAL • 100 kW
GUAM †KTWR-TRANS WORLD R, Merizo	E ASIA • 100 kW
NORTHERN MARIANA IS †KFBS-FAR EAST BC, Saipan Island	WEST USSR • 100 kW / M-F • WEST USSR • 100 kW / Sa/Su • WEST USSR • 100 kW
USSR RADIO MOSCOW	(D) • W NORTH AM • USB
11670 **FRANCE** †R FRANCE INTL, Issoudun-Allouis	E EUROPE & WEST USSR • 500 kW / (J) • E NORTH AM • 100/500 kW / E NORTH AM & C AMERICA • 100/500 kW / (D) • E EUROPE & WEST USSR • 500 kW / (J) • E EUROPE & WEST USSR • 500 kW
†R FRANCE INTL, Multiple Locations	C AMERICA • 100/500 kW / C AMERICA & S AMERICA • 100/500 kW
†R FRANCE INTL, Via French Guiana	C AMERICA • 500 kW / (D) • C AMERICA • 500 kW
USSR †BELORUSSIAN RADIO, Minsk	RUSSIAN, ETC • DS-2 • 20 kW
RADIO MOSCOW	(J) • E EUROPE
11675 **CHINA (PR)** RADIO BEIJING, Xi'an	(J) • S ASIA • 120 kW
ISRAEL †KOL ISRAEL, Tel Aviv	E EUROPE & WEST USSR • 300 kW
USSR †RADIO KIEV, Simferopol'	(J) • E NORTH AM • 240 kW
RADIO MOSCOW	(D) • S ASIA / (J) • E ASIA / (J) • EUROPE
†RADIO MOSCOW, Simferopol'	(J) • E NORTH AM & W EUROPE • 240 kW
†RADIO YEREVAN, Simferopol'	(J) • E NORTH AM • 240 kW
11680 **BULGARIA** †RADIO SOFIA, Sofia	(D) • E NORTH AM & C AMERICA • 250 kW
UNITED KINGDOM †BBC, Rampisham	(J) • WEST USSR • 500 kW / (J) • EUROPE & N AFRICA • 500 kW / (J) • E EUROPE • 500 kW / (J) Su • E EUROPE • 500 kW
†BBC, Skelton, Cumbria	(J) • N AFRICA • 300 kW / E EUROPE • 250/300 kW / W AFRICA • 300 kW / (D) • E EUROPE • 300 kW / W EUROPE • 300 kW / (J) • E EUROPE • 250 kW / (D) Su • E EUROPE • 300 kW / (J) Su • E EUROPE • 250 kW
USA †KGEI-VO FRIENDSHIP, Redwood City,Ca	WEST USSR • 250 kW / F-W • WEST USSR • 250 kW / M • WEST USSR • 250 kW / Su/M/W/F • WEST USSR • 250 kW / Th • WEST USSR • 250 kW / Tu-Su • WEST USSR • 250 kW / Tu/Th/Sa • WEST USSR • 250 kW
VOA, Greenville, NC	(D) • S AMERICA • 500 kW / (J) • S AMERICA • 500 kW
USSR RADIO MOSCOW, Ul'yanovsk	DS-1 • 100 kW
11680v **KOREA (DPR)** KOREAN CENTRAL BS, Pyongyang	DS • 100/200 kW
11685 **CHINA (PR)** RADIO BEIJING, Kunming	(J) • SE ASIA • 120 kW / S ASIA & SE ASIA • 120 kW / (D) • S ASIA • 120 kW
(con'd)	

ENGLISH ▬▬   ARABIC ∼∼∼   CHINESE □□□   FRENCH ▬▬   GERMAN ▬▬   RUSSIAN ══   SPANISH ══   OTHER ▬

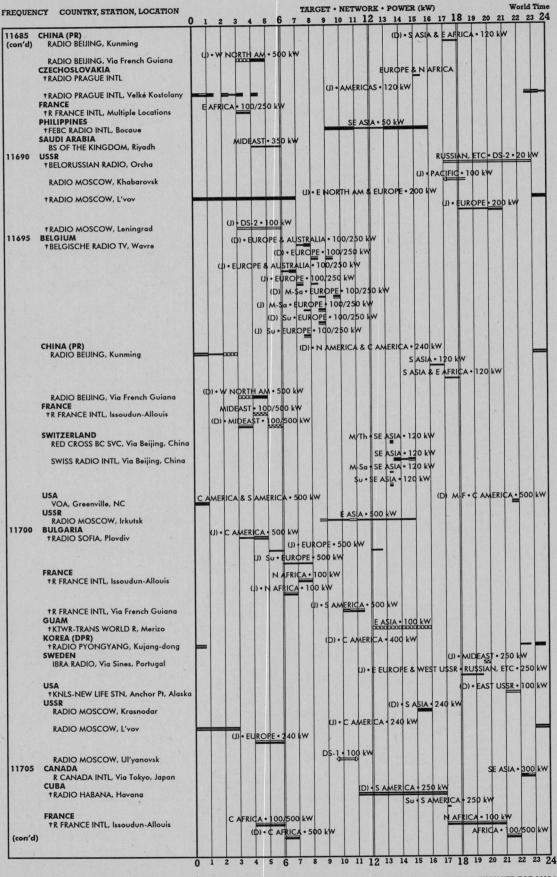

FREQUENCY   COUNTRY, STATION, LOCATION

TARGET • NETWORK • POWER (kW)   World Time

11685 **CHINA (PR)**
(con'd)   RADIO BEIJING, Kunming — (D) • S ASIA & E AFRICA • 120 kW

           RADIO BEIJING, Via French Guiana — (J) • W NORTH AM • 500 kW
CZECHOSLOVAKIA
           †RADIO PRAGUE INTL — EUROPE & N AFRICA
           †RADIO PRAGUE INTL, Velké Kostolany — (J) • AMERICAS • 120 kW
FRANCE
           †R FRANCE INTL, Multiple Locations — E AFRICA • 100/250 kW
PHILIPPINES
           †FEBC RADIO INTL, Bocaue — SE ASIA • 50 kW
SAUDI ARABIA
           BS OF THE KINGDOM, Riyadh — MIDEAST • 350 kW
11690 **USSR**
           †BELORUSSIAN RADIO, Orcha — RUSSIAN, ETC • DS-2 • 20 kW

           RADIO MOSCOW, Khabarovsk — (J) • PACIFIC • 100 kW

           †RADIO MOSCOW, L'vov — (J) • E NORTH AM & EUROPE • 200 kW
                                   — (J) • EUROPE • 200 kW

           †RADIO MOSCOW, Leningrad — (J) • DS-2 • 100 kW
11695 **BELGIUM**
           †BELGISCHE RADIO TV, Wavre — (D) • EUROPE & AUSTRALIA • 100/250 kW
                                        — (D) • EUROPE • 100/250 kW
                                        — (J) • EUROPE & AUSTRALIA • 100/250 kW
                                        — (J) • EUROPE • 100/250 kW
                                        — (D) • M-Sa • EUROPE • 100/250 kW
                                        — (J) • M-Sa • EUROPE • 100/250 kW
                                        — (D) • Su • EUROPE • 100/250 kW
                                        — (J) • Su • EUROPE • 100/250 kW

           CHINA (PR)
           RADIO BEIJING, Kunming — (D) • N AMERICA & C AMERICA • 240 kW
                                    — S ASIA • 120 kW
                                    — S ASIA & E AFRICA • 120 kW

           RADIO BEIJING, Via French Guiana — (D) • W NORTH AM • 500 kW
FRANCE
           †R FRANCE INTL, Issoudun-Allouis — MIDEAST • 100/500 kW
                                              — (D) • MIDEAST • 100/500 kW

           SWITZERLAND
           RED CROSS BC SVC, Via Beijing, China — M/Th • SE ASIA • 120 kW

           SWISS RADIO INTL, Via Beijing, China — SE ASIA • 120 kW
                                                  — M-Sa • SE ASIA • 120 kW
                                                  — Su • SE ASIA • 120 kW

           USA
           VOA, Greenville, NC — C AMERICA & S AMERICA • 500 kW
                                 — (D) • M-F • C AMERICA • 500 kW
           USSR
           RADIO MOSCOW, Irkutsk — E ASIA • 500 kW
11700 **BULGARIA**
           †RADIO SOFIA, Plovdiv — (J) • C AMERICA • 500 kW
                                   — (J) • EUROPE • 500 kW
                                   — (J) • Su • EUROPE • 500 kW

           FRANCE
           †R FRANCE INTL, Issoudun-Allouis — N AFRICA • 100 kW
                                              — (J) • N AFRICA • 100 kW

           †R FRANCE INTL, Via French Guiana — (J) • S AMERICA • 500 kW
           GUAM
           †KTWR-TRANS WORLD R, Merizo — E ASIA • 100 kW
           KOREA (DPR)
           †RADIO PYONGYANG, Kujang-dong — (D) • C AMERICA • 400 kW
           SWEDEN
           IBRA RADIO, Via Sines, Portugal — (J) • MIDEAST • 250 kW
                                             — (J) • E EUROPE & WEST USSR • RUSSIAN, ETC • 250 kW

           USA
           †KNLS-NEW LIFE STN, Anchor Pt, Alaska — (D) • EAST USSR • 100 kW
           USSR
           RADIO MOSCOW, Krasnodar — (D) • S ASIA • 240 kW

           RADIO MOSCOW, L'vov — (J) • C AMERICA • 240 kW
                                 — (J) • EUROPE • 240 kW

           RADIO MOSCOW, Ul'yanovsk — DS-1 • 100 kW
11705 **CANADA**
           R CANADA INTL, Via Tokyo, Japan — SE ASIA • 300 kW
           CUBA
           †RADIO HABANA, Havana — (D) • S AMERICA • 250 kW
                                   — Su • S AMERICA • 250 kW

           FRANCE
           †R FRANCE INTL, Issoudun-Allouis — C AFRICA • 100/500 kW
                                              — N AFRICA • 100 kW
                                              — (D) • C AFRICA • 500 kW
                                              — AFRICA • 100/500 kW
(con'd)

FREQUENCY   COUNTRY, STATION, LOCATION   TARGET • NETWORK • POWER (kW)   World Time

		0 1 2 3 4 5 6 7 8 9 10 11 12 13 14 15 16 17 18 19 20 21 22 23 24

11705 FRANCE
(con'd) †R FRANCE INTL, Multiple Locations — C AFRICA & E AFRICA • 100/250/500 kW   N AFRICA & W AFRICA • 250/500 kW
KOREA (DPR)
  †RADIO PYONGYANG, Kujang-dong — Alternative Frequency to 11760 kHz
NORTHERN MARIANA IS
  †KFBS-FAR EAST BC, Saipan Island — EAST USSR • 100 kW
SWEDEN
  †RADIO SWEDEN, Hörby — S AMERICA • 350 kW
    E NORTH AM & C AMERICA • 350 kW

USA
  CHRIST SCI MONITOR, Maine — (J) • EUROPE • 500 kW
    (J) M-F • EUROPE • 500 kW
    (J) Sa/Su • EUROPE • 500 kW

  †CHRIST SCI MONITOR, South Carolina — C AMERICA • 500 kW
    M-F • C AMERICA • 500 kW
    Sa/Su • C AMERICA • 500 kW

  VOA, Via Kaválla, Greece — (J) • WEST USSR • 250 kW

  †VOA, Via Sri Lanka — S ASIA • 35 kW
USSR
  RADIO MOSCOW, Khabarovsk — (J) • PACIFIC • 100 kW

  RADIO MOSCOW, Serpukhov — (D) • EUROPE • 240 kW
    (J) • EUROPE & ATLANTIC • 240 kW

11705v BANGLADESH
  †RADIO BANGLADESH, Dhaka — S ASIA • 100 kW
    MIDEAST • 250 kW

11710 ARGENTINA
  †R ARGENTINA-RAE, Buenos Aires — Tu-Sa • AMERICAS • 100 kW   M-F • E ASIA • 100 kW   M-F • AMERICAS • 100 kW

  †RADIO NACIONAL, Buenos Aires — Sa/Su • E ASIA • DS • 100 kW   Sa/Su • AMERICAS • DS • 100 kW
    Su/M • AMERICAS • DS • 100 kW

BULGARIA
  †RADIO SOFIA, Sofia — (J) • C AMERICA • 250 kW
CONGO
  †RTV CONGOLAISE, Brazzaville — FRENCH, ETC • DS • 50 kW
HOLLAND
  †RADIO NEDERLAND, Flevoland — (D) • EUROPE • 500 kW
    (J) • E EUROPE & MIDEAST • 500 kW

PHILIPPINES
  †RADIO VERITAS ASIA, Palauig — (D) • SE ASIA • 250 kW   SE ASIA • 250 kW
UNITED KINGDOM
  †BBC, Via Zyyi, Cyprus — (D) • E EUROPE • 250 kW
    (J) • E EUROPE • 250 kW

USA
  †VOA, Via Kaválla, Greece — (D) • WEST USSR • 250 kW

  †VOA, Via Tangier, Morocco — (D) • E EUROPE • 50 kW   (D) • E EUROPE • 100 kW

  †VOA, Via Woofferton, UK — WEST USSR • 250 kW
    (D) • WEST USSR • 250 kW
    (J) • WEST USSR • 250 kW

USSR
  RADIO MOSCOW, Moscow — (D) • N AFRICA & MIDEAST • 240 kW
    (J) • DS-1 • 100 kW

  RADIO MOSCOW, Petropavlovsk-K — (J) • W NORTH AM • 100 kW

  RADIO MOSCOW, Via Havana, Cuba — (J) • N AMERICA • 100 kW
11715 AFGHANISTAN
  RADIO AFGHANISTAN, Via USSR — (D) • MIDEAST
ALGERIA
  "VO PALESTINE", Via RTV Algerienne — EUROPE • PLO • 50 kW

  RTV ALGERIENNE, Algiers — EUROPE • DS • 50 kW
CHINA (PR)
  RADIO BEIJING, Via Bamako, Mali — N AMERICA • 100 kW   C AFRICA & E AFRICA • 50 kW
    (D) • N AMERICA • 100 kW

EGYPT
  RADIO CAIRO, Kafr Silim-Abis — S AMERICA • 250 kW
FRANCE
  †R FRANCE INTL, Via Tokyo, Japan — (D) • E ASIA • 300 kW
    (J) • E ASIA • 300 kW

HOLLAND
  †RADIO NEDERLAND, Flevoland — C AMERICA • 500 kW
    C AMERICA • 300 kW

INDIA
  †ALL INDIA RADIO, Aligarh — SE ASIA • 250 kW

  †ALL INDIA RADIO, Delhi — SE ASIA • 250 kW   AUSTRALIA • 250 kW
    DS • 100 kW
    ENGLISH, ETC • DS • 100 kW

IRAN
(con'd) †VO THE ISLAMIC REP, Tehrān — (J) • MIDEAST • 500 kW

	0 1 2 3 4 5 6 7 8 9 10 11 12 13 14 15 16 17 18 19 20 21 22 23 24

ENGLISH ▬   ARABIC ▨   CHINESE ▦   FRENCH ▬   GERMAN ▬   RUSSIAN ▭   SPANISH ▬   OTHER ▬

FREQUENCY   COUNTRY, STATION, LOCATION   TARGET • NETWORK • POWER (kW)   World Time

World Time scale: 0 1 2 3 4 5 6 7 8 9 10 11 12 13 14 15 16 17 18 19 20 21 22 23 24

Frequency	Country, Station, Location	Target • Network • Power
11715 (con'd)	**KOREA (REPUBLIC)** RADIO KOREA, Via Sackville, Can	S AMERICA • 250 kW; (J) • N AMERICA • 250 kW
	SWEDEN †RADIO SWEDEN, Hörby	Alternative Frequency to 9765 kHz; (J) • USSR • 350 kW
	UNITED KINGDOM †BBC, Via Singapore	(J) • SE ASIA • 100 kW
	USA KNLS-NEW LIFE STN, Anchor Pt, Alaska	(J) • E ASIA • 100 kW
	VOA, Via Philippines	AUSTRALIA • 50 kW
	†VOA, Via Portugal	(J) • WEST USSR • 250 kW
	USSR RADIO MOSCOW, Komsomol'sk 'Amure	(J) • E ASIA • 240 kW
	VATICAN STATE †VATICAN RADIO, Sta Maria di Galeria	Su • WEST USSR • 250/500 kW; (D) • S ASIA • 500 kW
11720	**AUSTRALIA** †RADIO AUSTRALIA, Shepparton	(J) • PACIFIC • 100 kW
	BULGARIA †RADIO SOFIA, Sofia	(J) • AFRICA • 250 kW; (J) • EUROPE • 250 kW
	†RADIO SOFIA, Stolnik	EUROPE, N AFRICA & MIDEAST • 150 kW; Su • EUROPE, N AFRICA & MIDEAST • 150 kW
	UNITED KINGDOM †BBC, Via Maṣirah, Oman	MIDEAST • 100 kW
	†BBC, Via Zyyi, Cyprus	MIDEAST • 100/250 kW
	USA VOA, Via Philippines	AUSTRALIA • 50 kW
	USSR RADIO MOSCOW, Tula	S ASIA • 240 kW
	RADIO MOSCOW, Via Havana, Cuba	(J) • AMERICAS • 100 kW
	RADIO MOSCOW, Yerevan	DS-MAYAK • 100 kW
11725	**CUBA** †RADIO HABANA, Havana	(D) • S AMERICA • 50 kW
	KOREA (REPUBLIC) RADIO KOREA, In-Kimjae	S AMERICA • 250 kW
	USA †RFE-RL, Via Germany	(J) • WEST USSR • 100 kW
	†RFE-RL, Via Portugal	(D) • WEST USSR • 250 kW; E EUROPE • 250 kW; (D) • E EUROPE • 250 kW; (J) • E EUROPE • 250 kW; (D) M-F • WEST USSR • 250 kW; (J) M-F • WEST USSR • 250 kW; (D) Sa/Su • E EUROPE • 250 kW; (J) Sa/Su • E EUROPE • 250 kW; (D) Su • E EUROPE • 250 kW
	†VOA, Via Germany	(J) • MIDEAST • 500 kW
	†WYFR-FAMILY RADIO, Okeechobee, Fl	(J) • EUROPE • 100 kW; C AMERICA • 100 kW
	USSR RADIO MOSCOW, Kazan'	(D) • MIDEAST, E AFRICA & S AFRICA • 100 kW
11730	**CANADA** R CANADA INTL, Sackville, NB	C AMERICA • 250 kW
	DENMARK †DANMARKS RADIO, Via Norway	(J) • N AMERICA • 500 kW
	HOLLAND RADIO NEDERLAND, Flevoland	(D) • E NORTH AM • 500 kW
	NORWAY †RADIO NORWAY INTL, Sveio	(J) Su/M • N AMERICA • 500 kW; (J) Tu-Sa • N AMERICA • 500 kW
	SAUDI ARABIA BS OF THE KINGDOM, Riyadh	MIDEAST & WEST USSR • DS-HOLY KORAN • 350 kW
	SPAIN R EXTERIOR ESPANA, Noblejas	AUSTRALIA • 350 kW
	UNITED KINGDOM †BBC, Via Seychelles	E AFRICA • 250 kW
	†BBC, Via Zyyi, Cyprus	MIDEAST & N AFRICA • 100/250 kW; (J) • N AFRICA • 100 kW
	USSR RADIO MOSCOW, Khabarovsk	(J) • E ASIA • 100 kW
	†RADIO MOSCOW, Orcha	DS-MAYAK • 20 kW
11734v	**TANZANIA** VOICE OF TANZANIA, Dole, Zanzibar	DS-SWAHILI • 50 kW
11735	**BULGARIA** RADIO SOFIA, Plovdiv	(D) • EUROPE • 500 kW
	†RADIO SOFIA, Sofia	(D) • AFRICA • 250 kW
	DENMARK (con'd) †DANMARKS RADIO, Via Norway	(D) • MIDEAST & E AFRICA • 350 kW

World Time scale: 0 1 2 3 4 5 6 7 8 9 10 11 12 13 14 15 16 17 18 19 20 21 22 23 24

SUMMER ONLY (J)   WINTER ONLY (D)   JAMMING / OR ∧   EARLIEST HEARD ◁   LATEST HEARD ▷   NEW OR CHANGED FOR 1992 †

FREQUENCY   COUNTRY, STATION, LOCATION   TARGET • NETWORK • POWER (kW)   World Time

0 1 2 3 4 5 6 7 8 9 10 11 12 13 14 15 16 17 18 19 20 21 22 23 24

Frequency	Country, Station, Location	Target • Network • Power
11735 (con'd)	**DENMARK** †DANMARKS RADIO, Via Norway	(D) • E EUROPE • 500 kW
		(D) • AFRICA • 350 kW
		(J) • E EUROPE • 350 kW
	GERMANY †DEUTSCHE WELLE, Via Sri Lanka	S ASIA • 250 kW
	INDIA †ALL INDIA RADIO, Delhi	S ASIA • 100 kW
	JAPAN †RADIO JAPAN/NHK, Via Moyabi, Gabon	EUROPE & N AFRICA • GENERAL • 500 kW
	KOREA (DPR) †RADIO PYONGYANG, Kujang-dong	E ASIA • 200 kW SE ASIA • 200 kW
	NORWAY †RADIO NORWAY INTL, Fredrikstad	(D) • MIDEAST & E AFRICA • 350 kW
		(D) • AFRICA • 350 kW
		(J) • E EUROPE • 350 kW
	†RADIO NORWAY INTL, Kvitsøy	(D) • E EUROPE • 500 kW
	TURKEY VOICE OF TURKEY, Ankara	WEST USSR • 500 kW
	URUGUAY †RADIO ORIENTAL, Montevideo	Irr • DS • 1.5 kW
		DS • 1.5 kW
	USA †RFE-RL, Via Germany	(J) • WEST USSR • 100 kW
	†VOA, Via Portugal	(J) • WEST USSR • 250 kW
	†VOA, Via Rhodes, Greece	(D) • MIDEAST • 50 kW
	USSR RADIO MOSCOW, Serpukhov	(J) • E EUROPE & W AFRICA • 240 kW
	YUGOSLAVIA †RADIO YUGOSLAVIA, Bijeljina	E NORTH AM • 500 kW (J) • EUROPE & E NORTH AM • 500 kW
11740	**CHINA (PR)** †CENTRAL PEOPLES BS, Beijing	DS-2 • 50 kW
	CHINA (TAIWAN) †BC CORP CHINA, Via Okeechobee, USA	C AMERICA • 100 kW
	VO FREE CHINA, Via Okeechobee, USA	C AMERICA • 100 kW
	ECUADOR †HCJB-VO THE ANDES, Quito	Alternative Frequency to 11925 kHz
	GERMANY †DEUTSCHE WELLE, Jülich	(D) • E ASIA • 100 kW
	†DEUTSCHE WELLE, Königswusterhausen	(J) • WEST USSR • 100 kW
	†DEUTSCHE WELLE, Via Sri Lanka	(D) • SE ASIA & AUSTRALIA • 250 kW SE ASIA • 250 kW
	HOLLAND †RADIO NEDERLAND, Via Madagascar	(D) • W AFRICA & C AFRICA • 300 kW
	†RADIO NEDERLAND, Via Neth Antilles	Alternative Frequency to 15560 kHz
	KOREA (REPUBLIC) RADIO KOREA, In-Kimjae	E ASIA • 100 kW
	PORTUGAL R PORTUGAL INTL, Lisbon	EUROPE • 100 kW
		M-F • EUROPE • 100 kW
		Sa/Su • EUROPE • 100 kW
	ROMANIA RADIO ROMANIA INTL, Bucharest	(D) • MIDEAST • 250 kW
	UNITED KINGDOM †BBC, Rampisham	(J) • EUROPE & WEST USSR • 500 kW
		(J) Sa/Su • EUROPE & WEST USSR • 500 kW
	BBC, Via Maşirah, Oman	MIDEAST • 100 kW
	†BBC, Via Zyyi, Cyprus	MIDEAST • 100 kW
	USA VOA, Via Kaválla, Greece	E AFRICA • 250 kW
		(D) • WEST USSR • 250 kW
	†VOA, Via Rhodes, Greece	(J) • MIDEAST • 50 kW
	USSR RADIO MOSCOW, Novosibirsk	DS-1 • 50 kW
	VATICAN STATE †VATICAN RADIO, Sta Maria di Galeria	EUROPE • 100 kW
		Su • EUROPE • 100 kW
		M-Sa • ENGLISH, FRENCH, SPANISH & ITALIAN • EUROPE • 100 kW
	YUGOSLAVIA †RADIO YUGOSLAVIA, Bijeljina	(J) • ATLANTIC & E NORTH AM • 500 kW
11745	**BRAZIL** †RADIO NACIONAL, Brasília	N AMERICA & C AMERICA • 250 kW
	CHINA (PR) RADIO BEIJING, Beijing	(J) • WEST USSR • 120 kW
		(J) • S AMERICA • 120 kW
	CHINA (TAIWAN) †VO FREE CHINA, T'ai-pei	SE ASIA • 50/100 kW E ASIA • 50/100 kW
(con'd)	**DENMARK** †DANMARKS RADIO, Via Norway	(J) • EUROPE • 500 kW

0 1 2 3 4 5 6 7 8 9 10 11 12 13 14 15 16 17 18 19 20 21 22 23 24

ENGLISH ▬   ARABIC ▨   CHINESE ▢▢▢   FRENCH ▬   GERMAN ▬   RUSSIAN ▬   SPANISH ▬   OTHER ▬

FREQUENCY   COUNTRY, STATION, LOCATION

TARGET • NETWORK • POWER (kW)   World Time

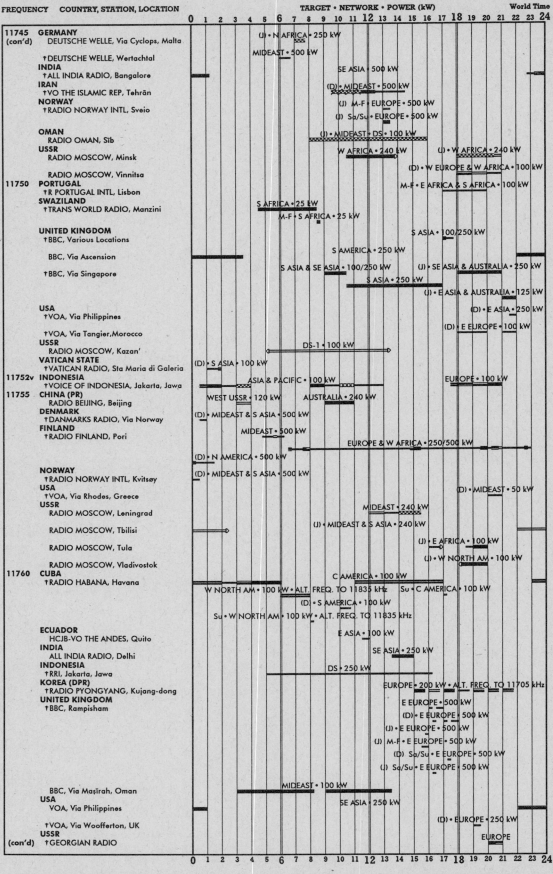

Frequency	Country, Station, Location	Details
11745 (con'd)	**GERMANY** DEUTSCHE WELLE, Via Cyclops, Malta	(J) • N AFRICA • 250 kW / MIDEAST • 500 kW
	†DEUTSCHE WELLE, Wertachtal	
	INDIA †ALL INDIA RADIO, Bangalore	SE ASIA • 500 kW
	IRAN †VO THE ISLAMIC REP, Tehrān	(D) • MIDEAST • 500 kW
	NORWAY †RADIO NORWAY INTL, Sveio	(J) • M-F EUROPE • 500 kW / (J) Sa/Su • EUROPE • 500 kW
	OMAN RADIO OMAN, Sīb	(J) • MIDEAST • DS • 100 kW
	USSR RADIO MOSCOW, Minsk	W AFRICA • 240 kW / (J) • W AFRICA • 240 kW
	RADIO MOSCOW, Vinnitsa	(D) • W EUROPE & W AFRICA • 100 kW
11750	**PORTUGAL** †R PORTUGAL INTL, Lisbon	M-F • E AFRICA & S AFRICA • 100 kW
	SWAZILAND †TRANS WORLD RADIO, Manzini	S AFRICA • 25 kW / M-F • S AFRICA • 25 kW
	UNITED KINGDOM †BBC, Various Locations	S ASIA • 100/250 kW
	BBC, Via Ascension	S AMERICA • 250 kW
	†BBC, Via Singapore	S ASIA & SE ASIA • 100/250 kW / (J) • SE ASIA & AUSTRALIA • 250 kW / S ASIA • 250 kW / (J) • E ASIA & AUSTRALIA • 125 kW
	USA †VOA, Via Philippines	(D) • E ASIA • 250 kW
	†VOA, Via Tangier, Morocco	(D) • E EUROPE • 100 kW
	USSR RADIO MOSCOW, Kazan'	DS-1 • 100 kW
	VATICAN STATE †VATICAN RADIO, Sta Maria di Galeria	(D) • S ASIA • 100 kW
11752v	**INDONESIA** †VOICE OF INDONESIA, Jakarta, Jawa	ASIA & PACIFIC • 100 kW / EUROPE • 100 kW
11755	**CHINA (PR)** RADIO BEIJING, Beijing	WEST USSR • 120 kW / AUSTRALIA • 240 kW
	DENMARK †DANMARKS RADIO, Via Norway	(D) • MIDEAST & S ASIA • 500 kW
	FINLAND †RADIO FINLAND, Pori	MIDEAST • 500 kW / EUROPE & W AFRICA • 250/500 kW
	NORWAY †RADIO NORWAY INTL, Kvitsøy	(D) • N AMERICA • 500 kW / (D) • MIDEAST & S ASIA • 500 kW
	USA †VOA, Via Rhodes, Greece	(D) • MIDEAST • 50 kW
	USSR RADIO MOSCOW, Leningrad	MIDEAST • 240 kW
	RADIO MOSCOW, Tbilisi	(J) • MIDEAST & S ASIA • 240 kW
	RADIO MOSCOW, Tula	(J) • E AFRICA • 100 kW
	RADIO MOSCOW, Vladivostok	(J) • W NORTH AM • 100 kW
11760	**CUBA** †RADIO HABANA, Havana	C AMERICA • 100 kW / W NORTH AM • 100 kW • ALT. FREQ. TO 11835 kHz / Su • C AMERICA • 100 kW / (D) • S AMERICA • 100 kW / Su • W NORTH AM • 100 kW • ALT. FREQ. TO 11835 kHz
	ECUADOR HCJB-VO THE ANDES, Quito	E ASIA • 100 kW
	INDIA ALL INDIA RADIO, Delhi	SE ASIA • 250 kW
	INDONESIA †RRI, Jakarta, Jawa	DS • 250 kW
	KOREA (DPR) †RADIO PYONGYANG, Kujang-dong	EUROPE • 200 kW • ALT. FREQ. TO 11705 kHz
	UNITED KINGDOM †BBC, Rampisham	E EUROPE • 500 kW / (D) • E EUROPE • 500 kW / (J) • E EUROPE • 500 kW / (J) M-F • E EUROPE • 500 kW / (D) Sa/Su • E EUROPE • 500 kW / (J) Sa/Su • E EUROPE • 500 kW
	BBC, Via Maṣīrah, Oman	MIDEAST • 100 kW
	USA VOA, Via Philippines	SE ASIA • 250 kW
	†VOA, Via Woofferton, UK	(D) • EUROPE • 250 kW
	USSR (con'd) †GEORGIAN RADIO	EUROPE

FREQUENCY   COUNTRY, STATION, LOCATION   TARGET • NETWORK • POWER (kW)   World Time

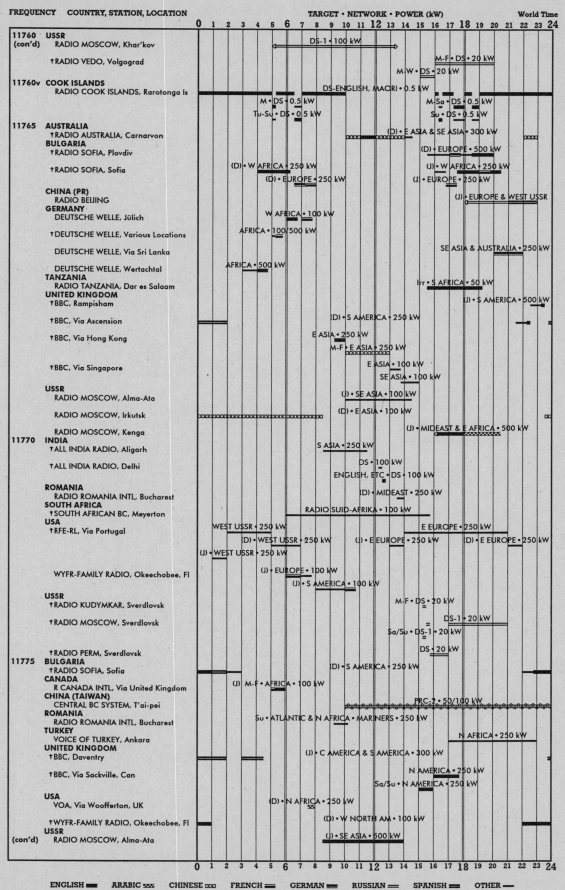

Frequency	Country, Station, Location	Target • Network • Power
11760 (con'd)	USSR RADIO MOSCOW, Khar'kov	DS-1 • 100 kW
	†RADIO VEDO, Volgograd	M-F • DS • 20 kW / M-W • DS • 20 kW
11760v	COOK ISLANDS RADIO COOK ISLANDS, Rarotonga Is	DS-ENGLISH, MAORI • 0.5 kW / M • DS • 0.5 kW / Tu-Su • DS • 0.5 kW / M-Sa • DS • 0.5 kW / Su • DS • 0.5 kW
11765	AUSTRALIA †RADIO AUSTRALIA, Carnarvon	(D) • E ASIA & SE ASIA • 300 kW
	BULGARIA †RADIO SOFIA, Plovdiv	(D) • EUROPE • 500 kW
	†RADIO SOFIA, Sofia	(D) • W AFRICA • 250 kW / (J) • W AFRICA • 250 kW / (D) • EUROPE • 250 kW / (J) • EUROPE • 250 kW
	CHINA (PR) RADIO BEIJING	(J) • EUROPE & WEST USSR
	GERMANY DEUTSCHE WELLE, Jülich	W AFRICA • 100 kW
	†DEUTSCHE WELLE, Various Locations	AFRICA • 100/500 kW
	DEUTSCHE WELLE, Via Sri Lanka	SE ASIA & AUSTRALIA • 250 kW
	DEUTSCHE WELLE, Wertachtal	AFRICA • 500 kW
	TANZANIA RADIO TANZANIA, Dar es Salaam	Irr • S AFRICA • 50 kW
	UNITED KINGDOM †BBC, Rampisham	(J) • S AMERICA • 500 kW
	†BBC, Via Ascension	(D) • S AMERICA • 250 kW
	†BBC, Via Hong Kong	E ASIA • 250 kW / M-F • E ASIA • 250 kW
	†BBC, Via Singapore	E ASIA • 100 kW / SE ASIA • 100 kW
	USSR RADIO MOSCOW, Alma-Ata	(J) • SE ASIA • 100 kW
	RADIO MOSCOW, Irkutsk	(D) • E ASIA • 100 kW
	RADIO MOSCOW, Kenga	(J) • MIDEAST & E AFRICA • 500 kW
11770	INDIA †ALL INDIA RADIO, Aligarh	S ASIA • 250 kW
	†ALL INDIA RADIO, Delhi	DS • 100 kW / ENGLISH, ETC • DS • 100 kW
	ROMANIA RADIO ROMANIA INTL, Bucharest	(D) • MIDEAST • 250 kW
	SOUTH AFRICA †SOUTH AFRICAN BC, Meyerton	RADIO SUID-AFRIKA • 100 kW
	USA †RFE-RL, Via Portugal	WEST USSR • 250 kW / E EUROPE • 250 kW / (D) • WEST USSR • 250 kW / (J) • E EUROPE • 250 kW / (D) • E EUROPE • 250 kW / (J) • WEST USSR • 250 kW
	WYFR-FAMILY RADIO, Okeechobee, Fl	(J) • EUROPE • 100 kW / (J) • S AMERICA • 100 kW
	USSR †RADIO KUDYMKAR, Sverdlovsk	M-F • DS • 20 kW
	†RADIO MOSCOW, Sverdlovsk	DS-1 • 20 kW / Sa/Su • DS-1 • 20 kW
	†RADIO PERM, Sverdlovsk	DS • 20 kW
11775	BULGARIA †RADIO SOFIA, Sofia	(D) • S AMERICA • 250 kW
	CANADA R CANADA INTL, Via United Kingdom	(J) M-F • AFRICA • 100 kW
	CHINA (TAIWAN) CENTRAL BC SYSTEM, T'ai-pei	PRC-2 • 50/100 kW
	ROMANIA RADIO ROMANIA INTL, Bucharest	Su • ATLANTIC & N AFRICA • MARINERS • 250 kW
	TURKEY VOICE OF TURKEY, Ankara	N AFRICA • 250 kW
	UNITED KINGDOM †BBC, Daventry	(J) • C AMERICA & S AMERICA • 300 kW
	†BBC, Via Sackville, Can	N AMERICA • 250 kW / Sa/Su • N AMERICA • 250 kW
	USA VOA, Via Woofferton, UK	(D) • N AFRICA • 250 kW
	†WYFR-FAMILY RADIO, Okeechobee, Fl	(D) • W NORTH AM • 100 kW
(con'd)	USSR RADIO MOSCOW, Alma-Ata	(J) • SE ASIA • 500 kW

ENGLISH ▬ ARABIC ≋ CHINESE ▫▫▫ FRENCH ▭ GERMAN ▬ RUSSIAN ═ SPANISH ▭▭ OTHER ▭

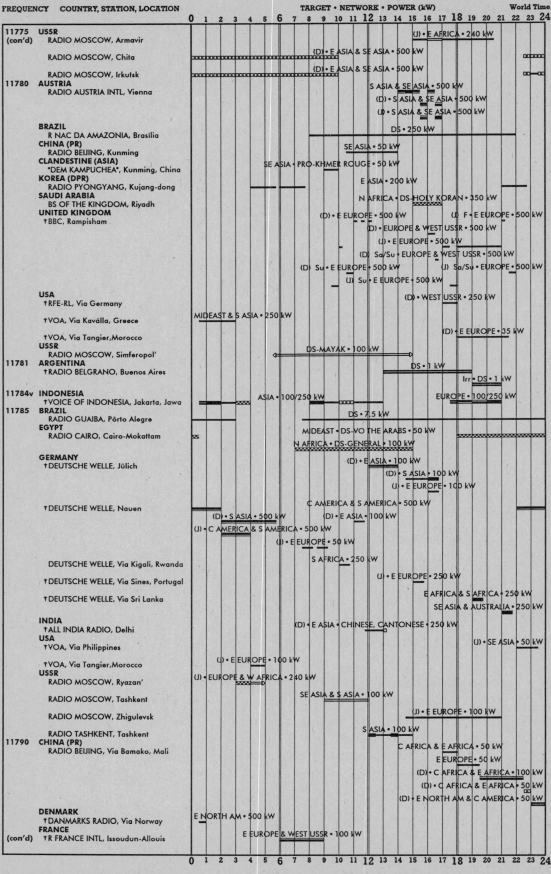

FREQUENCY   COUNTRY, STATION, LOCATION   TARGET • NETWORK • POWER (kW)   World Time

0 1 2 3 4 5 6 7 8 9 10 11 12 13 14 15 16 17 18 19 20 21 22 23 24

11790 FRANCE
(con'd)   ↑R FRANCE INTL, Issoudun-Allouis   (J) • E EUROPE & WEST USSR • 100 kW
IRAN
   ↑VO THE ISLAMIC REP, Tehrān   S ASIA • 500 kW   MIDEAST • 500 kW   WEST USSR • 500 kW   S ASIA • DS • 500 kW

NORWAY
   ↑RADIO NORWAY INTL, Sveio   E NORTH AM • 500 kW
PHILIPPINES
   ↑RADIO VERITAS ASIA, Palauig   SE ASIA • 250 kW   E ASIA • 250 kW
ROMANIA
   RADIO ROMANIA INTL, Bucharest   EUROPE • 250 kW   (D) • AFRICA • 250 kW
SPAIN
   ↑R EXTERIOR ESPANA, Arganda   EUROPE • 100 kW   N AFRICA • 100 kW   M-F • EUROPE • 100 kW
UNITED KINGDOM
   ↑BBC, Via Ascension   C AFRICA • 250 kW   S AFRICA • 250 kW   W AFRICA & C AFRICA • 250 kW
USA
   ↑WORLD HARVEST R, Noblesville,Indiana   C AMERICA • 100 kW   Su • C AMERICA • 100 kW
USSR
   ↑RADIO KIEV, Simferopol'   (J) • E NORTH AM • 500 kW
   RADIO MOSCOW, Ryazan'   (J) • W EUROPE & ATLANTIC • 240 kW
   ↑RADIO MOSCOW, Simferopol'   (J) • E NORTH AM • 500 kW   (J) • EUROPE • 500 kW
   ↑RADIO VILNIUS, Simferopol'   (J) • E NORTH AM • 500 kW
   RADIO YEREVAN, Simferopol'   (J) • E NORTH AM • 500 kW
   ↑SOVIET BELORUSSIA, Simferopol'   (J) • E NORTH AM • 500 kW
11795 CANADA
   ↑R CANADA INTL, Via Xi'an, China(PR)   (J) • E ASIA • 120 kW
CYPRUS
   ↑CYPRUS BC CORP, Zyyi   (J) F-Su • EUROPE • 250 kW
ECUADOR
   ↑HCJB-VO THE ANDES, Quito   S AMERICA • 100 kW
GERMANY
   ↑DEUTSCHE WELLE, Jülich   (J) • S ASIA • 100 kW   AUSTRALIA • 100 kW   AFRICA • 100 kW   (D) • S ASIA • 100 kW
   ↑DEUTSCHE WELLE, Königswusterhausen   (J) • E EUROPE • 100 kW
   ↑DEUTSCHE WELLE, Nauen   (D) • MIDEAST • 500 kW   (J) • N AMERICA • 500 kW
   DEUTSCHE WELLE, Via Antigua   S AMERICA • 250 kW
PHILIPPINES
   ↑RADIO VERITAS ASIA, Palauig   SE ASIA • 250 kW
UNITED ARAB EMIRATES
   ↑UAE RADIO, Dubai   EUROPE • 300 kW
UNITED KINGDOM
   ↑BBC, Via Zyyi, Cyprus   (J) M-F • EUROPE • 250 kW
USSR
   RADIO MOSCOW, Tbilisi   DS-MAYAK • 100 kW
11800 AUSTRALIA
   ↑RADIO AUSTRALIA, Shepparton   (D) • PACIFIC • 100 kW   (J) • PACIFIC • 100 kW
FRANCE
   R FRANCE INTL, Issoudun-Allouis   (D) • N AFRICA & W AFRICA • 500 kW
   R FRANCE INTL, Multiple Locations   N AFRICA & W AFRICA • 500 kW
ITALY
   RTV ITALIANA, Rome   E NORTH AM & C AMERICA • 100 kW   MIDEAST • 100 kW   (D) • WEST USSR • 100 kW   EUROPE • 100 kW   E ASIA • 100 kW
PORTUGAL
   ↑R PORTUGAL INTL, Lisbon   EUROPE • 100 kW   M-F • EUROPE • 100 kW   Sa/Su • EUROPE • 250 kW
SRI LANKA
   ↑SRI LANKA BC CORP, Colombo-Ekala   S ASIA • 100 kW   Su • S ASIA • 100 kW   MIDEAST • 100 kW
11805 CHINA (TAIWAN)
   VO FREE CHINA, Via Okeechobee,USA   (D) • EUROPE • 100 kW
GUAM
(con'd)   KTWR-TRANS WORLD R, Merizo   AUSTRALIA • 100 kW

0 1 2 3 4 5 6 7 8 9 10 11 12 13 14 15 16 17 18 19 20 21 22 23 24

ENGLISH ▬   ARABIC ▨   CHINESE ∞   FRENCH ▬   GERMAN ▬   RUSSIAN ═   SPANISH ▬   OTHER —

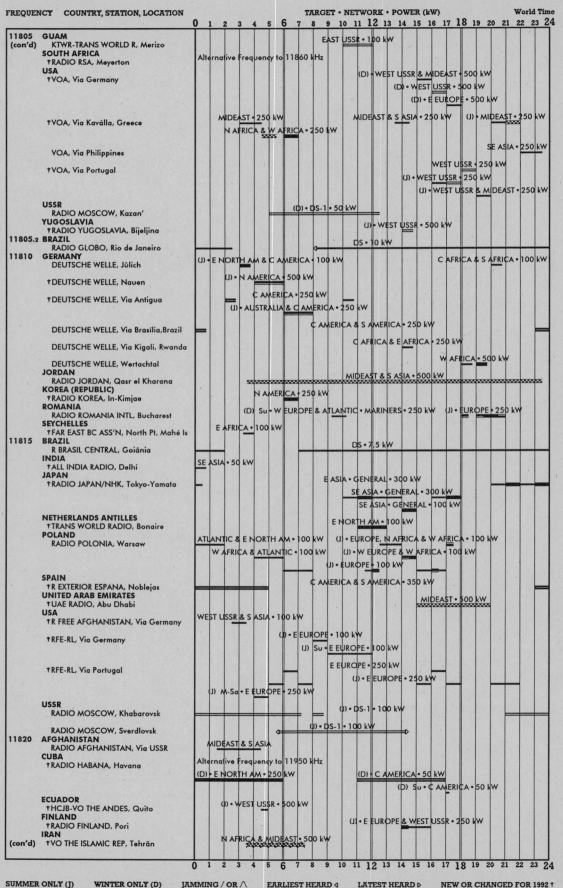

FREQUENCY   COUNTRY, STATION, LOCATION

TARGET • NETWORK • POWER (kW)

World Time

0 1 2 3 4 5 6 7 8 9 10 11 12 13 14 15 16 17 18 19 20 21 22 23 24

11805 GUAM
(con'd)   KTWR-TRANS WORLD R, Merizo — EAST USSR • 100 kW
SOUTH AFRICA
  †RADIO RSA, Meyerton — Alternative Frequency to 11860 kHz
USA
  †VOA, Via Germany — (D) • WEST USSR & MIDEAST • 500 kW / (D) • WEST USSR • 500 kW / (D) • E EUROPE • 500 kW
  †VOA, Via Kaválla, Greece — MIDEAST • 250 kW / N AFRICA & W AFRICA • 250 kW / MIDEAST & S ASIA • 250 kW / (J) • MIDEAST • 250 kW
  VOA, Via Philippines — SE ASIA • 250 kW
  †VOA, Via Portugal — WEST USSR • 250 kW / (J) • WEST USSR • 250 kW / (J) • WEST USSR & MIDEAST • 250 kW
  USSR
    RADIO MOSCOW, Kazan' — (D) • DS-1 • 50 kW
  YUGOSLAVIA
    †RADIO YUGOSLAVIA, Bijeljina — (J) • WEST USSR • 500 kW
11805.2 BRAZIL
    RADIO GLOBO, Rio de Janeiro — DS • 10 kW
11810 GERMANY
    DEUTSCHE WELLE, Jülich — (J) • E NORTH AM & C AMERICA • 100 kW / C AFRICA & S AFRICA • 100 kW
    †DEUTSCHE WELLE, Nauen — (J) • N AMERICA • 500 kW
    †DEUTSCHE WELLE, Via Antigua — C AMERICA • 250 kW / (J) • AUSTRALIA & C AMERICA • 250 kW
    DEUTSCHE WELLE, Via Brasilia, Brazil — C AMERICA & S AMERICA • 250 kW
    DEUTSCHE WELLE, Via Kigali, Rwanda — C AFRICA & E AFRICA • 250 kW
    DEUTSCHE WELLE, Wertachtal — W AFRICA • 500 kW
JORDAN
    RADIO JORDAN, Qasr el Kharana — MIDEAST & S ASIA • 500 kW
KOREA (REPUBLIC)
    †RADIO KOREA, In-Kimjae — N AMERICA • 250 kW
ROMANIA
    RADIO ROMANIA INTL, Bucharest — (D) Su • W EUROPE & ATLANTIC • MARINERS • 250 kW / (J) • EUROPE • 250 kW
SEYCHELLES
    †FAR EAST BC ASS'N, North Pt, Mahé Is — E AFRICA • 100 kW
11815 BRAZIL
    R BRASIL CENTRAL, Goiânia — DS • 7.5 kW
INDIA
    †ALL INDIA RADIO, Delhi — SE ASIA • 50 kW
JAPAN
    †RADIO JAPAN/NHK, Tokyo-Yamata — E ASIA • GENERAL • 300 kW / SE ASIA • GENERAL • 300 kW / SE ASIA • GENERAL • 100 kW
NETHERLANDS ANTILLES
    †TRANS WORLD RADIO, Bonaire — E NORTH AM • 100 kW
POLAND
    RADIO POLONIA, Warsaw — ATLANTIC & E NORTH AM • 100 kW / (J) • EUROPE, N AFRICA & W AFRICA • 100 kW / W AFRICA & ATLANTIC • 100 kW / (J) • W EUROPE & W AFRICA • 100 kW / (J) • EUROPE • 100 kW
SPAIN
    †R EXTERIOR ESPANA, Noblejas — C AMERICA & S AMERICA • 350 kW
UNITED ARAB EMIRATES
    †UAE RADIO, Abu Dhabi — MIDEAST • 500 kW
USA
    †R FREE AFGHANISTAN, Via Germany — WEST USSR & S ASIA • 100 kW
    †RFE-RL, Via Germany — (J) • E EUROPE • 100 kW / (J) Su • E EUROPE • 100 kW
    †RFE-RL, Via Portugal — E EUROPE • 250 kW / (J) • E EUROPE • 250 kW / (J) M-Sa • E EUROPE • 250 kW
USSR
    RADIO MOSCOW, Khabarovsk — (J) • DS-1 • 100 kW
    RADIO MOSCOW, Sverdlovsk — (J) • DS-1 • 100 kW
11820 AFGHANISTAN
    RADIO AFGHANISTAN, Via USSR — MIDEAST & S ASIA
CUBA
    †RADIO HABANA, Havana — Alternative Frequency to 11950 kHz / (D) • E NORTH AM • 250 kW / (D) • C AMERICA • 50 kW / (D) Su • C AMERICA • 50 kW
ECUADOR
    †HCJB-VO THE ANDES, Quito — (J) • WEST USSR • 500 kW
FINLAND
    †RADIO FINLAND, Pori — (J) • E EUROPE & WEST USSR • 250 kW
IRAN
(con'd) †VO THE ISLAMIC REP, Tehrān — N AFRICA & MIDEAST • 500 kW

0 1 2 3 4 5 6 7 8 9 10 11 12 13 14 15 16 17 18 19 20 21 22 23 24

SUMMER ONLY (J)   WINTER ONLY (D)   JAMMING / OR ∧   EARLIEST HEARD ◁   LATEST HEARD ▷   NEW OR CHANGED FOR 1992 †

| FREQUENCY | COUNTRY, STATION, LOCATION | TARGET • NETWORK • POWER (kW) | World Time |

World Time scale: 0 1 2 3 4 5 6 7 8 9 10 11 12 13 14 15 16 17 18 19 20 21 22 23 24

11820 (con'd) QATAR
QATAR BC SERVICE, Doha-Al Khaisah — N AFRICA • 250 kW

SEYCHELLES
FAR EAST BC ASS'N, North Pt, Mahé Is — E AFRICA • 100 kW

UNITED KINGDOM
†BBC, Via Ascension — (J) • S AMERICA • 250 kW
W AFRICA • 250 kW
C AFRICA • 250 kW

†BBC, Via Delano, USA — (J) • C AMERICA & S AMERICA • 250 kW

†BBC, Via Hong Kong — E ASIA • 250 kW

USA
KNLS-NEW LIFE STN, Anchor Pt, Alaska — (J) • E ASIA • 100 kW

USSR
RADIO MOSCOW, Bishkek — (D) • SE ASIA • 500 kW
(J) • S ASIA • 50 kW

RADIO MOSCOW, Voronezh — (J) • EUROPE • 100 kW

11820v MOZAMBIQUE
RADIO MOCAMBIQUE, Maputo — DS • 120 kW

11822v COLOMBIA
†RADIO NACIONAL, Bogotá — Irr • DS • 25 kW

11825 ALBANIA
RADIO TIRANA, Lushnjë — E NORTH AM & C AMERICA • 100 kW

CHINA (TAIWAN)
†VO FREE CHINA, T'ai-pei — SE ASIA

CLANDESTINE (AFRICA)
"VO LIBYAN PEOPLE", Southern Chad — Irr • N AFRICA • ANTI QADDAFI

"VO THE PEOPLE", Southern Chad — Irr • N AFRICA • ANTI QADDAFI

SAUDI ARABIA
†BS OF THE KINGDOM, Riyadh — S ASIA • 350 kW
MIDEAST • 350 kW

UNITED KINGDOM
†BBC, Via Zyyi, Cyprus — (J) • Su • WEST USSR • 250 kW

USA
†RFE-RL, Via Germany — (D) • WEST USSR & MIDEAST • 100 kW

†RFE-RL, Via Portugal — (J) • WEST USSR • 250 kW

†VOA, Via Germany — (D) • MIDEAST • 500 kW

†VOA, Via Portugal — (D) • WEST USSR • 250 kW

USSR
RADIO MOSCOW, Kenga — DS-1 • 100 kW

†RADIO MOSCOW, Orcha — DS-ORFEY • 20 kW

11827 FRENCH POLYNESIA
†RFO-TAHITI, Papeete — PACIFIC • DS-FRENCH, TAHITIAN • 20 kW

11830 BRAZIL
†RADIO ANHANGUERA, Goiânia — Irr • DS • 1 kW   DS • 1 kW

CLANDESTINE (AFRICA)
†"AV DO GALO NEGRO", Jamba, Angola — S AFRICA • UNITA

GUAM
KTWR-TRANS WORLD R, Merizo — E ASIA • 100 kW

INDIA
†ALL INDIA RADIO, Aligarh — DS • 250 kW
ENGLISH, ETC • DS • 250 kW

†ALL INDIA RADIO, Bombay — DS • 100 kW
Su • DS • 100 kW

ALL INDIA RADIO, Delhi — E AFRICA • 250 kW

ROMANIA
RADIO ROMANIA INTL, Bucharest — AMERICAS • 250 kW
(J) • MIDEAST • 250 kW

UNITED KINGDOM
†BBC, Via Zyyi, Cyprus — (J) • WEST USSR • 250 kW

USA
VOICE OF THE OAS, Cincinnati, Ohio — C AMERICA & S AMERICA • 250 kW
M-Sa • C AMERICA & S AMERICA • 250 kW
Su • C AMERICA & S AMERICA • 250 kW

†WYFR-FAMILY RADIO, Okeechobee, Fl — W NORTH AM • 100 kW
(D) • S AMERICA • 100 kW
(D) • W NORTH AM • 100 kW
(J) • S AMERICA • 100 kW

USSR
RADIO MOSCOW, Moscow — (J) • EUROPE • 240 kW

VATICAN STATE
†VATICAN RADIO, Sta Maria di Galeria — AUSTRALIA • 250/500 kW
E ASIA • 250 kW
E ASIA & SE ASIA • 250 kW
AUSTRALIA • 250 kW

11835 ALBANIA
†RADIO TIRANA, Lushnjë — AFRICA • 100 kW
SE ASIA & AUSTRALIA • 100 kW

(con'd)

World Time scale: 0 1 2 3 4 5 6 7 8 9 10 11 12 13 14 15 16 17 18 19 20 21 22 23 24

ENGLISH ▬ ARABIC ▩ CHINESE ▢▢▢ FRENCH ▬ GERMAN ▬ RUSSIAN ═ SPANISH ▬ OTHER ▬

FREQUENCY   COUNTRY, STATION, LOCATION

TARGET • NETWORK • POWER (kW)

World Time

0 1 2 3 4 5 6 7 8 9 10 11 12 13 14 15 16 17 18 19 20 21 22 23 24

FREQUENCY	COUNTRY, STATION, LOCATION	TARGET • NETWORK • POWER (kW)
11835 (con'd)	CUBA †RADIO HABANA, Havana	Alternative Frequency to 11760 kHz
	ECUADOR †HCJB-VO THE ANDES, Quito	EUROPE & WEST USSR • 500 kW / EUROPE • 500 kW
		(J) • EUROPE & WEST USSR • 500 kW
		(D) M-F • EUROPE & WEST USSR • 500 kW
		(J) M-F • WEST USSR • 500 kW
		(D) Sa/Su • EUROPE & WEST USSR • 500 kW
	GERMANY †DEUTSCHE WELLE, Nauen	E EUROPE • 50 kW
		(D) • E EUROPE • 50 kW
	SRI LANKA SRI LANKA BC CORP, Colombo-Ekala	SE ASIA & AUSTRALIA • 35 kW
	UNITED KINGDOM †BBC, Skelton, Cumbria	(D) • EUROPE • 300 kW
		(D) Sa/Su • EUROPE • 300 kW
	BBC, Via Zyyi, Cyprus	(J) • E EUROPE & WEST USSR • 250 kW
	URUGUAY R EL ESPECTADOR, Montevideo	Irr • DS • 5 kW
	USA †VOA, Greenville, NC	W AFRICA • 500 kW
		M-F • W AFRICA • 500 kW
	VOA, Via Kaválla, Greece	MIDEAST • 250 kW
	†VOA, Via Philippines	SE ASIA • 250 kW
		(D) • SE ASIA • 250 kW
	†VOA, Via Portugal	WEST USSR • 250 kW
	VOA, Via Woofferton, UK	(D) • WEST USSR • 250 kW
	USSR RADIO MOSCOW, Armavir	(J) • S ASIA • 100 kW
	RADIO MOSCOW, Tashkent	(J) • S ASIA & SE ASIA • 500 kW
	YUGOSLAVIA †RADIO YUGOSLAVIA, Bijeljina	S AMERICA • 500 kW / N AFRICA • 500 kW
		(D) • N AFRICA • 500 kW
11835v	MOZAMBIQUE RADIO MOCAMBIQUE, Maputo	Irr • S AMERICA • 120 kW
11840	ALBANIA †RADIO TIRANA, Lushnjë	S AMERICA • 100 kW
		C AMERICA & S AMERICA • 100 kW
	BULGARIA †RADIO SOFIA, Sofia	AFRICA • 250 kW
	CHINA (PR) RADIO BEIJING, Via Sackville, Can	S AMERICA • 250 kW
		(D) • N AMERICA • 250 kW
		(J) • N AMERICA • 250 kW
	DENMARK †DANMARKS RADIO, Via Norway	(J) • MIDEAST & E AFRICA • 500 kW
		(J) • MIDEAST • 500 kW
	GERMANY †DEUTSCHE WELLE, Nauen	(D) • N AFRICA • 500 kW
	JAPAN †RADIO JAPAN/NHK, Tokyo-Yamata	(J) • E ASIA • 100 kW / SE ASIA • 100 kW
		E ASIA • GENERAL • 300 kW / (J) • SE ASIA • GENERAL • 100 kW
		(J) • E ASIA • GENERAL • 100 kW
	†RADIO JAPAN/NHK, Via Sri Lanka	S ASIA • 300 kW
		S ASIA • GENERAL • 300 kW
	NORWAY †RADIO NORWAY INTL, Kvitsøy	(J) • MIDEAST & E AFRICA • 500 kW
		(J) • MIDEAST • 500 kW
	OMAN RADIO OMAN, Sïb	(J) • MIDEAST • DS • 100 kW
	POLAND RADIO POLONIA, Warsaw	EUROPE, ATLANTIC & E NORTH AM • 100 kW
		W EUROPE & W AFRICA • 100 kW
		EUROPE & N AFRICA • 100 kW
	PORTUGAL †R PORTUGAL INTL, Lisbon	S AMERICA • 100 kW
		Su/M • S AMERICA • 100 kW
		Tu-Sa • S AMERICA • 100 kW
	USA VOA, Via Germany	N AFRICA • 500 kW
	†VOA, Via Philippines	SE ASIA • 250 kW
		(D) • E ASIA • 250 kW
	USSR †BELORUSSIAN RADIO, Orcha	RUSSIAN, ETC • DS-1 • 20 kW
(con'd)	RADIO MOSCOW, Kenga	(J) • DS-1 • 50 kW

0 1 2 3 4 5 6 7 8 9 10 11 12 13 14 15 16 17 18 19 20 21 22 23 24

SUMMER ONLY (J)   WINTER ONLY (D)   JAMMING / OR ∧   EARLIEST HEARD ◁   LATEST HEARD ▷   NEW OR CHANGED FOR 1992 †

FREQUENCY	COUNTRY, STATION, LOCATION	TARGET • NETWORK • POWER (kW)	World Time

World Time scale: 0 1 2 3 4 5 6 7 8 9 10 11 12 13 14 15 16 17 18 19 20 21 22 23 24

11840 USSR
(con'd)
  RADIO MOSCOW, Via Havana, Cuba — N AMERICA • 100 kW
  RADIO MOSCOW, Vinnitsa — DS-MAYAK • 100 kW
  †Y-SAKHALINSK R, Yuzhno-Sakhalinsk — DS/TIKHIY OKEAN • 50 kW • USB

11845 CANADA
  †R CANADA INTL, Sackville, NB
    C AMERICA • 100 kW
    Su/M • C AMERICA • 100 kW
    Tu-Sa • C AMERICA • 100 kW

DENMARK
  †DANMARKS RADIO, Via Norway — (D) • E NORTH AM • 350 kW
FRANCE
  R FRANCE INTL, Issoudun-Allouis — N AFRICA • 100 kW
GERMANY
  †DEUTSCHE WELLE, Wertachtal — (J) • SE ASIA • 500 kW
KOREA (DPR)
  †RADIO PYONGYANG, Kujang-dong — SE ASIA • 200 kW / N AFRICA • 200 kW
NORWAY
  †RADIO NORWAY INTL, Fredrikstad — (D) • E NORTH AM • 350 kW
UNITED KINGDOM
  †BBC, Daventry
    (J) • E EUROPE & MIDEAST • 300 kW
    (J) • WEST USSR • 300 kW
    (J) M-Sa • E EUROPE & MIDEAST • 300 kW
  †BBC, Rampisham
    (D) M-F • E EUROPE • 500 kW
    (J) M-F • E EUROPE • 500 kW
    (D) Sa/Su • E EUROPE • 500 kW
  †BBC, Via Zyyi, Cyprus
    (D) • E AFRICA • 250 kW
    WEST USSR • 250 kW
    (D) • WEST USSR • 250 kW
    (D) M-F • EUROPE & WEST USSR • 250 kW
    (J) • WEST USSR • 250 kW
    (D) Su • WEST USSR • 250 kW
    (D) • MIDEAST & S ASIA • 250 kW

USA
  VOA, Via Kaválla, Greece
USSR
  RADIO MOSCOW, Kazan'
    S ASIA & SE ASIA • 100 kW
    (J) • S ASIA & SE ASIA • 100 kW

11850 CANADA
  †R CANADA INTL, Sackville, NB — (D) M-F • C AMERICA • 250 kW
CUBA
  †RADIO HABANA, Havana
    (D) • C AMERICA & S AMERICA • 100 kW
    (D) Su • C AMERICA & S AMERICA • 100 kW
  RADIO HABANA, Via USSR — (D) • MIDEAST & E AFRICA • 200 kW
DENMARK
  †DANMARKS RADIO, Via Norway
    (J) • MIDEAST • 500 kW
    (D) • ATLANTIC & E NORTH AM • 350 kW
    (J) • E AFRICA • 500 kW
    (D) • W AFRICA & S AMERICA • 500 kW
FINLAND
  RADIO FINLAND, Pori — (D) • MIDEAST • 500 kW
GERMANY
  DEUTSCHE WELLE, Wertachtal
    E EUROPE • 500 kW
    (D) • E EUROPE • 500 kW
JAPAN
  RADIO JAPAN/NHK, Tokyo-Yamata — AUSTRALIA • GENERAL • 100 kW
MONGOLIA
  †RADIO ULAANBAATAR, Ulaanbaatar
    E ASIA • 50 kW • ALT. FREQ. TO 9616 kHz / EUROPE • 250 kW
    AUSTRALIA • 50 kW / Tu/F • E ASIA • 250 kW
    M-Sa • E ASIA • 50 kW • ALT. FREQ. TO 9616 kHz
    Tu/F/Sa • E ASIA • 50 kW • ALT. FREQ. TO 9616 kHz
    W/Th/Sa-M • E ASIA • 250 kW

NETHERLANDS ANTILLES
  †TRANS WORLD RADIO, Bonaire — S AMERICA • 50 kW
NORWAY
  †RADIO NORWAY INTL, Fredrikstad
    (D) M-F • ATLANTIC & E NORTH AM • 350 kW
    (D) Sa/Su • ATLANTIC & E NORTH AM • 350 kW
  †RADIO NORWAY INTL, Kvitsøy
    (D) • E AFRICA • 500 kW
    (J) • MIDEAST • 500 kW
  †RADIO NORWAY INTL, Sveio — (D) • W AFRICA & S AMERICA • 500 kW
UNITED KINGDOM
  †BBC, Via Maşirah, Oman
    S ASIA • 100 kW
    MIDEAST • 100 kW
  †BBC, Via Singapore
    SE ASIA • 250 kW
    Su • S ASIA & SE ASIA • 100 kW
  BBC, Via Zyyi, Cyprus — N AFRICA • 100 kW
USSR
  †GEORGIAN RADIO — DS-1
  RADIO MOSCOW, Konevo — (D) • EUROPE • 240 kW
(con'd) †RADIO MOSCOW, Ryazan'
    (J) • N AFRICA & MIDEAST • 240 kW
    MIDEAST & E AFRICA • 200 kW

World Time scale: 0 1 2 3 4 5 6 7 8 9 10 11 12 13 14 15 16 17 18 19 20 21 22 23 24

ENGLISH ▬ ARABIC ▩ CHINESE ▭▭ FRENCH ═ GERMAN ▬ RUSSIAN ═ SPANISH ▬ OTHER ──

FREQUENCY	COUNTRY, STATION, LOCATION	TARGET • NETWORK • POWER (kW)	World Time

11850 USSR (con'd)
- †RADIO MOSCOW, Ryazan' — (J) • MIDEAST & E AFRICA • 240 kW
- RADIO MOSCOW, Via Havana, Cuba — (J) • N AMERICA • 100 kW

11855 AUSTRALIA
- †RADIO AUSTRALIA, Carnarvon — (D) • SE ASIA • 250 kW; (D) • SE ASIA • 100 kW

BRAZIL
- RADIO APARECIDA, Aparecida — DS • 7.5 kW

CANADA
- R CANADA INTL, Sackville, NB — (D) M-F • E NORTH AM • 250 kW; (J) M-F • E NORTH AM • 250 kW; Su • E NORTH AM • 100 kW; (D) Su • E NORTH AM • 100 kW; (J) Su • E NORTH AM • 100 kW

CHINA (PR)
- RADIO BEIJING, Jinhua — (J) • W NORTH AM • 500 kW; (J) • MIDEAST & N AFRICA • 500 kW

CHINA (TAIWAN)
- †VO FREE CHINA, Via Okeechobee, USA — (J) • W NORTH AM • 100 kW

USA
- †RFE-RL, Via Germany — WEST USSR • 100 kW; (D) • WEST USSR • 250 kW; (J) • WEST USSR • 100 kW
- VOA, Via Kaválla, Greece — (J) • MIDEAST & S ASIA • 250 kW
- †VOA, Via Portugal — (D) • WEST USSR • 250 kW; (J) • WEST USSR • 250 kW
- †VOA, Via Woofferton, UK — (J) • WEST USSR • 300 kW
- †WYFR-FAMILY RADIO, Okeechobee, Fl — (D) • C AMERICA • 100 kW; C AMERICA • 100 kW; (D) • EUROPE • 100 kW; (J) • W NORTH AM • 100 kW; (J) • S AMERICA • 100 kW

11860 BULGARIA
- †RADIO SOFIA, Sofia — EUROPE • 250 kW; Su • EUROPE • 250 kW
- †RADIO SOFIA, Stolnik — (D) • E EUROPE, MIDEAST & N AFRICA • 125 kW; (J) • E EUROPE, MIDEAST & N AFRICA • 125 kW

CHINA (TAIWAN)
- VO FREE CHINA, T'ai-pei — SE ASIA • 50 kW

DENMARK
- †DANMARKS RADIO, Via Norway — (D) • EUROPE • 500 kW; (D) • S AMERICA • 500 kW

INDIA
- †ALL INDIA RADIO, Aligarh — N AFRICA • 250 kW

NORWAY
- †RADIO NORWAY INTL, Kvitsøy — (D) • S AMERICA • 500 kW
- †RADIO NORWAY INTL, Sveio — (J) M-F • EUROPE • 500 kW; (J) Sa/Su • EUROPE • 500 kW

SEYCHELLES
- FAR EAST BC ASS'N, North Pt, Mahé Is — E AFRICA • 100 kW; W-Su • E AFRICA & S AFRICA • 100 kW

SOUTH AFRICA
- †RADIO RSA, Meyerton — S AFRICA • 100 kW • ALT. FREQ. TO 11805 kHz

UNITED KINGDOM
- †BBC, Via Ascension — W AFRICA • 250 kW; (J) • W AFRICA • 250 kW; (J) Sa/Su • W AFRICA • 250 kW
- BBC, Via Seychelles — E AFRICA & S AFRICA • 250 kW; E AFRICA • 250 kW

USA
- KNLS-NEW LIFE STN, Anchor Pt, Alaska — (J) • EAST USSR • 100 kW

USSR
- RADIO MOSCOW, Gor'kiy — (D) • S ASIA • 240 kW; (J) • MIDEAST & S ASIA • 240 kW
- RADIO MOSCOW, Krasnoyarsk — (J) • E ASIA • 100 kW
- †RADIO MOSCOW, Nizhniy Novgorod — (J) • EUROPE • 240 kW
- †SOVIET BELORUSSIA, Nizhniy Novgorod — (J) M/Tu/Th/F • EUROPE • 240 kW; (J) W/Sa/Su • EUROPE • 240 kW

11865 DENMARK
- †DANMARKS RADIO, Via Norway — (D) • W NORTH AM & PACIFIC • 350 kW; (J) • N AMERICA • 500 kW; (J) • EUROPE • 350 kW

GERMANY (con'd)
- DEUTSCHE WELLE, Jülich — S AMERICA • 100 kW

| FREQUENCY | COUNTRY, STATION, LOCATION | TARGET • NETWORK • POWER (kW) | World Time |

World Time scale: 0 1 2 3 4 5 6 7 8 9 10 11 12 13 14 15 16 17 18 19 20 21 22 23 24

11865 GERMANY
(con'd) DEUTSCHE WELLE, Jülich
- (D) • WEST USSR • 100 kW
- (J) • MIDEAST • 250 kW
- (J) • MIDEAST • 100 kW

†DEUTSCHE WELLE, Multiple Locations
- N AMERICA & C AMERICA • 100/250 kW
- C AMERICA & S AMERICA • 100/250 kW
- (D) • E ASIA • 100/500 kW

†DEUTSCHE WELLE, Nauen
- EUROPE • 500 kW

†DEUTSCHE WELLE, Via Antigua
- Alternative Frequency to 11960 kHz

†DEUTSCHE WELLE, Via Cyclops, Malta
- (D) • E ASIA • 250 kW

DEUTSCHE WELLE, Via Sines, Portugal
- (D) • E EUROPE • 250 kW

DEUTSCHE WELLE, Wertachtal
- (D) • MIDEAST & S ASIA • 500 kW
- (J) • WEST USSR • 500 kW

HOLLAND
RADIO NEDERLAND, Flevoland
- (J) • W EUROPE • 500 kW

JAPAN
†RADIO JAPAN/NHK, Tokyo-Yamata
- Alternative Frequency to 15195 kHz
- (J) • PACIFIC & W NORTH AM • GENERAL • 300 kW

NORWAY
†RADIO NORWAY INTL, Fredrikstad
- (D) • W NORTH AM & PACIFIC • 350 kW
- (J) • EUROPE • 350 kW

†RADIO NORWAY INTL, Sveio
- (J) • N AMERICA • 500 kW
- (J) Su/M • N AMERICA • 500 kW
- (J) Tu-Sa • N AMERICA • 500 kW

SEYCHELLES
†FAR EAST BC ASS'N, North Pt, Mahé Is
- S ASIA • 100 kW
- M • S ASIA • 100 kW
- M-Sa • S ASIA • 100 kW
- M/Sa • S ASIA • 100 kW
- Tu-Su • S ASIA • 100 kW

UNITED KINGDOM
†BBC, Via Singapore
- SE ASIA • 100/250 kW
- (D) • E ASIA • 250 kW
- (J) • E ASIA • 100 kW

USA
†VOA, Via Woofferton, UK
- E EUROPE & WEST USSR • 300 kW
- (D) • E EUROPE & WEST USSR • 300 kW
- (J) • E EUROPE & WEST USSR • 300 kW

USSR
RADIO MOSCOW, Novosibirsk
- (J) • DS-MAYAK • 100 kW

11869.8 COSTA RICA
ADVENTIST WORLD R, Alajuela
- C AMERICA • 5 kW
- Sa • C AMERICA • 5 kW
- Su-F • C AMERICA • 5 kW

11870 BULGARIA
†RADIO SOFIA, Plovdiv
- MIDEAST • 500 kW

†RADIO SOFIA, Sofia
- (D) • C AMERICA & S AMERICA • 250 kW • ALT. FREQ. TO 9655 kHz

CLANDESTINE (ASIA)
"DEM KAMPUCHEA", Kunming, China
- SE ASIA • PRO-KHMER ROUGE • 50 kW

DENMARK
†DANMARKS RADIO, Via Norway
- (J) • MIDEAST • 500 kW
- (D) • W NORTH AM • 500 kW

INDIA
†ALL INDIA RADIO, Delhi
- DS • 50 kW
- ENGLISH, ETC • DS • 50 kW

JAPAN
†RADIO JAPAN/NHK, Tokyo-Yamata
- (D) • W NORTH AM • GENERAL • 100 kW

LAOS
LAO NATIONAL RADIO, Via USSR
- (D) • EUROPE • 240 kW

NORWAY
†RADIO NORWAY INTL, Kvitsøy
- (J) • MIDEAST • 500 kW

†RADIO NORWAY INTL, Sveio
- (D) • W NORTH AM • 500 kW

USA
VOA, Via Philippines
- AUSTRALIA • 250 kW

USSR
RADIO MOSCOW, Khabarovsk
- (J) • E ASIA & SE ASIA • 240 kW

11875 CUBA
†RADIO HABANA, Havana
- (J) • S AMERICA • 250 kW
- (J) • S AMERICA • 100 kW
- (J) Su • S AMERICA • 100 kW

DENMARK
†DANMARKS RADIO, Via Norway
- (D) • MIDEAST • 500 kW

EGYPT
RADIO CAIRO, Kafr Silim-Abis
- S AFRICA • 250 kW

JAPAN
†RADIO JAPAN/NHK, Tokyo-Yamata
- Alternative Frequency to 15300 kHz
- S AMERICA • 300 kW

(con'd)

Bottom time scale: 0 1 2 3 4 5 6 7 8 9 10 11 12 13 14 15 16 17 18 19 20 21 22 23 24

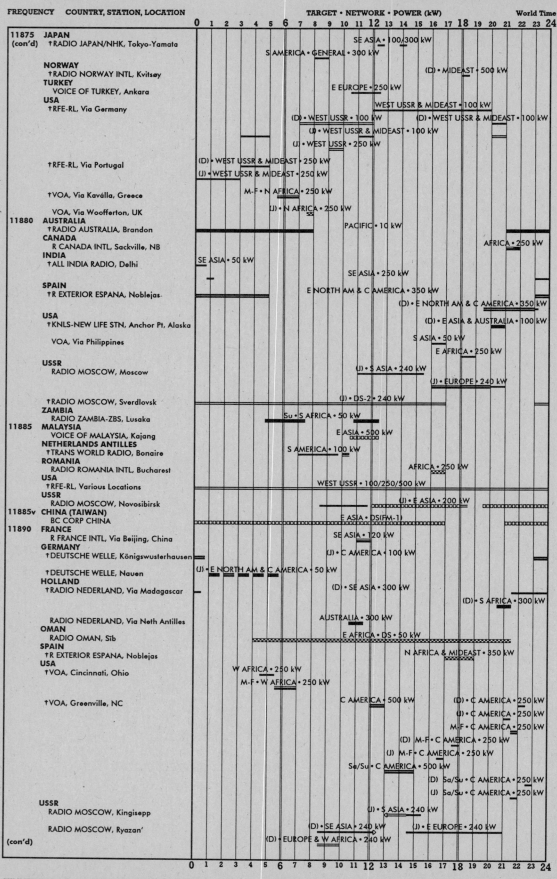

FREQUENCY   COUNTRY, STATION, LOCATION   TARGET • NETWORK • POWER (kW)   World Time

11875	JAPAN	
(con'd)	†RADIO JAPAN/NHK, Tokyo-Yamata	SE ASIA • 100/300 kW
		S AMERICA • GENERAL • 300 kW
	NORWAY	
	†RADIO NORWAY INTL, Kvitsøy	(D) • MIDEAST • 500 kW
	TURKEY	
	VOICE OF TURKEY, Ankara	E EUROPE • 250 kW
	USA	
	†RFE-RL, Via Germany	WEST USSR & MIDEAST • 100 kW
		(D) • WEST USSR • 100 kW (D) • WEST USSR & MIDEAST • 100 kW
		(J) • WEST USSR & MIDEAST • 100 kW
		(J) • WEST USSR • 250 kW
	†RFE-RL, Via Portugal	(D) • WEST USSR & MIDEAST • 250 kW
		(J) • WEST USSR & MIDEAST • 250 kW
	†VOA, Via Kaválla, Greece	M-F • N AFRICA • 250 kW
	VOA, Via Woofferton, UK	(J) • N AFRICA • 250 kW
11880	AUSTRALIA	
	†RADIO AUSTRALIA, Brandon	PACIFIC • 10 kW
	CANADA	
	R CANADA INTL, Sackville, NB	AFRICA • 250 kW
	INDIA	
	†ALL INDIA RADIO, Delhi	SE ASIA • 50 kW
		SE ASIA • 250 kW
	SPAIN	
	†R EXTERIOR ESPANA, Noblejas	E NORTH AM & C AMERICA • 350 kW
		(D) • E NORTH AM & C AMERICA • 350 kW
	USA	
	†KNLS-NEW LIFE STN, Anchor Pt, Alaska	(D) • E ASIA & AUSTRALIA • 100 kW
	VOA, Via Philippines	S ASIA • 50 kW
		E AFRICA • 250 kW
	USSR	
	RADIO MOSCOW, Moscow	(J) • S ASIA • 240 kW
		(J) • EUROPE • 240 kW
	†RADIO MOSCOW, Sverdlovsk	(J) • DS-2 • 240 kW
	ZAMBIA	
	RADIO ZAMBIA-ZBS, Lusaka	Su • S AFRICA • 50 kW
11885	MALAYSIA	
	VOICE OF MALAYSIA, Kajang	E ASIA • 500 kW
	NETHERLANDS ANTILLES	
	†TRANS WORLD RADIO, Bonaire	S AMERICA • 100 kW
	ROMANIA	
	RADIO ROMANIA INTL, Bucharest	AFRICA • 250 kW
	USA	
	†RFE-RL, Various Locations	WEST USSR • 100/250/500 kW
	USSR	
	RADIO MOSCOW, Novosibirsk	(J) • E ASIA • 200 kW
11885v	CHINA (TAIWAN)	
	BC CORP CHINA	E ASIA • DS(FM-1)
11890	FRANCE	
	R FRANCE INTL, Via Beijing, China	SE ASIA • 120 kW
	GERMANY	
	†DEUTSCHE WELLE, Königswusterhausen	(J) • C AMERICA • 100 kW
	†DEUTSCHE WELLE, Nauen	(J) • E NORTH AM & C AMERICA • 50 kW
	HOLLAND	
	†RADIO NEDERLAND, Via Madagascar	(D) • SE ASIA • 300 kW
		(D) • S AFRICA • 300 kW
	RADIO NEDERLAND, Via Neth Antilles	AUSTRALIA • 300 kW
	OMAN	
	RADIO OMAN, Sīb	E AFRICA • DS • 50 kW
	SPAIN	
	†R EXTERIOR ESPANA, Noblejas	N AFRICA & MIDEAST • 350 kW
	USA	
	†VOA, Cincinnati, Ohio	W AFRICA • 250 kW
		M-F • W AFRICA • 250 kW
	†VOA, Greenville, NC	C AMERICA • 500 kW (D) • C AMERICA • 250 kW
		(J) • C AMERICA • 250 kW
		M-F • C AMERICA • 250 kW
		(D) • M-F • C AMERICA • 250 kW
		(J) • M-F • C AMERICA • 250 kW
		Sa/Su • C AMERICA • 500 kW
		(D) Sa/Su • C AMERICA • 250 kW
		(J) Sa/Su • C AMERICA • 250 kW
	USSR	
	RADIO MOSCOW, Kingisepp	(J) • S ASIA • 240 kW
	RADIO MOSCOW, Ryazan'	(D) • SE ASIA • 240 kW (J) • E EUROPE • 240 kW
(con'd)		(D) • EUROPE & W AFRICA • 240 kW

FREQUENCY   COUNTRY, STATION, LOCATION   TARGET • NETWORK • POWER (kW)   World Time

0 1 2 3 4 5 6 7 8 9 10 11 12 13 14 15 16 17 18 19 20 21 22 23 24

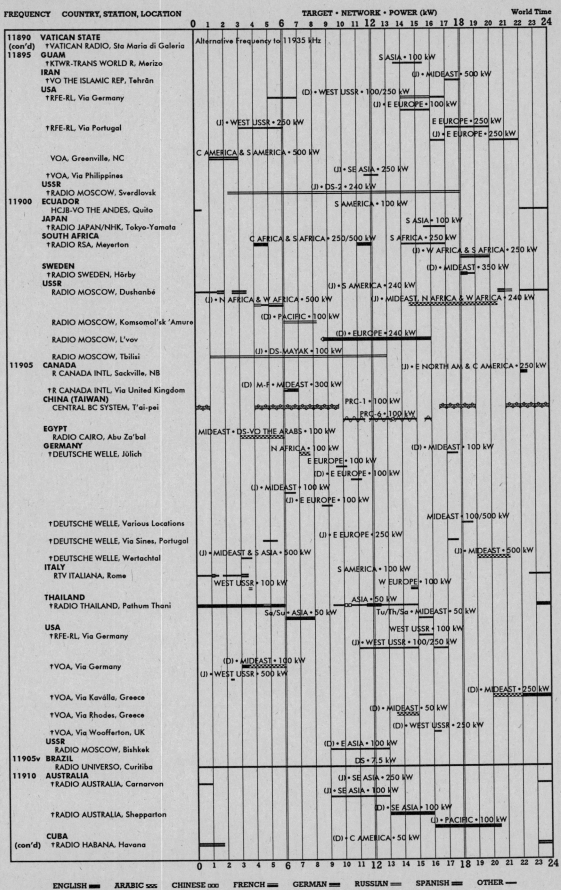

Frequency	Country, Station, Location	Target • Network • Power
11890 (con'd)	VATICAN STATE †VATICAN RADIO, Sta Maria di Galeria	Alternative Frequency to 11935 kHz
11895	GUAM †KTWR-TRANS WORLD R, Merizo	S ASIA • 100 kW
	IRAN †VO THE ISLAMIC REP, Tehrān	(J) • MIDEAST • 500 kW
	USA †RFE-RL, Via Germany	(D) • WEST USSR • 100/250 kW; (J) • E EUROPE • 100 kW
	†RFE-RL, Via Portugal	(J) • WEST USSR • 250 kW; E EUROPE • 250 kW; (J) • E EUROPE • 250 kW
	VOA, Greenville, NC	C AMERICA & S AMERICA • 500 kW
	†VOA, Via Philippines	(J) • SE ASIA • 250 kW
	USSR †RADIO MOSCOW, Sverdlovsk	(J) • DS-2 • 240 kW
11900	ECUADOR HCJB-VO THE ANDES, Quito	S AMERICA • 100 kW
	JAPAN †RADIO JAPAN/NHK, Tokyo-Yamata	S ASIA • 100 kW
	SOUTH AFRICA †RADIO RSA, Meyerton	C AFRICA & S AFRICA • 250/500 kW; S AFRICA • 250 kW; (J) • W AFRICA & S AFRICA • 250 kW
	SWEDEN †RADIO SWEDEN, Hörby	(D) • MIDEAST • 350 kW
	USSR RADIO MOSCOW, Dushanbé	(J) • S AMERICA • 240 kW; (J) • N AFRICA & W AFRICA • 500 kW; (J) • MIDEAST, N AFRICA & W AFRICA • 240 kW
	RADIO MOSCOW, Komsomol'sk 'Amure	(D) • PACIFIC • 100 kW
	RADIO MOSCOW, L'vov	(D) • EUROPE • 240 kW
	RADIO MOSCOW, Tbilisi	(J) • DS-MAYAK • 100 kW
11905	CANADA R CANADA INTL, Sackville, NB	(J) • E NORTH AM & C AMERICA • 250 kW
	†R CANADA INTL, Via United Kingdom	(D) • M-F • MIDEAST • 300 kW
	CHINA (TAIWAN) CENTRAL BC SYSTEM, T'ai-pei	PRC-1 • 100 kW; PRC-6 • 100 kW
	EGYPT RADIO CAIRO, Abu Za'bal	MIDEAST • DS-VO THE ARABS • 100 kW
	GERMANY †DEUTSCHE WELLE, Jülich	N AFRICA • 100 kW; (D) • MIDEAST • 100 kW; E EUROPE • 100 kW; (D) • E EUROPE • 100 kW; (J) • MIDEAST • 100 kW; (J) • E EUROPE • 100 kW
	†DEUTSCHE WELLE, Various Locations	MIDEAST • 100/500 kW
	†DEUTSCHE WELLE, Via Sines, Portugal	(J) • E EUROPE • 250 kW
	†DEUTSCHE WELLE, Wertachtal	(J) • MIDEAST & S ASIA • 500 kW; (J) • MIDEAST • 500 kW
	ITALY RTV ITALIANA, Rome	WEST USSR • 100 kW; S AMERICA • 100 kW; W EUROPE • 100 kW
	THAILAND †RADIO THAILAND, Pathum Thani	ASIA • 50 kW; Sa/Su • ASIA • 50 kW; Tu/Th/Sa • MIDEAST • 50 kW
	USA †RFE-RL, Via Germany	WEST USSR • 100 kW; (J) • WEST USSR • 100/250 kW
	†VOA, Via Germany	(D) • MIDEAST • 100 kW; (J) • WEST USSR • 500 kW
	†VOA, Via Kaválla, Greece	(D) • MIDEAST • 250 kW
	†VOA, Via Rhodes, Greece	(D) • MIDEAST • 50 kW
	†VOA, Via Woofferton, UK	(D) • WEST USSR • 250 kW
	USSR RADIO MOSCOW, Bishkek	(D) • E ASIA • 100 kW
11905v	BRAZIL RADIO UNIVERSO, Curitiba	DS • 7.5 kW
11910	AUSTRALIA †RADIO AUSTRALIA, Carnarvon	(J) • SE ASIA • 250 kW; (J) • SE ASIA • 100 kW
	†RADIO AUSTRALIA, Shepparton	(D) • SE ASIA • 100 kW; (J) • PACIFIC • 100 kW
	CUBA (con'd) †RADIO HABANA, Havana	(D) • C AMERICA • 50 kW

0 1 2 3 4 5 6 7 8 9 10 11 12 13 14 15 16 17 18 19 20 21 22 23 24

ENGLISH ▬ ARABIC ▨ CHINESE ▦ FRENCH ▬ GERMAN ▬ RUSSIAN ═ SPANISH ▬ OTHER ▬

FREQUENCY   COUNTRY, STATION, LOCATION

TARGET • NETWORK • POWER (kW)   World Time

World Time scale: 0 1 2 3 4 5 6 7 8 9 10 11 12 13 14 15 16 17 18 19 20 21 22 23 24

Frequency	Country / Station / Location	Schedule
11910 (con'd)	**CUBA** †RADIO HABANA, Havana	(D) Su • C AMERICA • 50 kW
	ECUADOR †HCJB-VO THE ANDES, Quito	S AMERICA • 500 kW / AMERICAS • 250 kW / Sa/Su • AMERICAS • 250 kW
	FRANCE †R FRANCE INTL, Via Xi'an, China	(J) • S ASIA • 150 kW
	HUNGARY †RADIO BUDAPEST	S AMERICA / N AMERICA / M • S AMERICA / M • N AMERICA / Su • EUROPE / EUROPE / M-Sa • EUROPE
	INDIA †ALL INDIA RADIO, Delhi	E ASIA • 250 kW / S ASIA • 250 kW / DS • 250 kW
	SPAIN †R EXTERIOR ESPANA, Via Xi'an, China	SE ASIA • 120 kW
	USA †KNLS-NEW LIFE STN, Anchor Pt, Alaska	(J) • E ASIA • 100 kW
11915	**BRAZIL** RADIO GAUCHA, Pôrto Alegre	DS • 7.5 kW
	CANADA †R CANADA INTL, Via Sines, Portugal	(D) • E EUROPE • 250 kW
	CHINA (TAIWAN) VO FREE CHINA, T'ai-pei	SE ASIA • 50/100 kW
	GERMANY DEUTSCHE WELLE, Multiple Locations	WEST USSR • 100/500 kW / (D) • WEST USSR • 100/500 kW / (J) • WEST USSR • 100/500 kW
	†DEUTSCHE WELLE, Via Cyclops, Malta	(D) • C AMERICA • 250 kW
	†DEUTSCHE WELLE, Via Sri Lanka	(J) • SE ASIA & AUSTRALIA • 250 kW
	SEYCHELLES FAR EAST BC ASS'N, North Pt, Mahé Is	MIDEAST • 100 kW / Su/Th/F • MIDEAST • 100 kW
	USA †RFE-RL, Via Germany	(J) • WEST USSR • 250 kW
	†RFE-RL, Via Portugal	(J) • WEST USSR • 250 kW
	VOA, Greenville, NC	C AMERICA • 250 kW
	†VOA, Via Rhodes, Greece	(J) • MIDEAST • 50 kW
	VOA, Via Tangier, Morocco	(J) • E EUROPE • 100 kW
11920	**MOROCCO** RTV MAROCAINE, Tangier	EUROPE & W AFRICA • 50 kW / M-Sa • EUROPE & W AFRICA • 50 kW / Su • EUROPE & W AFRICA • 50 kW
	SOUTH AFRICA †RADIO RSA, Meyerton	S AFRICA • 250 kW • ALT. FREQ. TO 11925 kHz
	SPAIN †R EXTERIOR ESPANA, Arganda	EUROPE • 100 kW
	UNITED KINGDOM †BBC, Via Maşirah, Oman	S ASIA • 100 kW
	†BBC, Via Singapore	SE ASIA • 100/250 kW / S ASIA • 250 kW / S ASIA & SE ASIA • 250 kW
	USA †VOA, Via Philippines	
	USSR RADIO MOSCOW, Novosibirsk	(J) • DS-MAYAK • 100 kW
	RADIO MOSCOW, Tashkent	(J) • S AMERICA • 500 kW / (J) M/W/Th/Sa • S AMERICA • 500 kW / (J) Su/Tu/F • S AMERICA • 500 kW
11925	**BRAZIL** RADIO BANDEIRANTES, São Paulo	DS • 10 kW / Irr • DS • 10 kW
	CANADA †R CANADA INTL, Via Vienna, Austria	MIDEAST • 300 kW / (D) • MIDEAST • 300 kW
	CHINA (PR) †CENTRAL PEOPLES BS, Beijing	CHINESE, ETC • TAIWAN-1 • 50 kW
	DENMARK †DANMARKS RADIO, Via Norway	E NORTH AM & C AMERICA • 500 kW / (D) • N AMERICA • 350 kW / (J) • W NORTH AM & PACIFIC • 500 kW
	ECUADOR †HCJB-VO THE ANDES, Quito	AUSTRALIA & PACIFIC • 100 kW / C AMERICA & E NORTH AM • 100 kW • ALT. FREQ. TO 11740 kHz / (D) • EUROPE & WEST USSR • 100 kW
(con'd)		

World Time scale: 0 1 2 3 4 5 6 7 8 9 10 11 12 13 14 15 16 17 18 19 20 21 22 23 24

SUMMER ONLY (J)   WINTER ONLY (D)   JAMMING / OR ∧   EARLIEST HEARD ◁   LATEST HEARD ▷   NEW OR CHANGED FOR 1992 †

FREQUENCY   COUNTRY, STATION, LOCATION

TARGET • NETWORK • POWER (kW)   World Time

0 1 2 3 4 5 6 7 8 9 10 11 12 13 14 15 16 17 18 19 20 21 22 23 24

Frequency	Country, Station, Location	Target • Network • Power
11925 (con'd)	ECUADOR †HCJB-VO THE ANDES, Quito	(D) • EUROPE • 100 kW
	GERMANY †DEUTSCHE WELLE, Königswusterhausen	(D) • MIDEAST • 100 kW
	MALTA VO MEDITERRANEAN, Cyclops	EUROPE, N AFRICA & MIDEAST • 250 kW
	NORWAY †RADIO NORWAY INTL, Fredrikstad	(D) Su/M • N AMERICA • 350 kW; (D) Tu-Sa • N AMERICA • 350 kW
	†RADIO NORWAY INTL, Sveio	(J) • W NORTH AM & PACIFIC • 500 kW; Su/M • E NORTH AM & C AMERICA • 500 kW; Tu-Sa • E NORTH AM & C AMERICA • 500 kW
	SOUTH AFRICA †RADIO RSA, Meyerton	Alternative Frequency to 11920 kHz
	SWEDEN RADIO SWEDEN, Hörby	(D) • USSR • 350 kW; (J) • USSR • 350 kW
	TURKEY †VOICE OF TURKEY, Ankara	WEST USSR • 250 kW
	UNITED KINGDOM †BBC, Via Ascension	W AFRICA & C AFRICA • 250 kW
	USA †RFE-RL, Via Germany	(D) • WEST USSR • 100 kW
	†RFE-RL, Via Portugal	(D) • WEST USSR • 50/250 kW; (J) • E EUROPE • 250 kW
	VOA, Via Philippines	E ASIA • 250 kW; (D) • E ASIA • 250 kW; (J) • E ASIA • 250 kW
	USSR RADIO MOSCOW, Krasnoyarsk	(D) • E ASIA & SE ASIA • 500 kW
11930	AUSTRALIA †RADIO AUSTRALIA, Brandon	(J) • PACIFIC • 10 kW; PACIFIC • 10 kW; (D) • PACIFIC • 10 kW
	CUBA †RADIO HABANA, Via USSR	(J) • EUROPE • 100 kW
	IRAN †VO THE ISLAMIC REP, Tehrān	(J) • C AMERICA • 500 kW
	†VO THE ISLAMIC REP, Zāhedān	(J) • MIDEAST • 500 kW
	MALAYSIA †RADIO MALAYSIA, Kajang	DS-1 (MALAY) • 100 kW
	NETHERLANDS ANTILLES †TRANS WORLD RADIO, Bonaire	C AMERICA • 100 kW; N AMERICA • 100 kW
	SEYCHELLES FAR EAST BC ASS'N, North Pt, Mahé Is	MIDEAST & S ASIA • 100 kW; Th-Sa • MIDEAST & S ASIA • 100 kW; S AFRICA • 100 kW
	USA RADIO MARTI, Greenville, NC	C AMERICA • 500 kW
	†VOA, Via Philippines	EAST USSR • 250 kW; (J) • EAST USSR • 250 kW; SE ASIA • 250 kW; E ASIA • 250 kW; (D) • EAST USSR • 250 kW
	USSR RADIO MOSCOW, Armavir	(D) • DS-1 • 100 kW
11935	CANADA †R CANADA INTL, Via United Kingdom	EUROPE • 300 kW; (D) • EUROPE • 300 kW; (J) • EUROPE • 300 kW
	GERMANY †DEUTSCHE WELLE, Leipzig	(D) • E ASIA • 100 kW
	HOLLAND †RADIO NEDERLAND, Flevoland	EUROPE • 500 kW; (J) • EUROPE • 500 kW
	INDIA ALL INDIA RADIO, Aligarh	WEST USSR • 250 kW
	ALL INDIA RADIO, Delhi	E AFRICA • 250 kW
	SAUDI ARABIA BS OF THE KINGDOM, Riyadh	N AFRICA • DS-HOLY KORAN • 350 kW
	USA †R FREE AFGHANISTAN, Via Portugal	(D) • WEST USSR & S ASIA • 250 kW
	†RFE-RL, Via Pals, Spain	WEST USSR • 250 kW; (J) • WEST USSR • 250 kW
	†RFE-RL, Via Portugal	(D) • WEST USSR • 250 kW
	†VOA, Greenville, NC	M-F • S AMERICA • 500 kW
	VATICAN STATE †VATICAN RADIO, Sta Maria di Galeria	(J) • S ASIA • 500 kW • ALT. FREQ. TO 11890 kHz
11937.8	CAMBODIA VO THE PEOPLE, Phnom Penh	SE ASIA • 50 kW

0 1 2 3 4 5 6 7 8 9 10 11 12 13 14 15 16 17 18 19 20 21 22 23 24

ENGLISH ▬   ARABIC ∞∞∞   CHINESE □□□   FRENCH ▬▬   GERMAN ═══   RUSSIAN ══   SPANISH ▬▬   OTHER ▬

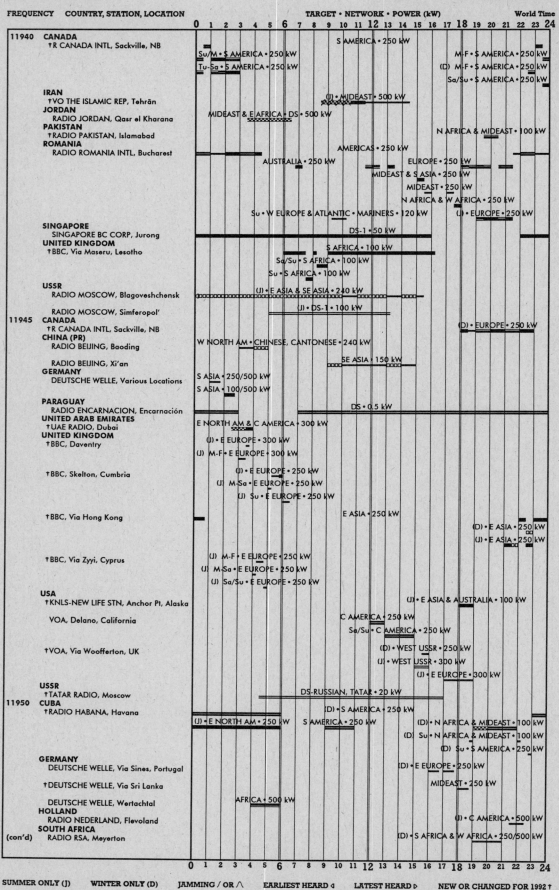

FREQUENCY   COUNTRY, STATION, LOCATION   TARGET • NETWORK • POWER (kW)   World Time

0 1 2 3 4 5 6 7 8 9 10 11 12 13 14 15 16 17 18 19 20 21 22 23 24

Frequency	Country, Station, Location	Target • Network • Power
11950 (con'd)	USSR — KAZAKH RADIO, Alma-Ata	M-F • DS-1 • 100 kW Th-Tu • DS-1 • 100 kW
		Sa • DS-1 • 100 kW W • DS-1 • 100 kW
		Sa-M/W • DS-1 • 100 kW
		Sa/Su • DS-1 • 100 kW
		Su-F • DS-1 • 100 kW
		Tu/Th/F • DS-1 • 100 kW
		RUSSIAN, ETC • DS-1 • 100 kW
	RADIO MOSCOW	(D) • EUROPE • 240/500 kW
	RADIO MOSCOW, Tula	(J) • MIDEAST & E AFRICA • 250 kW
11954.8	ANGOLA — †RADIO NACIONAL, Luanda	S AFRICA • 100 kW
11955	CANADA — R CANADA INTL, Sackville, NB	Su • E NORTH AM • 100 kW
		(D) Su • E NORTH AM • 100 kW
		(J) Su • E NORTH AM • 100 kW
	†R CANADA INTL, Via Tokyo, Japan	(D) • E ASIA • 300 kW
	HOLLAND — †RADIO NEDERLAND, Via Madagascar	AUSTRALIA • 300 kW
	JORDAN — RADIO JORDAN, Qasr el Kharana	E EUROPE & WEST USSR • DS • 500 kW
	SWITZERLAND — RED CROSS BC SVC, Schwarzenburg	Irr • M/Th • AFRICA • ENGLISH, FRENCH • 150 kW
	†SWISS RADIO INTL, Schwarzenburg	E EUROPE • 150 kW
		AFRICA • 150 kW
		M-Sa • AFRICA • 150 kW
		Su • AFRICA • 150 kW
	TURKEY — †VOICE OF TURKEY, Ankara	MIDEAST • 250/500 kW
	UNITED KINGDOM — †BBC, Rampisham	(D) • WEST USSR • 500 kW (J) • EUROPE & WEST USSR • 500 kW
		(J) • WEST USSR • 500 kW
	BBC, Via Maṣīrah, Oman	S ASIA • 100 kW
	†BBC, Via Singapore	E ASIA & AUSTRALIA • 100/125 kW
		E ASIA & SE ASIA • 250 kW
		S ASIA • 250 kW
		SE ASIA • 250 kW
		(D) • SE ASIA & AUSTRALIA • 125/250 kW
		M-F • S ASIA • 250 kW
		Sa/Su • S ASIA • 250 kW
	BBC, Via Zyyi, Cyprus	MIDEAST & S ASIA • 250 kW
	USA — †VOA, Via Philippines	(J) • E ASIA • 250 kW
	USSR — RADIO MOSCOW, Ivano-Frankovsk	(J) • W AFRICA • 240 kW
11960	ALBANIA — †RADIO TIRANA, Lushnjë	WEST USSR • 100 kW
	ECUADOR — HCJB-VO THE ANDES, Quito	AMERICAS • 100 kW
	GERMANY — DEUTSCHE WELLE, Jülich	(J) • E EUROPE • 100 kW
	†DEUTSCHE WELLE, Königswusterhausen	(J) • W EUROPE • 100 kW
	†DEUTSCHE WELLE, Via Antigua	C AMERICA • 250 kW • ALT FREQ. TO 11865 kHz
	DEUTSCHE WELLE, Via Sines, Portugal	(J) • E EUROPE • 250 kW
	INDIA — ALL INDIA RADIO, Bangalore	S ASIA • 500 kW
	SWEDEN — †RADIO SWEDEN, Hörby	(J) • USSR & SE ASIA • 350 kW
	USA — VOA, Via Kaválla, Greece	(J) • WEST USSR • 250 kW
	†VOA, Via Rhodes, Greece	(D) • MIDEAST • 50 kW
	USSR — RADIO MOSCOW, Armavir	(J) • E AFRICA & S AFRICA • 500 kW
	†RADIO MOSCOW, Orcha	(J) • EUROPE • 200 kW
	RADIO MOSCOW, Serpukhov	(J) • EUROPE & ATLANTIC • 240 kW
	†SOVIET BELORUSSIA, Orcha	(J) M/Tu/Th/F • EUROPE • 200 kW
		(J) W/Sa/Su • EUROPE • 200 kW
11960v	MALI — RTV MALIENNE, Bamako	FRENCH, ETC • DS • 50 kW
		Su • FRENCH, ETC • DS • 50 kW

0 1 2 3 4 5 6 7 8 9 10 11 12 13 14 15 16 17 18 19 20 21 22 23 24

FREQUENCY   COUNTRY, STATION, LOCATION   TARGET • NETWORK • POWER (kW)   World Time

```
0  1  2  3  4  5  6  7  8  9 10 11 12 13 14 15 16 17 18 19 20 21 22 23 24
```

11965 BRAZIL
RADIO RECORD, São Paulo — Irr • DS • 7.5 kW / DS • 7.5 kW

CANADA
↑R CANADA INTL, Via Germany — (D) • MIDEAST • 500 kW
FRANCE
R FRANCE INTL, Issoudun-Allouis — S AMERICA • 100 kW / (D) • W AFRICA • 500 kW

GERMANY
↑DEUTSCHE WELLE, Via Antigua — (D) • AUSTRALIA & C AMERICA • 250 kW

DEUTSCHE WELLE, Via Kigali, Rwanda — S AFRICA • 250 kW

↑DEUTSCHE WELLE, Via Sri Lanka — (J) • S ASIA • 250 kW
SEYCHELLES
↑FAR EAST BC ASS'N, North Pt, Mahé Is — S ASIA • 100 kW / Th-Su • S ASIA • 100 kW

UNITED ARAB EMIRATES
↑UAE RADIO, Abu Dhabi — EUROPE • 500 kW
UNITED KINGDOM
↑BBC, Via Delano, USA — (D) • C AMERICA & S AMERICA • 250 kW
USA
↑KNLS-NEW LIFE STN, Anchor Pt, Alaska — (J) • EAST USSR • 100 kW

VOA, Via Philippines — EAST USSR • 250 kW / (D) • E ASIA • 250 kW / (J) • EAST USSR • 250 kW / E ASIA • 250 kW / (D) • EAST USSR • 250 kW / (J) • E ASIA • 250 kW

11970 CUBA
↑RADIO HABANA, Havana — (D) • S AMERICA • 100 kW / (D) • Su • S AMERICA • 100 kW

GERMANY
↑DEUTSCHE WELLE, Nauen — (J) • EUROPE • 50 kW
INDIA
↑ALL INDIA RADIO, Delhi — DS • 50 kW / DS • 100 kW / ENGLISH & HINDI • DS • 100 kW

USA
↑RFE-RL, Via Germany — (D) • WEST USSR • 250 kW

↑RFE-RL, Via Pals, Spain — (J) • WEST USSR • 250 kW

↑RFE-RL, Via Portugal — (J) • WEST USSR • 250 kW / (D) • WEST USSR • 250 kW
USSR
RADIO MOSCOW, Irkutsk — (J) • E ASIA • 240 kW

11975 CHINA (PR)
RADIO BEIJING — (J) • S ASIA / (J) • MIDEAST & S ASIA / (J) • E AFRICA

EGYPT
RADIO CAIRO, Abu Za'bal — E AFRICA & S AFRICA • 100 kW
USSR
RADIO MOSCOW, Khar'kov — (J) • MIDEAST • 240 kW

↑RADIO TASHKENT, Tashkent — S ASIA • 100 kW / (D) • MIDEAST • 50 kW

11980 CHINA (PR)
RADIO BEIJING, Baoding — (D) • S AMERICA • 240 kW

RADIO BEIJING, Beijing — (D) • WEST USSR • 120 kW

RADIO BEIJING, Jinhua — (D) • W NORTH AM • 500 kW
EGYPT
RADIO CAIRO, Abu Za'bal — N AFRICA & MIDEAST • DS-VO THE ARABS • 100 kW

RADIO CAIRO, Kafr Silim-Abis — N AFRICA • DS-VO THE ARABS • 250 kW
GUAM
ADVENTIST WORLD R, Agat — E ASIA • 100 kW / (D) • E ASIA • 100 kW / S ASIA • 100 kW

11985 ALBANIA
↑RADIO TIRANA, Lushnjë — SE ASIA & AUSTRALIA • 100 kW
BELGIUM
↑BELGISCHE RADIO TV, Wavre — (D) • AFRICA • 100/250 kW / (J) • AFRICA • 100/250 kW

UNITED ARAB EMIRATES
↑UAE RADIO, Abu Dhabi — (D) • E NORTH AM & C AMERICA • 500 kW / (D) • EUROPE • 500 kW

11990 CHINA (PR)
↑RADIO BEIJING, Via USSR — (J) • EUROPE
CZECHOSLOVAKIA
↑RADIO PRAGUE INTL — (J) • EUROPE

↑RADIO PRAGUE INTL, Rimavská — AMERICAS • 250 kW
USSR
RADIO MOSCOW, Komsomol'sk 'Amure — DS-MAYAK • 100 kW

RADIO MOSCOW, Tula — (J) • W AFRICA • 100 kW

```
0  1  2  3  4  5  6  7  8  9 10 11 12 13 14 15 16 17 18 19 20 21 22 23 24
```

SUMMER ONLY (J)   WINTER ONLY (D)   JAMMING / OR ∧   EARLIEST HEARD ◁   LATEST HEARD ▷   NEW OR CHANGED FOR 1992 ↑

FREQUENCY   COUNTRY, STATION, LOCATION   TARGET • NETWORK • POWER (kW)   World Time

Time scale: 0 1 2 3 4 5 6 7 8 9 10 11 12 13 14 15 16 17 18 19 20 21 22 23 24

11995 **FRANCE**
  †R FRANCE INTL, Issoudun-Allouis
- (D) • E AFRICA • 100 kW
- E EUROPE • 100 kW
- (D) • E EUROPE • 100 kW
- (J) • E EUROPE • 100 kW

  †R FRANCE INTL, Multiple Locations
- (D) • MIDEAST & E AFRICA • 100/250 kW

  R FRANCE INTL, Via French Guiana
- S AMERICA • 500 kW

MONACO
  †TRANS WORLD RADIO, Monte Carlo
- Alternative Frequency to 12020 kHz

PHILIPPINES
  †FEBC RADIO INTL, Bocaue
- SE ASIA • 50 kW

USSR
  RADIO TASHKENT, Tashkent
- (J) • MIDEAST • 100 kW

12000 **AUSTRALIA**
  †RADIO AUSTRALIA, Carnarvon
- SE ASIA • 100 kW   SE ASIA • 250/300 kW
- (J) • SE ASIA • 100 kW
- (J) • E ASIA & SE ASIA • 250 kW

CUBA
  †RADIO HABANA, Havana
- (D) • C AMERICA • 50/100 kW

USSR
  RADIO MOSCOW
- (J) • W EUROPE & ATLANTIC
- (D) • W AFRICA & S AMERICA

  RADIO MOSCOW, Kazan'
- DS-MAYAK • 100 kW

  RADIO TASHKENT, Tashkent
- (D) • MIDEAST • 100 kW

12005 **MONACO**
  †TRANS WORLD RADIO, Monte Carlo
- (J) • F-M • WEST USSR • 500 kW
- (J) • F-W • WEST USSR • 500 kW

TUNISIA
  †RTV TUNISIENNE, Sfax
- Irr • DS-RAMADAN • 100 kW
- DS • 100 kW

USSR
  RADIO MOSCOW
- (J)
- (D)
- (D) • AFRICA
- (J) • AFRICA

12010 **AUSTRIA**
  RADIO AUSTRIA INTL, Vienna
- MIDEAST • 100 kW
- (D) • MIDEAST • 100 kW
- (J) • MIDEAST • 100 kW
- M-Sa • MIDEAST • 100 kW
- Su • MIDEAST • 100 kW

MONACO
  †TRANS WORLD RADIO, Monte Carlo
- Alternative Frequency to 12020 kHz

USSR
  RADIO MOSCOW
- (D)
- (J) • EUROPE
- (J)

  RADIO MOSCOW, Komsomol'sk 'Amure
- (D) • E ASIA • 240 kW

  RADIO MOSCOW, Petropavlovsk-K
- (D) • W NORTH AM • 100 kW

  RADIO MOSCOW, Serpukhov
- (J) • S AMERICA • 240 kW

12015 **CHINA (PR)**
  RADIO BEIJING, Xi'an
- SE ASIA • 120 kW

FRANCE
  R FRANCE INTL, Via Moyabi, Gabon
- AFRICA • 250 kW

MONGOLIA
  †RADIO ULAANBAATAR, Ulaanbaatar
- E ASIA • 250 kW
- AUSTRALIA • 250 kW
- (J) Su • E ASIA • 50/100 kW
- M-Sa • E ASIA • 250 kW
- Tu/F • E ASIA • 50/100 kW
- W/Th/Sa-M • E ASIA & AUSTRALIA • 250 kW

USSR
  RADIO MOSCOW
- (J)
- (D)
- (D) • E EUROPE
- (D) • DS-MAYAK

12018v **VIETNAM**
  †VOICE OF VIETNAM, Hanoi
- (D) • SE ASIA • 30 kW
- (D) • E ASIA & AMERICAS • 30 kW
- (D) • AFRICA • 30 kW
- (D) • EUROPE • 30 kW

12020 **MONACO**
  †TRANS WORLD RADIO, Monte Carlo
- USSR • 500 kW • ALT. FREQ. TO 11995 kHz
- MIDEAST • 500 kW • ALT. FREQ. TO 12010 kHz
- (J) • MIDEAST • 500 kW
- (J) M-F • MIDEAST • 500 kW
- Sa • USSR • 500 kW • ALT. FREQ. TO 11995 kHz

PHILIPPINES
(con'd) †FEBC RADIO INTL, Iba
- E ASIA • 100 kW

Time scale: 0 1 2 3 4 5 6 7 8 9 10 11 12 13 14 15 16 17 18 19 20 21 22 23 24

ENGLISH ▅▅   ARABIC ▨▨   CHINESE ▫▫▫   FRENCH ▭▭   GERMAN ▬▬   RUSSIAN ══   SPANISH ▪▪   OTHER ──

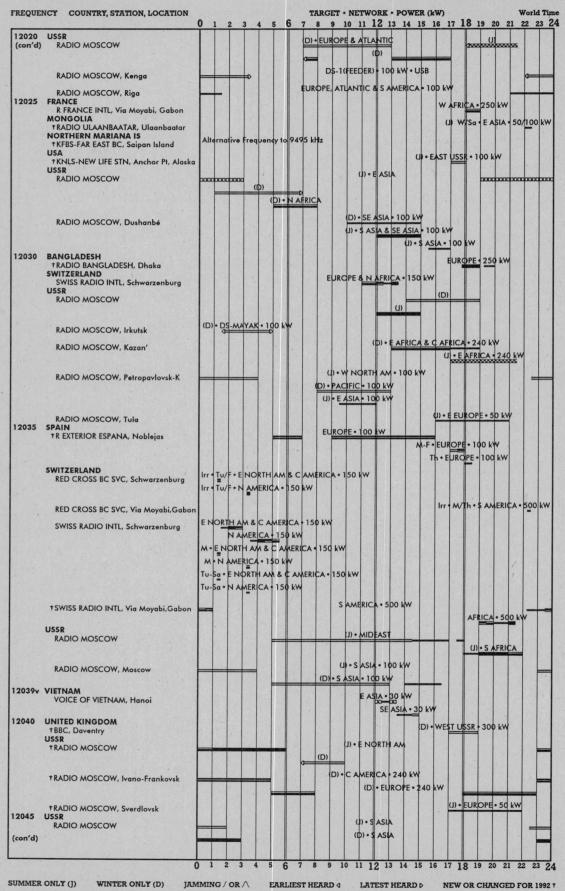

FREQUENCY   COUNTRY, STATION, LOCATION   TARGET • NETWORK • POWER (kW)   World Time

		0 1 2 3 4 5 6 7 8 9 10 11 12 13 14 15 16 17 18 19 20 21 22 23 24

12020 (con'd) USSR — RADIO MOSCOW — (D) • EUROPE & ATLANTIC — (J) — (D)

RADIO MOSCOW, Kenga — DS-1(FEEDER) • 100 kW • USB

RADIO MOSCOW, Riga — EUROPE, ATLANTIC & S AMERICA • 100 kW

12025 FRANCE — R FRANCE INTL, Via Moyabi, Gabon — W AFRICA • 250 kW
MONGOLIA — †RADIO ULAANBAATAR, Ulaanbaatar — (J) W/Sa • E ASIA • 50/100 kW
NORTHERN MARIANA IS — †KFBS-FAR EAST BC, Saipan Island — Alternative Frequency to 9495 kHz
USA — †KNLS-NEW LIFE STN, Anchor Pt, Alaska — (J) • EAST USSR • 100 kW
USSR — RADIO MOSCOW — (J) • E ASIA — (D) — (D) • N AFRICA

RADIO MOSCOW, Dushanbé — (D) • SE ASIA • 100 kW — (J) • S ASIA & SE ASIA • 100 kW — (J) • S ASIA • 100 kW

12030 BANGLADESH — †RADIO BANGLADESH, Dhaka — EUROPE • 250 kW
SWITZERLAND — SWISS RADIO INTL, Schwarzenburg — EUROPE & N AFRICA • 150 kW
USSR — RADIO MOSCOW — (D) — (J)

RADIO MOSCOW, Irkutsk — (D) • DS-MAYAK • 100 kW

RADIO MOSCOW, Kazan' — (D) • E AFRICA & C AFRICA • 240 kW — (J) • E AFRICA • 240 kW

RADIO MOSCOW, Petropavlovsk-K — (J) • W NORTH AM • 100 kW — (D) • PACIFIC • 100 kW — (J) • E ASIA • 100 kW

RADIO MOSCOW, Tula — (J) • E EUROPE • 50 kW

12035 SPAIN — †R EXTERIOR ESPANA, Noblejas — EUROPE • 100 kW — M-F • EUROPE • 100 kW — Th • EUROPE • 100 kW

SWITZERLAND — RED CROSS BC SVC, Schwarzenburg — Irr • Tu/F • E NORTH AM & C AMERICA • 150 kW — Irr • Tu/F • N AMERICA • 150 kW

RED CROSS BC SVC, Via Moyabi, Gabon — Irr • M/Th • S AMERICA • 500 kW

SWISS RADIO INTL, Schwarzenburg — E NORTH AM & C AMERICA • 150 kW — N AMERICA • 150 kW — M • E NORTH AM & C AMERICA • 150 kW — M • N AMERICA • 150 kW — Tu-Sa • E NORTH AM & C AMERICA • 150 kW — Tu-Sa • N AMERICA • 150 kW

†SWISS RADIO INTL, Via Moyabi, Gabon — S AMERICA • 500 kW — AFRICA • 500 kW

USSR — RADIO MOSCOW — (J) • MIDEAST — (J) • S AFRICA

RADIO MOSCOW, Moscow — (J) • S ASIA • 100 kW — (D) • S ASIA • 100 kW

12039v VIETNAM — VOICE OF VIETNAM, Hanoi — E ASIA • 30 kW — SE ASIA • 30 kW

12040 UNITED KINGDOM — †BBC, Daventry — (D) • WEST USSR • 300 kW
USSR — †RADIO MOSCOW — (J) • E NORTH AM — (D)

†RADIO MOSCOW, Ivano-Frankovsk — (D) • C AMERICA • 240 kW — (D) • EUROPE • 240 kW

†RADIO MOSCOW, Sverdlovsk — (J) • EUROPE • 50 kW

12045 USSR — RADIO MOSCOW — (J) • S ASIA — (D) • S ASIA
(con'd)

	0 1 2 3 4 5 6 7 8 9 10 11 12 13 14 15 16 17 18 19 20 21 22 23 24

FREQUENCY	COUNTRY, STATION, LOCATION	TARGET • NETWORK • POWER (kW)	World Time

World Time scale: 0 1 2 3 4 5 6 7 8 9 10 11 12 13 14 15 16 17 18 19 20 21 22 23 24

12045 USSR
(con'd) †RADIO MOSCOW, Voronezh, RSFSR — DS-1 • 50 kW

12050 EGYPT
RADIO CAIRO, Multiple Locations — EUROPE & E NORTH AM • DS-GENERAL • 250 kW
EUROPE, E NORTH AM & N AFRICA • DS-GENERAL • 100/250 kW
EUROPE, E NORTH AM & MIDEAST • DS-GENERAL • 100/250 kW

MONGOLIA
†RADIO ULAANBAATAR, Ulaanbaatar — EUROPE • 250 kW
Tu/F • EUROPE • 250 kW

USSR
†GEORGIAN RADIO — EUROPE

†RADIO MOSCOW, Bishkek — (D) • SE ASIA • 100 kW

†RADIO MOSCOW, Khabarovsk — PACIFIC & W NORTH AM • WORLD SVC/N A SVC • 100/240 kW
(J) • PACIFIC & W NORTH AM • 100/240 kW
(J) • PACIFIC & W NORTH AM • NORTH AMERICAN SVC • 100/240 kW
(J) • PACIFIC & W NORTH AM • TIKHIY OKEAN/DS-1 • 100/240 kW

†RADIO MOSCOW, Tbilisi — (J) • S AMERICA • 240/500 kW

†RADIO YEREVAN, Tbilisi — (J) • S AMERICA • ARMENIAN, SPANISH • 240/500 kW

12055 CHINA (PR)
RADIO BEIJING, Xi'an — S AMERICA • 120 kW
USSR
RADIO MOSCOW — E ASIA
(J) • MIDEAST
(J)

RADIO MOSCOW, Armavir — AFRICA • 120 kW
(D) • AFRICA • 120 kW
(J) • AFRICA • 120 kW

12056 USSR
†RADIO HOPE, Keila, Estonia — DS/ANTI-SEPARATIST • 0.5/1 kW
12060 USSR
†RADIO MOSCOW, Bishkek — (J) • W EUROPE & C AMERICA • 500 kW
(D) • S AMERICA • 500 kW

†RADIO MOSCOW, Kenga — (J) • DS-1 • 50/100 kW

†RADIO MOSCOW, Voronezh, RSFSR — (J) • DS-MAYAK • 240 kW

†RADIO YEREVAN, Bishkek — (D) • S AMERICA • ARMENIAN, SPANISH • 500 kW
12065 USSR
†RADIO MOSCOW — (J) • E NORTH AM
(J)

12070 USSR
†GEORGIAN RADIO — EUROPE

†R TIKHIY OKEAN, Khabarovsk — (J) • PACIFIC & W NORTH AM • 100 kW

†RADIO MOSCOW — (D) • AFRICA
(J)

†RADIO MOSCOW, Kenga — (J) • SE ASIA • 240 kW
DS-1 • 100 kW

†RADIO MOSCOW, L'vov — (D) • S AMERICA • 500 kW
(D) • W AFRICA • 240 kW
(J) • C AMERICA • 240 kW

12085 SYRIA
SYRIAN BC SERVICE, Adhra — S AMERICA • 500 kW
DS • 500 kW
MIDEAST • 500 kW
AUSTRALIA • 500 kW
EUROPE • 500 kW
(J) • DS • 500 kW

12095 UNITED KINGDOM
†BBC, Multiple Locations — EUROPE • 100/250/500 kW
EUROPE N AFRICA & W AFRICA • 100/250/500 kW

†BBC, Woofferton — (J) • N AMERICA • 250 kW
12100 USSR
RADIO MOSCOW — (D) • (FEEDER) • USB
12105 GREECE
FONI TIS HELLADAS, Kaválla — AFRICA • 250 kW
MIDEAST • 250 kW
(J) • E EUROPE & WEST USSR • 250 kW

12110 CHINA (PR)
RADIO BEIJING, Kunming — SE ASIA • 50 kW
12120 CHINA (PR)
†CENTRAL PEOPLES BS — DS-1
W-M • DS-1

12175 USSR
RADIO MOSCOW, Moscow — Irr • DS-1(FEEDER) • 20 kW • LSB
12205 USSR
RADIO MOSCOW, Alma-Ata — Irr • DS-MAYAK(FEEDER) • 15 kW • LSB

World Time scale: 0 1 2 3 4 5 6 7 8 9 10 11 12 13 14 15 16 17 18 19 20 21 22 23 24

ENGLISH ▬ ARABIC ▩ CHINESE ▭ FRENCH ▬ GERMAN ▬ RUSSIAN ═ SPANISH ▬ OTHER ▬

FREQUENCY   COUNTRY, STATION, LOCATION   TARGET • NETWORK • POWER (kW)   World Time

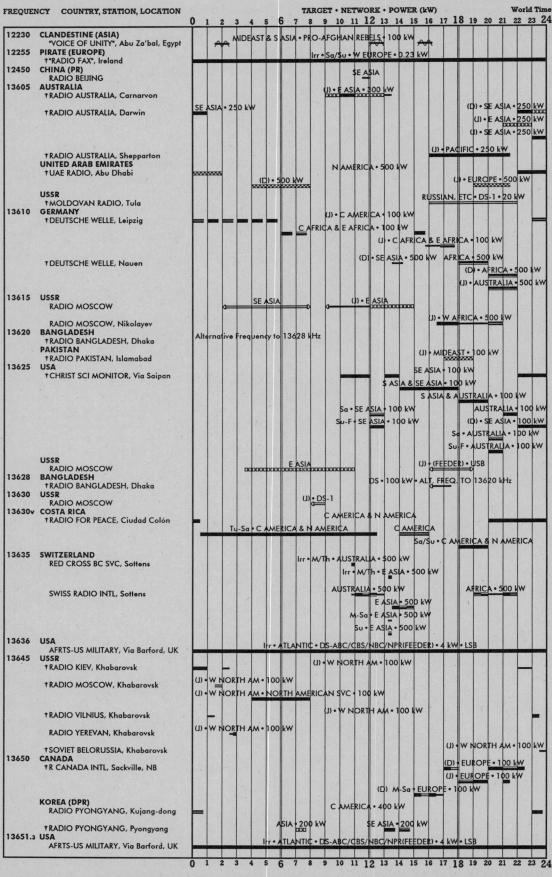

The chart lists the following frequencies, countries, stations, locations and transmission details:

- **12230** — CLANDESTINE (ASIA), "VOICE OF UNITY", Abu Za'bal, Egypt — MIDEAST & S ASIA • PRO-AFGHAN REBELS • 100 kW
- **12255** — PIRATE (EUROPE), †"RADIO FAX", Ireland — Irr • Sa/Su • W EUROPE • 0.23 kW
- **12450** — CHINA (PR), RADIO BEIJING — SE ASIA
- **13605** — AUSTRALIA, †RADIO AUSTRALIA, Carnarvon — (J) • E ASIA • 300 kW
  - †RADIO AUSTRALIA, Darwin — SE ASIA • 250 kW; (D) • SE ASIA • 250 kW; (J) • E ASIA • 250 kW; (J) • SE ASIA • 250 kW
  - †RADIO AUSTRALIA, Shepparton — (J) • PACIFIC • 250 kW
- UNITED ARAB EMIRATES, †UAE RADIO, Abu Dhabi — N AMERICA • 500 kW; (D) • 500 kW; (J) • EUROPE • 500 kW
- USSR, †MOLDOVAN RADIO, Tula — RUSSIAN, ETC • DS-1 • 20 kW
- **13610** — GERMANY, †DEUTSCHE WELLE, Leipzig — (J) • C AMERICA • 100 kW; C AFRICA & E AFRICA • 100 kW; (J) • C AFRICA & E AFRICA • 100 kW
  - †DEUTSCHE WELLE, Nauen — (D) • SE ASIA • 500 kW; AFRICA • 500 kW; (D) • AFRICA • 500 kW; (J) • AUSTRALIA • 500 kW
- **13615** — USSR, RADIO MOSCOW — SE ASIA; (J) • E ASIA
  - RADIO MOSCOW, Nikolayev — (J) • W AFRICA • 500 kW
- **13620** — BANGLADESH, †RADIO BANGLADESH, Dhaka — Alternative Frequency to 13628 kHz
- PAKISTAN, †RADIO PAKISTAN, Islamabad — (J) • MIDEAST • 100 kW
- **13625** — USA, †CHRIST SCI MONITOR, Via Saipan — SE ASIA • 100 kW; S ASIA & SE ASIA • 100 kW; S ASIA & AUSTRALIA • 100 kW; Sa • SE ASIA • 100 kW; AUSTRALIA • 100 kW; Su-F • SE ASIA • 100 kW; (D) • SE ASIA • 100 kW; Sa • AUSTRALIA • 100 kW; Su-F • AUSTRALIA • 100 kW
- USSR, RADIO MOSCOW — E ASIA; (J) • (FEEDER) • USB
- **13628** — BANGLADESH, †RADIO BANGLADESH, Dhaka — DS • 100 kW • ALT. FREQ. TO 13620 kHz
- **13630** — USSR, RADIO MOSCOW — (J) • DS-1
- **13630v** — COSTA RICA, †RADIO FOR PEACE, Ciudad Colón — C AMERICA & N AMERICA; Tu-Sa • C AMERICA & N AMERICA; C AMERICA; Sa/Su • C AMERICA & N AMERICA
- **13635** — SWITZERLAND, RED CROSS BC SVC, Sottens — Irr • M/Th • AUSTRALIA • 500 kW; Irr • M/Th • E ASIA • 500 kW
  - SWISS RADIO INTL, Sottens — AUSTRALIA • 500 kW; AFRICA • 500 kW; E ASIA • 500 kW; M-Sa • E ASIA • 500 kW; Su • E ASIA • 500 kW
- **13636** — USA, AFRTS-US MILITARY, Via Barford, UK — Irr • ATLANTIC • DS-ABC/CBS/NBC/NPR(FEEDER) • 4 kW • LSB
- **13645** — USSR, †RADIO KIEV, Khabarovsk — (J) • W NORTH AM • 100 kW
  - †RADIO MOSCOW, Khabarovsk — (J) • W NORTH AM • 100 kW; (J) • W NORTH AM • NORTH AMERICAN SVC • 100 kW
  - †RADIO VILNIUS, Khabarovsk — (J) • W NORTH AM • 100 kW
  - RADIO YEREVAN, Khabarovsk — (J) • W NORTH AM • 100 kW
  - †SOVIET BELORUSSIA, Khabarovsk — (J) • W NORTH AM • 100 kW
- **13650** — CANADA, †R CANADA INTL, Sackville, NB — (D) • EUROPE • 100 kW; (J) • EUROPE • 100 kW; (D) • M-Sa • EUROPE • 100 kW
- KOREA (DPR), RADIO PYONGYANG, Kujang-dong — C AMERICA • 400 kW
  - †RADIO PYONGYANG, Pyongyang — ASIA • 200 kW; SE ASIA • 200 kW
- **13651.3** — USA, AFRTS-US MILITARY, Via Barford, UK — Irr • ATLANTIC • DS-ABC/CBS/NBC/NPR(FEEDER) • 4 kW • LSB

World Time scale: 0 1 2 3 4 5 6 7 8 9 10 11 12 13 14 15 16 17 18 19 20 21 22 23 24

SUMMER ONLY (J)   WINTER ONLY (D)   JAMMING / OR ∧   EARLIEST HEARD ◁   LATEST HEARD ▷   NEW OR CHANGED FOR 1992 †

FREQUENCY   COUNTRY, STATION, LOCATION   TARGET • NETWORK • POWER (kW)   World Time

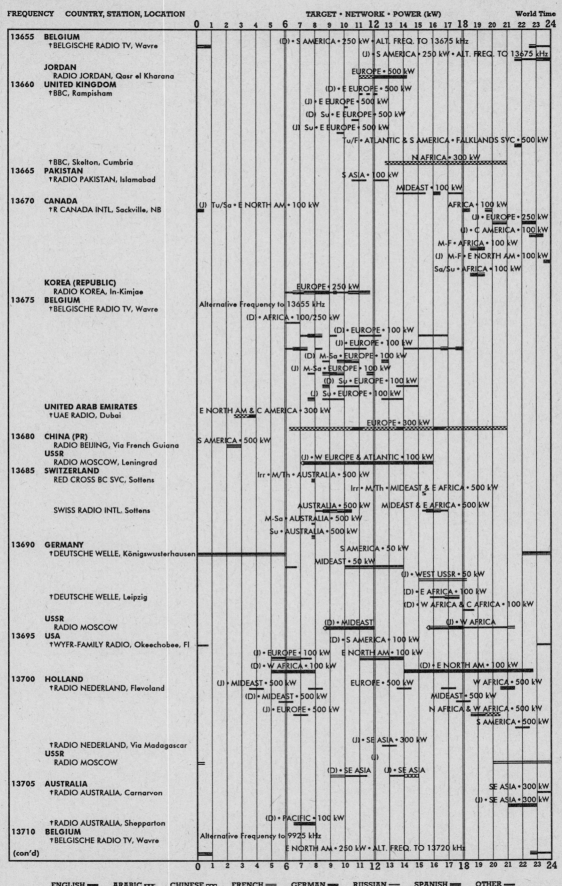

The following is the content of the schedule chart:

13655 BELGIUM
†BELGISCHE RADIO TV, Wavre
- (D) • S AMERICA • 250 kW • ALT. FREQ. TO 13675 kHz
- (J) • S AMERICA • 250 kW • ALT. FREQ. TO 13675 kHz

JORDAN
RADIO JORDAN, Qasr el Kharana
- EUROPE • 500 kW

13660 UNITED KINGDOM
†BBC, Rampisham
- (D) • E EUROPE • 500 kW
- (J) • E EUROPE • 500 kW
- (D) • Su • E EUROPE • 500 kW
- (J) • Su • E EUROPE • 500 kW
- Tu/F • ATLANTIC & S AMERICA • FALKLANDS SVC • 500 kW

†BBC, Skelton, Cumbria
- N AFRICA • 300 kW

13665 PAKISTAN
†RADIO PAKISTAN, Islamabad
- S ASIA • 100 kW
- MIDEAST • 100 kW

13670 CANADA
†R CANADA INTL, Sackville, NB
- (J) • Tu/Sa • E NORTH AM • 100 kW
- AFRICA • 100 kW
- (J) • EUROPE • 250 kW
- (J) • C AMERICA • 100 kW
- M-F • AFRICA • 100 kW
- (J) • M-F • E NORTH AM • 100 kW
- Sa/Su • AFRICA • 100 kW

KOREA (REPUBLIC)
RADIO KOREA, In-Kimjae
- EUROPE • 250 kW

13675 BELGIUM
†BELGISCHE RADIO TV, Wavre
- Alternative Frequency to 13655 kHz

13675 (Radio Korea)
- (D) • AFRICA • 100/250 kW
- (D) • EUROPE • 100 kW
- (J) • EUROPE • 100 kW
- (D) • M-Sa • EUROPE • 100 kW
- (J) • M-Sa • EUROPE • 100 kW
- (D) • Su • EUROPE • 100 kW
- (J) • Su • EUROPE • 100 kW

UNITED ARAB EMIRATES
†UAE RADIO, Dubai
- E NORTH AM & C AMERICA • 300 kW
- EUROPE • 300 kW

13680 CHINA (PR)
RADIO BEIJING, Via French Guiana
- S AMERICA • 500 kW

USSR
RADIO MOSCOW, Leningrad
- (J) • W EUROPE & ATLANTIC • 100 kW

13685 SWITZERLAND
RED CROSS BC SVC, Sottens
- Irr • M/Th • AUSTRALIA • 500 kW
- Irr • M/Th • MIDEAST & E AFRICA • 500 kW

SWISS RADIO INTL, Sottens
- AUSTRALIA • 500 kW
- MIDEAST & E AFRICA • 500 kW
- M-Sa • AUSTRALIA • 500 kW
- Su • AUSTRALIA • 500 kW

13690 GERMANY
†DEUTSCHE WELLE, Königswusterhausen
- S AMERICA • 50 kW
- MIDEAST • 50 kW
- (J) • WEST USSR • 50 kW

†DEUTSCHE WELLE, Leipzig
- (D) • E AFRICA • 100 kW
- (D) • W AFRICA & C AFRICA • 100 kW

USSR
RADIO MOSCOW
- (D) • MIDEAST
- (J) • W AFRICA

13695 USA
†WYFR-FAMILY RADIO, Okeechobee, Fl
- (D) • S AMERICA • 100 kW
- (J) • EUROPE • 100 kW
- E NORTH AM • 100 kW
- (D) • W AFRICA • 100 kW
- (D) • E NORTH AM • 100 kW

13700 HOLLAND
†RADIO NEDERLAND, Flevoland
- (J) • MIDEAST • 500 kW
- EUROPE • 500 kW
- W AFRICA • 500 kW
- (D) • MIDEAST • 500 kW
- MIDEAST • 500 kW
- (J) • EUROPE • 500 kW
- N AFRICA & W AFRICA • 500 kW
- S AMERICA • 500 kW

†RADIO NEDERLAND, Via Madagascar
- (J) • SE ASIA • 300 kW

USSR
RADIO MOSCOW
- (J)
- (D) • SE ASIA
- (J) • SE ASIA

13705 AUSTRALIA
†RADIO AUSTRALIA, Carnarvon
- SE ASIA • 300 kW
- (J) • SE ASIA • 300 kW

†RADIO AUSTRALIA, Shepparton
- (D) • PACIFIC • 100 kW

13710 BELGIUM
†BELGISCHE RADIO TV, Wavre
- Alternative Frequency to 9925 kHz
- E NORTH AM • 250 kW • ALT. FREQ. TO 13720 kHz

(con'd)

World Time scale: 0 1 2 3 4 5 6 7 8 9 10 11 12 13 14 15 16 17 18 19 20 21 22 23 24

ENGLISH ▬▬   ARABIC ⋙   CHINESE ░░░   FRENCH ▬▬   GERMAN ▬▬   RUSSIAN ══   SPANISH ▬▬   OTHER ——

FREQUENCY	COUNTRY, STATION, LOCATION	TARGET • NETWORK • POWER (kW)	World Time

TARGET • NETWORK • POWER (kW) — World Time scale: 0 1 2 3 4 5 6 7 8 9 10 11 12 13 14 15 16 17 18 19 20 21 22 23 24

13710 ITALY
(con'd)   VOICE OF EUROPE, Forni Alto — Alternative Frequency to 7538v kHz
USSR
†RADIO MOSCOW — DS-MAYAK
†RADIO VEDO, Volgograd — M-F • DS • 20 kW / M-W • DS • 20 kW

13715 CZECHOSLOVAKIA
†RADIO PRAGUE INTL — MIDEAST
USSR
RADIO MOSCOW — (D) • EUROPE

13720 BELGIUM
†BELGISCHE RADIO TV, Wavre — Alternative Frequency to 13710 kHz
CANADA
†R CANADA INTL, Sackville, NB — (D) M-F • S AMERICA • 250 kW
Su/M • S AMERICA • 250 kW
(J) Su/M • S AMERICA • 250 kW
Tu-Sa • S AMERICA • 250 kW

GUAM
†ADVENTIST WORLD R, Agat — E ASIA • 100 kW / S ASIA & SE ASIA • 100 kW
Sa/Su • E ASIA • 100 kW / SE ASIA • 100 kW / Sa/Su • E AFRICA • 100 kW
(J) • EAST USSR • 100 kW / Sa/Su • EAST USSR • 100 kW
Sa/Su • S ASIA & E AFRICA • 100 kW

USA
†CHRIST SCI MONITOR, Via Saipan — (D) Sa • S ASIA & SE ASIA • 100 kW
(D) Su-F • S ASIA & SE ASIA • 100 kW

13725 USSR
RADIO MOSCOW — (D) • SE ASIA

13730 AUSTRIA
RADIO AUSTRIA INTL, Vienna — N AMERICA • 100 kW / S AFRICA • 500 kW
EUROPE • 100 kW / S AMERICA • 100 kW
(D) • EUROPE • 100 kW
M-Sa • EUROPE • 100 kW / (D) • S AFRICA • 500 kW
(J) • EUROPE • 100 kW / (J) • S AFRICA • 500 kW
Su • EUROPE • 100 kW / M-Sa • S AFRICA • 500 kW
Su • S AFRICA • 500 kW

13735 USSR
†RADIO MOSCOW — (J) • WORLD SERVICE (FEEDER) • USB
WORLD SERVICE (FEEDER) • USB

13740 USA
†VOA, Cincinnati, Ohio — S AMERICA • 250 kW / (D) M-F • C AMERICA • 250 kW
(J) M-F • C AMERICA • 250 kW
†VOA, Delano, California — M-F • S AMERICA • 250 kW

13745 AUSTRALIA
†RADIO AUSTRALIA, Carnarvon — S ASIA & SE ASIA • 250/300 kW
UNITED KINGDOM
†BBC, Rampisham — (D) • E EUROPE • 500 kW
(D) • WEST USSR • 500 kW
(J) • E EUROPE • 500 kW
Su • E EUROPE • 500 kW
(D) Su • E EUROPE • 500 kW
(J) Su • E EUROPE • 500 kW

USSR
RADIO MOSCOW — (D) • EUROPE / (J) • S ASIA

13753 ISRAEL
†RASHUTH HASHIDUR, Tel Aviv — E EUROPE & WEST USSR • DS-B • 20/300 kW
Su-F • E EUROPE & WEST USSR • DS-B • 20/300 kW

13760 GERMANY
DEUTSCHE WELLE, Wertachtal — (D) • E ASIA • 500 kW
KOREA (DPR)
†RADIO PYONGYANG, Kujang-dong — C AMERICA • 400 kW
USA
†CHRIST SCI MONITOR, South Carolina — Alternative Frequency to 9455 kHz
S AMERICA • 500 kW / W NORTH AM & C AMERICA • 500 kW • ALT. FREQ. TO 17555 kHz
C AMERICA • 500 kW
C AMERICA & AUSTRALIA • 500 kW
M • S AMERICA • 500 kW / M-F • C AMERICA • 500 kW
M • C AMERICA • 500 kW / Sa/Su • C AMERICA • 500 kW
M-F • C AMERICA & AUSTRALIA • 500 kW
M-F • W NORTH AM & C AMERICA • 500 kW • ALT. FREQ. TO 17555 kHz
M-Sa • S AMERICA • 500 kW
Sa-M • S AMERICA • 500 kW
Sa-M • C AMERICA • 500 kW
Sa/Su • C AMERICA & AUSTRALIA • 500 kW
(con'd)   Sa/Su • W NORTH AM & C AMERICA • 500 kW • ALT. FREQ. TO 17555 kHz

World Time scale: 0 1 2 3 4 5 6 7 8 9 10 11 12 13 14 15 16 17 18 19 20 21 22 23 24

SUMMER ONLY (J)   WINTER ONLY (D)   JAMMING / OR ∧   EARLIEST HEARD ◁   LATEST HEARD ▷   NEW OR CHANGED FOR 1992 †

FREQUENCY   COUNTRY, STATION, LOCATION   TARGET • NETWORK • POWER (kW)   World Time

World Time scale: 0 1 2 3 4 5 6 7 8 9 10 11 12 13 14 15 16 17 18 19 20 21 22 23 24

Frequency	Country, Station, Location	Target • Network • Power
13760 (con'd)	**USA** †CHRIST SCI MONITOR, South Carolina	Su • S AMERICA • 500 kW
		Tu-F • S AMERICA • 500 kW
		Tu-F • C AMERICA • 500 kW
		Tu-Su • S AMERICA • 500 kW
		Tu-Su • C AMERICA • 500 kW
	†WORLD HARVEST R, Noblesville, Indiana	M-Sa • E NORTH AM & W EUROPE • 100 kW
		Su • E NORTH AM & W EUROPE • 100 kW
		ENGLISH, ETC • E NORTH AM & W EUROPE • 100 kW
	WYFR-FAMILY RADIO, Okeechobee, Fl	(J) • EUROPE • 100 kW
	USSR †RADIO MOSCOW, Moscow	(J) • DS-1 (FEEDER) • 15 kW • USB
13770	**GERMANY** †DEUTSCHE WELLE, Königswusterhausen	N AMERICA • 100 kW
		(J) • N AMERICA • 100 kW
	HOLLAND †RADIO NEDERLAND, Flevoland	(J) • E EUROPE & MIDEAST • 500 kW
		S ASIA • 500 kW
		MIDEAST • 500 kW
	USA †CHRIST SCI MONITOR, Maine	(J) Sa/Su • EUROPE • 500 kW
		(D) • EUROPE • 500 kW
		(D) M-F • EUROPE • 500 kW
		(D) Sa • EUROPE • 500 kW
		(D) Sa/Su • EUROPE • 500 kW
		(D) Su-F • EUROPE • 500 kW
	CHRIST SCI MONITOR, South Carolina	(J) M-F • E NORTH AM • 500 kW
		(J) Sa • E NORTH AM • 500 kW
		(J) Su-F • E NORTH AM • 500 kW
		(J) Su • E NORTH AM • 500 kW
13775	**USA** VOA, Greenville, NC	C AMERICA • 250 kW
		Sa/Su • C AMERICA • 250 kW
	USSR RADIO MOSCOW	(J) • E ASIA
13780	**GERMANY** †DEUTSCHE WELLE, Jülich	(D) • AUSTRALIA • 100 kW EUROPE • 100 kW (J) • E ASIA • 100 kW
		MIDEAST • 100 kW
		E NORTH AM & C AMERICA • 100 kW
		(J) • E NORTH AM & C AMERICA • 100 kW
	†DEUTSCHE WELLE, Königswusterhausen	(J) • MIDEAST • 100 kW
		(J) • 100 kW
	†DEUTSCHE WELLE, Nauen	(J) • MIDEAST • 100 kW
	†DEUTSCHE WELLE, Various Locations	MIDEAST • 250/500 kW
	DEUTSCHE WELLE, Wertachtal	(D) • E ASIA • 500 kW
	MONGOLIA †RADIO ULAANBAATAR, Ulaanbaatar	M-Sa • E ASIA • 50/100 kW
13785	**NEW ZEALAND** †R NEW ZEALAND INTL, Rangitaiki	Su-F • ENGLISH, ETC • PACIFIC • 100 kW
13790	**GERMANY** †DEUTSCHE WELLE, Jülich	W AFRICA • 100 kW
		(J) • MIDEAST • 100 kW
	†DEUTSCHE WELLE, Königswusterhausen	(J) • N AMERICA • 100 kW
	†DEUTSCHE WELLE, Various Locations	S AMERICA • 100/250 kW
	†DEUTSCHE WELLE, Wertachtal	AFRICA • 500 kW
13795	**USSR** †RADIO KIEV	EUROPE & WEST USSR
	†RADIO MOSCOW	DS-MAYAK
		DS-2
	†UKRAINIAN RADIO	
13810	**USSR** KAZAKH TELEGRAPH, Alma-Ata	M/W/F • DS-DICTATION NEWS • 15 kW
	KAZAKH TELEGRAPH, Alma-ata	M/W/F • DS-DICTATION NEWS • 15 kW
13820	**USSR** †RADIO MOSCOW, Moscow	DS-MAYAK (FEEDER) • 15 kW • ISL
		DS-1 (FEEDER) • 15 kW • ISU
13830	**ICELAND** †RIKISUTVARPID, Reykjavik	ATLANTIC & EUROPE • DS-1 • 10 kW • USB
13855	**ICELAND** †RIKISUTVARPID, Reykjavik	ATLANTIC & E NORTH AM • DS-1 • 10 kW • USB
		ATLANTIC & EUROPE • DS-1 • 10 kW • USB
14410	**USSR** †RADIO MOSCOW, Moscow	(J) • DS-MAYAK (FEEDER) • 15 kW • USB

World Time scale: 0 1 2 3 4 5 6 7 8 9 10 11 12 13 14 15 16 17 18 19 20 21 22 23 24

ENGLISH ▬▬   ARABIC ▨▨   CHINESE ▭▭   FRENCH ══   GERMAN ▬▬   RUSSIAN ═══   SPANISH ▬▬   OTHER ▬▬

FREQUENCY   COUNTRY, STATION, LOCATION

TARGET • NETWORK • POWER (kW)   World Time

0 1 2 3 4 5 6 7 8 9 10 11 12 13 14 15 16 17 18 19 20 21 22 23 24

FREQUENCY	COUNTRY, STATION, LOCATION	TARGET • NETWORK • POWER (kW)
14526	**USA** †VOA, Greenville, NC	EUROPE & MIDEAST • (FEEDER) • 40 kW • ISU
		EUROPE & MIDEAST • (FEEDER) • 40 kW • ISL
		(D) • EUROPE & MIDEAST • (FEEDER) • 40 kW • ISL
		(D) • EUROPE & MIDEAST • (FEEDER) • 40 kW • ISU
		(J) • EUROPE & MIDEAST • (FEEDER) • 40 kW • ISL
		(J) • EUROPE & MIDEAST • (FEEDER) • 40 kW • ISU
14850	**USSR** †RADIO MOSCOW, Moscow	DS-1 • 20 kW • USB
14917.7	**KIRIBATI** †RADIO KIRIBATI, Betio	Irr • ENGLISH, ETC • DS(FEEDER) • 10 kW • USB
		Irr • DS(FEEDER) • 10 kW • USB M-Sa • ENGLISH, ETC • DS(FEEDER) • 10 kW • USB
		Sa • ENGLISH, ETC • DS(FEEDER) • 10 kW • USB
15000	**USA** WWV, Ft Collins, Colorado	WEATHER/WORLD TIME • 10 kW
	WWVH, Kekaha, Hawaii	WEATHER/WORLD TIME • 10 kW
15009v	**VIETNAM** VOICE OF VIETNAM, Ha Son Binh	(J) • SE ASIA • 30 kW
		(J) • E ASIA & AMERICAS • 30 kW
		(J) • AFRICA • 30 kW
		(J) • EUROPE • 30 kW
15020	**INDIA** ALL INDIA RADIO, Aligarh	S ASIA • 250 kW
15030v	**COSTA RICA** †RADIO FOR PEACE, Ciudad Colón	N AMERICA
		Tu-Sa • N AMERICA Sa/Su • N AMERICA
15039.5	**CLANDESTINE (N AMER)** "VOICE OF TOMORROW", Virginia, USA	Irr • E NORTH AM • NEO-NAZI PARTY
15045v	**PIRATE (EUROPE)** †"WEEKEND MUSIC R", Scotland	Irr • Su • W EUROPE • 0.1 kW
15050	**INDIA** ALL INDIA RADIO, Aligarh	E ASIA • 250 kW
	PIRATE (EUROPE) †"RADIO TOWER"	Irr • E NORTH AM
15050v	**CLANDESTINE (M EAST)** "VO KURDISH PEOPLE, Middle East	Irr • Sa-Th • MIDEAST • ANTI-IRAQI GOVT MIDEAST • ANTI-IRAQI GOVT
		Irr • F • MIDEAST • ANTI-IRAQI GOVT
15060	**SAUDI ARABIA** †BS OF THE KINGDOM, Riyadh	MIDEAST • 350 kW
15070	**UNITED KINGDOM** †BBC, Daventry	(J) • C AMERICA • 300 kW
		N AFRICA • 300 kW
		(J) • N AFRICA • 300 kW
	†BBC, Multiple Locations	EUROPE • 250/300/500 kW
	†BBC, Woofferton	(J) • E NORTH AM • 250 kW
15084	**IRAN** †VO THE ISLAMIC REP, Tehrān	MIDEAST • 100/350 kW
		DS • 100/350 kW
15090	**VATICAN STATE** †VATICAN RADIO, Sta Maria di Galeria	E AFRICA • 100/250 kW
		AFRICA • 100/250 kW
		(J) • S ASIA • 500 kW S ASIA • 500 kW
15095	**PHILIPPINES** †FEBC RADIO INTL, Iba	E ASIA • 100 kW
	SYRIA SYRIAN BC SERVICE, Adhra	S AMERICA • 500 kW
		MIDEAST • 500 kW (J) • EUROPE • 500 kW
		DS • 500 kW (J) • WEST USSR • 500 kW
		(J) • N AMERICA • 500 kW
15100	**CHINA (PR)** RADIO BEIJING	(J) • N AFRICA
	RADIO BEIJING, Baoding	(D) • W NORTH AM, C AMERICA & S AMERICA • 240 kW
		(J) • E NORTH AM, C AMERICA & S AMERICA • 240 kW
	CLANDESTINE (M EAST) †"IRAN FREEDOM FLAG, Egypt	MIDEAST • ANTI-IRANIAN GOVT • 100 kW
	ISRAEL †KOL ISRAEL, Tel Aviv	(J) • E EUROPE & WEST USSR • 100 kW
		MIDEAST • DS-D
	PHILIPPINES †FEBC RADIO INTL, Bocaue	SE ASIA • 50 kW
		Sa • SE ASIA • 50 kW
		Sa-M • SE ASIA • 50 kW
	USSR †ARMENIAN RADIO, Serpukhov	RUSSIAN, ETC • DS-1 • 20 kW
15105	**CUBA** †RADIO HABANA, Havana	Alternative Frequency to 15230 kHz
(con'd)	**GERMANY** DEUTSCHE WELLE, Jülich	(J) • AUSTRALIA • 100 kW

0 1 2 3 4 5 6 7 8 9 10 11 12 13 14 15 16 17 18 19 20 21 22 23 24

SUMMER ONLY (J)   WINTER ONLY (D)   JAMMING / OR ∧   EARLIEST HEARD ◁   LATEST HEARD ▷   NEW OR CHANGED FOR 1992 †

FREQUENCY COUNTRY, STATION, LOCATION | TARGET • NETWORK • POWER (kW) | World Time

0 1 2 3 4 5 6 7 8 9 10 11 12 13 14 15 16 17 18 19 20 21 22 23 24

Frequency	Country, Station, Location	Target • Network • Power
15105 (con'd)	**GERMANY**	
	DEUTSCHE WELLE, Multiple Locations	S ASIA • 100/250 kW
	†DEUTSCHE WELLE, Various Locations	(D) • E ASIA • 100/500 kW
	DEUTSCHE WELLE, Via Antigua	S AMERICA • 250 kW
	DEUTSCHE WELLE, Via Cyclops, Malta	(J) • E NORTH AM & C AMERICA • 250 kW
	†DEUTSCHE WELLE, Via Sri Lanka	(J) • E ASIA • 250 kW S AFRICA • 250 kW
		(J) • SE ASIA • 250 kW
	†DEUTSCHE WELLE, Wertachtal	(J) • MIDEAST • 500 kW
	MOROCCO	
	RTV MAROCAINE, Tangier	E EUROPE, N AFRICA & MIDEAST • 50 kW
	UNITED KINGDOM	
	BBC, Daventry	(J) • WEST USSR • 100 kW
	†BBC, Via Ascension	C AFRICA • 250 kW W AFRICA • 250 kW S AFRICA • 250 kW
		W AFRICA & C AFRICA • 250 kW
	USA	
	VOA, Via Kaválla, Greece	(J) • MIDEAST & S ASIA • 250 kW
	†WORLD HARVEST R, Noblesville, Indiana	C AMERICA • 100 kW
		Su • C AMERICA • 100 kW
	VATICAN STATE	
	†VATICAN RADIO, Sta Maria di Galeria	(J) • E ASIA • 500 kW
		(J) • E ASIA & SE ASIA • 500 kW
		(J) • AUSTRALIA • 500 kW
		M-Sa • ENGLISH, FRENCH, SPANISH & ITALIAN • MIDEAST • 100 kW
15110	**BULGARIA**	
	†RADIO SOFIA, Sofia	(J) • S AMERICA • 250 kW
	CLANDESTINE (ASIA)	
	"DEM KAMPUCHEA", Beijing, China (PR)	SE ASIA • PRO-KHMER ROUGE • 120 kW
	INDIA	
	†ALL INDIA RADIO, Delhi	Alternative Frequency to 17830 kHz
	PHILIPPINES	
	RADIO VERITAS ASIA, Palauig	USSR • 250 kW
	SPAIN	
	†R EXTERIOR ESPANA, Noblejas	E NORTH AM & C AMERICA • 350 kW
	USSR	
	RADIO MOSCOW, Kazan	S ASIA • 100 kW
	RADIO MOSCOW, Tbilisi	MIDEAST & E AFRICA • 500 kW
15110v	**CHINA (PR)**	
	RADIO BEIJING, Via Bamako, Mali	N AMERICA • 50 kW (J) • W AFRICA & C AFRICA • 50 kW
		(J) • C AFRICA & E AFRICA • 50 kW
15114.4	**PAKISTAN**	
	†RADIO PAKISTAN, Karachi	S ASIA & SE ASIA • 50 kW
15115	**ECUADOR**	
	HCJB-VO THE ANDES, Quito	AMERICAS • 100 kW
	EGYPT	
	RADIO CAIRO, Abu Za'bal	W AFRICA • 100 kW
	FINLAND	
	RADIO FINLAND, Pori	EUROPE & W AFRICA • 500 kW
	KOREA (DPR)	
	RADIO PYONGYANG, Kujang-dong	C AMERICA • 400 kW
	UNITED KINGDOM	
	†BBC, Rampisham	(D) • E EUROPE • 500 kW
		(D) • EUROPE & WEST USSR • 500 kW
		(J) • EUROPE & WEST USSR • 500 kW
		(D) Su • WEST USSR • 500 kW
		(J) Su • WEST USSR • 500 kW
	†BBC, Skelton, Cumbria	(D) • EUROPE & WEST USSR • 250 kW
		(J) • EUROPE & WEST USSR • 250 kW
	USA	
	†RFE-RL, Via Portugal	E EUROPE • 250 kW
		(D) • E EUROPE • 250 kW
		(J) • E EUROPE • 250 kW
	†VOA, Greenville, NC	W AFRICA • 500 kW
	†VOA, Via Kaválla, Greece	(D) • MIDEAST • 250 kW
	†VOA, Via Tangier, Morocco	EUROPE • 100 kW
	USSR	
	RADIO MOSCOW	(J)
15120	**HOLLAND**	
	†RADIO NEDERLAND, Via Neth Antilles	Su • C AMERICA • 300 kW
	INDIA	
	†ALL INDIA RADIO, Aligarh	SE ASIA • 250 kW
		E AFRICA • 250 kW
		E ASIA • CHINESE, CANTONESE • 250 kW
	†ALL INDIA RADIO, Delhi	(J) • DS • 50 kW
(con'd)		(J) • ENGLISH, ETC • DS • 50 kW

0 1 2 3 4 5 6 7 8 9 10 11 12 13 14 15 16 17 18 19 20 21 22 23 24

ENGLISH ▬   ARABIC ▩   CHINESE ☐☐☐   FRENCH ═   GERMAN ▬   RUSSIAN ═   SPANISH ▬   OTHER ▬

FREQUENCY	COUNTRY, STATION, LOCATION	TARGET • NETWORK • POWER (kW)	World Time

15120 **PHILIPPINES**
(con'd) †RADIO VERITAS ASIA, Palauig — Alternative Frequency to 15215 kHz
SEYCHELLES
†FAR EAST BC ASS'N, North Pt, Mahé Is — MIDEAST • 100 kW
SOUTH AFRICA
†RADIO RSA, Meyerton — (D) • E AFRICA • 100 kW
SRI LANKA
†SRI LANKA BC CORP, Colombo-Ekala — E ASIA • 35 kW / EUROPE • 35/100 kW
USA
†VOA, Greenville, NC — (D) • C AMERICA • 500 kW
— (J) • C AMERICA • 500 kW
— M-F • C AMERICA & S AMERICA • 500 kW
— (D) Sa/Su • C AMERICA • 500 kW
— (J) Sa/Su • C AMERICA • 500 kW

†VOA, Via Philippines — (D) • E ASIA • 250 kW

15125 **CHINA (PR)**
RADIO BEIJING — (J) • SE ASIA
— (J) • S ASIA

CHINA (TAIWAN)
BC CORP CHINA — E ASIA • DS(FM-1)
UNITED KINGDOM
†BBC, Via Maşirah, Oman — SE ASIA • 100 kW
USA
†VOA, Via Kaválla, Greece — (J) • MIDEAST & S ASIA • 250 kW

†VOA, Via Philippines — SE ASIA • 250 kW

†VOA, Via Tangier, Morocco — (J) • E EUROPE • 100 kW / (D) • E EUROPE • 100 kW
USSR
RADIO MOSCOW, Moscow — EUROPE • 250 kW

15130 **CHINA (TAIWAN)**
VO FREE CHINA, Via Okeechobee, USA — S AMERICA • 100 kW
USA
†RFE-RL, Via Pals, Spain — (D) • WEST USSR • 250 kW

†RFE-RL, Via Portugal — (J) • WEST USSR • 250 kW

WYFR-FAMILY RADIO, Okeechobee, Fl — S AMERICA • 100 kW
— C AMERICA • 50 kW
— (D) • S AMERICA • 100 kW

15130v **CHINA (PR)**
RADIO BEIJING, Via Bamako, Mali — (J) • N AMERICA • 50 kW / (D) • C AFRICA & E AFRICA • 50 kW
— (D) • E NORTH AM & C AMERICA • 50 kW

15135 **CHINA (PR)**
RADIO BEIJING, Kunming — SE ASIA • 120 kW
FRANCE
†R FRANCE INTL, Issoudun-Allouis — E AFRICA • 100 kW
— (D) • E AFRICA • 100 kW
— (J) • E AFRICA • 100 kW

GERMANY
†DEUTSCHE WELLE, Wertachtal — (D) • AFRICA • 500 kW
INDIA
†ALL INDIA RADIO, Aligarh — SE ASIA • 250 kW
— MIDEAST • 250 kW

UNITED KINGDOM
†BBC, Rampisham — (J) • WEST USSR • 500 kW

†BBC, Skelton, Cumbria — (J) F • E EUROPE • 250 kW
— (J) • E EUROPE • 250 kW
— (J) Sa/Su • E EUROPE • 250 kW
— (J) Su • E EUROPE • 250 kW

15139v **CHILE**
†RADIO NACIONAL, Santiago — AMERICAS • VERY IRREGULAR • 60 kW
15140 **CANADA**
†R CANADA INTL, Sackville, NB — (D) • EUROPE • 250 kW
CUBA
†RADIO HABANA, Havana — (J) • C AMERICA & S AMERICA • 50 kW
— (J) • N AMERICA • 50 kW

INDIA
†ALL INDIA RADIO, Bangalore — (J) • WEST USSR • 500 kW
PHILIPPINES
†RADIO VERITAS ASIA, Palauig — MIDEAST • 250 kW
— Sa-M • MIDEAST • 250 kW

PORTUGAL
R PORTUGAL INTL, Lisbon — Sa/Su • C AMERICA • 100 kW
SAUDI ARABIA
BS OF THE KINGDOM, Jiddah — WEST USSR • DS-GENERAL • 50 kW
UNITED KINGDOM
†BBC, Via Ascension — M-F • C AMERICA • 250 kW
USSR
RADIO MOSCOW, Ryazan' — S ASIA & SE ASIA • 240 kW
— (J) • S ASIA & SE ASIA • 240 kW

RADIO MOSCOW, Tbilisi — (J) • W AFRICA • 500 kW
15145 **GERMANY**
(con'd) †DEUTSCHE WELLE, Nauen — C AFRICA & E AFRICA • 500 kW

World Time scale: 0 1 2 3 4 5 6 7 8 9 10 11 12 13 14 15 16 17 18 19 20 21 22 23 24

SUMMER ONLY (J)   WINTER ONLY (D)   JAMMING / OR ∧   EARLIEST HEARD ◁   LATEST HEARD ▷   NEW OR CHANGED FOR 1992 †

FREQUENCY	COUNTRY, STATION, LOCATION	TARGET • NETWORK • POWER (kW)	World Time

0 1 2 3 4 5 6 7 8 9 10 11 12 13 14 15 16 17 18 19 20 21 22 23 24

15145 GERMANY
(con'd) †DEUTSCHE WELLE, Nauen — (D) • C AFRICA & E AFRICA • 500 kW
UNITED KINGDOM
†BBC, Rampisham — (D) • EUROPE • 500 kW
†BBC, Via Zyyi, Cyprus — (D) Su • WEST USSR • 250 kW
USA
†RFE-RL, Via Pals, Spain — (D) • WEST USSR • 250 kW
†RFE-RL, Via Portugal — (J) • WEST USSR • 250 kW
†VOA, Via Kaválla, Greece — (D) • MIDEAST & S ASIA • 250 kW
— (J) • MIDEAST • 250 kW
†VOA, Via Tangier, Morocco — (D) • EUROPE • 35 kW
WINB-WORLD INTL BC, Red Lion, Pa — S AMERICA • 50 kW
M • S AMERICA • 50 kW
ENGLISH, ETC • EUROPE & N AFRICA • 50 kW
Su • S AMERICA • 50 kW
Su/M • S AMERICA • 50 kW
Tu-Sa • S AMERICA • 50 kW
†WYFR-FAMILY RADIO, Okeechobee, Fl — (J) • C AMERICA • 100 kW
USSR
RADIO MOSCOW — (J) • SE ASIA
15150 CANADA
R CANADA INTL, Sackville, NB — AFRICA • 250 kW
CHINA (PR)
RADIO BEIJING — (J) • SE ASIA
HOLLAND
RADIO NEDERLAND, Via Madagascar — S ASIA • 300 kW
USA
VOA, Via Philippines — M-F • E AFRICA • 250 kW
USSR
RADIO MOSCOW, Minsk — EUROPE, E NORTH AM & C AMERICA • 100 kW
RADIO MOSCOW, Multiple Locations — E AFRICA, EUROPE & ATLANTIC • 240/500 kW
15154.6 INDONESIA
†RRI, Jakarta, Jawa — DS • 250 kW
15155 ECUADOR
†HCJB-VO THE ANDES, Quito — N AMERICA & C AMERICA • 100 kW
N AMERICA & C AMERICA • 100 kW • ALT. FREQ. TO 6230 kHz
EGYPT
RADIO CAIRO, Abu Za'bal — E AFRICA • 100 kW
FRANCE
†R FRANCE INTL, Issoudun-Allouis — (J) • E AFRICA • 100 kW
E EUROPE & WEST USSR • 100 kW
(D) • E AFRICA • 100 kW
(D) • E EUROPE & WEST USSR • 100 kW
(J) • E EUROPE & WEST USSR • 100 kW
†R FRANCE INTL, Multiple Locations — E AFRICA • 100/250 kW
GERMANY
DEUTSCHE WELLE, Via Sines, Portugal — (J) • E EUROPE • 250 kW
HOLLAND
†RADIO NEDERLAND, Flevoland — S AMERICA • 500 kW
UNITED KINGDOM
†BBC, Rampisham — (J) • E EUROPE & MIDEAST • 500 kW
USA
†VOA, Via Philippines — E ASIA • 250 kW
USSR
†BELORUSSIAN RADIO, Minsk — RUSSIAN, ETC • DS-2 • 20 kW
RADIO MOSCOW, Kazan' — (J) • S ASIA • 250 kW
15160 ALGERIA
RTV ALGERIENNE, Algiers — Irr • S AMERICA • 100 kW
EUROPE • DS • 100 kW
AUSTRALIA
†RADIO AUSTRALIA, Shepparton — (J) • PACIFIC • 100 kW
PACIFIC • 100 kW
BULGARIA
†RADIO SOFIA, Sofia — W AFRICA • 250 kW
EUROPE • 250 kW
HUNGARY
†RADIO BUDAPEST, Jászberény — S AMERICA • 250 kW
M • S AMERICA • 250 kW
MEXICO
†LV AMERICA LATINA, México City — DS-VERY IRREGULAR • 10 kW
TURKEY
VOICE OF TURKEY, Ankara — N AFRICA • 250 kW
F • N AFRICA • 250 kW
UNITED KINGDOM
BBC, Via Ascension — S AFRICA • 250 kW
USA
†VOA, Via Kaválla, Greece — MIDEAST • 250 kW
(J) • S ASIA • 250 kW
VOA, Via Philippines — E ASIA • 250 kW
(con'd) VOICE OF THE OAS, Cincinnati, Ohio — C AMERICA & S AMERICA • 250 kW

0 1 2 3 4 5 6 7 8 9 10 11 12 13 14 15 16 17 18 19 20 21 22 23 24

ENGLISH ▬ ARABIC ∑∑∑ CHINESE □□□ FRENCH ═ GERMAN ▬ RUSSIAN ═ SPANISH ▬ OTHER ▬

FREQUENCY   COUNTRY, STATION, LOCATION

TARGET • NETWORK • POWER (kW)   World Time

15160 (con'd)	**USA** VOICE OF THE OAS, Cincinnati, Ohio	M-Sa • C AMERICA & S AMERICA • 250 kW Su • C AMERICA & S AMERICA • 250 kW	
15165	**CHINA (PR)** RADIO BEIJING		(J) • E AFRICA & S AFRICA (J) • C AFRICA & W AFRICA (J) • EUROPE
	RADIO BEIJING, Xi'an	SE ASIA • 150 kW S ASIA • 150 kW AUSTRALIA • CHINESE, CANTONESE • 150 kW	
	DENMARK †DANMARKS RADIO, Via Norway	EUROPE & W AFRICA • 500 kW ATLANTIC • 350 kW (D) • E NORTH AM & C AMERICA • 350 kW	(J) • ATLANTIC & E NORTH AM • 350 kW (J) • E NORTH AM & C AMERICA • 350 kW
	INDIA †ALL INDIA RADIO, Aligarh	E AFRICA • 250 kW	
	†ALL INDIA RADIO, Bangalore	SE ASIA • 500 kW	
	†ALL INDIA RADIO, Delhi	S ASIA • 100 kW DS • 100 kW ENGLISH & HINDI • DS • 100 kW	
	NORWAY †RADIO NORWAY INTL, Fredrikstad	ATLANTIC • 350 kW (D) • N AMERICA • 350 kW	(J) • E NORTH AM & C AMERICA • 350 kW (J) • M-F • ATLANTIC & E NORTH AM • 350 kW (J) • Sa/Su • ATLANTIC & E NORTH AM • 350 kW
	†RADIO NORWAY INTL, Kvitsøy	EUROPE & W AFRICA • 500 kW	
	UNITED KINGDOM †BBC, Via Zyyi, Cyprus	SE ASIA • 250 kW	
	USA VOA, Via Philippines		E AFRICA • 250 kW
	YUGOSLAVIA †RADIO YUGOSLAVIA, Bijeljina		W AFRICA • 500 kW S AFRICA • 500 kW (J) • N AFRICA • 500 kW
15170	**AUSTRALIA** †RADIO AUSTRALIA, Darwin	(D) • E ASIA & SE ASIA • 250 kW (J) • E ASIA & SE ASIA • 250 kW	(D) • E ASIA • 250 kW
	KOREA (REPUBLIC) †RADIO KOREA, In-Kimjae	N AMERICA • 250 kW	
	SAUDI ARABIA BS OF THE KINGDOM, Jiddah	C AFRICA • DS-HOLY KORAN • 50 kW	
	SWAZILAND †TRANS WORLD RADIO, Manzini	S ASIA • 100 kW	
	USA †RFE-RL, Via Germany	(J) • WEST USSR & MIDEAST • 100 kW	
	†RFE-RL, Via Portugal	(D) • WEST USSR & MIDEAST • 250 kW (J) • WEST USSR & MIDEAST • 250 kW	WEST USSR & MIDEAST • 250 kW
	†VOA, Via Portugal		(J) • E EUROPE • 250 kW
	†WYFR-FAMILY RADIO, Okeechobee, Fl	(J) • S AMERICA • 100 kW (D) • S AMERICA • 100 kW	
	USSR RADIO MOSCOW, Irkutsk	SE ASIA • 50 kW (J) • SE ASIA • 50 kW	
15171v	**FRENCH POLYNESIA** †RFO-TAHITI, Papeete	PACIFIC • DS-FRENCH, TAHITIAN • 20 kW	
15175	**DENMARK** †DANMARKS RADIO, Via Norway	(J) • SE ASIA & AUSTRALIA • 500 kW • ALT. FREQ. TO 15180 kHz (J) • MIDEAST • 500 kW (J) • MIDEAST & E AFRICA • 500 kW	(J) • EUROPE & AFRICA • 350 kW
	EGYPT RADIO CAIRO, Abu Za'bal	MIDEAST • DS-GENERAL • 100 kW	
	RADIO CAIRO, Kafr Silim-Abis		MIDEAST & S ASIA • 250 kW
	INDIA ALL INDIA RADIO, Aligarh	SE ASIA • 250 kW	
	NORWAY †RADIO NORWAY INTL, Fredrikstad		(J) • M-F • EUROPE & AFRICA • 350 kW (J) • Sa/Su • EUROPE & AFRICA • 350 kW
	†RADIO NORWAY INTL, Kvitsøy	(J) • SE ASIA & AUSTRALIA • 500 kW • ALT. FREQ. TO 15180 kHz (J) • MIDEAST • 500 kW (J) • MIDEAST & E AFRICA • 500 kW	
	USSR (con'd) †BELORUSSIAN RADIO, Minsk		RUSSIAN, ETC • DS-1 • 20 kW

SUMMER ONLY (J)   WINTER ONLY (D)   JAMMING / OR ∧   EARLIEST HEARD ◁   LATEST HEARD ▷   NEW OR CHANGED FOR 1992 †

FREQUENCY	COUNTRY, STATION, LOCATION	TARGET • NETWORK • POWER (kW) / World Time

0 1 2 3 4 5 6 7 8 9 10 11 12 13 14 15 16 17 18 19 20 21 22 23 24

15175 (con'd) **USSR**
RADIO MOSCOW, Armavir — (J) • EUROPE, ATLANTIC & E NORTH AM • 500 kW
(J) • W EUROPE • 500 kW

15180 DENMARK
†DANMARKS RADIO, Via Norway — Alternative Frequency to 15175 kHz
FRANCE
†R FRANCE INTL, Issoudun-Allouis — E EUROPE & WEST USSR • 500 kW
(J) • E EUROPE & WEST USSR • 500 kW
KOREA (DPR)
RADIO PYONGYANG, Kujang-dong — SE ASIA • 200 kW
NORWAY
†RADIO NORWAY INTL, Kvitsøy — Alternative Frequency to 15175 kHz
UNITED KINGDOM
†BBC, Rampisham — N AFRICA & W AFRICA • 500 kW
USA
VOA, Via Philippines — S ASIA & SE ASIA • 50 kW
USSR
†AZERBAIJANI RADIO, Tula — DS-2 • 20 kW
†R TIKHIY OKEAN, Komsomol'sk 'Amure — (J) • PACIFIC & W NORTH AM • MARINERS • 100 kW
†RADIO KIEV, Komsomol'sk 'Amure — W NORTH AM • 100 kW
†RADIO MOSCOW, Komsomol'sk 'Amure — W NORTH AM • 100 kW
W NORTH AM • NORTH AMERICAN SVC • 100 kW
(J) • W NORTH AM • NORTH AMERICAN SVC • 100 kW
†RADIO VILNIUS, Komsomol'sk 'Amure — W NORTH AM • 100 kW
RADIO YEREVAN, Komsomol'sk 'Amure — W NORTH AM • 100 kW
†SOV BELORUSSIA, Komsomol'sk 'Amure — W NORTH AM • 100 kW

15185 FINLAND
†RADIO FINLAND, Pori — (J) • N AMERICA • 500 kW
(D) • MIDEAST & E AFRICA • 500 kW
(J) • MIDEAST & E AFRICA • 500 kW
(J) • EUROPE & W AFRICA • 100 kW • USB
GERMANY
†DEUTSCHE WELLE, Jülich — (J) • WEST USSR • 100 kW
(D) • SE ASIA • 100 kW
†DEUTSCHE WELLE, Various Locations — E ASIA • 100/250 kW
†DEUTSCHE WELLE, Via Sri Lanka — (D) • E ASIA • 250 kW
DEUTSCHE WELLE, Wertachtal — W AFRICA • 500 kW
INDIA
†ALL INDIA RADIO, Aligarh — (J) • DS • 250 kW
(J) • ENGLISH, ETC • DS • 250 kW
†ALL INDIA RADIO, Bangalore — MIDEAST & N AFRICA • 500 kW
†ALL INDIA RADIO, Delhi — (J) • DS • 100 kW
(J) • ENGLISH & HINDI • DS • 100 kW
USA
VOA, Greenville, NC — M-F • C AMERICA • 250 kW
VOA, Via Philippines — SE ASIA • 50 kW
S ASIA • 250 kW
WINB-WORLD INTL BC, Red Lion, Pa — EUROPE & N AFRICA • 50 kW
USSR
RADIO MOSCOW, Zhigulevsk — S ASIA • 240 kW
DS-1 • 240 kW

15190 BRAZIL
R INCONFIDENCIA, Belo Horizonte — DS • 5 kW
FRANCE
R FRANCE INTL, Issoudun-Allouis — E EUROPE & WEST USSR • 100/500 kW
S AMERICA • 100 kW
(D) • E EUROPE & WEST USSR • 100/500 kW
(J) • S AMERICA • 100 kW
(J) • E EUROPE & WEST USSR • 100/500 kW
LAOS
LAO NATIONAL RADIO, Via USSR — (D) • EUROPE • 240 kW
PAKISTAN
†RADIO PAKISTAN, Islamabad — S ASIA & SE ASIA • 100 kW
UNITED KINGDOM
†BBC, Via Ascension — S AMERICA • 250 kW
USSR
RADIO MOSCOW, Khabarovsk — (J) • E ASIA & SE ASIA • 100 kW

15195 CHINA (PR)
RADIO BEIJING — (J) • WEST USSR
RADIO BEIJING, Baoding — (J) • S AMERICA • 240 kW
RADIO BEIJING, Jinhua — (J) • W NORTH AM • 500 kW
FRANCE
(con'd) R FRANCE INTL, Issoudun-Allouis — E EUROPE & WEST USSR • 100 kW

0 1 2 3 4 5 6 7 8 9 10 11 12 13 14 15 16 17 18 19 20 21 22 23 24

ENGLISH ▬ ARABIC ≋ CHINESE ∞ FRENCH ═ GERMAN ▭ RUSSIAN ═ SPANISH ▭ OTHER ▬

FREQUENCY   COUNTRY, STATION, LOCATION   TARGET • NETWORK • POWER (kW)   World Time

Frequency	Country / Station / Location	Schedule
15195 (con'd)	**FRANCE** R FRANCE INTL, Issoudun-Allouis	(D) • E EUROPE & WEST USSR • 100 kW; (J) • E EUROPE & WEST USSR • 100 kW
	JAPAN †RADIO JAPAN/NHK, Tokyo-Yamata	E ASIA • GENERAL • 100 kW; (J) • PACIFIC & N AMERICA • GENERAL • 100 kW; (J) • E ASIA • GENERAL • 100 kW; (J) • W NORTH AM & C AMERICA • GENERAL • 100 kW • ALT. FREQ. TO 11865 kHz
	USA †VOA, Delano, California	(J) • C AMERICA & S AMERICA • 250 kW • ALT. FREQ. TO 9815 kHz; (J) Tu-Sa • C AMERICA & S AMERICA • 250 kW • ALT. FREQ. TO 9815 kHz
	†VOA, Greenville, NC	W AFRICA & C AFRICA • 250 kW; M-F • W AFRICA & C AFRICA • 250 kW; Sa/Su • W AFRICA & C AFRICA • 250 kW
	†VOA, Via Germany	MIDEAST • 100 kW; (J) • MIDEAST • 100 kW
	VOA, Via Kaválla, Greece	(J) • MIDEAST & S ASIA • 250 kW
	†VOA, Via Philippines	E ASIA • 250 kW
	†VOA, Via Portugal	(J) • WEST USSR & MIDEAST • 250 kW; (J) • WEST USSR • 250 kW
	†VOA, Via Tangier, Morocco	(D) • WEST USSR & MIDEAST • 100 kW; (D) • E EUROPE & MIDEAST • 100 kW
	USSR RADIO MOSCOW	(J)
15200	**BANGLADESH** †RADIO BANGLADESH, Dhaka	Alternative Frequency to 15208 kHz
	FRANCE R FRANCE INTL, Via French Guiana	S AMERICA • 500 kW; C AMERICA • 500 kW
	GUAM †KTWR-TRANS WORLD R, Merizo	SE ASIA • 100 kW; F • SE ASIA • 100 kW; Sa-Th • SE ASIA • 100 kW
	SEYCHELLES †FAR EAST BC ASS'N, North Pt, Mahé Is	MIDEAST & S ASIA • 100 kW; MIDEAST • 100 kW; Th-Sa • MIDEAST & S ASIA • 100 kW
	USSR †BELORUSSIAN RADIO, Minsk	RUSSIAN, ETC • DS-1 • 20 kW
	RADIO MOSCOW, Kalach	S ASIA • 240 kW
	TATAR RADIO, Minsk	DS-RUSSIAN, TATAR • 20 kW
15205	**ALGERIA** RTV ALGERIENNE, Algiers	AFRICA • DS • 100 kW
	GERMANY †DEUTSCHE WELLE, Königswusterhausen	W AFRICA • 100 kW; (J) • W AFRICA • 100 kW
	DEUTSCHE WELLE, Via Antigua	S AMERICA • 250 kW
	DEUTSCHE WELLE, Via Cyclops, Malta	(J) • E NORTH AM & C AMERICA • 250 kW
	INDIA †ALL INDIA RADIO, Delhi	E AFRICA • 250 kW
	SEYCHELLES †FAR EAST BC ASS'N, North Pt, Mahé Is	S ASIA • 100 kW; F-Su • S ASIA • 100 kW
	UNITED KINGDOM †BBC, Via Antigua	(D) • E NORTH AM & S AMERICA • 125 kW
	†BBC, Via Zyyi, Cyprus	(J) • WEST USSR • 250 kW; (J) Su • WEST USSR • 250 kW
	USA VOA, Greenville, NC	C AMERICA & S AMERICA • 250 kW; Tu-Sa • C AMERICA & S AMERICA • 250 kW
	VOA, Via Kaválla, Greece	MIDEAST & S ASIA • 250 kW; (D) • MIDEAST & S ASIA • 250 kW; (J) • MIDEAST & S ASIA • 250 kW; (D) • WEST USSR • 250 kW
	VOA, Via Tangier, Morocco	EUROPE & N AFRICA • 35/100 kW
	VOA, Via Woofferton, UK	EUROPE & WEST USSR • 300 kW
15208	**BANGLADESH** †RADIO BANGLADESH, Dhaka	EUROPE • 250 kW • ALT. FREQ. TO 15200 kHz
15210	**EGYPT** RADIO CAIRO, Kafr Silim-Abis	W AFRICA • 250 kW
(con'd)	**JAPAN** †RADIO JAPAN/NHK, Via Sri Lanka	MIDEAST & N AFRICA • 300 kW

SUMMER ONLY (J)   WINTER ONLY (D)   JAMMING / OR ∧   EARLIEST HEARD ◁   LATEST HEARD ▷   NEW OR CHANGED FOR 1992 †

FREQUENCY   COUNTRY, STATION, LOCATION   TARGET • NETWORK • POWER (kW)   World Time

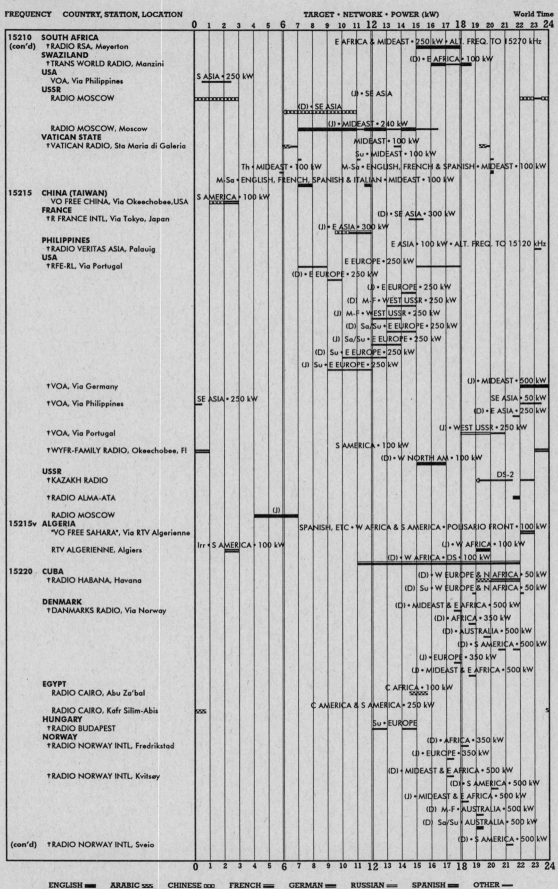

15210 (con'd)	**SOUTH AFRICA** †RADIO RSA, Meyerton — E AFRICA & MIDEAST • 250 kW • ALT. FREQ. TO 15270 kHz
	SWAZILAND †TRANS WORLD RADIO, Manzini — (D) • E AFRICA • 100 kW
	USA VOA, Via Philippines — S ASIA • 250 kW
	USSR RADIO MOSCOW — (J) • SE ASIA / (D) • SE ASIA
	RADIO MOSCOW, Moscow — (J) • MIDEAST • 240 kW
	VATICAN STATE †VATICAN RADIO, Sta Maria di Galeria — MIDEAST • 100 kW / Su • MIDEAST • 100 kW / Th • MIDEAST • 100 kW / M-Sa • ENGLISH, FRENCH & SPANISH • MIDEAST • 100 kW / M-Sa • ENGLISH, FRENCH, SPANISH & ITALIAN • MIDEAST • 100 kW
15215	**CHINA (TAIWAN)** VO FREE CHINA, Via Okeechobee, USA — S AMERICA • 100 kW
	FRANCE †R FRANCE INTL, Via Tokyo, Japan — (D) • SE ASIA • 300 kW / (J) • E ASIA • 300 kW
	PHILIPPINES †RADIO VERITAS ASIA, Palauig — E ASIA • 100 kW • ALT. FREQ. TO 15120 kHz
	USA †RFE-RL, Via Portugal — E EUROPE • 250 kW / (D) • E EUROPE • 250 kW / (J) • E EUROPE • 250 kW / (D) M-F • WEST USSR • 250 kW / (J) M-F • WEST USSR • 250 kW / (D) Sa/Su • E EUROPE • 250 kW / (J) Sa/Su • E EUROPE • 250 kW / (D) Su • E EUROPE • 250 kW / (J) Su • E EUROPE • 250 kW
	†VOA, Via Germany — (J) • MIDEAST • 500 kW
	†VOA, Via Philippines — SE ASIA • 250 kW / SE ASIA • 50 kW / (D) • E ASIA • 250 kW
	†VOA, Via Portugal — (J) • WEST USSR • 250 kW
	†WYFR-FAMILY RADIO, Okeechobee, Fl — S AMERICA • 100 kW / (D) • W NORTH AM • 100 kW
	USSR †KAZAKH RADIO — DS-2
	†RADIO ALMA-ATA
	RADIO MOSCOW — (J)
15215v	**ALGERIA** "VO FREE SAHARA", Via RTV Algerienne — SPANISH, ETC • W AFRICA & S AMERICA • POLISARIO FRONT • 100 kW
	RTV ALGERIENNE, Algiers — Irr • S AMERICA • 100 kW / (J) • W AFRICA • 100 kW / (D) • W AFRICA • DS • 100 kW
15220	**CUBA** †RADIO HABANA, Havana — (D) • W EUROPE & N AFRICA • 50 kW / (D) Su • W EUROPE & N AFRICA • 50 kW
	DENMARK †DANMARKS RADIO, Via Norway — (D) • MIDEAST & E AFRICA • 500 kW / (D) • AFRICA • 350 kW / (D) • AUSTRALIA • 500 kW / (D) • S AMERICA • 500 kW / (J) • EUROPE • 350 kW / (J) • MIDEAST & E AFRICA • 500 kW
	EGYPT RADIO CAIRO, Abu Za'bal — C AFRICA • 100 kW
	RADIO CAIRO, Kafr Silim-Abis — C AMERICA & S AMERICA • 250 kW
	HUNGARY †RADIO BUDAPEST — Su • EUROPE
	NORWAY †RADIO NORWAY INTL, Fredrikstad — (D) • AFRICA • 350 kW / (J) • EUROPE • 350 kW
	†RADIO NORWAY INTL, Kvitsøy — (D) • MIDEAST & E AFRICA • 500 kW / (D) • S AMERICA • 500 kW / (J) • MIDEAST & E AFRICA • 500 kW / (D) M-F • AUSTRALIA • 500 kW / (D) Sa/Su • AUSTRALIA • 500 kW
(con'd)	†RADIO NORWAY INTL, Sveio — (D) • S AMERICA • 500 kW

ENGLISH ▬▬   ARABIC ⧈⧈⧈   CHINESE ░░░   FRENCH ▬▬   GERMAN ▬▬   RUSSIAN ══   SPANISH ▬▬   OTHER ──

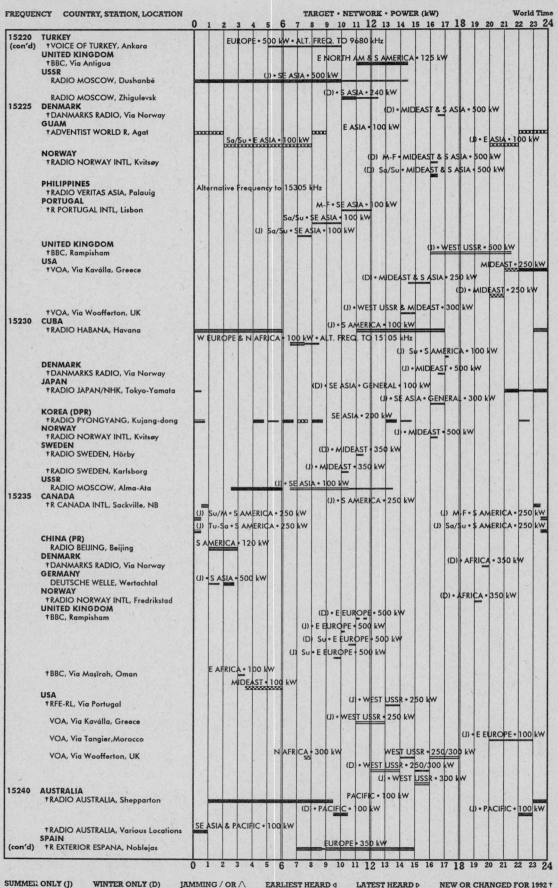

FREQUENCY	COUNTRY, STATION, LOCATION

TARGET • NETWORK • POWER (kW)

World Time

0 1 2 3 4 5 6 7 8 9 10 11 12 13 14 15 16 17 18 19 20 21 22 23 24

15220 TURKEY
(con'd) †VOICE OF TURKEY, Ankara — EUROPE • 500 kW • ALT. FREQ. TO 9680 kHz
UNITED KINGDOM
†BBC, Via Antigua — E NORTH AM & S AMERICA • 125 kW
USSR
RADIO MOSCOW, Dushanbé — (J) • SE ASIA • 500 kW

RADIO MOSCOW, Zhigulevsk — (D) • S ASIA • 240 kW
15225 DENMARK
†DANMARKS RADIO, Via Norway — (D) • MIDEAST & S ASIA • 500 kW
GUAM
†ADVENTIST WORLD R, Agat — E ASIA • 100 kW / (J) • E ASIA • 100 kW
Sa/Su • E ASIA • 100 kW

NORWAY
†RADIO NORWAY INTL, Kvitsøy — (D) M-F • MIDEAST & S ASIA • 500 kW
(D) Sa/Su • MIDEAST & S ASIA • 500 kW

PHILIPPINES
†RADIO VERITAS ASIA, Palauig — Alternative Frequency to 15305 kHz
PORTUGAL
†R PORTUGAL INTL, Lisbon — M-F • SE ASIA • 100 kW
Sa/Su • SE ASIA • 100 kW
(J) Sa/Su • SE ASIA • 100 kW

UNITED KINGDOM
†BBC, Rampisham — (J) • WEST USSR • 500 kW
USA
†VOA, Via Kaválla, Greece — MIDEAST • 250 kW
(D) • MIDEAST & S ASIA • 250 kW
(D) • MIDEAST • 250 kW

†VOA, Via Woofferton, UK — (J) • WEST USSR & MIDEAST • 300 kW
15230 CUBA
†RADIO HABANA, Havana — (J) • S AMERICA • 100 kW
W EUROPE & N AFRICA • 100 kW • ALT. FREQ. TO 15105 kHz
(J) Su • S AMERICA • 100 kW

DENMARK
†DANMARKS RADIO, Via Norway — (J) • MIDEAST • 500 kW
JAPAN
†RADIO JAPAN/NHK, Tokyo-Yamata — (D) • SE ASIA • GENERAL • 100 kW
(J) • SE ASIA • GENERAL • 300 kW

KOREA (DPR)
†RADIO PYONGYANG, Kujang-dong — SE ASIA • 200 kW
NORWAY
†RADIO NORWAY INTL, Kvitsøy — (J) • MIDEAST • 500 kW
SWEDEN
†RADIO SWEDEN, Hörby — (D) • MIDEAST • 350 kW

†RADIO SWEDEN, Karlsborg — (J) • MIDEAST • 350 kW
USSR
RADIO MOSCOW, Alma-Ata — (J) • SE ASIA • 100 kW
15235 CANADA
†R CANADA INTL, Sackville, NB — (J) • S AMERICA • 250 kW
(J) Su/M • S AMERICA • 250 kW / (J) M-F • S AMERICA • 250 kW
(J) Tu-Sa • S AMERICA • 250 kW / (J) Sa/Su • S AMERICA • 250 kW

CHINA (PR)
RADIO BEIJING, Beijing — S AMERICA • 120 kW
DENMARK
†DANMARKS RADIO, Via Norway — (D) • AFRICA • 350 kW
GERMANY
DEUTSCHE WELLE, Wertachtal — (J) • S ASIA • 500 kW
NORWAY
†RADIO NORWAY INTL, Fredrikstad — (D) • AFRICA • 350 kW
UNITED KINGDOM
†BBC, Rampisham — (D) • E EUROPE • 500 kW
(J) • E EUROPE • 500 kW
(D) Su • E EUROPE • 500 kW
(J) Su • E EUROPE • 500 kW

†BBC, Via Maṣīrah, Oman — E AFRICA • 100 kW
MIDEAST • 100 kW

USA
†RFE-RL, Via Portugal — (J) • WEST USSR • 250 kW

VOA, Via Kaválla, Greece — (J) • WEST USSR • 250 kW

VOA, Via Tangier, Morocco — (J) • E EUROPE • 100 kW

VOA, Via Woofferton, UK — N AFRICA • 300 kW / WEST USSR • 250/300 kW
(D) • WEST USSR • 250/300 kW
(J) • WEST USSR • 300 kW

15240 AUSTRALIA
†RADIO AUSTRALIA, Shepparton — PACIFIC • 100 kW
(D) • PACIFIC • 100 kW / (J) • PACIFIC • 100 kW

†RADIO AUSTRALIA, Various Locations — SE ASIA & PACIFIC • 100 kW
SPAIN
(con'd) †R EXTERIOR ESPANA, Noblejas — EUROPE • 350 kW

0 1 2 3 4 5 6 7 8 9 10 11 12 13 14 15 16 17 18 19 20 21 22 23 24

FREQUENCY   COUNTRY, STATION, LOCATION   TARGET • NETWORK • POWER (kW)   World Time

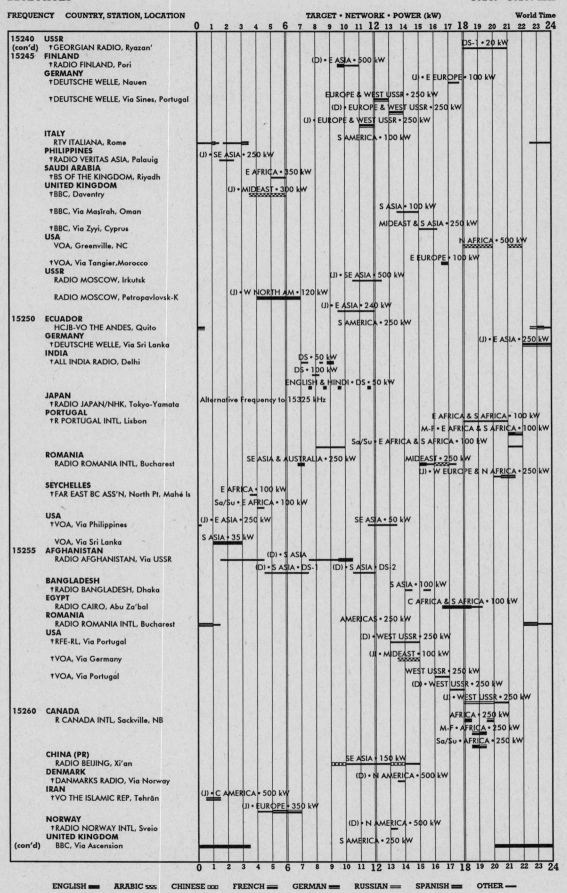

Frequency	Country / Station / Location	Target • Network • Power
15240 (con'd)	USSR †GEORGIAN RADIO, Ryazan'	DS-1 • 20 kW
15245	FINLAND †RADIO FINLAND, Pori	(D) • E ASIA • 500 kW
	GERMANY †DEUTSCHE WELLE, Nauen	(J) • E EUROPE • 100 kW
	†DEUTSCHE WELLE, Via Sines, Portugal	EUROPE & WEST USSR • 250 kW / (D) • EUROPE & WEST USSR • 250 kW / (J) • EUROPE & WEST USSR • 250 kW
	ITALY RTV ITALIANA, Rome	S AMERICA • 100 kW
	PHILIPPINES †RADIO VERITAS ASIA, Palauig	(J) • SE ASIA • 250 kW
	SAUDI ARABIA †BS OF THE KINGDOM, Riyadh	E AFRICA • 350 kW
	UNITED KINGDOM †BBC, Daventry	(J) • MIDEAST • 300 kW
	†BBC, Via Maşīrah, Oman	S ASIA • 100 kW
	†BBC, Via Zyyi, Cyprus	MIDEAST & S ASIA • 250 kW
	USA VOA, Greenville, NC	N AFRICA • 500 kW
	†VOA, Via Tangier, Morocco	E EUROPE • 100 kW
	USSR RADIO MOSCOW, Irkutsk	(J) • SE ASIA • 500 kW
	RADIO MOSCOW, Petropavlovsk-K	(J) • W NORTH AM • 120 kW / (J) • E ASIA • 240 kW
15250	ECUADOR HCJB-VO THE ANDES, Quito	S AMERICA • 250 kW
	GERMANY †DEUTSCHE WELLE, Via Sri Lanka	(J) • E ASIA • 250 kW
	INDIA †ALL INDIA RADIO, Delhi	DS • 50 kW / DS • 100 kW / ENGLISH & HINDI • DS • 50 kW
	JAPAN †RADIO JAPAN/NHK, Tokyo-Yamata	Alternative Frequency to 15325 kHz
	PORTUGAL †R PORTUGAL INTL, Lisbon	E AFRICA & S AFRICA • 100 kW / M-F • E AFRICA & S AFRICA • 100 kW / Sa/Su • E AFRICA & S AFRICA • 100 kW
	ROMANIA RADIO ROMANIA INTL, Bucharest	SE ASIA & AUSTRALIA • 250 kW / MIDEAST • 250 kW / (J) • W EUROPE & N AFRICA • 250 kW
	SEYCHELLES †FAR EAST BC ASS'N, North Pt, Mahé Is	E AFRICA • 100 kW / Sa/Su • E AFRICA • 100 kW
	USA †VOA, Via Philippines	(J) • E ASIA • 250 kW / SE ASIA • 50 kW
	VOA, Via Sri Lanka	S ASIA • 35 kW
15255	AFGHANISTAN RADIO AFGHANISTAN, Via USSR	(D) • S ASIA / (D) • S ASIA • DS-1 / (D) • S ASIA • DS-2
	BANGLADESH †RADIO BANGLADESH, Dhaka	S ASIA • 100 kW
	EGYPT RADIO CAIRO, Abu Za'bal	C AFRICA & S AFRICA • 100 kW
	ROMANIA RADIO ROMANIA INTL, Bucharest	AMERICAS • 250 kW
	USA †RFE-RL, Via Portugal	(D) • WEST USSR • 250 kW
	†VOA, Via Germany	(J) • MIDEAST • 100 kW
	†VOA, Via Portugal	WEST USSR • 250 kW / (D) • WEST USSR • 250 kW / (J) • WEST USSR • 250 kW
15260	CANADA R CANADA INTL, Sackville, NB	AFRICA • 250 kW / M-F • AFRICA • 250 kW / Sa/Su • AFRICA • 250 kW
	CHINA (PR) RADIO BEIJING, Xi'an	SE ASIA • 150 kW
	DENMARK †DANMARKS RADIO, Via Norway	(D) • N AMERICA • 500 kW
	IRAN †VO THE ISLAMIC REP, Tehrān	(J) • C AMERICA • 500 kW / (J) • EUROPE • 350 kW
	NORWAY †RADIO NORWAY INTL, Sveio	(D) • N AMERICA • 500 kW
	UNITED KINGDOM	
(con'd)	BBC, Via Ascension	S AMERICA • 250 kW

ENGLISH ▬   ARABIC ≈≈   CHINESE ▫▫▫   FRENCH ═══   GERMAN ▬▬▬   RUSSIAN ═══   SPANISH ▬▬   OTHER ▬

FREQUENCY   COUNTRY, STATION, LOCATION
TARGET • NETWORK • POWER (kW)
World Time

0 1 2 3 4 5 6 7 8 9 10 11 12 13 14 15 16 17 18 19 20 21 22 23 24

Frequency	Country, Station, Location	Target • Network • Power
15260 (con'd)	UNITED KINGDOM — BBC, Via Sackville, Can	N AMERICA • 250 kW
		Sa/Su • N AMERICA • 250 kW
	USA — VOA, Via Kaválla, Greece	(J) • MIDEAST • 250 kW
	USSR — RADIO MOSCOW, Baku	(J) • EUROPE • 240 kW
	RADIO MOSCOW, Kiev	(D) • EUROPE • 100 kW
		(D) M-Sa • EUROPE • 100 kW
	†UKRAINIAN RADIO, Kiev	DS-1 • 20 kW
15265	BRAZIL — †RADIO NACIONAL, Brasília	EUROPE & W AFRICA • 250 kW
	INDIA — †ALL INDIA RADIO, Bangalore	AUSTRALIA • 500 kW
	QATAR — QATAR BC SERVICE, Doha-Al Khaisah	(J) • EUROPE • DS • 250 kW
	TURKEY — †VOICE OF TURKEY, Ankara	(J) • EUROPE • 250 kW
	USA — VOA, Greenville, NC	M-F • S AMERICA • 500 kW
		Sa/Su • C AMERICA & S AMERICA • 500 kW
	†VOA, Via Tangier, Morocco	(D) • WEST USSR • 100 kW
	USSR — RADIO MOSCOW, Chita	(J) • S ASIA & SE ASIA • 100 kW
		(J) • S ASIA • 100 kW
15270	CANADA — R CANADA INTL, Via Tokyo, Japan	E ASIA • 100 kW
	CHINA (TAIWAN) — VO FREE CHINA, T'ai-pei	SE ASIA • 100 kW EUROPE • 100/250 kW
	ECUADOR — †HCJB-VO THE ANDES, Quito	(J) • EUROPE • 500 kW EUROPE • 500 kW
		(J) M-F • EUROPE • 500 kW
		(J) Sa/Su • EUROPE • 500 kW
		(J) Su/M/W/F • EUROPE • 500 kW
		Tu/Th/Sa • EUROPE • 500 kW
	GERMANY — †DEUTSCHE WELLE, Jülich	(J) • S ASIA • 100 kW
	DEUTSCHE WELLE, Via Kigali, Rwanda	W AFRICA & AMERICAS • 250 kW
	JAPAN — †RADIO JAPAN/NHK, Tokyo-Yamata	AUSTRALIA • 100 kW (D) • AUSTRALIA • GENERAL • 100 kW
	NORWAY — RADIO NORWAY INTL, Kvitsøy	(J) Su • E ASIA • 500 kW
	SOUTH AFRICA — †RADIO RSA, Meyerton	Alternative Frequency to 15210 kHz
	SWEDEN — †RADIO SWEDEN, Hörby	(J) • EUROPE & MIDEAST • 350 kW
	USA — VOA, Via Germany	(J) • WEST USSR • 500 kW
	VOA, Via Tangier, Morocco	(J) • WEST USSR • 100 kW
	VOA, Via Woofferton, UK	(J) • WEST USSR • 250 kW
	USSR — †BELORUSSIAN RADIO, Minsk	RUSSIAN, ETC • DS-1 • 20 kW
15275	CANADA — †R CANADA INTL, Via Vienna, Austria	(J) • MIDEAST • 300 kW
	FRANCE — R FRANCE INTL, Via Beijing, China	S ASIA • 120 kW
	GERMANY — †DEUTSCHE WELLE, Jülich	AFRICA • 100 kW
		MIDEAST • 100 kW
		(D) • AFRICA • 100 kW
		(J) • MIDEAST • 100 kW
	DEUTSCHE WELLE, Multiple Locations	MIDEAST & S ASIA • 100/500 kW
		AFRICA • 100/500 kW
	†DEUTSCHE WELLE, Various Locations	MIDEAST • 100/500 kW
	DEUTSCHE WELLE, Via Antigua	(D) • N AMERICA • 250 kW
	DEUTSCHE WELLE, Wertachtal	(J) • MIDEAST & S ASIA • 500 kW
	INDIA — †ALL INDIA RADIO, Aligarh	SE ASIA • 250 kW
		DS • 250 kW
		ENGLISH, ETC • DS • 250 kW
	SEYCHELLES — †FAR EAST BC ASS'N, North Pt, Mahé Is	MIDEAST • 100 kW
		M-Sa • MIDEAST • 100 kW
15280	CHINA (PR) — †RADIO BEIJING, Baoding	(J) • E NORTH AM, C AMERICA & S AMERICA • 240 kW
(con'd)	HOLLAND — RADIO NEDERLAND, Flevoland	N AFRICA & W AFRICA • 500 kW

0 1 2 3 4 5 6 7 8 9 10 11 12 13 14 15 16 17 18 19 20 21 22 23 24

SUMMER ONLY (J)   WINTER ONLY (D)   JAMMING / OR ∧   EARLIEST HEARD ◁   LATEST HEARD ▷   NEW OR CHANGED FOR 1992 †

FREQUENCY   COUNTRY, STATION, LOCATION

TARGET • NETWORK • POWER (kW)

World Time

0 1 2 3 4 5 6 7 8 9 10 11 12 13 14 15 16 17 18 19 20 21 22 23 24

Frequency	Country, Station, Location	Target • Network • Power
15280 (con'd)	JAPAN †RADIO JAPAN/NHK, Tokyo-Yamata	(J) • AUSTRALIA • GENERAL • 100 kW
	UNITED KINGDOM †BBC, Via Hong Kong	E ASIA • 250 kW
		Su • E ASIA • 250 kW
	†BBC, Via Singapore	E ASIA • 100 kW (D) • SE ASIA • 250 kW
	USA †KGEI-VO FRIENDSHIP, Redwood City, Ca	C AMERICA & S AMERICA • 50 kW
		M • C AMERICA & S AMERICA • 50 kW M-Sa • C AMERICA & S AMERICA • 50 kW
		Tu-Su • C AMERICA & S AMERICA • 50 kW Su • C AMERICA & S AMERICA • 50 kW
	VOA, Via Germany	(D) • WEST USSR • 500 kW
	†VOA, Via Tangier, Morocco	(J) • E EUROPE • 100 kW
	VOA, Via Woofferton, UK	(J) • WEST USSR • 300 kW
	USSR RADIO MOSCOW, Armavir	(J) • W EUROPE & ATLANTIC • 500 kW
	RADIO MOSCOW, Serpukhov	(J) • S ASIA • 240 kW
15280.3	CLANDESTINE (ASIA) †"VOICE OF CHINA", Taiwan	E ASIA • 100 kW
15285	CHINA (PR) RADIO BEIJING, Beijing	(J) • AUSTRALIA • 120 kW
	EGYPT RADIO CAIRO, Abu Za'bal	MIDEAST • DS-VO THE ARABS • 100 kW
	FRANCE R FRANCE INTL, Via Beijing, China	AUSTRALIA & PACIFIC • 120 kW
	PORTUGAL R PORTUGAL INTL, Lisbon	Sa/Su • E NORTH AM • 100 kW
	USA †VOA, Via Philippines	SE ASIA • 250 kW
	USSR RADIO MOSCOW, Irkutsk	E ASIA • 240 kW
	RADIO MOSCOW, Serpukhov	S ASIA • 100 kW
15290	BULGARIA †RADIO SOFIA, Plovdiv	(J) • EUROPE • 500 kW
		(J) Su • EUROPE • 500 kW
	CHINA (PR) RADIO BEIJING, Xi'an	(J) • E NORTH AM, C AMERICA & S AMERICA • 300 kW
	USA †R FREE AFGHANISTAN, Via Portugal	(J) • WEST USSR & S ASIA • 250 kW
	†RFE-RL, Via Pals, Spain	WEST USSR • 500 kW
		(J) • WEST USSR • 250 kW
	†RFE-RL, Via Portugal	(J) • WEST USSR • 250 kW (D) • WEST USSR • 50 kW
	†VOA, Greenville, NC	M-F • W AFRICA • 500 kW
	VOA, Via Philippines	E ASIA • 250 kW
	USSR RADIO MOSCOW, Via Plovdiv, Bulgaria	(J) • E NORTH AM & C AMERICA • 500 kW
15295	ECUADOR †HCJB-VO THE ANDES, Quito	S AMERICA • 100 kW
	MALAYSIA †VOICE OF MALAYSIA, Kajang	AUSTRALIA • 500 kW SE ASIA • 500 kW
		MIDEAST • 500 kW
	MOZAMBIQUE RADIO MOCAMBIQUE, Maputo	DS • 100 kW
	PAKISTAN †RADIO PAKISTAN, Islamabad	S ASIA & SE ASIA • 100 kW
	USA WINB-WORLD INTL BC, Red Lion, Pa	ENGLISH, ETC • EUROPE & N AFRICA • 50 kW
	USSR RADIO MOSCOW, Voronezh, RSFSR	S ASIA • 240 kW
15300	CUBA †RADIO HABANA, Havana	(J) • S AMERICA • 50 kW
	FRANCE †R FRANCE INTL, Issoudun-Allouis	AFRICA • 100/500 kW
		N AFRICA & W AFRICA • 100/500 kW
		(J) • AFRICA • 100/500 kW
	†R FRANCE INTL, Multiple Locations	(J) • MIDEAST • 100/250 kW AFRICA • 100/500 kW
	JAPAN †RADIO JAPAN/NHK, Tokyo-Yamata	SE ASIA • 100 kW
		SE ASIA • 100 kW • ALT. FREQ. TO 11875 kHz
	USSR RADIO MOSCOW, Novosibirsk	(J) • E ASIA • 500 kW
15305	CANADA †R CANADA INTL, Sackville, NB	(J) • EUROPE • 100 kW
		(J) M-Sa • EUROPE • 100 kW
	DENMARK †DANMARKS RADIO, Via Norway	Alternative Frequency to 15310 kHz
	NORWAY †RADIO NORWAY INTL, Fredrikstad	Alternative Frequency to 15310 kHz
(con'd)	†RADIO NORWAY INTL, Sveio	Alternative Frequency to 15310 kHz

0 1 2 3 4 5 6 7 8 9 10 11 12 13 14 15 16 17 18 19 20 21 22 23 24

ENGLISH ▬   ARABIC ▧   CHINESE ▭▭▭   FRENCH ▬   GERMAN ▬   RUSSIAN ═   SPANISH ▬   OTHER ▬

FREQUENCY   COUNTRY, STATION, LOCATION   TARGET • NETWORK • POWER (kW)   World Time

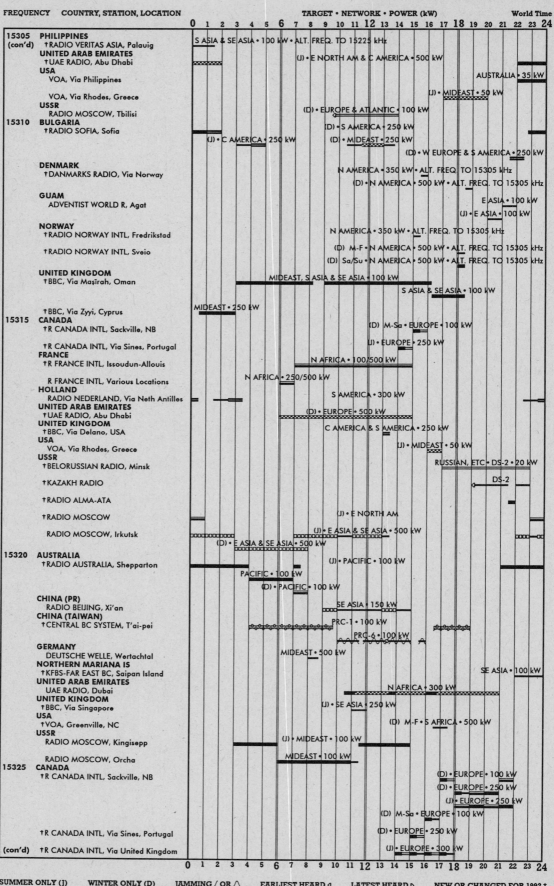

FREQUENCY	COUNTRY, STATION, LOCATION	TARGET • NETWORK • POWER (kW)
15305 (con'd)	PHILIPPINES †RADIO VERITAS ASIA, Palauig	S ASIA & SE ASIA • 100 kW • ALT. FREQ. TO 15225 kHz
	UNITED ARAB EMIRATES †UAE RADIO, Abu Dhabi	(J) • E NORTH AM & C AMERICA • 500 kW
	USA VOA, Via Philippines	AUSTRALIA • 35 kW
	VOA, Via Rhodes, Greece	(J) • MIDEAST • 50 kW
	USSR RADIO MOSCOW, Tbilisi	(D) • EUROPE & ATLANTIC • 100 kW
15310	BULGARIA †RADIO SOFIA, Sofia	(D) • S AMERICA • 250 kW (J) • C AMERICA • 250 kW (D) • MIDEAST • 250 kW (D) • W EUROPE & S AMERICA • 250 kW
	DENMARK †DANMARKS RADIO, Via Norway	N AMERICA • 350 kW • ALT. FREQ. TO 15305 kHz (D) • N AMERICA • 500 kW • ALT. FREQ. TO 15305 kHz
	GUAM ADVENTIST WORLD R, Agat	E ASIA • 100 kW (J) • E ASIA • 100 kW
	NORWAY †RADIO NORWAY INTL, Fredrikstad	N AMERICA • 350 kW • ALT. FREQ. TO 15305 kHz
	†RADIO NORWAY INTL, Sveio	(D) M-F • N AMERICA • 500 kW • ALT. FREQ. TO 15305 kHz (D) Sa/Su • N AMERICA • 500 kW • ALT. FREQ. TO 15305 kHz
	UNITED KINGDOM †BBC, Via Maşirah, Oman	MIDEAST, S ASIA & SE ASIA • 100 kW S ASIA & SE ASIA • 100 kW
	†BBC, Via Zyyi, Cyprus	MIDEAST • 250 kW
15315	CANADA †R CANADA INTL, Sackville, NB	(D) M-Sa • EUROPE • 100 kW
	†R CANADA INTL, Via Sines, Portugal	(J) • EUROPE • 250 kW
	FRANCE †R FRANCE INTL, Issoudun-Allouis	N AFRICA • 100/500 kW
	R FRANCE INTL, Various Locations	N AFRICA • 250/500 kW
	HOLLAND RADIO NEDERLAND, Via Neth Antilles	S AMERICA • 300 kW
	UNITED ARAB EMIRATES †UAE RADIO, Abu Dhabi	(D) • EUROPE • 500 kW
	UNITED KINGDOM †BBC, Via Delano, USA	C AMERICA & S AMERICA • 250 kW
	USA VOA, Via Rhodes, Greece	(J) • MIDEAST • 50 kW
	USSR †BELORUSSIAN RADIO, Minsk	RUSSIAN, ETC • DS-2 • 20 kW
	†KAZAKH RADIO	DS-2
	†RADIO ALMA-ATA	
	†RADIO MOSCOW	(J) • E NORTH AM
	RADIO MOSCOW, Irkutsk	(J) • E ASIA & SE ASIA • 500 kW (D) • E ASIA & SE ASIA • 500 kW
15320	AUSTRALIA †RADIO AUSTRALIA, Shepparton	(J) • PACIFIC • 100 kW PACIFIC • 100 kW (D) • PACIFIC • 100 kW
	CHINA (PR) RADIO BEIJING, Xi'an	SE ASIA • 150 kW
	CHINA (TAIWAN) †CENTRAL BC SYSTEM, T'ai-pei	PRC-1 • 100 kW PRC-6 • 100 kW
	GERMANY DEUTSCHE WELLE, Wertachtal	MIDEAST • 500 kW
	NORTHERN MARIANA IS †KFBS-FAR EAST BC, Saipan Island	SE ASIA • 100 kW
	UNITED ARAB EMIRATES UAE RADIO, Dubai	N AFRICA • 300 kW
	UNITED KINGDOM †BBC, Via Singapore	(J) • SE ASIA • 250 kW
	USA †VOA, Greenville, NC	(D) M-F • S AFRICA • 500 kW
	USSR RADIO MOSCOW, Kingisepp	(J) • MIDEAST • 100 kW
	RADIO MOSCOW, Orcha	MIDEAST • 100 kW
15325	CANADA †R CANADA INTL, Sackville, NB	(D) • EUROPE • 100 kW (D) • EUROPE • 250 kW (J) • EUROPE • 250 kW (D) M-Sa • EUROPE • 100 kW
	†R CANADA INTL, Via Sines, Portugal	(D) • EUROPE • 250 kW
(con'd)	†R CANADA INTL, Via United Kingdom	(J) • EUROPE • 300 kW

FREQUENCY	COUNTRY, STATION, LOCATION	TARGET • NETWORK • POWER (kW) — World Time

0 1 2 3 4 5 6 7 8 9 10 11 12 13 14 15 16 17 18 19 20 21 22 23 24

15325 FINLAND
(con'd)   RADIO FINLAND, Pori — EUROPE & W AFRICA • 100 kW • USB

JAPAN
†RADIO JAPAN/NHK, Tokyo-Yamata — EUROPE • 300 kW • ALT. FREQ. TO 15250 kHz
— EUROPE • 300 kW
— EUROPE • GENERAL • 300 kW • ALT. FREQ. TO 15250 kHz

RADIO JAPAN/NHK, Via French Guiana — C AMERICA • 500 kW
— C AMERICA • GENERAL • 500 kW

SEYCHELLES
†FAR EAST BC ASS'N, North Pt, Mahé Is — MIDEAST • 100 kW   S ASIA • 100 kW
— F • MIDEAST • 100 kW
— Su/F • MIDEAST • 100 kW

SPAIN
†R EXTERIOR ESPANA, Noblejas — 350 kW

TURKEY
†VOICE OF TURKEY, Ankara — Sa-Th • EUROPE • 250 kW

UNITED KINGDOM
†BBC, Via Zyyi, Cyprus — (D) • WEST USSR • 250 kW
— (D) • E EUROPE • 250 kW
— (J) • E EUROPE • 250 kW
— (D) M-Sa • E EUROPE • 250 kW
— (J) M-Sa • E EUROPE • 250 kW
— (D) Su • E EUROPE • 250 kW
— (J) Su • E EUROPE • 250 kW

USA
VOA, Via Philippines — EAST USSR • 250 kW
— (D) • EAST USSR • 250 kW
— (J) • EAST USSR • 250 kW

15330 BULGARIA
†RADIO SOFIA, Sofia — (J) • MIDEAST • 250 kW   (D) • EUROPE • 250 kW
— (J) • E NORTH AM • 250 kW
— (J) • EUROPE • 250 kW

CHINA (PR)
RADIO BEIJING, Beijing — SE ASIA • 120 kW

HOLLAND
RADIO NEDERLAND, Via Neth Antilles — C AMERICA • 300 kW

ITALY
RTV ITALIANA, Rome — E AFRICA & MIDEAST • 100 kW   (J) • E ASIA • 100 kW
— (J) • WEST USSR • 100 kW

MOROCCO
RTV MAROCAINE, Tangier — MIDEAST, E EUROPE & N AFRICA • DS • 50 kW

SEYCHELLES
†FAR EAST BC ASS'N, North Pt, Mahé Is — W-Sa • S ASIA • 100 kW

USA
†VOA, Greenville, NC — (D) • S AMERICA • 500 kW
— (J) • S AMERICA • 500 kW

VOA, Via Philippines — E AFRICA • 250 kW
— M-F • E AFRICA • 250 kW

USSR
RADIO MOSCOW — (J)
— (J) • W AFRICA & C AFRICA • 100 kW

RADIO MOSCOW, Kursk

RADIO MOSCOW, Tashkent — (D) • S ASIA & SE ASIA • 100 kW
— (D) • SE ASIA • 100 kW
— (J) • E ASIA • 500 kW

15335 EGYPT
RADIO CAIRO, Kafr Silim-Abis — W AFRICA • 250 kW

INDIA
†ALL INDIA RADIO, Aligarh — AUSTRALIA • 250 kW
— SE ASIA • 100 kW

†ALL INDIA RADIO, Madras

MOROCCO
RTV MAROCAINE, Tangier — EUROPE & W AFRICA • DS • 100 kW

ROMANIA
RADIO ROMANIA INTL, Bucharest — ASIA & AUSTRALIA • 250 kW   S ASIA • 250 kW
— Su • S ASIA & SE ASIA • MARINERS • 250 kW
— Su • W AFRICA & ATLANTIC • MARINERS • 250 kW

SAUDI ARABIA
†BS OF THE KINGDOM, Riyadh — W AFRICA • 350 kW

15340 CUBA
†RADIO HABANA, Havana — (J) • S AMERICA • 50 kW
— (D) • S AMERICA • 50 kW
— (D) Su • S AMERICA • 50 kW

ITALY
RTV ITALIANA, Rome — MIDEAST • 100 kW

KOREA (DPR)
RADIO PYONGYANG, Kujang-dong — E AFRICA • 200 kW

ROMANIA
RADIO ROMANIA INTL, Bucharest — W AFRICA • 250 kW
— SE ASIA • 250 kW   AFRICA • 250 kW

(con'd)

0 1 2 3 4 5 6 7 8 9 10 11 12 13 14 15 16 17 18 19 20 21 22 23 24

ENGLISH ▬▬ ARABIC ▨▨ CHINESE ▭▭▭ FRENCH ▬▬ GERMAN ▬▬ RUSSIAN ▬▬ SPANISH ▬▬ OTHER ▬

FREQUENCY   COUNTRY, STATION, LOCATION

TARGET • NETWORK • POWER (kW)

World Time

0 1 2 3 4 5 6 7 8 9 10 11 12 13 14 15 16 17 18 19 20 21 22 23 24

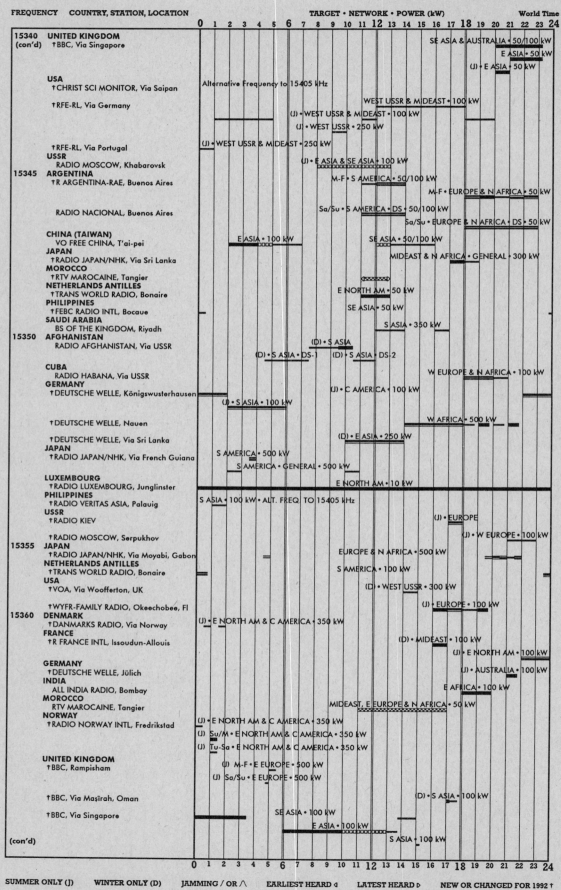

15340 **UNITED KINGDOM**
(con'd)   †BBC, Via Singapore — SE ASIA & AUSTRALIA • 50/100 kW / E ASIA • 50 kW / (J) • E ASIA • 50 kW

USA
†CHRIST SCI MONITOR, Via Saipan — Alternative Frequency to 15405 kHz
†RFE-RL, Via Germany — WEST USSR & MIDEAST • 100 kW / (J) • WEST USSR & MIDEAST • 100 kW / (J) • WEST USSR • 250 kW
†RFE-RL, Via Portugal — (J) • WEST USSR & MIDEAST • 250 kW

USSR
RADIO MOSCOW, Khabarovsk — (J) • E ASIA & SE ASIA • 100 kW

15345 **ARGENTINA**
†R ARGENTINA-RAE, Buenos Aires — M-F • S AMERICA • 50/100 kW / M-F • EUROPE & N AFRICA • 50 kW
RADIO NACIONAL, Buenos Aires — Sa/Su • S AMERICA • DS • 50/100 kW / Sa/Su • EUROPE & N AFRICA • DS • 50 kW

CHINA (TAIWAN)
VO FREE CHINA, T'ai-pei — E ASIA • 100 kW / SE ASIA • 50/100 kW

JAPAN
†RADIO JAPAN/NHK, Via Sri Lanka — MIDEAST & N AFRICA • GENERAL • 300 kW

MOROCCO
†RTV MAROCAINE, Tangier

NETHERLANDS ANTILLES
†TRANS WORLD RADIO, Bonaire — E NORTH AM • 50 kW

PHILIPPINES
†FEBC RADIO INTL, Bocaue — SE ASIA • 50 kW

SAUDI ARABIA
BS OF THE KINGDOM, Riyadh — S ASIA • 350 kW

15350 **AFGHANISTAN**
RADIO AFGHANISTAN, Via USSR — (D) • S ASIA / (D) • S ASIA • DS-1 / (D) • S ASIA • DS-2

CUBA
RADIO HABANA, Via USSR — W EUROPE & N AFRICA • 100 kW

GERMANY
†DEUTSCHE WELLE, Königswusterhausen — (J) • C AMERICA • 100 kW / (J) • S ASIA • 100 kW
†DEUTSCHE WELLE, Nauen — W AFRICA • 500 kW
†DEUTSCHE WELLE, Via Sri Lanka — (D) • E ASIA • 250 kW

JAPAN
†RADIO JAPAN/NHK, Via French Guiana — S AMERICA • 500 kW / S AMERICA • GENERAL • 500 kW

LUXEMBOURG
†RADIO LUXEMBOURG, Junglinster — E NORTH AM • 10 kW

PHILIPPINES
†RADIO VERITAS ASIA, Palauig — S ASIA • 100 kW • ALT. FREQ. TO 15405 kHz

USSR
†RADIO KIEV — (J) • EUROPE
†RADIO MOSCOW, Serpukhov — (J) • W EUROPE • 100 kW

15355 **JAPAN**
†RADIO JAPAN/NHK, Via Moyabi, Gabon — EUROPE & N AFRICA • 500 kW

NETHERLANDS ANTILLES
†TRANS WORLD RADIO, Bonaire — S AMERICA • 100 kW

USA
†VOA, Via Woofferton, UK — (D) • WEST USSR • 300 kW
†WYFR-FAMILY RADIO, Okeechobee, Fl — (J) • EUROPE • 100 kW

15360 **DENMARK**
†DANMARKS RADIO, Via Norway — (J) • E NORTH AM & C AMERICA • 350 kW

FRANCE
†R FRANCE INTL, Issoudun-Allouis — (D) • MIDEAST • 100 kW / (J) • E NORTH AM • 100 kW

GERMANY
†DEUTSCHE WELLE, Jülich — (J) • AUSTRALIA • 100 kW

INDIA
ALL INDIA RADIO, Bombay — E AFRICA • 100 kW

MOROCCO
RTV MAROCAINE, Tangier — MIDEAST, E EUROPE & N AFRICA • 50 kW

NORWAY
†RADIO NORWAY INTL, Fredrikstad — (J) • E NORTH AM & C AMERICA • 350 kW / (J) Su/M • E NORTH AM & C AMERICA • 350 kW / (J) Tu-Sa • E NORTH AM & C AMERICA • 350 kW

UNITED KINGDOM
†BBC, Rampisham — (J) M-F • E EUROPE • 500 kW / (J) Sa/Su • E EUROPE • 500 kW
†BBC, Via Maşīrah, Oman — (D) • S ASIA • 100 kW
†BBC, Via Singapore — SE ASIA • 100 kW / E ASIA • 100 kW / S ASIA • 100 kW

(con'd)

0 1 2 3 4 5 6 7 8 9 10 11 12 13 14 15 16 17 18 19 20 21 22 23 24

SUMMER ONLY (J)   WINTER ONLY (D)   JAMMING / OR ∧   EARLIEST HEARD ◁   LATEST HEARD ▷   NEW OR CHANGED FOR 1992 †

FREQUENCY	COUNTRY, STATION, LOCATION	TARGET • NETWORK • POWER (kW)	World Time

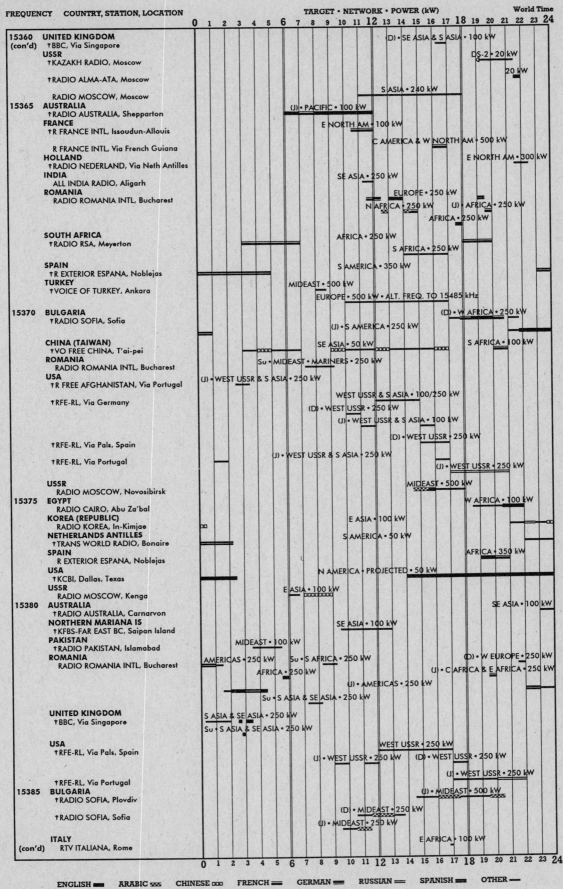

15360 (con'd)	UNITED KINGDOM †BBC, Via Singapore	(D) • SE ASIA & S ASIA • 100 kW
	USSR †KAZAKH RADIO, Moscow	DS-2 • 20 kW
	†RADIO ALMA-ATA, Moscow	20 kW
	RADIO MOSCOW, Moscow	S ASIA • 240 kW
15365	AUSTRALIA †RADIO AUSTRALIA, Shepparton	(J) • PACIFIC • 100 kW
	FRANCE †R FRANCE INTL, Issoudun-Allouis	E NORTH AM • 100 kW
	R FRANCE INTL, Via French Guiana	C AMERICA & W NORTH AM • 500 kW
	HOLLAND †RADIO NEDERLAND, Via Neth Antilles	E NORTH AM • 300 kW
	INDIA ALL INDIA RADIO, Aligarh	SE ASIA • 250 kW
	ROMANIA RADIO ROMANIA INTL, Bucharest	EUROPE • 250 kW
		N AFRICA • 250 kW (J) • AFRICA • 250 kW
		AFRICA • 250 kW
	SOUTH AFRICA †RADIO RSA, Meyerton	AFRICA • 250 kW
		S AFRICA • 250 kW
	SPAIN †R EXTERIOR ESPANA, Noblejas	S AMERICA • 350 kW
	TURKEY †VOICE OF TURKEY, Ankara	MIDEAST • 500 kW
		EUROPE • 500 kW • ALT. FREQ. TO 15485 kHz
15370	BULGARIA †RADIO SOFIA, Sofia	(D) • W AFRICA • 250 kW
		(J) • S AMERICA • 250 kW
	CHINA (TAIWAN) †VO FREE CHINA, T'ai-pei	SE ASIA • 50 kW S AFRICA • 100 kW
	ROMANIA RADIO ROMANIA INTL, Bucharest	Su • MIDEAST • MARINERS • 250 kW
	USA †R FREE AFGHANISTAN, Via Portugal	(J) • WEST USSR & S ASIA • 250 kW
	†RFE-RL, Via Germany	WEST USSR & S ASIA • 100/250 kW
		(D) • WEST USSR • 250 kW
		(J) • WEST USSR & S ASIA • 100 kW
	†RFE-RL, Via Pals, Spain	(D) • WEST USSR • 250 kW
	†RFE-RL, Via Portugal	(J) • WEST USSR & S ASIA • 250 kW
		(J) • WEST USSR • 250 kW
	USSR RADIO MOSCOW, Novosibirsk	MIDEAST • 500 kW
15375	EGYPT RADIO CAIRO, Abu Za'bal	W AFRICA • 100 kW
	KOREA (REPUBLIC) RADIO KOREA, In-Kimjae	E ASIA • 100 kW
	NETHERLANDS ANTILLES †TRANS WORLD RADIO, Bonaire	S AMERICA • 50 kW
	SPAIN R EXTERIOR ESPANA, Noblejas	AFRICA • 350 kW
	USA †KCBI, Dallas, Texas	N AMERICA • PROJECTED • 50 kW
	USSR RADIO MOSCOW, Kenga	E ASIA • 100 kW
15380	AUSTRALIA †RADIO AUSTRALIA, Carnarvon	SE ASIA • 100 kW
	NORTHERN MARIANA IS †KFBS-FAR EAST BC, Saipan Island	SE ASIA • 100 kW
	PAKISTAN †RADIO PAKISTAN, Islamabad	MIDEAST • 100 kW
	ROMANIA RADIO ROMANIA INTL, Bucharest	AMERICAS • 250 kW Su • S AFRICA • 250 kW (D) • W EUROPE • 250 kW
		AFRICA • 250 kW (J) • C AFRICA & E AFRICA • 250 kW
		(J) • AMERICAS • 250 kW
		Su • S ASIA & SE ASIA • 250 kW
	UNITED KINGDOM †BBC, Via Singapore	S ASIA & SE ASIA • 250 kW
		Su • S ASIA & SE ASIA • 250 kW
	USA †RFE-RL, Via Pals, Spain	WEST USSR • 250 kW
		(J) • WEST USSR • 250 kW (D) • WEST USSR • 250 kW
	†RFE-RL, Via Portugal	(J) • WEST USSR • 250 kW
15385	BULGARIA †RADIO SOFIA, Plovdiv	(J) • MIDEAST • 500 kW
	†RADIO SOFIA, Sofia	(D) • MIDEAST • 250 kW
		(J) • MIDEAST • 250 kW
	ITALY (con'd) RTV ITALIANA, Rome	E AFRICA • 100 kW

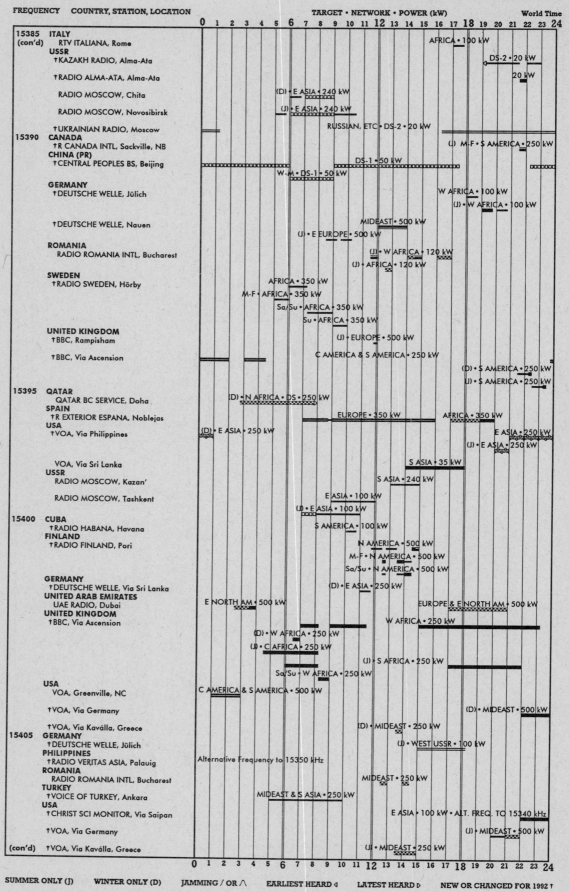

FREQUENCY   COUNTRY, STATION, LOCATION   TARGET • NETWORK • POWER (kW)   World Time

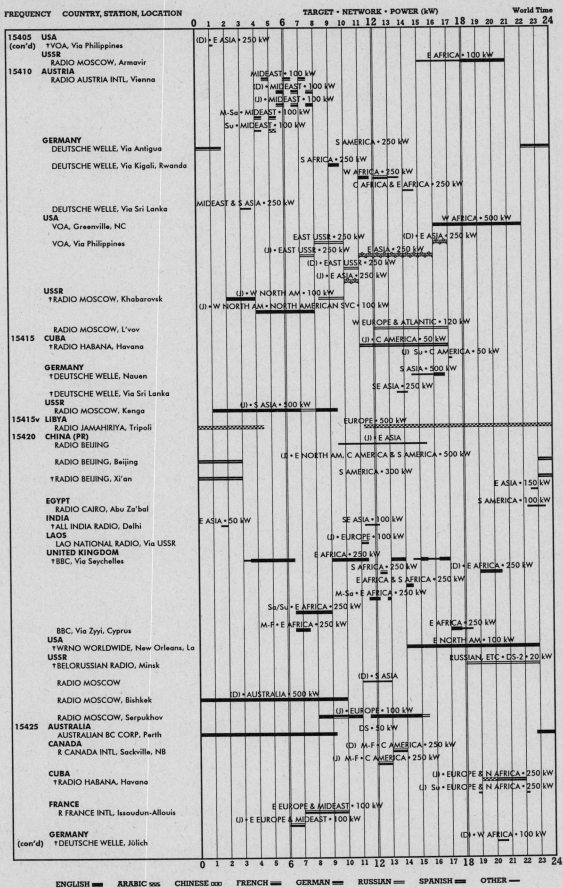

FREQUENCY	COUNTRY, STATION, LOCATION	TARGET • NETWORK • POWER (kW)
15405 (con'd)	USA †VOA, Via Philippines	(D) • E ASIA • 250 kW
	USSR RADIO MOSCOW, Armavir	E AFRICA • 100 kW
15410	AUSTRIA RADIO AUSTRIA INTL, Vienna	MIDEAST • 100 kW / (D) • MIDEAST • 100 kW / (J) • MIDEAST • 100 kW / M-Sa • MIDEAST • 100 kW / Su • MIDEAST • 100 kW
	GERMANY DEUTSCHE WELLE, Via Antigua	S AMERICA • 250 kW
	DEUTSCHE WELLE, Via Kigali, Rwanda	S AFRICA • 250 kW / W AFRICA • 250 kW / C AFRICA & E AFRICA • 250 kW
	DEUTSCHE WELLE, Via Sri Lanka	MIDEAST & S ASIA • 250 kW
	USA VOA, Greenville, NC	W AFRICA • 500 kW
	VOA, Via Philippines	EAST USSR • 250 kW / (D) • E ASIA • 250 kW / (J) • EAST USSR • 250 kW / E ASIA • 250 kW / (D) • EAST USSR • 250 kW / (J) • E ASIA • 250 kW
	USSR †RADIO MOSCOW, Khabarovsk	(J) • W NORTH AM • 100 kW / (J) • W NORTH AM • NORTH AMERICAN SVC • 100 kW
	RADIO MOSCOW, L'vov	W EUROPE & ATLANTIC • 120 kW
15415	CUBA †RADIO HABANA, Havana	(J) • C AMERICA • 50 kW / (J) • Su • C AMERICA • 50 kW
	GERMANY †DEUTSCHE WELLE, Nauen	S ASIA • 500 kW
	†DEUTSCHE WELLE, Via Sri Lanka	SE ASIA • 250 kW
	USSR RADIO MOSCOW, Kenga	(J) • S ASIA • 500 kW
15415v	LIBYA RADIO JAMAHIRIYA, Tripoli	EUROPE • 500 kW
15420	CHINA (PR) RADIO BEIJING	(J) • E ASIA
	RADIO BEIJING, Beijing	(J) • E NORTH AM, C AMERICA & S AMERICA • 500 kW
	†RADIO BEIJING, Xi'an	S AMERICA • 300 kW / E ASIA • 150 kW / S AMERICA • 100 kW
	EGYPT RADIO CAIRO, Abu Za'bal	
	INDIA †ALL INDIA RADIO, Delhi	E ASIA • 50 kW / SE ASIA • 100 kW
	LAOS LAO NATIONAL RADIO, Via USSR	(J) • EUROPE • 100 kW
	UNITED KINGDOM †BBC, Via Seychelles	E AFRICA • 250 kW / S AFRICA • 250 kW / (D) • E AFRICA • 250 kW / E AFRICA & S AFRICA • 250 kW / M-Sa • E AFRICA • 250 kW / Sa/Su • E AFRICA • 250 kW / M-F • E AFRICA • 250 kW / E AFRICA • 250 kW
	BBC, Via Zyyi, Cyprus	E NORTH AM • 100 kW
	USA †WRNO WORLDWIDE, New Orleans, La	
	USSR †BELORUSSIAN RADIO, Minsk	RUSSIAN, ETC • DS-2 • 20 kW
	RADIO MOSCOW	(D) • S ASIA
	RADIO MOSCOW, Bishkek	(D) • AUSTRALIA • 500 kW
	RADIO MOSCOW, Serpukhov	(J) • EUROPE • 100 kW
15425	AUSTRALIA AUSTRALIAN BC CORP, Perth	DS • 50 kW
	CANADA R CANADA INTL, Sackville, NB	(D) • M-F • C AMERICA • 250 kW / (J) • M-F • C AMERICA • 250 kW
	CUBA †RADIO HABANA, Havana	(J) • EUROPE & N AFRICA • 250 kW / (J) • Su • EUROPE & N AFRICA • 250 kW
	FRANCE R FRANCE INTL, Issoudun-Allouis	E EUROPE & MIDEAST • 100 kW / (J) • E EUROPE & MIDEAST • 100 kW
(con'd)	GERMANY †DEUTSCHE WELLE, Jülich	(D) • W AFRICA • 100 kW

ENGLISH ▬ ARABIC ⋙ CHINESE ░ FRENCH ▬ GERMAN ═ RUSSIAN ═ SPANISH ▬ OTHER ▬

FREQUENCY   COUNTRY, STATION, LOCATION   TARGET • NETWORK • POWER (kW)   World Time

0 1 2 3 4 5 6 7 8 9 10 11 12 13 14 15 16 17 18 19 20 21 22 23 24

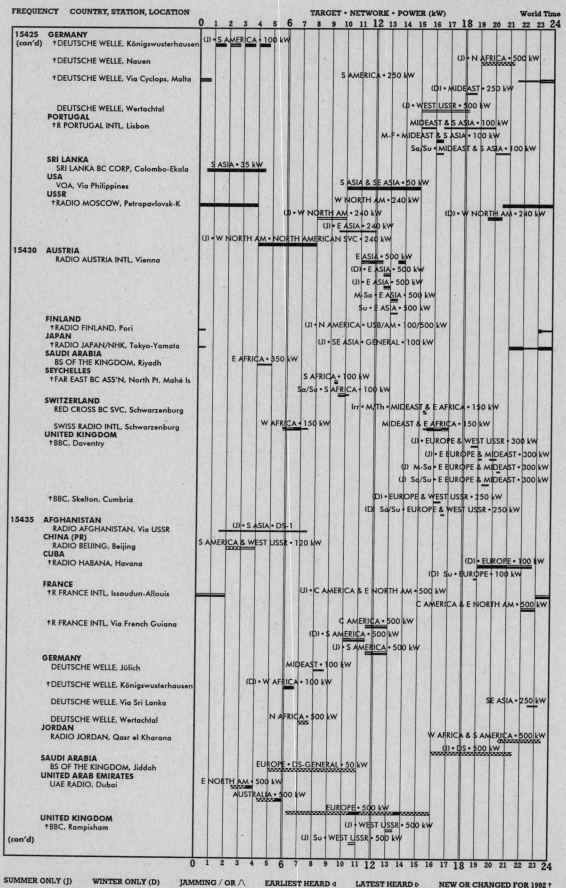

15425 GERMANY
(con'd) †DEUTSCHE WELLE, Königswusterhausen — (J) • S AMERICA • 100 kW
 †DEUTSCHE WELLE, Nauen — (J) • N AFRICA • 500 kW
 †DEUTSCHE WELLE, Via Cyclops, Malta — S AMERICA • 250 kW
 — (D) • MIDEAST • 250 kW
 DEUTSCHE WELLE, Wertachtal — (J) • WEST USSR • 500 kW
PORTUGAL
 †R PORTUGAL INTL, Lisbon — MIDEAST & S ASIA • 100 kW
 — M-F • MIDEAST & S ASIA • 100 kW
 — Sa/Su • MIDEAST & S ASIA • 100 kW
SRI LANKA
 SRI LANKA BC CORP, Colombo-Ekala — S ASIA • 35 kW
USA
 VOA, Via Philippines — S ASIA & SE ASIA • 50 kW
USSR
 †RADIO MOSCOW, Petropavlovsk-K — W NORTH AM • 240 kW
 — (J) • W NORTH AM • 240 kW
 — (D) • W NORTH AM • 240 kW
 — (J) • E ASIA • 240 kW
 — (J) • W NORTH AM • NORTH AMERICAN SVC • 240 kW

15430 AUSTRIA
 RADIO AUSTRIA INTL, Vienna — E ASIA • 500 kW
 — (D) • E ASIA • 500 kW
 — (J) • E ASIA • 500 kW
 — M-Sa • E ASIA • 500 kW
 — Su • E ASIA • 500 kW
FINLAND
 †RADIO FINLAND, Pori — (J) • N AMERICA • USB/AM • 100/500 kW
JAPAN
 †RADIO JAPAN/NHK, Tokyo-Yamata — (J) • SE ASIA • GENERAL • 100 kW
SAUDI ARABIA
 BS OF THE KINGDOM, Riyadh — E AFRICA • 350 kW
SEYCHELLES
 †FAR EAST BC ASS'N, North Pt, Mahé Is — S AFRICA • 100 kW
 — Sa/Su • S AFRICA • 100 kW
SWITZERLAND
 RED CROSS BC SVC, Schwarzenburg — Irr • M/Th • MIDEAST & E AFRICA • 150 kW
 SWISS RADIO INTL, Schwarzenburg — W AFRICA • 150 kW
 — MIDEAST & E AFRICA • 150 kW
UNITED KINGDOM
 †BBC, Daventry — (J) • EUROPE & WEST USSR • 300 kW
 — (J) • E EUROPE & MIDEAST • 300 kW
 — (J) M-Sa • E EUROPE & MIDEAST • 300 kW
 — (J) Sa/Su • E EUROPE & MIDEAST • 300 kW
 †BBC, Skelton, Cumbria — (D) • EUROPE & WEST USSR • 250 kW
 — (D) Sa/Su • EUROPE & WEST USSR • 250 kW

15435 AFGHANISTAN
 RADIO AFGHANISTAN, Via USSR — (J) • S ASIA • DS-1
CHINA (PR)
 RADIO BEIJING, Beijing — S AMERICA & WEST USSR • 120 kW
CUBA
 †RADIO HABANA, Havana — (D) • EUROPE • 100 kW
 — (D) Su • EUROPE • 100 kW
FRANCE
 †R FRANCE INTL, Issoudun-Allouis — (J) • C AMERICA & E NORTH AM • 500 kW
 — C AMERICA & E NORTH AM • 500 kW
 †R FRANCE INTL, Via French Guiana — C AMERICA • 500 kW
 — (D) • S AMERICA • 500 kW
 — (J) • S AMERICA • 500 kW
GERMANY
 DEUTSCHE WELLE, Jülich — MIDEAST • 100 kW
 †DEUTSCHE WELLE, Königswusterhausen — (D) • W AFRICA • 100 kW
 DEUTSCHE WELLE, Via Sri Lanka — SE ASIA • 250 kW
 DEUTSCHE WELLE, Wertachtal — N AFRICA • 500 kW
JORDAN
 RADIO JORDAN, Qasr el Kharana — W AFRICA & S AMERICA • 500 kW
 — (J) • DS • 500 kW
SAUDI ARABIA
 BS OF THE KINGDOM, Jiddah — EUROPE • DS-GENERAL • 50 kW
UNITED ARAB EMIRATES
 UAE RADIO, Dubai — E NORTH AM • 500 kW
 — AUSTRALIA • 500 kW
 — EUROPE • 500 kW
UNITED KINGDOM
 †BBC, Rampisham — (J) • WEST USSR • 500 kW
(con'd) — (J) Su • WEST USSR • 500 kW

0 1 2 3 4 5 6 7 8 9 10 11 12 13 14 15 16 17 18 19 20 21 22 23 24

SUMMER ONLY (J)   WINTER ONLY (D)   JAMMING / OR ∧   EARLIEST HEARD ◁   LATEST HEARD ▷   NEW OR CHANGED FOR 1992 †

FREQUENCY	COUNTRY, STATION, LOCATION	TARGET • NETWORK • POWER (kW) / World Time

15435 (con'd) USA
  †VOA, Via Kavála, Greece — (J) • MIDEAST • 250 kW
USSR
  RADIO MOSCOW, Bishkek — SE ASIA & E ASIA • 500 kW
  (J) • SE ASIA & E ASIA • 240 kW

15440 CHINA (PR)
  RADIO BEIJING, Kunming — AUSTRALIA • 120 kW
CHINA (TAIWAN)
  †BC CORP CHINA, Via Okeechobee, USA — C AMERICA • 100 kW
  VO FREE CHINA, Via Okeechobee, USA — (D) • EUROPE • 100 kW
GERMANY
  †DEUTSCHE WELLE, Königswusterhausen — (D) • SE ASIA • 100 kW
USA
  †VOA, Via Portugal — (J) • WEST USSR • 250 kW
  †WYFR-FAMILY RADIO, Okeechobee, Fl — C AMERICA • 100 kW / (D) • EUROPE • 100 kW

15445 CHINA (PR)
  †RADIO BEIJING, Via Brasilia, Brazil — C AMERICA & S AMERICA • 250 kW
NETHERLANDS ANTILLES
  TRANS WORLD RADIO, Bonaire — S AMERICA • 100 kW
PAKISTAN
  †RADIO PAKISTAN, Islamabad — N AFRICA & MIDEAST • 100 kW
UNITED KINGDOM
  †BBC, Daventry — (J) • EUROPE & WEST USSR • 300 kW
  (J) Sa/Su • EUROPE & WEST USSR • 300 kW
USA
  †R FREE AFGHANISTAN, Via Portugal — WEST USSR & S ASIA • 250 kW
  †RFE-RL, Via Portugal — (D) • WEST USSR • 250 kW
  †VOA, Via Kavála, Greece — (D) • MIDEAST • 250 kW
  †VOA, Via Tangier, Morocco — (J) • E EUROPE • 35 kW

15450 AUSTRIA
  RADIO AUSTRIA INTL, Vienna — AUSTRALIA • 500 kW
  (D) • AUSTRALIA • 500 kW
  (J) • AUSTRALIA • 500 kW
PHILIPPINES
  †FEBC RADIO INTL, Bocaue — S ASIA & SE ASIA • 50 kW
  M-F • S ASIA & SE ASIA • 50 kW
TUNISIA
  RTV TUNISIENNE, Sfax — DS • 100 kW
USSR
  RADIO MOSCOW, Serpukhov — (J) • S ASIA • 100 kW

15450v LIBYA
  RADIO JAMAHIRIYA, Tripoli — AFRICA • 500 kW

15455 CHINA (PR)
  RADIO BEIJING, Jinhua — (D) • W NORTH AM • 500 kW
USSR
  †RADIO KIEV, Petropavlovsk-K — (J) • W NORTH AM • 100 kW
  †RADIO MOSCOW — (D) / (J)
  †RADIO MOSCOW, Petropavlovsk-K — (J) • W NORTH AM • 100 kW / (J) • W NORTH AM • NORTH AMERICAN SVC • 100 kW
  †RADIO VILNIUS, Petropavlovsk-K — (J) • W NORTH AM • 100 kW
  †RADIO YEREVAN, Kiev — (D) Su • EUROPE • 100 kW
  RADIO YEREVAN, Petropavlovsk-K — (J) • W NORTH AM • 100 kW
  †SOVIET BELORUSSIA, Petropavlovsk-K — (J) • W NORTH AM • 100 kW

15460 FRANCE
  †R FRANCE INTL, Issoudun-Allouis — E AFRICA • 100 kW / (J) • E AFRICA • 100 kW
PHILIPPINES
  †FEBC RADIO INTL, Bocaue — S ASIA & SE ASIA • 50 kW
  S ASIA & SE ASIA • 50 kW • ALT. FREQ. TO 15465 kHz
  Sa/Su • S ASIA & SE ASIA • 50 kW • ALT. FREQ. TO 15465 kHz
USSR
  RADIO MOSCOW, Krasnoyarsk — DS-1 • 50 kW
  RADIO MOSCOW, Moscow — (D) • S ASIA • 100 kW
  RADIO TASHKENT, Tashkent — (J) • S ASIA • 100 kW

15465 AUSTRALIA
  †RADIO AUSTRALIA, Shepparton — (D) • PACIFIC • 100 kW
PHILIPPINES
  †FEBC RADIO INTL, Bocaue — Alternative Frequency to 15460 kHz
USSR
  RADIO MOSCOW — (J) • W AFRICA & S AMERICA

15470 GERMANY
  †DEUTSCHE WELLE, Via Cyclops, Malta — (J) • MIDEAST • 250 kW
  DEUTSCHE WELLE, Via Sines, Portugal — E EUROPE • 250 kW / (D) • E EUROPE • 250 kW

(con'd)

ENGLISH ▬ ARABIC ▩ CHINESE ▭▭▭ FRENCH ═ GERMAN ▬▬ RUSSIAN ══ SPANISH ▬▬ OTHER ▬

FREQUENCY   COUNTRY, STATION, LOCATION

TARGET • NETWORK • POWER (kW)   World Time

0 1 2 3 4 5 6 7 8 9 10 11 12 13 14 15 16 17 18 19 20 21 22 23 24

Frequency	Country, Station, Location	Target • Network • Power
15470 (con'd)	GERMANY — DEUTSCHE WELLE, Via Sines, Portugal	(J) • E EUROPE • 250 kW
	USSR — RADIO MOSCOW	(J) • E ASIA
	RADIO MOSCOW, Dushanbé	(J) • SE ASIA • 100 kW
	RADIO MOSCOW, Vladivostok	(D) • SE ASIA • 100 kW
		(J) • SE ASIA • 100 kW
15475	RADIO TASHKENT, Tashkent	(D) • S ASIA • 100 kW
	GABON — †AFRIQUE NUMERO UN, Moyabi	W AFRICA & E NORTH AM • 250 kW
	USSR — RADIO MOSCOW	AFRICA
		(J) • W EUROPE & E NORTH AM
15475v	ANTARCTICA — R NACIONAL-LRA36, Base Esperanza	S AMERICA • DS • TEMP INACTIVE • 1.5 kW
15480	ISRAEL — †KOL ISRAEL, Tel Aviv	MIDEAST • DS-D
	USSR — RADIO MOSCOW, Khar'kov	MIDEAST • 120 kW
15485	FRANCE — †R FRANCE INTL, Issoudun-Allouis	MIDEAST • 100/500 kW
		(J) • MIDEAST • 100/500 kW
	GUAM — †KTWR-TRANS WORLD R, Merizo	E ASIA • 100 kW
		(J) • E ASIA • 100 kW
	TURKEY — †VOICE OF TURKEY, Ankara	Alternative Frequency to 15365 kHz
	USSR — †RADIO KIEV, Simferopol'	(J) • E NORTH AM • 240 kW
	†RADIO MOSCOW, Kiev	ATLANTIC • 100 kW
	†RADIO VILNIUS, Simferopol'	(J) • E NORTH AM • 240 kW
	†RADIO YEREVAN, Simferopol'	(D) Su • EUROPE • 240 kW
	†SOVIET BELORUSSIA, Simferopol'	(J) • E NORTH AM • 240 kW
15490	USSR — RADIO MOSCOW	(J) • W AFRICA & S AMERICA
	RADIO MOSCOW, Irkutsk	DS-1 (FEEDER) • 15 kW • USB
	RADIO MOSCOW, Minsk	MIDEAST • 100 kW
	RADIO MOSCOW, Moscow	(J) • E AFRICA & S AFRICA • 240 kW
	RADIO MOSCOW, Tula	S ASIA & SE ASIA • 240 kW
		(J) • S ASIA & SE ASIA • 240 kW
15495	USSR — RADIO MOSCOW, Kiev	W EUROPE & W AFRICA • 100 kW
15500	CHINA (PR) — †CENTRAL PEOPLES BS, Beijing	DS-2 • 120 kW
		Th/Sa-Tu • DS-2 • 120 kW
	PHILIPPINES — †FEBC RADIO INTL, Iba	MIDEAST • 100 kW
	USSR — †R TIKHIY OKEAN	(D) • E ASIA & PACIFIC • MARINERS
	†RADIO MOSCOW	(J) • C AMERICA
		(D) • E ASIA
		(J)
	†RADIO MOSCOW, Moscow	MIDEAST • 240 kW
		(D) • MIDEAST • 240 kW
		(J) • MIDEAST • 240 kW
15510	AFGHANISTAN — †RADIO AFGHANISTAN, Via USSR	(J) • EUROPE
	GERMANY — DEUTSCHE WELLE, Via Cyclops, Malta	(J) • S ASIA • 250 kW
	DEUTSCHE WELLE, Wertachtal	E EUROPE • 500 kW
		(D) • E EUROPE • 500 kW
		(J) • E EUROPE • 500 kW
	USSR — †RADIO MOSCOW, Zhigulevsk	(J) • S AMERICA • 100 kW
	†RADIO YEREVAN, Yerevan	Su • EUROPE • 100 kW
		(J) • EUROPE • 100 kW
		(D) Su • EUROPE • 100 kW
		(J) M-Sa • EUROPE • 100 kW
		(J) • Su • EUROPE • 100 kW
15510v	BANGLADESH — †RADIO BANGLADESH, Dhaka	DS • 100 kW • ALT. FREQ. TO 17730 kHz
15514.3	PAKISTAN — †RADIO PAKISTAN, Karachi	S ASIA • 50 kW
15515 (con'd)	BELGIUM — †BELGISCHE RADIO TV, Wavre	(D) • AFRICA • 100/250 kW

0 1 2 3 4 5 6 7 8 9 10 11 12 13 14 15 16 17 18 19 20 21 22 23 24

SUMMER ONLY (J)   WINTER ONLY (D)   JAMMING / OR ∧   EARLIEST HEARD ◁   LATEST HEARD ▷   NEW OR CHANGED FOR 1992 †

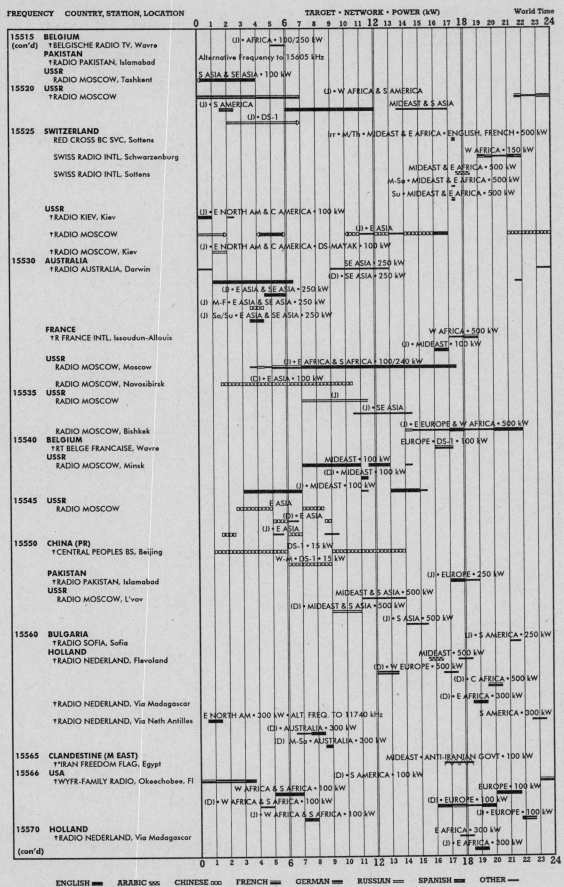

FREQUENCY   COUNTRY, STATION, LOCATION

TARGET • NETWORK • POWER (kW)

World Time

15515	**BELGIUM**
(con'd)	†BELGISCHE RADIO TV, Wavre
	PAKISTAN
	†RADIO PAKISTAN, Islamabad
	USSR
	RADIO MOSCOW, Tashkent
15520	**USSR**
	†RADIO MOSCOW
15525	**SWITZERLAND**
	RED CROSS BC SVC, Sottens
	SWISS RADIO INTL, Schwarzenburg
	SWISS RADIO INTL, Sottens
	USSR
	†RADIO KIEV, Kiev
	†RADIO MOSCOW
	†RADIO MOSCOW, Kiev
15530	**AUSTRALIA**
	†RADIO AUSTRALIA, Darwin
	FRANCE
	†R FRANCE INTL, Issoudun-Allouis
	USSR
	RADIO MOSCOW, Moscow
	RADIO MOSCOW, Novosibirsk
15535	**USSR**
	RADIO MOSCOW
	RADIO MOSCOW, Bishkek
15540	**BELGIUM**
	†RT BELGE FRANCAISE, Wavre
	USSR
	RADIO MOSCOW, Minsk
15545	**USSR**
	RADIO MOSCOW
15550	**CHINA (PR)**
	†CENTRAL PEOPLES BS, Beijing
	PAKISTAN
	†RADIO PAKISTAN, Islamabad
	USSR
	RADIO MOSCOW, L'vov
15560	**BULGARIA**
	†RADIO SOFIA, Sofia
	HOLLAND
	†RADIO NEDERLAND, Flevoland
	†RADIO NEDERLAND, Via Madagascar
	†RADIO NEDERLAND, Via Neth Antilles
15565	**CLANDESTINE (M EAST)**
	†"IRAN FREEDOM FLAG, Egypt
15566	**USA**
	†WYFR-FAMILY RADIO, Okeechobee, Fl
15570	**HOLLAND**
	†RADIO NEDERLAND, Via Madagascar
(con'd)	

Annotations within the chart area:

- (J) • AFRICA • 100/250 kW
- Alternative Frequency to 15605 kHz
- S ASIA & SE ASIA • 100 kW
- (J) • W AFRICA & S AMERICA
- (J) • S AMERICA
- MIDEAST & S ASIA
- (J) • DS-1
- Irr • M/Th • MIDEAST & E AFRICA • ENGLISH, FRENCH • 500 kW
- W AFRICA • 150 kW
- MIDEAST & E AFRICA • 500 kW
- M-Sa • MIDEAST & E AFRICA • 500 kW
- Su • MIDEAST & E AFRICA • 500 kW
- (J) • E NORTH AM & C AMERICA • 100 kW
- (J) • E ASIA
- (J) • E NORTH AM & C AMERICA • DS-MAYAK • 100 kW
- SE ASIA • 250 kW
- (D) • SE ASIA • 250 kW
- (J) • E ASIA & SE ASIA • 250 kW
- (J) M-F • E ASIA & SE ASIA • 250 kW
- (J) Sa/Su • E ASIA & SE ASIA • 250 kW
- W AFRICA • 500 kW
- (J) • MIDEAST • 100 kW
- (J) • E AFRICA & S AFRICA • 100/240 kW
- (D) • E ASIA • 100 kW
- (J)
- (J) • SE ASIA
- (J) • E EUROPE & W AFRICA • 500 kW
- EUROPE • DS-1 • 100 kW
- MIDEAST • 100 kW
- (D) • MIDEAST • 100 kW
- (J) • MIDEAST • 100 kW
- E ASIA
- (D) • E ASIA
- (J) • E ASIA
- DS-1 • 15 kW
- W-M • DS-1 • 15 kW
- (J) • EUROPE • 250 kW
- MIDEAST & S ASIA • 500 kW
- (D) • MIDEAST & S ASIA • 500 kW
- (J) • S ASIA • 500 kW
- (J) • S AMERICA • 250 kW
- MIDEAST • 500 kW
- (D) • W EUROPE • 500 kW
- (D) • C AFRICA • 500 kW
- (D) • E AFRICA • 300 kW
- E NORTH AM • 300 kW • ALT FREQ. TO 11740 kHz
- S AMERICA • 300 kW
- (D) • AUSTRALIA • 300 kW
- (D) M-Sa • AUSTRALIA • 300 kW
- MIDEAST • ANTI-IRANIAN GOVT • 100 kW
- (D) • S AMERICA • 100 kW
- W AFRICA & S AFRICA • 100 kW
- EUROPE • 100 kW
- (D) • W AFRICA & S AFRICA • 100 kW
- (D) • EUROPE • 100 kW
- (J) • W AFRICA & S AFRICA • 100 kW
- (J) • EUROPE • 100 kW
- E AFRICA • 300 kW
- (J) • E AFRICA • 300 kW

0 1 2 3 4 5 6 7 8 9 10 11 12 13 14 15 16 17 18 19 20 21 22 23 24

ENGLISH ▬▬   ARABIC ⧈⧈⧈   CHINESE □□□   FRENCH ═══   GERMAN ▬▬   RUSSIAN ══   SPANISH ▬▬   OTHER ──

FREQUENCY	COUNTRY, STATION, LOCATION	TARGET • NETWORK • POWER (kW)	World Time

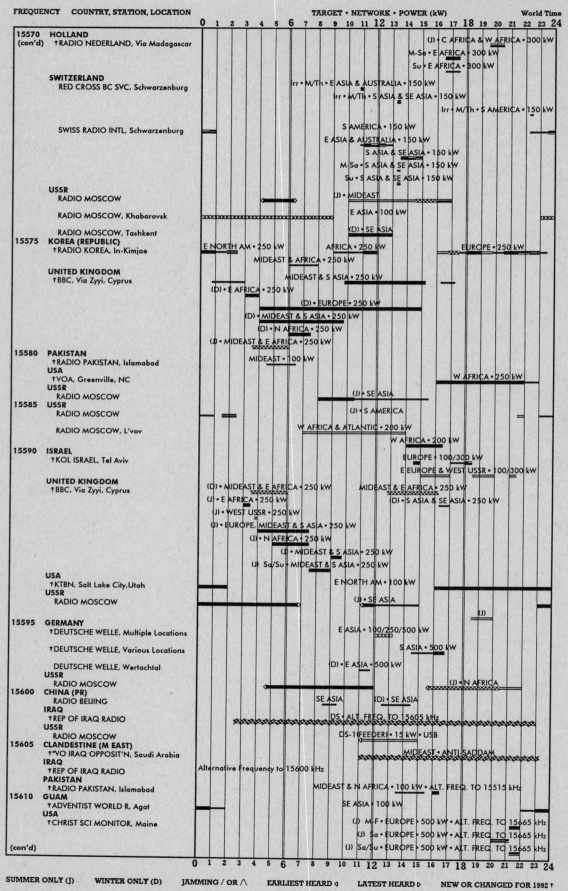

15570 HOLLAND
(con'd) †RADIO NEDERLAND, Via Madagascar — (J) • C AFRICA & W AFRICA • 300 kW / M-Sa • E AFRICA • 300 kW / Su • E AFRICA • 300 kW

SWITZERLAND
RED CROSS BC SVC, Schwarzenburg — Irr • M/Th • E ASIA & AUSTRALIA • 150 kW / Irr • M/Th • S ASIA & SE ASIA • 150 kW / Irr • M/Th • S AMERICA • 150 kW

SWISS RADIO INTL, Schwarzenburg — S AMERICA • 150 kW / E ASIA & AUSTRALIA • 150 kW / S ASIA & SE ASIA • 150 kW / M-Sa • S ASIA & SE ASIA • 150 kW / Su • S ASIA & SE ASIA • 150 kW

USSR
RADIO MOSCOW — (J) • MIDEAST

RADIO MOSCOW, Khabarovsk — E ASIA • 100 kW

RADIO MOSCOW, Tashkent — (D) • SE ASIA

15575 KOREA (REPUBLIC)
†RADIO KOREA, In-Kimjae — E NORTH AM • 250 kW / AFRICA • 250 kW / EUROPE • 250 kW / MIDEAST & AFRICA • 250 kW

UNITED KINGDOM
†BBC, Via Zyyi, Cyprus — MIDEAST & S ASIA • 250 kW / (D) • E AFRICA • 250 kW / (D) • EUROPE • 250 kW / (D) • MIDEAST & S ASIA • 250 kW / (D) • N AFRICA • 250 kW / (J) • MIDEAST & E AFRICA • 250 kW

15580 PAKISTAN
†RADIO PAKISTAN, Islamabad — MIDEAST • 100 kW
USA
†VOA, Greenville, NC — W AFRICA • 250 kW
USSR
RADIO MOSCOW — (J) • SE ASIA

15585 USSR
RADIO MOSCOW — (J) • S AMERICA

RADIO MOSCOW, L'vov — W AFRICA & ATLANTIC • 200 kW / W AFRICA • 200 kW

15590 ISRAEL
†KOL ISRAEL, Tel Aviv — EUROPE • 100/300 kW / E EUROPE & WEST USSR • 100/300 kW

UNITED KINGDOM
†BBC, Via Zyyi, Cyprus — (D) • MIDEAST & E AFRICA • 250 kW / MIDEAST & E AFRICA • 250 kW / (J) • E AFRICA • 250 kW / (D) • S ASIA & SE ASIA • 250 kW / (J) • WEST USSR • 250 kW / (J) • EUROPE, MIDEAST & S ASIA • 250 kW / (J) • N AFRICA • 250 kW / (J) • MIDEAST & S ASIA • 250 kW / (J) Sa/Su • MIDEAST & S ASIA • 250 kW

USA
†KTBN, Salt Lake City, Utah — E NORTH AM • 100 kW
USSR
RADIO MOSCOW — (J) • SE ASIA / (J)

15595 GERMANY
†DEUTSCHE WELLE, Multiple Locations — E ASIA • 100/250/500 kW

†DEUTSCHE WELLE, Various Locations — S ASIA • 500 kW

DEUTSCHE WELLE, Wertachtal — (D) • E ASIA • 500 kW
USSR
RADIO MOSCOW — (J) • N AFRICA
15600 CHINA (PR)
RADIO BEIJING — SE ASIA / (D) • SE ASIA
IRAQ
†REP OF IRAQ RADIO — DS • ALT. FREQ. TO 15605 kHz
USSR
RADIO MOSCOW — DS-1 (FEEDER) • 15 kW • USB
15605 CLANDESTINE (M EAST)
†"VO IRAQ OPPOSIT'N, Saudi Arabia — MIDEAST • ANTI-SADDAM
IRAQ
†REP OF IRAQ RADIO — Alternative Frequency to 15600 kHz
PAKISTAN
†RADIO PAKISTAN, Islamabad — MIDEAST & N AFRICA • 100 kW • ALT. FREQ. TO 15515 kHz
15610 GUAM
†ADVENTIST WORLD R, Agat — SE ASIA • 100 kW
USA
†CHRIST SCI MONITOR, Maine — (J) M-F • EUROPE • 500 kW • ALT. FREQ. TO 15665 kHz / (J) Sa • EUROPE • 500 kW • ALT. FREQ. TO 15665 kHz / (J) Sa/Su • EUROPE • 500 kW • ALT. FREQ. TO 15665 kHz

(con'd)

SUMMER ONLY (J)   WINTER ONLY (D)   JAMMING / OR ∧   EARLIEST HEARD ◁   LATEST HEARD ▷   NEW OR CHANGED FOR 1992 †

FREQUENCY   COUNTRY, STATION, LOCATION   TARGET • NETWORK • POWER (kW)   World Time

```
                                            0  1  2  3  4  5  6  7  8  9 10 11 12 13 14 15 16 17 18 19 20 21 22 23 24
```

Frequency	Country, Station, Location	Schedule
15610 (con'd)	USA †CHRIST SCI MONITOR, Maine	(J) Su-F • EUROPE • 500 kW • ALT. FREQ. TO 15665 kHz
	†CHRIST SCI MONITOR, South Carolina	(D) M-F • EUROPE • 500 kW
		(D) Sa • E NORTH AM & C AMERICA • 500 kW
		(D) Sa • EUROPE • 500 kW
		Sa/Su • E NORTH AM & C AMERICA • 500 kW
		(D) Sa/Su • E NORTH AM & C AMERICA • 500 kW
		(D) Su-F • EUROPE • 500 kW
		(D) Su • E NORTH AM & C AMERICA • 500 kW
		(D) Su • EUROPE • 500 kW
	†CHRIST SCI MONITOR, Via Saipan	AUSTRALIA • 100 kW
		(D) • AUSTRALIA • 100 kW
		M-F • AUSTRALIA • 100 kW
		(D) Sa • AUSTRALIA • 100 kW
		Sa/Su • AUSTRALIA • 100 kW
		(D) Su-F • AUSTRALIA • 100 kW
15617	ISRAEL †RASHUTH HASHIDUR, Tel Aviv	EUROPE & E NORTH AM • DS-B • 50/300 kW
		Su-F • EUROPE & E NORTH AM • DS-B • 50/300 kW
15625	GREECE FONI TIS HELLADAS, Athens	AUSTRALIA • 100 kW (J) • AFRICA • 100 kW
		(J) • ATLANTIC • 100 kW
		(J) • E ASIA • 100 kW
		(J) • MIDEAST • 100 kW
	FONI TIS HELLADAS, Kaválla	(J) • N AMERICA & EUROPE • 250 kW
15630	GREECE FONI TIS HELLADAS, Athens	(D) • ATLANTIC • 100 kW
		(D) • E ASIA • 100 kW
		(D) • N AMERICA & EUROPE • 100 kW
		(D) • AFRICA • 100 kW
	USSR †RADIO MOSCOW	DS-2 (FEEDER) • USB
15640	ISRAEL †KOL ISRAEL, Tel Aviv	WEST USSR • 300 kW EUROPE • 300 kW
		E EUROPE & WEST USSR • 100/300 kW
		AFRICA • 300 kW
		E NORTH AM & C AMERICA • 300 kW
15650	CLANDESTINE (M EAST) "RADIO IRAN", Abu Za'bal, Egypt	MIDEAST • ANTI-IRANIAN GOVT • 100 kW (J) • MIDEAST • ANTI-IRANIAN GOVT • 100 kW
	GREECE FONI TIS HELLADAS, Athens	(J) • N AMERICA & EUROPE • 100 kW
15665	USA †CHRIST SCI MONITOR, Maine	Alternative Frequency to 15610 kHz
		(J) • EUROPE • 500 kW
		(J) M-F • EUROPE • 500 kW
		(D) Sa • EUROPE • 500 kW
		(J) Su • EUROPE • 500 kW
		(J) Sa/Su • EUROPE • 500 kW
		(J) Su-F • EUROPE • 500 kW
15670	CHINA (PR) †CENTRAL PEOPLES BS, Kunming	DS-MINORITIES • 50 kW
	UNITED KINGDOM †BRITISH FORCES BS	(J) • MIDEAST • (FEEDER) • USB
15685	CLANDESTINE (ASIA) "VOICE OF UNITY", Abu Za'bal, Egypt	MIDEAST & S ASIA • PRO-AFGHAN REBELS • 100 kW
15690	USA †WWCR, Nashville, Tennessee	E NORTH AM & EUROPE • 100 kW
15710	CHINA (PR) †CENTRAL PEOPLES BS, Beijing	CHINESE, ETC • TAIWAN-1 • 10 kW
15720	USSR RADIO MOSCOW	(J) • (FEEDER) • USB
15750	USSR †RADIO MOSCOW	DS-2 (FEEDER) • USB
15752	USA VOA, Cincinnati, Ohio	(J) • N AFRICA • (FEEDER) • 50 kW • ISU
15770	ICELAND †RIKISUTVARPID, Reykjavik	ATLANTIC & EUROPE • DS-1 • 10 kW • USB
		ATLANTIC & E NORTH AM • DS-1 • 10 kW • USB
15775	USA †RFE-RL, Via Holzkirchen, GFR	Irr • W EUROPE • (FEEDER) • 10 kW • ISL
		Irr • W EUROPE • (FEEDER) • 10 kW • ISU
15790	ICELAND †RIKISUTVARPID, Reykjavik	ATLANTIC & EUROPE • DS-1 • 10 kW • USB
15880	CHINA (PR) †CENTRAL PEOPLES BS, Beijing	CHINESE, ETC • TAIWAN-2 • 15 kW
		Th-Tu • CHINESE ETC • TAIWAN-2 • 15 kW

```
                                            0  1  2  3  4  5  6  7  8  9 10 11 12 13 14 15 16 17 18 19 20 21 22 23 24
```

ENGLISH ▬   ARABIC �   CHINESE ▭▭▭   FRENCH ▬▬   GERMAN ▬▬   RUSSIAN ▬▬   SPANISH ▬▬   OTHER ▬

FREQUENCY	COUNTRY, STATION, LOCATION	TARGET • NETWORK • POWER (kW) — World Time
16041.3	USA †AFRTS-US MILITARY, Via Barford, UK	Irr • ATLANTIC • DS-ABC/CBS/NBC/NPR(FEEDER) • 4 kW • LSB
16065	USA RFE-RL, Via Holzkirchen, GFR	Irr • W EUROPE • (FEEDER) • 10 kW • ISL Irr • W EUROPE • (FEEDER) • 10 kW • ISU Irr • (J) • W EUROPE • (FEEDER) • 10 kW • ISL Irr • (J) • W EUROPE • (FEEDER) • 10 kW • ISU
16330	USSR †RADIO MOSCOW	DS-2(FEEDER) • USB
16454.3	USA †AFRTS-US MILITARY, Via Barford, UK	Irr • ATLANTIC • DS-ABC/CBS/NBC/NPR(FEEDER) • 4 kW • LSB
17387	INDIA †ALL INDIA RADIO, Aligarh	AUSTRALIA • 250 kW SE ASIA • 250 kW ENGLISH, ETC • DS • 250 kW
17500	TUNISIA †RTV TUNISIENNE, Sfax	DS • 100 kW
17510	USA †CHRIST SCI MONITOR, South Carolina	(J) M-F • E NORTH AM & EUROPE • 500 kW (J) Sa • E NORTH AM & EUROPE • 500 kW (J) Sa/Su • E NORTH AM & EUROPE • 500 kW (J) Su • E NORTH AM & EUROPE • 500 kW
17525	USA †WWCR, Nashville, Tennessee	E NORTH AM & EUROPE • 100 kW
	VATICAN STATE †VATICAN RADIO, Sta Maria di Galeria	C AMERICA & S AMERICA • 250/500 kW E ASIA • 250/500 kW • ALT. FREQ. TO 17535 kHz SE ASIA & AUSTRALIA • 250/500 kW • ALT. FREQ. TO 17535 kHz
17533	CHINA (PR) RADIO BEIJING, Kunming	(D) • S AMERICA • CHINESE, CANTONESE • 120 kW
	CLANDESTINE (ASIA) "DEM KAMPUCHEA", Kunming, China	(J) • SE ASIA • PRO-KHMER ROUGE • 50 kW
17535	GREECE FONI TIS HELLADAS, Athens	(D) • N AMERICA & EUROPE • 100 kW (J) • AUSTRALIA • 100 kW (J) • E ASIA • 100 kW (J) • N AMERICA & EUROPE • 100 kW
	VATICAN STATE †VATICAN RADIO, Sta Maria di Galeria	Alternative Frequency to 17525 kHz
17540	CLANDESTINE (ASIA) "VOICE OF UNITY", Abu Za'bal, Egypt	MIDEAST & S ASIA • PRO-AFGHAN REBELS • 100 kW
17545	ISRAEL †RASHUTH HASHIDUR, Tel Aviv	EUROPE • DS-B • 50/300 kW
17550	BELGIUM †BELGISCHE RADIO TV, Wavre	(D) • AFRICA • 100/250 kW (J) • AFRICA • 100/250 kW (D) M/Tu/Th/F • AFRICA • 100/250 kW (J) M/Tu/Th/F • AFRICA • 100/250 kW (D) W/Sa/Su • AFRICA • 100/250 kW (J) W/Sa/Su • AFRICA • 100/250 kW
	GREECE FONI TIS HELLADAS, Athens	(D) • AUSTRALIA • 100 kW (D) • N AMERICA & EUROPE • 100 kW
17554v	PAKISTAN †RADIO PAKISTAN, Karachi	MIDEAST • 50 kW
17555	PAKISTAN †RADIO PAKISTAN, Islamabad	MIDEAST & N AFRICA • 100 kW
	USA †CHRIST SCI MONITOR, South Carolina	Alternative Frequency to 13760 kHz S AMERICA • 500 kW M-Sa • S AMERICA • 500 kW Sa • C AMERICA & W NORTH AM • 500 kW Sa • S AMERICA • 500 kW Sa/Su • C AMERICA & W NORTH AM • 500 kW Su • C AMERICA & W NORTH AM • 500 kW Su • S AMERICA • 500 kW Su-F • S AMERICA • 500 kW
	†CHRIST SCI MONITOR, Via Saipan	SE ASIA • 100 kW M-Sa • SE ASIA • 100 kW (J) • E ASIA • 100 kW Sa/Su • SE ASIA • 100 kW Su • SE ASIA • 100 kW
17560	USSR †RADIO MOSCOW	(D) • SE ASIA (J) • S ASIA
17565	USSR †RADIO MOSCOW	(J) • S AMERICA (D) • AFRICA

FREQUENCY　　COUNTRY, STATION, LOCATION

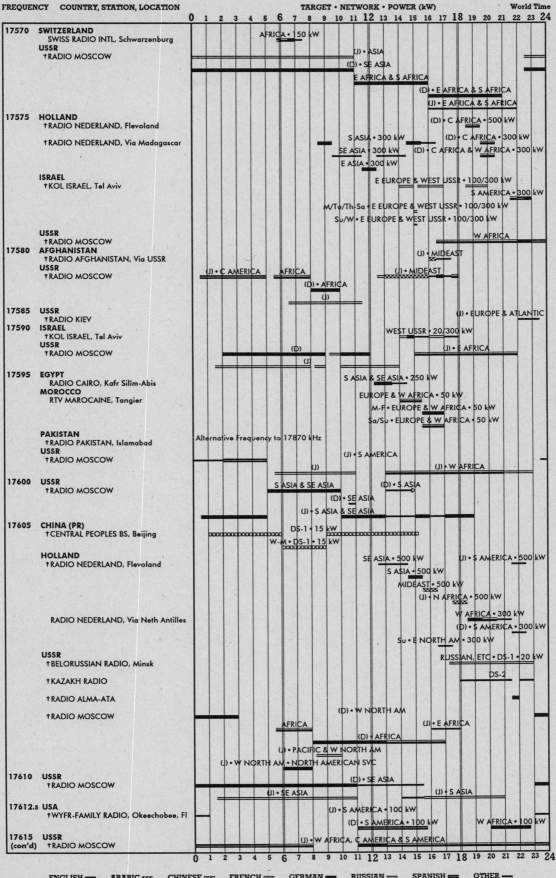

FREQUENCY	COUNTRY, STATION, LOCATION	TARGET • NETWORK • POWER (kW)
17570	SWITZERLAND	
	SWISS RADIO INTL, Schwarzenburg	AFRICA • 150 kW
	USSR	
	†RADIO MOSCOW	(J) • ASIA
		(D) • SE ASIA
		E AFRICA & S AFRICA
		(D) • E AFRICA & S AFRICA
		(J) • E AFRICA & S AFRICA
17575	HOLLAND	
	†RADIO NEDERLAND, Flevoland	(D) • C AFRICA • 500 kW
	†RADIO NEDERLAND, Via Madagascar	S ASIA • 300 kW　(D) • C AFRICA • 300 kW
		SE ASIA • 300 kW　(D) • C AFRICA & W AFRICA • 300 kW
		E ASIA • 300 kW
	ISRAEL	
	†KOL ISRAEL, Tel Aviv	E EUROPE & WEST USSR • 100/300 kW
		S AMERICA • 300 kW
		M/Tu/Th/Sa • E EUROPE & WEST USSR • 100/300 kW
		Su/W • E EUROPE & WEST USSR • 100/300 kW
	USSR	
	†RADIO MOSCOW	W AFRICA
17580	AFGHANISTAN	
	†RADIO AFGHANISTAN, Via USSR	(J) • MIDEAST
	USSR	
	†RADIO MOSCOW	(J) • C AMERICA　AFRICA　(J) • MIDEAST
		(D) • AFRICA
		(J)
17585	USSR	
	†RADIO KIEV	(J) • EUROPE & ATLANTIC
17590	ISRAEL	
	†KOL ISRAEL, Tel Aviv	WEST USSR • 20/300 kW
	USSR	
	†RADIO MOSCOW	(J) • E AFRICA
		(D)
		(J)
17595	EGYPT	
	RADIO CAIRO, Kafr Silim-Abis	S ASIA & SE ASIA • 250 kW
	MOROCCO	
	RTV MAROCAINE, Tangier	EUROPE & W AFRICA • 50 kW
		M-F • EUROPE & W AFRICA • 50 kW
		Sa/Su • EUROPE & W AFRICA • 50 kW
	PAKISTAN	
	†RADIO PAKISTAN, Islamabad	Alternative Frequency to 17870 kHz
	USSR	
	†RADIO MOSCOW	(J) • S AMERICA
		(J)　(J) • W AFRICA
17600	USSR	
	†RADIO MOSCOW	S ASIA & SE ASIA　(D) • S ASIA
		(D) • SE ASIA
		(J) • S ASIA & SE ASIA
17605	CHINA (PR)	
	†CENTRAL PEOPLES BS, Beijing	DS-1 • 15 kW
		W-M • DS-1 • 15 kW
	HOLLAND	
	†RADIO NEDERLAND, Flevoland	SE ASIA • 500 kW　(J) • S AMERICA • 500 kW
		S ASIA • 500 kW
		MIDEAST • 500 kW
		(J) • N AFRICA • 500 kW
	RADIO NEDERLAND, Via Neth Antilles	W AFRICA • 300 kW
		(D) • S AMERICA • 300 kW
		Su • E NORTH AM • 300 kW
	USSR	
	†BELORUSSIAN RADIO, Minsk	RUSSIAN, ETC • DS-1 • 20 kW
	†KAZAKH RADIO	DS-2
	†RADIO ALMA-ATA	
	†RADIO MOSCOW	(D) • W NORTH AM
		AFRICA　(J) • E AFRICA
		(D) • AFRICA
		(J) • PACIFIC & W NORTH AM
		(J) • W NORTH AM • NORTH AMERICAN SVC
17610	USSR	
	†RADIO MOSCOW	(D) • SE ASIA
		(J) • SE ASIA　(J) • S ASIA
17612.5	USA	
	†WYFR-FAMILY RADIO, Okeechobee, Fl	(J) • S AMERICA • 100 kW
		(D) • S AMERICA • 100 kW　W AFRICA • 100 kW
17615 (con'd)	USSR	
	†RADIO MOSCOW	(J) • W AFRICA, C AMERICA & S AMERICA

ENGLISH ▬　ARABIC ▒▒▒　CHINESE ▫▫▫　FRENCH ▬▬　GERMAN ▬▬　RUSSIAN ═══　SPANISH ▬▬　OTHER ▬

FREQUENCY   COUNTRY, STATION, LOCATION

TARGET • NETWORK • POWER (kW)

World Time

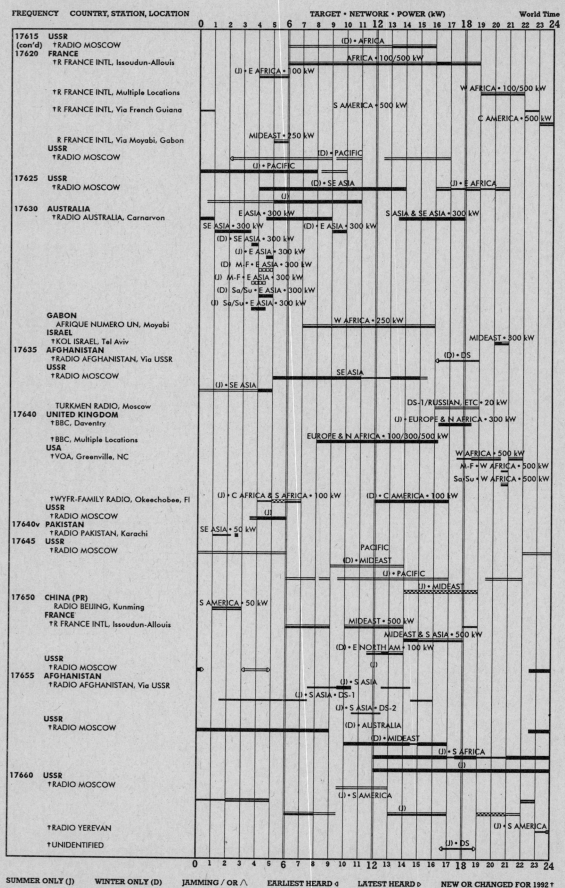

17615 USSR
(con'd) †RADIO MOSCOW
17620 FRANCE
        †R FRANCE INTL, Issoudun-Allouis
        †R FRANCE INTL, Multiple Locations
        †R FRANCE INTL, Via French Guiana
        R FRANCE INTL, Via Moyabi, Gabon
        USSR
        †RADIO MOSCOW
17625 USSR
        †RADIO MOSCOW
17630 AUSTRALIA
        †RADIO AUSTRALIA, Carnarvon
        GABON
        AFRIQUE NUMERO UN, Moyabi
        ISRAEL
        †KOL ISRAEL, Tel Aviv
17635 AFGHANISTAN
        †RADIO AFGHANISTAN, Via USSR
        USSR
        †RADIO MOSCOW
        TURKMEN RADIO, Moscow
17640 UNITED KINGDOM
        †BBC, Daventry
        †BBC, Multiple Locations
        USA
        †VOA, Greenville, NC
        †WYFR-FAMILY RADIO, Okeechobee, Fl
        USSR
        †RADIO MOSCOW
17640v PAKISTAN
        †RADIO PAKISTAN, Karachi
17645 USSR
        †RADIO MOSCOW
17650 CHINA (PR)
        RADIO BEIJING, Kunming
        FRANCE
        †R FRANCE INTL, Issoudun-Allouis
        USSR
        †RADIO MOSCOW
17655 AFGHANISTAN
        †RADIO AFGHANISTAN, Via USSR
        USSR
        †RADIO MOSCOW
17660 USSR
        †RADIO MOSCOW
        †RADIO YEREVAN
        †UNIDENTIFIED

Chart labels (target • network • power):
- (D) • AFRICA
- AFRICA • 100/500 kW
- (J) • E AFRICA • 100 kW
- W AFRICA • 100/500 kW
- S AMERICA • 500 kW
- C AMERICA • 500 kW
- MIDEAST • 250 kW
- (D) • PACIFIC
- (J) • PACIFIC
- (D) • SE ASIA
- (J) • E AFRICA
- (J)
- E ASIA • 300 kW
- S ASIA & SE ASIA • 300 kW
- SE ASIA • 300 kW
- (D) • E ASIA • 300 kW
- (D) • SE ASIA • 300 kW
- (J) • E ASIA • 300 kW
- (D) M-F • E ASIA • 300 kW
- (J) M-F • E ASIA • 300 kW
- (D) Sa/Su • E ASIA • 300 kW
- (J) Sa/Su • E ASIA • 300 kW
- W AFRICA • 250 kW
- MIDEAST • 300 kW
- (D) • DS
- SE ASIA
- (J) • SE ASIA
- DS-1/RUSSIAN, ETC • 20 kW
- (J) • EUROPE & N AFRICA • 300 kW
- EUROPE & N AFRICA • 100/300/500 kW
- W AFRICA • 500 kW
- M-F • W AFRICA • 500 kW
- Sa/Su • W AFRICA • 500 kW
- (J) • C AFRICA & S AFRICA • 100 kW
- (D) • C AMERICA • 100 kW
- (J)
- SE ASIA • 50 kW
- PACIFIC
- (D) • MIDEAST
- (J) • PACIFIC
- (J) • MIDEAST
- S AMERICA • 50 kW
- MIDEAST • 500 kW
- MIDEAST & S ASIA • 500 kW
- (D) • E NORTH AM • 100 kW
- (J)
- (J) • S ASIA
- (J) • S ASIA • DS-1
- (J) • S ASIA • DS-2
- (D) • AUSTRALIA
- (D) • MIDEAST
- (J) • S AFRICA
- (J)
- (J) • S AMERICA
- (J)
- (J) • S AMERICA
- (J) • DS

FREQUENCY   COUNTRY, STATION, LOCATION   TARGET • NETWORK • POWER (kW)   World Time

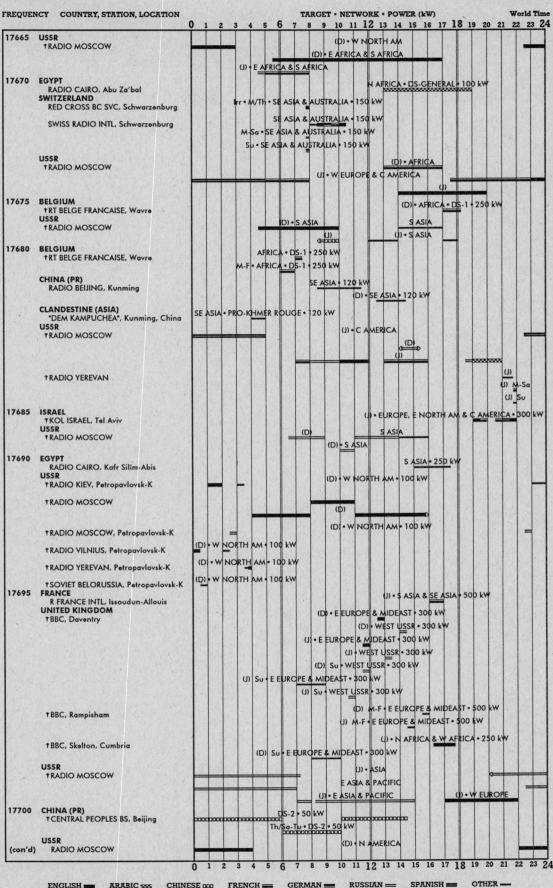

17665	**USSR**
	†RADIO MOSCOW
17670	**EGYPT**
	RADIO CAIRO, Abu Za'bal
	SWITZERLAND
	RED CROSS BC SVC, Schwarzenburg
	SWISS RADIO INTL, Schwarzenburg
	USSR
	†RADIO MOSCOW
17675	**BELGIUM**
	†RT BELGE FRANCAISE, Wavre
	USSR
	†RADIO MOSCOW
17680	**BELGIUM**
	†RT BELGE FRANCAISE, Wavre
	CHINA (PR)
	RADIO BEIJING, Kunming
	CLANDESTINE (ASIA)
	"DEM KAMPUCHEA", Kunming, China
	USSR
	†RADIO MOSCOW
	†RADIO YEREVAN
17685	**ISRAEL**
	†KOL ISRAEL, Tel Aviv
	USSR
	†RADIO MOSCOW
17690	**EGYPT**
	RADIO CAIRO, Kafr Silim-Abis
	USSR
	†RADIO KIEV, Petropavlovsk-K
	†RADIO MOSCOW
	†RADIO MOSCOW, Petropavlovsk-K
	†RADIO VILNIUS, Petropavlovsk-K
	†RADIO YEREVAN, Petropavlovsk-K
	†SOVIET BELORUSSIA, Petropavlovsk-K
17695	**FRANCE**
	R FRANCE INTL, Issoudun-Allouis
	UNITED KINGDOM
	†BBC, Daventry
	†BBC, Rampisham
	†BBC, Skelton, Cumbria
	USSR
	†RADIO MOSCOW
17700	**CHINA (PR)**
	†CENTRAL PEOPLES BS, Beijing
(con'd)	**USSR**
	RADIO MOSCOW

FREQUENCY	COUNTRY, STATION, LOCATION	TARGET • NETWORK • POWER (kW)	World Time

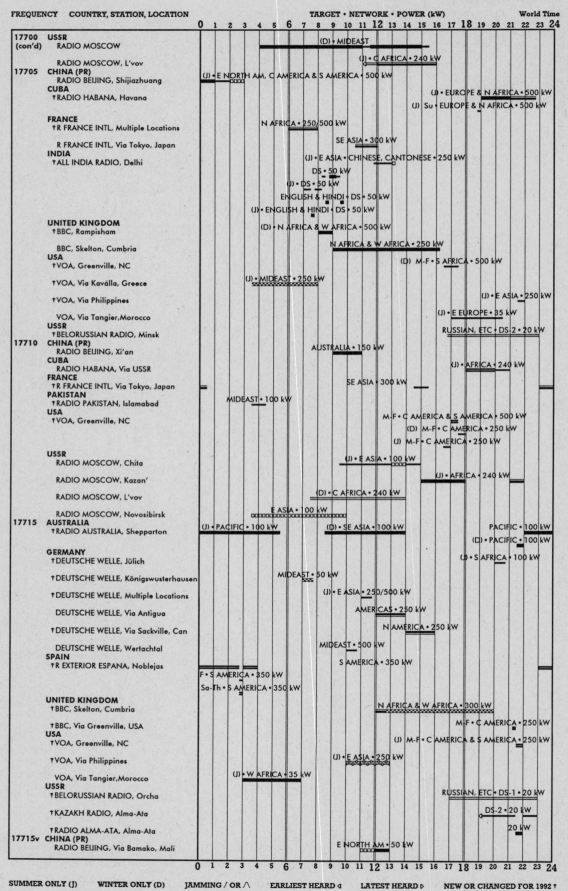

17700 (con'd) — **USSR** — RADIO MOSCOW — (D) • MIDEAST
RADIO MOSCOW, L'vov — (J) • C AFRICA • 240 kW
17705 — **CHINA (PR)** — RADIO BEIJING, Shijiazhuang — (J) • E NORTH AM, C AMERICA & S AMERICA • 500 kW
CUBA — †RADIO HABANA, Havana — (J) • EUROPE & N AFRICA • 500 kW
(J) • Su • EUROPE & N AFRICA • 500 kW
FRANCE — †R FRANCE INTL, Multiple Locations — N AFRICA • 250/500 kW
R FRANCE INTL, Via Tokyo, Japan — SE ASIA • 300 kW
INDIA — †ALL INDIA RADIO, Delhi — (J) • E ASIA • CHINESE, CANTONESE • 250 kW
DS • 50 kW
(J) • DS • 50 kW
ENGLISH & HINDI • DS • 50 kW
(J) • ENGLISH & HINDI • DS • 50 kW
UNITED KINGDOM — †BBC, Rampisham — (D) • N AFRICA & W AFRICA • 500 kW
BBC, Skelton, Cumbria — N AFRICA & W AFRICA • 250 kW
USA — †VOA, Greenville, NC — (D) • M-F • S AFRICA • 500 kW
†VOA, Via Kavála, Greece — (J) • MIDEAST • 250 kW
†VOA, Via Philippines — (J) • E ASIA • 250 kW
VOA, Via Tangier, Morocco — (J) • E EUROPE • 35 kW
USSR — †BELORUSSIAN RADIO, Minsk — RUSSIAN, ETC • DS-2 • 20 kW
17710 — **CHINA (PR)** — RADIO BEIJING, Xi'an — AUSTRALIA • 150 kW
CUBA — RADIO HABANA, Via USSR — (J) • AFRICA • 240 kW
FRANCE — †R FRANCE INTL, Via Tokyo, Japan — SE ASIA • 300 kW
PAKISTAN — †RADIO PAKISTAN, Islamabad — MIDEAST • 100 kW
USA — †VOA, Greenville, NC — M-F • C AMERICA & S AMERICA • 500 kW
(D) • M-F • C AMERICA • 250 kW
(J) • M-F • C AMERICA • 250 kW
USSR — RADIO MOSCOW, Chita — (J) • E ASIA • 100 kW
RADIO MOSCOW, Kazan' — (J) • AFRICA • 240 kW
RADIO MOSCOW, L'vov — (D) • C AFRICA • 240 kW
RADIO MOSCOW, Novosibirsk — E ASIA • 100 kW
17715 — **AUSTRALIA** — †RADIO AUSTRALIA, Shepparton — (J) • PACIFIC • 100 kW
(D) • SE ASIA • 100 kW
PACIFIC • 100 kW
(D) • PACIFIC • 100 kW
GERMANY — †DEUTSCHE WELLE, Jülich — (J) • S AFRICA • 100 kW
†DEUTSCHE WELLE, Königswusterhausen — MIDEAST • 50 kW
†DEUTSCHE WELLE, Multiple Locations — (J) • E ASIA • 250/500 kW
DEUTSCHE WELLE, Via Antigua — AMERICAS • 250 kW
†DEUTSCHE WELLE, Via Sackville, Can — N AMERICA • 250 kW
DEUTSCHE WELLE, Wertachtal — MIDEAST • 500 kW
SPAIN — †R EXTERIOR ESPANA, Noblejas — S AMERICA • 350 kW
F • S AMERICA • 350 kW
Sa-Th • S AMERICA • 350 kW
UNITED KINGDOM — †BBC, Skelton, Cumbria — N AFRICA & W AFRICA • 300 kW
†BBC, Via Greenville, USA — M-F • C AMERICA • 250 kW
USA — †VOA, Greenville, NC — (J) • M-F • C AMERICA & S AMERICA • 250 kW
†VOA, Via Philippines — (J) • E ASIA • 250 kW
VOA, Via Tangier, Morocco — (J) • W AFRICA • 35 kW
USSR — †BELORUSSIAN RADIO, Orcha — RUSSIAN, ETC • DS-1 • 20 kW
†KAZAKH RADIO, Alma-Ata — DS-2 • 20 kW
†RADIO ALMA-ATA, Alma-Ata — 20 kW
17715v — **CHINA (PR)** — RADIO BEIJING, Via Bamako, Mali — E NORTH AM • 50 kW

SUMMER ONLY (J)   WINTER ONLY (D)   JAMMING / OR ∧   EARLIEST HEARD ◁   LATEST HEARD ▷   NEW OR CHANGED FOR 1992 †

FREQUENCY   COUNTRY, STATION, LOCATION   TARGET • NETWORK • POWER (kW)   World Time

0 1 2 3 4 5 6 7 8 9 10 11 12 13 14 15 16 17 18 19 20 21 22 23 24

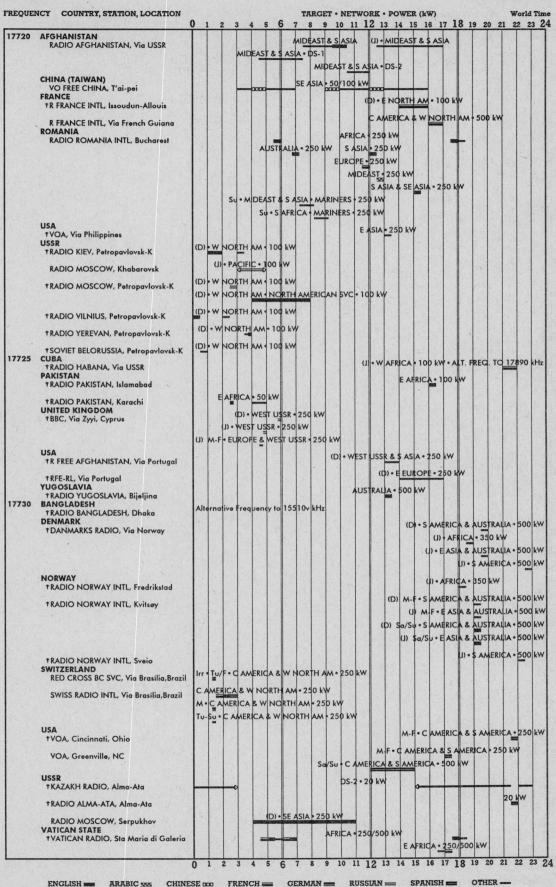

Frequency	Country, Station, Location	Target • Network • Power
17720	**AFGHANISTAN**	
	RADIO AFGHANISTAN, Via USSR	MIDEAST & S ASIA (J) • MIDEAST & S ASIA
		MIDEAST & S ASIA • DS-1
		MIDEAST & S ASIA • DS-2
	CHINA (TAIWAN)	
	VO FREE CHINA, T'ai-pei	SE ASIA • 50/100 kW
	FRANCE	
	†R FRANCE INTL, Issoudun-Allouis	(D) • E NORTH AM • 100 kW
		C AMERICA & W NORTH AM • 500 kW
	R FRANCE INTL, Via French Guiana	
	ROMANIA	
	RADIO ROMANIA INTL, Bucharest	AFRICA • 250 kW
		AUSTRALIA • 250 kW S ASIA • 250 kW
		EUROPE • 250 kW
		MIDEAST • 250 kW
		S ASIA & SE ASIA • 250 kW
		Su • MIDEAST & S ASIA • MARINERS • 250 kW
		Su • S AFRICA • MARINERS • 250 kW
	USA	
	†VOA, Via Philippines	E ASIA • 250 kW
	USSR	
	†RADIO KIEV, Petropavlovsk-K	(D) • W NORTH AM • 100 kW
	RADIO MOSCOW, Khabarovsk	(J) • PACIFIC • 100 kW
	†RADIO MOSCOW, Petropavlovsk-K	(D) • W NORTH AM • 100 kW
		(D) • W NORTH AM • NORTH AMERICAN SVC • 100 kW
	†RADIO VILNIUS, Petropavlovsk-K	(D) • W NORTH AM • 100 kW
	†RADIO YEREVAN, Petropavlovsk-K	(D) • W NORTH AM • 100 kW
	†SOVIET BELORUSSIA, Petropavlovsk-K	(D) • W NORTH AM • 100 kW
17725	**CUBA**	
	†RADIO HABANA, Via USSR	(J) • W AFRICA • 100 kW • ALT. FREQ. TO 17890 kHz
	PAKISTAN	
	†RADIO PAKISTAN, Islamabad	E AFRICA • 100 kW
	†RADIO PAKISTAN, Karachi	E AFRICA • 50 kW
	UNITED KINGDOM	
	†BBC, Via Zyyi, Cyprus	(D) • WEST USSR • 250 kW
		(J) • WEST USSR • 250 kW
		(J) M-F • EUROPE & WEST USSR • 250 kW
	USA	
	†R FREE AFGHANISTAN, Via Portugal	(D) • WEST USSR & S ASIA • 250 kW
	†RFE-RL, Via Portugal	(D) • E EUROPE • 250 kW
	YUGOSLAVIA	
	†RADIO YUGOSLAVIA, Bijeljina	AUSTRALIA • 500 kW
17730	**BANGLADESH**	
	†RADIO BANGLADESH, Dhaka	Alternative Frequency to 15510v kHz
	DENMARK	
	†DANMARKS RADIO, Via Norway	(D) • S AMERICA & AUSTRALIA • 500 kW
		(J) • AFRICA • 350 kW
		(J) • E ASIA & AUSTRALIA • 500 kW
		(J) • S AMERICA • 500 kW
	NORWAY	
	†RADIO NORWAY INTL, Fredrikstad	(J) • AFRICA • 350 kW
	†RADIO NORWAY INTL, Kvitsøy	(D) M-F • S AMERICA & AUSTRALIA • 500 kW
		(J) M-F • E ASIA & AUSTRALIA • 500 kW
		(D) Sa/Su • S AMERICA & AUSTRALIA • 500 kW
		(J) Sa/Su • E ASIA & AUSTRALIA • 500 kW
	†RADIO NORWAY INTL, Sveio	(J) • S AMERICA • 500 kW
	SWITZERLAND	
	RED CROSS BC SVC, Via Brasília, Brazil	Irr • Tu/F • C AMERICA & W NORTH AM • 250 kW
	SWISS RADIO INTL, Via Brasília, Brazil	C AMERICA & W NORTH AM • 250 kW
		M • C AMERICA & W NORTH AM • 250 kW
		Tu-Su • C AMERICA & W NORTH AM • 250 kW
	USA	
	†VOA, Cincinnati, Ohio	M-F • C AMERICA & S AMERICA • 250 kW
	VOA, Greenville, NC	M-F • C AMERICA & S AMERICA • 250 kW
		Sa/Su • C AMERICA & S AMERICA • 500 kW
	USSR	
	†KAZAKH RADIO, Alma-Ata	DS-2 • 20 kW
	†RADIO ALMA-ATA, Alma-Ata	20 kW
	RADIO MOSCOW, Serpukhov	(D) • SE ASIA • 250 kW
	VATICAN STATE	
	†VATICAN RADIO, Sta Maria di Galeria	AFRICA • 250/500 kW
		E AFRICA • 250/500 kW

0 1 2 3 4 5 6 7 8 9 10 11 12 13 14 15 16 17 18 19 20 21 22 23 24

ENGLISH ▬▬   ARABIC ⧓⧓⧓   CHINESE ▫▫▫   FRENCH ▭▭   GERMAN ▬▬   RUSSIAN ▬▬   SPANISH ▬▬   OTHER ▬

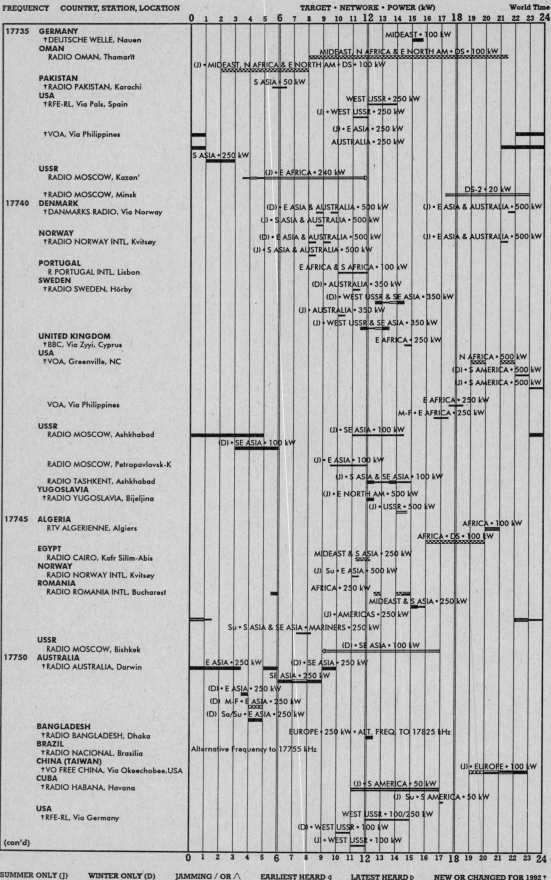

FREQUENCY   COUNTRY, STATION, LOCATION   TARGET • NETWORK • POWER (kW)   World Time

0 1 2 3 4 5 6 7 8 9 10 11 12 13 14 15 16 17 18 19 20 21 22 23 24

17750   **USA**
(con'd)   †RFE-RL, Via Portugal   (J) • WEST USSR • 250 kW

      †WYFR-FAMILY RADIO, Okeechobee, Fl   (J) • S AMERICA • 100 kW
                                 EUROPE • 100 kW
                                 (J) • C AMERICA • 100 kW

17755   **BRAZIL**
      †RADIO NACIONAL, Brasilia   AFRICA • 250 kW • ALT. FREQ. TO 17750 kHz
      DENMARK
      †DANMARKS RADIO, Via Norway   N AMERICA • 500 kW
                                 (J) • N AMERICA • 500 kW
      GERMANY
      †DEUTSCHE WELLE, Königswusterhausen   W AFRICA • 100 kW
      KOREA (DPR)
      †RADIO PYONGYANG, Pyongyang   SE ASIA • 200 kW
      NORWAY
      †RADIO NORWAY INTL, Fredrikstad   N AMERICA • 350 kW
      †RADIO NORWAY INTL, Sveio   (J) • N AMERICA • 500 kW
                              (J) • M-F • N AMERICA • 500 kW
                              (J) • Sa/Su • N AMERICA • 500 kW
      SPAIN
      †R EXTERIOR ESPANA, Noblejas   AFRICA • 350 kW
      SURINAME
      †R SURINAME INTL, Via Brasilia, Brazil   Alternative Frequency to 17835 kHz
      USA
      VOA, Via Philippines   E AFRICA • 250 kW

17760   **DENMARK**
      †DANMARKS RADIO, Via Norway   N AMERICA • 500 kW
      HOLLAND
      †RADIO NEDERLAND, Via Neth Antilles   S AMERICA • 300 kW
      NORWAY
      †RADIO NORWAY INTL, Sveio   M-F • N AMERICA • 500 kW
                               (D) Sa/Su • N AMERICA • 500 kW
                               (J) Sa/Su • N AMERICA • 500 kW
      SAUDI ARABIA
      †BS OF THE KINGDOM, Riyadh   E AFRICA • 350 kW
      USA
      †RFE-RL, Via Germany   WEST USSR & MIDEAST • 100 kW
                    (J) • WEST USSR • 100 kW
                         (J) • WEST USSR & MIDEAST • 100 kW
                         (D) • WEST USSR & MIDEAST • 100 kW
      †RFE-RL, Via Portugal

17765   **DENMARK**
      †DANMARKS RADIO, Via Norway   (J) • MIDEAST & E AFRICA • 500 kW
                    (J) • AFRICA • 500 kW
                    (J) • W AFRICA • 500 kW
      GERMANY
      DEUTSCHE WELLE, Via Sri Lanka   AFRICA • 250 kW
      DEUTSCHE WELLE, Wertachtal   W AFRICA • 500 kW
                        E AFRICA • 500 kW
                        AFRICA • 500 kW
                 (D) • S AFRICA • 500 kW   S AFRICA • 500 kW
      JAPAN
      RADIO JAPAN/NHK, Tokyo-Yamata   E ASIA • 300 kW
                      E ASIA • GENERAL • 300 kW
      KOREA (DPR)
      †RADIO PYONGYANG, Pyongyang   SE ASIA • 200 kW
                      E AFRICA • 200 kW
      NORWAY
      †RADIO NORWAY INTL, Kvitsøy   (J) • MIDEAST & E AFRICA • 500 kW
                    (J) • AFRICA • 500 kW
                    (J) • W AFRICA • 500 kW
      SOUTH AFRICA
      †RADIO RSA, Meyerton   (D) • W AFRICA & S AFRICA • 250 kW
      USA
      †VOA, Via Philippines   (D) • E ASIA • 250 kW
                                 E ASIA • 250 kW
                               (J) • E ASIA • 250 kW
      USSR
      †BELORUSSIAN RADIO, Minsk   RUSSIAN, ETC • DS-2 • 20 kW
      RADIO MOSCOW, Armavir   (J) • S ASIA & SE ASIA • 500 kW
      RADIO MOSCOW, Tula   (D) • S ASIA & SE ASIA • 240 kW

17770   **CUBA**
      †RADIO HABANA, Havana   (J) • EUROPE & N AFRICA • 250 kW
                               (J) Su • EUROPE & N AFRICA • 250 kW
      EGYPT
      RADIO CAIRO, Kafr Silim-Abis   S AMERICA • 250 kW
                        SE ASIA • 250 kW
      GERMANY
      †DEUTSCHE WELLE, Nauen   (J) • E ASIA • 100 kW
                    (J) • SE ASIA • 100 kW
(con'd)

0 1 2 3 4 5 6 7 8 9 10 11 12 13 14 15 16 17 18 19 20 21 22 23 24

ENGLISH ▬   ARABIC ⋙   CHINESE ∞   FRENCH ═   GERMAN ▬   RUSSIAN ═   SPANISH ▬   OTHER ▬

FREQUENCY	COUNTRY, STATION, LOCATION	TARGET • NETWORK • POWER (kW)	World Time

17770
(con'd) **NEW ZEALAND**
†R NEW ZEALAND INTL, Rangitaiki — ENGLISH, ETC • PACIFIC • DS • 100 kW
QATAR
QATAR BC SERVICE, Doha-Al Khaisah — (J) • EUROPE • 100/250 kW
USA
†VOA, Via Philippines — (D) • E ASIA • 250 kW

17775 **FRANCE**
R FRANCE INTL, Issoudun-Allouis — M-Sa • E AFRICA • MEDIAS FRANCE • 100 kW
HOLLAND
†RADIO NEDERLAND, Flevoland — (J) • C AFRICA • 500 kW
USA
†KVOH-VO HOPE, Rancho Simi, Ca — W NORTH AM & C AMERICA • 50 kW
Su • W NORTH AM & C AMERICA • 50 kW
USSR
RADIO MOSCOW, Bishkek — S ASIA & SE ASIA • 100 kW
(J) • E AFRICA • 500 kW
(J) • S ASIA & SE ASIA • 100 kW

17780 **BULGARIA**
†RADIO SOFIA, Sofia — MIDEAST • 250 kW / (D) • EUROPE • 250 kW
GERMANY
†DEUTSCHE WELLE, Jülich — (D) • E ASIA • 100 kW
DEUTSCHE WELLE, Via Sri Lanka — MIDEAST & S ASIA • 250 kW
†DEUTSCHE WELLE, Wertachtal — AUSTRALIA • 500 kW
ITALY
†RTV ITALIANA, Rome — E AFRICA • 100 kW
E NORTH AM • 100 kW
UNITED KINGDOM
†BBC, Daventry — (J) • WEST USSR • 300 kW
BBC, Rampisham — (D) • WEST USSR • 500 kW
†BBC, Via Maşīrah, Oman — (D) Su • WEST USSR • 100 kW
(J) Su • WEST USSR • 100 kW
USA
CHRIST SCI MONITOR, Via Saipan — E ASIA • 100 kW
†R FREE AFGHANISTAN, Via Portugal — (J) • WEST USSR & S ASIA • 250 kW
VOA, Via Kaválla, Greece — (D) • WEST USSR • 250 kW
†VOA, Via Philippines — S ASIA • 250 kW
(J) • E ASIA • 250 kW

17785 **FRANCE**
R FRANCE INTL, Issoudun-Allouis — AFRICA • MEDIAS FRANCE • 500 kW
M-Sa • W AFRICA • MEDIAS FRANCE • 500 kW
INDIA
†ALL INDIA RADIO, Aligarh — MIDEAST • 250 kW
JAPAN
RADIO JAPAN/NHK, Tokyo-Yamata — (J) • SE ASIA • 100 kW
PAKISTAN
†RADIO PAKISTAN, Karachi — SE ASIA • 50 kW
UNITED KINGDOM
BBC, Via Zyyi, Cyprus — MIDEAST • 250 kW
USA
†VOA, Greenville, NC — W AFRICA • 250 kW
M-F • W AFRICA • 250 kW
(D) M-F • S AFRICA • 250 kW
Sa/Su • W AFRICA • 250 kW
USSR
†KYRGYS RADIO, Nizhny Novgorod — RUSSIAN, ETC • DS-1 • 20 kW

17790 **DENMARK**
†DANMARKS RADIO, Via Norway — (J) • C AMERICA & S AMERICA • 500 kW
(J) • E NORTH AM & C AMERICA • 500 kW • ALT. FREQ. TO 17795 kHz
(J) • E NORTH AM & C AMERICA • 500 kW
(J) • W NORTH AM • 500 kW
(J) • N AMERICA • 500 kW
ECUADOR
†HCJB-VO THE ANDES, Quito — EUROPE • 500 kW
M-F • EUROPE • 500 kW
Sa/Su • EUROPE • 500 kW
NORWAY
†RADIO NORWAY INTL, Sveio — (J) • C AMERICA & S AMERICA • 500 kW
(J) • E NORTH AM & C AMERICA • 500 kW • ALT. FREQ. TO 17795 kHz
(J) • E NORTH AM & C AMERICA • 500 kW
(J) • N AMERICA • 500 kW
(J) M-F • W NORTH AM • 500 kW
(J) Sa/Su • W NORTH AM • 500 kW
ROMANIA
RADIO ROMANIA INTL, Bucharest — W AFRICA • 250 kW
Su • MIDEAST & S ASIA • MARINERS • 250 kW
Su • W AFRICA • MARINERS • 250 kW

(con'd)

SUMMER ONLY (J)   WINTER ONLY (D)   JAMMING / OR ∧   EARLIEST HEARD ◁   LATEST HEARD ▷   NEW OR CHANGED FOR 1992 †

FREQUENCY   COUNTRY, STATION, LOCATION   TARGET • NETWORK • POWER (kW)   World Time

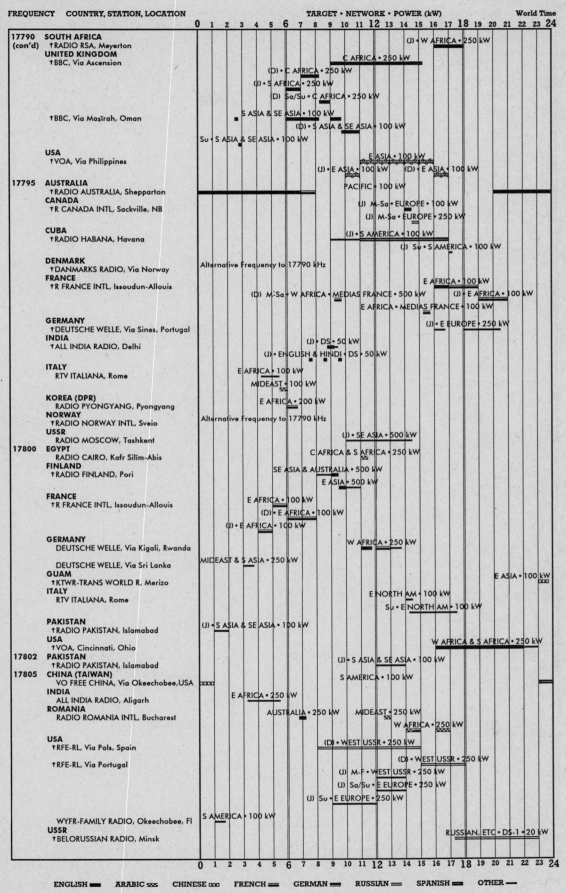

ENGLISH ▬▬   ARABIC ⟩⟩⟩   CHINESE ▫▫▫   FRENCH ▬▬   GERMAN ▬▬   RUSSIAN ══   SPANISH ▬▬   OTHER ▬

FREQUENCY   COUNTRY, STATION, LOCATION   TARGET • NETWORK • POWER (kW)   World Time

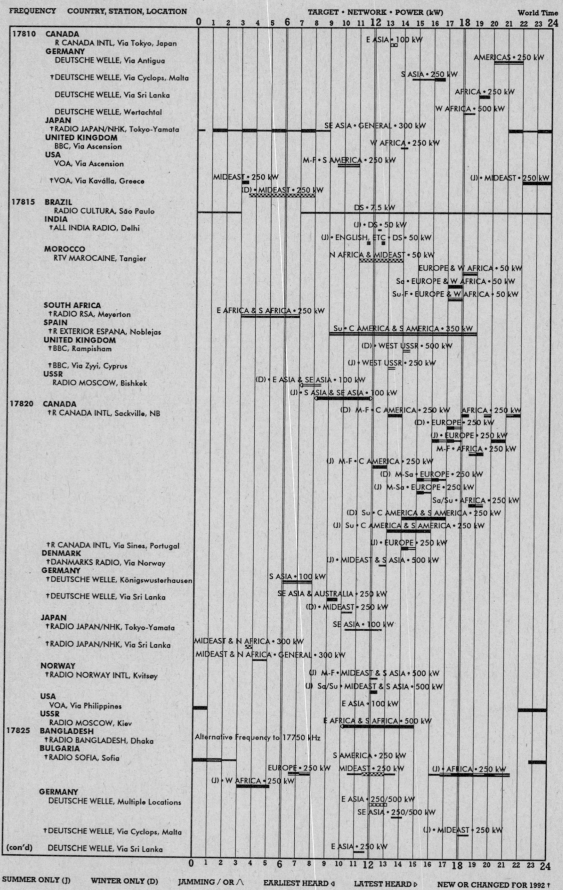

SUMMER ONLY (J)   WINTER ONLY (D)   JAMMING / OR /\   EARLIEST HEARD ◁   LATEST HEARD ▷   NEW OR CHANGED FOR 1992 †

FREQUENCY	COUNTRY, STATION, LOCATION	TARGET • NETWORK • POWER (kW)	World Time

World Time scale: 0 1 2 3 4 5 6 7 8 9 10 11 12 13 14 15 16 17 18 19 20 21 22 23 24

17825 (con'd) GERMANY
DEUTSCHE WELLE, Wertachtal
- MIDEAST & S ASIA • 500 kW
- (J) • AFRICA • 500 kW

JAPAN
†RADIO JAPAN/NHK, Tokyo-Yamata
- W NORTH AM, C AMERICA & S AMERICA • 300 kW
- W NORTH AM, C AMERICA & S AMERICA • GENERAL • 300 kW

17830 GERMANY
DEUTSCHE WELLE, Jülich
- (J) • W AFRICA • 100 kW

INDIA
†ALL INDIA RADIO, Delhi
- SE ASIA • 250 kW • ALT. FREQ. TO 15110 kHz
- SE ASIA • 50 kW
- DS • 50 kW
- ENGLISH, ETC • DS • 50 kW

SWITZERLAND
RED CROSS BC SVC, Schwarzenburg
- Irr • M/Th • SE ASIA & AUSTRALIA • 150 kW
- Irr • M/Th • S ASIA & SE ASIA • 150 kW
- Irr • M/Th • MIDEAST & E AFRICA • 150 kW
- Irr • M/Th • MIDEAST & E AFRICA • ENGLISH, FRENCH • 150 kW

SWISS RADIO INTL, Schwarzenburg
- SE ASIA & AUSTRALIA • 150 kW
- S ASIA & SE ASIA • 150 kW
- MIDEAST & E AFRICA • 150 kW
- M-Sa • S ASIA & SE ASIA • 150 kW
- M-Sa • MIDEAST & E AFRICA • 150 kW
- Su • S ASIA & SE ASIA • 150 kW
- Su • MIDEAST & E AFRICA • 150 kW

UNITED ARAB EMIRATES
UAE RADIO, Dubai
- E ASIA • 300 kW

UNITED KINGDOM
†BBC, Via Ascension
- E AFRICA • 250 kW
- C AFRICA • 250 kW
- W AFRICA & C AFRICA • 250 kW

†BBC, Via Hong Kong
- E ASIA • 250 kW

†BBC, Via Maşīrah, Oman
- SE ASIA • 100 kW
- (J) • E EUROPE • 100 kW

†BBC, Via Singapore
- SE ASIA & AUSTRALIA • 125/250 kW
- (D) • E ASIA • 125 kW
- (D) • SE ASIA & AUSTRALIA • 125 kW

USA
VOA, Via Ascension
- Sa/Su • S AMERICA • 250 kW

VOA, Via Kaválla, Greece
- (J) • MIDEAST • 250 kW

†WORLD HARVEST R, Noblesville, Indiana
- C AMERICA • 100 kW
- M-Sa • C AMERICA • 100 kW
- Su • C AMERICA • 100 kW

17835 CUBA
†RADIO HABANA, Havana
- (J) • S AMERICA • 100 kW
- (J) • Su • S AMERICA • 100 kW

GERMANY
†DEUTSCHE WELLE, Königswusterhausen
- (D) • EUROPE • 100 kW

JAPAN
†RADIO JAPAN/NHK, Tokyo-Yamata
- E ASIA • 100 kW
- E ASIA • GENERAL • 100 kW
- E ASIA • GENERAL • 300 kW

SOUTH AFRICA
†RADIO RSA, Meyerton
- E AFRICA • 250 kW
- (D) • W AFRICA • 250 kW

SURINAME
†R SURINAME INTL, Via Brasília, Brazil
- M-F • EUROPE • 250 kW • ALT. FREQ. TO 17755 kHz

UNITED KINGDOM
†BBC, Skelton, Cumbria
- (D) • EUROPE • 250 kW
- (J) • EUROPE • 250 kW

USA
†R FREE AFGHANISTAN, Via Portugal
- (J) • WEST USSR & S ASIA • 250 kW

†RFE-RL, Via Portugal
- (D) • WEST USSR • 250 kW
- (J) • WEST USSR • 250 kW

†VOA, Via Portugal
- (D) • WEST USSR & MIDEAST • 250 kW

USSR
RADIO MOSCOW, Zhigulevsk
- MIDEAST & E AFRICA • 200 kW

17840 CANADA
R CANADA INTL, Via United Kingdom
- (J) • M-F • AFRICA • 300 kW

CZECHOSLOVAKIA
RADIO PRAGUE INTL, Rimavská
- AUSTRALIA • 250 kW

USSR
RADIO MOSCOW, Bishkek
- (D) • SE ASIA • 500 kW

UZBEK RADIO, Moscow
- DS-2/RUSSIAN, UZBEK • 20 kW

ENGLISH ▬ ARABIC ≋ CHINESE ▭▭▭ FRENCH ═ GERMAN ▬ RUSSIAN ═ SPANISH ▬ OTHER ▬

FREQUENCY   COUNTRY, STATION, LOCATION   TARGET • NETWORK • POWER (kW)   World Time

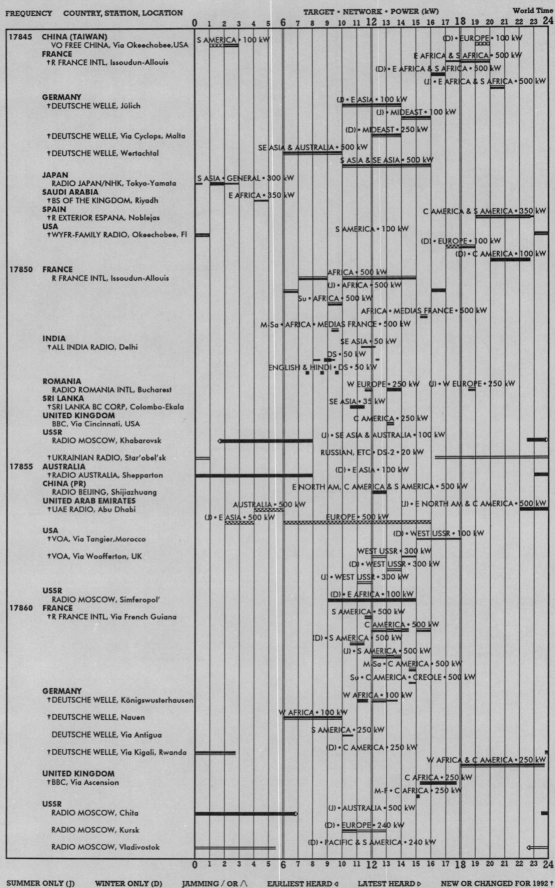

FREQUENCY	COUNTRY, STATION, LOCATION	Schedule
17845	CHINA (TAIWAN) VO FREE CHINA, Via Okeechobee, USA	S AMERICA • 100 kW / (D) • EUROPE • 100 kW
	FRANCE ↑R FRANCE INTL, Issoudun-Allouis	E AFRICA & S AFRICA • 500 kW / (D) • E AFRICA & S AFRICA • 500 kW / (J) • E AFRICA & S AFRICA • 500 kW
	GERMANY ↑DEUTSCHE WELLE, Jülich	(J) • E ASIA • 100 kW / (J) • MIDEAST • 100 kW
	↑DEUTSCHE WELLE, Via Cyclops, Malta	(D) • MIDEAST • 250 kW
	↑DEUTSCHE WELLE, Wertachtal	SE ASIA & AUSTRALIA • 500 kW / S ASIA & SE ASIA • 500 kW
	JAPAN RADIO JAPAN/NHK, Tokyo-Yamata	S ASIA • GENERAL • 300 kW
	SAUDI ARABIA ↑BS OF THE KINGDOM, Riyadh	E AFRICA • 350 kW
	SPAIN ↑R EXTERIOR ESPANA, Noblejas	C AMERICA & S AMERICA • 350 kW
	USA ↑WYFR-FAMILY RADIO, Okeechobee, Fl	S AMERICA • 100 kW / (D) • EUROPE • 100 kW / (D) • C AMERICA • 100 kW
17850	FRANCE R FRANCE INTL, Issoudun-Allouis	AFRICA • 500 kW / (J) • AFRICA • 500 kW / Su • AFRICA • 500 kW / AFRICA • MEDIAS FRANCE • 500 kW / M-Sa • AFRICA • MEDIAS FRANCE • 500 kW
	INDIA ↑ALL INDIA RADIO, Delhi	SE ASIA • 50 kW / DS • 50 kW / ENGLISH & HINDI • DS • 50 kW
	ROMANIA RADIO ROMANIA INTL, Bucharest	W EUROPE • 250 kW / (J) • W EUROPE • 250 kW
	SRI LANKA ↑SRI LANKA BC CORP, Colombo-Ekala	SE ASIA • 35 kW
	UNITED KINGDOM BBC, Via Cincinnati, USA	C AMERICA • 250 kW
	USSR RADIO MOSCOW, Khabarovsk	(J) • SE ASIA & AUSTRALIA • 100 kW
	↑UKRAINIAN RADIO, Star'obel'sk	RUSSIAN, ETC • DS-2 • 20 kW
17855	AUSTRALIA ↑RADIO AUSTRALIA, Shepparton	(D) • E ASIA • 100 kW
	CHINA (PR) RADIO BEIJING, Shijiazhuang	E NORTH AM, C AMERICA & S AMERICA • 500 kW
	UNITED ARAB EMIRATES ↑UAE RADIO, Abu Dhabi	AUSTRALIA • 500 kW / (J) • E NORTH AM & C AMERICA • 500 kW / (J) • E ASIA • 500 kW / EUROPE • 500 kW
	USA ↑VOA, Via Tangier, Morocco	(D) • WEST USSR • 100 kW
	↑VOA, Via Woofferton, UK	WEST USSR • 300 kW / (D) • WEST USSR • 300 kW / (J) • WEST USSR • 300 kW
	USSR RADIO MOSCOW, Simferopol'	(D) • E AFRICA • 100 kW
17860	FRANCE ↑R FRANCE INTL, Via French Guiana	S AMERICA • 500 kW / C AMERICA • 500 kW / (D) • S AMERICA • 500 kW / (J) • S AMERICA • 500 kW / M-Sa • C AMERICA • 500 kW / Su • C AMERICA • CREOLE • 500 kW
	GERMANY ↑DEUTSCHE WELLE, Königswusterhausen	W AFRICA • 100 kW
	↑DEUTSCHE WELLE, Nauen	W AFRICA • 100 kW
	DEUTSCHE WELLE, Via Antigua	S AMERICA • 250 kW / (D) • C AMERICA • 250 kW / W AFRICA & C AMERICA • 250 kW
	↑DEUTSCHE WELLE, Via Kigali, Rwanda	
	UNITED KINGDOM ↑BBC, Via Ascension	C AFRICA • 250 kW / M-F • C AFRICA • 250 kW
	USSR RADIO MOSCOW, Chita	(J) • AUSTRALIA • 500 kW
	RADIO MOSCOW, Kursk	(D) • EUROPE • 240 kW
	RADIO MOSCOW, Vladivostok	(D) • PACIFIC & S AMERICA • 240 kW

FREQUENCY   COUNTRY, STATION, LOCATION   TARGET • NETWORK • POWER (kW)   World Time

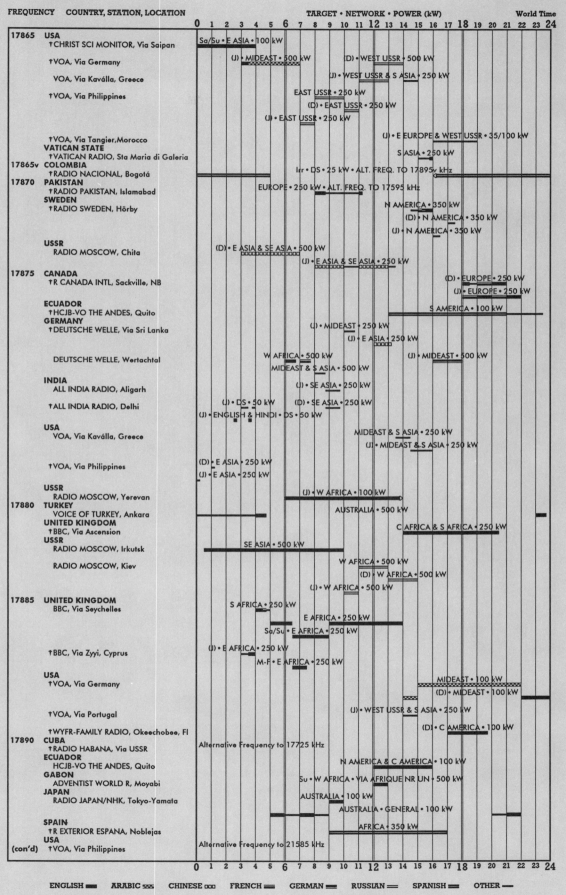

FREQUENCY	COUNTRY, STATION, LOCATION
17865	**USA**
	†CHRIST SCI MONITOR, Via Saipan
	†VOA, Via Germany
	VOA, Via Kaválla, Greece
	†VOA, Via Philippines
	†VOA, Via Tangier, Morocco
	VATICAN STATE
	†VATICAN RADIO, Sta Maria di Galeria
17865v	**COLOMBIA**
	†RADIO NACIONAL, Bogotá
17870	**PAKISTAN**
	†RADIO PAKISTAN, Islamabad
	SWEDEN
	†RADIO SWEDEN, Hörby
	USSR
	RADIO MOSCOW, Chita
17875	**CANADA**
	†R CANADA INTL, Sackville, NB
	ECUADOR
	†HCJB-VO THE ANDES, Quito
	GERMANY
	†DEUTSCHE WELLE, Via Sri Lanka
	DEUTSCHE WELLE, Wertachtal
	INDIA
	ALL INDIA RADIO, Aligarh
	†ALL INDIA RADIO, Delhi
	USA
	VOA, Via Kaválla, Greece
	†VOA, Via Philippines
	USSR
	RADIO MOSCOW, Yerevan
17880	**TURKEY**
	VOICE OF TURKEY, Ankara
	UNITED KINGDOM
	†BBC, Via Ascension
	USSR
	RADIO MOSCOW, Irkutsk
	RADIO MOSCOW, Kiev
17885	**UNITED KINGDOM**
	BBC, Via Seychelles
	†BBC, Via Zyyi, Cyprus
	USA
	†VOA, Via Germany
	†VOA, Via Portugal
	†WYFR-FAMILY RADIO, Okeechobee, Fl
17890	**CUBA**
	†RADIO HABANA, Via USSR
	ECUADOR
	HCJB-VO THE ANDES, Quito
	GABON
	ADVENTIST WORLD R, Moyabi
	JAPAN
	RADIO JAPAN/NHK, Tokyo-Yamata
	SPAIN
	†R EXTERIOR ESPANA, Noblejas
	USA
(con'd)	†VOA, Via Philippines

Sa/Su • E ASIA • 100 kW
(J) • MIDEAST • 500 kW   (D) • WEST USSR • 500 kW
(J) • WEST USSR & S ASIA • 250 kW
EAST USSR • 250 kW
(D) • EAST USSR • 250 kW
(J) • EAST USSR • 250 kW
(J) • E EUROPE & WEST USSR • 35/100 kW
S ASIA • 250 kW
Irr • DS • 25 kW • ALT. FREQ. TO 17895v kHz
EUROPE • 250 kW • ALT. FREQ. TO 17595 kHz
N AMERICA • 350 kW
(D) • N AMERICA • 350 kW
(J) • N AMERICA • 350 kW
(D) • E ASIA & SE ASIA • 500 kW
(J) • E ASIA & SE ASIA • 250 kW
(D) • EUROPE • 250 kW
(J) • EUROPE • 250 kW
S AMERICA • 100 kW
(J) • MIDEAST • 250 kW
(J) • E ASIA • 250 kW
W AFRICA • 500 kW
MIDEAST & S ASIA • 500 kW
(J) • SE ASIA • 250 kW
(J) • DS • 50 kW   (D) • SE ASIA • 250 kW
(J) • ENGLISH & HINDI • DS • 50 kW
(J) • MIDEAST • 500 kW
MIDEAST & S ASIA • 250 kW
(J) • MIDEAST & S ASIA • 250 kW
(D) • E ASIA • 250 kW
(J) • E ASIA • 250 kW
(J) • W AFRICA • 100 kW
AUSTRALIA • 500 kW
C AFRICA & S AFRICA • 250 kW
SE ASIA • 500 kW
W AFRICA • 500 kW
(D) • W AFRICA • 500 kW
(J) • W AFRICA • 500 kW
S AFRICA • 250 kW
E AFRICA • 250 kW
Sa/Su • E AFRICA • 250 kW
(J) • E AFRICA • 250 kW
M-F • E AFRICA • 250 kW
MIDEAST • 100 kW
(D) • MIDEAST • 100 kW
(J) • WEST USSR & S ASIA • 250 kW
(D) • C AMERICA • 100 kW
Alternative Frequency to 17725 kHz
N AMERICA & C AMERICA • 100 kW
Su • W AFRICA • VIA AFRIQUE NR UN • 500 kW
AUSTRALIA • 100 kW
AUSTRALIA • GENERAL • 100 kW
AFRICA • 350 kW
Alternative Frequency to 21585 kHz

ENGLISH ▬   ARABIC ▧▧   CHINESE ▭▭   FRENCH ▬   GERMAN ▬   RUSSIAN ═   SPANISH ▬   OTHER ▬

FREQUENCY   COUNTRY, STATION, LOCATION   TARGET • NETWORK • POWER (kW)   World Time

FREQUENCY	COUNTRY, STATION, LOCATION	TARGET • NETWORK • POWER (kW)
17890 (con'd)	USSR RADIO MOSCOW, Moscow	SE ASIA • 250 kW
	†TATAR RADIO, Moscow	DS • 20 kW
17895	HOLLAND †RADIO NEDERLAND, Flevoland	S AMERICA • 500 kW
	INDIA †ALL INDIA RADIO, Delhi	E ASIA • 250 kW
	PAKISTAN †RADIO PAKISTAN, Islamabad	(D) • S ASIA & SE ASIA • 100 kW
		(J) • MIDEAST • 100 kW
	SAUDI ARABIA BS OF THE KINGDOM, Riyadh	SE ASIA • 350 kW
	USA †R FREE AFGHANISTAN, Via Germany	(J) • WEST USSR & S ASIA • 100 kW
	†RFE-RL, Via Germany	(D) • WEST USSR • 100 kW
	†RFE-RL, Via Portugal	(J) • WEST USSR & S ASIA • 100 kW
	†VOA, Via Germany	(D) • MIDEAST • 500 kW
	ZAMBIA RADIO ZAMBIA-ZBS, Lusaka	Su • S AFRICA • 50 kW
17895v	COLOMBIA †RADIO NACIONAL, Bogotá	Alternative Frequency to 17865v kHz
17940	IRAQ †REP OF IRAQ RADIO	DS • ALT. FREQ. TO 17960 kHz
17950	CLANDESTINE (M EAST) †"VO IRAQ OPPOSIT'N, Saudi Arabia	MIDEAST • ANTI-SADDAM
17960	IRAQ †REP OF IRAQ RADIO	Alternative Frequency to 17940 kHz
18195	USSR †RADIO MOSCOW	(J) • DS-MAYAK
18275	USA †VOA, Greenville, NC	EUROPE • (FEEDER) • 50 kW • ISU
		EUROPE • (FEEDER) • 50 kW • ISL
		(D) • EUROPE • (FEEDER) • 50 kW • ISL
		(D) • EUROPE • (FEEDER) • 50 kW • ISU
		(J) • EUROPE • (FEEDER) • 50 kW • ISL
18511	USA †VOA, Delano, California	SE ASIA • (FEEDER) • 50 kW • ISU
		SE ASIA • (FEEDER) • 50 kW • ISL
		(J) • SE ASIA • (FEEDER) • 50 kW • ISL
		(J) • SE ASIA • (FEEDER) • 50 kW • ISU
		(J) • M-F • SE ASIA • (FEEDER) • 50 kW • ISU
18525	USA †VOA, Delano, California	SE ASIA • (FEEDER) • 50 kW • ISL
		SE ASIA • (FEEDER) • 50 kW • ISU
		(D) • SE ASIA • (FEEDER) • 50 kW • ISU (J) • SE ASIA • (FEEDER) • 50 kW • ISL
		(J) • SE ASIA • (FEEDER) • 50 kW • ISU
18730	USSR †RADIO MOSCOW	WORLD SVC/MAYAK(FEEDER) • USB
18782.5	USA †VOA, Greenville, NC	EUROPE & MIDEAST • (FEEDER) • 40 kW • ISL
		EUROPE & MIDEAST • (FEEDER) • 40 kW • ISU
		(D) • EUROPE & MIDEAST • (FEEDER) • 40 kW • ISU
		(D) • EUROPE & MIDEAST • (FEEDER) • 40 kW • ISL
		(J) • EUROPE & MIDEAST • (FEEDER) • 40 kW • ISL
		(J) • EUROPE & MIDEAST • (FEEDER) • 40 kW • ISU
18870	USSR †RADIO MOSCOW	(J) • DS-MAYAK(FEEDER) • USB
19261.5	USA †VOA, Cincinnati, Ohio	N AFRICA • (FEEDER) • 50 kW • USB
20000	USA †WWV, Ft Collins, Colorado	WEATHER/WORLD TIME • 2.5 kW
21455	ECUADOR †HCJB-VO THE ANDES, Quito	EUROPE & PACIFIC • 10 kW • USB
	USA †VOA, Via Germany	(D) • MIDEAST • 500 kW
	†VOA, Via Kaválla, Greece	(D) • MIDEAST • 250 kW
21460	BELGIUM †RT BELGE FRANCAISE, Wavre	AFRICA • DS-1 • 250 kW • ALT. FREQ. TO 25645 kHz
		(J) • AFRICA • DS-1 • 250 kW
	COSTA RICA †RADIO FOR PEACE, Ciudad Colón	Alternative Frequency to 7375 kHz
	SWEDEN †RADIO SWEDEN, Hörby	Alternative Frequency to 21720 kHz
21465	GERMANY †DEUTSCHE WELLE, Leipzig	MIDEAST & S ASIA • 100 kW
		SE ASIA • 100 kW
		(D) • W AFRICA • 100 kW
		(D) • S ASIA • 100 kW
		(J) • E ASIA • 100 kW

SUMMER ONLY (J)   WINTER ONLY (D)   JAMMING / OR ∧   EARLIEST HEARD ◁   LATEST HEARD ▷   NEW OR CHANGED FOR 1992 †

| FREQUENCY | COUNTRY, STATION, LOCATION | TARGET • NETWORK • POWER (kW) | World Time |

0 1 2 3 4 5 6 7 8 9 10 11 12 13 14 15 16 17 18 19 20 21 22 23 24

21470 UNITED KINGDOM
BBC, Via Ascension — C AFRICA • 250 kW
†BBC, Via Zyyi, Cyprus — E AFRICA • 250 kW
(D) • E AFRICA • 250 kW
(J) Sa/Su • E AFRICA • 250 kW

21474v PAKISTAN
†RADIO PAKISTAN, Karachi — SE ASIA • 50 kW
21475 USA
VOA, Via Philippines — S ASIA • 250 kW
21480 ECUADOR
†HCJB-VO THE ANDES, Quito — MIDEAST • 500 kW
EUROPE • 100 kW
(J) • EUROPE • 100 kW
M-F • MIDEAST • 500 kW
Sa/Su • MIDEAST • 500 kW

HOLLAND
†RADIO NEDERLAND, Flevoland — SE ASIA • 500 kW
(J) • SE ASIA • 500 kW

RADIO NEDERLAND, Via Madagascar — E ASIA • 300 kW   S ASIA • 300 kW
SE ASIA • 300 kW
(D) • SE ASIA • 300 kW

PAKISTAN
†RADIO PAKISTAN, Islamabad — E AFRICA & S AFRICA • 100 kW
21485 HOLLAND
RADIO NEDERLAND, Via Madagascar — ASIA • 300 kW
SE ASIA • 300 kW

USA
†VOA, Greenville, NC — W AFRICA & S AFRICA • 250 kW
W AFRICA • 250 kW
M-F • S AFRICA • 250 kW

VATICAN STATE
†VATICAN RADIO, Sta Maria di Galeria — S AMERICA • 500 kW
21490 AUSTRIA
RADIO AUSTRIA INTL, Vienna — MIDEAST • 300 kW   W AFRICA • 100 kW
AUSTRALIA • 100 kW   (D) • W AFRICA • 100 kW
M-Sa • MIDEAST • 300 kW   E NORTH AM • 100 kW
(D) • MIDEAST • 300 kW   (J) • W AFRICA • 100 kW
(D) • AUSTRALIA • 100 kW
Su • MIDEAST • 300 kW   (D) • E NORTH AM • 100 kW
(J) • MIDEAST • 300 kW   M-Sa • W AFRICA • 100 kW
(J) • AUSTRALIA • 100 kW
(J) • E NORTH AM • 100 kW
Su • W AFRICA • 100 kW

UNITED KINGDOM
†BBC, Via Ascension — S AMERICA • 250 kW
C AFRICA & E AFRICA • 250 kW

USA
VOA, Via Ascension — M-F • S AMERICA • 250 kW
Sa/Su • S AMERICA • 250 kW

USSR
†KAZAKH RADIO — DS-2
†RADIO ALMA-ATA
RADIO MOSCOW, Irkutsk — (J) • SE ASIA • DS-MAYAK • 250 kW
21495 PORTUGAL
†R PORTUGAL INTL, Lisbon — Alternative Frequency to 21500 kHz
SPAIN
†R EXTERIOR ESPANA, Noblejas — S AMERICA • 350 kW
21500 HOLLAND
†RADIO NEDERLAND, Flevoland — (D) • SE ASIA • 500 kW
(D) Su • S ASIA • 500 kW

PORTUGAL
†R PORTUGAL INTL, Lisbon — W AFRICA & S AMERICA • 100 kW • ALT. FREQ. TO 21495 kHz
(D) • W AFRICA & S AMERICA • 100 kW • ALT. FREQ. TO 21495 kHz
(J) • W AFRICA & S AMERICA • 100 kW • ALT. FREQ. TO 21495 kHz
Sa/Su • W AFRICA & S AMERICA • 100 kW • ALT. FREQ. TO 21495 kHz
(D) Sa/Su • W AFRICA & S AMERICA • 100 kW • ALT. FREQ. TO 21495 kHz
(J) Sa/Su • W AFRICA & S AMERICA • 100 kW • ALT. FREQ. TO 21495 kHz

SWEDEN
†RADIO SWEDEN, Hörby — E NORTH AM • 350 kW • ALT. FREQ. TO 21655 kHz
USA
†VOA, Via Germany — (J) • MIDEAST • 500 kW

†WYFR-FAMILY RADIO, Okeechobee, Fl — (J) • EUROPE • 100 kW
21505 SAUDI ARABIA
BS OF THE KINGDOM, Riyadh — N AFRICA • DS-GENERAL • 350 kW
E ASIA • DS-HOLY KORAN • 350 kW

(con'd)

0 1 2 3 4 5 6 7 8 9 10 11 12 13 14 15 16 17 18 19 20 21 22 23 24

ENGLISH ▬ ARABIC ░ CHINESE ▫▫▫ FRENCH ══ GERMAN ▬▬ RUSSIAN ═ SPANISH ▬▬ OTHER ▬

FREQUENCY   COUNTRY, STATION, LOCATION   TARGET • NETWORK • POWER (kW)   World Time

0 1 2 3 4 5 6 7 8 9 10 11 12 13 14 15 16 17 18 19 20 21 22 23 24

21505　SAUDI ARABIA
(con'd)　　BS OF THE KINGDOM, Riyadh — ASIA • DS-HOLY KORAN • 350 kW

21510　USA
　　†R FREE AFGHANISTAN, Via Portugal — WEST USSR & S ASIA • 250 kW
　　†RFE-RL, Via Portugal — WEST USSR & S ASIA • 250 kW
　　　— (D) • WEST USSR • 250 kW
　　　— (D) • WEST USSR & S ASIA • 250 kW
　　　— (J) • WEST USSR & S ASIA • 250 kW

21515　HOLLAND
　　　RADIO NEDERLAND, Via Neth Antilles — C AFRICA • 300 kW
　　ITALY
　　　RTV ITALIANA, Rome — Su • E AFRICA • 100 kW
　　UNITED ARAB EMIRATES
　　†UAE RADIO, Abu Dhabi — (J) • E ASIA • 500 kW — (J) • EUROPE • 500 kW
　　USSR
　　　RADIO MOSCOW, Bishkek — (J) • E ASIA • 50 kW
　　VATICAN STATE
　　　VATICAN RADIO, Sta Maria di Galeria — (D) • Su • E ASIA • 500 kW
　　　— (J) • Su • E ASIA • 500 kW

21520　FRANCE
　　　R FRANCE INTL, Via Moyabi, Gabon — S AFRICA • 250 kW
　　HOLLAND
　　　RADIO NEDERLAND, Flevoland — S ASIA • 500 kW
　　　— C AFRICA • 500 kW
　　PAKISTAN
　　†RADIO PAKISTAN, Islamabad — EUROPE • 250 kW
　　USA
　　†VOA, Via Kaválla, Greece — S ASIA • 250 kW
　　　— (D) • MIDEAST & S ASIA • 250 kW

21525　AUSTRALIA
　　†RADIO AUSTRALIA, Darwin — E ASIA & SE ASIA • 250 kW
　　　— (D) • E ASIA & SE ASIA • 250 kW
　　USA
　　　WYFR-FAMILY RADIO, Okeechobee, Fl — C AFRICA & S AFRICA • 100 kW

21530　FRANCE
　　†R FRANCE INTL, Issoudun-Allouis — MIDEAST • 500 kW
　　　— (J) • MIDEAST • 500 kW
　　HOLLAND
　　†RADIO NEDERLAND, Flevoland — (J) • C AFRICA & S ASIA • 500 kW

21535　FRANCE
　　†R FRANCE INTL, Issoudun-Allouis — MIDEAST & S ASIA • 500 kW
　　†R FRANCE INTL, Via Moyabi, Gabon — MIDEAST • 250 kW
　　ITALY
　　†RTV ITALIANA, Rome — Su • S AMERICA • 100 kW
　　TUNISIA
　　†RTV TUNISIENNE, Sfax — (J) • MIDEAST & N AFRICA • DS • 100 kW
　　USA
　　†VOA, Via Germany — MIDEAST • 500 kW

21540　GERMANY
　　†DEUTSCHE WELLE, Nauen — ASIA • 500 kW

21545　CANADA
　　†R CANADA INTL, Sackville, NB — EUROPE • 250 kW
　　　— (D) • EUROPE • 250 kW
　　　— (J) • EUROPE • 250 kW
　　USA
　　†CHRIST SCI MONITOR, Maine — Alternative Frequency to 21640 kHz
　　　VOA, Via Philippines — S ASIA • 250 kW

21550　FINLAND
　　†RADIO FINLAND, Pori — SE ASIA & AUSTRALIA • USB/AM • 100/500 kW
　　　— N AMERICA • USB/AM • 100/500 kW
　　　— (J) • E ASIA • USB/AM • 100/500 kW
　　　— (J) • MIDEAST • USB/AM • 100/500 kW
　　　— M-F • N AMERICA • USB/AM • 100/500 kW
　　　— Sa/Su • N AMERICA • USB/AM • 100/500 kW
　　ROMANIA
　　　RADIO ROMANIA INTL, Bucharest — SE ASIA & AUSTRALIA • 250 kW
　　　— W EUROPE • 250 kW
　　USA
　　†VOA, Via Philippines — E AFRICA & S AFRICA • 50 kW
　　USSR
　　　RADIO MOSCOW — (D) • MIDEAST

21555　SPAIN
　　†R EXTERIOR ESPANA, Noblejas — C AMERICA & S AMERICA • 350 kW
　　YUGOSLAVIA
　　　VARIOUS LOCAL STNS, Bijeljina — (J) • Sa/Su • E ASIA & AUSTRALIA • DS • 500 kW

21560　GERMANY
　　†DEUTSCHE WELLE, Jülich — MIDEAST • 100 kW
　　　— (J) • MIDEAST • 100 kW
　　†DEUTSCHE WELLE, Via Sri Lanka — C AFRICA & E AFRICA • 250 kW • ALT. FREQ. TO 21570 kHz
　　　DEUTSCHE WELLE, Wertachtal — (J) • E ASIA • 500 kW
　　ITALY
(con'd)　　RTV ITALIANA, Rome — E AFRICA • 100 kW — E NORTH AM • 100 kW

0 1 2 3 4 5 6 7 8 9 10 11 12 13 14 15 16 17 18 19 20 21 22 23 24

SUMMER ONLY (J)　　WINTER ONLY (D)　　JAMMING / OR ∧　　EARLIEST HEARD ◁　　LATEST HEARD ▷　　NEW OR CHANGED FOR 1992 †

FREQUENCY	COUNTRY, STATION, LOCATION	TARGET • NETWORK • POWER (kW)	World Time

World Time scale: 0 1 2 3 4 5 6 7 8 9 10 11 12 13 14 15 16 17 18 19 20 21 22 23 24

21560 PHILIPPINES
(con'd) †RADIO VERITAS ASIA, Palauig — (J) • S ASIA • 100 kW

21570 GERMANY
†DEUTSCHE WELLE, Via Sri Lanka — Alternative Frequency to 21560 kHz

SPAIN
†R EXTERIOR ESPANA, Noblejas — C AMERICA & S AMERICA • 350 kW

SWEDEN
†RADIO SWEDEN, Karlsborg — (D) • SE ASIA & AUSTRALIA • 350 kW
(D) • S ASIA & SE ASIA • 350 kW
(J) • SE ASIA & AUSTRALIA • 350 kW
(J) • S ASIA & SE ASIA • 350 kW

USA
†VOA, Via Germany — MIDEAST • 500 kW
(J) • MIDEAST • 500 kW

†VOA, Via Kaválla, Greece — (D) • MIDEAST • 250 kW

†VOA, Via Philippines — (J) • E ASIA • 250 kW

VOA, Via Tangier, Morocco — (J) • MIDEAST & WEST USSR • 35 kW

21575 JAPAN
†RADIO JAPAN/NHK, Via Moyabi, Gabon — Alternative Frequency to 21690 kHz

PAKISTAN
†RADIO PAKISTAN, Karachi — E AFRICA • 50 kW

21580 FRANCE
R FRANCE INTL, Issoudun-Allouis — AFRICA • 500 kW
(J) • AFRICA • 500 kW

†R FRANCE INTL, Via French Guiana — (J) • W AFRICA • 500 kW

GERMANY
†DEUTSCHE WELLE, Via Sri Lanka — MIDEAST • 250 kW

PAKISTAN
†RADIO PAKISTAN, Islamabad — MIDEAST & N AFRICA • 250 kW   (J) • MIDEAST & N AFRICA • 250 kW

USA
VOA, Greenville, NC — C AMERICA & S AMERICA • 250 kW
Sa/Su • C AMERICA & S AMERICA • 250 kW

21585 USA
†VOA, Via Philippines — E ASIA • 250 kW
E ASIA • 250 kW • ALT. FREQ. TO 17890 kHz
(D) • E ASIA • 250 kW • ALT. FREQ. TO 17890 kHz
(J) • E ASIA • 250 kW

USSR
RADIO MOSCOW, Dushanbé — (J) • SE ASIA • 100 kW

21590 GERMANY
†DEUTSCHE WELLE, Nauen — (J) • SE ASIA • 500 kW

HOLLAND
†RADIO NEDERLAND, Via Neth Antilles — (J) • N AFRICA & W AFRICA • 300 kW

UNITED KINGDOM
†BBC, Rampisham — SE ASIA • 500 kW
(D) • WEST USSR • 500 kW

21595 SPAIN
†R EXTERIOR ESPANA, Noblejas — N AFRICA & MIDEAST • 350 kW

21600 AFGHANISTAN
†RADIO AFGHANISTAN, Via USSR — (J) • S ASIA

GERMANY
DEUTSCHE WELLE, Jülich — AFRICA • 100 kW
E AFRICA • 100 kW

DEUTSCHE WELLE, Via Sri Lanka — MIDEAST & S ASIA • 250 kW

DEUTSCHE WELLE, Wertachtal — AFRICA • 500 kW

USA
†VOA, Via Philippines — S ASIA & SE ASIA • 250 kW

YUGOSLAVIA
†RADIO YUGOSLAVIA, Bijeljina — Alternative Frequency to 21605 kHz

21605 UNITED ARAB EMIRATES
UAE RADIO, Dubai — EUROPE • 300 kW

YUGOSLAVIA
†RADIO YUGOSLAVIA, Bijeljina — (J) • S ASIA • 500 kW • ALT. FREQ. TO 21600 kHz

21610 DENMARK
†DANMARKS RADIO, Via Norway — W AFRICA • 500 kW

JAPAN
†RADIO JAPAN/NHK, Tokyo-Yamata — PACIFIC & S AMERICA • 100 kW
SE ASIA • GENERAL • 100 kW

NORWAY
†RADIO NORWAY INTL, Sveio — W AFRICA • 500 kW

USA
VOA, Greenville, NC — Sa/Su • C AMERICA & S AMERICA • 250 kW

VOA, Via Kaválla, Greece — (J) • MIDEAST & S ASIA • 250 kW

21615 USA
†VOA, Via Kaválla, Greece — (J) • MIDEAST • 250 kW

WYFR-FAMILY RADIO, Okeechobee, Fl — EUROPE • 100 kW
(J) • EUROPE • 100 kW

USSR
RADIO MOSCOW, Tashkent — S ASIA & SE ASIA • 100 kW

21620 FRANCE
(con'd) †R FRANCE INTL, Issoudun-Allouis — E AFRICA • 100 kW

World Time scale: 0 1 2 3 4 5 6 7 8 9 10 11 12 13 14 15 16 17 18 19 20 21 22 23 24

ENGLISH ▬ ARABIC ≈≈≈ CHINESE □□□ FRENCH ═ GERMAN ▬ RUSSIAN ═ SPANISH ▬ OTHER ▬

FREQUENCY   COUNTRY, STATION, LOCATION   TARGET • NETWORK • POWER (kW)   World Time

Time scale: 0 1 2 3 4 5 6 7 8 9 10 11 12 13 14 15 16 17 18 19 20 21 22 23 24

Frequency	Country / Station / Location	Target • Network • Power
21620 (con'd)	**FRANCE** †R FRANCE INTL, Issoudun-Allouis	(J) • E AFRICA • 100 kW
21625	**USA** †VOA, Via Germany	(J) • WEST USSR • 500 kW
	†VOA, Via Portugal	(D) • WEST USSR & S ASIA • 250 kW
	†VOA, Via Tangier, Morocco	W AFRICA • 35 kW
21630	**GERMANY** †DEUTSCHE WELLE, Via Sri Lanka	(D) • MIDEAST • 250 kW
	HOLLAND RADIO NEDERLAND, Via Neth Antilles	(D) • N AFRICA & W AFRICA • 300 kW
	SWITZERLAND RED CROSS BC SVC, Schwarzenburg	Irr • M/TH • MIDEAST • 150 kW
	SWISS RADIO INTL, Schwarzenburg	MIDEAST • 150 kW
	USSR RADIO MOSCOW, Star'obel'sk	(J) • MIDEAST, E AFRICA & S AFRICA • 100 kW
21635	**FRANCE** †R FRANCE INTL, Issoudun-Allouis	E NORTH AM • 100 kW
	JAPAN RADIO JAPAN/NHK, Via Moyabi, Gabon	S AMERICA • GENERAL • 500 kW
	USSR RADIO MOSCOW, Kalinin	SE ASIA • 240 kW
21640	**GERMANY** †DEUTSCHE WELLE, Via Sri Lanka	AUSTRALIA • 250 kW
		(J) • E ASIA • 250 kW
	JAPAN RADIO JAPAN/NHK, Via Moyabi, Gabon	EUROPE & N AFRICA • GENERAL • 500 kW
	NORWAY RADIO NORWAY INTL, Fredrikstad	(J) • S AMERICA • 350 kW
		(J) • C AMERICA • 350 kW
	RADIO NORWAY INTL, Kvitsøy	(J) • AFRICA • 500 kW
	SAUDI ARABIA †BS OF THE KINGDOM, Riyadh	SE ASIA • 350 kW
	UNITED KINGDOM BBC, Rampisham	W AFRICA • 500 kW
	BBC, Via Ascension	C AFRICA • 250 kW
	USA †CHRIST SCI MONITOR, Maine	AFRICA • 500 kW
		AFRICA • 500 kW • ALT. FREQ. TO 21545 kHz
		M-F • AFRICA • 500 kW
		M-F • AFRICA • 500 kW • ALT. FREQ. TO 21545 kHz
		Sa • AFRICA • 500 kW
		Sa • AFRICA • 500 kW • ALT. FREQ. TO 21545 kHz
		Sa/Su • AFRICA • 500 kW
		Sa/Su • AFRICA • 500 kW • ALT. FREQ. TO 21545 kHz
		Su-F • AFRICA • 500 kW
		Su-F • AFRICA • 500 kW • ALT. FREQ. TO 21545 kHz
21645	**FRANCE** R FRANCE INTL, Issoudun-Allouis	C AMERICA • 500 kW
		(J) • C AMERICA • 500 kW
	R FRANCE INTL, Via French Guiana	C AMERICA • 500 kW
		M-Sa • C AMERICA • 500 kW
		Su • C AMERICA • CREOLE • 500 kW
21650	**GERMANY** DEUTSCHE WELLE, Jülich	MIDEAST & S ASIA • 100 kW
		SE ASIA & AUSTRALIA • 100 kW
	†DEUTSCHE WELLE, Königswusterhausen	MIDEAST • 100 kW
	DEUTSCHE WELLE, Multiple Locations	E ASIA • 250/500 kW
		SE ASIA • 250/500 kW
		(J) • E ASIA • 250/500 kW
	DEUTSCHE WELLE, Via Sri Lanka	MIDEAST & S ASIA • 250 kW
	VATICAN STATE VATICAN RADIO, Sta Maria di Galeria	(D) Su • AFRICA • 500 kW
		(J) Su • AFRICA • 500 kW
21655	**SWEDEN** †RADIO SWEDEN, Hörby	Alternative Frequency to 21500 kHz
21660	**UNITED KINGDOM** †BBC, Via Ascension	S AFRICA • 250 kW
		Sa/Su • S AFRICA • 250 kW
		(D) • S AFRICA • 250 kW
	†BBC, Woofferton	(J) M-F • C AMERICA • 300 kW
21665	**ROMANIA** RADIO ROMANIA INTL, Bucharest	(J) • AFRICA • 250 kW
	USA †RFE-RL, Via Portugal	(J) • WEST USSR • 250 kW
21670 (con'd)	**CUBA** RADIO HABANA, Via USSR	(J) • AFRICA • 100 kW

Time scale: 0 1 2 3 4 5 6 7 8 9 10 11 12 13 14 15 16 17 18 19 20 21 22 23 24

SUMMER ONLY (J)   WINTER ONLY (D)   JAMMING / OR ∧   EARLIEST HEARD ◁   LATEST HEARD ▷   NEW OR CHANGED FOR 1992 †

FREQUENCY   COUNTRY, STATION, LOCATION   TARGET • NETWORK • POWER (kW)   World Time

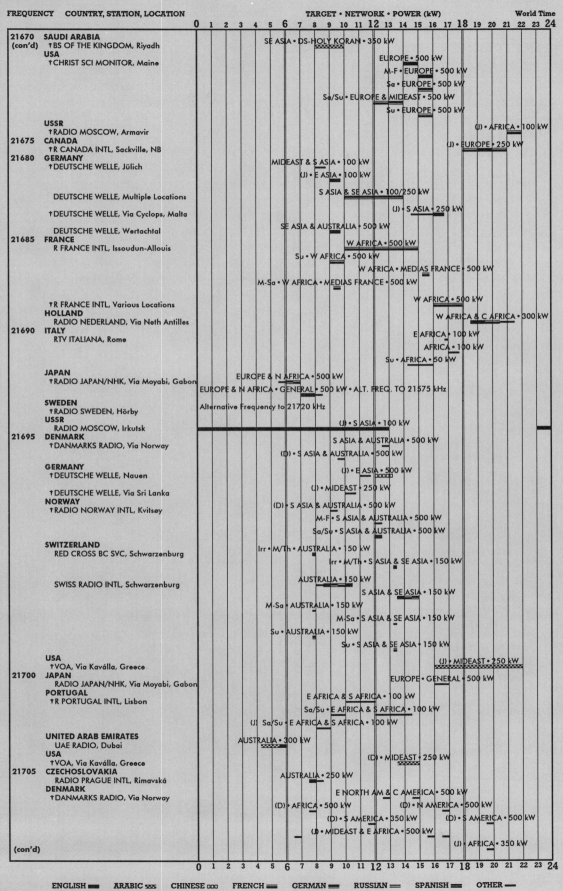

0 1 2 3 4 5 6 7 8 9 10 11 12 13 14 15 16 17 18 19 20 21 22 23 24

21670 **SAUDI ARABIA**
(con'd)   †BS OF THE KINGDOM, Riyadh — SE ASIA • DS-HOLY KORAN • 350 kW
      USA
      †CHRIST SCI MONITOR, Maine — EUROPE • 500 kW
        M-F • EUROPE • 500 kW
        Sa • EUROPE • 500 kW
        Sa/Su • EUROPE & MIDEAST • 500 kW
        Su • EUROPE • 500 kW
      USSR
      †RADIO MOSCOW, Armavir — (J) • AFRICA • 100 kW
21675 **CANADA**
      †R CANADA INTL, Sackville, NB — (J) • EUROPE • 250 kW
21680 **GERMANY**
      †DEUTSCHE WELLE, Jülich — MIDEAST & S ASIA • 100 kW
        (J) • E ASIA • 100 kW
      DEUTSCHE WELLE, Multiple Locations — S ASIA & SE ASIA • 100/250 kW
      †DEUTSCHE WELLE, Via Cyclops, Malta — (J) • S ASIA • 250 kW
      DEUTSCHE WELLE, Wertachtal — SE ASIA & AUSTRALIA • 500 kW
21685 **FRANCE**
      R FRANCE INTL, Issoudun-Allouis — W AFRICA • 500 kW
        Su • W AFRICA • 500 kW
        W AFRICA • MEDIAS FRANCE • 500 kW
        M-Sa • W AFRICA • MEDIAS FRANCE • 500 kW
      †R FRANCE INTL, Various Locations — W AFRICA • 500 kW
      HOLLAND
      RADIO NEDERLAND, Via Neth Antilles — W AFRICA & C AFRICA • 300 kW
21690 **ITALY**
      RTV ITALIANA, Rome — E AFRICA • 100 kW
        AFRICA • 100 kW
        Su • AFRICA • 50 kW
      JAPAN
      †RADIO JAPAN/NHK, Via Moyabi, Gabon — EUROPE & N AFRICA • 500 kW
        EUROPE & N AFRICA • GENERAL • 500 kW • ALT. FREQ. TO 21575 kHz
      SWEDEN
      †RADIO SWEDEN, Hörby — Alternative Frequency to 21720 kHz
      USSR
      RADIO MOSCOW, Irkutsk — (J) • S ASIA • 100 kW
21695 **DENMARK**
      †DANMARKS RADIO, Via Norway — S ASIA & AUSTRALIA • 500 kW
        (D) • S ASIA & AUSTRALIA • 500 kW
      GERMANY
      †DEUTSCHE WELLE, Nauen — (J) • E ASIA • 500 kW
      †DEUTSCHE WELLE, Via Sri Lanka — (J) • MIDEAST • 250 kW
      NORWAY
      †RADIO NORWAY INTL, Kvitsøy — (D) • S ASIA & AUSTRALIA • 500 kW
        M-F • S ASIA & AUSTRALIA • 500 kW
        Sa/Su • S ASIA & AUSTRALIA • 500 kW
      SWITZERLAND
      RED CROSS BC SVC, Schwarzenburg — Irr • M/Th • AUSTRALIA • 150 kW
        Irr • M/Th • S ASIA & SE ASIA • 150 kW
      SWISS RADIO INTL, Schwarzenburg — AUSTRALIA • 150 kW
        S ASIA & SE ASIA • 150 kW
        M-Sa • AUSTRALIA • 150 kW
        M-Sa • S ASIA & SE ASIA • 150 kW
        Su • AUSTRALIA • 150 kW
        Su • S ASIA & SE ASIA • 150 kW
      USA
      †VOA, Via Kaválla, Greece — (J) • MIDEAST • 250 kW
21700 **JAPAN**
      RADIO JAPAN/NHK, Via Moyabi, Gabon — EUROPE • GENERAL • 500 kW
      PORTUGAL
      †R PORTUGAL INTL, Lisbon — E AFRICA & S AFRICA • 100 kW
        Sa/Su • E AFRICA & S AFRICA • 100 kW
        (J) Sa/Su • E AFRICA & S AFRICA • 100 kW
      UNITED ARAB EMIRATES
      UAE RADIO, Dubai — AUSTRALIA • 300 kW
      USA
      †VOA, Via Kaválla, Greece — (D) • MIDEAST • 250 kW
21705 **CZECHOSLOVAKIA**
      RADIO PRAGUE INTL, Rimavská — AUSTRALIA • 250 kW
      DENMARK
      †DANMARKS RADIO, Via Norway — E NORTH AM & C AMERICA • 500 kW
        (D) • AFRICA • 500 kW
        (D) • N AMERICA • 500 kW
        (D) • S AMERICA • 350 kW
        (D) • S AMERICA • 500 kW
        (J) • MIDEAST & E AFRICA • 500 kW
        (J) • AFRICA • 350 kW

(con'd)

0 1 2 3 4 5 6 7 8 9 10 11 12 13 14 15 16 17 18 19 20 21 22 23 24

ENGLISH ▬   ARABIC ▒   CHINESE □□□   FRENCH ▬   GERMAN ▬   RUSSIAN ═   SPANISH ▬   OTHER ▬

FREQUENCY   COUNTRY, STATION, LOCATION   TARGET • NETWORK • POWER (kW)   World Time

		0 1 2 3 4 5 6 7 8 9 10 11 12 13 14 15 16 17 18 19 20 21 22 23 24

21705 DENMARK
(con'd) †DANMARKS RADIO, Via Norway   (J) • W AFRICA & S AMERICA • 500 kW
                                        (J) • S AMERICA & AUSTRALIA • 500 kW

   NORWAY
      †RADIO NORWAY INTL, Fredrikstad   (D) • S AMERICA • 350 kW   (J) • AFRICA • 350 kW

      †RADIO NORWAY INTL, Kvitsøy   (D) • AFRICA • 500 kW   (J) • W AFRICA & S AMERICA • 500 kW
                                        (J) • MIDEAST & E AFRICA • 500 kW
                                        (J) M-F • MIDEAST & E AFRICA • 500 kW
                                        (J) M-F • S AMERICA & AUSTRALIA • 500 kW
                                        (J) Sa/Su • MIDEAST & E AFRICA • 500 kW
                                        (J) Sa/Su • S AMERICA & AUSTRALIA • 500 kW

      †RADIO NORWAY INTL, Sveio   E NORTH AM & C AMERICA • 500 kW
                                        (D) • N AMERICA • 500 kW
                                        (D) • S AMERICA • 500 kW
                                        (J) • E NORTH AM & C AMERICA • 500 kW
                                        (J) • W AFRICA & S AMERICA • 500 kW

21710 DENMARK
      †DANMARKS RADIO, Via Norway   S ASIA & AUSTRALIA • 500 kW
   NORWAY
      †RADIO NORWAY INTL, Kvitsøy   S ASIA & AUSTRALIA • 500 kW
21715 UNITED KINGDOM
      †BBC, Via Hong Kong   E ASIA • 250 kW
                                        (D) • E ASIA • 250 kW
                                        Su • E ASIA • 250 kW

      BBC, Via Singapore   E ASIA • 100 kW
21720 AUSTRALIA
      †RADIO AUSTRALIA, Darwin   (J) • S ASIA & SE ASIA • 250 kW
   CHINA (TAIWAN)
      VO FREE CHINA, Via Okeechobee, USA   (J) • EUROPE • 100 kW
   SWEDEN
      †RADIO SWEDEN, Hörby   AFRICA • 350 kW • ALT. FREQ. TO 21460 kHz
                                        EUROPE & MIDEAST • 350 kW • ALT. FREQ. TO 21690 kHz
                                        M-F • AFRICA • 350 kW • ALT. FREQ. TO 21460 kHz
                                        Sa/Su • AFRICA • 350 kW • ALT. FREQ. TO 21460 kHz
                                        Su • AFRICA • 350 kW • ALT. FREQ. TO 21460 kHz

      USA
      †VOA, Via Kaválla, Greece   (J) • MIDEAST • 250 kW

      †WYFR-FAMILY RADIO, Okeechobee, Fl   (J) • EUROPE • 100 kW
21725 USSR
      RADIO MOSCOW, Tbilisi   (D) • W AFRICA • 100 kW
21730 DENMARK
      †DANMARKS RADIO, Via Norway   (D) • MIDEAST & E AFRICA • 500 kW
                                        (J) • E ASIA & AUSTRALIA • 500 kW   (D) • AFRICA • 500 kW
                                        (J) • S ASIA & AUSTRALIA • 500 kW

   FRANCE
      R FRANCE INTL, Issoudun-Allouis   M-Sa • E AFRICA • MEDIAS FRANCE • 100 kW
   NORWAY
      †RADIO NORWAY INTL, Kvitsøy   (J) • E ASIA & AUSTRALIA • 500 kW   (D) • AFRICA • 500 kW
                                        (J) • S ASIA & AUSTRALIA • 500 kW
                                        (D) M-F • MIDEAST & E AFRICA • 500 kW
                                        (D) Sa/Su • MIDEAST & E AFRICA • 500 kW

      PAKISTAN
      †RADIO PAKISTAN, Islamabad   S ASIA & SE ASIA • 100 kW
21735 INDIA
      ALL INDIA RADIO, Delhi   E ASIA • 250 kW
                                        SE ASIA • 250 kW

      UNITED ARAB EMIRATES
      †UAE RADIO, Abu Dhabi   AUSTRALIA • 500 kW
                                        (D) • E ASIA • 500 kW   EUROPE • 500 kW

      UNITED KINGDOM
      †BBC, Rampisham   (J) • WEST USSR • 500 kW
      USA
      WYFR-FAMILY RADIO, Okeechobee, Fl   (D) • EUROPE • 100 kW
21740 AUSTRALIA
      †RADIO AUSTRALIA, Shepparton   PACIFIC • 100 kW
                                        (J) • PACIFIC • 100 kW

21745 HOLLAND
      †RADIO NEDERLAND, Flevoland   Su • MIDEAST • 500 kW

      RADIO NEDERLAND, Via Madagascar   MIDEAST • 300 kW
      UNITED KINGDOM
      †BBC, Multiple Locations   (J) • EUROPE & WEST USSR • 300/500 kW

      †BBC, Rampisham   (D) • WEST USSR • 500 kW
                                        (D) Su • WEST USSR • 500 kW
                                        (J) Su • WEST USSR • 500 kW

      USA
(con'd) †RFE-RL, Via Portugal   (J) • E EUROPE • 250 kW

	0 1 2 3 4 5 6 7 8 9 10 11 12 13 14 15 16 17 18 19 20 21 22 23 24

SUMMER ONLY (J)   WINTER ONLY (D)   JAMMING / OR ∧   EARLIEST HEARD ◁   LATEST HEARD ▷   NEW OR CHANGED FOR 1992 †

FREQUENCY   COUNTRY, STATION, LOCATION   TARGET • NETWORK • POWER (kW)   World Time

```
                                          0 1 2 3 4 5 6 7 8 9 10 11 12 13 14 15 16 17 18 19 20 21 22 23 24
```

21745	USA
(con'd)	†VOA, Cincinnati, Ohio — M-F • C AMERICA & S AMERICA • 250 kW
21750	USSR — RADIO MOSCOW — (J) • MIDEAST
21765	FRANCE — †R FRANCE INTL, Issoudun-Allouis — S ASIA & SE ASIA • 500 kW • ALT. FREQ. TO 21770 kHz
	R FRANCE INTL, Via French Guiana — (J) • S AMERICA • 500 kW
21770	FRANCE — †R FRANCE INTL, Issoudun-Allouis — Alternative Frequency to 21765 kHz
	SWITZERLAND — †RED CROSS BC SVC, Schwarzenburg — Irr • M/Th • S ASIA & SE ASIA • 150 kW / Irr • M/Th • W AFRICA • ENGLISH, FRENCH • 150 kW
	†SWISS RADIO INTL, Schwarzenburg — S ASIA & SE ASIA • 150 kW / W AFRICA • 150 kW / M-Sa • W AFRICA • 150 kW / Su • W AFRICA • 150 kW
	†SWISS RADIO INTL, Sottens — AFRICA • 500 kW
21775	AUSTRALIA — †RADIO AUSTRALIA, Carnarvon — S ASIA • 250 kW / (D) • S ASIA • 250 kW
21780	USA — †CHRIST SCI MONITOR, South Carolina — E NORTH AM • 500 kW / M-Sa • E NORTH AM • 500 kW / Sa • E NORTH AM • 500 kW / Sa/Su • EUROPE • 500 kW / Su • E NORTH AM • 500 kW / Su-F • E NORTH AM • 500 kW
21785	USSR — RADIO MOSCOW — (J) • E AFRICA
21790	USSR — RADIO MOSCOW — (J)
21795	USSR — RADIO MOSCOW — (J)
21800	USSR — RADIO MOSCOW — (J) • E AFRICA
21810	BELGIUM — †BELGISCHE RADIO TV, Wavre — Alternative Frequency to 21815 kHz
21815	BELGIUM — †BELGISCHE RADIO TV, Wavre — (D) • AFRICA • 100/250 kW • ALT. FREQ. TO 21810 kHz / (D) • E NORTH AM & SE ASIA • 250 kW • ALT. FREQ. TO 21810 kHz / (J) • AFRICA • 100/250 kW • ALT. FREQ. TO 21810 kHz / (J) • E NORTH AM & SE ASIA • 250 kW • ALT. FREQ. TO 21810 kHz / (D) M-Sa • AFRICA • 100/250 kW • ALT. FREQ. TO 21810 kHz / (D) M-Sa • E NORTH AM & SE ASIA • 250 kW • ALT. FREQ. TO 21810 kHz / (J) M-Sa • AFRICA • 100/250 kW • ALT. FREQ. TO 21810 kHz / (J) M-Sa • E NORTH AM & SE ASIA • 250 kW • ALT. FREQ. TO 21810 kHz / (D) Su • AFRICA • 100/250 kW • ALT. FREQ. TO 21810 kHz / (D) Su • E NORTH AM & SE ASIA • 250 kW • ALT. FREQ. TO 21810 kHz / (J) Su • AFRICA • 100/250 kW • ALT. FREQ. TO 21810 kHz / (J) Su • E NORTH AM & SE ASIA • 250 kW • ALT. FREQ. TO 21810 kHz
21820	USSR — RADIO MOSCOW — (J)
21825	AUSTRALIA — †RADIO AUSTRALIA, Darwin — (D) • E ASIA • 250 kW
	FRANCE — †R FRANCE INTL, Via Moyabi, Gabon — (D) • MIDEAST • 250 kW
21840	USA — †WORLD HARVEST R, Noblesville, Indiana — M-Sa • E NORTH AM & W EUROPE • 100 kW
21845	VATICAN STATE — †VATICAN RADIO, Sta Maria di Galeria — S AMERICA • 250/500 kW
25645	BELGIUM — †RT BELGE FRANCAISE, Wavre — Alternative Frequency to 21460 kHz
25690	UNITED ARAB EMIRATES — †UAE RADIO, Abu Dhabi — EUROPE • 500 kW / (D) • AUSTRALIA • 500 kW
25730	DENMARK — †DANMARKS RADIO, Via Norway — S AMERICA • 350 kW / (D) • E ASIA & AUSTRALIA • 500 kW / (D) • S ASIA & AUSTRALIA • 500 kW / (D) • MIDEAST & E AFRICA • 500 kW / (J) • S ASIA & AUSTRALIA • 500 kW
	NORWAY — †RADIO NORWAY INTL, Fredrikstad — S AMERICA • 350 kW
	†RADIO NORWAY INTL, Kvitsøy — (D) • E ASIA & AUSTRALIA • 500 kW / (D) • MIDEAST & E AFRICA • 500 kW / (J) • S ASIA & AUSTRALIA • 500 kW / (D) M-F • S ASIA & AUSTRALIA • 500 kW / (D) Sa/Su • S ASIA & AUSTRALIA • 500 kW

```
  0 1 2 3 4 5 6 7 8 9 10 11 12 13 14 15 16 17 18 19 20 21 22 23 24
```

ENGLISH ▬ ARABIC ▨ CHINESE ▭▭▭ FRENCH ▬ GERMAN ▬ RUSSIAN ═ SPANISH ▬ OTHER ▬

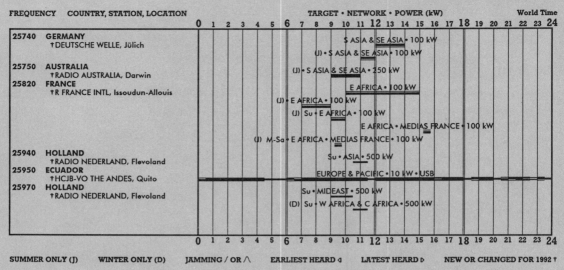

SUMMER ONLY (J)   WINTER ONLY (D)   JAMMING / OR ∧   EARLIEST HEARD ◁   LATEST HEARD ▷   NEW OR CHANGED FOR 1992 †

Directory of Advertisers

Advertising Representative:
Mary Kroszner
IBS, Ltd.
Box 300
Penn's Park, PA 18943 USA
Telephone: 215/794-8252
Fax: 215/598-3794

GLOSSARY

Terms and Abbreviations Used in World Band Radio

A wide variety of terms and abbreviations is used in world band radio. Some are specialized and need explanation; a few are foreign words that need translation; and yet others are simply adaptations of common usage. Here, then, is *Passport's* guide to what's what in world band terminology and abbreviations—including what each one means. For a thorough writeup on what determines how well a world band radio performs, please see the *RDI White Paper*, "How to Interpret Receiver Specifications and Lab Tests."

Adjacent-Channel Rejection. *See* Selectivity.

AGC. *See* Automatic Gain Control.

Alt. Alternative frequency or channel. Frequency or channel that may be used unexpectedly in place of the regularly scheduled frequency or channel.

Amateur Radio. *See* Hams.

AM Band. The local radio band, which currently runs from 520 to 1611 kHz (530–1705 kHz in the Western Hemisphere), within the Medium Frequency (MF) range of the radio spectrum. In many countries it is called the mediumwave (MW) band.

Analog Frequency Readout. Needle-and-dial tuning, greatly inferior to synthesized tuning for world band use. *See* Synthesizer.

Artificial Intelligence (AI). The ability of a computer to operate similarly to the human brain.

Audio Quality, Audio Fidelity. *See* High Fidelity.

Automatic Gain Control. Smoothes out fluctuations in signal strength brought about by fading, a regular occurrence with world band signals.

AV. A Voz—Portuguese for Voice of.

Bandwidth. The main variable to determine selectivity (*see*), bandwidth is the amount of radio signal at -6 dB a set will let pass through, and thus be heard. With world band channel spacing at 5 kHz, the best single bandwidths are usually in the vicinity of 3 to 6 kHz. Better radios offer two or more selectable bandwidths: one of 5 to 7 kHz or so for when a station is in the clear, and one or more others between 2 to 4 kHz for when a station is hemmed in by other stations next to it. Proper selectivity is a key determinant of the aural quality of what you hear.

BC, BS. Broadcasting, Broadcasting Company, Broadcasting Corporation, Broadcasting Station, Broadcasting Service.

Broadcast. A radio or TV transmission meant for the general public. *Compare* Utility Stations.

Cd. Ciudad—Spanish for City.

Channel. An everyday term to indicate where a station is supposed to be located on the dial. World band channels are exactly 5 kHz apart. Stations operating outside this norm are "off channel" (for these, *Passport* provides resolution to better than one kHz to aid in station identification). Measured in units of 5 kHz; that is, world band channels, unlike some other radio/TV channels, aren't assigned sequentially, like street numbers, in an *n + 1* fashion.

Chuffing. The sound made by some synthesized tuning systems when the tuning knob is being turned. Called "chuffing," as it is suggestive of the rhythmic "chuff, chuff" sound of steam locomotives.

Cl. Club, Clube.

Cu, Cult. Cultura, Cultural, Culture.

(D). December. Frequency operates at this time winters only. Not heard summers.

Default. The setting a radio normally operates at, and to which it normally will eventually return if that default setting is changed by the operator.

Digital Frequency Display. *See* Synthesizer.

DS. Domestic Service—Broadcasting intended primarily for audiences in the broadcaster's home country. However, some DS programs are relayed on world band to expatriates and officials abroad. *Compare* ES.

DXers. From an old telegraph term "to DX"; that is, to communicate over a great distance. Thus, DXers are those who specialize in finding distant or exotic stations. Only 1% or so of those tuning world band are considered to be regular DXers, but many others seek DX stations every now and then, usually by bandscanning, which is made easier by using *Passport's* Blue Pages.

Dynamic Range. The ability of a set to handle weak signals in the presence of strong competing signals within the same world band segment (*see* World Band Spectrum). Sets with inferior dynamic range sometimes "overload," causing a mishmash of false signals mixed together up and down—and even beyond—the band segment being received.

Earliest Heard (or Latest Heard). See key at the bottom of each "Blue Page." If the *Passport* monitoring team cannot establish the definite sign-on (or sign-off) time of a station, the earliest (or latest) time the station could be traced is indicated, instead, by a triangular "flag." This means that the station almost certainly operates beyond the time shown by that "flag." It also means that, unless you live relatively close to the station, you're unlikely to be able to hear it beyond that "flagged" time.

ECSS. *See* Synchronous Detector.

Ed, Educ. Educational , Educação, Educadora.

Em. Emissora, Emisora, Emissor, Emetteur—In effect, station in various languages.

Enhanced Fidelity. *See* High Fidelity.

EP. Emissor Provincial—Portuguese for Provincial Station.

ER. Emissor Regional—Portuguese for Regional Station.

Ergonomics. How handy and comfortable a set is to operate, especially if you're adjusting the controls hour after hour.

ES. External Service—Broadcasting intended primarily for audiences abroad. *Compare* DS.

F. Friday.

Feeder. A utility station that transmits programs from the broadcaster's home country to a relay site some distance away. Although these highly specialized stations carry world band programming, they are not intended to be received by the general public. Many world band radios can process these quasi-broadcasts anyway. Feeders operate in lower sideband (LSB), upper sideband (USB) or independent sideband (termed ISL if heard on the lower side, ISU if heard on the upper side) modes. *See* Single Sideband, Utility Stations.

Frequency. The standard term to indicate where a station is located on the dial—regardless of whether it's "on-channel" or "off-channel" (*see* Channel). Measured in kilohertz (kHz) or Megahertz (MHz). Either measurement is equally valid, but to minimize confusion *Passport* designates frequencies only in kHz.

GMT. Greenwich Mean Time—*See* UTC.

Hams. Government-licensed amateur radio hobbyists who communicate with each other by radio for pleasure within special amateur bands. Many of these bands are within the shortwave spectrum (see). This is the same spectrum used by world band, but world band radio and ham radio are two very separate entities.

High Fidelity, Enhanced Fidelity. World band reception is usually of only mediocre audio quality, or fidelity, with some stations sounding even worse. Advanced radios with good audio performance and certain high-tech circuits already can improve on this, and radios of the 21st century may provide genuine high fidelity; i.e., smooth, relatively wideband audio, and freedom from excessive distortion. Among the newer fidelity-enhancing techniques already available is Synchronous Detection (see).

Image Rejection. A variant of spurious-signal rejection (see).

Independent Sideband. See Single Sideband.

Interference. Sounds from other stations that are disturbing the station you're trying to hear. Worthy radios reduce interference by having good selectivity (see).

Ionosphere. See Propagation.

Irr. Irregular operation or hours of operation; i.e., schedule tends to be unpredictable.

ISB. Independent sideband. See Single Sideband.

ISL. Independent sideband, lower. See Feeder.

ISU. Independent sideband, upper. See Feeder.

(J). June. Frequency operates at this time summers only. Not heard winters.

Jamming. Deliberate interference to a transmission with the intent of making reception impossible. With the rollback of the Cold War, this impediment has become far less commonplace, making world band reception easier, clearer and more enjoyable.

kHz. Kilohertz, the most common unit for measuring where a station is on the world band dial. Formerly known as "kilocycles/second." 1,000 kilohertz equals one Megahertz.

kW. Kilowatt(s), the most common unit of measurement for transmitter power (see).

LCD. Liquid-crystal display. LCDs are fairly easily seen in bright light, but require backlighting under darker conditions. LCDs, being gray on gray, also tend to have mediocre contrast, and sometimes can be seen from only a certain angle or angles, but they consume nearly no battery power.

LED. Light-emitting diode. LEDs are very easily seen in the dark or in normal room light.

Loc. Local.

Location. The physical location of a station's transmitter, which may be different from the studio location. Transmitter location is useful as a guide to reception quality. For example, if you're in Eastern North America and wish to listen to Radio Moscow, a transmitter located in the Ukraine will almost certainly provide better reception than one located in Siberia, and one located in Cuba will probably be better yet.

Longwave Band. The 148.5–283.5 kHz portion of the low-frequency (LF) radio spectrum used in Europe, the Near East, North Africa, the USSR and Mongolia for domestic broadcasting. In general, these longwave signals, which have nothing to do with world band or shortwave signals, are not audible in other parts of the world.

LSB. Lower Sideband. See Feeder, Single Sideband.

LV. La Voix, La Voz—French and Spanish for The Voice.

M. Monday.

Mediumwave Band. See AM Band.

Memory(ies). See Preset.

Meters. An outdated unit of measurement used for individual world band segments of the shortwave spectrum. The frequency range covered by a given meters designation—also known as "wavelength"—can be gleaned from the following formula: frequency (kHz) = 299,792/meters. Thus, 49 meters comes out to a frequency of 6118 kHz—well within the range of frequencies included in that segment (see World Band Spectrum). Inversely, meters can be derived from the following: meters = 299,792/frequency (kHz).

MHz. Megahertz, a common unit to measure where a station is on the dial. Formerly known as "Megacycles/second." One Megahertz equals 1,000 kilohertz.

Mode. Method of transmission of radio signals. World band radio broadcasts are almost always in the AM mode, the same mode that's also used in the mediumwave AM band. The AM mode consists of three components: two "sidebands" and one "carrier." Each sideband contains the same programming as the other, and the carrier carries no programming, so a few stations are experimenting with the single-sideband (SSB) mode. SSB contains only one sideband, either the lower sideband (LSB) or upper sideband (USB), and no carrier. It requires special radio circuitry to be demodulated, or made intelligible. There are yet other modes used on shortwave, but not for world band. These include CW (Morse-type code), fax, RTTY (radioteletype) and narrow-band FM used by utility and ham stations. Narrow-band FM is not used for music, and is different from the usual FM. See Single Sideband, ISB, ISL, ISU, LSB and USB.

N. New, Nueva, Nuevo, Nouvelle, Nacional, National, Nationale.

Nac. Spanish and Portuguese for Nacional.

Narrow-Band Facsimile Video. A technique in which pictures can be transmitted without taking up a great deal of radio spectrum space.

Nat, Natl. National, Nationale.

Other. Programs are in a language other than one of the world's primary languages.

Overloading. See Dynamic Range.

PBS. People's Broadcasting Station.

Power. Transmitter power before amplification by the antenna, expressed in kilowatts (kW). The present range of world band powers is 0.01 to 600 kW.

PR. People's Republic.

Preset. Allows you to push one button, as on a car radio, to select a station.

Propagation. World band signals travel, like a basketball, up and down from the station to your radio. The "floor" below is the earth's surface, whereas the "player's hand" on high is the ionosphere, a gaseous layer that envelops the earth. While the earth's surface remains pretty much the same from day to day, the ionosphere—nature's own passive "satellite"—varies in how it propagates radio signals, depending on how much sunlight hits the "bounce points."

This is why some world band segments do well mainly by day, whereas others are best by night. During winter there's less sunlight, so the "night bands" become unusually active, while the "day bands" become correspondingly less useful (see World Band Spectrum). Day-to-day changes in the sun's weather also cause short-term changes in world band radio reception; this explains why some days you can hear rare signals. Additionally, the 11-year sunspot cycle has a long-term effect on propagation.

PS. Provincial Station, Pangsong.

Pto. Puerto, Pôrto.

QSL. A card or letter from a station verifying that a listener indeed heard that particular station.

R. Radio, Radiodiffusion, Radiodifusora, Radiofusão, Radiofonikos, Radiostansiya, Radyo, Radyosu, and so forth.

Receiver. Synonym for a radio. In practice, "receiver" is often used to designate a set—usually a tabletop model—with superior ability to ferret out weak, hard-to-hear signals.

Reduced Carrier. See Single Sideband.

Reg. Regional.

Relay. A retransmission facility, shown in **bold** in "Worldwide Broadcasts in English" and "Voices from Home" in Passport's Worldscan section. Relay facilities are considered to be located outside the broadcaster's country. Being closer to the target audience, they usually provide superior reception. See Feeder.

Rep. Republic, République, República.

RN. See R and N.

RS. Radio Station, Radiostansiya, Radiofonikos Stathmos.

RT, RTV. Radiodiffusion Télévision, Radio Télévision, and so forth.

S. San, Santa, Santo, São, Saint, Sainte.

Sa. Saturday.

Scanner. Circuitry within a radio that allows it to tune automatically in one or more of a number of possible ways. Useful for such non-world band applications as listening to police and fire calls on VHF and UHF. Of dubious value for world band listening.

Selectivity. The ability of a radio to reject interference from signals on adjacent channels. Thus, also known as adjacent-channel rejection. A key variable in radio quality.

Sensitivity. The ability of a radio to receive weak signals. Also known as weak signal sensitivity. Of special importance if you're listening during the day, or if you're located in such parts of the world as Western North America and the Pacific, where signals tend to be relatively weak.

Shortwave Spectrum. The shortwave spectrum—also known as the High Frequency (HF) spectrum—is, strictly speaking, that portion of the radio spectrum from 3–30 MHz (3,000–

30,000 kHz). However, common usage places it from 2.3-30 MHz (2,000–30,000 kHz). World band operates on short-wave, but most of the shortwave spectrum is occupied by Hams (see) and Utility Stations (see)—not world band. Also, see World Band Spectrum.

Single Sideband, Independent Sideband. Spectrum- and power-conserving modes of transmission commonly used by utility stations and hams. Few broadcasters—world band or other—use these modes, but this may change early in the 21st century. Many world band radios are already capable of demodulating single sideband transmissions, and some can even process independent sideband transmissions. Certain single sideband signals operate with reduced carrier, which allows them to be listened to, albeit with some distortion, on ordinary radios not equipped to demodulate single sideband. Properly designed synchronous detectors (see) prevent such distortion. See Feeder, Mode.

Slew Controls. Up and down controls, usually pushbuttons, to tune a radio. On some radios with synthesized tuning, slew controls are used in lieu of a tuning knob. Better is when slew controls are complemented by a tuning knob, which is more versatile.

Spurious-Signal Rejection. The ability of a radio receiver not to produce false, or "ghost," signals that might otherwise interfere with the clarity of the station you're trying to hear.

St, Sta, Sto. Saint.

Su. Sunday.

Synchronous Detector. World band radios are increasingly coming equipped with this high-tech circuit that reduces fading distortion. Better synchronous detectors also allow for selectable sideband; that is, the ability to select the clearer of the two sidebands of a world band or other AM-mode signal. See Mode.

Synthesizer. Simple radios usually use archaic needle-and-dial tuning that makes it difficult to find a desired channel or to tell which station you are hearing, except by ear. Advanced models utilize a digital frequency *synthesizer* to tune in signals without your having to hunt and peck. Among other things, synthesizers allow for push-button tuning and presets, and display the exact frequency digitally—pluses that make tuning in the world considerably easier.

Target. Where a transmission is beamed if it is intended to be heard outside the country.

Th. Thursday.

Travel Power Lock. Control to disable the on/off switch so as to prevent a radio from switching on accidentally in transit.

Tu. Tuesday.

Universal Time. See UTC.

USB. Upper Sideband. See Feeder, Single Sideband.

UTC. Coordinated Universal Time, also known as World Time, Greenwich Mean Time and Zulu time. With around 150 countries on world band radio, if each announced its own local time you would need a calculator to figure it all out. To get around this, a single international time—UTC—is used. The difference between UTC and local time is determined simply by listening to UTC time announcements given on the hour by world band broadcasters—or minute by minute by WWV and WWVH in the United States on such frequencies as 5000, 10000, 15000 and 20000 kHz. A 24-hour clock is used, so "1800 UTC" means 6:00 PM UTC. If you're in North America, Eastern Time is five hours behind UTC winters and four hours behind UTC summers, so 1800 UTC would be 1:00 PM EST or 2:00 PM EDT. The easiest solution is to use a 24-hour clock set to UTC. Many radios already have these built in, and UTC clocks are also available as inexpensive accessories.

UTC also applies to the days of the week. So if it's 9:00 PM (21:00) Wednesday in New York during the winter, it's 0200 UTC *Thursday*.

Utility Stations. Most signals within the shortwave spectrum are not world band stations. Rather, they are utility stations—radio telephones, ships at sea, aircraft and the like—that transmit point-to-point and are not intended to be heard by the general public. *Compare* Broadcast, Hams and Feeders.

v. Variable frequency; i.e., one that is unstable or drifting because of a transmitter malfunction.

Vo. Voice of.

W. Wednesday.

Wavelength. *See* Meters.

World Band Radio. Similar to regular AM band and FM band radio, except that world band broadcasters can be heard over enormous distances and thus often carry news, music and entertainment programs created especially for audiences abroad. Some world band stations have audiences of over 100 million worldwide each day.

World Band Spectrum. The collected segments of the short-wave spectrum set aside by the International Telecommunication Union (ITU) for broadcasting. The ITU also allows some world band broadcasting to take place outside these segments. The official world band segment—along with, when appropriate, the "real world" segments [in brackets]—are detailed below, with general guides as to when reception should be best. Remember, these are only *general* guides—actual reception will vary according to your location, station location, time of year, and other factors (*see* Propagation).

Exceedingly Rare, Faint Reception Winter Nights in Most Countries

*2 MHz (120 Meters):
   2300–2498 kHz (Tropical domestic transmissions only)

Poor Reception Winter Nights

*3 MHz (90 Meters):
   3200–3400 kHz (Tropical domestic transmissions only)

Fair-to-Good Reception Winter Nights except in Americas

**4 MHz (75 Meters):
   3900-3950 kHz (Asian & Pacific transmissions only)
   3950-4000 kHz (European, African, Asian & Pacific transmissions only)

Weak-to-Fair Reception Winter Nights

*5 MHz (60 Meters):
   4750–4995 kHz [4600–4996 kHz] (Tropical domestic transmissions only)
   5005-5060 kHz [5004-5100 kHz] (Tropical domestic transmissions only)

Strong Night Reception, Some Day Reception

6 MHz (49 Meters):
   5950–6200 kHz [5850–6250 kHz]
***7 MHz (41 Meters):
   7100–7300 kHz [7100–7600 kHz] (No American transmissions below 7300 kHz)

Strong Night and Day Reception

9 MHz (31 Meters):
   9500–9775 kHz [9250–9995 kHz]
11 MHz (25 Meters):
   11700–11975 kHz [11500–12100 kHz]

Strong Day Reception, Some Night Reception

*13 MHz (22 Meters):
   [13600–13800 kHz]
15 MHz (19 Meters):
   15100–15450 kHz [15005–15700 kHz]
17 MHz (16 Meters):
   17700–17900 kHz [17500–17900 kHz]
21 MHz (13 Meters):
   21450–21750 kHz [21450–21850 kHz]

Variable Day Reception

25 MHz (11 Meters):
   25600–26100 kHz

World Time. *See* UTC.

WS. World Service.

---

*Shared with utility stations.
**Shared with ham stations.
***7100-7300 kHz shared with hams; 7300-7600 kHz shared with utility stations.

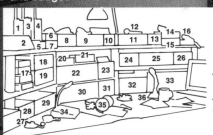